STUDIES IN ANTIQUITY AND CHRISTIANITY

The Roots of Egyptian Christianity
Birger A. Pearson and James E. Goehring, editors

The Formation of Q: Trajectories in Ancient Wisdom Collections
John S. Kloppenborg

Saint Peter of Alexandria: Bishop and Martyr
Tim Vivian

Images of the Feminine in Gnosticism
Karen L. King, editor

Gnosticism, Judaism, and Egyptian Christianity
Birger A. Pearson

Ascetic Behavior in Greco-Roman Antiquity
Vincent L. Wimbush, editor

Elijah in Upper Egypt
David Frankfurter

The Institute for Antiquity and Christianity
Claremont Graduate School
Claremont, California

A fresco, *The Prophet Ilija in the Desert,* from thirteenth-century Moraca.

STUDIES IN ANTIQUITY & CHRISTIANITY

ELIJAH IN UPPER EGYPT

THE APOCALYPSE OF ELIJAH AND EARLY EGYPTIAN CHRISTIANITY

David Frankfurter

FORTRESS PRESS   **MINNEAPOLIS**

For

Eleanor, Jack, and Anath

ELIJAH IN UPPER EGYPT
The Apocalypse of Elijah and Early Egyptian Christianity

Library of Congress Cataloging-in-Publication Data

Frankfurter, David, 1961–
    Elijah in Upper Egypt : the apocalypse of Elijah and early
  Egyptian Christianity / David Frankfurter.
      p. cm. — (Studies in antiquity and Christianity)
  Includes bibliographical references and index.
  ISBN 0–8006–3106–4 (alk. paper)
    1. Apocalypse of Elijah—Criticism, interpretation, etc.
  2. Egypt—Religion. I. Title. II. Series.
  BS1830.E46F73   1992
  229'.913—dc20   92–17353
                                       CIP

Manufactured in the U.S.A.   AF 1–3106

97   96   95   94   93   1   2   3   4   5   6   7   8   9   10

Contents

PART TWO
Envisioning the Collapse of Things:
The Convergence of Egyptian and Christian Worldviews
in the Apocalypse of Elijah

PART THREE

A Silhouette of the Millennium:
Toward a Historical and Social Context
for the Apocalypse of Elijah

Foreword

We are delighted to welcome the publication of David Frankfurter's volume *Elijah in Upper Egypt* in the Studies in Antiquity and Christianity series. As he himself notes in his Introduction, this monograph addresses themes of significance for the study of the development of Egyptian Christianity, and thus his work contributes to the discussions taken up within the Roots of Egyptian Christianity Project of the Institute for Antiquity and Christianity. The particular concern of Dr. Frankfurter's book for rural Egyptian Christianity distinguishes his work from other studies of Christianity and religious traditions in Egypt. Dr. Frankfurter is also a member of and a contributor to the Coptic Magical Texts Project of the Institute for Antiquity and Christianity, and his evaluation in this book and other publications of the figure of Elijah in Egyptian texts of ritual power advances the study of Egyptian magical traditons. Dr. Frankfurter uses the Coptic Apocalypse of Elijah as a window through which we may glimpse aspects of the troubled and creative world of third-century Egypt. In that world, with its preoccupation with prophecy, apocalyptic, millennialism, asceticism, and sacred power and knowledge, we may recognize social anxieties that continue to call for the response of thoughtful people.

MARVIN MEYER
Director, Coptic Magical Texts Project, Claremont
Associate Professor of Religion, Chapman University

BIRGER PEARSON
Director, Roots of Egyptian Christianity Project
Professor of Religious Studies
University of California, Santa Barbara

Acknowledgments

It was in John Strugnell's Pseudepigrapha Seminar at Harvard Divinity School that I first encountered the Elijah Apocalypse and came to write about the problems it entailed; he has since remained an interested mentor and critic. My growing interest in the text and its Egyptian background culminated in a dissertation, directed by Martha Himmelfarb and John Gager and presented to Princeton University's Department of Religion in 1990. This book is a revision and expansion of that dissertation.

I am deeply indebted to Martha Himmelfarb, who encouraged the project from the beginning, patiently read undigested drafts and delivered finely detailed criticisms, and guided me through a maze of apocryphal writings and religious remains with generosity and interest. And I thank John Gager for demonstrating the importance of social-scientific theory, of articulating historical context, and of the "alternative" data represented in the magical corpora, all vital contributions to the present project.

Roman Egypt is the shared domain of historians, classicists, Egyptologists, and religionists; and each must work in conversation with the others to gather a full impression of this remote and complex world. Yet to cross fields with integrity is a skill few of us are taught, and I am deeply indebted to the patient advice, open encouragement, and inspiring academic ecumenism of Ludwig Koenen and David Potter of the classics department of the University of Michigan, Garth Fowden of the Research Center for Greek and Roman Antiquity in Athens, Janet Johnson of the Oriental Institute of the University of Chicago, and John

Gwyn Griffiths of the Department of Classics and Ancient History of the University of Wales. I also thank Peter Brown, Adela Yarbro Collins, John Collins, Evasio DeMarcellis, Richard Valentasis, Jacques van de Vliet, and Richard Lim, invaluable consultants and critics at various points along the way.

I owe my deep appreciation to Marvin Meyer, a generous and patient sponsor; the Institute for Antiquity and Christianity, for accepting this work and granting funds for indexing and production; and Birger Pearson and James Goehring, for helpful suggestions. Finally, I thank the College of Charleston for a summer research grant, and particularly Michael Phillips and Shirley Davidson, interlibrary loan staff of Robert Scott Small Library, for being my indefatigable and good-humored links to the rest of the world.

I dedicate these studies to my parents, Eleanor Munro and Jack Kahn, models of dedication and self-discipline, and to Anath Golomb who witnessed the very germination of this project, who intertwined her graduate career with mine, and who consented in 1988 to join her life with mine too.

Abbreviations

AARSR	American Academy of Religion Studies in Religion
AB	Anchor Bible
Acts And. Matt.	*Acts of Andrew and Matthew*
Acts Paul	*Acts of Paul*
Adomnan	*Vision of Adomnan*
Adv. haer.	Irenaeus *Adversus haereses*
AnBoll	Analecta Bollandiana
ANF	*The Ante-Nicene Fathers* (10 vols.), ed. Alexander Roberts and James Donaldson (Edinburgh: T. & T. Clark, 1885–97)
ANRW	*Aufstieg und Niedergang der römischen Welt*, ed. Hildegard Temporini and Wolfgang Haase (Berlin: De Gruyter, 1972–)
Ant.	Josephus *Antiquities*
AOH	*Acta Orientalia Hungaricae*
AOT	*The Apocryphal Old Testament*, ed. H.F.D. Sparks (Oxford: Clarendon, 1984)
Apion	Josephus *Against Apion*
Apoc. Ab.	*The Apocalypse of Abraham*
ApocEl	The Apocalypse of Elijah
Apoc. Paul	*The Apocalypse of Paul*
Apoc. Pet.	*The Apocalypse of Peter*
Apoc. Sed.	*The Apocalypse of Sedrach*
Apopth. patr.	*Apopthegmata patrum*
Asc. Is.	*Ascension of Isaiah*

As. Mos.	*Assumption of Moses*
ATLA	American Theological Library Association
2 Bar.	*2 Baruch*
BASOR	*Bulletin of the American Schools for Oriental Research*
BASP	*Bulletin of the American Society of Papyrologists*
BIFAO	*Bulletin de l'institut français d'archéologie orientale*
BJRL	*Bulletin of the John Rylands University Library of Manchester*
Borghouts	J. F. Borghouts, *Ancient Egyptian Magical Texts*, Nisaba 9 (Leiden: Brill, 1978)
BWANT	Beiträge zur Wissenschaft vom Alten und Neuen Testament
BZNW	Beihefte zur Zeitschrift für die neutestamentliche Wissenschaft
CAH	*The Cambridge Ancient History* (12 vols.), ed. S. A. Cook (Cambridge: Cambridge University Press, 1st ed. 1923–39; 2d ed. 1970–)
CBQ	*Catholic Biblical Quarterly*
2 Clem.	*2 Clement*
Comm. Eccles.	Didymus the Blind, *Commentary on Ecclesiastes*
Comm. Matt.	Origen *Commentary on Matthew*
Corp. Herm.	*Corpus Hermeticum*
CP	*Classical Philology*
CPJ	*Corpus Papyrorum Judaicarum* (3 vols.), ed. Victor Tcherikover and Alexander Fuks (Cambridge: Harvard University Press, 1957–64)
CQR	*Church Quarterly Review*
Crum	W. E. Crum, *A Coptic Dictionary* (Oxford: Clarendon, 1939)
CSCO	Corpus scriptorum christianorum orientalium (Louvain)
De fuga	Tertullian *De fuga in persecutione*
Dem. Chr.	*Demotic Chronicle*
De Spec. leg.	Philo, *De Specialibus legibus*
Disc. 8–9	*Discourse on the Eighth and Ninth*
Div. inst.	Lactantius *Divinae institutae*
1, 2 En	*1, 2 Enoch*
Epis. apost.	*Epistula apostolorum*

Epis. Aristeas	*Epistle of Aristeas*
Epis. Barn.	*Epistle of Barnabas*
EPRO	Études préliminaires aux religions orientales dans l'empire romain
ER	*Encyclopedia of Religion* (6 vols.), ed. M. Eliade (New York: Macmillan, 1987)
ERE	*Encyclopedia of Religion and Ethics* (13 vols.), ed. James Hastings (New York: Scribners, 1911)
ETL	*Ephemerides theologicae lovanienses*
Exh. ad mart.	Origen *Exhortatio ad martyrum*
Gos. Thom.	*Gospel of Thomas*
GRBS	*Greek, Roman, and Byzantine Studies*
HDR	Harvard Dissertations in Religion
Herm. Sim.	Hermas *Similitude(s)*
Herm. Vis.	Hermas *Vision(s)*
Hist. eccles.	Eusebius of Caesarea *Historia ecclesiastica*
Hist. mon.	*Historia monachorum in Aegypto*
Hom.	Pseudo-Clement *Homilies*
HR	*History of Religions*
HSCP	*Harvard Studies in Classical Philology*
HSM	Harvard Semitic Monographs
HTR	*Harvard Theological Review*
HUCA	*Hebrew Union College Annual*
JA	*Journal asiatique*
JAAR	*Journal of the American Academy of Religion*
JAC	*Jahrbuch für Antike und Christentum*
JAOS	*Journal of the American Oriental Society*
JBL	*Journal of Biblical Literature*
JEA	*Journal of Egyptian Archaeology*
JEH	*Journal of Ecclesiastical History*
Jerome, *Comm. Is.*	*Commentary on Isaiah*
JHS	*Journal of Hellenic Studies*
JJP	*Journal of Juristic Papyrology*
JJS	*Journal of Jewish Studies*
JNES	*Journal of Near Eastern Studies*
JQR	*Jewish Quarterly Review*
JRS	*Journal of Roman Studies*

JSJ	*Journal for the Study of Judaism in the Persian, Hellenistic and Roman Period*
JSNT	*Journal for the Study of the New Testament*
JTS	*Journal of Theological Studies*
Kropp	Angelicus M. Kropp, *Ausgewählte koptische Zaubertexte* (3 vols; Brussels: Fondation reine Élisabeth, 1931)
Kuhn	K. H. Kuhn, "The Apocalypse of Elijah," *AOT* 753–73
LCL	Loeb Classical Library
Lichtheim	Miriam Lichtheim, *Ancient Egyptian Literature* (3 vols.; Berkeley: University of California Press, 1973–80)
LSJ	H. G. Liddell, R. Scott, and H. S. Jones, *A Greek–English Lexicon*, 9th ed. (Oxford: Clarendon, 1925–40; Suppl. 1968)
LXX	Septuagint
Neferti	*Prophecy of Neferti*
NHC	Nag Hammadi Codices
NHL	*The Nag Hammadi Library*, 3d ed., ed. James M. Robinson (San Francisco: Harper & Row, 1988)
NHS	Nag Hammadi Studies
NPNF	*Nicene and Post-Nicene Fathers*, series 2 (14 vols.), ed. Philip Schaff and Henry Wace (Edinburgh: T. & T. Clark)
NTA	E. Hennecke, *New Testament Apocrypha* (2 vols.), ed. W. Schneemelcher; English translation ed. R. McL. Wilson (Philadelphia: Fortress Press, 1963)
NTS	*New Testament Studies*
NumenSupp	*Numen* Supplements
Or. Lamb.	*Oracle of the Lamb*
Or. Pot.	*Oracle of the Potter*
Orig. World	*On the Origin of the World*
OTP	*The Old Testament Pseudepigrapha* (2 vols.), ed. James H. Charlesworth (Garden City, N.Y.: Doubleday, 1983–86)
Paraph. Shem	*The Paraphrase of Shem*
PG	*Patrologia graeca*, ed. J.-P. Migne
PGM	*Papyri graecae magicae: Die griechischen Zauberpapyri*, 2d ed., ed. K. Preisendanz et al. (Stuttgart:

	Teubner, 1973–74), tr. and extended in *The Greek Magical Papyri in Translation*, vol. 1, ed. Hans Dieter Betz (Chicago: University of Chicago Press, 1986)
Pietersma	Albert Pietersma, Susan Turner Comstock, and Harold A. Attridge, *The Apocalypse of Elijah*, SBLTT 19 (Missoula, Mont.: Scholars Press, 1981)
PL	*Patrologia latina*, ed. J.-P. Migne
Pss. Sol.	*Psalms of Solomon*
PTA	Papyrologische Texte und Abhandlungen
PW	Pauly-Wissowa, *Real-Encyclopädie der classischen Altertumswissenschaft*
RB	*Revue biblique*
REA	*Revue des études anciennes*
REg	*Revue d'égyptologie*
RHPR	*Revue d'histoire et de philosophie religieuses*
RHR	*Revue de l'histoire des religions*
Rosenstiehl	Jean-Marc Rosenstiehl, *L'Apocalypse d'Élie: Introduction, traduction, et notes*, Textes et études pour servir a l'histoire du Judaisme intertestamentaire 1 (Paris: Paul Guethner, 1972)
RSO	*Rivista degli studii orientale*
SAC	Studies in Antiquity and Christianity
SBL	Society of Biblical Literature
SBLDS	SBL Dissertation Series
SBLMS	SBL Monograph Series
SBLSP	SBL Seminar Papers
SBLTT	SBL Tests and Translations
SC	Sources chrétiennes
Schrage	Wolfgang Schrage, "Die Elia-Apokalypse," in *Apokalypsen*, ed. Werner Georg Kümmel et al., Jüdische Schriften aus hellenistisch-römischer Zeit 5 (Gütersloh: Gerd Mohn, 1980)
Sib. Or.	*Sibylline Oracles*
Slav. Vis. Dan.	*Slavonic Vision of Daniel*
Steindorff	Georg Steindorff, *Die Apokalypse des Elias, eine unbekannte Apokalypse, und Bruchstücke der Sophonias-Apokalypse* (Leipzig: J. C. Hinrichs, 1899)
Stone/ Strugnell	Michael E. Stone and John Strugnell, *The Books of*

	Elijah, Parts 1–2, SBLTT 18 (Missoula, Mont.: Scholars Press, 1979)
Strom.	Clement of Alexandria *Stromata*
SVTP	Studia in Veteris Testamenti Pseudepigrapha
T. Adam	*Testament of Adam*
TDNT	*Theological Dictionary of the New Testament* (Grand Rapids: Eerdmans, 1964)
T. Isaac	*Testament of Isaac*
T. Job	*Testament of Job*
T. Levi	*Testament of Levi*
TPAPA	*Transactions and Proceedings of the American Philological Association*
TZ	*Theologische Zeitschrift*
VigChr	*Vigiliae Christianae*
War	Josephus *The Jewish War*
Wintermute	O. S. Wintermute, "Apocalypse of Elijah," *OTP* 1:721–53
WUNT	Wissenschaftliche Untersuchungen zum Neuen Testament
ZÄS	*Zeitschrift für ägyptische Sprache und Altertumskunde*
ZKG	*Zeitschrift für Kirchengeschichte*
ZNW	*Zeitschrift für die neutestamentliche Wissenschaft*
ZPE	*Zeitschrift für Papyrologie und Epigraphik*

DEAD SEA SCROLLS

CD	Cairo *Damascus Document*
1QH	*Thanksgiving Hymns*
1QM	*War Scroll*
1QS	*Rule of the Community*
4QSb	Appendix B *(Blessings)* to 1QS
4QpNah	*Commentary on Nahum*

Sed priusquam ille veniat,
prophetabit Helias
tempore partito
medio hebdomadis axe.

But before that happens,
Elijah will prophesy
in time divided,
in the middle of the week.

—Commodian *Carmen apologeticum* 833–34

Introduction

The editors of the first volume of Studies in Antiquity and Christianity, *The Roots of Egyptian Christianity*, explained its contribution as follows: "By studying the development of Egyptian Christianity as an expression of Egyptian culture, one is better able to understand what makes Egyptian Christianity Egyptian."[1] But, as historically critical as the collected papers aimed to be, every paper focused on the religious cultures of either Alexandria or established monasticism. Strikingly absent from discussion was the suburban and rural Christianity of Greco-Egyptians and native Egyptians from the period before Pachomius, a Christianity that would form a complex of links between Alexandria and the rural monastery, between apocalyptic Judaism and apocalyptic Egyptian Christianity, between epichoric folk religion and fanatical Egyptian martyrs, between the scribal traditions of the native Egyptian priesthood and Coptic literature, and between Alexandrian ecumenism and the nationalism of Egyptian monastic culture.

The Apocalypse of Elijah is unique evidence of this phase in the development of Egyptian Christianity and of Egyptian religions of the Roman period as a whole.[2] The text, which can be dated both paleo-

1. Birger A. Pearson and James E. Goehring, Foreword, *The Roots of Egyptian Christianity*, ed. Birger A. Pearson and James E. Goehring, SAC 1 (Philadelphia: Fortress, 1986), xvii.
2. Cf. Tito Orlandi ("Coptic Literature," in *Roots of Egyptian Christianity*), who notes that the Apocalypse of Elijah was "written in a milieu characterized by the mixture of Jewish and Christian elements in the presence of some form of Egyptian nationalism. This is precisely the type of milieu where one can imagine that Coptic literature had its beginnings" (p. 58). Ewa Wipszycka's recent article "La christianisation de l'Égypte aux IVe–VIe siècles: Aspects sociaux et ethniques" (*Aegyptus* 68 [1988]:117–65) shows in

graphically and historically to a fairly definite period—the latter half of the third century C.E.—reflects in its sustained eschatological details a social group outside an urban setting, whose members were over-whelmingly concerned with the end of the world as they knew it, namely, of Egypt itself. Insofar as the text shows general influence from the book of Revelation, this group was one of the first truly "millennialist" movements; yet it seems their ideals lay not in overthrowing an increasingly oppressive Roman establishment but rather in acquiring eschatological salvation and sacred power through martyrdom.

These were not people who were entirely accustomed to the topography, lore, and genres of biblical literature; nor do they exhibit any commitment to the Gospel tradition. The places in which they oriented themselves and envisioned future events lay in Egypt; the narrative materials by which they defined themselves as Christian came not so much from the reading and recollection of actual texts as from a thriving oral lore (inherited, presumably, from Egyptian Jews as well as diverse Christian evangelists). The most striking aspect of the Apocalypse of Elijah, however, is its author's deep acquaintance with native Egyptian prophetic tradition, a world of motifs and oracles reflecting the ideology of the pharaoh. No other Christian text of this period represents such a thorough synthesis of indigenous and Christian ideas and traditions. Thus the Apocalypse of Elijah can be seen as a precursor to the Coptic "nationalism" of the later monasteries. Similarly, when placed in the context of the many other Egyptian prophetic texts copied and composed in this period, the Apocalypse of Elijah represents a Christian offshoot of this native millennialist literature—the hopes and fantasies of temple priests that a true pharaoh would return and cleanse the land.

Finally, the Coptic Apocalypse of Elijah may now stand as our best attested Elijah apocryphon from antiquity, whose historical importance is shown by the varied uses to which both Byzantine and Irish apocalyptic traditions subsequently put its contents. But what, then, do we learn about the biblical pseudonym "Elijah" from a text whose initial currency lay largely in Christian Egypt? The Apocalypse of Elijah demonstrates vividly how the heroes and authorities of biblical tradition

---

detail that the countryside was far more resistant to conversion than were the cities (not least because the language of conversion was, initially, Greek), but this does not excuse a perspective on Christianity that concentrates exclusively upon Alexandria until the rise of monastic culture.

were as meaningful to Egyptian Christians with little or no acquaintance with Judaism as they were to Jews of Palestine.

Thus, composed in the midst of the political and social turmoil of the third century, the Apocalypse of Elijah is evidence for an early Egyptian Christianity that lay outside the religious world of Alexandria and its various, interpenetrating Christianities, gnostic sects, and Hermetic groups. This Christianity was, for all intents and purposes, eschatologically oriented. In its sustained concern about deceivers and a "Lawless One" (a prototype for the Antichrist tradition), the Apocalypse of Elijah also opens a window upon the social anxieties of a millennialist sect to discern legitimate charismatic authority in a new religion fraught with diverse teachings and "deception."

The method throughout this book represents a combination of social history, literary criticism, and history of religions, focusing on how certain types of literary forms and genres function within particular social and historical situations. As contemporary historians have begun to demonstrate, the literary collection, the book or scroll, the legend or prophecy, the metaphor, and the word itself all assume vastly different meanings and values in different—and differently literate—cultures.[3] The following chapters therefore attempt to take full account of the nature of literacy, the circulation of texts, and traditional concepts of language and the written word in the Roman Egyptian culture that spawned the Elijah Apocalypse and influenced its rapid circulation over the fourth century.

3. Cf. J. Goody and I. Watt, "The Consequences of Literacy," *Comparative Studies in Society and History* 5 (1962–63):304–45; J. Goody, *The Interface between the Written and the Oral* (Cambridge: Cambridge University Press, 1987), esp. 125–208; Natalie Zemon Davis, "Printing and the People" and "Proverbial Wisdom and Popular Errors," in *Society and Culture in Early Modern France* (Stanford: Stanford University Press, 1975), 189–267, 326–46; and Carlo Ginzburg, *The Cheese and the Worms*, tr. John Tedeschi and Anne Tedeschi (Harmondsworth, Eng.: Penguin, 1982).

PART ONE

THE APOCALYPSE
OF ELIJAH
AS RELIGIOUS LITERATURE

1

The Coptic Apocalypse
of Elijah

CONTENTS OF THE APOCALYPSE OF ELIJAH

The general topic of the Apocalypse of Elijah involves deception and false leaders in the last days—how deception will manifest itself, how it will be exposed at the end, and how the righteous and the "saints" can expect vindication in an eschatological judgment and rest in a millennial paradise. Six relatively discrete sections are woven together in eschatological sequence to reflect this theme.

Opening with a prophetic commission formula—"The word of the Lord came to me saying, 'Say to this people, "Why do you add sin to your sins and anger the Lord God who created you?"'" (1:1)—which lacks any indication of identity or setting, the Apocalypse of Elijah turns quickly to a discussion in dualistic terms of the devil and the world, the coming of Christ, angelic status, and the invincibility and rewards of those professing Christ (1:2-12). This section reflects the most direct influence of early Christian (particularly Johannine) texts in the Apocalypse of Elijah. A discussion of this introduction in chapter 4 of this book addresses its contextual and rhetorical effects upon the rest of the text; chapter 3 discusses the relationship of the opening formula to Elijah pseudepigraphy.

Addressed in homiletical style to the "wise men of the land," the discussion turns to "deceivers who will multiply in the last times" and who preach that "the fast does not exist, nor did God create it" (1:13-14). The speaker argues instead for the spiritual and concrete benefits of fasting, then turns abruptly to the dangers of spiritual "double-mindedness" (1:23-27). Chapter 11 in this book proposes a historical context for this fasting passage.

Chapter 2 of the Apocalypse of Elijah (henceforth ApocEl 2) is an extended prediction of political "times of woe," similar in genre to the so-called apocalypse in Mark 13 and to the tradition of the *Sibylline Oracles* but deriving more directly from the native Egyptian apocalyptic tradition, which describes "times of distress" and their resolution under a new, God-sent pharaoh. This Egyptian tradition and its literature are outlined in chapter 7 of this book, following which chapter 8 provides a commentary on this section of the Apocalypse of Elijah, demonstrating its Egyptian inheritance and literary context. The conclusion of ApocEl 2 predicts a time of (temporary) peace and beneficence, preparing the way for the advent of the eschatological adversary.

The third chapter (ApocEl 3) consists of a series of signs and attributes of the eschatological Adversary, who is called the "Lawless One" (ⲡϣⲏⲣⲉ ⲛ̄ⲧⲁⲛⲟⲙⲓⲁ), occasionally the "Shameless One" (ⲡⲁⲧϣⲓⲡⲉ), and once the "Destructive One" (ⲡϣⲏⲣⲉ ⲙ̄ⲡⲧⲁⲕⲟ), and who functions as the antihero of the Apocalypse of Elijah. The chapter begins by comparing the advent of this deceiver to the parousia of Christ (3:1-4). A description of the true parousia is followed by a list of the miracles that the Adversary is able to perform (3:6-13). The chapter ends with a physiognomic description of the Adversary, emphasizing his ability to change appearance (3:14-18). An analysis of the nature and sources of these signs of the Adversary can be found in chapter 5 below.

The text's fourth chapter (ApocEl 4) discusses the activities of the eschatological Adversary as his influence spreads upon the earth, emphasizing his cruelty toward those who try to unveil him and concluding with a description of the decline of the earth as the saints depart and he is left in dominion.

Three successive martyrdoms are expected, having a common literary pattern: (1) "The virgin whose name is Tabitha" arises to expose and harry the Lawless One, but he throws her upon a temple platform and sucks her blood. In the morning she resurrects herself and continues her diatribe, announcing her spiritual inviolability (4:1-6).[1] (2) Enoch and Elijah return as the "two witnesses" of Revelation 11 to condemn the Lawless One. He kills them, but they arise on the fourth day to declare

---

1. For an extended discussion of this passage, see David T. M. Frankfurter, "Tabitha in the Apocalypse of Elijah," *JTS* 44 (1990):13–25.

their spiritual inviolability and the Adversary's impending doom (4:7-19).[2]

An interlude describing the gruesome tortures applied on the Lawless One's orders to "the priests of the land" follows the first two martyrdoms (4:20-23). Other priests are described as fleeing into the desert (4:24-29). Then, (3) "sixty righteous ones" wage a massive assault on the Adversary, consequently to suffer martyrdom (4:30-33).[3] Both the imagery and the ideology of martyrdom in this section of the text suggest that the author was composing in response to rumors and legends of actual executions, which flourished after the Decian or Valerian religious edicts. The interface between history and a martyrdom *ideology* obviously engendered by apocalyptic beliefs is analyzed in chapter 6 of this book.

The last chapter (ApocEl 5) may be divided into three sequential eschatological "movements," enlarging the scope of action from the terrestrial (that is, the land of Egypt) to the cosmic. The first section combines the realization by the deceived masses that their leader is the Adversary and ultimately powerless with a description of angels taking up or leading away the saints (5:1-20). Lacking the saints, the earth dries up and loses its fertility, and animals die (5:7-9, 14, 18). At this point begins the battle between the Adversary and the angels of Christ (5:20-21).

The second section begins with conflagration: God sends fire upon the earth and judges sinners (5:22-31), and the earth and mountains bear witness at this judgment (Is 1:2; Mi 6:2). Enoch and Elijah return to strike the deathblow to the Adversary, who "will perish like a serpent which has no breath in it" (5:32-35). The Adversary and his minions are locked into "the abyss."

The third section also begins with conflagration: at his parousia, modeled generally on Revelation 20–21 (5:36-39), Christ also scorches

2. The Apocalypse of Elijah doubles the eschatological return of Enoch and Elijah in a manner unique in early Christian literature: at 4:7-19 they are martyred, resurrected, and assumed up to heaven; and at 5:32 they return to kill the Adversary. Richard Bauckham has shown, in an exhaustive study of the Enoch/Elijah tradition ("The Martyrdom of Enoch and Elijah: Jewish or Christian?" *JBL* 95, 3 [1976]:447–58), that the former image was a Christian tradition influenced but not based on Rv 11:4-12 (to which ApocEl 4:7-19 closely conforms), while the latter image of their simple return at the eschaton was Jewish. Whereas each of the texts he analyzes represents either the Jewish or the Christian tradition, only the Apocalypse of Elijah has both (see also idem, "Enoch and Elijah in the Coptic Apocalypse of Elijah," *Studia Patristica* 16, 2 [1985]:69–76).

3. This scene perhaps recalls the legend of the sixty *hasidim* in 1 Macc 7:16-17.

the earth (5:37). A "new heaven and new earth," between which the saints can pass easily, are established. The time period of Christ's rule is specified as a millennium, although what follows this millennium is not mentioned.

HISTORIES OF THE APOCALYPSE OF ELIJAH:
A REVIEW OF RESEARCH

Previous scholarship on the Coptic Elijah Apocalypse has adhered to two principal fields of inquiry: the relationship of this Elijah apocryphon to those cited by rabbinic and patristic sources, and the historical interpretation of its "political" prophecies (in ApocEl 2).

When Georg Steindorff first published the Berlin and Paris codices as distinct apocalypses of Elijah and Zephaniah, he stated (with no particular argument) that "the Apocalypse of Elijah derives from a Jewish *Grundschrift* which referred particularly to the Jerusalem Temple and the re-establishment of the holy places."[4] He then concluded, from the profusion of Egyptian references, that the text arose among Egyptian Jews. Finally, Steindorff ventured two historical identifications of figures in ApocEl 2: (1) that an "Assyrian King" described in the beginning of the oracles represents Antiochus Epiphanes; and (2) that a "King of Peace" who succeeds him refers to Popillius Laenus, the Roman ambassador who forced Antiochus to leave Egypt.[5]

Immediately following Steindorff's edition, Wilhelm Bousset made a detailed study of the Apocalypse of Elijah.[6] Agreeing that the first part of ApocEl 2 must be Jewish (largely on the basis of the slogan "The name of God is One," present in 2:10; cf. 2:49), he suggested as a *terminus post quem* for the *Grundschrift* the period of Trajan and Hadrian—that is, the era of the Jewish revolt (116-117 C.E.).[7] The text therefore constituted a series of different redactions. The second layer, indicated by the description of Assyrians and Persians and a king from "the City of the Sun" (2:42-53), referred (through comparison to *Sib. Or.* 13:151) to Odenath of Palmyra and thus established a third-century C.E. Jewish redaction.

4. Georg Steindorff, *Die Apokalypse des Elias, eine unbekannte Apokalypse, und Bruchstücke der Sophonias-Apokalypse* (Leipzig: J. C. Hinrichs, 1899), 19.
5. Ibid., 75 n. 7, 77 n. 3. On Antiochus and Popillius, see Edwyn R. Bevan, *House of Ptolemy* (Chicago: Ares, 1968), 286.
6. Wilhelm Bousset, "Beiträge zur Geschichte der Eschatologie: Die Apokalypse des Elias," *ZKG* 20 (1899):103–12.
7. Ibid., 105.

Because the text seemed to place considerable hope in the Persians *against* the Assyrians, Bousset concluded that the context of this redaction was Jewish fears of Odenath, trust in Persian deliverance, and anticipation of a messianic king during the last quarter of the third century C.E.[8] The description of Christ immediately after the mention of the messianic king (3:2-4) therefore signified a subsequent Christian redaction, whose intention was in part to show the false hopes of the prior Jewish editor.[9]

But although some oracles could be understood as portraying the circumstances and eschatological hopes of third-century Jews (e.g., "liberation" of Jews, 2:39), others bore no direct correspondences.[10] Indeed, Bousset could only connect such oracles as "four kings will fight with three" (2:43b) with "the confusion of pretenders during that period of the Roman Empire."[11] Thus Bousset's certainty in redaction criticism and historical correspondence only went so far—and then only for Egyptian Judaism. The rest of the oracles were either attenuated to the point of incomprehensibility or deliberately vague.

At the same time as Bousset's analysis of the Apocalypse of Elijah, there appeared a short review of the Steindorff edition by the great French Egyptologist Gaston Maspero.[12] Although agreeing that the text was probably Jewish with a considerable Christian overlay, Maspero was the first scholar to point out the native Egyptian background of many of the oracles.[13] He concluded by suggesting that

> perhaps one might come to think, without too much horror, that the Jewish apocalypses [from Egypt] which were adapted or imitated by Christians were themselves preceded by rudimentary sorts of apocalypses composed by Pagans, some in Greek, others in the native language of Egypt.[14]

---

8. Ibid., 106–8. Bousset's assumption that the king from the City of the Sun is opposed to the Persians in ApocEl 2:46 does not fit the text. As O. S. Wintermute ("Apocalypse of Elijah," in *OTP* 1:743 n. 13) and Wolfgang Schrage ("Die Elia-Apokalypse," in *Apokalypsen*, Jüdische Schriften aus hellenistisch-römischer Zeit 5, ed. Werner Georg Kümmel et al. [Gütersloh: Gerd Mohn, 1980], 222) show, the king from the City of the Sun must be identified with the Righteous King of 2:51 rather than with the Assyrian King of 2:47b.

9. Bousset, "Beiträge," 111.

10. Ibid., 107–8.

11. Ibid.

12. Gaston Maspero, review of *Die Apokalypse des Elias*, by Georg Steindorff, *Journal des savants* (1899):31–43.

13. Ibid., 38, 40–43.

14. Ibid., 43.

Maspero's intuition of a native Egyptian background to various elements of the text has since been corroborated through publications and discussions of Egyptian prophetic literature of the Roman period, and the second section of this book is partly meant to bear out Maspero's idea.

Oscar von Lemm continued the German predilection for historical decoding in his 1904 philological discussion of the Apocalypse of Elijah, suggesting a Jewish *Grundschrift* from the early post-Exilic period.[15] The wars between Persian and Assyrian kings in 2:39-50, he imagined, must reflect Cyrus's assault on Nebuchadnezzar in 540 B.C.E., which led to the restoration of Palestine to the Jews and the building of the Second Temple. Presuming—as von Lemm did—that this section of the Apocalypse of Elijah represents a Jewish author's perspective, this interpretation would explain the passage's depiction of Assyrians (thus denoting Babylonians!) as evil and Persians as salvific. Such a "literal" historical understanding of "Persian" and "Assyrian," however, conflicts with the Egyptian locus of the events described: Memphis, Kos, the Nile. It was Cambyses, not Cyrus, who invaded Egypt, and he was hardly lauded for this act in Egyptian and Coptic tradition. Further, von Lemm did not address the meaning such an ancient recollection would have had in an Egyptian Christian composition.

Consequently, Emil Schürer discussed the Coptic Apocalypse of Elijah in the context of "Lost Pseudepigrapha" in his *History of the Jewish People in the Time of Jesus Christ* (1909). Demonstrating the text's saturation with Christian elements, he expressed doubt that a Jewish *Grundlage* lay beneath it, or that the text was in any way a development of another Elijah apocalypse. The historical ApocEl 2 that describes Persian battles Schürer ascribed generally to the political fears of the late third century C.E.[16]

When it has been cited, Schürer's more conservative assessment of the Apocalypse of Elijah has been viewed as an extreme and unpenetrating opinion that could be disregarded in the interest of showing Jewish origins.[17] Yet it represents the beginning of a restrained current of scholarly views, one that will be followed in this study.

15. Oscar von Lemm, "Kleine koptische Studien—XXVI: Bemerkungen zu einigen Stellen der koptischen Apokalypsen, 13–18," *Bulletin de l'académie impériale des sciences de St.-Pétersbourg* 21 (1904):228.

16. Émil Schürer, *Geschichte des jüdischen Volkes im Zeitalter Jesu Christi*, 4 vols. (4th ed.; Leipzig: Hinrischs'sche, 1909), 3:368.

17. E.g., see Jean-Marc Rosenstiehl, *L'Apocalypse d'Élie: Introduction, traduction, et notes*, Textes et études pour servir à l'histoire du Judaisme intertestamentaire 1 (Paris:

Jean-Marc Rosenstiehl's 1972 commentary on the Apocalypse of Elijah argued in most detail for an early Jewish "core."[18] Acknowledging a third-century Jewish layer to the text, Rosenstiehl began with Bousset's theory that the end of ApocEl 2 reflects events in Palmyra. Indeed, he claimed to identify even closer correspondences than Bousset did between the oracles of the text and historical events during the reign of Valerian and its aftermath.[19] As support for the theory that a Jewish author was placing messianic hopes in the Palmyrenes after Odenath's devastation of Babylonian Jewry, Rosenstiehl referred to the evidence that Odenath's wife, Zenobia (who was inclined toward exotic religions), reconstructed an Egyptian synagogue during her invasion.[20] Thus Jews had reason to extol Zenobia's forces as liberating, he reasoned, reversing Bousset's original theory that the Jewish author feared the Syrians and hoped for the Persians.[21]

Rosenstiehl's most radical theory about the origins of the Apocalypse of Elijah, however, was his reading of Essene traditions in the beginning of ApocEl 2 and much of ApocEl 3.[22] This interpretation, influenced by the research of Marc Philonenko, viewed ApocEl 3 as composed largely of allegories for the Qumran community's experiences: Tabitha represented the Essene sect, the adversarial Lawless One represented Hyrcanus II (the hypothetical persecutor of the Qumran Essenes), and the two kings in the beginning of ApocEl 2 stood for Pompey and Caesar, the Roman rulers at the time of the Essenes. Thus Rosenstiehl put the first draft of the text in a first-century Egyptian Jewish milieu, with strong connections to the Qumran Essenes.[23] But with no more certain indications of a date in the first century than the roughest historical analogies and coming as it did from a school that has tended to see Essene influence in virtually all Second Temple literature, Rosenstiehl's Essene theory has found few followers.[24]

Paul Guethner, 1972), 61–62. James H. Charlesworth (*The Pseudepigrapha and Modern Research, with a Supplement*, Septuagint and Cognate Studies 7 [Chico, Calif.: Scholars Press, 1981], 95), who decided that "most scholars concur that [ApocEl] derives from an earlier Jewish work," did not even cite Schürer.

18. Rosenstiehl. The sixty-year hiatus in ApocEl scholarship is doubtless due to the discovery of the Qumran library (a considerable influence on Rosenstiehl) and the consequent projects to collect all the pseudepigrapha in translations and commentaries.

19. Ibid., 64–67.

20. *CPJ* 3:144 (= no. 1449); Rosenstiehl, 67; cf. Jacques Schwartz, "Les palmyréniens et l'Égypte," *Bulletin de la société archéologique d'Alexandrie* 40 (1953):77.

21. Bousset, "Beiträge," 108.

22. Rosenstiehl, 68–73.

23. Ibid., 76.

24. See the review of Rosenstiehl by P. M. Parvis, *JTS* 24 (1973):588–89; cf. Adela

Nevertheless, Rosenstiehl's serious discussion of Egyptian literary and mythological influences on the Apocalypse of Elijah established the necessity of considering native materials when interpreting the Apocalypse of Elijah.[25] Such a literary–historical perspective has since been offered by Wolfgang Schrage.[26] Citing not only the Hellenistic Egyptian *Potter's Oracle* and its associated texts but also Greco-Egyptian legends of Alexander, Schrage showed in even more detail than Maspero the complex of literary traditions in which the Apocalypse of Elijah participated.[27]

However, these literary observations hardly qualified Schrage's assumption that the text must pivot upon *ex eventu* references to historical figures and his consequent search for specific correspondences at the end of ApocEl 2. While attributing particular details—for example, numerology—to literary traditions inherited from the Bible and other sources, Schrage identified the king from the "City of the Sun" as Zenobia, a significant correction of Bousset and Rosenstiehl, and argued that the author had already witnessed her expulsion by Aurelian in 272. This reinterpretation depended on (1) the identification of the "king from the sun" not, as Bousset thought, with the Assyrian King—that is, an evil ruler—but with the "Righteous King"; (2) the correspondence of "Persians" with the Palmyrenes; and (3) the "Assyrians" signifying Rome.[28]

Schrage's implication that a woman could be symbolized as a "king" and the Palmyrenes—Syrians—as Persians (who were the enemies of Palmyra during the third century) obviously assumes that the writer had such a limited selection of allegorical signifiers at his disposal that these contradictory representations were necessary, an assumption made rather doubtful by the large repertoire of symbols characteristic of the *Sibylline Oracles* (to which Schrage often refers for parallels to his identifications).[29] But if the dramatis personae are so deliberately limited in

---

Yarbro Collins, "The Early Christian Apocalypses," *Semeia* 14 (1979):99. Charlesworth alone follows Rosenstiehl (*Pseudepigrapha and Modern Research*, 95).

25. Rosenstiehl, 43–47. Rosenstiehl's uncritical use of R. Reitzenstein and H. H. Schaeder ('Das Töpferorakel," in idem, *Studien zum antiken Synkretismus aus Iran und Griechenland* [Leipzig: Teubner, 1926], 38–51) in interpreting the *Potter's Oracle* led him to see Iranian traditions influencing the Apocalypse of Elijah (Rosenstiehl, 43–46).

26. Schrage, 194–288.

27. Ibid., 212–17.

28. Ibid., 222–25.

29. A third-century pseudonymous author who "predicted" Zenobia (who presented herself as the new Cleopatra) as a savior–king would have had a considerable "eschatological woman" tradition from which to draw appropriate symbols (cf. *Sib. Or.* 3.75-82, 356-62; 8.75-80, 194-212; Valentin Nikiprowetzky, *La troisième Sibylle*, Études

this section, what certain indications are there that historical events are portrayed *ex eventu*—that the entire episode is not a prophetic fantasy? Moreover, Schrage's suggestion of such detailed correspondences presumes a considerable degree of political awareness on the part of the author, a presumption that might be said to contrast with the overtly fantastic nature of most of the text. Thus Schrage's analysis begs certain important historical and theoretical questions.

Schrage follows Schürer in considering the Apocalypse of Elijah, as it stands, to be the composition (not redaction) of a Christian author who himself made use of diverse early Jewish traditions.[30] Schrage's commentary therefore represents a step away from facile "core" theories but demonstrates the problems inherent in cursory attempts to associate an Egyptian oracular or prophetic text too closely with events of any period.

O. S. Wintermute's 1983 edition of the text sought for the first time to *prove* a Jewish "core," this time through redaction criticism.[31] Limiting himself to the parallel martyrdom stories of ApocEl 4, Wintermute suggested that the most "primitive" one, describing the martyrdom of the "sixty righteous" (4:30-33), must have been original, and that it functioned as the model for the description of Tabitha's and Enoch/Elijah's previous martyrdoms (4:1-6, 7-19).[32] Many factors might have led to the parallel construction of ApocEl 4, however, above all the compositional style of the author;[33] and such a small portion of a stylistically complex text is hardly the basis for a general redactional theory of Jewish origins. Indeed, Wintermute was then led to make such statements as "we are inclined to confront the present section with the *a priori* assumption that it contains an early Jewish stratum that has been supplemented by a Christian editor."[34]

Still, Wintermute refrained from proposing any historical correspondences and instead summarized the perspectives on ApocEl 2 in three different hermeneutical interpretations:

---

juives 9 (Paris: Mouton, 1970), 143–50). Schrage suggests that a hypothetical, brief alliance that Zenobia forged with Shapur (reflected in *Sib. Or.* 13.111) might have led some Jews to see Palmyrenes and Persians as one entity (223). Not only is this perspective doubtful within the more general historical circumstances of Palmyrene–Persian animosity, but the historicity of this alliance has itself been questioned (cf. A. Alföldi, "The Crisis of the Empire," *CAH* 12 [1939], 178–79).

30. Schrage, 206.
31. Wintermute, 721–53.
32. Ibid., 725.
33. See Rosenstiehl, 28–37, and Schrage's more extensive argument, 217–20.
34. Wintermute, 726.

1. All of the kings are drawn from a literary tradition, and the author himself believes or speculates that at some future date the first of these kings will appear.
2. Some of the kings had already appeared, but the author casts his work in the style of a seer who desires to warn his contemporaries of the imminent end of the age by joining their own history to that of the final age and casting it all in the form of a future prophecy.
3. The author has made use of a prior literary tradition or even a complete apocalypse from an earlier time, which he brought up to date by modifying details of the predicted future to conform more accurately to the actual course of history as he knew it.[35]

Interpretations 2 and 3 represent those made by previous scholars in search of historical and redactional specificity. By contrast, scholarly attention to native Egyptian literary tradition opened up the first alternative.[36]

Rollin Kearns's 1986 discussion of the influence of Egyptian prophecy on the Christian "son of man" tradition again imposed a rigid historical determinism on the symbolism and narrative of the Apocalypse of Elijah.[37] Kearns attempted to improve upon Schrage's correspondence between the king from the "City of the Sun" and Zenobia by referring this messianic figure to Waballath, Zenobia's son and puppet ruler during the Palmyrene occupation of Alexandria.[38] The application of the oracle to this new king constituted a traditional use of "Isis–Horus" propaganda to justify a foreign kingship.[39]

Kearns's detailed history of Egyptian prophetic and oracular literature does exhibit the background against which the Apocalypse of Elijah should be read. He has been criticized, however, for drawing his historical correspondences too closely,[40] and this use of Waballath is a case in point. Evidence exists neither for Waballath's significance as a ruler nor for propaganda arguing his legitimacy.[41] Finally, Kearns's

---

35. Ibid., 723.
36. Cf. ibid., 723–24.
37. Rollin Kearns, *Das Traditionsgefüge um den Menschensohn* (Tübingen: Mohr [Siebeck], 1986).
38. Ibid., 96–100.
39. Ibid., 98–99.
40. See remarks by John Collins in his review of Kearns, in *JBL* 107 (1988):538.
41. Cf. Schwartz, "Les palmyréniens," 76. Waballath's appearance on coins with Aurelian in 270 showed not his coimperial pretensions but Zenobia's arrogating of his father's title, Corrector Orientis, for her son. There is evidence that Zenobia conciliated certain Greco-Egyptian sentiments (and devoted considerable propaganda to enhance this effect by appearing as a new Cleopatra; cf. Arthur Stein, "Kallinikos von Petrai," *Hermes* 58 [1923]:454–55; Glen W. Bowersock, "The Miracle of Memnon," *BASP* 21

answer to the gender of the "king from the sun" still does not account for the other problems involved in making a close connection between the Palmyrene invasion and the Apocalypse of Elijah.

The history of scholarship on the Apocalypse of Elijah, and on ApocEl 2 especially, represents a series of attempts to prove a preconceived Jewish core and—in the service of these attempts—to associate the oracles of ApocEl 2 to any series of historical events that would have had an immediate impact upon Jews.[42] Coincidentally, the historical period that has achieved some scholarly consensus in this regard, the last quarter of the third century C.E., also agrees with the *terminus ante quem* posed by the manuscripts of the Apocalypse of Elijah, so one cannot fault it on textual grounds.

Because of the explicit references to Egypt and the manifest use of Egyptian oracle tradition, all commentators have acknowledged that the text took its form in Egypt; however, no commentators seeking a Jewish *Grundschrift* or even a Jewish redaction in the late third century have addressed the virtually complete lack of evidence for any Jewish activity in Egypt at this time.[43]

Finally, all but Wintermute have assumed that the major function of oracles and their symbols is to recast historical events allegorically, as *vaticinia ex eventus*, and that the text itself can always be dated by the last "historical" reference before the text lurches into imaginary eschatology.

DATING

Early attempts at dating the Apocalypse of Elijah presupposed that it was a Christian redaction of a Jewish Elijah apocalypse—presumably the one cited by Origen as the source of 1 Cor 2:9—and that therefore it contained a "core" deriving from the first century C.E. or B.C.E.; but those who propose Jewish origins for texts that express any degree of Christian self-definition carry the burden of proof. Inevitably, the "Chris-

---

[1984]:31–32), but we cannot deduce from this and from the existence of the prediction of a "king from the sun" that the Apocalypse of Elijah was designed as propaganda for Waballath.

42. See the wise remarks by B. Dehandschutter, "Les Apocalypses d'Élie," in *Élie le prophète: Bible, tradition, iconographie,* ed. Gerard F. Willems (Louvain: Peeters, 1988), 64–66.

43. See *CPJ* 1:94, although cf. A. Kasher, "The Jewish Community of Oxyrhynchus in the Roman Period," *JJS* 32 (1981):153–57, who perhaps draws too much from CPJ 473.

tianization" of preexisting Jewish texts is a continuous process rather than a cross-cultural plundering; and it is precisely in this cultural continuity between Judaism and Christianity—a continuity that allowed such Christian compilations as 2 Esdras and the *Testaments of the Twelve Patriarchs*—that one should expect the composition of biblical pseudepigrapha by professing Christians.[44] Such classic attempts as that by R. H. Charles to dissect apocalyptic texts for their cores and interpolations have been shown to rest on dubious presuppositions,[45] and similar analyses of the Apocalypse of Elijah have demonstrated little development in redaction-critical methodology. Thus the following discussion of the date of the Apocalypse of Elijah will focus on the Coptic (once Greek) text at hand, rather than a putative Jewish core lying within this text.

Terminus ante quem

An Achmimic manuscript of the Apocalypse of Elijah is the earliest evidence of the text, dating from the beginning of the fourth century C.E.[46] This would suggest that the latest period in which the present Apocalypse of Elijah might have been composed in Greek would be the last quarter of the third century.[47]

Terminus post quem

Wintermute has rightly noted that the earliest date the Apocalypse of Elijah (in its present form) could have been composed is bound by the

44. See James H. Charlesworth, "Christian and Jewish Self-Definition in Light of the Christian Additions to the Apocryphal Writings," in *Jewish and Christian Self-Definition,* vol. 2: *Aspects of Judaism in the Greco-Roman Period,* ed. E. P. Sanders et al. (Philadelphia: Fortress, 1981), 27–55, 310–15; and the apt remarks by Marinus de Jonge, "The Testaments of the Twelve Patriarchs: Christian and Jewish," in *Jewish Eschatology, Early Christian Christology, and the Testaments of the Twelve Patriarchs* (Leiden: Brill, 1991), 233–43.

45. Cf. James Barr, "Jewish Apocalyptic in Recent Scholarly Study," *BJRL* 58 (1975):9–35; and John J. Collins, "Apocalyptic Literature," in *Early Judaism and Its Modern Interpreters,* ed. Robert A. Kraft and George W. E. Nickelsburg (Atlanta: Scholars Press, 1986), 348–50.

46. Berlin staatl. Museen, Abteil. P.1862 and Paris, Bibl. Nat. Copte. 135 (see pp. 21–23, below, on manuscripts). On its dating, cf. Steindorff, 6 (late fourth/early fifth century); Carl Schmidt, "Der Kolophon des Ms. Orient. 7594 des Britischen Museums," *Sitzungsberichte der preussischen Akademie der Wissenschaften, Philosophisch-Historisch Klasse* (1925):317 (fourth century); and Viktor Stegemann, *Koptische Paläographie* (Heidelberg: Im Selbstverlag, von F. Bilabel, 1936), 11b–12a, fig. 1 (third century). Rosenstiehl (20); Schrage (201); and Pietersma (1) all place the ms. at late third/early fourth century.

47. Steindorff, 18.

availability of the New Testament texts reflected in its composition.[48] The recollection of Johannine literature and the book of Revelation would thus signal the middle of the second century as the earliest date.[49]

The introductory passage of the Apocalypse of Elijah is shared by the *Apocalypse of Paul* (*Apoc. Paul* 3) and might conceivably derive from a text or fragment that existed before either of these texts.[50] If so, the *terminus ante quem* of such a source would be the approximate date of these texts: the second half of the third century C.E.[51] There is no possible *terminus post quem* for such a fragment; nor can one presume that its biblical phraseology indicates Jewish authorship. If each text employed the passage as a fragment, moreover, there is no necessary historical relationship between its lost continuation and the texts that made use of it. But if the fragment did belong to an Elijah apocryphon, then it may not be a coincidence that the apocalypses of Paul and Elijah both contain the type of materials attributed to lost Elijah apocrypha by rabbinic and patristic sources (respectively, a tour of hell and eschatological details). That is, both apocalypses could have been composed as new revelations in an "Elianic revelation" tradition.

Chapter 8 will discuss in detail the debt that ApocEl 2 owes to Egyptian prophetic literary tradition, particularly to the native oracles that were circulating during the time of its composition. Chief among these are the Oracles of the Lamb and the Potter, which have been dated in origin to the Hellenistic period but are extant only in papyri of the Roman period.[52] While the Apocalypse of Elijah participates in the same literary and ideological tradition as these "pagan" texts, however, there is no specific evidence of dependence upon actual manuscripts of these texts.[53] Therefore one can date the ideology, sentiments, imagery, and even oracular sayings of this chapter of the Apocalypse of Elijah to the Hellenistic period (and even much earlier) without affecting the date of the complete Apocalypse of Elijah as a historical composition.

48. Wintermute, 729–30.

49. Manuscript evidence for these latter texts' circulation in Egypt does not begin until the third century, however.

50. See below, pp. 28–29 and Appendix.

51. On dating *Apoc. Paul*, see R. P. Casey, "The Apocalypse of Paul," *JTS* 34 (1933):28, 31.

52. See C. C. McCown, "Hebrew and Egyptian Apocalyptic Literature," *HTR* 18 (1925):392–401; and Ludwig Koenen, "Die Prophezeiungen des 'Töpfers,'" *ZPE* 2 (1968):186–94.

53. *Pace* Françoise Dunand, "L'Oracle du Potier et la formation de l'apocalyptique en Égypte," in *L'Apocalyptique*, ed. M. Philonenko and M. Simon, Études d'histoire des religions 3 (Paris: Paul Geuthner, 1977), 56.

Attempts at Closer Dating

Most scholars have seen the present form of ApocEl 2 as reflecting—even if not directly—the political turmoil of the late third century C.E. and therefore have placed the text's extant form toward its later terminus: that is, around 260–295. Debate, as we have seen, has concerned the dating of earlier *Vorlagen*. Chapters 9–11 discuss in detail the external reasons for a later third-century date.

A *terminus post quem* may also be inferred from the details and ideology of martyrdom in ApocEl 4. These materials probably reflect the martyrological lore that circulated around the Decian edict in 249–251 C.E., with the concomitant development of the ideal of martyrdom among Egyptian Christians.[54]

QUESTIONS OF PROVENANCE AND MILIEU

The abundant references to Egypt and Egyptian cities make an Egyptian milieu certain. The favorable view of Memphis and the use of a negative Hellenistic euphemism for Alexandria, discussed below in chapter 8, suggest that the composition took place in Egypt proper; the presence of one Achmimic and three different Sahidic Coptic manuscripts also suggests that the text had particular popularity among Coptic speakers. The knowledge of and ability to use Egyptian prophetic traditions suggest that the author, and presumably his audience, were accustomed to such language and traditions; and because these traditions tended to have nationalist overtones, it is conceivable that the text's milieu shared such sentiments toward Egypt and its mythological status. Therefore any reconstruction of the milieu must take into account both traditional and Christian aspects of the text.

The eschatological focus of the text, its use of sectarian nomenclature for both dramatis personae and audience (see chapter 4, pp. 98–101), and its apparent use of the book of Revelation (see chapter 2, pp. 37–38) all suggest a millennialist social setting. Evidence for one such millennialist movement in Egypt at this time corroborates this sociological inference, as is further discussed in chapter 10. The attention to fasting and the cultivation of psychic "single-mindedness" (1:23-27), combined

---

54. See below, chap. 6. Bauckham has sought to corroborate the text's "later" dating by pointing out the relatively late stage of the Enoch/Elijah legend in ApocEl 4:7-19 ("Martyrdom of Enoch and Elijah," 458).

with the text's fascination with martyrdom, may indicate ascetic tendencies (see chapter 11), and the reference to "deceivers" who deny fasting may be a hyperbolic attempt to describe a recent dispute over the proper limits of ascetic practice (see chapter 11). Yet no social organization or hierarchy (such as is found in established monasticism) is apparent; the text shows no specific interest, positive or negative, in Alexandrian ecclesiastical hierarchy or authority; and there are no reflections of (purely) theological disputes.

MANUSCRIPT CHARACTER

Five manuscripts or fragments witness to the Apocalypse of Elijah, although their variations are significant enough to suggest a number of different recensions and (in light of the state of the manuscripts) even the independent circulation of fragments of the text without authority or title.[55] Although four of these manuscripts are in Coptic, the presence of a Greek fragment of the text verifies that the Apocalypse was originally written, or took its present form, in Greek. The manuscripts themselves range in date (on paleographical grounds) from the early fourth through the fifth centuries C.E.

One manuscript in Achmimic Coptic (designated Ach), collated and edited by Steindorff from Berlin, staatl. Museen, Abteilung P.1862 and Paris, Bibl. Nat. Copte 135, came from the library of Shenoute's White Monastery.[56] Included in the same codex was a recension of the *Apocalypse of Zephaniah*, and at one time the two texts were understood together to constitute the Apocalypse of Elijah.[57] This manuscript, from the early fourth century C.E., contains the beginning and end of the Apocalypse of Elijah but is missing significant portions of the middle. It provides the only text of the Apocalypse's conclusion. But though it has ordinarily been taken as the earliest text,[58] the Achmimic manuscript has

55. For a detailed discussion of the texts and their relationships, see Pietersma, 1, 7–18.

56. Steindorff, 66–107. See Maspero's account of the find in his review of Steindorff, 1–2 n. 5.

57. Urbain-Bouriant, "Les papyrus d'Akhmim (Fragments de manuscrits en dialectes bachmourique et thébain)," *Mémoires publiés par les membres de la mission archéologique française au Caire* 1, 2 (1885):245–46, 260–79; and L. Stern, "Die koptische Apocalypse des Sophonias, mit einem Anhang über den untersahidischen Dialekt," *ZÄS* (1886):115–35. See H.F.D. Sparks, "Introduction to the Apocalypse of Elijah," *AOT*, 753–54. This view is followed by Wilhelm Bousset, *The Antichrist Legend*, trans. A. H. Keane (London: Hutchinson, 1896), 87–91.

58. This is the text given precedence in the translations of Kuhn, Schrage, and

been shown more recently to represent an independent Coptic recension of, presumably, a common Greek *Vorlage*.[59]

The recently published fourth/fifth-century Chester Beatty manuscript (P.Chester Beatty 2018) in Sahidic Coptic is now our most complete copy of the Apocalypse of Elijah, and on text-critical grounds may lie closest to an "original" Greek text.[60] The text stops considerably short of the end, however, and line fillers at this point suggest that the scribe himself may not have known the end.[61] This text has been designated Sa³.

The most interesting aspect of Sa³ is its unique use of a punctuation system that distinguishes not grammatical units but rather syllabic units, evidently to facilitate reading aloud. Such punctuation must have been fairly novel in the ancient Mediterranean world, where written documents generally lacked such visual conveniences as word separation, punctuation, or demarcated sections.[62] Often readers with even a moderate degree of literacy were unable to make sense of a manuscript: Hermas, for example, describes copying an entire book, yet says, "I was unable to distinguish the syllables" until granted divine *gnōsis* (*Herm. Vis.* 2.1.4–2.2.1). The several punctuation systems deployed in Sa³, however, divided the words even further, into phonemes.[63] This fact should illuminate the performative context of the Apocalypse of Elijah and presumably other early Coptic texts not obviously homiletic in nature: the text was to be read aloud to an audience, rather than privately by an individual; and reading such a text did not require a high degree of literacy.[64]

Another manuscript of the Apocalypse of Elijah in fourth/fifth-century Sahidic Coptic (designated Sa¹), also found in the White Monas-

Wintermute. Rosenstiehl gives a simultaneous translation of the Achmimic text and Steindorff's Sahidic text (discussed below, pp. 299–300).

59. See Pietersma, 12–15; also Pierre Lacau, "Remarques sur le manuscrit akhmimique des apocalypses de Sophonie et d'Élie," *Journal asiatique* 254 (1966):169–70, 187–95.

60. Pietersma, 18.

61. See Pietersma, 6, 88 (facsimile of last page).

62. See Paul J. Achtemeier, "*Omne verbum sonat:* The New Testament and the Oral Environment of Western Antiquity," *JBL* 109 (1990):10–11.

63. Pietersma, 2. See the linguistic analysis of this phenomenon by Nathalie Beaux, "Pour une paléographie du papyrus Chester Beatty 2018," *Études coptes* 3, Cahiers de la bibliothèque copte 4 (Louvain: Peeters, 1988), 46–47.

64. See Herbert C. Youtie's discussion of the "illiterate" lector in P.Oxy 2673 ("AGRAMMATOS: An Aspect of Greek Society in Egypt," *HSCP* 75 [1971]:163); although cf. Ewa Wipszycka's counterhypothesis ("Un lecteur qui ne sait pas écrire ou un chrétien qui ne veut pas souiller? [P.Oxy. XXXIII 2673]," *ZPE* 50 [1983]:117–21). On

tery, shares the manuscript inventory Paris copte 135 with the Achmimic text. Also collated and edited by Steindorff,[65] this manuscript included another, Sahidic recension of the *Apocalypse of Zephaniah;* however, it lacks the beginning, the end, and part of the middle of the Apocalypse of Elijah.

A colophon to a biblical codex in the British Museum (BM 7594), written in a Greek script but in Sahidic Coptic, was found in 1925 to represent the opening passages of the Apocalypse of Elijah, although the title was not included.[66] The script is dated to the mid-fourth century. There is no evidence that the scribe knew much more than this beginning of the text; therefore this manuscript may provide evidence that fragments of the Apocalypse of Elijah circulated independently in third- and fourth-century Egypt. This colophon text is designated Sa[2].

Of special significance is a fourth-century papyrus fragment with several lines of Greek (PSI 7, designated Grk), which matches on the verso the Achmimic text of one of the final scenes of the Apocalypse of Elijah.[67] The recto side, however, cannot be reconstructed to parallel any other part of the Achmimic text, which suggests that the Greek fragment contains another or earlier recension of the Apocalypse of Elijah than that of the Achmimic manuscript. Because the conclusion of the text is missing in all of the Sahidic manuscripts, it is impossible to say whether this different recension matches any of the Sahidic versions.

The evidence of the manuscripts shows that a variety of recensions of the Apocalypse of Elijah already existed by the end of the fourth century (Grk, Ach, Sa[3]) and that the Apocalypse of Elijah also circulated in fragments (Sa[2], Sa[3]). The binding together of the apocalypses of Elijah and Zephaniah in Ach and Sa[1] codices further suggests an early historical association between the texts, a hypothesis corroborated by their tandem appearance in medieval canon lists.

---

public performance of Scripture, see William A. Graham, *Beyond the Written Word: Oral Aspects of Scripture in the History of Religion* (Cambridge: Cambridge University Press, 1987), 129. The recognition of syllables was the first stage in the teaching of literacy in Pachomian monasticism; see the Pachomian *Praecepta* 139b, in Armand Veilleux, ed. and tr., *Pachomian Koinonia*, 3 vols., Cistercian Studies Series 45–47 (Kalamazoo, Mich.: Cistercian Press, 1980–82), 2:166.

65. Steindorff, 115–45.

66. E. A. Wallis Budge, *Coptic Biblical Texts in the Dialect of Upper Egypt* (London: British Museum, 1912; reprint, New York: AMS, 1977), lv–lvii, 270–71; and Schmidt, "Der Kolophon," 312–21.

67. PSI 7, in *Papiri Greci e Latini* 1 (Florence: Ariani, 1912), 16–17; and "Appendix: The Greek *Apocalypse of Elijah,*" in Pietersma, 91–94.

WITNESSES

Several rabbinic and patristic sources refer to Elijah apocrypha that are no longer extant. Only four sources, however, betray a definite knowledge of the Apocalypse of Elijah as gleaned from the Coptic texts; and several other texts seem to have known either the extant Apocalypse of Elijah or its traditions.

Didymus the Blind

The earliest source referring directly to the extant Apocalypse of Elijah is Didymus the Blind (fourth century). In his *Commentary on Ecclesiastes* (235, ll. 26–28) concerning Qoh 8:4b-5a, Didymus says:

> It is true that nobody says of the truth of God, "What will you do?" as also of the shameless [ἀναιδής] and impudent king. And this shameless one perhaps can take the countenance of the Antichrist. For in this regard, in the Prophecy of Elijah, a certain girl [κόρη], having risen up and accused him, called him "Shameless."[68]

This allusion clearly matches the description of the heroine and martyr Tabitha, who pursues and harries the Shameless One in ApocEl 4:1-6. It is important to note, however, that Didymus calls his source the "Prophecy of Elijah" whereas elsewhere he ascribes to an "Apocalypse of Elijah" a vision that does not exist in the extant text of the same name.[69]

The Tiburtine Sibyls

The Greek Tiburtine Sibyl, which was expanded in 503–504 C.E. from an earlier Sibylline prophecy of ca. 378–390, contains a final description of the eschaton whose details (among which is another, anonymous reference to the eschatological Tabitha) show a clear dependence on the Apocalypse of Elijah.[70] The author assigned oracles, signs, and eschatological events from the Apocalypse of Elijah (particularly ApocEl 2) in somewhat rearranged order to a "ninth generation" of the world.

---

68. Didymus the Blind, *Commentary on Ecclesiastes*, tr. and ed. Bärbel Krebber and Johannes Kramer, *Didymos der Blinde: Kommentar zum Ecclesiastes (Tura-Papyrus)*, vol. 4: *Kommentar zu Eccl. Kap. 7–8, 8, 16* (Bonn: Rudolf Habelt, 1972), 136–37. On Didymus's knowledge of ApocEl generally, see ibid., 159–61.
69. Didymus, *Comm. Eccles.* 92.5.
70. Paul J. Alexander, *The Oracle of Baalbek: The Tiburtine Sibyl in Greek Dress*, Dumbarton Oaks Studies 10 (Washington, D.C.: Dumbarton Oaks, 1967), 19–22 (text), 28–29 (translation), 38–40 (discussion). On the late fourth-century *Vorlage*, see ibid., 48–65, 136–37.

The original, fourth-century Sibylline prophecy, according to Paul Alexander, also gave rise to the briefer Latin Tiburtine Sibyl, a text that shows many of the same parallels to the Apocalypse of Elijah as does the Greek, along with some that are different.[71] In this Latin recension the sequence of the eschatological woes and signs from the Apocalypse of Elijah has been entirely rearranged, but the Christian vocabulary and emphasis have been retained more consistently than in the extant (508 C.E.) Greek Tiburtine Sibyl.

The Latin recension also gives unique emphasis to the figure of the "last Roman emperor," the earliest appearance of what was to become a standard *topos* of Byzantine apocalypses. Although it remains unclear whether this idea derives from the text of the fourth-century Tiburtine Sibyl, the function of this final beneficent ruler in the eschatological timetable bears a striking similarity to that of the "king from the city . . . of the Sun" in ApocEl 2:46-53, such that one could imagine this latter figure as one of the "last emperor's" ideological roots.[72]

The independent proximity in word and image of both the Greek and the Latin Tiburtine Sibyls to the Apocalypse of Elijah suggests that the late fourth-century *Vorlage* (which Alexander calls the "Theodosian Sibyl") must have been intended as an expansion of the Apocalypse of Elijah.[73]

The "Apocalypse" of Shenoute

A visionary narrative and eschatological discourse added to Besa's *Life of Shenoute* in the Arabic version of that text also contains details whose most probable source was the Apocalypse of Elijah. This passage has been dated to 685–690 C.E.[74] It is interesting to note that the two

71. Latin Tiburtine Sibyl, in *Sibyllinische Texte und Forschungen*, ed. Ernst Sackur (Halle: Max Niemeyer, 1898), 177–87, esp. 185–86; translated in Bernard McGinn, *Visions of the End*, Records of Civilization, Sources and Studies 46 (New York: Columbia University Press, 1979), 49–50.

72. See Paul J. Alexander, "The Diffusion of Byzantine Apocalypses in the Medieval West and the Beginnings of Joachimism," in *Prophecy and Millenarianism: Essays in Honour of Marjorie Reeves*, ed. Ann Williams (Essex: Longman, 1980), 58–59, 93–94 n. 9. See also below, p. 202.

73. See Alexander, *Oracle of Baalbek*, 60, 137.

74. E. Amélineau, *Monuments pour servir à l'histoire de l'Égypte chrétienne aux IVᵉ et Vᵉ siècles* (*Mémoires publiés par les membres de la mission archéologique française au Caire* 4 [Paris: Ernest Leroux, 1888]), 342–43 (text and translation), lii–lviii (discussion and dating; although cf. David N. Bell, trans., *The Life of Shenoute by Besa*, Cistercian Studies 73 [Kalamazoo, Mich.: Cistercian Press, 1983], 4–5). On the dependence upon ApocEl, see Rosenstiehl, 40–41, (40 n. 54); Bauckham, "Enoch and Elijah in the Coptic Apocalypse," 73.

manuscripts of the Apocalypse of Elijah that Steindorff edited (Ach and Sa[1]) were both found in the White Monastery of Shenoute, where this Arabic *Life* was doubtless edited.

Canon Lists

Three medieval lists of books mention an Elijah apocryphon in immediate association with a Zephaniah apocryphon: the *Synopsis scripturae sacrae* of Pseudo-Athanasius (sixth century?) and the *Stichometry of Nicephorus* (patriarch of Constantinople 806–815) both mention a book of Elijah followed by a book of Zephaniah; the *Catalogue of Sixty Canonical Books* separates the two by the *Vision of Isaiah*.[75] Although the number of stichoi listed for the Elijah apocryphon in the *Stichometry* does not precisely match what can be reconstructed for the Apocalypse of Elijah,[76] the close association of the Elijah and Zephaniah apocrypha matches the manuscript form in which both Sa[1] and Ach were found.

Tabitha References

Two additional texts mentioning an eschatological heroine Tabitha may be dependent on the fuller exposition of her legend in ApocEl 4:1-6 or, alternately, may provide independent attestations of a Tabitha legend.

1. A Coptic Enoch apocryphon in the Pierpont Morgan Library (Coptic Theological Texts 3, fols. 1–9) reveals that "[two] will be taken up to [heaven] in their bodies, one Elijah, and another Tabitha [. . ."] (9ᵛ).[77]

2. A final prediction in the Arabic recension of the *History of Joseph the Carpenter* more explicitly reflects the martyrdom scenes of the Apocalypse of Elijah: "Who are those four, those of whom you have said that the Antichrist shall slay them because of their reproaching? The Saviour answered: 'They are Enoch, Elijah, Schila, and Tabitha'" (32).[78]

---

75. Lists reproduced in Rosenstiehl, 13–16.
76. Steindorff, 14–15.
77. W. E. Crum, *Theological Texts from Coptic Papyri*, Anecdota Oxoniensia, Semitic Series 12 (Oxford: Oxford University Press, 1913), 3–11 (= no. 3); and Birger A. Pearson, "The Pierpont Morgan Fragments of a Coptic Enoch Apocryphon," in *Studies on the Testament of Abraham*, ed. George W. E. Nickelsburg, Septuagint and Cognate Studies 6 (Missoula, Mont.: Scholars Press, 1976), 227–83, esp. 243, 270–71. See Frankfurter, "Tabitha," 23–25.
78. Constantine Tischendorff, *Evangelia apocrypha* (Leipzig: Avenarius & Mendel-

MANUSCRIPTS, RECENSIONS, FRAGMENTS:
THE IDENTITY OF THE APOCALYPSE
OF ELIJAH

As with any text that is extant in a number of different versions or recensions (including those of the New Testament), the question remains, On what basis do we assume or infer "the" text? Multiple theories of scribal procedure and error may account for many of the differences among texts as "variations" from an "original" form. Yet such theories can only account for some variations; considerable differences may remain among manuscripts that are nearly identical in title and contents, requiring the responsible editor or translator to print the divergent passages in parallel columns.

Occasionally it is possible to account for differences in wording or for duplicated phrases;[79] more often it is difficult to argue for one original form or, when passages are missing from a manuscript, that one manuscript has added the passages or another has left them out.[80] Do such differences suggest an ideological tendency in one or the other manuscript or recension? Albert Pietersma has shown that the Achmimic and Sahidic manuscripts really belong to two different recensions, whereas

---

ssohn, 1853), 133; see A. Battista and B. Bagatti, *Edizione critico del testo Arabo della historia Iosephi Fabri Lignarii,* Studium Biblicum Franciscanum, collectio minor 20 (Jerusalem: Franciscan Press, 1978), 176. The identity of "Schila" is unclear; W. E. Crum suggests it is a corruption of "Sibyl" ("Schila und Tabitha," *ZNW* 12 [1911]:352), but cf. Grk. Tib. Sib. l. 140: "There will arise *Skylla,* wife of the ruling wild beast, and she will bring forth two wombs" (Alexander, *Oracle of Baalbek,* 17, 27).

79. E.g., the image of people desiring death in the times of woe (ApocEl 2:5, 32). In both Ach and Sa³ the second passage includes a chiastic second strophe, "and death will flee from them" (cf. Rv 9:6; the relationship to the phrase in Revelation is not direct, however: see further, chapter 2, p. 37, below); but only in Ach does this second strophe appear also in the first passage. One may account for the difference as the Achmimic scribe's addition to the first passage, based on that scribe's recollection of Rv 9:6 and doubtless on his more immediate memory (from previous reading) of the phrase in the second passage.

80. E.g., the prophetic introduction to Ach has God addressing the narrator, "Son of Man, say to this people," whereas that of Sa² and Sa³ reads simply, "Say to this people" (1:1). Although the appellation "Son of Man" is appropriate to a divine figure's address to a prophet—the scenario presupposed in the introduction—one can only guess whether it belonged to the Greek original of ApocEl or seemed an "appropriate addition" to the Achmimic scribe. Likewise, in the eschatological discourse in ApocEl 2, the "Persians" are described as ransacking Egypt; but whereas Sa³ describes their taking "the wealth in that place," Ach gives more detail in indicating "the wealth *of the temple* in that place" (2:43). Does Ach add or Sa³ leave out? Such methodological questions are somewhat avoided in the extensive review of manuscript pluses and minuses in Pietersma, 16–18. See Jean-Marc Rosenstiehl's astute comments in "L'Apocalypse d'Élie," *Le muséon* 95 (1982):275–76.

Rosenstiehl has suggested two families of one recension.[81] How does this help one to understand the origin and development of the Apocalypse of Elijah? What can be said about the extent of these recensions in light of the Greek fragment, whose recto side does not correspond to anything in the extant Achmimic text?

Rosenstiehl has advanced the striking hypothesis that the two families or recensions derive from a divergence already present in the Greek manuscript tradition.[82] This hypothesis assumes that the wording and contents of the Apocalypse of Elijah could have been fluid fairly soon after the text's initial composition. Only a scribal context of dynamic creativity, highly influenced by situations of oral reading and interpretation, would account for such early divergence in the manuscripts.

But the problem is further manifest in the circulation of fragments. It has been mentioned that line fillers following the abrupt end of Sa³ indicate that the scribe had neither an ending such as we find in Ach nor even a title before him. Similarly, in Sa² the opening passages of the Apocalypse of Elijah, without much more than 1:1-16, appear to have been added in script to a biblical codex. Thus by the mid-fourth century, pieces of the Apocalypse of Elijah circulated independently.

This can also be seen in external parallels to the text. The close parallel between the introductions of ApocEl 1:1-4 and *Apocalypse of Paul* 3-4, displayed in the Appendix, implies some literary relationship; and traditionally scholars have viewed the Apocalypse of Elijah and the *Apocalypse of Zephaniah* as sources for the *Apocalypse of Paul*.[83] The visionary materials that follow in the *Apocalypse of Paul*, however, may themselves derive from an earlier period than those of the subsequent chapters of the Apocalypse of Elijah, which betray a third-century origin. Moreover, *Apocalypse of Paul* 3-4 lacks the collection of Johan-

---

81. Pietersma, 12-13, 18; Rosenstiehl, "L'Apocalypse d'Élie," 270-72.

82. Rosenstiehl, "L'Apocalypse d'Élie," 273-74. His most convincing evidence is the alternative wording ⲛⲛⲙ̄ⲡⲟⲗⲉⲙⲟⲥ in Sa³ and ⲛⲙ̄ⲡⲟⲗⲓⲥ in Ach, for 2:36. Rather than regarding this to be a Coptic scribe's conflation of ⲡⲟⲗⲉⲙⲟⲥ to ⲡⲟⲗⲟⲥ, whence ⲡⲟⲗⲓⲥ (see ibid., 273 n. 21), Rosenstiehl finds the explanation at the Greek level: $\tau\hat{\omega}\nu$ $\pi o\lambda\acute{\epsilon}\mu\omega\nu$ could easily be written as $\tau\hat{\omega}\nu$ $\pi\acute{o}\lambda\epsilon\omega\nu$ (ibid., 273). The hypothesis would tentatively explain why the recto of the Greek does not match anything in the extant Coptic text, because the only ms. containing this final section of ApocEl is Ach. By Rosenstiehl's hypothesis, the lost parallel section in Sahidic might give a translation of the Greek's recto.

83. M. R. James, *The Apocryphal New Testament* (Oxford: Clarendon, 1924), 527 n. 1; R. P. Casey, "The Apocalypse of Paul," *JTS* 34 (1933):7-8; Theodore Silverstein, *Visio Sancti Pauli*, Studies and Documents 4 (London: Christophers, 1935), 3, 92 n. 3.

nine phrases employed in ApocEl 1:1-7, suggesting that the form in which this introduction occurs in the *Apocalypse of Paul* is more primitive. And the use in the *Apocalypse of Paul* of only this introductory passage, without anything else of the Apocalypse of Elijah, requires some explanation, for certainly the *Apocalypse of Paul* has an interest in eschatological judgment.[84] The most likely historical reason for the co-incidental opening passages is either that the *Apocalypse of Paul* or the Apocalypse of Elijah used an unattributed fragment of the other, or that each employed an unattributed fragment from some other text. Yet the fragment theory brings one no closer to a historical lineage than these two alternatives.

How might such fragments have entered circulation? The state of our major texts of the Apocalypse of Elijah provides an answer: sizable leaves of codex, such as are missing from Ach and Sa[1], simply dropped out in circulation. The material on these loose leaves, albeit unattributed in authority, may well have provided valuable visions of the eschaton, unique descriptions of the Antichrist, underworld scenes, or biblical lore to a scribe engaged in the composition of a new text. This "free" and ad hoc use of unattributed material resembles the transmission and reuse of early Jewish rabbinic and mystical texts, as Peter Schäfer has shown:

> Most of the manuscripts hand them down in the form of only loosely structured "raw material," without a title (and if with a title, then with phantasy titles interchangeable almost at will), with no recognizeable beginning and no recognizeable end (and if with a beginning or an end, then not very uniform in the various manuscripts).[85]

The analysis of ancient literature, Schäfer argues, "is not a matter of static texts, but rather of the documentation and description of a dynamic manuscript tradition."[86] In the case of the Apocalypse of Elijah this statement is amply demonstrated by the text's free use in the Tiburtine Sibylline tradition: the prophecies themselves were authoritative but their sequence and literary context were evidently not.

The fragmentary and divergent transmission of the manuscripts of the Apocalypse of Elijah following its initial compilation may indeed provide a fair illustration of the literary milieu in which an Elijah text

---

84. E.g., *Apoc. Paul* 18, 21; cf. Collins, "Early Christian Apocalypses," 86.

85. Peter Schäfer, "Research into Rabbinic Literature: An Attempt to Define the *Status Quaestionis*," *JJS* 37 (1986):149. Cf. also idem, "Tradition and Redaction in Hekhalot Literature," *JSJ* 14 (1983):180–81.

86. Schäfer, "Research into Rabbinic Literature," 151.

was first composed in Roman Egypt. That is, the manuscript record expresses a world in which fragmentary sources and a liberal (and perhaps less direct) use of prior texts and traditions were normative to literary culture. Such a cultural scenario is corroborated by the historical evidence for general illiteracy, semiliteracy, and the eclecticism evident among those who were actually able to compose texts.

2

The Apocalypse of Elijah
in Its Biblical Context

As an Old Testament pseudepigraphon appealing to the authority of the biblical prophet Elijah, presuming to reveal the layout of the times of woe and the eschaton, employing biblical phraseology and motifs, and drawing upon the world of Jewish and Christian lore, the Apocalypse of Elijah demonstrates a complex relationship to Scripture. Its author was evidently acquainted as much with oral traditions and phrases as with actual texts. Its attribution in the memory of Didymus the Blind and in the library of the White Monastery was to Elijah, and yet Elijah is not mentioned as the narrator. Finally, there is evidence for a number of Elijah apocrypha in circulation in late antiquity; does this text reflect an original or a later version of the others? Was it composed in conscious relationship with the others? Approaching the Apocalypse of Elijah with these issues in mind, we can gain a sense of how literary composition in early Christian Egypt reflected indigenous notions of Scripture and scriptural authority.

THE APOCALYPSE OF ELIJAH'S USE OF SOURCES

Although the papyrological evidence shows a diversity of biblical and Christian texts circulating in Egypt by the third century, the particular selection of these texts—and later, their particular collection in codices—allows no basis for assuming what Scripture a third-century Christian might have known.[1] Not only were texts inconsistently available to

1. See H. Idris Bell, "Evidences of Christianity in Egypt during the Roman Period,"

different Christian congregations, but the congregations developed their own orientations and preferences from among the available texts. Sozomen gives a valuable assessment of this chronic diversity in the public canon as it continued even in the fifth century, when the New Testament had become established:

> The same prayers and psalms are not recited nor the same lections read on the same occasions in all churches. Thus the book entitled "The Apocalypse of Peter," which was considered altogether spurious by the ancients, is still read in some of the churches of Palestine, on the day of preparation, when the people observe a fast in memory of the passion of the Savior. So the work entitled "The Apocalypse of the Apostle Paul," though unrecognized by the ancients, is still esteemed by most of the monks. . . . Many other customs are still to be observed in cities and villages; and those who have been brought up in their observance would, from respect to the great men who instituted and perpetuated these customs, consider it wrong to abolish them.[2]

Here we have a vivid illustration of the way local traditions determined the variety of texts to which congregants were accustomed and that they venerated as inspired: Scripture was, in effect, a regional phenomenon. When we examine a text from the era before the New Testament's completion, then, we should expect this regional diversity to extend even to texts that became canonized. It would be methodologically unsound to marshal a stream of parallels from Jewish and Christian texts on the assumption that a scribe or a Christian community was familiar with the entire Bible and New Testament (as we know these collections) or even a substantial portion of them.

Eusebius offers a different glimpse of how Scripture circulated in this period, citing an Egyptian martyr, deported to Palestine, who had apparently memorized "whole books of scripture." Eusebius describes how he could, at will, recite

> like some treasury of discourses, now a text from the Law and the Prophets, now from the Writings, and other times a gospel or apostolic text . . . : standing before a large assembly in a church he recited certain parts of holy scripture. While I could only hear his voice I thought that

---

HTR 37 (1944):199–203, esp. 202 n. 57; and Colin H. Roberts, *Manuscript, Society, and Belief in Early Christian Egypt* (London: British Academy, 1979), chap. 1. The evidence shows far more biblical than Christian scriptures were used by Christians in Egypt and, among those Christian scriptures used, a fairly even distribution of New Testament and noncanonical texts.

2. Sozomen, *Historia ecclesiastica* 7.19 (tr. Chester D. Hartranft, in *NPNF* 2:390).

someone was reading aloud [ἀναγινώσκειν], as is the custom in the meet-
ings, but when I came closer I saw at once what was going on: all the
others stood with clear eyes in a circle around him; and he, using only his
mind's eye, spoke plainly, without flourish, like some prophet, over-
coming many of them in their strong bodies.[3]

Obviously such scenarios were typical of Christian use of Scripture in
Egypt: sparse literacy, memorized texts, vibrant performances of oral
"scripture"—indeed, where were the texts themselves? It is quite probable that most who participated in Christian ceremony in Roman Egypt
were familiar with biblical and other sacred materials *only* through their
public reading or recitation.[4] This oral dissemination of "texts" and ideas
would have informed the repertoire and compositional abilities of
Christian scribes at least as much as did actual texts. In the words of
Gustav Bardy,

> The first translations [of the New Testament into Coptic] owe their origin
> in Egypt to oral explications, given on behalf of those who could not
> follow the passages read in church in the sacred tongue; and naturally
> matters were not preserved in the same way everywhere.[5]

It would therefore be incorrect to assume that a particular idea or
image expressed in an Egyptian Christian writing should owe its origin
to the author's use of a written text. Instead, ideas and images derive
from the author's synthesis of traditions within an oral milieu, where the
texts themselves invariably had an oral or public nature.

Notwithstanding this uncertainty as to the circulation and influence
of texts, it is quite apparent that somehow (presumably through oral
traditions, such as preaching) a "biblical culture" arose in Egypt, consisting of the veneration of biblical heroes, the use of biblical formulas
and phrases in new compositions, and the magical use of scriptural
phrases and fragments. This biblical culture would account not only for
the choice of Elijah as pseudonymous authority (in ApocEl as well as
other Old Testament pseudepigrapha composed in Egypt) but also for

---

3. Eusebius, *Martyrs of Palestine* [Grk.] 13.7, 8 in *Eusèbe de Césarée: Histoire
ecclésiastique, Livres VIII–X et les martyrs en Palestine*, ed. and tr. Gustav Bardy, SC 55
[Paris: Éditions du Cerf, 1958], 169–72).

4. Cf. Roberts, *Manuscript, Society, and Belief*, 20; William V. Harris, *Ancient Literacy*
(Cambridge: Harvard University Press, 1989), 305; and see further discussion below,
chapter 10.

5. Gustav Bardy, "Les premiers temps du christianisme de langue copte en Égypte,"
in *Mémorial LaGrange* (Paris: J. Gabalda, 1940), 209.

the type of language the author uses for the Apocalypse of Elijah.[6] Much of the text is composed in biblical phraseology, employing parallelisms—"she will pursue him up to Judea, scolding him up to Jerusalem" (ApocEl 4:2; cf. 2:37-38)—and phraseology drawn particularly from the Prophets—"sixty righteous ones who are prepared for this hour will hear; and they will gird on the breastplate of God" (4:30f).[7] The formulaic introduction to the text is unique in this regard, explicitly recalling a prophetic commission formula from Ezekiel and Jeremiah, which must have entered the repertoire of Egyptian Christian scribes as a typical prophetic opening.[8] Prophetic imagery also contributes to the composition of the final chapter of the Apocalypse of Elijah: the judgment of "the shepherds of the people"[9] and of the heavens and the earth, the witness of the mountains and byways, and the separation of the righteous. But this style is characteristic of pseudepigrapha and of milieus acquainted even to a modest degree with biblical texts; it does not at all imply the author's close literary attention to particular texts.

The most obvious use of extant Christian Scripture would appear to be ApocEl 1:2, which echoes 1 Jn 2:15; yet only the first part of the verse is a quotation. The rest of the verse— "for the pride of the world and its destruction are the devil's"—seems rather to be a rough recollection of 1 Jn 2:16-17,[10] suggesting the text's historical distance from a text of 1

6. See B. R. Rees, "Popular Religion in Graeco-Roman Egypt, 2: The Transition to Christianity," *JEA* 36 (1950):96–97. On the reverence for and popularity of biblical texts, see also Roberts, *Manuscript, Society, and Belief*, 12–21. Roberts sees a historical continuity between Jewish and early Christian scribalism in Egypt, which would account for the intra-Christian development of the *nomina sacra*, by which the scribe of a biblical manuscript can be identified as Jewish or Christian (ibid., 44–47).

7. Cf. Is 59:17; Wis 5:18; Eph 6:10-17.

8. "The word of the Lord came to me saying, 'Say to this people, "Why do you add sin to your sins and anger the Lord God who created you?"'" (ApocEl 1:1). This pericope, perhaps drawn from an independent fragment in circulation (cf. *Apoc. Paul* 3, in Appendix and above, pp. 28–29), receives more extensive discussion below, chapter 4, p. 82.

9. "He will judge the shepherds of the people; he will ask about the flock of sheep" (ApocEl 5:31). Although the scriptural source of this metaphor is Ezekiel 34 (cf. Zec 13:7), it achieved wider currency in Greco-Roman Judaism with the association made in *1 Enoch* ("Dream Visions") 89–90 with the "angels of the nations" (cf. Dn 10:13; see discussions in R. H. Charles, *Apocrypha and Pseudepigrapha of the Old Testament*, 2 vols. (Oxford: Clarendon, 1913), 2:255 n. 59; and Martin Hengel, *Judaism and Hellenism*, 2 vols., tr. John Bowden [Tübingen: Mohr, 1973; 2d ed., Philadelphia: Fortress, 1974], 1:187). In *1 En* 90:25, the seventy angelic "shepherds," having destroyed their "sheep," are "judged and found guilty, and they were cast into that fiery abyss" (tr. R. H. Charles, *The Book of Enoch or 1 Enoch* [Oxford: Clarendon, 1912], 213). In the *Shepherd of Hermas* the metaphor is reversed: wayward sheep are flogged by a "shepherd of punishment" (*Herm. Sim.* 6.2–3).

10. See below, p. 83.

John. This inference gathers considerable weight with the fact that, whereas 1 John introduces (and even promotes) the title "Antichrist" in a millennialist context similar to that of the Apocalypse of Elijah,[11] the Apocalypse of Elijah never uses this title at all, preferring "Lawless One" or "Shameless One" to designate a clearly defined eschatological adversary. It would appear that in the author's mind, at least, local titles for eschatological adversaries had gained precedence over the authority of this particular scripture.

Likewise, the vividly dualistic cosmology, into which the Son is sent "to save us from the captivity" (1:5), may have been inspired by such language in the Gospel of John (e.g., 3:17)—a text of early and prominent circulation in Egypt—or other Johannine literature (cf. 1 Jn 2:15-17) but was probably not based on them.

The angelological account of Christ's descent in ApocEl 1:5-7 echoes not only Phil 2:6-8 and Hebrews (e.g., 1:4-6; 2:7-9), but, more vividly, the *Ascension of Isaiah* and *Epistula Apostolorum* 13. This variety of parallels reflects the rich store of apocalyptic angelological traditions current in late antiquity and available to an Egyptian author through both esoteric and exoteric channels.

It would be equally difficult to posit a direct source for the brief heavenly ascent narrative in ApocEl 1:8-10, where the righteous are described as passing hostile "Thrones" on their way up to the heavenly city, simply by virtue of bearing the correct divine "seal." Those who have sinned and therefore lack the seal, the text proceeds to say (1:11-12), cannot pass by the "Thrones of death." A traditional vocabulary seems to be *assumed* here; for although Thrones are listed as an angelic rank in Col 1:16 and *T. Levi* 3:8, there seem to be no other references to Thrones as the specific rank that prohibited access to heaven. The structure of ascent itself—displaying one's seal to what seem to be angelic gatekeepers—finds general attestation in gnostic and Jewish *Hekhalot* literature of the Roman period. Origen, for example, discusses what the Ophites "are taught to say at the eternally chained gates of the Archons after passing through what they call 'the Barrier of Evil,'" whereas the *Ascension of Isaiah* describes the angels of the three lowest

---

11. See Gregory C. Jenks's analysis of ἀντίχριστος in 1 John in connection with the development of Adversary traditions (*The Origins and Early Development of the Antichrist Myth*, BZNW 59 [Berlin: de Gruyter, 1991], 339–47. Jenks notes that although the title "Antichrist" gained ascendancy in patristic literature of the third century, the Johannine epistles themselves were rarely employed (347).

heavens requiring a "password" of Christ during his *descent*—"so that he might not be recognized" (10:23-28).[12] Irenaeus knows of actual ascent rituals in which neophytes are trained to respond in rote formulas to the different heavenly ranks, so that they "may become incapable of being seized by the principalities and powers. . . . And they affirm that by saying these things, [the utterer] escapes from the powers."[13] Handbooks of this sort have actually come down to us in the two *Books of Jeu*.

Seals as the means of entrance or passage are specified in *Hekhalot*, gnostic, and ritual ("magical") texts, the latter two types often providing iconographic diagrams of the various seals required for complete ascent.[14] This iconographic development of the tradition of heavenly passage, which essentially transformed the descriptive text into an apotropaic passport, demonstrates the legacy of the Egyptian *Book of the Dead*, particularly in those texts with an Egyptian provenance (such as the *Books of Jeu*).[15]

But the ascent narrative in the Apocalypse of Elijah presents an anomaly. By itself, the ascent to the heavenly city derives from the Jewish apocalyptic tradition, particularly the books of *Enoch*, which captured the interest of Egyptian Christians from an early date.[16] Similarly, the technical designation of an angelic rank as Thrones should be ascribed to current apocalyptic lore, expanding as such Christian texts as Colossians began to circulate. It may be appropriate, however, to view the Thrones' "hostility" and the implication that they would destroy sinners who try to pass in the context of Egyptian mortuary mythology, whose imagery was widely known (and even on view in temples) throughout the Roman period. It is the Egyptian tradition that most

---

12. Origen, *Contra Celsum* 6.31 (in *Origen: Contra Celsum*, tr. H. Chadwick [Cambridge: Cambridge University Press, 1953], 346). In general, see Kurt Rudolph, *Gnosis*, tr. and ed. R. McL. Wilson (San Francisco: Harper & Row, 1983), 171–75; and Martha Himmelfarb, "Heavenly Ascent and the Relationship of the Apocalypses and the *Hekhalot* Literature," *HUCA* 59 (1988):82–85.

13. Irenaeus, *Contra haereses* 1.21.5, tr. A. Roberts and J. Donaldson, *ANF* 1:346.

14. See Himmelfarb, "Heavenly Ascent," 80–82; Rudolph, *Gnosis*.

15. See L. Kákosy, "Gnosis und ägyptische Religion," in *The Origins of Gnosticism: Colloquium of Messina*, ed. U. Bianchi (Leiden: Brill, 1970), 241–43. By itself the "sealing" of the righteous (cf. 4 Ez 6:5; Rv 7:2-8, 13:16-18) is a biblical motif (Ezek 9:4-5; Is 44:5; see Michael Stone, *Fourth Ezra: A Commentary on the Book of Fourth Ezra*, Hermeneia [Minneapolis: Fortress, 1990], 158 n. 107), but its strongly iconographic and apotropaeic uses in early Jewish mysticism and Coptic Gnosticism clearly incorporate ritual traditions outside the Bible.

16. See George W. E. Nickelsburg, "Two Enochic Manuscripts: Unstudied Evidence for Egyptian Christianity," in *Of Scribes and Scrolls: Studies on the Hebrew Bible, Intertestamental Judaism, and Christian Origins, Presented to John Strugnell*, ed. Harold W. Attridge, John J. Collins, and Thomas H. Tobin, College Theology Society Resources in Religion 5 (Lanham, Md.: University Press of America, 1990), 252–60.

vividly emphasized the threat posed by the "gatekeepers" to the un-righteous soul.[17] The Apocalypse of Elijah may not be consciously syn-thesizing these traditions but may rather envision Jewish ascent motifs through the lens of native mythology.

A more immediate resource or inspiration for eschatological and other imagery in the Apocalypse of Elijah may be the book of Rev-elation. The Elect will have the name of God written on their foreheads and therefore "will not hunger or thirst" (ApocEl 1:9; 5:6; cf. Rv 3:12; 7:3, 16; 14:1); and they "will walk with the angels up to [God's] city" (ApocEl 1:10; cf. Rv 21:10-27; Heb 11:16). An image of people fruitlessly seeking to die in the days of woe (ApocEl 2:5, 32-33) may come either from Rv 9:6 or from native Egyptian tradition.[18] The first narrative of Enoch and Elijah's return appears to be one of the earliest combinations of Jewish Enoch/Elijah tradition with the "two witnesses" passage in Rv 11:3-12, although it is more likely that the author received a tradition already synthesized than that he edited the text of Revelation 11.[19] Finally, the conclusion of the text, culminating in a "millennium" (5:22-24, 35-39), reflects the author's familiarity with an eschatological sequence pre-sumably derived from Revelation 20–22 (although he has notably left out the postmillennial "return" of Satan described in Rv 20:7-10). Al-though all these echoes of the book of Revelation demonstrate a general awareness in the Apocalypse of Elijah of the former's teachings and themes, H.F.D. Sparks has aptly cautioned that "it is possible to discount some of the [proposed] contacts with Revelation . . . as no more than part of the common stock-in-trade of apocalyptic literature, whether Jewish or Christian."[20]

---

17. See Jan Zandee, *Death as an Enemy, according to Ancient Egyptian Conceptions,* NumenSupp 5 (Leiden: Brill, 1960), 114-25 (cf. 316-18); J. Gwyn Griffiths, *The Divine Verdict: A Study of Divine Judgement in the Ancient Religions,* NumenSupp 52 (Leiden: Brill, 1991), 210-13; cf. Rudolph, *Gnosis,* 179-85, on gnostic images of the punishment of the unrighteous ascender. Himmelfarb notes that "instances of angelic hostility in the apocalypses are rare" ("Heavenly Ascent," 84) and refers to Johann Maier's explanation of the hostile powers in *Hekhalot* texts as due to the fear involved in imagining or "practicing" their esoteric ascents (84–85, citing Johann Maier, "Das Gefährdungsmotiv bei der Himmelsreise in der jüdischen Apokalyptik und 'Gnosis,'" *Kairos* 5 [1963]:22–24, 28–30). Although useful psychologically, this explanation avoids the question of Egyptian influence posed (at least) by the gnostic texts.

18. Cf. *Admonitions of Ipuwer* 4.3; *Sib. Or.* 8.353. See below, chapter 8, pp. 183–84.

19. See Joachim Jeremias, "ʿΗλ(ε)ίας," ed. Gerhard Kittel, tr. and ed. Geoffrey W. Bromiley, *TDNT* 2:940; Richard Bauckham, "The Martyrdom of Enoch and Elijah: Jewish or Christian?" *JBL* 95, 3 (1976):457–58; idem, "Enoch and Elijah in the Coptic Apocalypse of Elijah," *Studia Patristica* 16, 2 (1985):73–75.

20. H.F.D. Sparks, "Introduction to the Apocalypse of Elijah," *AOT,* 758. Sparks's caution has been given extensive foundation in Gonzalo Aranda, "Ideas escatológicas

Still, it is not surprising that Revelation would have had such an influence, directly or indirectly, on the composition of early Christian pseudepigrapha in Egypt. André Grabar observed the influence of Revelation throughout the iconography of Coptic chapels.[21] More importantly, evidence from Eusebius shows this text and the image of the heavenly city exerting considerable power on Upper Egyptian communities in the third century.[22] There is good reason to believe that the Apocalypse of Elijah was composed in just such a community.

Like the book of Revelation, the *Shepherd of Hermas* achieved considerable popularity in Egyptian Christianity from an early date.[23] It is perhaps from this text's short discourse against "double-mindedness" in *Herm. Vis.* 4.2.5–6, which associates psychic preparation with eschatological resilience, that the author of the Apocalypse of Elijah drew ideological inspiration for the discourse on the same topic (1:23-27). Yet the rustic metaphors the author of the Elijah Apocalypse employs to describe "doubt" and "single-mindedness" show that he has integrated the ideology thoroughly into local terms and therefore was probably not dependent upon a text of *Hermas*.

The Apocalypse of Elijah bears significant parallels to two other important Egyptian Christian apocalypses, the apocalypses of Peter and of Paul; yet none of these parallels is verbatim and few are sufficiently idiosyncratic to prove the use of one or another as sources. The abbreviated judgment scene in ApocEl 5:26-29 recalls the more extensive scenes in *Apoc. Pet.* 6 and *Apoc. Paul* 13-51; but the pronounced interest

judías en el Apocalípsis copto de Elías," in *Simposio bíblico español,* ed. N. Fernandez Marcos, J. Trebolle Barrera, and J. Fernandez Vallina (Madrid: Universidad Complutense, 1984), 663–79.

21. André Grabar, *Martyrium: Recherches sur le culte des reliques et l'art chrétien antique,* 2 vols. (Paris: Collège de France, 1946), 2:231 (cf. 2:210, on Jewish apocalyptic visions in general).

22. See Eusebius, *Hist. eccles.* 7.24; *Martyrs of Palestine* 11. 9–10 (cf. Heb 11:15f); Gerhard Maier, *Die Johannesoffenbarung und die Kirche,* WUNT 25 (Tübingen: Mohr [Siebeck], 1981), 86–107. James Charlesworth notes a lack of influence from Revelation upon early Christian apocalypses, except for the apocalypses of Elijah and Paul (*The New Testament Apocrypha and Pseudepigrapha: A Guide to Publications, with Excurses on Apocalypses,* ATLA Bibliography Series 17 [Metuchen, N.J., and London: ATLA/Scarecrow Press, 1987], 34–36, 39–40). Because the latter two texts are distinctly Egyptian in origin, the relative influence of Revelation may indeed be based on regional proclivities. Paul Alexander has pointed out a similar absence of Revelation's influence in Byzantine apocalypses ("The Diffusion of Byzantine Apocalypses in the Medieval West and the Beginnings of Joachimism," in *Prophecy and Millenarianism: Essays in Honour of Marjorie Reeves,* ed. Ann Williams [Essex: Longman, 1980], 59).

23. P.Mich. 130 (late second century); see Roberts, *Manuscript, Society, and Belief,* 21–22.

in afterlife materials in Egyptian Christian texts makes a simple source hypothesis untenable. Indeed, within the context of this afterlife tradition it is quite remarkable that the judgment scene in the Apocalypse of Elijah is so short.

The striking parallel between the introductory passages in *Apoc. Paul* 3 and ApocEl 1:1-4 represents an instance of common sources rather than the immediate dependence of one upon the other, as we discuss below. The Apocalypse of Elijah's relationship to the apocalypses of Peter and of Paul demonstrates no more than that the literary culture of early Egyptian Christianity was beginning to focus on particular topics (such as the afterlife).

Hence, except for the problem of the introductory passage and the possible use of the book of Revelation, the Apocalypse of Elijah does not display any evidence of having made direct use of prior textual sources. Yet it is evident that the oral scriptural culture, which influenced the composition of the Apocalypse of Elijah, was richly influenced by (primarily) biblical and (to a lesser extent) Christian texts.

THE "APOCALYPSE" OF ELIJAH

There is reason to believe that, rather than pertaining to a distinct, historically self-conscious literary genre, the word "apocalypse" gained popularity and even conventionality through the great notoriety of the book of Revelation, which described itself as an ἀποκάλυψις in its incipit (Rv 1:1).[24] Not only were Jewish revelatory pseudepigrapha thus titled retroactively, but subsequent, Christian attempts at composing revelatory texts came to be designated "apocalypses."[25] The history of the use of the title shows the importance of the book of Revelation in early Christian literature, and that it stands as an archetype behind subsequent Christian revelatory texts.[26] By contrast, the fact that titles in late antiquity conventionally followed the texts themselves suggests that in performance they had little importance in establishing the genre of a

24. Cf. Philip Vielhauer, "Apocalypses and Related Subjects: Introduction," tr. David Hill, *NTA* 2:582 ("This literary genre does not appear originally to have had any common title").

25. See Morton Smith, "On the History of ΑΠΟΚΑΛΥΠΤΩ and ΑΠΟΚΑΛΥΨΙΣ," in *Apocalypticism in the Mediterranean World and the Near East*, ed. David Hellholm (Tübingen: Mohr [Siebeck], 1983), 19.

26. Vielhauer, "Apocalypses," 582. On the varying impact of Revelation on subsequent apocalypses, see Charlesworth, *New Testament Apocrypha*, 34–36.

text for an audience and may have been added merely to facilitate library reference or, occasionally, to classify texts by authority and canon.[27]

Although the Apocalypse of Elijah may be outlined as having sequential sections, it does not have an overall structure of supernatural revelation to a particular, legendary recipient. Unlike Daniel, 4 Ezra, 2 *Baruch,* and Revelation (for example), the Apocalypse of Elijah contains no opening story that might describe how, when, and where its contents—almost exclusively eschatology—were revealed to (presumably) Elijah or a closing story that would account for the present, literary nature of the revelations (cf. Dn 12:5-13; 4 Ezr 14:37-48; 2 *Baruch* 77-87; Rv 22:6-19).[28] The "spoken" character of the Apocalypse of Elijah contrasts with the vividly textual or scribal self-consciousness of traditional apocalypses (e.g., Dn 12:4, 9; 1 *En* 14:1; 92:1; 93:1; Rv 22:18).

Furthermore, the text of the Apocalypse of Elijah lacks all indication of the identity of the implied narrator, although the voice is highly personalized through the use of first-person pronouns and exclamatory interjections. A first-person voice to deliver revelation was characteristic of many apocalypses—establishing the literary conceit that the hero himself beheld the cosmic secrets, that the audience was receiving his true disclosures—and allowed for some flexibility and exchange among the literary genres of apocalypse, epistle (e.g., Rv 1:4; 22:21), and testament (1 *En* 83:1; 91:1-3).[29] It was customary, however, for these genres to identify this voice, even in the first person: "I, Enoch [/Ezekiel/Abraham/John]." The Apocalypse of Elijah contains no such identification

---

27. In Egypt the titles themselves came to acquire a power independent of their function as reference rubrics. P.Mich. inv. 1559 is only one of many talismanic φυλακτήρια containing only the titles and first words of biblical texts (in this case, the four canonical Gospels); cf. Gerald M. Browne, *Michigan Coptic Texts* (Barcelona: Papyrologia Castroctaviana, 1979), 43-45. See, in general, E. A. Judge, "The Magical Use of Scripture in the Papyri," in *Perspectives on Language and Text: Essays and Poems in Honor of Francis J. Andersen's Sixtieth Birthday,* ed. Edgar W. Conrad and Edward G. Newing (Winona Lake, Ind.: Eisenbrauns, 1987), 339-49.

28. See the analysis of the literary framing elements in Revelation by Lars Hartman, "Form and Message: A Preliminary Discussion of 'Partial Texts' in Rev 1-3 and 22:6ff," in *L'apocalypse johannique et l'apocalyptique dans le Nouveau Testament,* ed. J. Lambrecht (Louvain: Louvain University Press, 1980), 129-49.

29. Cf. Anitra Bingham Kolenkow, "The Genre Testament and Forecasts of the Future in the Hellenistic Jewish Milieu," *JSJ* 6 (1975):57-71. On Revelation, see John J. Collins, "Pseudonymity, Historical Reviews, and the Genre of the Revelation of John," *CBQ* 39 (1977):340-41, 342 n. 47; Elisabeth Schüssler Fiorenza, *The Book of Revelation: Justice and Judgment* (Philadelphia: Fortress, 1985), 165-70.

and therefore lacks both the conceit of an ancient revelation and the implicit authority of a legendary figure.

As such, the Apocalypse of Elijah cannot be included under the literary category "apocalypse," whether this category is defined exclusively by its frame narrative or in addition by eschatological interests.[30] A genre apocalypse must represent the essential contextualizing framework by which subsidiary contents are presented and authorized, and the Apocalypse of Elijah lacks this framework.

However, the attribution and title, the opening discourse, the parenetic section that follows the incipit, and the markedly Christian eschatology that concludes the text of the Apocalypse of Elijah all recall the *type* of materials found in many apocalypses. We therefore must presume on the part of the composer some rudimentary familiarity with apocalypses, although without an awareness of an apocalyptic genre such as was apparently current in Second Temple Judaism and which we now employ as a taxonomic category.

Under these circumstances, one must assess the significance of the Apocalypse of Elijah's title both in the history and for the classification of the text; for the title and its relative antiquity have implications both for the intentionality of the author[31] and for the local significance of the word "apocalypse." Because Elijah is explicitly missing as dramatis persona during the course of the text,[32] the only indication that this text *is*

30. Cf. Vielhauer, "Apocalypses," 582–87; John J. Collins, "Introduction: Towards the Morphology of a Genre," *Semeia* 14 (1979):9; idem, "Apocalyptic Literature," in *Early Judaism and Its Modern Interpreters*, ed. Robert A. Kraft and George W. E. Nickelsburg (Atlanta: Scholars Press, 1986), 346–47; and Adela Yarbro Collins, "Introduction: Early Christian Apocalypticism," *Semeia* 36 (1986):5–6. The emphasis on eschatology has been criticized by Christopher Rowland, *The Open Heaven: A Study of Apocalyptic in Judaism and Early Christianity* (New York: Crossroad, 1982), 48, 70–72; and Martha Himmelfarb, "The Experience of the Visionary and Genre in the Ascension of Isaiah 6–11 and the Apocalypse of Paul," *Semeia* 36 (1986):106.

31. Although any text transcends structurally and historically the author's intentions, the choice of genre and the subsequent effects of the genre upon the text's contents should be recognized as the author's vital historical act as medium between the literary culture in which the text is composed and the message intended; and it is a choice with recurrent effects on the reception and interpretation of the text as it is transmitted in history. On the importance of authorial intentionality with respect to genre criticism, see E. D. Hirsch, Jr., *Validity in Interpretation* (New Haven and London: Yale University Press, 1967), 100–101, 123–26, and passim; and David Hellholm, "The Problem of Apocalyptic Genre," *Semeia* 36 (1986):31 (= §3.3.5.1).

32. The two episodes describing Elijah's eschatological return in tandem with Enoch (ApocEl 4:7-19; 5:32) constitute typical components of early Jewish eschatology, with no more intrinsic connection to an implied author than Tabitha or the Lord. See Emil Schürer (*Geschichte des jüdischen Volkes in Zeitalter Jesu Christi*, 3 vols. [4th ed.; Leipzig: Hinrichs'sche, 1909], 3:368), who doubts an Elijah apocalypse *Grundlage* on this very

an "Apocalypse of Elijah" appears in the Achmimic manuscript, which alone contains the end of the text. If Sa[1] were a Sahidic version of the same codex (because both contain the Apocalypse of Elijah and what appears to be a portion of the *Apocalypse of Zephaniah*), then Sa[1] would also have contained the title "Apocalypse of Elijah" after the same text.[33]

The hypothesis that our Apocalypse of Elijah circulated under this name in conjunction with the *Apocalypse of Zephaniah* gains strength in light of the Byzantine canon lists, the *Catalogue of Sixty Canonical Books* and the *Stichometry of Nicephorus*, which list the two titles together or in close proximity.[34]

In the two manuscripts that did not include the *Apocalypse of Zephaniah*, Sa[2] and Sa[3], however, there is no indication that the text was known as the "Apocalypse of Elijah." Appended in script to a codex containing Deuteronomy, Jonah, Acts, and Revelation,[35] Sa[2] is missing all but the first, homiletic section. It might be inferred that the Apocalypse of Elijah, in whatever length, was added in connection with the codex's book of Revelation, for this early section of the Apocalypse of Elijah contains many references to Revelation. This inference, however, requires that the scribe knew neither the rest of the Apocalypse of Elijah nor the name of the text he was copying down.

By contrast, Sa[3] seems to have been missing its end and title already at the copyist stage: line fillers on page 20[r] suggest that no more of the text was known to the scribe.[36] We therefore cannot presume that the text was necessarily copied as the "Apocalypse of Elijah."

Such manuscript evidence offers no more concerning the nature of the title than that the text circulated as the "Apocalypse of Elijah" only in conjunction with the *Apocalypse of Zephaniah*, and even then not necessarily from the compositional stage of the text.

---

basis; cf. Heinrich Weinel, "Die spätere christliche Apokalyptik," in EΥΧΑΡΙΣΤΗΡΙΟΝ, ed. Hans Schmidt (Göttingen: Vandenhoeck & Ruprecht, 1923), 166.

33. Urbain Bouriant, "Les papyrus d'Akhmim (Fragments de manuscrits en dialectes bachmourique et thébain)," *Mémoires publiés par les membres de la mission archéologique française au Caire*, vol. 1, fasc. 2 (1885):261. The recent analysis of the Sahidic and Achmimic versions of the Apocalypse of Elijah by Pietersma et al. suggests that, if Ach and Sa[1] do in fact have a historical relationship, Sa[1] was probably the codex from which Ach was copied. Pietersma et al. have noted a general agreement among the Sahidic mss., from which Ach stands at a substantial distance (its somewhat greater age notwithstanding). See Pietersma, 12–18.

34. See above, p. 26.

35. See E. A. Wallis Budge, *Coptic Biblical Texts in the Dialect of Upper Egypt* (London: British Museum, 1912; reprint, New York: AMS, 1977), ix–x, lv–lvii.

36. Pietersma, 6, 88.

Didymus the Blind, presently the earliest witness to the text, is quite enigmatic as to its title. In his Ecclesiastes commentary he cites the extant Apocalypse of Elijah as the "Prophecy of Elijah" but refers to another apocryphon, which apparently disclosed secrets of the underworld, as "the Apocalypse of Elijah."[37] In his Zechariah commentary, Didymus seems to recall the passage describing the arrival of Enoch and Elijah (ApocEl 4:7-19) but only as "an apocryphal book."[38]

While it is conceivable that Didymus was referring to the same text under several names—that the precise title of the text was unimportant to him—there is reason to believe he knew more than one Elijah apocryphon. The text that he calls the "Apocalypse of Elijah" seems to contain such "tours of hell" material as is ascribed to Elijah apocrypha by the *Pseudo-Titus Epistle* and several rabbinic sources.[39] The text that he calls the "Prophecy of Elijah" and "an apocryphal book" appears to be the extant Apocalypse of Elijah. Didymus wrote at approximately the same time that the Achmimic manuscript of the Apocalypse of Elijah was copied (early or mid-fourth century), and by the end of the fourth century the various recensions of the text ran significantly parallel to one another. Because there is no indication that any of these recensions ever contained a tour of hell, it is doubtful that Didymus could have known one Elijah apocryphon with both a tour of hell and the heroic persecution materials now in the Apocalypse of Elijah.

Didymus therefore probably knew both a Prophecy of Elijah and an Apocalypse of Elijah, and the text that he calls the "Prophecy of Elijah" is what we now call the Apocalypse of Elijah, whereas his "Apocalypse of Elijah" is now lost.[40] But how fixed and distinct were these titles for

---

37. Didymus the Blind, Commentary on Ecclesiastes 235.26–28, on Qoh 8:4-5: "Prophecy of Elijah" (in *Didymos der Blinde: Kommentar zum Ecclesiastes (Tura-Papyrus)*, vol. 4: *Kommentar zu Eccl. Kap. 7–8, 8*, tr. and ed. Johannes Kramer and Bärbel Krebber, PTA 16 [Bonn: Rudolf Habelt, 1972], 136–37): cf. *ApocEl* 4:1-6; and *Comm. Eccles.* 92.5, on Qoh 3:16: "Apocalypse of Elijah" (ed. Michael Gronewald, *Didymos der Blinde: Kommentar zum Ecclesiastes*, vol. 2, PTA 22 [Bonn: Rudolf Habelt, 1977], 130–31).

38. *Commentary on Zechariah* 77.19 (342), on Zech 4:11-14 (ed. Louis Doutreleau, SC 83 [Paris: Editions du Cerf, 1962], 1:374–77). See discussion by Krebber, *Didymos der Blinde*, 4:160. It is worth noting that both this reference to ApocEl and the one to "the Prophecy of Elijah" concern the episodes of heroic persecution from ApocEl 4.

39. See Michael Stone and John Strugnell, *The Books of Elijah*, SBLTT 18 (Missoula, Mont.: Scholars Press, 1979), 14–26; and below, pp. 45–46.

40. Although he may have been simply copying Origen, who attributed Paul's quotation in 1 Cor 2:9 to the "*secretum* of Elijah the Prophet" (Origen, *Comm. Matt.* 23.37), Jerome claimed to have known an "*Apocalypsus* of Elijah" where the passage could be found (Jerome, *Comm. Is.* 17, on 64:4; and *Ep. 57* to Pammachius). See

Didymus? How do we account for the fact that he and the scribe of the Achmimic manuscript gave the same text different names?

It is no coincidence that the Elijah apocryphon from which Didymus recalls a vision of the underworld is called ἀποκάλυψις, whereas the Elijah apocryphon from which he recalls Tabitha in her eschatological assault on the Antichrist is called προφητεία. The former material does constitute a revelation or "unveiling" (of a secret cosmic realm), whereas the latter would more properly be called "prophecy." Titles of apocrypha were evidently rather fluid for Didymus and (we might suppose) his contemporaries, and a single text might be referred to by a variety of analogous titles, depending on the primary association a scholar, scribe, or librarian might have with it.

Although the text of the Apocalypse of Elijah derives originally from the later third century, there is no evidence to ascribe a fixed title of "apocalypse" to this initial stage of composition. Quite the contrary: there is evidence for a fluidity of titles—under the pseudonym Elijah— at least until the creation of the Achmimic codex in the mid-fourth century. The "Apocalypse of Elijah" must therefore be considered without the constraints of the rubric "apocalypse."

Still, it is important to consider that during the fourth century this text came to be called an "apocalypse," at least in some manuscripts. Merely as a recollection of the book of Revelation, this title would not have been entirely extraordinary as applied to the Apocalypse of Elijah. Parts of the text recall the book of Revelation, while more generally the eschatological focus of the text might have reminded some millennialist scribe of the similarly dramatic prophecies in Revelation. In Egypt, where the extant Apocalypse of Elijah was especially popular in some areas, it is conceivable the text came to be called an "apocalypse" because certain scribes, in light of Revelation, associated the title ἀποκάλυψεις specifically with eschatological contents (as do many modern scholars).

THE APOCALYPSE OF ELIJAH AND OTHER ELIJAH PSEUDEPIGRAPHA

A valuable collection of patristic and rabbinic references to Elijah apocrypha, edited by Michael Stone and John Strugnell, illustrates the

---

Stone/Strugnell, 64–71. Because Jerome provides no further information about this text, it cannot be certain that he had ever read it.

extent of the pseudepigraphic Elijah tradition.[41] Few of these references
can be connected with the Apocalypse of Elijah discussed here, but they
do illustrate the interests and tendencies of literature written under the
name of Elijah and therefore supply the context in which the present
Apocalypse of Elijah would have developed.

Tours of Hell

The fifth-century *Epistle of Pseudo-Titus* contains the earliest and
most extended "quotation" from an Elijah apocalypse, describing the
torments of sinners in Gehenna (ll. 400–417).[42] The rabbinic *Chronicle of
Jerachmeel* also attributes such a vision to Elijah.[43] But whereas the
Hebrew apocryphon *Sefer Eliahu* does describe Elijah's journey "to the
west of the world [where] I saw souls being judged in pain, each
according to his deeds,"[44] the Apocalypse of Elijah nowhere mentions
even the existence of an underworld, merely suggesting a vertical
separation of saints and sinners in 5:26-28.[45]

---

41. See Stone/Strugnell. Cf. Albert-Marie Denis, *Introduction aux pseudépigraphes
grecs d'ancien testament*, SVTP 1 (Leiden: Brill, 1970), 163–69; and Emil Schürer, *History
of the Jewish People in the Age of Jesus Christ*, 3 vols., ed. Geza Vermes, Fergus Millar,
and Martin Goodman (rev. ed.; Edinburgh: T. & T. Clark, 1987), 3:799–803.

42. See Stone/Strugnell, 14–15; also *Epistle of Pseudo-Titus*, tr. A. de Santos Otero
(Eng. translation by George Ogg) in *NTA* 2:158. Cf. the brief discussion in Montague
Rhodes James, *The Lost Apocrypha of the Old Testament: Their Titles and Fragments*
(London: SPCK, 1920), 55–56, 61.

43. A nearly identical vision to that in *Jerachmeel* is also found, attributed to Elijah, in
Reshith Chokmah. For both, see Stone/Strugnell, 16–26 (cf. James, *Lost Apocrypha*, 56).
Jean-Marc Rosenstiehl discusses another early tour led by Elijah, which makes use of a
popular folklore motif of the ancient world for its frame, that of the unequal fates of
rich and poor: "Les révélations d'Élie: Élie et les tourments des damnés," in *La littérature
intertestamentaires: Collogne de Strasbourg* (Strasbourg: Presses universitaires de France,
1985), 99–107. On the relationship of these texts to other apocalyptic visions of
underworld punishments, see Martha Himmelfarb, *Tours of Hell: An Apocalyptic Form in
Jewish and Christian Literature* (Philadelphia: University of Pennsylvania Press, 1983)
34–37, 127–39.

44. In Moses Buttenwieser, *Die hebräische Elias-Apokalypse* (Leipzig: Eduard Pfeiffer,
1897), 15. The "west" as the land of the dead is an Egyptian tradition, ⲀⲘⲚⲦⲈ or "west"
being the standard term for Hades in Coptic literature. Richard Bauckham has argued
that the visit to Gehenna in *Sefer Eliahu*, which he dates to the first century C.E., at the
latest, is a "summary" of the more elaborate accounts of Hell attributed to Elijah in the
Pseudo-Titus Epistle and the *Chronicle of Jerachmeel* (see below, pp. 49–50), implying that
the Pseudo-Titus Elijah fragment would be "probably the oldest extant tour of hell"
(Bauckham, "Early Jewish Visions of Hell," *JTS* 41 [1990]:375; cf. 363–65). While
Bauckham appropriately derives visions of hell from the Jewish heavenly tours tradition
(cf. Himmelfarb, *Tours of Hell*, chap. 2), this particular proposition rests on quite
insecure dating.

45. It is strange that Ach commences ApocEl 2 with the phrase "regarding the
dissolution of heaven and earth *and that which is under the earth*," whereas the Sahidic

It is thus of considerable interest that Didymus the Blind, who cites the Coptic Elijah Apocalypse accurately in one passage—as the Prophecy of Elijah—refers elsewhere to an "Apocalypse of Elijah" that contains information about Hades.[46] Bärbel Krebber, the editor of Didymus's Ecclesiastes commentary, has assumed that a single apocryphon must lie behind both citations;[47] but in light of the present evidence, it is more likely that Didymus knew two Elijah apocrypha, one describing a tour of Hades and the other describing the eschaton. The latter has come down as the Coptic Elijah Apocalypse.

Origen's Attribution of 1 Corinthians 2:9

Origen claimed that Paul had taken the verse, "what no eye has seen, nor ear heard, nor the heart of man conceived, what God has prepared for those who love him," from "no canonical book, except in the apocryphon of Elijah the prophet."[48] Jerome also knew of such a phrase in "the Apocalypse of Elijah."[49]

This phrase appears nowhere in the extant Apocalypse of Elijah. Two significant instances of the phrase—in Clement of Alexandria's *Protrepticus* and the *Apostolic Constitutions*—place it in the context of a "description" of eschatological rewards, destined for the righteous after the last judgment.[50] Although the Apocalypse of Elijah demonstrates an overwhelming interest in the ultimate fate of the righteous, not a single manuscript bears a trace of the phrase; and it would be difficult to determine where it might most appropriately have fit, as the Apocalypse

---

texts have only ". . . heaven and earth." But because the phrase—and the chapters that follow—concerns the eschatological dissolution of these places, it is doubtful that a description of the underworld such as we find in the Elijah fragments could have been alluded to here.

The image of eschatological judgment in ApocEl 5:26-28 poses the righteous and the condemned observing each other from their respective places, a scene paralleled in the story of Lazarus (Q/Lk 16:23-26) and the Egyptian story of Setne-Khamwas (cf. *1 En* 62:11-12; 108:14-15; Jb 23:30). Yet at an earlier point (1:11) the Apocalypse of Elijah describes judgment as occurring as all people attempt to ascend to the heavenly Jerusalem in the eschaton: only the righteous can safely pass the "Thrones of death."

46. Didymus the Blind, *Comm. Eccles.* 235.26–28 (on Tabitha; tr. and ed. Kramer and Krebber); 92.5 (on Hades; tr. Gronewald).

47. Krebber, "Die Eliasapokalypse bei Didymos," in Kramer and Krebber, eds., *Didymos der Blinde*, 4:159–61.

48. Origen, *Comm. Matt.*, on Mt 27:9; see Stone/Strugnell, 64–73.

49. Jerome, *Comm. Is.*, book 17, on 64:4; *Ep. 57* to Pammachius; see Stone/Strugnell, 68–71.

50. Clement of Alexandria, *Protrepticus* 44; *Apos. Cons.* 7.32.5 (both in Stone/Strugnell, 44–46, frags. III.f–g). See James, *Lost Apocrypha*, 54; Denis, *Introduction aux pseudépigraphes grecs*, 163–64 and n. 2.

of Elijah tends to give more concrete images of reward than "what eye has not seen, nor ear heard."[51]

Furthermore, the phrase circulated widely as an unattributed, formulaic logion.[52] Thus although its content—unimaginable heavenly rewards—suggests the type of material offered by an apocalyptic vision, the phrase would hardly be a distinctive feature of any text.[53]

Paul himself probably drew the phrase from the store of formulas and expressions arising from ancient liturgical tradition, as Pierre Prigent has argued.[54] Deriving as it must from such general origins, it is understandable why the phrase would have circulated so widely in late antiquity.[55] But then what value has Origen as a witness to an Elijah apocalypse contemporaneous with Paul? None whatsoever; it is more likely that Origen and Jerome were familiar—although not necessarily directly familiar—with an Elijah apocalypse in their own historical periods. Whether they knew that this apocalypse contained the phrase, or (equally likely) whether they associated the phrase with contents they ascribed to this apocalypse, Origen and Jerome decided that this apocalypse must be Paul's scriptural source at 1 Cor 2:9. It must be realized, however, that their only reason for seeking a source for 1 Cor 2:9 among the apocrypha circulating in their cultures was that Paul himself indicated that the phrase was quoted from elsewhere.

Origen therefore can be a witness not to an Elijah apocryphon of the first century C.E. or earlier but rather to one from his own time and place, third-century Alexandria and Caesarea. Because Didymus the Blind

---

51. E.g., ApocEl 1:8-10; 4:27-29; 5:6, 39. Denis would make the Clement passage the possible conclusion to ApocEl (*Introduction aux pseudépigraphes grecs*, 164); and it is true that here there is only one ms. witness (Ach), allowing the possibility of an alternative ending. But because Clement does not claim to be quoting an apocryphon here, least of all one of Elijah, it would be a forced and convoluted argument, speculating on the original place in ApocEl of a passage from Clement, in order to support *Origen's* claim. Cf. B. Dehandschutter, "Les Apocalypses d'Élie," in *Élie le prophète: Bible, tradition, iconographie*, ed. Gerard F. Willems (Louvain: Peeters, 1988), 60–61.

52. See Stone/Strugnell, 42–63; Eusebius, *De laudibus Constantini* 6.21 (*PG* 20:1549); and, in general, Pierre Prigent, "Ce que l'oeil n'a pas vu, I Cor. 2,9: Histoire et préhistoire d'une citation," *TZ* 14 (1958):416–29.

53. See Hans Conzelmann's discussion of the phrase as a combination of wisdom and apocalyptic theologies (*1 Corinthians*, tr. James W. Leitch [Philadelphia: Fortress, 1975], 63–64).

54. Prigent, "Ce que l'oeil n'a pas vu," 424–29.

55. Paul's opening καθὼς γέγραπται, does not imply that Paul knew the source but only that the source was at least occasionally found in textual form. Cf. Archibald Robertson and Alfred Plummer, *A Critical and Exegetical Commentary on the First Epistle of St. Paul to the Corinthians* (Edinburgh: T. & T. Clark, 1911), 41–43.

knew two Elijah apocalypses in fourth-century Alexandria, of which only ours remains in Coptic, it is likely that Origen knew at least one of them. Jerome may have become familiar with this second Elijah apocalypse either through its wide circulation or, more likely, through his interest in Egyptian monastic culture, which circulated and transcribed an abundance of apocryphal literature. In this respect it is interesting to note a passage of the biblical pseudepigraphon *Testament of Jacob*, probably compiled among Egyptian Christians of an "Old Testament" orientation after the third century:[56]

> He was taken up into the heavens to visit the resting-places. And behold, a host of tormentors came out. The appearance of each one was different; and they were ready to torment the sinners—that is the fornicators, and the harlots, and the catamites . . . [etc.]. In short, many are the punishments for all the sins we have mentioned: the unquenchable fire, the outer darkness, the place where there shall be weeping and grinding of teeth, and the worm that does not sleep. And it is a terrible thing for you to be brought before the judge, and it is a terrible thing to come into the hands of the living God. Woe to all sinful men for whom these tortures and these tormentors are prepared. And afterwards he took me and showed me the place where my fathers Abraham and Isaac were, a place that was all light; and they were glad and rejoiced in the kingdom of the heavens, in the city of the beloved. And he showed me all the resting-places and all the good things prepared for the righteous, and the things that eye has not seen nor ear heard, and have not come into the heart of men, that God has prepared for those who love him and do his will on earth (for, if they end well, they do his will).[57]

Although at one time briefly discussed as the source of 1 Cor 2:9, the passage is fairly obviously built out of a number of quotations or recollections from Christian Scripture.[58] Its contents, however, curiously combine the phrase from 1 Cor 2:9 and a tour of hell, two "Elianic" attributions missing from the Coptic Elijah Apocalypse but evidently part of the lost Elijah apocalypse. The *Testament of Jacob* nowhere implies an association with Elijah; nor is it apparent that the above

56. The text assumes the existence of an established liturgical calendar. Cf. James H. Charlesworth, *The Pseudepigrapha and Modern Research, with a Supplement*, Septuagint and Cognate Studies 7 (Chico, Calif.: Scholars Press, 1981), 131–33; Schürer, *History of the Jewish People*, 3.2:766.

57. *T. Jacob* 8 (tr. K. S. Kuhn, *AOT* 447–48).

58. See H.F.D. Sparks, "1 Kor 2⁹: A Quotation from the Coptic Testament of Jacob?" *ZNW* 67 (1976):267–76, esp. 273–75, responding to Eckhard von Nordheim, "Das Zitat des Paulus in 1 Kor 2⁹ und seine Beziehung zum koptischen Testament Jakobs," *ZNW* 65 (1974):112–20.

passage derives from another source. As the sole heavenly tour in the text, however, the passage certainly depended on some model for its contents, particularly as the composer was relying on phrases from Christian Scripture to fill in the details. It is conceivable that an Elijah apocalypse with a tour of hell and "eye has not seen" phrase distantly provided this model.

The Physiognomy of Antichrist

Although descriptions of the appearance of the eschatological Adversary circulated widely in late antiquity and eventually became a standard component of both Jewish and Christian apocalyptic literature,[59] a Greek manuscript fragment attributes the Adversary's description to "secrets that Elijah the prophet said."[60] Both the Apocalypse of Elijah and *Sefer Eliahu* contain short physiognomies of Adversaries; yet there is not a common detail among the three descriptions. This would suggest that only the concept of accurate descriptions of the eschatological Adversary may have been associated with the authority of Elijah.[61]

Sefer Eliahu

This Hebrew text,[62] written in the name of Elijah, was coincidentally also dated to the rise of Palmyra in the third century C.E. by its editor, Moses Buttenweiser. The text's obvious references to events in the seventh century, however, make the theory of a third-century core difficult to sustain critically.[63] The text is manifestly an apocalypse,

59. See Jean-Marc Rosenstiehl, "Le portrait de l'Antichrist," in *Pseudépigraphes de l'ancien testament et manuscrits de la mer morte,* ed. Marc Philonenko (Paris: Presses universitaires, 1967), 45–60; Stone/Strugnell, 28–39; and Bernard McGinn, "Portraying Antichrist in the Middle Ages," in *The Use and Abuse of Eschatology in the Middle Ages,* ed. Werner Verbeke et al., Mediaevalia Lovaniensia Series 1, Studia 15 (Louvain: Louvain University Press, 1988), 1–13.

60. Paris Greek 4, f.228ʳ, in Stone/Strugnell, 28–29.

61. Cf. James, *Lost Apocrypha,* 57–60.

62. Text and German translation in Buttenweiser, *Die hebräische Elias-Apokalypse;* text and Hebrew commentary in *Midrᵉshei Gᵉulah,* ed. Yehudah Eben-Shmuel (Jerusalem: Mosad Bialik, 1954), 41–48.

63. Buttenweiser, *Die hebräische Elias-Apokalypse,* 68–77, summarized in idem, *Outline of the Neo-Hebraic Apocalyptic Literature* (Cincinnati: Jennings & Pye, 1901), 30–31. Buttenweiser's dating has been criticized in Schürer, *History of the Jewish People,* 3:803. On the historical context of *Sef. El.,* see M. Avi-Yonah, *The Jews under Roman and Byzantine Rule* (New York: Schocken, 1976), 261, cf. 257–60; and Salo Wittmayer Baron, *A Social and Religious History of the Jews,* vol. 5: *Religious Controls and Dissensions* (2d ed.; New York: Columbia University Press, 1957), 138–69.

revealed by Michael to Elijah on Mount Carmel (cf. 1 Kings 19). A very brief tour of the regions of the world,[64] including Gehenna, moves quickly to a discussion of ominous battles, the precise names of the last kings, and an eschatological timetable culminating in conflagration, judgment, resurrection, and a new world.

There are few parallels in *Sefer Eliahu* to the Apocalypse of Elijah. The former focuses exclusively on Palestine, whereas the latter describes events in Egypt. Whereas the Apocalypse of Elijah only alludes to biblical passages, *Sefer Eliahu* cites them explicitly, along with certain rabbinic authorities. The discussion of kings—Persian and Roman— hardly resembles the battles between Persians and Assyrians in ApocEl 2. Although each text contains a physiognomic description of an eschatological Adversary, the details are not parallel.[65] Finally, *Sefer Eliahu's* attribution to Elijah can be understood within the context of Jewish mysticism, where his eschatological status as the final legal authority lent him unparalleled authority as the bearer of revelation. Gershom Scholem observed that "at important turning points in the history of Jewish mysticism—precisely at those times when something new appeared—constant reference was made to revelations of the prophet Elijah."[66] As much as one can account for the Elijah pseudonym also in an Egyptian Christian context (see chapter 3, below), one can see the pseudonym as a distinctive outgrowth of early Byzantine Judaism in the case of *Sefer Eliahu*. It therefore becomes difficult to account for the coincidence of pseudepigraphic authorities on the basis of a common *Vorlage*. It is scarcely possible that the two texts have a common origin, although their obvious sharing of themes allows the possibility of an Elijah revelation "tradition" of some sort, a subject to which we will return.

---

64. This tour, which is organized by direction, seems to reflect a larger tradition of Elijah's traverses of the world; see Louis Ginzberg, *The Legends of the Jews,* 7 vols. (Philadelphia: Jewish Publication Society, 1909–38), 4:203; 6:326 n. 46 (*b. Berakot* 4b). The tradition is amply witnessed in a Kurdistani Jewish havdalah hymn: "Elijah (dwells) among the angels. He soars (over) the entire world in four orbits. . . . He travels (to) the four corners of the world" (4, 7), in Yona Sabar, *The Folk Literature of the Kurdistani Jews: An Anthology,* Yale Judaica Series 23 (New Haven: Yale University Press, 1982), 68–70. Bauckham sees this tour in *SefEl* as a "summary" of a prior Jewish apocalypse ("Early Jewish Visions of Hell," 362–65).

65. See Rosenstiehl, "Le portrait de l'antichrist," 52.

66. Gershom Scholem, *Origins of the Kabbalah,* ed. R. J. Werblowsky, tr. Allan Arkush (Philadelphia: Jewish Publication Society, 1987), 36; cf. 238–46. See also Aharon Wiener, *The Prophet Elijah in the Development of Judaism: A Depth-Psychological Study* (London: Routledge & Kegan Paul, 1978), 53–59; Ginzberg, *Legends of the Jews,* 4:229–33; and Moshe Idel, *Kabbalah: New Perspectives* (New Haven: Yale University Press, 1988), 100, 241.

The Two Sorrows of the Kingdom of Heaven
and the Irish Apocryphal Tradition

The considerable secondary literature on Irish biblical apocrypha has shown in detail not only the indigenous folkloric sources of some of the legends but also the early circulation in Ireland of a substantial corpus of ancient Jewish and Christian literature from the Mediterranean.[67] Early Irish Christianity's interest in the figures of Elijah and Enoch and their destined opposition to the Antichrist is reflected in a number of indigenous compositions; but Elijah apparently held a special position in legend.[68] Therefore we read in a text entitled *The Two Sorrows of the Kingdom of Heaven*, apparently dating from the tenth or eleventh century,[69] how Elijah preached before the birds of paradise after his ascension:[70]

> He preached to them about the Day of Judgement, in particular, about the tortures to be meted out to the souls of certain persons on Doomsday. The four rivers around Mount Sion would be assigned to burn souls for ten thousand years. . . . Thus, a great amount of distress awaits the sinner. Fortunate is he who has accumulated goodly merit, even on that day itself. . . ,
>
> The host assembled there will be enormous. Moreover, it is in the presence of that host that all will set forth their deeds, both good and bad. . . . Christ, son of God, along with the angels of heaven, and the inhabi-

67. The diversity of late antique texts and of new compositions based upon late antique texts in manuscripts dating as early as the eighth century suggests that such texts began to enter Ireland with the beginning of Irish monasticism in the fourth century C.E. Cf. M. R. James, "Learning and Literature Till Pope Sylvester II," *Cambridge Medieval History* 3 (1922):504–6; St. John D. Seymour, "The Bringing Forth of the Soul in Irish Literature," *JTS* 22 (1921):16–20; idem, "Notes on Apocrypha in Ireland," *Proceedings of the Royal Irish Academy* 37C (1925–27):107–17; D. N. Dumville, "Biblical Apocrypha and the Early Irish: A Preliminary Investigation," *Proceedings of the Royal Irish Academy* 73C (1973):299–338; Martin McNamara, *The Apocrypha in the Irish Church* (Dublin: Institute for Advanced Studies, 1975); Jane Stevenson, "Ascent through the Heavens, from Egypt to Ireland," *Cambridge Medieval Celtic Studies* 5 (1983):21–35; and Máire Herbert and Martin McNamara, eds., *Irish Biblical Apocrypha: Selected Texts in Translation* (Edinburgh: T. & T. Clark, 1989).

68. See Dumville, "Biblical Apocrypha," 308–11 (Elijah *and* Enoch). Elijah and Enoch lore was apparently even more widespread in medieval Europe: e.g., the semi-Christian eschatological saga in Old German, the *Muspilli*, wherein Elijah alone fights with the Antichrist. See translation and discussion in Ursula Dronke, "Beowulf and Ragnarok," *Saga-Book of the Viking Society* 17 (1969):317–21.

69. McNamara, "Introduction," in Herbert and McNamara, eds., *Irish Biblical Apocrypha*, xxii.

70. On multiforms of this frame narrative, see Seymour, "Notes on Apocrypha in Ireland," 110. There are obvious indigenous folkloric roots to the story, as no analogs exist in Mediterranean or Jewish texts (cf. Ginzberg, *Legends of the Jews*, 4:202–11).

tants of earth and of hell, will be listening to all until the revelations are
completed. . . .

[A judgement process is described, where each person is witnessed by
an accompanying angel and demon and sent to heaven or hell, depending
on the "measure" of good or evil.] At last, when the decisions about the
fate of the children are completed, then Christ will bid those who have
chosen thus to depart with the devil and his rabble, to be cast into his
company in the eternal abyss. . . .

. . . [The author describes the cry] uttered by the souls in their delight at
escaping from the devil, and the cry of the denizens of hell left behind.
[Another] cry is that of the souls of those who merit hell, as they are being
dragged off to the eternal dwelling of pain and torture, which has no end.
Those, however, chosen by God, will go to the eternal kingdom with
Christ, son of God, to remain there forever among the hosts of archangels.[71]

The discourse concludes with the frame-ending "Thus Elijah
preaches of the distress of Doomsday," and then the text proceeds to
discuss Enoch and Elijah's eschatological battle with Antichrist (§8).
Here we come upon the statement that "there is no miracle performed
by Christ on earth that he [Antichrist] will not perform, *except for the
raising of the dead.*"[72]

This idea finds its first and most detailed expression in ApocEl 3:11-
13; 4:31 but it does not appear to have been typical of Antichrist signs
thereafter.[73] Further, the inability to resurrect was not a common expectation of the Antichrist in Irish Christian tradition, for another apocryphon devoted exclusively to the origins and appearance of the Antichrist says that "he will raise the dead in imitation of Christ."[74] Thus
where M. R. James once proposed that the *Two Sorrows* derived from "an

---

71. *Two Sorrows*, §§3–6, tr. Máire Herbert, in Herbert and McNamara, eds., *Irish
Biblical Apocrypha*, 19–21. See also text and introduction in G. Dottin, "Les deux
chagrins du royaume du ciel," *Revue celtique* 21 (1909):349–87; and discussion by
McNamara, *Apocrypha in the Irish Church*, 24–27.

72. *Two Sorrows* §8, in *Irish Biblical Apocrypha*, 21.

73. Cf. Wilhelm Bousset, *The Antichrist Legend*, tr. A. H. Keane (London: Hutchinson,
1896), 177–79. An eschatological tract attributed to Ephraem Syrus is the only other
significant early source (*De fine extremo* 9; see Bousset, *Antichrist Legend*, 178, 282 n. 14),
but it is doubtful that this was the text used by the author of the *Two Sorrows*.

74. *Antichrist* §3, in *Irish Biblical Apocrypha*, 149. So also in the Antichrist discourse in
the *Book of Lismore*; f.110; RIA ms. 23.N.15, translated in Dottin, "Les deux chagrins,"
355; and Douglas Hyde, "Mediaeval Account of Antichrist," in *Medieval Studies in
Memory of Gertrude Schoepperle Loomis* (Paris: Champion, 1927), 391–98. B. O'Cuív has
published a Middle Irish poem from a fourteenth century ms., which predicts,
"Everything that fair Christ did while He was on earth Antichrist does without
difficulty except raise people from the dead" ("Two Items from Irish Apocryphal
Tradition: 1. The Conception and Characteristics of Antichrist," *Celtica* 10 [1973]:98).

apocryphon which it is safe to say, belongs to Eastern Christendom," there is now good reason to believe that it is the Apocalypse of Elijah, in its Greek form, that lies somewhere behind the *Two Sorrows*.[75]

Yet the only substantial thematic overlaps between the *Two Sorrows* and the Apocalypse of Elijah lie in (1) the judgment scene, which is considerably less detailed and demonological in ApocEl 5:24-31 than in *Two Sorrows*;[76] (2) the general theme of the return of Enoch and Elijah; and (3) the basic idea of the "distress of Doomsday," which is articulated in terms of underworld punishment in the *Two Sorrows* and in terms of terrestrial woes and signs in the Apocalypse of Elijah.[77] There is a narrative *correlation* between the texts: the Apocalypse of Elijah is essentially an extended homiletic discourse, whereas the *Two Sorrows* is a story *about* such an extended discourse;[78] but this correlation represents no more than a common tradition (of which the Apocalypse of Elijah might be the ultimate source). Under such circumstances, it is doubtful that the Apocalypse of Elijah lay *immediately* before the author of the *Two Sorrows*.

The most striking aspect of the *Two Sorrows* is its coincidental combination of the very two traditions—eschatology and underworld pun-

75. James, "Learning and Literature," 505; cf. 502–3 on circulation and reading of Greek apocrypha in Ireland. Cf. McNamara, who insists that Irish apocrypha with Eastern Mediterranean origins derive from Latin versions (*Apocrypha in the Irish Church*, 2–3, 128). The Latin sources he has suggested, however—e.g., Pseudo-Hippolytus, *De consummatione mundi* (see McNamara, *Apocrypha in the Irish Church*, 25; cf. Dottin, "Les deux chagrins," 357–58)—are late, with no apparent parallels to the *Two Sorrows*. Circulation of Greek lore and texts in early Irish Christianity may be manifest in Saint Patrick's association of the name Ἡλίας with the sun, ἥλιος, in his *Confessions* (chap. 20). This name tradition is otherwise attested only in the eastern Mediterranean world (see below, pp. 71–72), suggesting that early Irish monks may have had a particular interest in the lore of Elijah. On early Coptic missions to Ireland, see Aziz S. Atiya, *History of Eastern Christianity* (Notre Dame, Ind.: University of Notre Dame Press, 1968), 150–51.

76. There is a close parallel between the *Two Sorrows*'s image of the accompanying angel and demon, who testify to a person's measure of good or evil, and the enigmatic statement in ApocEl 5:26 that "the sins of each one will stand against him in the place where they were committed, whether of the day or of the night."

77. A separation between underworld punishment and terrestrial distress seems to be implied in another Irish apocryphon *The Vision of Adomnán*, a tour apocalypse manifestly influenced by Enochic and apocalyptic Pauline literatures, which epitomizes the story of the *Two Sorrows*: Elijah is described as telling the inhabitants of Paradise "of the punishments and tortures of hell, *and* the terrors of Doomsday" (*Adomnán* 43, ed. and tr. Herbert, in Herbert and McNamara, eds., *Irish Biblical Apocrypha*, 147).

78. In the Ethiopian Jewish text *Abba Elijah*, an extended homily on diverse subjects (including, at the end, eschatology) is framed as the words of "preacher Abba Elijah, of the city of Rome"; see text in Wolf Leslau, *Falasha Anthology*, Yale Judaica Series 6 (New Haven: Yale University Press, 1951; reprint, New York: Schocken, 1969), 40–49.

ishments—ascribed to an Elijah apocryphon by late antique sources, as discussed above. Punishment of sinners is given much more emphasis in the Irish text than in the Apocalypse of Elijah (where it is largely implied that sinners will die in the reign of, or with, the Lawless One). The *Two Sorrows* casts its underworld punishments into the aftermath of an eschatological judgment, in contrast to the *Pseudo-Titus Epistle* and the *Chronicle of Jerachmeel,* which both reveal punishments as the status quo of an (ongoing) underworld.[79] The *Two Sorrows* does not discuss methods of punishment, whereas the two Elijah "quotations" dwell luridly on measure-for-measure deserts. And there are many differences between the eschatology of the Apocalypse of Elijah and that of the *Two Sorrows.* Yet somehow the author has envisioned the proper topics of an Elijah discourse to be eschatology and punishments. Could it, therefore, reflect the original, core Elijah apocryphon?

This is doubtful. Knowledge of the transmission of manuscripts between the Greek world and Ireland is exceedingly primitive, and the most responsible appraisal of such apparent textual affiliations should neither require immediate textual dependence nor extrapolate from one medieval Irish text to explain the diverse Elijah apocrypha of late antiquity. It is more plausible to suggest that the author of the *Two Sorrows* had once heard or read the Apocalypse of Elijah but was more interested in (or remembered with more relish) its symbolism of the judgment than in all the cosmic and social distress portrayed as leading up to that judgment. Although he might have encountered the tradition of Elijah's underworld visions through Christian folklore, the discussion of punishments in the *Two Sorrows* can be better understood as an expansion of the corresponding section of the Apocalypse of Elijah than as an eschatologizing epitome of the lurid *Pseudo-Titus Epistle.*

Conclusion: Apocalypse of Elijah and Elianica

M. R. James concluded after his 1920 survey of such Elianic references and writings:

> It is quite probable, I think, that the original Apocalypse [of Elijah] contained all the ingredients that the fragments show us, descriptions of

---

79. Explicit descriptions of underworld punishments are cast in the context of eschatological prophecy in *Apoc. Pet.* 7–13 (Eth.). There is an indication in such literature of a tension between traditions of eschatological judgment and recompense (perhaps native to sectarian eschatology) and traditions of afterdeath judgment and recompense (perhaps native to less sectarian and eschatologically oriented groups).

hell-torments, eschatological prophecy, descriptions of Antichrist and didactic matter. But neither of the extant Apocalypses can be supposed to represent the old book faithfully. The Coptic has been Christianized, the Hebrew abridged, and additions made to both.[80]

In 1979, Stone and Strugnell expressed a more equivocal opinion: "The editors believe that, in antiquity there was *at least* one Elijah apocryphon"; and yet the "fragments . . . may, as literary pieces, go back to, or reflect knowledge of, *an* early Greek apocryphal work on Elijah."[81] Sparks alone has taken the restrained position that "there were probably several 'Elijahs' circulating in the early centuries in various languages, some of which were only distantly related to one another, if at all."[82] This is the view assumed in this book. If there was ever an original text disclosing the revelations of Elijah—and there is no evidence that there ever was—it is inextricable from the profusion of Elianic texts and, more importantly, Elianic lore that circulated in the Greco-Roman period.[83]

We have concrete evidence, therefore, for (1) an Elijah apocryphon composed in Greek in the latter half of the third century C.E., consisting almost entirely of eschatology and known both as Elijah's "prophecy" (Didymus the Blind) and Elijah's "apocalypse" (Ach)—the subject of this study; and (2) an Elijah apocryphon composed in Hebrew in the seventh century C.E., perhaps on the basis of a prior version. We also have good reason, on the testimony of Didymus, to consider the existence of (3) a Greek Elijah apocryphon containing a tour of hell. If Origen had heard of or read this apocryphon, then its *terminus ante quem* would be around 244 C.E. (the period of his commentary on the Gospel of Matthew). Its earliest date would be impossible to establish, but given this hypothetical text's absence so far among Egyptian manuscript archives, it would perhaps be unsafe to push the *terminus post quem* back further than the second century C.E. or to assume Jewish origin.[84] Further, one cannot presume a literary connection between this hypothetical Greek tour-apocalypse of Elijah and the Elijah tour fragments in the *Epistle of*

80. James, *Lost Apocrypha*, 61. This assumption is again reflected in Richard Bauckham, "The Apocalypses in the New Pseudepigrapha," *JSNT* 26 (1986):109–10.

81. Stone/Strugnell, 1, 6 (emphasis mine). John Strugnell reiterated his conviction in the existence of an *Ur*-Elijah apocryphon in a conversation with the author in April 1989.

82. Sparks, "Introduction to the Apocalypse of Elijah," 759.

83. Cf. Dehandschutter, "Les Apocalypses d'Élie," 64–67.

84. This would place the text in the early period of Christian tour-of-hell apocalypses; cf. Himmelfarb, *Tours of Hell*, 169–70.

Pseudo-Titus and the *Chronicle of Jerachmeel*. So Didymus's "Apocalypse of Elijah" may simply be one more imaginative retelling of the lore of Elijah, this time written in Alexandria.

Finally, because Origen's theory of 1 Cor 2:9 is incorrect and no source-critical dissections of the Coptic Elijah apocalypse have succeeded convincingly in demonstrating a Jewish *Vorlage*, we have no reason to assume or even to seek a pre-Christian Elijah apocalypse. Certainly, the argument from silence cannot be pushed too far; but when only sheer conjecture proposes Hellenistic Jewish writing in the name of Elijah, we would be mistaken to seek proof in such obviously late texts as the three Elijah apocrypha mentioned above.

The diverse Elianica that we have discussed do indicate the parameters within which revelations of Elijah were composed throughout late antiquity. If we except the "eye has not seen" saying as too widespread to be indicative, then these parameters would be constituted by (1) revelations of the underworld and (2) revelations of the eschaton, with particular attention to the appearance of the eschatological Adversary. No doubt the parameters functioned in the following way: a text, or even a fragment, that dealt with either or both of these subjects would be attributed to Elijah, who was understood to be an authority on such matters (presumably insofar as he was supposed to have traveled through the heavens from Mount Horeb and to return to expose the eschatological Adversary in the eschaton).[85] Precisely how such texts or fragments were thereby understood as the revelations of Elijah—generally and in the specific context of early Egyptian Christianity—occupies chapter 3. This theory would allow for the possibility that the authors of the *Pseudo-Titus Epistle* and the *Chronicle of Jerachmeel* may have inserted in their works, as traditional Elianica, unattributed fragments containing underworld descriptions. That is, they would have labeled them as visions of Elijah because these represented the type of revelation that these authors associated with Elijah.[86] Of course, other figures were credited with both underworld and eschatological rev-

---

85. Himmelfarb proposes that "in the late Second Temple period tours with a particular interest in the punishment of the wicked after death must have circulated . . . the heroes were probably Isaiah and Elijah" (*Tours of Hell*, 169), although her basis for this conjecture is the much later use of these figures as guides among the earlier extant tour texts. Cf. Bauckham, "Early Jewish Visions of Hell," 362–65, 375–76.

86. Himmelfarb proposes that the Pseudo-Titus Elijah fragment was itself interpolated with Christian imagery (*Tours of Hell*, 36). If so, it would demonstrate the continuing authority of the Elianic vision for some Christians.

elations, and we must therefore explain why Elijah is the seer in some cases and Paul, Peter, Ezra, or Mary in others. The answer probably lies in the relative authority or "traditionality" that one name (and his or her legend) held in any particular place and time. The dominant status of Elijah in early Coptic asceticism is discussed in the next chapter.

Even when the abundance of Elijah attributions and texts are accounted for through the acknowledgment of a historically fluid tradition, questions remain about the extant texts: If the Elijah tradition encompassed both eschatological and underworld visions, why do the three extant Elijah texts—Apocalypse of Elijah, *Sefer Eliahu,* and the *Two Sorrows*—only *allude* to the underworld (vividly, in the case of the *Two Sorrows*) without incorporating or inventing an underworld tour? Did the two traditions of Elijah's revelations continue independently? Was there ever the desire on the part of an early scribe—as there was in the case of Enoch literature—to compile (or compose) a complete apocalypse of Elijah out of the diverse traditions circulating in late antiquity? At the present state of availability of Elijah texts, these questions cannot be answered. It is conceivable that, as more Elijah texts are found and more non-Elijah texts are explored for Elijah traditions, the tendencies of traditions and composition will increasingly be fleshed out. It is hoped that the observations and hypotheses advanced in this book will sustain the evidence afforded by further discoveries.

3

The Context of Christian Elijah Pseudepigraphy in Egypt

The discussion of an Elianic revelation tradition raises a more general issue—the meaning of Elijah pseudepigraphy itself. Why write a book in the name of Elijah? What significance did his name carry and for whom? What is the relationship between the legendary Elijah and the contents of a text written in his name?

Although reverence for biblical heroes such as Elijah, Enoch, and Moses was widespread in antiquity, these questions must be asked separately of each Elijah pseudepigraphon we have discussed, for each is a product of its immediate environment and religious culture. Thus just as the pseudepigraphy of *Sefer Eliahu* must be explained in the context of sixth- and seventh-century Palestine, so one must understand the motivations of Elianic composition and attribution in third- and fourth-century Egypt to explain the pseudepigraphy of the Apocalypse of Elijah.[1]

This chapter was presented in shorter form to the Consultation in Christian Apocrypha of the SBL 1989 Annual Meeting, Chicago, November 1989.
1. Pseudepigraphy per se has been studied from a number of different angles, particularly that of psychological motivation. This topic has been bracketed in this study and the anachronistic question of "deception" through pseudepigraphy has been avoided. Pseudepigraphy was a cultural phenomenon, and its motivations ranged from the need for a hero's authority to the literary conventions of some scribal group. See, e.g., L. H. Brockington, "The Problem of Pseudonymity," *JTS* 4 (1953):15–22; Kurt Aland, "The Problem of Anonymity and Pseudonymity in Christian Literature of the First Two Centuries," *JTS* 12 (1961):39–49; Wolfgang Speyer, "Religöse Pseudepigraphie und literarische Fälschung im Altertum," *JAC* 8/9 (1965/66):88–125; Bruce M. Metzger, "Literary Forgeries and Canonical Pseudepigrapha," *JBL* 91 (1972):3–24; Morton Smith, "Pseudepigraphy in the Israelite Literary Tradition," in *Pseudepigrapha I*, ed. Kurt von Fritz, Entretiens sur l'antiquité classique 18 (Geneva: Vandoeuvres, 1972), 191–227;

Because the means by which a text might gain authority through a pseudonym are twofold, the issue in the Apocalypse of Elijah will be approached in two ways: first, by examining the social and religious milieu that might give rise to Elijah pseudepigraphy; and second, by considering the ways in which the pseudonymous authority is constructed within the text. These two contexts will be referred to as, respectively, the religious context and the narrative context. The religious context represents the cultural or practical significance of a pseudonymous authority (in this case, Elijah). The narrative context denotes the story of revelation—whatever connects the substance of revelation with the scriptural (or legendary) traditions of the pseudonymous authority.

NARRATIVE CONTEXT
OF ELIJAH PSEUDEPIGRAPHY
IN THE APOCALYPSE OF ELIJAH

The Apocalypse of Elijah does not discuss the manner or recipient of revelation; hence there are no explicit indications of its Elijah pseudepigraphy, apart from the title. It will be necessary, therefore, to examine other Elijah materials to form some idea of how this text might have been considered an "Apocalypse of Elijah," whether by the author or a later scribe. Would an audience in Upper Egypt have assumed a particular frame-story telling the circumstances of Elijah's revelation?

The Apocalypse of Elijah opens: "The word of the Lord came to me saying, 'Say to this people, "Why do you add sin to your sins and anger the Lord God who created you?"'" This prophetic commission formula, coupled with a remonstrative oracle, seems to be built out of similar formulas in Ezekiel and Jeremiah; these formulas would have been easily remembered by Egyptian Christian scribes. But the introduction also recalls the language of the biblical Elijah legend: "Then the word of the Lord came to Elijah the Tishbite, saying, 'Go down, . . . and you shall say to him'" (1 Kgs 21:17, 19). Likewise, on Carmel, Elijah uses the same kind of rhetorical question against the masses: "How long will you go limping with two different opinions?" (1 Kgs 18:21). The language of the

---

Martin Hengel, "Anonymität, Pseudepigraphie und 'Literarische Fälschung' in der jüdisch-hellenistischen Literatur," in *Pseudepigrapha I*, ed. von Fritz, 231–329; Christopher Rowland, *The Open Heaven: A Study of Apocalyptic in Judaism and Early Christianity* (New York: Crossroad, 1982), 61–70, 240–47.

introduction therefore would allow some connection between the text of the Apocalypse of Elijah and the Elijah of biblical legend.

The contents of the Apocalypse of Elijah provide information about the eschaton and its preceding woes and therefore could constitute an eschatological revelation, given by or to some legendary figure. Furthermore, the Elianic revelation tradition represented by the *Chronicle of Jerachmeel*, the *Pseudo-Titus Epistle*, and other texts discussed above provide evidence that Elijah was believed (in some Jewish and Christian circles of late antiquity) to have received revelations concerning the underworld and the judgment. Yet the biblical story of Elijah does not mention a particular occasion for revelation of any kind. Once again one may ask, Why were these revelations attributed to Elijah?

No legend of Elijah's revelations appears in the earliest *Lives of the Prophets*,[2] but in two later recensions he is said to have "traversed the heavens [οὐρανοπολῶν] with angels"[3] and to have been "reckoned worthy of the greatest mysteries and divine gifts [χαρισμάτων]."[4] Both passages refer to Elijah's lifetime rather than to events following his ascent by chariot (cf. 2 Kgs 2:11).[5] A similar tradition is reported by the fourth-century Syriac writer Aphraat, who states that "the Holy One transported [Elijah] into the abode of the saints, where those who love impurity have no power."[6] These texts show the existence of a tradition in which Elijah received revelations, thus supplementing the tradition already discussed of the content of Elijah's revelations. These texts do not indicate, however, the precise narrative context in which the Apocalypse of Elijah might have been heard.[7]

The clearest indication of this narrative context is in *Sefer Eliahu*. To

2. *Vitae Prophetarum*, Codex Marchalianus, Elijah (tr. D.R.A. Hare, *OTP* 2:396-97).

3. Recension Dorothei, in Stone/Strugnell, 95.

4. Recension Epiphanii, in Stone/Strugnell, 97. Dating estimates from Schürer, *The History of the Jewish People in the Age of Jesus Christ*, ed. Geza Vermes, Fergus Millar, and Martin Goodman, 3 vols. (Edinburgh: T. & T. Clark, 1973–87), 3:785.

5. Presumably any revelations received after this point in the legend would require some account of Elijah's descent or reappearance, so that the revelations could be transmitted as literary apocalypse. While there existed a vast lore concerning Elijah's eschatological return (as per Malachi 4), a revelation that depended upon this lore to explain its existence would also imply that the eschaton itself had come. To a certain extent, this is the case in the Apocalypse of Elijah (see below, pp. 265–66, 296–98), but the Elijah revelations in general do not reflect this implication about the times of the reader.

6. Aphraat, *De virginitate et sanctitate*, Patrologia syriaca 1, 1:833–34.

7. Cf. the narrative contexts in which gnostic revelations were attributed to Jesus: "The favourite period for such revelations is the forty days between the resurrection and the (final) ascension, but other events from the life of Jesus are also used, such as the transfiguration scene" (Kurt Rudolph, *Gnosis*, tr. R. McL. Wilson [San Francisco: Harper & Row, 1983], 151).

its eschatological prophecies *Sefer Eliahu* adds two literary elements: (1) it begins with a quotation of 1 Kgs 19:5-9, the description of Elijah's journey to Mount Horeb; and (2) it contains the following frame story:

> Michael the great Prince of Israel revealed this mystery to Elijah the prophet on Mount Carmel: the End and the age which is to come at the end of days, at the end of the fourth kingdom, in the days of the fourth king who is to come:

> "The spirit of the Lord lifted me up and took me to the east of the world, and I saw there a high place in flames, such that no-one could enter in there. Again the spirit lifted me up and took me to the south of the world."[8]

In each direction Elijah beholds secret places, one of which is hell; following these brief tours of the cosmos, the archangel Michael tells him of the eschaton. Although originating in a distinctly different place and time from the Apocalypse of Elijah, *Sefer Eliahu* expresses a tradition associating Elijah's revelations with a particular point in his legend: his ascent of a mountain. It should be noted that *Sefer Eliahu* contradicts itself by giving both Horeb and Carmel as the mountain; but in addition to Elijah's intimacy there with the "still, small voice" (1 Kgs 19:12-13), there is another reason to believe that Horeb was the originally intended locus of Elijah's revelations. According to the ninth- or tenth-century *Midrash Tanhuma*, God revealed to Elijah that the four phenomena that he beheld on Horeb represented the four worlds that humankind must traverse: life on earth (as the storm), death (as the earthquake), hell (as fire), and judgment (as the small voice).[9] This haggadah does not only correspond to the four worlds that Elijah tours in *Sefer Eliahu*; it also suggests a connection between the eschatological content of many Elianic revelations and the symbolic phenomena of 1 Kgs 19:11-12.[10]

---

8. *Sefer Eliahu*, in *Midrᵉshei Gᵉulah*, ed. Eben-Shmuel (Jerusalem: Mosad Bialik, 1954), 41; cf. Moses Buttenweiser, *Die Hebräische Elias-Apokalypse* (Leipzig: Eduard Pfeiffer, 1897), 15 (directions reversed).

9. *Midrash Tanhuma*, Pekude 2; Yezirat ha-Valad 155; cited in Louis Ginzberg, *The Legends of the Jews*, 7 vols. (Philadelphia: Jewish Publication Society, 1909–38), 4:200; 6:322 n. 30. On the dating of this tractate, see Moshe David Herr, "Tanhuma Yelammedenu," in *Encyclopedia Judaica* (New York: Macmillan, 1971), 15:795. In the Targum to the Kings passage, Elijah beholds *angels* of wind, storm, and fire before seeing God himself.

10. A twelfth-century Coptic encomium to Elijah, attributed to John Chrysostom, gives an extensive discourse on right piety and rewards, apparently delivered by God to Elijah while he is on Mount Horeb. See E. A. Wallis Budge, "On the Fragments of a Coptic Version of an Encomium on Elijah the Tishbite, attributed to Saint John

But what use might *Sefer Eliahu,* with its frame-story and hence more apocalyptic format, have for Egyptian Christianity? A connection can be made through Coptic healing, binding, and amulet spells from the Byzantine period. It became conventional in Greco-Egyptian "magic" to identify or authorize a set of ritual instructions or even a mere spell under an authoritative pseudonym, much like a miniature apocalypse. The *Testament of Solomon* and the *Eighth Book of Moses* (PGM XIII.1-343) are good examples of this device. It was also common in Coptic ritual spells to make an oblique or cursory reference to some legend associated with Christ, Mary, Peter, or Hebrew figures—called a *historiola*—to invoke the power to perform a particular feat or cure. The *historiola,* a cross-cultural speech phenomenon, consists of an invocation of a mythical prototype for a desired act, expressed in an often enigmatic shorthand. *Historiolae* in Coptic spells draw upon the paradigmatic narratives of biblical and Christian legend as myths, in order to invoke the same power in contemporary times.[11] The *historiola* constitutes, in Bronislaw Malinowski's terms, "the historical statement of one of those events which once for all vouch for the truth of a certain form of magic."[12]

The legend of Elijah was also used as such a framing device. A line of powerful χαρακτῆρες on a Coptic papyrus of the sixth or seventh century is introduced with the phrase "This is the φυλακατήριον of the prayer of Elijah."[13] A complex spell from the same period begins, "The Prayer of Elijah the Tishbite: (It is) the chariot of Christ that he has prayed: Jesus is the name; he has raised up the one who seeks(?) after him [ετεκτναϥ]."[14] Here the reference to Elijah is drawn out through an

---

Chrysostom," *Transactions of the Society of Biblical Archaeology* 9 (1893):367–69, 393–94.

In his brief review of "Apocalypses dans le Talmud" (*Revue des études juives* 1 [1880]:108–14), Israel Lévi proposed that a passage in *b. Sanhedrin* 9, in which Elijah is questioned about the age of the world, derives from a larger apocalyptic work in which Elijah is the revealer (110). The postulated text might be an early form of *Sefer Eliahu,* or another, independent Elijah apocalypse.

11. Cf. Kropp, 3:5–9, 51–63, 218–24.

12. Bronislaw Malinowski, *Magic, Science, and Religion, and Other Essays* (Garden City, N.Y.: Doubleday, 1954), 84. Gerardus Van der Leeuw calls it the "magical antecedent"; see his *Religion in Essence and Manifestation,* tr. J. E. Turner (2d ed.; Princeton: Princeton University Press, 1964), 423.

13. P.London Hay 10434ᵛ, in W. E. Crum, "Magical Texts in Coptic—II," *JEA* 20 (1934):199.

14. P.Rainer 108, spell 2, in Viktor Stegemann, *Die koptischen Zaubertexte der Sammlung Papyrus Erzherzog Rainer in Wien,* Sitzungsberichte der heidelberger Akademie der Wissenschaften, Philos.-hist. Klasse (Heidelberg: Carl Winters Universitätsbuchhandlung, 1934), 73–76, cf. ibid., 26. Stegemann derives ετεκτναϥ from κωτε.

oblique reference to the chariot of fire in which Elijah was assumed. One may infer from these texts that a tradition of "Elijah's prayer" was current in Coptic ritual tradition, and that therefore the clients of "magic"—which included everybody in Roman Egypt and beyond—considered a correspondence between Elijah and powerful speech to be conceivable.[15]

A third spell provides further evidence of an Elijah "folklore" that assimilated biblical legend for pragmatic applications. It invokes the legend of Elijah splitting the Jordan River to dry up a hemorrhage. Moreover, like the first two spells' reference to a prayer of Elijah, this one refers to Elijah's magic "command."

> For a flow or discharge of blood:
> (As) Elijah, being about to cross over the Jordan,
> upon the water, on foot, held up his staff in commands
> that the Jordan be like the dry land,
> so also, Lord, cast the flow from NN,
> through the power of the One
> in whose hands are the keys of the heavens,
> LAGAR GAR GAR AROMARKAR[16]

In the fourth text, from the tenth century, Elijah's powerful speech is invoked as a frame for the spell that follows, but this time in the context of a legendary "holy mountain":

> The binding words, which Elijah the prophet spoke
> upon the holy mountain,
> of which the names are these:
> CHAKOURI CHABNEI CHABNA SHORANI SHOUIONA
> Let this binding be upon the male organ
> of NN (entering) into NN[17]

The text does not specify with which mountain the spell should be associated (presumably Carmel or Horeb). If Carmel, it should be associated with Elijah's prayer to bring down fire from heaven (1 Kgs 18:36-38); if Horeb, it should be understood as words that were "revealed" to

---

15. This idea of Elijah's words of power is still prominent in Syriac tradition; see Michel Hayek, "Élie dans la tradition syriaque," in *Élie le prophète*, vol. 1: *Selon les écritures et les traditions chrétiennes* (Bruges: Les études carmélitaines, 1956), 170.

16. P.London Hay 10391ᵛ, ll. 1–4, in Kropp 1:59.

17. P.Heidelberg 1682, ll. 29–34, in Friederich Bilabel and Adolf Grohman, *Griechische, koptische, und arabische Texte zur Religion und religiösen Literatur in Ägyptens Spätzeit*, Veröffentlichungen aus den badischen Papyrus-Sammlungen 5 (Heidelberg: Verlag der Universitätsbibliothek, 1934), 394.

Elijah as part of a larger revelation. Because the text does not specify which of these two, however, it is equally likely that Carmel and Horeb had symbolically merged in the practical context of the magical *historiola*, that is, there was one mountain with which Elijah's powerful speech and his knowledge of spells was associated.[18]

When a ritual text attributed its spells or formulas to a hero in late antiquity, there was invariably a story presupposed of how that hero might have come by such magical words. The *Testament of Solomon* and the *Eighth Book of Moses* again are good examples of this literary presupposition, but the Greek Magical Papyri are full of attributions to such lesser-known figures as Astrapsoukos (PGM VIII.1), Zminis of Tentyra (PGM XII.121), and Pythagoras (PGM VII.795).[19]

Similarly, it may be argued from the fourth Elijah spell cited above and its association of Elijah with a holy mountain and with words of power that this spell presupposed a story—a wider tradition—that Elijah received a revelation on top of a mountain. Although the full extent of this tradition is retained only in *Sefer Eliahu*, there are indications that a legend of Elijah's mountaintop revelation lies behind the additions to Elijah section of the *Lives of the Prophets*. Moreover, the attestation of this tradition in the sphere of practical ritual, or "magic," suggests (1) that there was a sizable Elijah folklore in Coptic Egypt, and (2) that the legend of Elijah's mountaintop revelation was a part of this folklore. Indeed, the idea of his powerful speech and the diversity of subjects to which it was applied probably arose from such a revelation tradition, rather than from the prayer in 1 Kings 18.[20]

Can one indeed infer from such a culturally and historically broad sampling of texts to the Apocalypse of Elijah? It should be remembered that the issue here is the narrative context by which an audience, with its store of Elijah legends, could comprehend the nature of an Elianic

18. On the symbolism of Horeb and its synthesis with other mountains in biblical tradition, see Robert L. Cohn, *The Shape of Sacred Space*, AARSR (Chico, Calif.: Scholars Press, 1981), 43–45, 54–61. The centrality of mountaintops in the visionary traditions of ancient Judaism has also been discussed by George W.E. Nickelsburg, "Enoch, Levi, and Peter: Recipients of Revelation in Upper Galilee," *JBL* 100 (1981):586, 589, 599.

19. See Hans Dieter Betz, "The Formation of Authoritative Tradition in the Greek Magical Papyri," in *Jewish and Christian Self-Definition*, vol. 3: *Self-Definition in the Greco-Roman World*, ed. Ben F. Meyer and E. P. Sanders (Philadelphia: Fortress, 1982), 161–70, 236–38.

20. Medieval (and perhaps earlier) Jewish magical tradition employed another, apocryphal Elijah legend for magical purposes: his opposition to Lilith and protection of a birthing woman. Gershom Scholem sees this *historiola* as a late importation from Byzantine Christian tradition (*Kabbalah* [New York: New American Library, 1978], 359–60), although Richard Greenfield views the Christian tradition itself as late (*Traditions of Belief in Late Byzantine Demonology* [Amsterdam: Hakkert, 1988], 187 n. 565).

revelation. While it is conceivable that the apocalyptic narrative frame here reconstructed arose during the later Byzantine period, closer to the time of the extant sources, there are compelling reasons to take the later evidence as witness to a tradition current in the third century. First, such a diverse selection of texts nonetheless reflects a fairly consistent legend of Elijah's revelations. Second, from the Elijah cycle in the books of Kings to the prophecy of an eschatological Elijah in Malachi to the discussions of Elijah's return in connection with John the Baptist and Jesus,[21] it is quite evident that the legend of his revelations came out of a folklore both rich and of tremendous antiquity. Although interest in Elijah underwent changes over the long history of this folklore, such a basic motif as his mountaintop revelations would probably have arisen well before the Byzantine period. Third, one would assume that the many apocalyptic and ascetic circles, both Jewish and Christian, in the eastern Mediterranean world that venerated Elijah would have treasured such a legend. If the Apocalypse of Elijah derives from such a milieu, then there is good reason to believe that some tradition whereby Elijah received secret revelations to pass on to his followers would have been of keen interest. Under these circumstances, a seventh-century Jewish text and a tenth-century Coptic spell carry considerable relevance for the Elianic nature of the Apocalypse of Elijah.

The narrative context of the Apocalypse of Elijah and its pseudepigraphic attribution may thus be outlined: the text would have been heard and understood in light of the legend of Elijah's revelations on a mountaintop. In a predominately illiterate culture, such legends would have carried authority equal to that of biblical stories.[22] Hence the audience would have been able to provide the narrative frame for the Apocalypse of Elijah and any other Elijah pseudepigrapha they heard, as if the introduction to the text were to read, "These are the revelations that the angel Michael disclosed to Elijah while he was praying on the mountain."

RELIGIOUS CONTEXT
OF ELIJAH PSEUDEPIGRAPHY

The currency of Elijah traditions in Coptic magic and folklore in general implies that Egyptian Christians held Elijah in special regard. In

---

21. Cf. Mk 6:15; 8:28; 9:4-5, 11-13; Jn 1:21, 25; Lk 9:54.
22. Epiphanius reports the didactic use of apocryphal (and rather derogatory) Elijah legends among the Borborite sect (*Panarion* 26.13.4–5).

investigating the religious context of Elijah pseudepigraphy, the questions become: Why write an apocalypse of *Elijah* in Egypt? What was the degree of his authority?

Eusebius reports a story in which a large number of Christians from the Egyptian countryside, deported to Palestine under Diocletian's edicts, came to trial under one Firmilian:

> [Firmilian] brought forward the first of them into the midst, and asked him what was his name; but instead of his real name he heard from them the name of a prophet. Also the rest of the Egyptians who were with him, instead of those names which their fathers had given them after the name of some idol, had taken for themselves the names of the prophets, such as these—Elias, Jeremiah, Isaiah, Samuel, Daniel.[23]

Frend has rightly inferred from this story that biblical prophets in early Christian Egypt had much more than legendary significance.[24] Apparently, they were forms of supernatural identity for some.[25]

The same identification with prophets—in this case, Elijah—is apparent in fourth-century traditions of the lives of Antony and Paul of Thebes. Athanasius mentions that Antony "said in himself that the Ascetic ought to learn closely from the *politeia* of the great Elijah, as a mirror of his own life" (7).[26] Even if unattributable to Antony's self-

---

23. Eusebius, *Martyrs in Palestine* [Syr.] 11.8 (ed. and tr. William Cureton, *History of the Martyrs of Palestine by Eusebius* [London: Williams & Norgate,, 1861], 40). The Greek texts vary only slightly: see Eusebius, *Martyrs in Palestine* [Grk.], ed. and tr. Gustav Bardy, *Eusèbe de Césarée: Histoire ecclésiastique livres VIII–X et les martyrs en Palestine*, SC 55 [Paris, 1958], 158–59). The Syriac text adds the same description to the martyrdoms of Paul, Valentina, and Hatha under Firmilian (*Martyrs in Palestine* [Syr.] 29, tr. Cureton, 27), whereas the Greek text omits it ([Grk.] 8.1, tr. Bardy, 144). Eusebius gives a similar account of this event in his Isaiah commentary (II.25) as the fulfillment of Is 44:5.

24. W.H.C. Frend, *Martyrdom and Persecution in the Early Church* (London: Basil Blackwell, 1965; reprint, Grand Rapids: Baker Book House, 1981), 466–67; and "The Winning of the Countryside," *JEH* 18 (1967):6.

25. On martyrs named Elijah, see Hippolyte Delehaye, *Les martyrs d'Égypte*, AnBoll 40 (Brussels: Société des Bollandistes, 1922), 74, 77-78, 80; and De Lacy O'Leary, *The Saints of Egypt* (London: Church Historical Society, 1937; reprint, Amsterdam: Philo Press, 1974), 128–29. On the distribution of Hebrew names among early Egyptian Christians, see Annick Martin, "Aux origines de l'église copte: L'implantation et le développement du christianisme en Égypte (Iᵉ–IVᵉ siècles)," *REA* 83 (1981):49 n. 89.

26. Athanasius, *Vita Antonii* 7 (*PG* 26:853). The Syriac version changes this gloss to "He said that the monk should be known, by his life and by his performance, to be a stranger to the world and the companion of the Watchers" (*La Vie primitive de S. Antoine*, tr. and ed. René Draguet, CSCO 418, S. Syri 184 [Louvain: Secrétariat du CSCO, 1980], 14), reflecting the Syriac Christian preference for angelological paradigms over biblical paradigms. T. D. Barnes's recent attempt to argue the Syriac text's priority raises more problems than it solves ("Angel of Light or Mystic Initiate? The Problem of

conception, it is likely that Athanasius's gloss reflects an early monastic tradition associating *anachoresis* with Elijah. The *Life of Pachomius*, for example, links Antony and Elijah directly.[27]

In Jerome's story of Paul of Thebes, the imitation of Elijah is even more explicit:

> And as [Paul and Antony] talked they perceived that a crow had settled on a branch of the tree, and softly flying down, deposited a whole loaf before their wondering eyes. And when he had withdrawn, "Behold," said Paul, "God hath sent us our dinner, God the merciful, God the compassionate. It is now sixty years since I have had each day a half loaf of bread; but at thy coming, Christ hath doubled his soldiers' rations.[28]

The incident recalls Elijah's being fed by crows in the beginning of his biblical cycle (1 Kgs 17:6). Such miraculous feedings became a motif of monastic legend, invariably implying a parallel with Elijah.[29] Again, later in Jerome's *Life of Paul*, Antony declares to his disciples when he has returned from visiting Paul just before the latter's death, "I have seen Elijah, I have seen John in the desert, truly I have seen Paul in Paradise!"[30] In this way Jerome puts Paul of Thebes in a lineage with Elijah and John the Baptist.

John the Baptist, himself an Elianic figure in the Gospels,[31] is rarely mentioned alone in Egyptian monastic literature as an anchoritic paradigm. This suggests that his name appeared as reinforcement of an Elijah paradigm: he expressed the continuity and validity of the anchoritic model of Elijah in the lore of Christian origins.

Thus a tradition of Elijah as the paradigm of *anachoresis* circulated even outside monastic literature. John Cassian reports that "anchorites . . . feared not to penetrate the vast recesses of the desert, imitating, to wit, John the Baptist, who passed all his life in the desert, and Elijah and Elisha.[32] Sozomen wrote that the Pachomian monks at Tabennesi "were clothed in skins in remembrance of Elias, it appears to me, because they thought that the virtue of the prophet would be thus always retained in

---

the *Life of Antony*," *JTS* 37 [1986]:353–68); see David Brakke, "St. Athanasius and Ascetic Christians in Egypt" (Ph.D. diss., Yale University, 1992).

27. *Vita Pachomius* 2; cf. John Cassian, *Conferences* 14.4.

28. Jerome *Vita Paul* 10 (*PL* 23:25; also in Helen Waddell, tr., *The Desert Fathers* [London: Constable, 1936; reprint, Ann Arbor: University of Michigan, 1957 (1936)], 35).

29. Cf. *Historia monachorum in Aegypto* 1.47 (tr. Norman Russell), and Benedicta Ward, "Introduction," both in *The Lives of the Desert Fathers* (London: Mowbray, 1981), 44.

30. Jerome *Vita Paul* 13 (*PL* 23:26).

31. E.g., Matthew's clarification of Mk 9:13 (Mt 17:12-13).

32. John Cassian, *Conferences* 18.6 (tr. E. Gibson, *NPNF* 11:481).

their memory."[33] Jerome suggests that monks may have considered these rough, Elijah-like garments to represent the human body—as concrete "garments of shame"—because "after driving us from the paradise of virginity [the serpent] tries to clothe us in tunics of skin, such as Elijah on his return to paradise threw upon the ground."[34]

Within the literary culture of *anachoresis* and monasticism, however, the figure of Elijah looms even greater. One monk, who had taken the name Elijah and retreated well into the desert of Antinoë, attracted popular rumors that "the spirit of Elijah rested upon him. He was famous for having spent seventy years in the terrible desert"; and thus "every day he worked many miracles and did not cease healing the sick."[35]

The *Panegyric on Makarios of Tkôw* largely concerns this Egyptian bishop's struggles against both native religion in Upper Egypt and "heretics" at church councils. The language of this opposition, however, explicitly reflects Elijah's confrontation with the priests of Baal in 1 Kings 18. During the scene of his extermination of the still-thriving Temple of Kothos, Makarios tells his attendant monks,

> "Let us stand and pray together, and we will bring fire from heaven and it will consume this temple." And when they stood at prayer with the brothers who were with them, a voice came down from heaven to them: "Save yourselves (by going) outside the door of the temple." And when we had come away from the temple and had not yet turned our gaze back, a great wall of fire surrounded the temple. And an hour had not yet elapsed before the fire had devoured the foundations of the temple. And the walls of the temple fell down, its walls and its stones. The fire consumed them right down to its foundations. [Makarios] looked back and cursed even its land, saying: "Let there be no tree giving shade on it, nor any seed be found in it for ever. And it shall be parched, with wild beasts and serpents breeding in it."[36]

---

33. Sozomen, *Historia ecclesiastica* 3.14 (*PG* 67:1069; tr. Chester D. Hartranft, *NPNF* 2:291–92. Cf. Palladius, *Historia lausiaca* 32.3, who merely reports that each monk must wear a coat of goatskin at all times and that an angel delivered this decree.

34. Jerome, *Epistle* 22.18.2 (tr. F. A. Wright, *Select Letters of St. Jerome* [LCL], 91). Clement of Alexandria may also be thinking of contemporaneous imitators of biblical saints when he asks about the Carpocratians, "Which of them goes about like Elijah, clad in a sheepskin and a leather girdle? Which of them goes about like Isaiah, naked except for a piece of sacking and without shoes? Or clothed merely in a loincloth like Jeremiah? Which of them will imitate John [the Baptist's] gnostic way of life?" (*Stromata* 3.6.53; tr. Henry Chadwick, *Alexandrian Christianity* [London: SCM, 1954], 65).

35. *Hist. mon.* 7 (tr. Russell, in *Lives of the Desert Fathers*, 69).

36. Dioscorus of Alexandria (attrib.), *Panegyric on Macarius of Tkôw*, V.9, ed. and tr. D. W. Johnson, CSCO 415–16, Scriptores Coptici 41–42 (Louvain: Sécretariat du CSCO, 1980), 2:27–28.

That this scene is meant to recall the descent of "the fire of YHWH" in 1 Kgs 18:38 is shown at the end of the text, when Makarios opposes heretics, saying, "Why indeed would I count myself among the priests of Baal, and not count myself with Elijah?"[37] Dioscorus himself praises Makarios: "The prophets are coming out to meet you because a prophetic spirit is what dwells in you. Elijah is coming out to meet you because you have been zealous for God like he was."[38] Consequently, at the end of his life Makarios is invited by Elisha and John the Baptist to share their Egyptian martyrium, presumably as Elijah's representative.[39]

Makarios's contemporary, Abbot Shenoute of Atripe, was said to have received Elijah's very mantle:

> When apa Pjol [Shenoute's boyhood superior] raised his eyes to heaven, he saw an angel of the Lord guarding the young boy Shenoute while he was sleeping, and the angel said to apa Pjol: "When you get up in the morning, put the mantle which you will find before you upon the young boy Shenoute, for it is the mantle of Elijah the Tishbite which the Lord Jesus has sent to you to put upon him. Truly, he will be a righteous and illustrious man, and after him, no-one like him will arise in any country."[40]

Indeed, following a description of Shenoute's ascetic regime, the biographer acclaims, "The whole of his life and his intention were like [those of] Elijah the Tishbite, the charioteer of Israel," and he refers to Shenoute as "prophet" throughout the rest of the Life.[41]

In his seventh-century description of a tour of the monasteries and gatherings of anchorites in the Egyptian desert, the monk Paphnouti describes a meeting with Apa Benofer, during which the old monk tells of his own youthful training in an Upper Egyptian monastery:

> I learned the divine work from these divine and perfect elders who lived in the manner of angels of God, and I heard from their mouth a discourse [ⲉⲩⲥⲁⲝⲓ] on Elijah the Tishbite—that at the moment when he had the most power in God of any sort, he was in the desert. Similarly John the Baptist, whom nobody could imitate, lived in the desert without showing himself in Jerusalem.[42]

---

37. *Panegyric* XV.8 (ibid., 2:95). That the power to bring down fire was considered a mark of Elianic power is shown in Lk 9:54.

38. *Panegyric* XIII.5 (ibid., 2:84).

39. *Panegyric* XVI.1–4, (ibid., 96–98). John the Baptist and Elisha themselves appear in a dream to Dioscorus to invite this deposition of Makarios's remains, VI.1–3.

40. Besa, *Life of Shenoute* 8 (tr. David N. Bell, *The Life of Shenoute by Besa*, Cistercian Studies Series 73 [Kalamazoo, Mich.: Cistercian Press, 1983], 44).

41. *Life of Shenoute* 10 (tr. Bell, 45). On the title προφήτης as applied to anchorites, see Bell, tr., *Life of Shenoute*, 93 n. 1.

42. *Vita Benofer*, tr. E. Amélineau, "Voyage d'un moine égyptien dans le désert,"

Several aspects of piety directed toward Elijah can be gleaned from this passage. First, we may note that the model of Elijah was considered basic to the practice of desert asceticism in the minds of the holy elders. Second, Elijah was not simply mentioned, but an entire discourse or homily would be composed (spontaneously, we must assume in this case) on his importance.[43] Third, in both the models of Elijah and John the Baptist here the city is specifically opposed to the desert; the desert is viewed as the locus for the attainment of power, as in the case of the anchorite named Elijah. Finally, John the Baptist is mentioned in immediate connection to Elijah, thus corroborating the suggestion that these two figures constituted one ascetic paradigm—John the Baptist viewed essentially as a later representative of Elijah.[44]

In all these cases, then, Elijah (and John the Baptist as his alter ego) constituted the reason, the paradigm, of *anachoresis*. Moreover, the idea is consistently expressed that if one withdraws into the desert like Elijah, one will gain the powers that Elijah had in the desert: powers of healing (Elijah the anchorite), powers of punishment (Makarios, Shenoute), but also, we may infer, powers of vision and revelation; for not only Shenoute but also the anchorite John of Lycopolis was credited with prophetic abilities.[45]

Recueil de travaux relatifs à la philologie et à l'archéologie égyptiennes et assyriennes 6 (1885):175.

43. A significant analog to such Elijah conferences can be found in the *Apophthegmata Patrum* (Alphabetical): a discussion of the humanity or divinity of Melchizedek between Apa Daniel and Cyril of Jerusalem (Daniel 8) and a virtual symposium on Melchizedek held by the monks of Scetis (Copres 3). Early Jewish Melchizedek traditions held this figure to be a holy wild man, called back to civilization by Abraham; and it is likely that this legend was embraced by Egyptian desert hermits as an identity with traditional authority. See Gustav Bardy, "Melchisédech dans la tradition patristique," *RB* 35 (1926):496–509, 36 (1927):25–45; and S. E. Robinson, "The Apocryphal Story of Melchizedek," *JSJ* 18 (1987). Cf. Birger A. Pearson, "The Figure of Melchizedek in Gnostic Literature," in idem, *Gnosticism, Judaism, and Egyptian Christianity*, SAC 5 (Minneapolis: Fortress, 1990), 108–23.

44. See E. Amélineau, "Le christianisme chez les anciens coptes," *RHR* 14 (1886):339–41.

45. Cf. Palladius, *Historia lausiaca* 35.9; and *Hist. mon.* 1.28, 64. Shenoute's abilities as a seer are evident in the addition of an "Apocalypse"—revealed by Christ—to the Besa's *Life* in the Arabic recension. A Coptic ostracon apparently sent by an important ascetic near the monastery of St. Epiphanius in Thebes begins a sentence, "If his deeds equal those of Elijah and [John] the Baptist" (MMA ostracon 12.180.150, ed. and tr. W. E. Crum in idem; and H. G. Evelyn White, *The Monastery of Epiphanius at Thebes*, 2 vols. [New York: Metropolitan Museum of Art, 1926], 2:33 [txt], 179 [trans.], = ostracon no. 103). The fourth-century Syrian Ephrem attributed Elijah's powers to "withhold the rain from the adulterers" and to "restrain the dew from the whoremongers" to the prophet's virginity; indeed, "since on earth he conquered fleshly desire, he went up to [the place] where holiness dwells and is at peace" (Hymn 14, tr. Kathleen E. McVey, *Ephrem the Syrian: Hymns* [New York: Paulist Press, 1989], 144). The language clearly presents both

As in the case of the narrative context of Elijah pseudepigraphy, the use of fourth- and fifth-century monastic sources to account for a third-century phenomenon might appear anachronistic, until one notices that such a wide selection of late texts seems again to reflect a consistent phenomenon in the case of anchoritic Elijahs. In some cases the Elijah paradigm is "marketed" for an extramonastic or even censorious audience: Jerome's Paul and Athanasius's Antony might fall into such a category;[46] but even when Besa casts Shenoute as Elijah's direct heir, he is evidently employing a parallel of considerable local authority, whose roots must antedate the fourth century. Finally, Eusebius's description of the Egyptians in Palestine suggests that such biblical paradigms invoked by anchorites continued from the third century, when many of these same anchorites entered the desert to escape the edicts—in many cases probably in explicit recollection of Elijah the Tishbite in his flight from the dominion of Ahab (1 Kgs 17:3).[47]

The powers immanent in an anchorite who emulated Elijah may also have been understood in a more ancient context. An encomium on a martyr named Elijah describes how the power and nature of the sun, $\H{\eta}\lambda\iota o\varsigma$, are immanent in the Greek name ʽHλίας:

> For the significance of Elijah, in the Greek language, is "sun." In the first place, this name came to him at his birth at the same time as his body. Then his life manifested itself in conformity with his name. And just as the saint had his name, so also he had his virtues, as it is written in the Psalms. But while the sun, insofar as it is perceptible, has an end to its light, the light of the martyrs has no end. After the sun (sets in) the west, it rises again. Thus the vanquished martyrs "set" in the body at their death; but they enter anew, with the Lord, into the glory because they are delivered from the cycle of their sufferings.[48]

Elijah's virginity and his resulting powers as imitable (cf. McVey, *Ephrem the Syrian*, 45–46).

46. Cf. Michael A. Williams, "The *Life of Antony* and the Domestication of Charismatic Wisdom," in idem, ed., *Charisma and Sacred Biography*, JAAR Thematic Studies 48, 3–4 (Chico, Calif.: American Academy of Religion, 1982), 23–45; discussed in more detail below, chapter 11, pp. 289–90.

47. Cf. Oliver Nicholson ("Flight from Persecution as Imitation of Christ: Lactantius' Divine Institutes IV.18, 1–2," *JTS* 40 [1989]:48–65), who proposes "that the spirituality of the refugees survived the end of the persecutions in the desert places where Christians had fled" (64).

48. *Martyrdom of St. Elijah* f. 35ʳ⁻ᵛ, in Geo. P. G. Sobhy, *Le martyre de saint Hélias et l'encomium de l'évêque Stéphanos de Hnès sur saint Hélias*, Bibliothèque d'études coptes 1 (Cairo: IFAO, 1919), 69–70 [trans. was modified from that of Sobhy on p. 114 of *Le martyre de saint Hélias*]. A homily on Elijah attributed to John Chrysostom reflects a similar theme (*PG* 63:464). There is probably no relationship in this case to the appearance of Elijah on a heavenly chariot in *Sib. Or.* 2.187–89, as the latter is not

The embodiment of the self's essence in one's name was a basic belief of classical Egyptian religion and a common theme of Egyptian mythology and magic.[49] The Greco-Egyptian and Coptic magical corpora, moreover, show that the considerable power attributed to names in Egypt—personal, legendary, and secret—continued throughout the Roman period. Finally, solar symbolism had a particular legacy in Egyptian tradition, denoting the power behind kingship (originally) and cosmic stability (more generally). This solar sense of the name Elijah would only have been accessible to an audience that understood Greek; yet it is clear that the name Elijah and its expression in the figure of a holy man or martyr had assumed indigenous connotations and achieved a peculiar degree of veneration in the milieu of the above encomium's author.[50]

In light of Elijah's great stature in Coptic tradition and the types of piety associated with his name, it is right to ask how an "Elijah charisma" was integrated into the Christian life of the hermits. Was this degree of veneration of a biblical prophet accepted in all quarters?

In fact, there is evidence in Egyptian monastic literature that Elijah veneration fell under some censure. In two stories from the *Historia monachorum*, demons call overzealous monks "Elijah." When Apa Apollo manages to save both his Thebaid monastery and the people of the region from a famine by multiplying a few baskets of bread, "Satan appeared to him and said, 'Are you not Elijah, or one of the prophets or apostles, that you have the confidence to do these things?'"[51] The second story is told by Apa Or:

---

explicitly solar; but cf. Jean Daniélou, *Primitive Christian Symbols*, tr. Donald Attwater (Baltimore: Helicon, 1964), 86–87.

49. Cf. George Foucart, "Names (Egyptian)," *ERE* 9:151–55; E. A. Wallis Budge, *Egyptian Magic*, Books on Egypt and Chaldea, vol. 2 (London: Kegan Paul, Trench, Trübner, 1901; reprint, New York: Dover, 1971), 157–81; Siegfried Morenz, *Egyptian Religion*, tr. Ann E. Keep (Ithaca, N.Y., and London: Cornell University Press, 1973), 9–10. For other Coptic examples, see Wolfgang Kosack, *Die Legende im Koptischen: Untersuchungen zur Volksliteratur Ägyptens*, Habelts Dissertationsdrucke, Reihe klassische Philologie 8 (Bonn: Habelt, 1970), 73.

50. As is briefly noted by Sobhy, *Martyre de saint Hélias*, 114 n. 2. It is significant that the *Confession* of St. Patrick (§20) records the same solar connotation to ʿΗλίας: "I saw the sun rising in the sky and . . . I was crying out 'Elijah! Elijah!' with all my strength" (tr. R.P.C. Hanson, *The Life and Writings of the Historical Saint Patrick* [New York: Seabury, 1983], 90). Hanson suggests that Patrick was able to make such an association while himself knowing little Greek (91), but the ʿΗλίας or ἥλιος connection may rather testify to the legacy of Greco-Egyptian Christianity in Irish monastic tradition. On veneration for Elijah in Ireland and Gaul, see D. B. Botte, "Une fête du prophète Élie en Gaule au VIᵉ siècle," *Cahiers sioniens* 3 (1950):170–77, esp. 174–75.

51. *Hist. mon.* 8.46 (tr. Russell, *Lives of the Desert Fathers*, 77).

> I know a man in the desert who did not taste any earthly food for three days; every three days an angel used to bring him heavenly food and put it in his mouth. For him this took the place of food and drink. And I know with regard to this same man that the demons appeared to him in a vision and showed him hosts of angels and a chariot of fire and a great escort of guards, as if an emperor was making a visit. And the 'emperor' said, "You have succeeded in attaining every virtue, my good man; prostrate yourself before me and I shall take you up like Elijah."[52]

He manages to expel the demons by invoking Christ.

Such tales of the sarcastic exaltation of hermits as Elijah must reflect a real situation and a real controversy in early Coptic culture: that hermits claimed explicitly to be Elijah and thus directed veneration away from Christ and attention away from churches. A similar situation may have occupied fourth-century Jerusalem, where Cyril's fourteenth catechetical lecture appears to respond to strong local sentiment preferring Hebrew figures—Elijah in particular—to the heroes of Christian legend:

> Elijah raised the dead, but demons are not driven out in the name of Elijah. We do not speak ill of the prophets, but we celebrate more magnificently their master. . . .
> . . . Remember that Enoch was transported to heaven, but Jesus ascended. Remember what was said yesterday about Elijah: that Elijah was taken up in a chariot of fire, but (it was) the chariot of Christ, of which thousands and thousands were singing praises; that Elijah was taken up to the east of the Jordan, while Christ ascended to the east of the river of Kidron; the former ascended *as it were* into heaven, but Jesus ascended (truly) into heaven; that (Elijah) said that he would give his holy disciple a double portion in Spirit, but Christ bestowed such an abundance of grace in the Holy Spirit to his own disciples that not only would they possess it in themselves, but by the laying-on of their hands they would be able to transfer it to believers. . . .
> . . . A servant of Christ ascended to the third heaven. So if Elijah only arrived at the first, while Paul the third, the latter then has the greater dignity. Do not put to shame the Apostles; they are not inferior to Moses, nor are they second to the prophets. They are noble with the noble, and nobler still. Elijah was taken up to heaven, but Peter received the keys to the Kingdom of Heaven. . . . Elijah went only to heaven, but Paul was in heaven and in Paradise.[53]

Such obvious rivalry is perhaps more understandable in a city surrounded by the holy spots of biblical heroes than in the Egyptian *chora*;[54]

---

52. *Hist. mon.* 2.9 (ibid., 64).
53. Cyril of Jerusalem, *Catecheses* 14.16, 25–26 (*PG* 33:845, 857, 860).
54. The immediate reason for such a crisis of legendary authorities in fourth-century

but Cyril's defense of Christian heroes provides general evidence for Elijah's tremendous significance in the Eastern empire, as a model of ascetic *anachoresis*, magical power, and heavenly privilege.[55]

This tremendous significance of Elijah, then, constitutes the religious context of Elijah pseudepigraphy in Christian Egypt. It is clear that this religious context goes beyond the world of the anchorites, who modeled themselves after Elijah. Not only did Elijah come to be viewed as the prototype and archetype of *anachoresis* around the Mediterranean world through the dissemination of the Greek *Vita Antonii* and Jerome's *Vita Pauli*, but even for the folk of the *chora* Elijah carried power: *"The people said the spirit of Elijah rested upon him . . . he did not cease healing the sick."* The charisma of Elijah was also a popular charisma, attracting and serving villagers and townspeople.[56] The ritual spells themselves show the importance of Elijah outside the walls of the monastery, for Elijah appears in them as the archetypal speaker of magic words.

John Collins and George W. E. Nickelsburg once suggested that "the willingness to use the [biblical] tradition, and conceive one's identity in terms derived from it, constitutes, perhaps, the most comprehensive definition of Judaism."[57] It is evident, however, that the veneration and imitation of biblical figures had also become a customary form of piety among early Coptic anchorites.

Jerusalem may have been the increase in pilgrimages to the holy sites of Elijah and John the Baptist in the Judean hills. See the detailed analysis of Cyril's audience by Joseph Tracy Rivers III, "Pattern and Process in Early Christian Pilgrimage" (Ph.D. diss., Duke University, 1983), 238–52; and Gedaliahu Stroumsa's argument for a large Jewish-Christian community in Jerusalem, to whose alternative "Christologies" Cyril would here be responding ("'Vetus Israel': Les Juifs dans la littérature hiérosolymitaine d'époque byzantine," *RHR* 205 [1988]:115–31).

55. A hymn attributed to Ephraim and appended to an eighth-century Syriac collection of *Vitae* of holy women casts Elijah as a metaphor for Christ: "As the earthly form in the chariot descended, thus our Lord descended clothed in a body by His grace; and being clothed in a cloud, He rode and ascended to reign above and beneath. Angels of fire and of wind wondered at the Elijah whom they saw, for in Him was hidden the gentle wisdom" (in Agnes Smith Lewis, tr., *Select Narratives of Holy Women*, Studia Sinaitica 10 [London: Clay, 1900]), 205 [= f.180ʳ]). On Elijah as descending angel, see also Ginzberg, *Legends of the Jews*, 6:325 nn. 39–40.

56. To a certain extent this would have been true of the Egyptian anchorite saint generally: the narrator of the *Historia monachorum* "saw there many great fathers who possessed various charisms, some in their speech, some in their manner of life, and others in the wonders and signs they performed" (*Hist. mon.* 5.7, tr. Russell, *Lives of the Desert Fathers*, 67).

57. John J. Collins and George W. E. Nickelsburg, "Introduction," in *Ideal Figures in Ancient Judaism*, ed. John J. Collins and George W. E. Nickelsburg, Septuagint and Cognate Studies 12 (Chico, Calif.: Scholars Press, 1980), 10.

CONCLUSION: UNDERSTANDING
ELIJAH PSEUDEPIGRAPHY IN EGYPT

Through identifying the narrative and religious contexts, one can understand the cultural significance of the title "Apocalypse of Elijah." There was a tradition of Elijah's revelations on Horeb; therefore an apocalyptic text might be cogently attributed to the legend of Elijah. And Elijah himself was so important as a paradigm and as a source of power for hermits as well as lay people that any text purporting to contain the revelations of Elijah would be met with considerable interest.

The intention of the author who applied the pseudonym can also be discerned, for under these circumstances to produce a text under the name Elijah would have been a holy act. A late Byzantine encomium attributed to John Chrysostom depicts God saying to Elijah, "Whosoever shall take the pains to have a book made and written in thy [Elijah's] name, and shall dedicate it to thy shrine, I will write his name in the book of life, and will make him to inherit the good things of the kingdom of heaven."[58]

It is also conceivable, in light of the evidence for anchorites' identification with Elijah and of the prophetic pretensions that arose in some hermits, that an author of an apocalypse of Elijah might actually have believed himself to be "channeling" the words of the ascended prophet.[59] The Coptic Apocalypse of Elijah is, for all intents and purposes, a prophecy of the end and may indeed have been delivered as the words of Elijah incarnate to an audience quite prepared for such a conceit.

---

58. Budge, "Fragments of a Coptic Version of an Encomium," 369, 394. The manuscript is dated to 1199 C.E. and was found in a church dedicated to Elijah (ibid., 355–56). On Chrysostom pseudepigraphy see Johannes Quasten, *Patrology*, vol. 3 (Utrecht: Spectrum, 1950; Westminster, Md.: Christian Classics, 1983), 470. The practice of blessing the scribe within the narrative or revelation is not unique in late antique literature: e.g., *Apoc. Sed.* 16:3, "the sin of him who copies this admirable sermon will not be reckoned for ever and ever" (tr. S. Agourides, *OTP* 1:613); cf. *T. Isaac* 6:21; and, in general, Violet MacDermot, *The Cult of the Seer in the Ancient Middle East* (London: Wellcome Institute of the History of Medicine, 1971), 195.

59. This is a common hypothesis of apocalyptic pseudepigraphy: Metzger speaks of "a vivid sense of kinship which the apocalyptist shared with the one in whose name he wrote" ("Literary Forgeries," 19), and John J. Collins believes that "the practice of pseudepigraphy automatically assumes a measure of identification of the real author with his pseudonymous hero" (*The Apocalyptic Vision of the Book of Daniel*, HSM 16 [Missoula, Mont.: Scholars Press, 1977], 27, cf. 72–73); cf. also D. S. Russell, *The Method and Message of Jewish Apocalyptic* (Philadelphia: Westminster, 1964), 133; Hengel, "Anonymität, Pseudepigraphie," 277–78; Rowland, *Open Heaven*, 62–66, 245.

It is in this context that the eschatological Elijah tradition from Malachi 4 assumes relevance. In the development of this tradition in Jewish and Christian apocalyptic circles of the first three centuries C.E., Elijah—and Enoch—returns not primarily to reconcile families and define laws (Mal 4:6) but to expose the eschatological Adversary and thus preserve the righteous during the woes before the judgment: "Nero shall be raised up from hell," Commodian declares, but "Elias shall first come to seal the beloved ones."[60] Insofar as the Apocalypse of Elijah offers its audience precisely the information needed to recognize the time, acts, and appearance of this Adversary (ApocEl 3), a "prophet–composer" of the Elijah apocalypse would implicitly stand in the role of the unveiler Elijah of the end times. It is precisely this unveiler Elijah who, in second-century Christian circles, became, along with Enoch, Elijah the martyr.[61] Indeed, we find Cyprian invoking Elijah as exemplary martyr along with Mattathias (of 2 Maccabees), Daniel, and the Three Young Men.[62] An intrinsic connection thus arises between the martyrological concerns of the text and the pseudonym "Elijah."[63]

It is not implausible that an Egyptian Christian of the third century might assume the role of prophet and the task of exposing an eschatological Adversary in the person of a religious or civil authority—and thus consider himself (or suggest to others the persona of) Elijah redivivus. In times of catastrophe and millennialist rumors—that is, in the right historical context—such a prophet might well be so recognized and gather a following. There were, indeed, two Elijah traditions in apocalyptic lore, that of the revealer of heavenly mysteries and that of the exposer of the eschatological Adversary. Neither was entirely exclusive of the other, and either might have been drawn upon as a paradigm for prophetic status and self-definition in early Christianity.[64]

A safer theory of pseudepigraphy for the Apocalypse of Elijah than that proposing outright identification with the pseudonymous authority has been proposed by Kurt Aland.[65] When a prophet presents a dis-

60. Commodian, *Instructions* 41 (tr. Robert Ernest Wallis, *ANF* 4:211). Cf. *Apoc. Pet.* 2 (Eth.); ApocEl 4:7-19, 5:32-35. Elijah also arrives alone in *Sib. Or.* 2.187-88 and in early rabbinic tradition (cf. Ginzberg, *Legends of the Jews*, 4:233–35). See, in general, Richard Bauckham, "The Martyrdom of Enoch and Elijah: Jewish or Christian?" *JBL* 95, 3 (1976) 453.

61. Ibid., 457–58.

62. Cyprian, *Epistle* 67.8.2.

63. See below, chapter 6.

64. Cf. B. Dehandschutter, "Les Apocalypses d'Élie," in *Élie le prophète: Bible, tradition, iconographie*, ed. Gerard F. Willems (Louvain: Peeters, 1988), 66–67.

65. Aland, "Problem of Anonymity," 43–45.

course to an audience in an oral setting, authorship is not strictly identified: the "prophecy" is understood as divinely inspired, while the identity (or individuality) of the prophet is apparent to the audience. The nature of the discourse is established by setting, therefore, rather than by title and attribution. When the discourse is written down, however, its status as prophecy—as divine word—requires an appropriate attribution, for the setting is henceforth the text itself and its subsequent public readings. Thus it is the scribe who attaches a pseudonym of local or general authority to a discourse that had been delivered orally without the insistence of individual authorship. "What happened in pseudonymous literature of the early period," concludes Aland, "was nothing but the shift of the message from the spoken to the written word."[66]

Aland's positivistic view of the role of the Holy Spirit notwithstanding,[67] his theory is eminently applicable to the Apocalypse of Elijah. First, it is appropriate to Greco-Roman Egypt to emphasize that texts passing from oral to written settings (and, indeed, between scribal settings) might undergo such formal and ideological changes as title and frame-narrative additions. Second, the text betrays evidence of having been intended as prophecy and (as is argued in chapter 4, below) of having been composed for, or in, an oral setting. Third, the evidence adduced in this chapter for the dominance of the figure of Elijah in early rural Egyptian Christianity accounts for the application of the name "Elijah" to a prophecy apparently delivered in such a milieu.

Would the audience of the text's first performance understand the performer—the prophet—to be Elijah to some extent, and the discourse itself to be Elijah's words? The evidence presented here suggests that some individuals in the *chora* (particularly desert ascetics) were locally considered to incarnate "the spirit of Elijah" in several ways (desert solitude, healing, vision). If the composer of the Apocalypse of Elijah held such a charisma preceding the actual delivery of the prophecy, then it is quite possible that the audience heard the prophecy as the words of Elijah himself: that is, they beheld him in his prophetic performance as, essentially, Elijah himself. But it is also possible that any individual who appeared prophetlike in third-century rural Egypt may have been regarded as "an Elijah" or "a second Elijah" (or a "second John the Baptist"), in which case a rural audience might have regarded *any* prophetic discourse as the "words of Elijah."

66. Ibid., 43.
67. E.g., "It needs no argument that it is the Spirit who speaks in the apocalypses" (ibid., 46). See other criticisms in Metzger, "Literary Forgeries," 14–16.

4

Literary Aspects of the Apocalypse of Elijah: Genre, Self-Presentation, and Audience

Both the private reading and the public performance of a text are diachronic processes: that is, the text is accepted and interpreted in progressive stages, from the first sentence to the last. It follows that the beginning of the text will always function as an introduction to the rest, thereby establishing context, authority, and tradition, those vital aspects of a text that determine how it will be understood from the beginning of any given reading. Genre is, in effect, the grounding in the traditions and literary conventions of a culture from which any text must start and to which any text must refer for it to be meaningful to an audience. The contents of a text—eschatology, parenesis, legend—can function in any genre, under a variety of rubrics, and can assume meaning and authority depending on the literary genre (or subgenre) through which they are communicated.

The opening segment of a text thus will, by and large, determine the significance of the rest of the text. In Hirsch's words, "An interpreter's preliminary conception of a text is constitutive of everything that he subsequently understands, and . . . this remains the case unless and until that generic conception is altered."[1] Likewise the closure of a text will either reinforce or redefine the context and significance established in its opening. It is therefore the total frame of the text—its opening and closing segments[2]—that functions in reading and performance as the

---

1. E. D. Hirsch, Jr., *Validity in Interpretation* (New Haven and London: Yale University Press, 1967), 74.
2. The frame is reinforced through the course of the text by the use of internal narrative elements referring back to the introduction: e.g., the narrative interludes in 2 *Bar.* 13:1; 21:1-4; 36:1; 44:1; etc.

78

chief indication of literary genre.[3] One cannot discuss the Apocalypse of Elijah as an apocalypse because the primary criterion for classifying a text under this genre is not the contents of its revelation but the story of its revelation, which establishes both tradition (i.e., the patriarch or hero's legend) and authority (his privilege in receiving revelation) as a link between the audience (or reader) and the author–performer.

It is still possible, however, to discuss the "intrinsic genre" of the text, that is, the manner in which it systematically presented itself to an audience in dialectic with the audience's own literary categories and expectations. Moreover, it must be admitted that when an author employs the conventions of a genre for the production of a new text, the author may not repeat the genre's abstract structure but rather may imitate recollectively an existing text. In this case—a case of what we might call "historical influence"—the scribe may well consider aspects of the content of the previous text to be as worthy of imitation as the basic revelatory structure.[4]

ORAL PERFORMANCE AND
THE PROGRESSIVE ASSEMBLING OF FORMS

In his letter "On Virginity," Jerome offers a rare glimpse of how an eschatological discourse functioned in a fourth-century Egyptian monastery:

3. This "progressive"/performative understanding of literary genre relies largely on Hirsch, *Validity in Interpretation*, 68–126; and Roger D. Abrahams, "The Complex Relations of Simple Forms," in *Folklore Genres*, ed. Dan Ben-Amos, Publications of the American Folklore Society 26 (Austin: University of Texas Press, 1976), 193–214. Cf. Northrop Frye, *Anatomy of Criticism* (Princeton: Princeton University Press, 1957), 246–50; Lars Hartman, "Survey of the Problem of Apocalyptic Genre," in *Apocalypticism in the Mediterranean World and the Near East*, ed. David Hellholm (Tübingen: Mohr, 1983), 329–43; and David Hellholm, "The Problem of Apocalyptic Genre and the Apocalypse of John," *Semeia* 36 (1986):29–33. Obviously, once the reading of the text is underway, certain traditional elements that would be properly classified under content, rather than genre criteria, may also provide literary indication as to genre, authority, and religious tradition. E.g., such images during the course of the text as angel descriptions, fire and light in heaven, angelic armies, zoomorphic accounts of history, and the special recognition of the patriarch all would corroborate that a text is an apocalypse (but would not in themselves establish the genre). On motifs and themes characteristic to particular genres, see Hartman, "Problem of Apocalyptic Genre," 333–36.
4. It can be suggested that John of Patmos created his apocalypse in this way, recalling details of Daniel as more important—or more contributive of authority—than pseudonymity (or the suppression of his own individual authorship); certainly his text could have appeared as a deutero-Daniel. Cf. John J. Collins, "Pseudonymity, Historical Reviews, and the Genre of the Revelation of John," *CBQ* 39 (1977):332.

When [the abbot, at the end of a long homily,] begins to announce the kingdom of Christ, the future happiness, and the coming glory, you may see everyone with a gentle sigh and lifted gaze saying to himself: "Oh that I had the wings of a dove. For then I would fly away and be at rest."[5]

The topics Jerome lists as typically so moving to the monks are precisely those that stand out at several points in the Apocalypse of Elijah: parousia, millennium, heavenly rewards for the righteous. We might note, in the passage by Jerome, that not only is such an eschatological discourse presented every evening but it is apparently presented orally: *coeperit adnuntiare.*[6] A discourse on such topics was probably considered an oral genre among Egyptian Christians, whether it was inspired by a text or, perhaps most relevant for the Apocalypse of Elijah, led subsequently to the composition of a text. And if one can take Jerome's somewhat romanticized description of the "gentle sigh" to indicate the audience's active interest and participation, it becomes clear that the eschatological discourse had a consistently strong impact on audiences in Egypt—offering not only hopes, to be sure, but also horrors.

It is a historically appropriate assumption that any "new" text in third-century Egypt would have been read aloud and composed with this performative setting in mind.[7] This assumption becomes all the more applicable to the Apocalypse of Elijah because of its recurrent use of imperative verbs and apostrophic addresses to "you wise men of the land" (e.g., 1:13) or "you priests of the land" (e.g., 2:40). This text has an oral quality that goes beyond the oral conceits of most other apocalyptic discourses.[8] The punctuation of the Chester Beatty manuscript (Sa³)

---

5. Jerome, *Epistle* 22, 35.3 (tr. F. A. Wright, *Select Letters of St. Jerome* [LCL], 139).

6. Earlier the abbot is described as "beginning to expound" *(incipit disputare).*

7. Cf. Rv 1:3; in general, see Josef Balogh, "'Voces Paginarum': Beiträge zur Geschichte des lauten Lesens und Schreibens," *Philologus* 82 (1926):84–109, 202–40; Paul J. Achtemeier, "*Omne verbum sonat:* The New Testament and the Oral Environment of Late Western Antiquity," *JBL* 109 (1990):3–27, esp. 15–19; William V. Harris, *Ancient Literacy* (Cambridge: Harvard University Press, 1989), 35–36, 125–26, 224–26, 231–32, 304–5; David L. Barr, "The Apocalypse of John as Oral Enactment," *Interpretation* 40 (1986):243–56; and William A. Graham, *Beyond the Written Word: Oral Aspects of Scripture in the History of Religion* (Cambridge: Cambridge University Press, 1987), chap. 11. Although he emphasizes the fourth century, Graham's general observations would hold even more for the premonastic period. On literary composition for public reading in contemporaneous Christian cultures, see M. van Uytfanghe, "L'hagiographie et son public à l'époque mérovingienne," *Studia patristica* 16, 2 (1985):54–62, and Ramsay MacMullen, "The Preacher's Audience (A.D. 350–400)," *JTS* 40 (1989):503–11, esp. 508–9.

8. Compare homiletic asides in Mk 13:14—"let the 'reader' understand" (where ἀναγινώσκω carries the sense of "perceiving by means of a text," whether privately or publicly)—and Rv 13:10, 18; 14:13. Cf. Rv 17:9, on which, R. H. Charles observes, "our

strongly suggests an orientation toward public reading.[9] Finally, the text's associative rather than systematic sequences of themes might even suggest that the text's first performance was spontaneous, like a prophecy. At the very least we may conclude that the text was written specifically for public performance and that this function continued in its Coptic translations.[10]

A public reading is an episodic event, as the audience hears material sequentially from a single source (the reader) and assesses subsequent material in light of prior material. Such an assessment occurs not only on the level of making progressive sense of narrative or argument but also with regard to the significance and authority of the material, its relationship with other materials (literary and oral) encountered in the past, and the nature of both performer and implied narrator of the text. The following analysis therefore approaches the Apocalypse of Elijah as a sequence of individual sections, each of which conforms to a particular literary form—or, in this case, speech type—and sets up a particular relationship between the public reader of the text and the audience (as mediated through an ambiguous implied speaker and implied audience).[11] These sections are discrete both form-critically and in terms of the effects they might have had on audiences if performed individually. Yet in the Apocalypse of Elijah they should have a reciprocal effect on each other as far as authority, traditionality, and the relationship between the audience and the performer (the public reader) are concerned.[12]

---

author abandons his role as Seer and addresses words of admonition directly to his readers" (*A Critical and Exegetical Commentary on Revelation of St. John*, 2 vols. [Edinburgh: T. & T. Clark, 1920], 1:368).

9. See above, p. 22.

10. Cf. Wintermute, 735 n. h., 737 n. n2. On the persistence of oral performative markers in written literature, see Walter J. Ong, *Orality and Literacy: The Technologizing of the Word* (London and New York: Methuen, 1982), 171.

11. On the difference between implied and historical audience and author, see Seymour Chatman, *Story and Discourse: Narrative Structure in Fiction and Film* (Ithaca, N.Y., and London: Cornell University Press, 1978), 146–51.

12. Cf. Roger D. Abrahams, "Complex Relations of Simple Forms," 194, 198–99; idem, "Introductory Remarks to a Rhetorical Theory of Folklore," *Journal of American Folklore* 81 (1968):144–46; the dialectical process between "author" and reader/audience, as outlined by Hirsch, *Validity in Interpretation*, 78–88; and issues in the assessment of social setting discussed by William G. Doty, "The Concept of Genre in Literary Analysis," in SBLSP (1972), ed. Lane C. McGaughy, 2 vols., 2:422–28. Similar interpretations of texts have been proposed by Menakhem Perry, "Literary Dynamics: How the Order of a Text Creates Its Meanings, I. Theory of Literary Dynamics," *Poetics Today* 1 (1979):35–61; and the contributors to Dennis E. Smith, ed., *How Gospels Begin, Semeia* 52 (1991).

The Apocalypse of Elijah begins, "The word of the Lord came to me saying to me, '[Son of Man,] say to this people, "Why do you add sin to your sins and anger the Lord God who created you?"'" This pericope reproduces a first-person narrative introduction used—in slightly abbreviated forms—in the prophetic books of Ezekiel and Jeremiah and also recalls formulaic narrative in the biblical Elijah cycle (1 Kgs 17:2, 8; 18:1; 21:17, 19). The form is generally classified as a "prophetic commission (or revelation) formula."[13] In analyzing the self-presentation of the text, however, it is useful to consider the function of this formula as it is intended to have an impact on the audience. Borrowing a concept from J. L. Austin's theory of speech acts, one might designate the commission formula's *illocutionary* function as establishing a first-person claim to divine authority (whereas its *locutionary* function is merely to inform an audience of the event of a god's contact).[14]

The "Son of Man" address appears only in the Achmimic text, but because its presence gives little nuance to the pericope (apart from the reinforcement of archaic phraseology) it is difficult to attribute much significance to its absence. It is clear nonetheless that the passage was meant to recall, if not Ezekiel specifically, the glorified claims of a biblical prophet.[15] The passage's almost identical fivefold repetition in Ezekiel would certainly have facilitated its memorization and subsequent recollection as a typical prophetic formula, suitable for the introduction of a new text.

13. Ez 6:1; 12:1; 13:1; 14:2; 33:1-2; Jer 1:4, 11, 13; 2:1; 16:1; 24:4; cf. Is 30:1d; Sir 3:27b. On the form, see Claus Westermann, *The Basic Forms of Prophetic Speech*, tr. Hugh Clayton White (Philadelphia: Westminster, 1967), 100–115; Klaus Koch, *The Growth of the Biblical Tradition*, tr. S. M. Cupitt (2d ed.; New York: Scribner's, 1969), 202, 216–17; David E. Aune, *Prophecy in Early Christianity and the Ancient Mediterranean World* (Grand Rapids: Eerdmans, 1983), 90–91, 328–31.

14. J. L. Austin, *How to Do Things with Words*, ed. J. O. Urmson and Marina Sbisà (2d ed.; Cambridge: Harvard University Press, 1975); John R. Searle, "A Taxonomy of Illocutionary Acts," in *Language, Mind, and Knowledge*, ed. Keith Gunderson, Minnesota Studies in the Philosophy of Science 7 (Minneapolis: University of Minnesota Press, 1975), 344–69; and Richard Ohmann, "Literature as Act," *Approaches to Poetics*, ed. Seymour Chatman (New York: Columbia University Press, 1973), 81–108, who approaches literature from the perspective of mimesis.

15. Arguments could be made both for the originality and for the later addition of "Son of Man," and so no assumptions will be made either way in this analysis. Functionally, it merely reinforces the Ezekelian language of the introduction. "Add sin to sins" appears not in Ezekiel but in Is 30:1d and Sir 3:27b, but in neither book in a context that seems to have influenced ApocEl. Therefore it is probable that the phrase circulated autonomously in the repertoire of stock biblical phrases from which Christian preachers and authors drew for their compositions and homilies. On the popularization of biblical phraseology in early Egyptian Christianity, see above, chap. 2, pp. 33–35.

There follows an admonition that begins with a fairly exact quotation of 1 Jn 2:15a—"Do not love the world or the things in the world"—but that appears to improvise an elaboration on this theme: "for the pride of the world and its destruction are the devil's." The content of this elaboration does not differ significantly from its analog in 1 Jn 2:16-17:

> For all that is in the world, the lust of the flesh and the lust of the eyes and the pride of life, is not of the Father but is of the world. And the world passes away, and the lust of it; but he who does the will of God abides for ever.

There is good reason to believe, therefore, that the author was recalling his source from memory and was only able to recall the first part exactly.[16]

From a careful consideration of the nature of scriptural citations in this introduction, therefore, it appears that the author intended to create a sense of biblical authority through the use of stock phraseology, rather than drawing carefully from set texts for the purpose of systematic exegesis. This would suggest that from its conception the Apocalypse of Elijah was designed for oral performance—where biblical phraseology and quotations would have an effect regardless of context and accuracy—rather than private reading—where accuracy and context could be checked against other texts and considered systematically.[17]

What effect might such an introduction have on the subsequent text and its oral reception? What clues does the audience receive as to implied speaker, authority, and genre? The claim established by the revelation/commission formula presents itself in the first person. Although many apocalypses employ the first-person voice for introduction or narration, the Apocalypse of Elijah lacks the journal-like commission formulas conventional to apocalypses such as 4 Ezra ("In the thirtieth year . . . I was troubled as I lay on my bed. . . . Then the angel that had been sent to me, whose name was Uriel, answered" [3:1, 4:1]) and Revelation ("I John . . . was on the island called Patmos. . . . I was in the Spirit on the Lord's day, and I heard behind me a loud voice like a trumpet

---

16. The special emphasis Wintermute puts on "pride, boasting" (ϣⲟⲩϣⲟⲩ; 735 n. g.) is perhaps unwarranted in the context of ApocEl. The "pride" seems not so much to refer to a personified *kosmos* as to the worldly and materialistic attitudes of nonascetics, as perceived by the author and his audience (a perspective identical to that in 1 Jn 2:15-17).

17. On the private reader's ability to check and "back-loop" to earlier text, see Ong, *Orality and Literacy*, 39–40.

saying, 'Write'" [1:9-11]).[18] The echo of the prophetic voice from Ezekiel and Jeremiah would probably have established the text in the mind of the audience as a prophetic discourse, a genre that customarily employed first-person narrative to indicate the context and authority of its contents. Although the "I" is not identified by name, we must suppose that the audience would have shared with the author a familiarity with the language and lore of prophets.[19]

This prophetic introduction therefore implies that the audience should consider what follows as divinely directed, if not inspired. The introduction's *perlocutionary* effect would presumably be the audience's sense of awed anticipation before the delivery of divine prophecies.[20] The immediate use of a scriptural quotation might have functioned to reinforce the divine authority of the text.

Of greatest importance is the reflexive effect that this introduction (and its implications for the nature of the first-person speaker) would have had on the public reader and, it is to be assumed, on the author who composed it for public reading. Without any third-person introduction to establish a separate implied speaker (e.g., Enoch, Abraham, Moses), without any systematic distinction between this introductory claim of divine direction and the rest of the Apocalypse of Elijah, the location of the emphatic "me" in the first verse falls necessarily upon the performer or public reader (as the implied author).[21] That is, this em-

18. Cf. 2 *Bar.* 1:1; *1 En* ("Parables") 37:1-5; Rv 1:1. See Aune, *Prophecy in Early Christianity*, 115–16, 330–31. Ezekiel anticipates this emphasis on the physical "text" of the revelation in 2:8—3:3.

19. Aune's analysis of the continuation and transformation of these formulas in first- and second-century Christianity (and, presumably, Judaism) aims ultimately at portraying a social and religious phenomenon of itinerant Christian "shamans" and their ecstatic utterances. No such context can be deduced from the Apocalypse of Elijah; indeed, Aune's acknowledgment of "literary oracles" (*Prophecy in Early Christianity*, 318–20) shows that formulas from an ecstatic or otherwise oral religious context might also be used in literature to give the pretense of the author's ecstasy and inspiration. Another plausible origin of prophetic formulas and language in the Apocalypse of Elijah and elsewhere is the "ecstatic" *anticipation of delivery* experienced by a religious leader as that leader composes the text of a homily or other inspirational discourse in private. From this state the composer might write an authentically ecstatic style into the text, even though the eventual performance derives from a prepared text.

20. Austin explains the perlocutionary act thus: "Saying something will often, or even normally, produce certain consequential effects upon the feelings, thoughts, or actions of the audience, or of the speaker, or of other persons: and it may be done with the design, intention, or purpose of producing them. . . . We shall call the performance of an act of this kind the performance of a 'perlocutionary' act" (*How to Do Things with Words*, 101).

21. Cf. Barr, "Apocalypse of John," 251–52. On the charisma of performance, see William Hugh Jansen, "Classifying Performance in the Study of Verbal Folklore," in

phatic "me" of the implied author–speaker would subsume the identity of the historical speaker (who, in the first performance of the text, may also have been the historical author or ad hoc oral composer). This would suggest that the authority of the text in its first performance(s) was borne not only by the biblical phraseology and the stated claim of divine direction but also by the prior charisma of the speaker. Indeed, there is probably a historical relationship between the typically prophetic voice employed in this introduction, the text's attribution to Elijah, and the particular form of the author's charisma in his community (e.g., as a prophet).

The manuscript tradition implies that the Apocalypse of Elijah had a dynamic presence in public readings well after its composition. One can infer this kind of popularity from both the punctuation in Sa[3] and the early diversification of recensions or text "families," evidently in the process of readings and applications. It is therefore appropriate to consider whether the performance and illocutions reviewed here would continue effectively over the course of a series of historical readings. David Barr has argued that the epistolary frame used in the beginning of the book of Revelation (1:11)—a text manifestly intended for oral performance (1:3)—actually preserves the orally authoritative voice of the prophet John as written literature after the historical prophet was gone.[22] One might observe similar attempts to couch oral prophecy within recognized literary genres, in order to endow them with permanent scriptural authority, in Mark 13, *Apocalypse of Peter* 2–6, and throughout the eschatological portions of Jewish apocalypses. If the composer or a subsequent redactor of the Elijah Apocalypse had added a literary frame to locate the parenesis and warnings in historical legend—to explain how the prophecy had been preserved through the time of the present audience—then the text would have become a "true" apocalypse whose authority would reside in its literary nature, not in its performative effect

---

Studies in Folklore, ed. W. Edson Richmond (Bloomington, Ind.: Indiana University Press, 1957), 110–18; and Abrahams, "Rhetorical Theory of Folklore," 147–48. Ong notes the incident of an African epic performer psychologically and dramatically identifying with his hero during the course of performance (*Orality and Literacy,* 46). One would assume this to be the case in public reading too, as any discourse will intrinsically put the historical reader in the position of the implied speaker (such a principle might be demonstrated with the Gospel of John and the Nag Hammadi tractate *Thunder, Perfect Mind*).

22. Barr, "Apocalypse of John," 249–50. Cf. Aune, *Prophecy in Early Christianity,* 275: "It is very possible that [Revelation's] public reading would replace a prophetic address to the congregations by one or more of their local prophets."

and "presence." The (so-named) Apocalypse of Elijah, however, preserves the immediacy of the first performer (the composer or prophet) as an authoritative presence in each reading: Elijah becomes not merely a visionary of biblical legend but, even more, the revealer of the present.

Thus the first-person introduction would continually have had a powerful effect on the somewhat disjointed homily that follows it, by creating in audiences the (perlocutionary) understanding that the homily is a continuation of the Lord's word, in spite of the fact that God is occasionally mentioned in subsequent verses in the third person.[23] It is not unusual for narrative religious literature to contain at some point a parenetic discourse that represents the ideology of the text's composer or compositional community.[24] The vividly homiletic nature of ApocEl 1:3-27, however, contrasts with those parenetic discourses written specifically for expression within the narrative context of an apocalypse, testament, or gospel.[25]

This homily contains a variety of subjects: cosmic Christology (ApocEl 1:3-7), an exposition on the eschatological fate of the audience—the saints—versus that of sinners (1:8-12), a defense of fasting and discussion of its benefits (apparently an issue of immediate significance to the audience—1:13-22), and, finally, an exhortation against doubt (1:23-27). But the links between these topics are not made explicitly. The hortatory and even urgent way in which topics commence should dissuade us from seeking aporias—gaps between artificially linked texts. Instead, there are implicit associations between topics, which would have been apparent to the first audiences (e.g., the relationship between powers of

23. The confusion created by this transition from Lord's voice to homily is exhibited by various translators' attempts to punctuate the end of the initial speech. While Wintermute (735) and Rosenstiehl (79) end the quotation before the verse from 1 John, Pietersma (21) carries it to the end of the latter verse. Schrage (231) and Kuhn (762) forgo quotation marks altogether, thus representing accurately the implicit nature of the text's voice.

24. Philip Vielhauer, "Apocalypses and Related Subjects: Introduction," tr. David Hill, in *NTA* 2:587.

25. The major distinction between the second-person addresses of a homily designed for public performance and a parenetic discourse designed for inclusion in a literary text is the presence in the latter of a narrated audience to whom the discourse is (apparently) directed (although it is implicitly directed to the reader or public audience). In the homily, which as a form lacks a narrative context, the object of the discourse is explicitly the historical audience. Although the homiletic section of the Elijah Apocalypse develops its themes much more than do the clipped parenetic utterances ascribed to early Jewish and Christian prophets, the authority by which parenesis might be woven into oracular and eschatological speech derives from the tradition of the prescriptive oracle. See Aune, *Prophecy in Early Christianity*, 321–22.

fasting and single-mindedness). Yet the unsystematic arrangement of the Apocalypse of Elijah as compared to, for example, the progressive visions of the book of Revelation is quite apparent and lends support to a compositional origin in public or even spontaneous prophecy.[26]

The author has reinforced the illocutionary effect of the first-person introduction—that the homily continues to represent the divine word—through his alternation of prophetic descriptions of God's intentions and "quotations" of God's own words. For example, the second segment of the homily appears almost entirely in God's voice:

> Remember that he has prepared for you [plural] thrones and crowns in heaven. For everyone who will obey [me (Ach)] [his voice (Sa³)] will receive thrones and crowns. Among those who are mine, says the Lord, I will write my name upon their foreheads and seal their right hands. They will not be hungry, nor will they thirst, nor will the Lawless One prevail over them, nor will the Thrones hinder them, but they will go with the angels to my city. (ApocEl 1:8-10)

Even when the next homiletic segment opens with the address, "Hear, O wise men of the land" (1:13a), the speaker does not clearly change until God is himself invoked in the third person (1:13b), when we understand the prophet–author to be speaking in human voice. But then the divine voice apparently breaks in again during the discourse on the powers of fasting (1:16):

Sa³	Ach
so that the evil one	so that the evil one
will not **deceive** you	will not **consume** you
But a holy fast is what	But a holy fast is what
he has established.	**I** have established,
The Lord says,	the Lord says,
He who fasts **continually**	He who fasts
will never sin	will never sin[27]

Once again, no change of speakers is indicated until, several verses later, God is mentioned in the third person (1:18).

Thus throughout the homiletic section the pretense of the divine voice, which was initiated in the first verse of the text, is maintained through a consistent confusion of implied speakers. In the context of

26. Cf. Barr, "Apocalypse of John," 244–49.
27. Cf. Wintermute, 738 n. d3. In ApocEl 1:20 the Achmimic ms. quotes God again—"But a holy fast is what I have created"—where Sa³ continues in third person—"a holy fast is what the Lord created."

public performance, the illocutionary nature of this confusion of voices would have been twofold: (1) a casting of divine authority over the entire discourse (the third-person references to God merely establishing the nature of the supernatural speaker), and (2) the implication that the performer—the public reader—himself spoke the voice of God.[28] This would again suggest that the author and original speaker of the text meant to cast himself as a prophet with divine authority, and one may presume that this effect continued in subsequent readings. One might say that the Apocalypse of Elijah was conceived for the type of enthusiastic Upper Egyptian assemblies in which Eusebius beheld the prodigious reciter of Scripture in the early fourth century.[29]

The confusion of speakers and authorities continues in the Apocalypse of Elijah 2: "[Those who are mine (Sa³)] [Now, therefore, they (Ach)] will not be overcome, says the Lord, nor will they fear in battle. And when they see a king who has arisen in the north" (ApocEl 2:2-3a). By not indicating a new speaker, the author has created the impression that it is God himself who delivers the sequence of political and social oracles in ApocEl 2, an impression that would be reinforced by the continued use of "oral" markers: the use of first-person singular and second-person plural pronouns and of exclamatory interjections ("Woe to you!").

While obviously maintaining the implication of oral address, ApocEl 2 changes in speech type from homily to oracular prophecy. The content and motifs of these oracles come directly from native Egyptian oracle tradition, rather than from the immediate ideology and concerns of the rural Christian movement; and there is reason to believe that, in third-century Egypt, an audience would have recognized the traditional language and imagery of the oracles.[30] Furthermore, while listening to the particular descriptions and predictions constituting ApocEl 2, the audience would hear and understand the whole text in light of its experiences of Egyptian oracles, which had considerable circulation in Greek during the Roman period. A text that had begun in the voice and authority of biblical prophecy and maintained this voice through a series of homilies would now acquire the voice, the authority, and even the concerns and dramatic scope of traditional Egyptian oracles.

28. On the illocutionary effect of "oral" markers, see Roger Fowler, *Literature as Social Discourse* (London: Batsford Academic, 1981), 88–91.
29. See above, pp. 32–33.
30. See chaps. 7–8.

The obscure imagery and language of ApocEl 2 also recall the symbolism and forms of speech used in Hellenistic oracular literature such as the *Sibylline Oracles*. Often such enigmatic language refers obliquely—but systematically—to actual historical events of the era of the writer; the oracles are thereby called *vaticinia ex eventus*, "prophecies (written) out of the events (that they seem to predict)." In the case of ApocEl 2, this function of allusively documenting contemporaneous events is not so clear; indeed, it is argued in chapter 8, below, that there is no *ex eventu* reference intended in this chapter of the Elijah Apocalypse. The audience is left, however, with such tantalizing oracles as "A king will rise up in the west, whom they will call the King of Peace. . . . He will kill the Unrighteous King" (2:6-7) and "For here are his signs—I will tell you so you will recognize him: for he has two sons, one on his right and one on his left" (2:17-18). Without an explanation (which is not forthcoming in the text) the audience might be left with the opaque ravings of a temple seer. But how does the opacity of this material operate in the context set up by the prior homily?

In anticipation of ApocEl 2, the author has introduced the homily on fasting with the address "Hear, O wise men [ⲛ̄ⲥⲁⲃⲉⲟⲩ] of the land, concerning the deceivers who will multiply in the end times [ⲛ̄ⲧⲅⲁⲏ ⲛ̄ⲛⲉⲟⲩⲟⲉⲓϣ]" (1:13a). The "deceivers" are subsequently identified as those opposing the fast. Because the oracular ApocEl 2 does discuss the eschaton, the "wisdom" ascribed to the audience in the address should indicate their special ability to understand the oracles. This is not to imply that the audience might actually have perceived a systematic correspondence between the oracles and their own period; but they may have been able to connect the "deceivers" to individuals who had been recently criticizing excessive fasting in the region.[31] A specific motif of eschatological opponents to fasting cannot be found elsewhere in Jewish and Christian literature. The audience could therefore locate itself in the eschaton, realize the author's pronouncement upon it of "wise men,"[32] and understand the oracles in ApocEl 2 to be a vivid portrayal of imminent events.

It is in ApocEl 2 that a corporate dramatis persona of "priests of the land" (ⲛⲟⲩⲏⲏⲃ ⲙ̄ⲡⲕⲁⲅ) begins to appear: as a reign is good or bad (or as

---

31. See below, chap. 11.

32. The illocutionary force of this address is both to separate the audience from outsiders hierarchically, as the "wise" against the "unwise," and to create in the audience the experience of unique and privileged understanding.

a sign bodes evil), so the "priests" gain or suffer or "tear their garments" (2:28). Because there is a historical correlation between the forms[33] of ApocEl 2—which arose in native Egyptian temple settings—and the relative fortune of the Egyptian priesthood under various historical rulers (whether Egyptian, Greek, or Roman), the author may have intended his use of ογΗΗΒ (or, originally, ἱερεῖς) to signify the audience's status in relation to the oracles he was delivering.[34] When he addresses the "priests" in the second person in 2:40, there is even further reason to take this term as a designation of the audience in the latter's projected eschatological experience: as the woes begin and the audience members recognize the signs, they will be like the temple priests who interpret chaotic events in the Egyptian kingship as preordained. Thus this enigmatic term for an eschatological group (which seems to reflect the implied audience) may derive from the very literary form employed in ApocEl 2; and consequently the audience, identifying with the "priests of the land," is placed in a more traditional relationship to the "pagan" imagery and language in ApocEl 2 than the more "Christian" sections in ApocEl 1 might have allowed.

The exhortation against doubt, which concluded the homiletic section and followed the fasting homily through the theme of "impassioned concentration," connects to this oracular section with the following words (1:27—2:3):

Sa	*Ach*
If you are always single-minded in the Lord, **be wise to the Time,** so that you might comprehend all things concerning the Assyrian kings and the destruction of heaven and earth.	**Therefore, be** always single-minded in the Lord, so that you might comprehend all things. **Therefore,** concerning the Assyrian kings and the destruction of heaven and earth **and the things under the earth.**

33. I prefer J. Arthur Baird's distinction of "form"—"small individual units representing the materials out of which the literary work is composed . . . usually said to be a product of the use to which the transmitting community put the oral material"—from "genre"—"a collective category that requires many individual units often, but not always, of different types. . . . It is basically a literary designation" ("Genre Analysis as a Method of Historical Criticism," in SBLSP [1972], 2:386–87).

34. Moreover, the perspective in ApocEl 2, which expresses a sympathetic interest in Memphis (2:21; cf. 2:44, 46-47) and sentiments against Alexandria (2:15; cf. 2:31), can be attributed to the ideology of the Egyptian priesthood, particularly during Roman times: as Garth Fowden observes, "Memphis was a potent symbol in Egyptian eyes, an antitype, . . . of the Greek metropolis of Alexandria" (*The Egyptian Hermes* [Cambridge: Cambridge University Press, 1987], 41).

Those who are mine will not be overcome, says the Lord, nor will they fear in battle. And when they see a king who has arisen in the north they will call him the King of the Assyrians and the Unrighteous King.	**Now, therefore, they** will not be overcome, says the Lord, nor will they fear in battle. And when they see a king who has arisen in the north they will call him the King of the Assyrians and the Unrighteous King.

As in ApocEl 1:13, wisdom is here associated with perception of the onset of eschatological woes; but here such wisdom is also characterized as lack of "double-mindedness," which apparently denoted a state of uncertainty preventing one's absolute conviction in legitimate authority.[35] Moreover, the audience's implicit capacity for discerning the nature of things is now focused on two themes or events: the eradication of the cosmos for a "new heaven and new earth"—a theme that the audience would presumably have recognized from Revelation, other eschatological literature, or an oral lore of cosmic cataclysm—and "the Assyrian kings."

The "Assyrians" function as the *dramatis personae maleficiorum* both in the beginning and the conclusion of ApocEl 2 (2:3b, 42-47). Thus the above passage does indeed focus the notion of wisdom with material anticipating the eschatological oracles. In the late third century, however, "kings of the Assyrians" would not have represented a readily apparent contemporary historical reference to most Egyptians. Indeed, the author (notably in the Lord's voice) indicates that this rather vague appellative is to be applied to an even vaguer "king arising in the north" (2:3a). Neither appellative brings the character any closer to historical identifiability. But the compounding of oracular references, particularly in the voice of God, was a traditional device both in Egyptian and early Christian prophetic literature, which functioned to give the reader or audience the sense of the oracle's interpretation and historical reference without completely unveiling it.[36]

Following ApocEl 2, the text turns progressively toward Christian images of eschatological woes, reflecting the tradition of eschatological discourse inherited from Enoch literature, Daniel, Revelation, and pre-

---

35. Cf. Oscar J. F. Seitz, "Antecedents and Signification of the Term DIPSYCHOS," *JBL* 66 (1947):211–19; and idem, "Afterthoughts on the Term 'Dipsychos,'" *NTS* 4 (1958):327–34.

36. Cf. Aune, *Prophecy in Early Christianity*, 327; and Janet H. Johnson and Robert K. Ritner, "Multiple Meaning and Ambiguity in the 'Demotic Chronicle,'" in *Studies in Egyptology Presented to Miriam Lichtheim*, 2 vols., ed. Sarah Israelit-Groll (Jerusalem: Magnes Press, 1990), 1:494–506.

sumably an oral tradition of eschatological preaching. The text continues to be punctuated with the speech devices of a public delivery, of oral performance; and the illocutionary authority of the voice likewise continues to be divine or prophetic (for what human leader, indeed, would have the knowledge to disclose these materials?):

> Then if you should hear that there is security and safety in Jerusalem, tear your garments, O priests of the land, because the Destructive One will not be long in coming! (2:40)

> In the fourth year of that king there will appear [someone (Sa³)] [the Lawless One (Ach)] saying, "I am the Christ." But he is not—do not believe him! (3:1)

> For behold, I will tell you his signs so that you might recognize him. (3:14)

From the almost familiar voice of the oracles and the signs of the Lawless One, the Apocalypse of Elijah changes abruptly in speech type to a series of dramatic narratives describing: (1) martyrdoms of eschatological heroes; (2) martyrdoms of "saints" and the "righteous"; (3) evacuation of saints and the righteous; (4) the decline of earth without saints; (5) final battle, judgment, and parousia. But though straight narrative does not require the degree of audience recognition or participation that the direct address does, the author of the Apocalypse of Elijah has nevertheless achieved a rhetorical effect similar to that of the earlier sections. In this case, rather than employing homiletic and oral performative devices, he constructs the narrative around a series of dramatic monologues delivered by the heroes and antiheroes of the narrative (ApocEl 4:2, 5, 8-12, 15, 16, 31; 5:10-19, 25-27). Thus the audience participates in the verbal exchanges between the Lawless One and his opponents at the same time as the drama of the eschatological events is "realized" in the immediate historical setting of the public reading.

In one of these monologues the participation of the audience in the events of the end times becomes strikingly explicit. "Sixty righteous ones" accuse the Lawless One before they die at his hands (4:31):

> Every feat which the prophets performed, you have performed [from the beginning (Ach)], but you were quite unable to raise a corpse, because you lack the power [to give life (Ach)]—by this we have recognized that you are the Lawless One!

This claim by the "righteous" immediately recalls an earlier passage in the Apocalypse of Elijah wherein the divine or oracular voice instructs the audience on the signs of the Lawless One (3:11-13):

> He will multiply his signs and his wonders in the presence of everyone. He will do the things which the Christ did, except only for raising a dead person—by this you will know that he is the Lawless One: he has no power to give life!

The "Righteous Ones" who have this knowledge in the eschaton are therefore identified with the audience of the Apocalypse of Elijah, who have just been informed of this crucial distinguishing "sign." Once again the immediate audience of the text in performance is represented in the narrative; whereas earlier it appeared through second-person plural addresses and through the image of apocalyptic wisdom, here audience members appear as actual *dramatis personae* in the eschatological narrative. This presence of the audience within the text is furthermore reinforced by the narrative theme of ApocEl 4, namely, martyrdom. Particularly gruesome details of the execution of the "saints . . . and the priests of the land" (4:21-23), an obvious reference to flight from persecution into the desert (4:24), and an apparently well-developed "martyr ideology" (4:26-29)[37] all reflect the practice and lore of martyrdom that began with the Decian edicts in the mid-third century in Egypt. Because any Egyptian Christian congregation with eschatological leanings would have been familiar with the lore of martyrdom (if not with the experience of fleeing or refusing the edicts) by the time the Apocalypse of Elijah was written, the text's audience would have found these narratives of eschatological martyrdoms familiar. Seeing themselves in the saints, priests, and "sixty righteous" would consequently follow the audience members' recognition of the martyrdom imagery.

The final scenes of eschatological destruction not only maintain the dialogue format but are punctuated with the refrain "on that day,"[38] a rhetorical device highly effective in (and probably distinctive of) an oral context, where the repetition of lines, phrases, and interjections serves to

---

37. The passage describes what must be a prior belief system: (1) desert refugees who die will not be eaten by animals (4:26); (2) refugees as well as martyrs will be granted a blessed eschatological status (4:26b-27a, 28-29), (3) but actual martyrs will have a higher status in the eschatological kingdom than the refugees (4:27b); and (4) a formulaic "promise" that martyrs would eventually "sit on God's right hand" (cf. *Herm. Vis.* 3.2.1) had circulated in Egypt and was used to justify the martyr–refugee hierarchy.

38. ϨⲘ ⲠⲈϨⲞⲞⲨ ⲈⲦⲘⲘⲀϨ (Sa³)/ ϨⲘ ⲠⲈϨⲞⲞⲨⲈ ⲈⲦⲘⲘⲞ (Ach): ApocEl 4:30; 5:1a, 2a, 7a, 15, 22, 25, 29b, 30, 33, 36a. Cf. 2:5, "many people will long for death in those days [ϨⲚ ⲚⲈϨⲞⲞⲨ ⲈⲦⲚⲈⲘⲀⲨ]."

reinforce the content and importance of a text and to raise the emotional participation of an audience.[39] In the case of the end of the Apocalypse of Elijah, the repetition of this particular formula synchronizes the events of eschatological judgment and cataclysm that follow the more (apparently) identifiable period of the eschatological martyrdoms.[40] The composer activates the more fantastic imagery of the end of the text and makes it available to his audience with a rhetorical device—the repetition of a formula—that emphasizes the culmination of a prophetic, eschatological discourse.

FROM GENRE TO "INTRINSIC" GENRE
IN THE DESCRIPTION OF THE
APOCALYPSE OF ELIJAH

E. D. Hirsch has described the process of literary interpretation as the progressive search for the "intrinsic" genre of the text.[41] The critic, reader, or audience commences an encounter with a text with a certain series of assumptions about the text as a whole, which concern context, authority, and literary type—that is, genre in the most general sense—based on previous literary encounters.[42] During the course of the reading,[43] these assumptions are gradually defined, corrected, substituted, or jettisoned until, at the end, the text has taken on a particular significance and context for the "reader(s)," one much more specific than their initial impression. This particular sense of a text is the "intrinsic genre," and Hirsch argues further that it is "a conception shared by the speaker and the interpreter."[44]

---

39. See Ong, *Orality and Literacy*, 39–41; and Aune, *Prophecy in Early Christianity*, 335–37. The emotional effect of prophetic rhetorical devices upon an audience is perlocutionary, that is, it is intentional as far as the "ritual" of prophetic audience implies emotive or ecstatic participation and as the function of prophet is to facilitate this participation, but this intention is not explicit in the prophetic utterances.

40. There is no basis to A. T. Olmstead's general claim "that the phrases 'in that day,' in those days,' usually introduce obvious interpolations" ("Intertestamental Studies," *JAOS* 56 [1936]:255).

41. Hirsch, *Validity in Interpretation*, 78–89.

42. Cf. ibid., 71–77. Abrahams's performative model would require that the performative situation of audience, performer, or reader be added here as a necessary constraint upon the preliminary sense of a text.

43. "Reading" here is meant to denote any encounter with a prepared text, whether private or public.

44. Hirsch, *Validity in Interpretation*, 81.

Applying this progressive model to the situation in which the Apocalypse of Elijah was composed and read, we can see that, although it would not have been heard as an apocalypse, the text's audience would have perceived forms of speech conventional to apocalypses, oracles, homilies, and both Egyptian and biblical prophecy and would have based its understanding of the text on prior experiences with and respect for these genres. That is, the "intrinsic genre" of the Apocalypse of Elijah is a conglomerate of several literary genres and traditions that were historically contemporaneous to the audience.

The initial "sense of the whole" would have been that of the biblical prophetic utterance, conditioned by the opening passage; and alternating prophetic and divine voices continue the illocutionary effect of this initial sense throughout a parenetic section. Subsequently, while maintaining the prophetic voice, the text moves into the language and imagery of Egyptian prophetic oracles. The prophetic authority is thus "situated" in the symbolic world of native Egyptian literature, while the use of this native oracular language gives increased scope and authority to the "prophet"—as if a biblical prophet were now speaking in the manner of a priest of Khnum, the oracular ram god of Elephantine.

The subsequent sections on the signs, acts, and demise of the Lawless One change the prophetic voice to one of relative intimacy with the audience: the prophet directly informs the audience of signs and dramatically enacts the conflicts between the "saints" and the Lawless One and the latter's pathetic demise. Here it is probable that the audience's acquaintance with an oral (homiletic) tradition of eschatological events and perhaps its experience of other eschatological texts (such as Revelation, Mark 13, 2 Thessalonians 2, 1 and 2 John) would have allowed it to understand these materials in the Apocalypse of Elijah as conceivable events of the end time. Certain passages in these last chapters, however, also make more particular reference either to the time and events of the audience (i.e., martyrdom, *anachoresis*) or to epichoric Egyptian concerns.[45] The particular eschatological traditions inherited from Jewish and Christian groups were thus explained and situated for the benefit of an Egyptian audience.

By the end, the audience has heard—nay, witnessed—a description

45. E.g., Tabitha (ApocEl 4:1-6; see David T. M. Frankfurter, "Tabitha in the Apocalypse of Elijah," *JTS* 41 [1990]:13–25); decline of fertility (5:7-14); saints' power over fertility (5:18); Lawless One compared to serpent (5:33b; cf. 1:4).

of the end of the world from an Egyptian perspective: the Egyptian Christian audience's particular historical situation is addressed as the onset of eschatological woes, and the signs of the end actually begin in Egypt. Yet the revealer is a biblical prophet, his allegiance—ultimately— to an angelic Christ figure and his heavenly city, and his "voice" the direct and even intimate style of a homilist.

THE IMPLIED AUDIENCE AND IMPLIED AUTHOR OF THE APOCALYPSE OF ELIJAH

An inference has been surfacing gradually in the present analysis of the Apocalypse of Elijah, that the text was composed for a specific audience in a concrete historical situation. If one were to take this as an assumption, then what indications might be gleaned from the text about the nature and self-definition of this audience? Likewise, how does the image of the implied speaker elucidate a historical author?

Implied and Historical Audience

Orality and Literacy

In contrast to the literary self-consciousness in apocalypses—evinced by the narrative frame describing the historical reason for the text—the Apocalypse of Elijah reveals itself as highly oral and performance-oriented, both in its speech types and its associative progression of themes. Nowhere are there mentions of books, scribes, or writing, details that characterized apocalypses in circulation at that time (e.g., 2 *Enoch* 22-23; *2 Bar.* 84:9; Rv 22:7, 18-19).[46] Further, scriptural allusions (e.g., to 1 John or Revelation) are neither explicit nor exactly cited and seem to be drawn from the memory of the author, if he was at all acquainted with the texts themselves. Some of these aspects can be partly accounted for by the homily genre; but considering that few people in Roman Egypt had the ability to read, comprehend, and use books, the oral nature of the Apocalypse of Elijah suggests that the audience itself was, at most, semiliterate.

46. This characteristic aspect of literary apocalypses has been seldom discussed. Cf. Theodore A. Bergren, "Accounts in the Apocalypses of Their Literary Origin" (paper presented to the SBL Pseudepigrapha Group, Chicago, November 1989).

Eschatology and Millennialism

The second indication of audience lies in the eschatological subject matter of the Elijah Apocalypse. Many apocalypses from the Second Temple period contain eschatological details but do not suggest a necessarily millennialist or eschatologically oriented social milieu. The overwhelmingly eschatological interest of the Apocalypse of Elijah, however, would seem to be a good indication of the audience's orientation. That the eschaton is said to begin with the arrival of the "Deceivers" opposing the fast (1:13) strengthens the case that the audience considered its own period to be premillennial.

Conversely, one might propose that the text represents the author-performer's endeavor to *convince* an audience of its eschatological status, where the audience was familiar enough with millennialist ideology and apocalyptic "signs" to be so convinced. Because there is evidence for millennialist activity in Upper Egypt during the second half of the third century c.e.,[47] either reconstruction of the audience's relationship to millennialist ideology would be historically plausible.

When the Apocalypse of Elijah is compared to other Egyptian Christian pseudepigrapha of the Roman period, it emerges as even more unusual in this eschatological focus. The *Apocalypse of Peter* opens with an eschatological section based on Mark 13 (*Apoc. Pet.* 1–2), Jewish eschatological lore (2–4; 6), and Greco-Roman ideas of cosmic ἐκπύρωσις (5) but then proceeds to Peter's extensive tourlike preview of the hell and heaven of the final judgment. The *Apocalypse of Paul* is almost entirely devoted to tours of hell and heaven, making only passing reference to an eventual "great day of judgment" (*Apoc. Paul* 16; 18; cf. 21). The *Testament of Abraham*, which may be taken as Christian for present purposes,[48] focuses exclusively on personal death and afterlife. And texts from the Nag Hammadi corpus rarely include eschatological narratives of any length.[49] It is therefore clear that an extended escha-

---

47. See chap. 10

48. Substantial scholarly opinion regards this text as Jewish, presumably pre-117 c.e., but its circulation, influence, and (most importantly) *preservation* in Egyptian Christianity make it an important document of Egyptian Christian literature of the Roman period—as this literature naturally developed from a uniquely Egyptian Jewish literature of the early Roman period.

49. When they are present, eschatological descriptions use cosmic rather than terrestrial details: e.g., *Orig. World* (NHC II, 5) 125–27; *Paraph. Shem* (NHC VII, 1) 43–45.

tological discourse was not a literary form typical of early Alexandrian and Greco-Egyptian Christian cultures[50] and may therefore represent an entirely different social milieu from those milieus that composed tours and discussions of death and afterlife. One might expect that communities interested in issues of individual death and afterlife were stable and relatively harmonious in their collective situations, whereas a community focusing exclusively on eschatological woes with dualistic, collective consequences would be in some crisis.

Rural Environment

The exhortation against doubt (ApocEl 1:23-27) employs imagery from Egyptian rural life: a farmer with his tool, a soldier with his breastplate, the implications of royal "service." Assuming that these rustic metaphors for the well-equipped psyche were meant to inspire familiarity in the audience, we might infer that the original audience was composed of people with rural backgrounds.[51]

"Wise Men"

The speaker addresses "wise men" (ⲛⲥⲁⲃⲉⲟⲩ) in ApocEl 1:13a, with regard to the arrival of the opponents of fasting, and follows this address with the exhortation to "be wise [ⲁⲣⲓ ⲥⲁⲃⲉ] to the times," which serves to introduce ApocEl 2, the Egyptian oracle section. Because the word is used in direct connection with both the audience's immediate situation (critics of fasting) and the eschatological significance of imminent events (the subject of the text as a whole), it is obvious that the use of ⲥⲁⲃⲉ (or, originally, σόφος) is not gratuitous but is meant to characterize the audience and the text's immediate milieu. That is, the audience is rendered "wise" through its reception of the author's revelations of eschatological signs.

To reinforce the audience's sense of this "sign-interpreting wisdom"

See George MacRae, "Apocalyptic Eschatology in Gnosticism," in *Apocalypticism in the Mediterranean World*, ed. Hellholm, 317–25.

50. It is possible, however, that the extended form of eschatological discourse among early Christians derived ultimately from earlier texts such as Revelation, Mark 13, and biblical prophecy (in dialectic with the Sibylline tradition).

51. Speech types that draw their imagery and reference from quotidian activities—besides this passage from the Apocalypse of Elijah, one might mention the parable, the joke, and the aphorism—originate by nature in an oral setting (cf. Ong, *Orality and Literacy*, 42–43; Werner Kelber, *The Oral and the Written Gospel* [Philadelphia: Fortress, 1983], 57–64). It is equally possible, however, that such imagery functioned as "quaint" rustic stereotypes rather than reflecting the audience's socioeconomic background.

and its self-definition as ⲛ̄ⲥⲁⲃⲉⲟⲩ, near the end of the text the author juxtaposes the fate of the *undiscerning* followers of the Lawless One as the land dries up (5:10-14): "You performed [vain (Sa³)] signs before us until you estranged us from the Christ," they wail, "Woe to us because we listened to you!" (5:11b). Similarly, the sixty martyrs who attempt to unveil the Lawless One mention a specific sign that the author has already revealed to his audience: the Lawless One cannot raise the dead (4:31; cf. 3:12-13).

Hence one might infer that the author was posing the audience of the Apocalypse of Elijah as "wise men," where wisdom means the specific ability to recognize the signs of eschatological woes and deceit based on information delivered by the author. It is furthermore conceivable that the original audience members held such wisdom to be their particular capacity and power beyond the immediate context of the reading.

"Saints"

More often than "wise men," the Apocalypse of Elijah refers in the course of narrative to a group called the "saints" (ⲛⲉⲧⲟⲩⲁⲁⲃ). The variety of situations in which saints are described implies a considerably developed ideology surrounding holy people and their status in this world and in the eschaton. It is unclear, however, to what degree "saint" was a term of self-definition for the social milieu of the Apocalypse of Elijah.

The author and his audience evidently consider their landscape and its fertility to be controlled by the presence of "saints" (5:18) and their "holy places," which will be alternately demolished and rebuilt during the eschatological woes (2:11, 41, 48b).

Saints are also the objects of the Lawless One's hostility (4:2, 21-29) and are thereby to be identified with the "sixty righteous ones" who recognize the Lawless One by his inability to resurrect. That is, "saints" are martyrs and ἀναχώρητες who are not deceived by the Lawless One's pretenses to authority. Once again, because it is ApocEl 3 that reveals the ability to recognize this figure, it would appear that the "saints" who are to suffer persecution are to be identified with the audience of the text. Further evidence for this identification appears in 1:8-10, where the audience (addressed in second person) is promised a heavenly end similar to that described for martyrs (4:27-29).

It appears, however, that there were at least two senses in which "saint" was understood in the social milieu of the Apocalypse of Elijah:

the martyred saint, whose remains and shrine offered power and fertility in the landscape (cf. 4:6); and the "holy persons" who resist "evil," suffer persecution, and are supposed to enter the heavenly city of Christ. Because the latter sense would have functioned more aptly as a model for religious life, the audience probably identified itself more with this kind of saint. Even in later Coptic tradition, however, there was a continuum between a persecuted or ascetic "sainthood" in life and the rewards and concrete powers of saints in their shrines and martyrologies.[52]

"Priests"

Finally, the Apocalypse of Elijah refers to a body called the "priests of the land" (ⲛⲟⲩⲏⲏⲃ ⲙ̄ⲡⲕⲁϩ—2:24, 28, 40; 4:21 [Ach]). It has been suggested that this appellative may have indicated the audience's hermeneutical status in relation to the native Egyptian "priestly" literary form of ApocEl 2.[53] There is the implication of this "syncretistic" meaning when ⲟⲩⲏⲏⲃ is used twice to refer, apparently, to priests of native or Greco-Roman temples (2:14b, 48).[54] Yet the term obviously designates groups in an orthodox relationship to the "Christian" Apocalypse of Elijah. Twice the text refers to "priests" and "saints" (2:24; 4:21 [Ach]) in such combination as to indicate that these are presumed to be two distinct bodies.

At one point the "priests" are addressed in the second person: "If you should hear that there is security and safety in Jerusalem, tear your garments, O priests of the land, because the Destructive One will not delay (his) coming!" (2:40). Earlier they are said to perform the same act in response to a different sign of woe: "On that day the priests of the land will tear their garments" (2:28).[55] Thus "priests" seems to designate a

---

52. See Peter Brown, *The Making of Late Antiquity* (Cambridge: Harvard University Press, 1975), chaps. 3–4; Violet MacDermot, *The Cult of the Seer in the Ancient Middle East* (London: Wellcome Institute of the History of Medicine, 1971), esp. 179–88, 201–19.

53. That is, just as the nationalist oracle derived from the temple priesthood in Egypt, so the understanding of such oracles (or participation in them) implied one's membership in a "priesthood."

54. Two lines corresponding to Sa³ are missing from Ach: "He will command that the temples of the pagans [ⲛ̄ϩⲉⲑⲛⲟⲥ] be plundered and their priests killed" (cf. Pietersma, 40). For alternate interpretations of this section, see Wintermute 743 n. n3; and Kuhn, 766.

55. Any relation to Mk 14:63 would have to be distant, because ApocEl shows no other knowledge of Mark, and the legendary high priest of Jerusalem who interrogated Jesus could hardly have been a positive paradigm for a third-century apocalyptic Christian community in Egypt.

particular holy group as dramatis personae of the eschatological woes—
their fortunes are indications of positive and negative signs—and it
designates the audience itself (as implied in the second-person address).

The precise distinction evidently assumed by the author between
"priests" and "saints" remains enigmatic, however, as does the extent of
the usage of the term "priests" in the milieu of the Apocalypse of Elijah.
We can only guess that the audience used "priests" as a self-designation,
because (1) "priests of the land" are addressed in the second person, and
(2) the cognate relationship (in Coptic) between "priest" (ⲟⲩⲏⲏⲃ) and
"saint" (ⲟⲩⲁⲁⲃ)—both signifying holiness and purity, a common self-
representation of religious sects—may reflect the use of ἱερ- in the
original Greek.[56] If there is some correlation between "priests" and the
originally (native) priestly literary form of nationalist oracle that the
author employs in ApocEl 2, then the use of ⲟⲩⲏⲏⲃ would represent an
interesting continuity between indigenous and Christian religious self-
definition.

Implied Speaker–Historical Author

Because the text is composed in an oral mode of expression, the first
author is likely to have been also the first performer of the text before an
audience. Based on inferences from Elijah pseudepigraphy and from the
use of the prophetic commission formula, there is reason to believe that
this author had a community designation as "prophet" before he presented the text; and the charisma that this designation reflected may
have derived from the author's status as ascetic anchorite or hermit and,
possibly, refugee from a religious edict.

The author has drawn on highly traditional oracular language and
imagery in the composition of ApocEl 2. As there is no reason to consider literary dependence upon such classical Egyptian oracular texts as
the *Oracle of the Potter* and its multiforms, it is likely that the author's
knowledge of such traditional Egyptian forms of expression came by
some other means.[57] Under these circumstances, it is conceivable that
the author's background included some activity in the Egyptian priest-

---

56. Cf. Crum, 487–88, s.v. ⲟⲩⲟⲡ. Compare the priestly self-definitions among the
Qumran Essenes and in the book of Revelation (e.g., Rv 1:6; 5:10; 6:9; 20:6); the author
of the Apocalypse of Elijah also might have sought to import archaic Jewish terms of
sacred privilege to characterize a heroic group in the drama of eschatological woes.

57. Cf. Jean-Pierre Mahé, *Hermès en Haute-Égypte*, 2 vols., Bibliothèque copte de Nag
Hammadi 3 and 7 (Quebec: Presses de l'Université Laval, 1978–82), 2:111–13, on the
similar issue in relation to the *Perfect Discourse*.

hood, which was the source of Egyptian oracle compositions. In the priesthood he would have had regular contact with the literary tradition of Egyptian oracles and their forms and motifs and thus been able to achieve the capability of composing such tracts, rather than merely being familiar with some of them (a familiarity that, to be sure, would apply to most Egyptians and Greco-Egyptians of this time). As Lactantius's liberal use of both Hermetic literature and the *Oracle of Hystaspes* expresses, there is no reason why an author defining himself as a Christian would not have looked to native ("pagan") literatures as being useful and authoritative.[58]

The priesthood had many classes, and there is some evidence that members on the lower rungs achieved popular leadership roles—including prophetic roles—independently of (and often contrary to) the higher priesthoods, who generally cooperated with Greco-Roman rulers.[59] Both the form and the sentiments—a modified religious nationalism—of ApocEl 2 reflect the perspectives of this lower priesthood and its insurgent and prophetic activities. To move from this status to the type of millennialist Christianity expressed in the Apocalypse of Elijah therefore may not have represented a great ideological change. This hypothesis of the author's origins would also account for his literacy, a skill that was normative only among the Egyptian priesthood.[60]

58. Fowden, *Egyptian Hermes*, 205–12. Fowden also has proposed the Egyptian priesthood as the font of other religious movements during the Roman period (166–68, 186–95).

59. See Samuel K. Eddy, *The King Is Dead* (Lincoln: University of Nebraska Press, 1961), 314–20; Françoise Dunand, *Religion populaire en Égypte romaine*, EPRO 77 (Leiden: Brill, 1979), 125–28; idem, "Grecs et égyptiens en Égypte lagide: Le problème de l'acculturation," in *Modes de contacts et processus de transformation dans les sociétés anciennes*, Collection de l'école française de Rome 67 (Pisa and Rome: École française de Rome, 1983), 59–62; and Glen W. Bowersock, "The Mechanics of Subversion in the Roman Provinces," in *Opposition et résistances à l'empire d'Auguste à Trajan*, Entretiens sur l'antiquité classique 33 (Geneva: Vandoeuvres, 1986), 291–317 (and discussion, 318–20).

60. Fourth-century and later monastic literature provides instances of Christianized *sons* of priests: *Apophthegmata patrum* (anonymous) no. 191 (ed. Nau, "Histoires des solitaires égyptiens," *Revue de l'orient chrétien* 13 [1908]:275) = no. 59 (tr. Benedicta Ward, *The Wisdom of the Desert Fathers* [Fairacres, Oxford: SLG Press, 1975], 20); and *Vita Mosis Abydi* 4 (ed. E. Amélineau, *Monuments*, 687).

5

The Lawless One
and the Fate of the Saints:
Major Themes and Traditions
in the Apocalypse of Elijah

DECEIT AND RECOGNITION AS
PRACTICAL CONCERNS

The organizing theme of the Apocalypse of Elijah is the manifestation and configuration of deceit and false leadership in the last days. The aim of the text is therefore to inform the audience how to distinguish legitimate from illegitimate charismatic leadership and to describe the imminent rewards for those who can maintain their powers of discernment through the eschatological woes.

This theme commences with the homily on fasting: "Hear now, you wise men of the land, concerning the deceivers who will multiply in the end time . . . who say 'The fast does not exist, nor did God create it'" (ApocEl 1:13). Therefore, when the audience members encounter opponents of fasting, they should know that the eschatological woes have started—that these are the deceptive leaders they should avoid. The audience must already be familiar with one or more individuals holding significant ecclesiastical positions who have criticized the practice of fasting in the audience's region; hence the time of the onset of deceit (according to the author–performer of the Apocalypse of Elijah) is "now," the time of the performance of the text. Thus what unfolds as the pathetic story of the Lawless One is actually a projection of imminent events and their dramatic resolution.

Apocalypse of Elijah 2 provides a foil to the subsequent, more focused account of the Lawless One by describing the alternately beneficial and evil reigns of kings in Egypt. A "King of Peace" follows a "king of injustice," but himself causes depredations in Egypt and is followed

103

by a demon-faced son (2:6-22). The violence that this son, subsequently also called a king, inflicts upon the land (2:24-38) culminates in invasions and the establishment of a king "from the city which is called 'The City of the Sun'" (2:39-50), whose reign is so beneficial to Egypt that "the living will go to the dead (saying), 'Rise up and be with us in this rest'" (2:53). At this point—when things are at their best—the Lawless One will appear. Thus the falseness of terrestrial peace and prosperity anticipates the subsequent falseness of the Lawless One.

The Lawless One is not identified with an Antichrist. Indeed, the term "Antichrist" should not be used to represent every instance of an eschatological Adversary, especially when "Antichrist" is not used explicitly. Although both Wilhelm Bousset and Gregory Jenks have convincingly shown that an Antichrist tradition has roots in Jewish tradition,[1] the Jewish sources tend to describe either a false prophet with supernatural powers or a royal figure manifesting delusory prophetic traits.[2] "Antichrist" in early Christian sources (that is, after Mk 13:22 and 1 John) has a more literal meaning: anti-Christ. The figure has a demonic character, more monstrous than deceitful, and resembles—if not derives from— the Jewish *Beliar*.[3] The lack of the term in the Apocalypse of Elijah, in spite of the considerable *semeia* and prophecies that the author has collected about the Lawless One, demonstrates that in the milieu of the author neither the term "Antichrist" nor a doctrine of his eschatological status had taken root. The author was assembling the tradition himself out of diverse Jewish and early Christian traditions of eschatological adversaries. Moreover, there is no reason to assume this nomenclature was drawn directly from the New Testament (e.g., from 2 Thessalonians 2 for "Destructive One"), because such nomenclature had entered oral circulation by the second century C.E.[4] In a similar (and probably con-

1. Wilhelm Bousset, *The Antichrist Legend*, tr. A. H. Keane (London: Hutchinson, 1896); and Gregory C. Jenks, *The Origins and Early Development of the Antichrist Myth*, BZNW 59 (Berlin: de Gruyter, 1991). Cf. R. H. Charles, *A Critical and Exegetical Commentary on the Revelation of St. John*, 2 vols. (Edinburgh: T. & T. Clark, 1920), 2:76–83; D. S. Russell, *The Method and Message of Jewish Apocalyptic* (Philadelphia: Westminster, 1964), 276–80.

2. Jenks tends to deemphasize the influence of the false prophet in the development of the Antichrist myth (cf. *Antichrist Myth*, 17–18, 202, 218, 341–43) to concentrate on the image of the "Endtyrant" (175–83, 193–328).

3. Cf. Bousset, *Antichrist Legend*, 153–56. Jenks subsumes *Beliar* alternately under the categories of "Satan" (*Antichrist Myth*, 139–49) and "Endtyrant" (119, 257–59), without addressing whether there existed a coherent *Beliar* tradition.

4. Cf. Colin H. Roberts, *Manuscript, Society, and Belief in Early Christian Egypt* (London: British Academy, 1979), 20; William V. Harris, *Ancient Literacy* (Cambridge: Harvard University Press, 1989), 298–99.

temporaneous) text from the Coptic monastery of Saint Macarius, the Adversary is named not only "Shameless One" but "Great Devil," "Lawless One," and "Antichrist."[5]

The author initially discusses the critical features of the Lawless One (implicitly posing the audience as the "wise men" and "saints" of the later narrative): he has powers that mirror those of Moses and Jesus, except that he cannot resurrect; there are physiognomic details to look for; he will appear "in the holy place" (ApocEl 3:5-18). His powers and his location suggest that this figure might be recognized as false only with great difficulty. He is a veritable $\psi\epsilon\upsilon\delta o\pi\rho o\phi\eta\tau\eta\varsigma$, although not so much by his ultimate evil as by his semblance of legitimacy.

Three eschatological heroes or teams of heroes (including Tabitha, Enoch, and Elijah) arise to accuse the Lawless One and expose his illegitimacy (4:1-19, 30-33), and in the course of these harangues we learn that the Lawless One has sought to associate himself with "the saints" (4:8)—a detail that shows the earnestness of his disguise. Yet he kills all these heroic exposers, as well as the "saints" and the "priests of the land": the Lawless One now assumes the role of persecutor.

This new role might be said to be his hubris (5:1):

Sa	Ach
And in that time the hearts of many will **turn away and withdraw** from him, saying	And in that time the hearts of many will **harden and they will flee** from him, saying,
This is not the Christ! For the Christ does not kill the Righteous, nor does he pursue people of truth. **Will he not (rather) seek** to persuade them with signs and wonders?	This is not the Christ! The Christ does not kill the Righteous, nor does he pursue people **when he will seek (them), but he persuades** them with signs and wonders.

Those who have thus recognized the Lawless One for what he is are consequently led from the earth to a liminal "holy place" by angels (5:2-6).

The Apocalypse of Elijah then describes in vivid terms the demise of the earth, now bereft of saints; and in traditional Egyptian style, the author uses drought imagery (5:7-10, 14).[6] Confronted with this situ-

---

5. Tr. Hugh G. Evelyn White, "Fragments of an Apocalyptic Gospel," in *Monasteries of Wadi 'N Natrun*, vol. 1: *New Coptic Texts from the Monastery of St. Macarius*, ed. Hugh G. Evelyn White (New York: Metropolitan Museum of Art, 1926), 20–21.
6. Cf. Bousset, *Antichrist Legend*, 195–99.

ation, the "sinners" who remained with the Lawless One realize their fatal error and cry, "What have you done to us, O Lawless One? . . . Woe to us because we listened to you!" (5:10-11). With a rapidly drying earth, the Lawless One himself realizes his imminent downfall and calls for the forcible return of the saints (5:15-20). When he (apparently) drags them back from their "holy place" (5:20), however, angels join to fight against him; and there follows a divine ἐκπύρωσις and judgment of the earth and its people (5:21-31). But it is Enoch and Elijah, returning a second time (cf. 4:7-19), who finally conquer the Lawless One and cast him into an abyss (5:32-35). Then, with a short description of parousia and millennium, the Apocalypse of Elijah ends.

From the onset of illegitimate, deceitful critics of fasting in ApocEl 1 to the disposal of the Lawless One in ApocEl 5, the text details the vicissitudes of falsehood in the progression of eschatological events. Just as the text's concentration on eschatology might imply a millennialist audience, so also this dominant theme of eschatological deceit probably indicates that the distinction between legitimate and illegitimate charismata was for the author an issue of critical contemporary importance.[7] Therefore he presented the inevitability of the eschatological woes, their imminence to the period of the audience, and the signs and features critical for the audience's correct understanding of events.

In all, the author was imposing a greater urgency and wider implications on his audience's choices between leaders and teachings—for these choices must have been numerous to inspire such a crisis over legitimacy.

A MAP THROUGH THE WOES:
SIGNS IN THE APOCALYPSE OF ELIJAH

The Tradition of the Eschatological Sign

In reconciling an anticipated crisis of legitimate leadership, the Apocalypse of Elijah provides signs by which deception can be discerned, wisdom gained, and a state of psychic resilience maintained throughout the eschatological woes. These signs continue and must be understood in the context of wider traditions of signs in the Greco-Roman world.

---

7. This is by no means a novel observation with regard to an early Christian text: 2 Thessalonians, 1 John, and the book of Revelation all express a similar social–religious context. See Neil Forsyth, *The Old Enemy: Satan and the Combat Myth* (Princeton: Princeton University Press, 1987), 309–17; Jenks, *Antichrist Myth*, 60–64, 115.

Two traditions informed the meaning of σημεῖον ("sign") in Greco-Roman Judaism and nascent Christian sects. One was the classical Hellenistic sense of the word, designating a divine omen—the very voice of a god or presage of an important event—that could (and must) be interpreted by professional seers. In this sense the σημεῖον itself—a flight of birds or shooting star—corresponded fundamentally to something else imminent in the human or cosmic environment.[8] The other pertinent tradition of σημεῖον derived from the Septuagint's translation of the Hebrew אות and denoted the function of a trait or action to demonstrate authority and legitimacy for a secondary act, primarily a command or one's speech in general: in R. Formesyn's words, "Le signe est au service de la parole."[9] Although there might certainly be a "cosmic" σημεῖον (e.g., Gn 1:14; 1 Sm 14:10; Ps 74:9), such a sign would function specifically to demonstrate this god's power and authority (as opposed to others'). Following the primary biblical use of אות (e.g., Ex 4:8), however, σημεῖον (and its plural form, occasionally combined with τέρατα—"wonders") came largely to refer to a prophet's authority, especially prophets expressing Mosaic traits and powers.[10] As elsewhere in the Greco-Roman world, there was a necessarily thaumaturgical aspect to establishing prophetic authority and charisma; the biblical tradition had merely encoded this aspect in traditions of Moses and his successors.[11]

Fundamental to both senses of σημεῖον—that legitimate supernatural

---

8. Cf. R. Formesyn, "Le sèmeion johannique et le sèmeion hellénistique," *ETL* 38 (1962):863–69.

9. Ibid., 874; cf. 869–81. Herbert C. Youtie has also discussed a sense of σημεῖον as "proof": (1) that a person knows the situation of which she or he presumes to speak, through reference to a specific detail that that person would not otherwise know; or (2) in a letter, that the author is who she or he says she or he is through reference to a specific detail (apparently agreed-upon), the knowledge of which is shared only by author and recipient. See Herbert C. Youtie, "SEMEION in the Papyri and Its Significance for Plato, Epistle 13 (360a–b)," in idem, *Scriptiunculae,* 2 vols. (Amsterdam: Hakkert, 1973), 2:963–75. But though this sense is characterized by the principle of legitimation and accurate recognition, the lack of a supernatural element removes it from the sphere of meaning under discussion.

10. Cf. Josephus, *Ant.* 2.284–328 and 20.168; Formesyn, "Le sèmeion," 870; and Otto Betz, "Miracles in the Writings of Flavius Josephus," in *Josephus, Judaism, and Christianity,* ed. Louis H. Feldman and Gohei Hata (Detroit: Wayne State University Press, 1987), 222–31. Note the phrase in Deuteronomy concerning prophets who attain legitimacy through the demonstration of "a sign [אות; LXX: σημεῖον] or a wonder [מופת; LXX, τέρας]" but who then use this authority to steer followers away from the traditional religion (Dt 13:1-3).

11. See, in general, Anitra Bingham Kolenkow, "Relationships between Miracle and Prophecy in the Greco-Roman World and Early Christianity," *ANRW* 2.22.2 (1980):1470–1506.

authority might be recognized and that a great event must be preceded by portent—was the belief not so much that a determinism permeated the universe but that a kind of certainty might be attained regardless of the vicissitudes of history. One gained such certainty through fore-knowledge of signs and events and through the consequent ability to recognize things when the time arrived. "How often," describes Cicero,

> has our senate enjoined the decemvirs to consult the books of the Sibyls! For instance, when two suns had been seen, or when three moons had appeared. . . . On all these occasions the diviners and their auspices were in perfect accordance with the prophetic verses of the Sibyl. . . . Or again, when the Tiber was discoloured with blood . . . did not the soothsayers in reply announce the events which subsequently took place, and were not similar predictions found in the Sibylline books? . . . In what important affairs, and how often has [the senate] not been guided wholly by the answers of the soothsayers![12]

The critical need for certainty and accurate recognition—the inspiration for seeking signs—rises in direct proportion to the sense of immanent chaos, whether in the realm of leadership (hence the promulgation of signs of legitimacy) or in the realm of cosmos and politics (hence the promulgation of signs of imminent disaster or beneficence). In the dramatically polarized world envisioned by sectarian Judaism and na-scent Christianity, any blurring of borders or unclarity in recognition might give rise to crisis.[13]

In such a context we can understand the evolution and systemati-zation of eschatological signs from Sibylline to Jewish apocalyptic texts.[14] The signs of the end, as Lars Hartman has argued, do not provide a chronology of eschatological events but rather a sense that a rigid determinism governs the sequence of the end times.[15] Revealed as they were by angels, these eschatological signs provided the audience with a sense of certainty and a conviction that the chaos that progressed out-side was unfolding in an inevitable pattern. Thus the "signs" were presented in details stereotyped from classical oracle literature, as in 4 Ezra:

12. Cicero, *On Divination* 1 (tr. Naphtali Lewis, *The Interpretation of Dreams and Portents* [Toronto and Sarasota, Fla.: Samuel Stevens, 1976], 104).

13. Cf. Ramsay MacMullen, "Two Types of Conversion to Early Christianity," *VigChr* 37 (1983):181–83.

14. See the review of the apocalyptic "signs of the end" tradition in Russell, *Method and Message*, 271–76.

15. Lars Hartman, "The Functions of Some So-called Apocalyptic Timetables," *NTS* 22 (1976):1–14.

Now concerning the signs: Behold, the days are coming when those who dwell on earth shall be seized with great terror, and the way of truth shall be hidden . . . and the sun shall suddenly shine forth at night, and the moon during the day. Blood shall drip from wood, and the stone shall utter its voice. . . . These are the signs which I am permitted to tell you. . . .

For behold, the time will come when the signs which I have foretold to you will come to pass; the city which is now seen shall appear, and the land which now is hidden shall be disclosed. And everyone who has been delivered from the evils that I have foretold shall see my wonders.[16]

Here, in the sectarian context of 4 Ezra (as opposed to the professional context of Cicero's civic soothsayers), the authoritative prophecy of the unfolding of eschatological events allows the immediate audience (and even subsequent readers) a sense of power in its certainty and text-bestowed ability to recognize these events.[17] But the distinction between those who have the privilege and ability to recognize events and those who do not is only implied in 4 Ezra through the "esoteric" context of the prophecy's revelation.[18] Other texts, following the theme of general chaos, detail the confusion of the eschatological woes for those who do not have the knowledge of signs. Lactantius stresses the confusing nature of eschatological portents:

> *Strange* prodigies in the sky will *confound* the minds of men with the greatest terror: the tails of comets, the eclipses of the sun, the color of the moon, and the fallings of stars. These things, however, will *not happen in their customary manner,* but there will suddenly arise *unknown* stars and those *not seen* by the eyes.[19]

An evil king will seek to attain power and authority over all; and by *"changing* his name and *transferring* the seat of empire, he will bring about the *confusion and disturbance* of the human race."[20] Second Thes-

---

16. 4 Ezr 5:1, 4-5, 13a; 7:26-27 (rsv). Cf. *As. Mos.* 10:4-6, where the signs of the end are portrayed as the reversal of the normal cosmic order: "The sun will not give light. And in darkness the horns of the moon will flee. Yea, they will be broken in pieces. It will be turned wholly to blood. Yea, even the circle of the stars will be thrown into disarray" (10:5; J. Priest, tr., *OTP* 1:932).

17. Cf. *2 Bar.* 27:1-14; Mk 13:5-37. On the social context of 4 Ezra, see Michael Edward Stone, *Fourth Ezra,* Hermeneia (Minneapolis: Fortress Press, 1990), 41–42; cf. 106–14 on the "signs of the end" passage.

18. Cf. Stone, *Fourth Ezra,* 113–14; although 4 Ezr 5:6 suggests a rudimentary social distinction in the ability to recognize things: "And one shall reign whom those who dwell on earth *do not expect,* and the birds shall fly away together" (rsv). The exodus of the birds undoubtedly functions as the portent of this ruler.

19. Lactantius *Divinae institutae* 7.16 (Mary Francis McDonald, tr., *Lactantius: Divine Institutes,* The Fathers of the Church 49 [Washington, D.C.: Catholic University Press, 1964], 516, emphasis mine).

20. Lactantius *Div. inst.* 7.16 (tr. McDonald, 515; emphasis mine).

salonians describes in even stronger language how the eschatological Adversary will come "with all wicked *deception* for those who are to perish, because they refused to love the truth and so be saved"; and then the author considers a different cause for the fate of the unenlightened: "God sends upon them a strong *delusion,* to make them *believe what is false"* (2 Thes 2:10-11; emphasis mine).

It is significant that in both Lactantius and 2 Thessalonians (as in Mk 13:21-23 and 1 Jn 2:18-19; 4:1-6) the advent and signs of illegitimate charismatic authority ("false teachers") become the paramount symbols of eschatological confusion.[21] The ability to see through this particular confusion and thereby to avoid deceitful allegiances becomes the paramount power that the "saints" hold in preparation for the last days. Thus to a certain extent the Apocalypse of Elijah's theme of eschatological deceit, and indeed the whole Antichrist tradition as a literary theme of the eschatological discourse, is an extension of the basic tradition of "signs of the end," focused upon one particular crisis and confusion.[22]

The theme of eschatological deceit thus derives from the general theme of eschatological signs. Indeed, the Apocalypse of Elijah, one of the earliest and most focused discussions of the eschatological Adversary in an apocalyptic setting, treats the two levels of signs as interrelated. The text provides various lists of signs by which the audience might recognize illegitimacy, thereby avoid deceit, and participate in the millennium. The signs of the Lawless One are one especially emphasized list. But both levels of signs—signs of the end in general and signs of the Lawless One in particular—offer the audience certainty and security in the midst of eschatological chaos. As the transition from ApocEl 1 to ApocEl 2 makes clear, the foreknowledge and understanding of signs is a privilege of those in the audience who remain "single-minded" (1:27—2:1).

The concept of eschatological signs embraces a wider array of motifs and literary forms than does simply the word σημεῖον; it is significant, however, that the Apocalypse of Elijah uses ⲙⲁⲉⲓⲛ, the standard Coptic translation of σημεῖον, seven times during the course of the text. In one instance σημεῖον carries the Hellenistic sense of a visible celestial portent: the returning Christ appears "with the sign of the cross preced-

---

21. Cf. Jenks, *Antichrist Myth,* 60–64, 115.

22. Presumably the origin and subsequent appeal of the tradition derived specifically from real or imagined crises of authority and charismatic legitimacy in the milieus of the authors. In many cases (particularly 2 Thessalonians and 1 John) this context can be demonstrated.

ing him" (3:2).[23] Twice it appears in tandem with ϣⲡ̄ⲏⲣⲉ—"wonders"—to denote the "false" miracles that the Lawless One is able to perform in front of the multitudes (3:11; 5:1b).[24] The phrase "signs and wonders" was often used in a sarcastic sense to describe false or alleged miracles performed by a pretender to Mosaic prophethood, and the author of the Apocalypse of Elijah evidently wants to invoke this understanding of false miracles.[25]

The other uses of the word ⲙⲁⲉⲓⲛ, however, refer specifically to the personal and physical characteristics by which one might recognize a specific individual. A passage offering a physiognomic description of the Lawless One commences: "For behold, I will tell you his signs so that you might recognize him" (3:14). The identical words open the earlier passage detailing the "King of Peace," his two sons, and their activities (2:17), suggesting that this passage was meant to anticipate and work in correspondence with the subsequent descriptions of the Lawless One. Indeed, as the chief sign of the most ruthless son is his polymorphism (2:19),[26] so also the Lawless One

> will transform himself [before you (Sa)] [in the presence of those who see him (Ach)]: at one time he will be an [old man (Sa)][young boy (Ach)]; but at another time he will be a [young boy (Sa)][old man (Ach)]. He will transform himself in every sign [in his signs (Sa¹)], but the sign of his head he will not be able to change. (3:16-17)

Thus signs in the Apocalypse of Elijah, while drawing on wider Jewish and Hellenistic traditions of heavenly portent and false miracles, more specifically encompass the minute details of an eschatological Adversary's behavior and appearance, which would allow precise identification; the audience's certainty in this domain would ensure its complete avoidance of unholy allegiances in the end times. The Apocalypse of Elijah takes its systematic predictions of woes and accumulation of

---

23. The complex of parallels adduced by Bousset (*Antichrist Legend,* 232–36) makes clear that the word here refers to more than simply the cross symbol itself. Indeed, the text proceeds to describe this parousiac image as a celestial event: "the whole world sees him like the sun which shines from east to west."

24. The word ⲙⲁⲉⲓⲛ is used similarly, but alone, in ApocEl 5:11.

25. See, e.g., Josephus, *Ant.* 20.168; *War* 7.438 (σημεῖα καὶ φάσματα); cf. *War* 1:28 (in positive sense); Mk 13:22; Jn 4:48. The list of miracles in ApocEl 3:6-10 is essentially Mosaic, i.e., the types of powers and beneficial acts exhibited by a salvific "new Moses," and the sixty righteous ones themselves refer to the Lawless One's miracles as "every feat which the prophets performed"; see below, pp. 112–17.

26. "Demonic face" is probably a translator's interpretation of "changed shape" (μορφὴν ἔχων ἠλλοιωμένην), as it appears in the corresponding episode in the Tiburtine Sibyl 191 (in Paul J. Alexander, *The Oracle of Baalbek: The Tiburtine Sibyl in Greek Dress,* Dumbarton Oaks Studies 10 [Washington, D.C.: Dumbarton Oaks, 1967], 20, 28).

details about the Lawless One to an obsessive degree, evidently addressing an audience's desperate need for "real" information. The following
pages address the two kinds of information the text provides: false signs
in performance of miracles and signs denoting personal appearance.

Signs and Wonders of the Lawless One

The signs of the Lawless One are confined, in the form of two lists, to
ApocEl 3. The first delineates the miracles he is expected to be able to
perform; the second, discussed in the next section, identifies his physiognomic features.

The list of miracles can be divided into three constitutive parts: (1) an
introduction, which places the list in the context of previous references
to the Lawless One and to what stage in the eschatological timetable he
is expected to appear (2:40; 3:1); (2) miracles that portray his power over
heavenly bodies; and (3) miracles that establish his powers and authority as akin to those of Jesus (and, as will be discussed, Moses before him).
The third part concludes with a directive to the audience on how to use
this list and its final clue.

1. Introduction (3:5):

The Lawless One will again begin to stand in the holy [place (Sa)] [places
(Ach)].

2. Cosmic powers (3:6-8a):

Sa	Ach
He will say to the sun,	He will say to the sun,
"Fall," and it will fall;	"Fall," and it will fall;
"Darken!" and it does so,	**He will say, "Shine!"—it does so,**
"Shine!" and it does so,	**He will say, "Darken!"—it does so**
	He will say to the moon,
	"Become blood!"—it does so,

He will accompany them through the sky.[27]

3. Imitatio Mosei et Christi (3:8b-13):

Saying, "Walk upon the sea	**He will** walk upon the sea
and the rivers	and the rivers
as if upon dry land."	as if upon dry land.

He will make the lame walk,
He will make the deaf hear,
He will make the dumb speak,

---

27. See notes on this line in Appendix, p. 314 n.58.

> He will make the blind see,
> Lepers he will purify,
> The sick he will heal,
> The demons he will cast out—

He will multiply his signs and wonders in the presence of everyone. He will do the things which the Christ did [will do (Sa¹)], except only for raising a corpse—by this you will know that he is the Lawless One: he has no power to give life!

The importance of this list for the structure and function of the Apocalypse of Elijah is evident in later references to it in some of the text's dramatic monologues. The "sixty righteous ones" recognize the Lawless One because, in their words, "you were [quite (Sa³)] unable to raise a corpse" (4:31b). Immediately before the final exodus of the saints, a last group realizes that the Lawless One has been trying "to persuade them with signs and wonders" (5:1b); and later, while the earth is drying up, those who followed the Lawless One lament that "you produced signs in our presence" (5:11). The list of the Lawless One's signs thus functions as the means by which the audience of the Apocalypse of Elijah can recognize and avoid the Lawless One's seductive power, can claim the fate of the saints, and thus can be evacuated from the earth by angels before eschatological conflagration.

The miracle list (part 3, above) itself derives from an early Jewish tradition of those miracles that, when performed by a prophet in the style of Moses, would inaugurate a time of redemption and a kind of terrestrial millennium. The scriptural basis of this tradition is Dt 18:15-19, a promise that Moses conveys from God to Israelites that "YHWH your God will raise up for you a prophet like me"; but the tradition would have had popular roots as well.[28] Around the Mosaic foundations of the promise there accumulated traditions of what such a "new Moses" would do; and the sources of such traditions came logically from the miracles in the Exodus legend (e.g., Ex 4:2-11; 17:1-6) and prophetic imagery of the "new Exodus" (e.g., Is 35:5-6).[29] It is in the latter texts that the authenticating miracles of the Mosaic prophet begin to take the form of a "list."

---

28. The legend of Elijah already bears Mosaic traits in its river-crossing episode (2 Kgs 2:8).

29. On the "new exodus" theme in Isaiah, see Frank Moore Cross, *Canaanite Myth and Hebrew Epic* (Cambridge: Harvard University Press, 1973), 170–74. The use of a similar miracle list to portray a millennium in *Sib. Or.* 8.205–8 probably derives from such popular Jewish tradition, rather than directly from a text such as Q/Lk 7:22.

The popularity of these miracle lists—which certainly circulated in oral as well as written form—in the early Roman period is shown not only in the reported activities of prophets in first-century Palestine[30] but also in early propaganda for Jesus. A unique pericope in the Synoptic Sayings Source (Q/Lk 7:22) presents such a list as a claim of Jesus,[31] and the miracle sources of both Mark and John appear to have been composed along such lists.[32] Still more representative of this tradition is the profusion of short accounts of Jesus' miracles, delivered in a list format with no common order or wording, throughout early Christian apocryphal literature. For example, in the *Acts of Paul* the apostle gives the following account:

> And he did great and wonderful works, so that he chose from the tribes twelve men whom he had with him in understanding and faith, as he raised the dead, healed diseases, cleansed lepers, healed the blind, made cripples whole, raised up paralytics, cleansed those possessed by demons.[33]

30. See above, p. 111 n.25; and Richard A. Horsley, "'Like One of the Prophets of Old': Two Types of Popular Prophets at the Time of Jesus," *CBQ* 47 (1985):435–63. The popularity of the Moses paradigm for the attainment of religious charisma is also manifest in the Qumran Essene sect: cf. N. Wieder, "The 'Law-Interpreter' of the Sect of the Dead Sea Scrolls: The Second Moses," *JJS* 4 (1953):158–75. See, in general, Geza Vermes, *Jesus the Jew* (Philadelphia: Fortress, 1973), 95–99. On the continuity of the Moses aretalogical paradigm in second- and third-century Judaism (and Jewish Christianity), see Jarl Fossum, *The Name of God and the Angel of the Lord* (Tübingen: Mohr [Siebeck], 1985), 112–55, 159–62.

31. Cf. Mt 11:5. Mark 7:37, in which a witnessing crowd acclaims that Jesus "has done all things well; he even makes the deaf hear and the dumb speak," undoubtedly also comes from such a tradition of Mosaic miracle lists. Although the narrative context is indeed the healing of a deaf mute (Mk 7:32-36), the plural nouns in 7:37 suggest that the phrase derives from elsewhere and may have led to the construction of the miracle story, rather than vice versa.

32. Cf. Paul J. Achtemeier, "Toward the Isolation of Pre-Markan Miracle Catenae," *JBL* 89 (1970):265–91; and idem, "The Origin and Function of the Pre-Marcan Miracle Catenae," *JBL* 91 (1972):198–221.

33. *Acts Paul* 10 (Eng. tr. R. Mcl. Wilson [Ger. tr. W. Schneemelcher]), *NTA* 2:382. Other lists are found in *Acts And. Matt.* 10; *Epis. Apost.* 5:9; *Sib. Or.* 1.351–59; *T. Adam* 3:1. See Paul J. Achtemeier, "Gospel Miracle Tradition and the Divine Man," *Interpretation* 26 (1972):189–94; Julian Hills, *Tradition and Composition in the Epistula Apostolorum*, HDR 24 (Philadelphia: Fortress, 1990), 39–44, 49–50; and David Frankfurter, "The Origin of the Miracle-List Tradition and Its Medium of Circulation," SBLSP (1990), ed. David J. Lull (Atlanta: Scholars Press, 1990), 344–74. There is no basis to Stephen E. Robinson's claim that the list in the *Testament of Adam* is the source of the Apocalypse of Elijah section under discussion (so as to provide a *terminus ante quem* for the former text; see Stephen Edward Robinson, *The Testament of Adam*, SBLDS 52 (Chico, Calif.: Scholars Press, 1982), 150–51. There is not one parallel that is not generic to the miracle-list tradition. Inheriting this tradition independently, the authors of the Elijah Apocalypse and the *Testament of Adam* developed their respective lists in relation to their own literary genres and cultures.

Associated with this tradition of Mosaic miracles—the signs such a prophet would perform in authentication of himself and inauguration of the new age—was a corresponding tradition of the miracles performed by one who claimed such prophetic status but who actually was illegitimate and deceptive. A warning in Dt 13:1-3 gave scriptural foundation to this false prophet tradition; thus in such "crisis literature" as 2 Thes 2:9-10, Mk 13:22, and Rv 13:13-14, the performance of "signs and wonders" is the primary mode of an eschatological Adversary's self-presentation.[34] That is, he tries to appear as a legitimate Mosaic prophet, but (in the ideology of these early Christian texts) he is only the false prophet of Deuteronomic instructions. Although the miracle-list traditions both of Jesus and of the eschatological Adversary arose out of the Mosaic prophet tradition, they mutually influenced each other throughout late antiquity.[35] Indeed, as the portrayal of Christ himself became more cosmic in scope, so also the portrayal of the eschatological Adversary gained cosmic powers.[36]

However, the Adversary's powers over the celestial bodies are consistently represented as those of changing the normal course of those bodies: for example, making the sun appear at night and the moon

---

34. These observations hold true for Jewish Adversary traditions also. An unpublished Hebrew manuscript from Yemen, probably with early medieval roots, applies the Mosaic list tradition (along with explicit references to biblical signs of redemption such as Is 35:5-6; 42:7) to the eschatological Adversary:

His feet will be like the feet of a bear,
   and his hands like the jaws of a panther.
He will be beautiful of eyes,
   and will break jaws,
will roar like a young lion
   and growl like a lion.
He will make the dead come alive,
   and will set free the prisoners of the pit,
and open the eyes of the blind.
   And he will bring manna down from heaven for them,
and will make rivers of honey flow in the valleys.
   And he will reign forty days.

(Cambridge University ms.890 add.3381, tr. Raphael Patai, in *The Messiah Texts* [Detroit: Wayne State University Press, 1979], 162).

35. See *Sib. Or.* 2.165-69; Hippolytus, *De Antichristo* 6; *Apocalypse of Daniel* 13; Pseudo-Clement *Hom.* 2.17-18; and, in general, Bousset, *Antichrist Legend*, 25-26; Jenks, *Antichrist Myth*, 57-60. For one theory of this mutual influence, see David J. Halperin, "Ascension or Invasion: Implications of the Heavenly Journey in Ancient Judaism," *Religion* 18 (1988):60-61; cf. Bernard McGinn, *Visions of the End*, Records of Civilization, Sources and Studies 46 (New York: Columbia University Press, 1979), 17.

36. Cf. Bousset, *Antichrist Legend*, 175-83; P. J. Alexander, *The Byzantine Apocalyptic Tradition*, ed. Dorothy deF. Abrahamse (Berkeley: University of California Press, 1985), 202-3.

during the day; blotting out the sun; causing the moon to become bloody and the stars to fall.[37] This tendency would suggest that traditional Hellenistic oracular portents, as discussed above, have become associated with the Adversary's own powers, perhaps by virtue of their "paganness" or opposition to natural order.[38] The Adversary's miracles therefore represent a synthesis of the catalog of celestial portents in oracular literature and the lists of Mosaic miracles that were circulating under the name of Jesus in Christian missionary tradition; the result is an eschatological Adversary who threatens the natural cosmic order. This synthesis is evident in the Apocalypse of Elijah's combination of cosmic powers and Mosaic miracles (parts 2 and 3 of the miracle list above).

The Lawless One's inability to resurrect, given as the mark crucial for his recognition in the Mosaic miracles, is quite unusual in Antichrist literature. Most lists of the eschatological Adversary's signs, particularly those that cleave closely to the Mosaic prophet tradition, include resurrection as simply one more of his powers.[39] Among Bousset's collection of late antique texts describing the Adversary's miracles, Pseudo-Ephraem is the only other early source (besides the Apocalypse of Elijah) stating that the Adversary will not be able to raise the dead.[40] The source

37. See also *Asc. Is.* 4:5; Pseudo-Methodius (in Alexander, *Byzantine Apocalyptic Tradition*, 51); *Slav. Vis. Dan.* 11 (ibid., 72); Erythraean Sibyl (ibid., 203). See, in general, Alexander, *Byzantine Apocalyptic Tradition*, 202–3.

38. The use of such imagery as portent continues in 4 Ezr 5:4b-5; *Sib. Or.* 2.6-7; 3.796-807; 8.202-205; *As. Mos.* 10:4-6; and elsewhere. Cf. biblical use of such "cosmic reversal" portents in Is 13:10; Ez 32:7-8; and, esp. Dn 8:10, which describes a mythic eschatological Adversary causing stars to fall. Lactantius's prophecy that the Adversary "will close heaven and hold back the rains . . . will order fire to descend from heaven, and the sun to stand still in its course" (*Div. inst.* 7.17; tr. McDonald, 517, 518) also expresses the use of portent as miracle (but may also reflect miracles from the legend of Elijah).

39. Esp. *Sib. Or.* 3.66; the Syriac Pseudo-Methodius apocalypse, published by F. Nau ("Révélations et légendes: Méthodius—Clément—Andronicus," *JA* 9 [1917]:442 [chap. 6]); and other late antique sources in Bousset, *Antichrist Tradition*, 176–77, 282; to which might be added the Irish apocryphon on the Antichrist published in Máire Herbert and Martin McNamara, eds., *Irish Biblical Apocrypha: Selected Texts in Translation* (Edinburgh: T. & T. Clark, 1989), 149 (chap. 3).

40. Pseudo-Ephraem, *De fine extremo* 9, 11 (in Bousset, *Antichrist Tradition*, 178–79; Grk texts: 277 n. 14, 278 n. 20. On doubtfulness of attribution, see Adela Yarbro Collins, *The Combat Myth in the Book of Revelation*, HDR 9 (Missoula, Mont.: Scholars Press, 1976) 168–69, 197 n. 74. Cf. Cyril of Jerusalem, *Catecheses* 15.14: "The multitudes may think that they see a dead man raised, who is not raised, and lame men walking, and blind men seeing, when the cure has not been wrought" (Gifford, tr., *NPNF* 7:108). A Daniel apocryphon describes how the Israelites warn a false messiah: "If you are the Messiah you must bring the dead to life, by which we will be persuaded." But he is unable to do it and becomes enraged (H. Zotenberg, ed. and tr., "Geschichte Daniels: Ein Apokryph," *Archiv für wissenschaftliche Erforschung des Alten Testaments* 1, 4 [1869]:416–19).

or origins of this idea are unclear and, because of the paucity and diversity of its witnesses, probably lie in the realm of oral tradition. Its prominence in the Apocalypse of Elijah as a critical sign of the Lawless One reflects the text's special interest in promoting the recognition of signs as a proper strategy of life in the end times.

The author of the Apocalypse of Elijah, then, integrates a highly structured list of (illegitimate) miracles—and one form of impotence— into the text both to establish the text's function (recognition of signs) and to create a core teaching to which subsequent narrative will refer. The strong similarity of this list to others promulgated to legitimize Jesus suggests the author's acquaintance with a general miracle-list tradition, whose immediate cultural origins may have been Jewish rather than Christian: as the "sixty righteous" announce, the Lawless One performs "every feat which *the prophets* performed" (ApocEl 4:31).

The isolation of the Lawless One's inability to resurrect, however, implies the author's knowledge of an extension of this miracle-list tradition, used to prophesy the miracles of the eschatological Adversary. The author's interest in emphasizing the Lawless One's impotence in this miracle suggests that his motivations go beyond a mere comparison of "Christ and Antichrist"; rather, the signs of the Adversary must be functional for a community living in the shadow of the parousia.

The Appearance of the Lawless One

Directly following the description of the Lawless One's "signs and wonders" is a detailing of features of his appearance. Like the signs and wonders, these physiognomic details are constructed in a list format; and just as the signs and wonders passage could be outlined with obvious introduction, conclusion, and thematic groups of signs, so even more can the physiognomic details.

1. Introduction (3:14):

For behold, I will tell you his signs so that you might recognize him:

2. Physiognomy (3:15):[41]

He is a small *pelēc*, thin-legged, tall, with a tuft of grey hair on his forehead, which is bald, while his eyebrows[42] reach to his ears,[43] (and) there is a leprous spot on the front of his hands.

---

41. On translation and interpretation difficulties in this physiognomic section, see notes *ad loc.* in Appendix, pp. 315–16.

42. Sa[3] has ⲃⲟⲩⳅⲉ, "eyelids," but this makes little sense in the context, which concerns the hair arrangement of the Lawless One. Cf. Wintermute, 746 n. z.

43. Cf. the Hebrew recension of the *Secretum secretorum,* a medieval miscellany: "Of

3. Polymorphism (3:16-18):

Sa	Ach

He will transform himself
  before **you:**
	He will transform himself
	  in the presence of **those**
	  who see him

at one time he will be
  an old man
	at one time he will be
	  a young boy

but at another time he will be
  a young boy.
	but at another time he will be
	  an old man

4. Conclusion (3:17-18):

He will transform himself in every sign,
but the sign of his head he will not be able to change.
By this you will know that he is the Lawless One!

The author is delivering two fundamental details: part 2 describes the hair on the Lawless One's head as configured in a certain way;[44] and part 3 states that he is polymorphic. The conclusion (4) then reconciles these two features: although the audience might think the Lawless One incapable of being recognized (3), his hair configuration (2) will always remain the same (4). The author was thus drawing on a tradition in which the peculiarities of facial and cranial hair constituted a sign of internal supernatural nature and potential.

The word σημεῖον itself carried the sense of distinctive physiognomic features.[45] Writers in late antiquity paid considerable attention to the physical appearances of holy persons (philosophers, heroes, saints) as a

---

brows:—Much hair on the eyebrows betokens weakness, and boldness of speech; when the eyebrows extend sidewards (to the temple) they betoken vainglory (pride), and he who has eyebrows wide apart, equal in length and shortness, and black, is alert and wise" (11.89; M. Gaster, tr., *Studies and Texts*, 3 vols. [1928; reprint, New York: Ktav, 1971], 2:800–801).

44. The "leprous spot [ογτο ⲛⲥⲱⲃϩ]" obviously constitutes a place of discolored or no hair. Cf. Wintermute: "A leprous bare spot" (746). The sign of the tuft of gray hair (ⲥϭⲓⲙ) is found, to my knowledge, only in two other texts: a medieval Irish ms. says, "There is a grey tuft (?) in the exact middle of his forehead," but goes on to describe "one eye protruding from his head in the middle of that tuft" (PH 7270-3, in B. O'Cuív, "Two Items from Irish Apocryphal Tradition: 1: The Conception and Characteristics of Antichrist," *Celtica* 10 [1973]:89); and a fourteenth-century Latin ms. describes a face "in the upper (part) marked with leprosy, having a white part in the hair on his forehead" (Corpus Christi College, Cambridge, ms. 404, fol. 7, in Montague Rhodes James, *The Lost Apocrypha of the Old Testament: Their Titles and Fragments* [London: SPCK, 1920], 59). A final verse of the latter text implies some relationship to the Apocalypse of Elijah: "These his marks will be unchangeable, but in the others he will be able to change himself" (James, *Lost Apocrypha*, 59).

45. LSJ, s.v. σημεῖον, 1593B, 1.9; Youtie, "SEMEION in the Papyri," 972–73.

visible expression of their inner natures and powers. By this idea, holiness and wisdom would by necessity be recognizable in one who held these powers.[46] Rabbinic tradition held that the biblical prophets and tannaitic sages manifested their holiness through exceptional beauty.[47] Hellenistic tradition tended to create odd features for heroes' attributes, to express their superhuman natures. Alexander, according to Pseudo-Callisthenes, "had the mane of a lion and eyes of different colors—the right eye black, the left grey—and teeth as sharp as a serpent's."[48] Lucian describes the Egyptian priest and sage Pancrates as "tall, flat-nosed, with protruding lips and thinnish legs."[49] In early Christian tradition one finds the following physiognomy of Paul: "A man small of stature, with a bald head and crooked legs, in a good state of body, with eyebrows meeting and nose somewhat hooked, full of friendliness."[50] In the context in which it appears, this description is supposed to epitomize Paul's nature as holy man and emissary of God; indeed, such features are "full of friendliness."[51]

Just as the miraculous signs of the Mosaic prophet could be assigned to identify illegitimate as well as legitimate leaders, so also this interest in physiognomy applied to tyrants, sorcerers, and other types of evil leadership. The Greek Tiburtine Sibyl adds a physiognomy to its

---

46. E.g., Ammianus Marcellinus: "Gazing long and earnestly at eyes at once delightful and awe-inspiring, and a face to which animation added charm, they tried to deduce what sort of man he would prove to be; it was as if they were examining those old books which interpret physical characteristics as a revelation of the spirit within" (15.8.16; Walter Hamilton, tr., *Ammianus Marcellinus* [Harmondsworth: Penguin, 1986], 82f). Cf. Origen, *Contra Celsum* 1.33. Patricia Cox describes the use of "physiognomic manuals that attached definite moral attitudes to specific bodily features. This method of typecasting was not so esoteric as it might seem, for physiognomical theory had captured the imagination of a broad spectrum of the Graeco-Roman literati" (*Biography in Late Antiquity* [Berkeley: University of California Press, 1983], 15). In general, see Elizabeth Cornelia Evans, "Roman Descriptions of Personal Appearance in History and Biography," *HSCP* 46 (1935):43–84; and idem, "The Study of Physiognomy in the Second Century A.D.," *TPAPA* 72 (1941):96–108.

47. Cf. Henry A. Fischel, "Martyr and Prophet (A Study in Jewish Literature)," *JQR* 37 (1947):379–81. In general, on rabbinic physiognomic speculation, see Emil Schürer, *The History of the Jewish People in the Age of Jesus Christ*, ed. Geza Vermes, Fergus Millar, and Martin Goodman, 3 vols. (Edinburgh: T. & T. Clark, 1973–87), 3:366–69.

48. Pseudo-Callisthenes, *Alexander Romance*, 13.3 (Ken Dowden, tr., "Pseudo-Callisthenes: The Alexander Romance," in *Collected Ancient Greek Novels*, ed. B. P. Reardon [Berkeley: University of California Press, 1989], 662).

49. Lucian, *Philopseudes* 34.

50. *Acts of Paul and Thecla* 3 (Eng tr. Wilson [Ger. tr. W. Schneemelcher], *NTA* 2:354).

51. E. Preuschen's assumption that the description is "not very flattering" is anachronistic, and his attempt to link it directly to the Apocalypse of Elijah passage under discussion somewhat strained ("Paulus als Antichrist," *ZNW* 2 (1901):191–94).

"prophecy" of the emperor Anastasius: "He is bald, handsome, his forehead (shines) like silver, he has a long right arm."[52] Tacitus reports that when a pretended Nero *redivivus* was executed in about 69 C.E., "his body, which was remarkable for its eyes, hair, and grim face, was carried to Asia and from there to Rome."[53] It would not have been his resemblance to the original Nero that would have inspired so many viewers as much as the expression in such features of Nero's legendary powers (or evils).[54]

The Qumran astrological text (4Q186) links physiognomic attributes both to horoscope and to one's "portions" of light and darkness:

> and his head . . . [and his cheeks are] fat. His teeth are of uneven length (?). His fingers are thick, and his thighs are thick and very hairy, each one. His toes are thick and short. His spirit consists of eight (parts) in the House of Darkness and one from the House of Light.[55]

Another horoscope for an individual holding "eight parts" in the House of Light indicates that "his fingers are thin and long. And his thighs are smooth."[56] As the *Acts of Paul* and the Apocalypse of Elijah also seem to

---

52. Greek Tiburtine Sibyl 166–67 (Alexander, tr., *Oracle of Baalbek*, 27; cf. 41–42, 111).

53. Tacitus, *Histories* 2.9 (Clifford H. Moore, tr., *Tacitus*, 5 vols. (Cambridge, 1925), 2:175.

54. Seneca (*De constantia sapientis* 18) and Suetonius (*De vita Caesarum: Caligula* 3) show an interest in physiognomic detail (and, implicitly, its symbolism) in describing the emperor Caligula; see Evans, "Roman Descriptions of Personal Appearance," 64–65; Jean-Marc Rosenstiehl, "Le portrait de l'antichrist," in *Pseudépigraphes de l'ancien testament et manuscrits de la mer morte*, ed. Marc Philonenko (Paris: Presses universitaires, 1967), 53–54 and notes *ad loc*.

Between Rome and Asia, Nero's powers would have been understood as both evil and salvific. On the diverse Mediterranean sentiments toward and mythic views of Nero, see John J. Collins, *The Sibylline Oracles of Egyptian Judaism*, SBLDS 13 (Missoula, Mont.: Scholars Press, 1974), 80–85; A. Yarbro Collins, *Combat Myth in Revelation*, 176–90; Martin Bodinger, "Le mythe de Néron de l'Apocalypse de Saint Jean au Talmud de Babylone," *RHR* 206 (1989):23–30.

55. 4Q186, 1, frag. (John M. Allegro, ed., *Discoveries in the Judaean Desert*, vol. 5: *Qumrân Cave 4* [Oxford: Clarendon, 1968], 88–91 [cf. Pl. 31]; also in G. Vermes, tr., *The Dead Sea Scrolls in English* [2d ed.; Harmondsworth: Penguin, 1975], 269). These horoscopes assume an anthropological scheme explained in the *Serek* scroll: "During their life all the hosts of men have a portion in their divisions [of light and darkness] and walk in (both) their ways. And the whole reward for their deeds shall be, for everlasting ages, according to whether each man's portion in their two divisions is great or small. For God has established the spirits [of light and darkness] in equal measure until the final age" (1QS 4.15–16; tr. Vermes, 77). In general, on Jewish physiognomic traditions, see Ithamar Gruenwald, *Apocalyptic and Merkavah Mysticism*, Arbeiten zur Geschichte des antiken Judentums und des Urchristentums 14 (Leiden: Brill, 1980), 218–24.

56. 4Q186, 2 (tr. Vermes, ibid., 269).

agree on this feature of their subjects, it is quite possible that "thinness" of limbs was a positive attribute for some circles during the Greco-Roman period.[57] Cranial and facial hair, another consistent detail of these physiognomies and the critical feature of the Lawless One, also seems to have carried special meaning for a subject's character and authority.[58]

Thus the attention to the eschatological Adversary's physical attributes functioned within a wider context of human appearance and its expression of inner nature. Rather than being a fantastic speculation on monstrosity, such physiognomies represented systematic deductions on the signs of deceitfulness and megalomania in the face and body. Only by the medieval period had the physiognomic description of the eschatological Adversary become monstrous, perhaps as his advent and deceptions seemed no more imminent and imaginable than the beasts of Daniel and Revelation.[59] The author of the Apocalypse of Elijah presents the physiognomy of the Lawless One as a plausible and functional list of signs.

As two other physiognomic descriptions of the eschatological Adversary have come down in the name of Elijah, what can be said about literary interdependence on this theme among Elijah texts? In *Sefer Eliahu* the evil king Gigit is described with a long face, a bald spot (?) between his eyes, tall stature, highly arched soles,[60] and thin legs.[61] In

---

57. Cf. Vermes, *Dead Sea Scrolls*, 268. The descriptions of Caligula and Nero in Suetonius and Seneca (see above, p. 120 n. 54) also mention their thin legs, but there it is evidently an emblem of malproportion, a physiognomic sign of evil nature; see Evans, "Roman Descriptions of Personal Appearance," 64–65, 67.

58. Cf. *Acts of John* 89, where Jesus' changing appearances are signaled in terms of hair: "rather bald-⟨headed⟩ but with a *thick* flowing beard . . . a young man whose beard was just beginning [ἀρχιγενείος]" (Eng. tr. G. C. Stead; [Ger. tr. Schäferdiek], NTA 2:225).

59. E.g., the Irish apocryphon on the Antichrist: "He will have a single eye protruding from his forehead, with a flat-surfaced face, and a mouth extending as far as his chest. He will have no upper teeth, nor will he have knees" (tr. Herbert, in Herbert and McNamara, eds., *Irish Biblical Apocrypha*, 149). Bousset's central thesis in the *Antichrist Legend* is that the eschatological Adversary derives from the ancient Near Eastern chaos monster (cf. 144, 164–66, 184, and passim). On the basis of this physiognomy tradition, it is more likely that a tradition of the eschatological Adversary that derived from the Jewish idea of false prophets merged with the Semitic chaos monster at a later point, perhaps in light of implications to this effect in Daniel and Revelation. See Bernard McGinn, "Portraying Antichrist in the Middle Ages," *The Use and Abuse of Eschatology in the Middle Ages*, ed. Werner Verbeke, et al., Mediaevalia lovaniensia series 1, study 15 (Louvain: Louvain University Press, 1988), 1–13.

60. כפות רגליו גבוהים.

61. *Sefer Eliahu*, in Yehudah Eben-Shmuel, ed., *Midrᵉshei Gᵉulah* (Jerusalem: Mosad

the Paris Greek fragment, the Antichrist is described as having a flaming head, a bloody right eye, a grayish (or glad [χαροπός]) left eye with two pupils, white eyelids, a big lower lip, thin right thigh, flat feet, but the big toe of his foot crushed.[62]

Apart from a pronounced interest in facial details, the only element shared by both these "Elianic" physiognomies and the section of the Apocalypse of Elijah is the attribute of thin legs. It has been noted, however, that this attribute was a standard "positive" sign in many ancient physiognomies, and a survey of the diverse physiognomies of the eschatological Adversary in Christian literature of late antiquity shows that thinness of legs had become a standard "negative" sign too.[63] There is no reason, therefore, to assume either that these physiognomies in the name of Elijah derived from a common origin or that there was any more historical relationship among them than there was among otherwise attributed physiognomies.

Like physiognomic signs, polymorphism as a power and attribute could characterize both good and evil forces. The most general context in which the polymorphism of the eschatological Adversary would have been understood in late antiquity—and in Egypt in particular—is demonology. Demons' abilities to change into any form were precisely their most dangerous power, as the Egyptian desert monks knew well: demons appeared to them as monsters, reptiles, native gods, heretics, beautiful women, and even monks.[64] In the urban Byzantine world of the sixth century, Procopius reports stories circulating that the emperor Justinian had been seen changing into a monstrous demon.[65] Procopius's reason for citing these stories echoes the function of the descriptions of the Lawless One in the Apocalypse of Elijah:

Bialik, 1954), 42; cf. Moses Buttenweiser, *Die hebräische Elias-Apokalypse* (Leipzig: Eduard Pfeiffer, 1897), 16, 62. The interpretation "bald spot" from the Hebrew גבפות is unclear and based largely on the parallel with ApocEl (cf. Buttenweiser, *Die hebräische Elias-Apokalypse*, 16 n. 12). As the text itself refers to Daniel's vision, Eben-Shmuel inserts קרן ("horn") into the text; thus "between his eyes a spiring horn" (Eben-Shmuel, *Midrᵉshei Gᵉulah*, 42 n. *ad loc.*).

62. Paris Greek 4, f.228ʳ, in Stone/Strugnell, 28–29; cf. Nau, "Méthodius—Clément—Andronicus," 453–62.

63. See Rosenstiehl, "Le portrait de l'antichrist," 59; Stone/Strugnell, 36–37.

64. Cf. E. Amélineau, "The Rôle of the Demon in the Ancient Coptic Religion," *The New World* 2 (1893):518–35; and Norman H. Baynes, "St. Antony and the Demons," *JEA* 40 (1954):7–10.

65. Procopius, *Anecdota* 12.20-27.

There is a clear difference between what is human and what is super-natural [τὰ δαιμόνια]. There have been many enough men, during the whole course of history, who by chance or by nature have inspired great fear, ruining cities or countries or whatever else fell into their power; but to destroy all men and bring calamity on the whole inhabited earth remained for these two [Justinian and Theodora] to accomplish, whom Fate aided in their schemes of corrupting all mankind. . . . *Thus not by human, but by some other kind of power they accomplished their dreadful designs.*[66]

In Procopius's mind, rumors of Justinian's demonic polymorphism account for the depredations and catastrophes of his rule: he is demonic by nature, and demons must inevitably manifest their true form.[67] Similarly, the Lawless One of the Apocalypse of Elijah, under whose dominion the saints will be killed and the land will dry up, may be known to the saints by his physiognomic signs and (or in spite of) his old–young polymorphism.

Yet there was also a "positive" tradition of polymorphism in antiquity, and it is this tradition that provides the context for the particular bi-morphic appearance of the Lawless One. In biblical tradition the ability to change form was a power and attribute of angels (e.g., Genesis 18–19), becoming a source of interest in Jewish apocalyptic speculation (but sometimes with terrifying effects on humans who observed the phenomenon).[68] Furthermore, through their ascents and heavenly "initiations" in apocalyptic literature, legendary Hebrew patriarchs and prophets also became, in a sense, polymorphic, as they assumed angelic characteristics.[69] Early Jesus traditions drew on this idea both in the image of the transfiguration (Mk 9:2-10 and parallels), where Jesus

66. Procopius, *Anecdota* 12.15–17 (tr. Atwater, in *Procopius: Secret History* [Ann Arbor: University of Michigan Press, 1961], 63–64).

67. On Procopius's use of contemporaneous popular traditions of the eschatological Adversary, see Berthold Rubin, who rightly sees this portrayal of Justinian in a long tradition of viewing evil rulers as incarnations of the demonic (*Das Zeitalter Iustinians* [Berlin: de Gruyter, 1960], 204–14, 441–54).

68. E.g., *Apoc. Ab.* 15:6-7: "A great crowd in the likeness of men . . . all were changing in aspect and shape, running and changing form and prostrating themselves and crying aloud words I did not know" (tr. R. Rubinkiewicz, *OTP* 1:696).

69. Cf. James H. Charlesworth, "The Portrayal of the Righteous as an Angel," in *Ideal Figures in Ancient Judaism*, ed. George W. E. Nickelsburg and John J. Collins, Septuagint and Cognate Studies 12 (Chico, Calif.: Scholars Press, 1980), 135–51; Martha Himmelfarb, "From Prophecy to Apocalypse: The *Book of the Watchers* and Tours of Heaven," in *Jewish Spirituality from the Bible through the Middle Ages*, ed. Arthur Green (New York: Crossroad, 1986), 145–65. Fischel generalizes this theme to encompass the apotheosis of martyrs ("Martyr and Prophet," 381–83).

appears in tandem with the angelicized Moses and Elijah, and in docetic ideas extending from the Gospel of John to the *Ascension of Isaiah*, the *Acts of John*, and the Coptic *Apocalypse of Peter* (NHC VII, 3).[70] The *Acts of Paul* says also of the apostle that "now he appeared like a man, and now he had the face of an angel."[71]

One of Christ's metamorphoses with special relevance for the Lawless One's peculiar polymorphism is his alternate appearance as a child, a youth, and an old man.[72] In the *Apocryphon of John*, the disciple is presented with a luminescent youth (ⲁⲗⲟⲩ) who turns into an old man, who then becomes like a slave boy (ϩⲁⲗ)[73]—"the [likenesses] appeared through each other, [and] the [likeness] had three forms."[74] In the *Acts of John*, the disciple James sees a child beckoning to him, while John himself sees a "man standing there who is handsome, fair and cheerful looking." As they follow him he appears to John "as rather bald-⟨headed⟩ but with a thick flowing beard, but to James as a young man whose beard was just beginning."[75] In the *Acts of Peter*, a group of widows whom Christ has healed from blindness claim they saw "'an old man . . .'; but others (said), 'we saw a growing lad'; and others said, 'we saw a boy.'"[76] Indeed, a hymn in this text describes Christ as "both great and little, beautiful and ugly, young and old."[77] In the *Apocalypse of Paul* (NHC V, 2) the apostle encounters a young child who reveals himself to be the Holy Spirit.

It is doubtful that the similar portrayal of the Lawless One in the

70. Cf. Gedaliahu G. Stroumsa, "Polymorphie divine et transformations d'un mythologème: L''Apocryphon de Jean' et ses sources," *VigChr* 35 (1981):412–34; Kurt Rudolph, *Gnosis*, tr. R. McL. Wilson (San Francisco: Harper & Row, 1983), 157–71; and David R. Cartlidge, "Transfigurations of Metamorphosis Traditions in the Acts of John, Thomas, and Peter," *Semeia* 38 (1986):53–66.

71. *Acts of Paul and Thecla* 3 (Eng. tr. R. Wilson [Ger. tr. W. Schneemelcher], *NTA* 2:354).

72. See the detailed discussion in Stroumsa ("Polymorphie divine," 416–19), who suggests that this trimorphism is rooted in a more ancient esoteric Jewish tradition of God as bimorphic—youth and old man—after the characters of the lover in Song of Solomon 5 and the "ancient of days" in Daniel 7 (420–21, 426–27).

73. Bentley Layton translates the three forms as "child," "elderly person," and "young person" to accentuate the trimorphism (*Gnostic Scriptures* [Garden City, N.Y.: Doubleday, 1987], 29), but Stroumsa ("Polymorphie divine," 418–19) argues that while ⲁⲗⲟⲩ has the ambivalent sense of child or young man, ϩⲁⲗ has the definite meaning of "servant, slave" (for which he finds a significant prototype in Phil 2:7 [425, 433 n. 76]).

74. NHC II, 1.2 (tr. Wisse, *NHL*, 105).

75. *Acts of John* 88–89 (Eng. tr. G. C. Stead [Ger. tr. K. Schäferdiek], *NTA* 2:225).

76. *Acts of Peter* 21 (Eng. tr. G. C. Stead [Ger. tr. W. Schneemelcher], *NTA* 2:304).

77. *Acts of Peter* 20 (Eng. tr. G. C. Stead [Ger. tr. W. Schneemelcher], *NTA* 2:302).

Apocalypse of Elijah and later apocalyptic literature[78] comes directly from this popular tradition of Jesus' epiphanies, for Jesus' child and old man aspects carried specific mythological and theological meanings that would not transfer to an eschatological Adversary. According to the *Gospel of Philip*, Jesus' varied appearances were supposed to mirror the spiritual levels of his beholders.[79] In the Apocalypse of Elijah, the Lawless One's alternating appearance as old and young is meant to indicate both the difficulty involved in his recognition and his supernatural power; and the immediate context of these motives is demonology of late antiquity.[80] The nearest prototype in Christian folklore for this particular power of the Lawless One, this "polymorphism of ages," however, would most probably be the similar metamorphoses of Jesus. Simon Magus, for example, was also said to hold this power: "He began suddenly to change his forms, so as instantly to become a child, and after a little an old man, and again a youth."[81] Thus once again the portrayal of the eschatological Adversary follows closely upon that of the prophet or, in this case, heavenly redeemer.

RECOGNITION OF SIGNS AS A SOLUTION TO DISORDER AND ANXIETY

The preceding pages have addressed what might be called the ideological core of the Apocalypse of Elijah as an apocalyptic document,

78. Cf. Bousset, *Antichrist Legend*, 150–51. Cf. also ApocEl 2:19, where the prince destined to devastate Egypt and its inhabitants has "a demonic face." The original form of Coptic ογϩο ⲛⲇⲓⲁⲃⲟⲗⲟⲥ may well be preserved in the Greek Tiburtine Sibyl: "a king who has a changed shape [μορφὴν ἔχων ἠλλοιωμένην]" (l. 191).

79. NHC II, 3.57.29–58.10.

80. Cf. Paul's conception of his opponents in 2 Cor 11:13-15: they are only disguised (μετασχηματιζόμενοι) as true, righteous apostles but are actually "deceitful workmen" (ἐργάται δόλιοι), and in this cover they mimic Satan himself, who "disguises himself as an angel of light."

81. *Martyrdom of Saints Peter and Paul* 14, in Bousset, *Antichrist Legend*, 275 n. 38 (text), 150 (translation). This tradition may be based on teachings, imputed upon Simon's followers by church fathers, that Simon himself was a docetic savior (Irenaeus *Adv. haer.* 1.23.3) and that Simon manifested himself as transfigured, one time as the Father and once as the Son (Cyril of Jerusalem, *Catecheses* 6.14); cf. Fossum, *Name of God*, 128–29. On traditions of Simon Magus as the eschatological Adversary, see Bousset, *Antichrist Legend*, 147–50. The trimorphism of Jesus and Simon may also be understood in the context of Greco-Roman omen traditions: Libanius reports that, in the midst of the Antiochene riots of 354 C.E., an old man pulling down an imperial statue "changed, first, into a youth, then into a child, and finally vanished; and [the crowd] felt no small alarm upon seeing the transformations" (*Or.* 19.30, ed. and tr. A. F. Norman, *Libanius: Selected Works*, 3 vols. LCL [Cambridge: Harvard, 1977], 2:286–87).

namely, the structure and meaning of the signs it provides to the audience. The Apocalypse of Elijah's use of the word and concept "sign" fits into wider traditions of the eschatological sign in the Greco-Roman world: as cosmic omen, as proof of charismatic authority through the performance of traditional miracles, as distinguishing feature in physical appearance. In each case, it has been argued, the interest in the sign—and even more, the providing of signs in literature—betrays a need for certainty of recognition when the forecast time arrives. Through this certainty the confusion and deceit that characterize the premillennial woes are avoided, an eschatological resilience is achieved, and the passage into the millennium is guaranteed.

The foreknowledge of signs thus also had a social aspect: those who know signs are saved, whereas those who do not are doomed to confusion in the end times. These social ramifications appear clearly in the descriptions of the onset of persecution and martyrdom in ApocEl 4. Although this theme was quite traditional to Jewish and Christian eschatology, consistently functioning in such a way as to separate and define historical audiences,[82] its articulation in the Apocalypse of Elijah was rendered vivid and effective through direct links between audience and characters (the persecuted saints) and through the use of Enoch, Elijah, and Tabitha as "first sacrifices" in the sequence of martyrdoms.

Crucial to the resilience of these saints—the projected audience—is the foreknowledge of two lists of signs of the Lawless One, provided in ApocEl 3. One, drawing on the tradition of ancient miracle lists of Jesus—and before him, Moses—describes the signs the Lawless One will perform ("sign" meaning proof); the second, drawing on Greco-Roman physiognomy and polymorphism traditions—customarily referring to both good and bad figures whose natures might be known by their appearances—describes the signs by which the Lawless One might be physically recognized ("sign" meaning physiognomic aspect). Each of these lists conforms to a strict structure of introduction, thematic organization, and conclusion.

Indeed, the use of such systematic structuring devices, which stand out from the narrative courses of chapters 2 and 4 in the Elijah Apocalypse, could imply that the author has used sources for both sections. The presence of miracle lists and physiognomies of eschatological Ad-

82. See chap. 6, below.

versaries throughout apocryphal literature of late antiquity allows the possibility that such lists circulated in written form and could have been used by the author of the Apocalypse of Elijah. However, the author's evident interest in communicating directly to an audience about such eschatological signs might also account for his change of style in the particular chapter where the details of signs are concentrated.

One striking aspect of the Apocalypse of Elijah's eschatological signs is their diversity: the extensive clues to the end times in ApocEl 2; the various signs the Lawless One can and cannot perform; the arrangement of his cranial and facial hair; and his ability to transform. The Apocalypse of Elijah seeks to prepare its audience with a variety of "media" of eschatological signs. Given the peculiar emphasis on the appearance of the Lawless One in particular, one might infer desperation in the author and his milieu in achieving this eschatological certainty.

THE TEXT AS ITS OWN SOLUTION:
THE APOCALYPSE OF ELIJAH
AS RITUAL EXECRATION

In his study *The Origins and Early Development of the Antichrist Myth*, Gregory Jenks placed the Apocalypse of Elijah with Irenaeus and Hippolytus as the main witnesses to an Antichrist "myth" developing in the third century c.e.[83] The literary genres of these texts differ considerably, however: literary treatises by named Christian authors on the one hand, and a biblical pseudepigraphon of an oral, prophetic nature on the other hand. Nevertheless, this very juxtaposition of witnesses to the Christian Antichrist tradition brings the Apocalypse of Elijah's approach to an eschatological Adversary into high relief. Rather than a discussion of Antichrist based upon imaginative biblical exegesis, as the third-century church authorities constructed their treatises,[84] the Apocalypse of Elijah constructs a dramatic narrative set in the definite future, punctuated with diatribes and laments by the opposing sides of the eschaton. Having analyzed the Apocalypse of Elijah as a repository of specific traditions concerning an eschatological Adversary and having established an interpretive framework for the text (as well as assumptions regarding

83. Jenks, *Antichrist Myth,* esp. 27–38.
84. Cf. ibid., 41–48.

its historical performance) in chapter 4, the next task is to examine the literary function of the Apocalypse of Elijah's description of the demise of the Lawless One.

The parallelism between the legends of Tabitha (4:1-6), Elijah and Enoch (4:7-19), and the sixty righteous ones (4:30-33) is quite noticeable: each heroic party (1) "hears" of the Lawless One's activity, (2) prepares itself (Tabitha: pure garment; righteous ones: breastplate), and (3) shifts location in order (4) to oppose the Lawless One with (5) a specific diatribe; (6) the Lawless One becomes angry and (7) kills the heroic party; but (8) in the cases of Tabitha and Elijah and Enoch, the heroic party resurrects itself to continue the diatribe.[85]

In each legend the dynamic focus is (5), the diatribe. Within the narrative, the diatribes consist of unveiling the Lawless One despite his pretensions, a function that the Apocalypse of Elijah itself serves for its audience by giving the Lawless One's signs in ApocEl 3. Within the overall performative context of the Apocalypse of Elijah, the diatribes, along with the several monologues in ApocEl 5, create a living drama of the end times within which the audience can participate through hearing the very words spoken by the dramatis personae—the heroes of the end.

Within the narrative, the heroic parties deliver the diatribes to—that is, *in the presence of*—the Lawless One. In the context of the performance or public reading, however, it is the performer who has taken over the heroic parties' roles, for he is the one who enacts the monologues, using the second-person singular voice. In the homily on fasting (1:13-22), the second-person plural pronouns acknowledged and established a role and a variety of identities for the audience; now, similarly, the second-person singular pronouns in these diatribe situations invoke their reference—the Lawless One—as a reality. Because the diatribes are addresses, there is the implication of a dual "address situation"—both addressor and addressee.[86] Thus the Lawless One is "present" in the situation set up by the performance in order to be rhetorically opposed

---

85. Cf. Rosenstiehl, 32–37; and Schrage, 218–19. Wintermute's attempt at source criticism on the basis of these intratextual parallels (724–26) is difficult to sustain methodologically.

86. This principle is true for any apostrophic speech but particularly in the context of prayer and exorcism (the address to otherworldly beings). From a speech-acts perspective, the conjuring or calling into being of a nonexisting situation constitutes "situating speech," a customary component of ritual. See Wade T. Wheelock, "The Problem of Ritual Language: From Information to Situation," *JAAR* 50 (1982):49–71.

by Tabitha, Elijah and Enoch, and the sixty righteous ones—and by the public reader in their voices.

Therefore it is important to recognize that the diatribes have a *perlocutionary* force in dramatizing the end times, their conflicts, and their spiritual realities within the immediate world of the audience; but the diatribes also have an *illocutionary* force as formal devices of combat. In the latter legends of Enoch and Elijah and the sixty righteous, the heroic parties rush "to do battle" (ⲛ̅ⲥⲉⲡⲟⲗⲉⲙⲉⲓ; 4:7) or "in combat" (ⲉⲩⲙⲓϣⲉ; 4:31) with the Lawless One, and at that point begin their diatribes. The militant significance is compounded in the case of the sixty righteous ones, who "gird themselves with the breastplate of God" (4:31) before beginning their speech.[87] Tabitha's "garment of linen" (4:1), while bearing archaic significance in the context of her healing blood, carries the overt meaning here of armor in the sense of garb for holy war;[88] and her "rebuking" (ⲥⲟⲟϩⲉ; 4:2) of the Lawless One has a clearly polemical sense. Thus the diatribes are positioned as weapons that the heroes employ against the Lawless One.

Several other circumstances offer further illustration of the function of hostile language in the Apocalypse of Elijah. In ApocEl 4:16, Elijah and Enoch promise that "we will . . . kill you, as you are powerless to speak on that day"; and in 5:32 it is fulfilled: "They kill him without his being able to utter a word." Evidently the ability to speak and military potency were conceived as reciprocal powers. Elijah and Enoch themselves are never said to bear any weapons except their own diatribes, and yet here they perform the final execution of the Lawless One; and the Lawless One dies when or because he is unable to speak.

A divergence in the Sahidic and Achmimic manuscripts continues this theme of dangerous speech. Where the Sahidic manuscript begins ApocEl 4:16 as part of Elijah and Enoch's diatribe, "Whenever you [the Lawless One] say 'I have overpowered them,'" the Achmimic manuscript interjects narrative "When the words were spoken, they over-

---

87. The biblical metaphor of spiritual armor (Is 11:5; 59:17; Wis 5:17-20; Eph 6:10-17) gained popularity among cultures through which biblical texts and formulas circulated. During the third century, however, it is likely that the metaphor would have assumed specific meaning within the ideology of martyrdom, as ApocEl 4:30-33 seems to reflect.

88. Cf. Jdt 16:8-9. The legend of Tabitha appears to be based on a figure from Egyptian healing spells, Tabitjet, the wife of Horus, who also had healing blood. In this sense the linen garment carries associations with the goddess Isis, who absorbed many such minor goddesses during the Greco-Roman period while rising to considerable prominence in Egyptian religion even during the third century; see David T. M. Frankfurter, "Tabitha in the Apocalypse of Elijah," *JTS* 41 (1990):16-19.

powered him" and then begins again with the diatribe. Curiously, in the Achmimic version the plural pronoun of "they overpowered" (ⲁⲩϭⲛ̄ϭⲁⲙ) seems to refer not to Elijah and Enoch but to their words: that is, the words in themselves bore the power to vanquish the enemy.[89]

The notion that a specific utterance might carry the power to harm or transform an object was axiomatic to Egyptian mythology and ritual practice.[90] Indeed, it was so deeply traditional to the culture that spawned Coptic Christianity that there is little surprise in finding the notion assumed in an early pseudepigraphon; the same concept of effective utterances continued to underlie the massive collections of ritual spells being gathered at the same time (e.g., the Demotic Papyrus of London and Leiden or the Paris Greek papyrus) and even the cryptographic inscriptions of sacred words and passages found on the walls of Coptic monasteries.[91] Certainly, such effective utterances in Egyptian religion (and, for that matter, in most religions) traditionally took place in highly stylized ritual situations, issuing from the mouths of designated authorities or priests.[92] The three legends that surround the diatribes under discussion offer important analogs. The verbal weapons—the diatribes—seem to draw part of their power from the figures who speak them: heroic prophetic figures whose respective martyrdoms in each legend actually seem to grant them further authority and power. As the speakers of the diatribes are, therefore, specially designated, so also the form in which the diatribes are delivered is clearly ritualized by virtue of its formal repetition in each legend. The diatribes must be delivered by the right figure in the right way, and thereby draw their power.

What, then, were the specific illocutionary effects of the diatribes—what constituted their weaponry? Along with references to the Lawless One's acts of cruelty and deception, the diatribes declare both his impotence against the heroes ("You have no power over my spirit or my

---

89. Cf. the similar image in Est 7:8.

90. See Jan Zandee, "Das Schöpferwort im alten Ägypten," in *Verbum: Essays on Some Aspects of the Religious Function of Words* (Utrecht: Kemink, 1964), 33–66; J. F. Borghouts, "Magie," in *Lexikon der Ägyptologie*, ed. Wolfgang Melck and Wolfhart Westendorf (Wiesbaden: Harrassowitz, 1980), 3:1139–41; and, esp., Robert K. Ritner, "The Mechanics of Ancient Egyptian Magical Practice" (Ph.D. diss., University of Chicago, 1987), 37–62.

91. See Frederik Wisse, "Language Mysticism in the Nag Hammadi Texts and in Early Coptic Monasticism 1: Cryptography," *Enchoria* 9 (1977):101–20.

92. Cf., in general, Stanley J. Tambiah, "The Magical Power of Words," *Man* 3 (1968):175–208; and Benjamin Ray, "'Performative Utterances' in African Rituals," *HR* 13 (1973):16–35.

body because I live in the Lord always," proclaims Tabitha; ApocEl 4:5) and his estrangement from heavenly powers (ApocEl 4:8-12):

1 you are always estranged
   [when you associate yourself
      with the saints (Sa¹)].
2 You have become an enemy to
      the heavenly ones
3 and you have (even) acted
      against those on earth.
4 You are an enemy of the
      Thrones and the angels.
5 You are always a stranger.
6 You have fallen from heaven
      like the morning star.
7 You changed (and) [your (Sa³)] lineage
      became dark to you.
8 Are you indeed not ashamed,
      as you establish yourself against God?
9 You, oh Devil!

The structure is repetitive, and in a way it *forces* the separation of the Lawless One from the powers of the cosmos. The verb tenses refer to the Adversary's status as a fait accompli: as desirable as they might be from the perspective of the audience, these are not wishes Elijah and Enoch are expressing but declarations, realities. Through their very utterances, the words of Tabitha, Elijah, and Enoch would effect this precise situation of impotence and estrangement, which they describe as reality. For example, in referring to the Lawless One as an "enemy" (ϫⲁϫⲉ) of the Thrones and the angels in line four, the diatribe invokes the prior image of Thrones as the heavenly gatekeepers who will "seize [sinners who try to ascend to heaven] and prevail over them because the angels do not trust them, and they have estranged themselves from his dwelling places" (1:11-12). It is not the animosity of the Lawless One against heaven that the diatribe describes but the animosity of the heavenly powers against the Lawless One as the archsinner, an animosity that should turn to seizing and overpowering him in his hubris.[93] So also lines two, six, seven, and eight all demarcate ways in which the Lawless One is separated from heaven.[94] Through these multiple allusions the

---

93. On this sense of "estrangement" (cf. 4 Ezr 6:5), see Stone, *Fourth Ezra*, 158.
94. Line six probably invokes Is 14:12 as a *historiola* (i.e., "as Lucifer fell, so may you"). On the interpretation of line seven, see note in the Appendix.

diatribe seeks to "fix" him in a safely unambiguous status outside the heavenly realm, as punished by heavenly powers.

Even line nine has such an "effective" or illocutionary function. "You, oh Devil"[95] is a thought unique to the Apocalypse of Elijah thus far, for the Lawless One has not been identified as the devil;[96] and so it appears to function as a conclusory statement, as if it were deduced from the preceding descriptions. In the context of the monologue's performative function, however, the words might be more aptly characterized as an exorcistic pronouncement: a second-person statement of identity ("you are X"), whose illocutionary function is to claim recognition and, through recognition, power over the subject of reference. It reinforces the dualistic opposition of the previous lines by naming the Lawless One as a (or the) traditional opponent of God, heavenly beings, and earthly saints. The words also isolate him in his "true nature"—he can no longer have the power of disguise, and he becomes subject to the punishments intended for the devil.

Do the diatribes work within the context of the narrative? Certainly, the Lawless One proceeds to slaughter more righteous people and to reign over the earth as it declines (5:1-20), so the contemporary reader is unable to perceive the lethal nature of the words within the text. But, as Stanley Tambiah has aptly noted,

> all ritual, whatever the idiom, is addressed to the *human participants* and uses a technique which attempts to re-structure and integrate the minds and emotions of the actors [i.e., in this case the lector and audience]. . . . Language is an artificial construct and its strength is that its form owes nothing to external reality: it thus enjoys the power to invoke images and comparisons, refer to time past and future and relate events which cannot be represented in action.[97]

---

95. Sa[1] clearly has ⲟⲩⲇⲓⲁⲃⲟⲗⲟⲥ; Sa[3] has a lacuna here, but the stem of some letter that could not be ⲟⲩ- is visible immediately before the break (cf. Pietersma, 83 [facsimile of ms., in ibid., 15]). Whereas Pietersma reads this letter as ⲡ- (thus: "you are *the* devil; 48), it seems more likely to be a *dalda*, the first letter of ⲇⲓⲁⲃⲟⲗⲟⲥ. The use of ⲛⲧⲟⲕ in the last two lines is an intensification of the primary noun.

96. The cosmic actions of the devil are mentioned in ApocEl 1:2, 4; and a character in the oracles of ApocEl 2 is said to "assume a demonic face" (ⲝⲛⲁⲝⲓ ⲛⲛⲟϩⲍⲟ ⲛⲇⲓⲁⲃⲟⲗⲟⲥ; 2:19). The fate of the Lawless One (dropped into the abyss—5:35) appears to be vaguely modeled on that of the devil in Revelation 20, yet the text never makes the identification explicit. A later scribe, as shown in the Achmimic manuscript, changed "Lawless One" to "Devil" to reflect this implication: "'What have you done to us, O Lawless One, saying "I am the Christ" when you are the Lawless One [Devil (Ach)]'" (5:10). Sa[1] and Sa[3] both have ⲡϣⲏⲣⲉ ⲛⲧⲁⲛⲟⲙⲓⲁ.

97. Tambiah, "Magical Power of Words," 202; emphasis mine.

The "world" in which these diatribes would have meaning as lethal utterances would be the performative situation, with its fabric of the needs and concerns that a third-century Egyptian Christian audience might bring into this world. The text itself establishes anxieties about deceit, legitimacy of power, and the need for certainty, and presumably these anxieties would have been generally contiguous with those of the audience itself, particularly if, as chapters 9 and 10 will demonstrate, the text grew out of and continued to address an audience with millennialist inclinations during a historical period of social and economic disintegration. Furthermore, in the public reading of the Elijah Apocalypse these diatribes and their object gained a certain reality: the Lawless One became the victim of the speeches in the very room in which the reader mimicked them. Indeed, the narration and the diatribes, read aloud to an audience, would have operated on a level more basic than that of a simple recounting of future events. In their dramatic structure, desperate reality, and illocutionary force, the diatribes conform to Bronislaw Malinowski's image of the magical rite, whose essence, he argues, is "the dramatic expression of emotion":

> In war magic, anger, the fury of attack, the emotions of combative passion, are frequently expressed in a more or less direct manner. In the magic of terror, in the exorcism directed against powers of darkness and evil, the magician behaves as if himself overcome by the emotion of fear, or at least violently struggling against it. . . . Or else in an act, recorded by myself, to ward off the evil powers of darkness, a man has ritually to tremble, to utter a spell slowly as if paralyzed by fear. . . .
>
>   All such acts, usually rationalized and explained by some principle of magic, are *prima facie* expressions of emotion.[98]

In the Apocalypse of Elijah Apocalypse emotion is expressed by the lector in the role of Tabitha, Elijah and Enoch, and the sixty righteous ones. Standing somewhere between Malinowski's "war" and "terror magic," then, the diatribes draw their lethal nature from their cathartic function within the performative situation: they "kill" the Lawless One at each reading. Within the text the diatribes stand as powerful weapons with which certain heroes are endowed and which, in the performative context of the public reading, effectively transform the Lawless One into an impotent demon.

In this way the Apocalypse of Elijah *itself* held such a function of

---

98. Bronislaw Malinowski, *Magic, Science and Religion, and Other Essays* (Garden City, N.Y.: Doubleday, 1954), 72; cf. 71–74.

chastizing the Lawless One, of conveying lethal words against an intensely "real" Adversary, merely through the text's narrative of his eschatological demise. By *describing* and *declaring* the eschatological events of the destruction of the Lawless One (the representative, locutionary function of ApocEl 1, 4–5), the Apocalypse of Elijah seeks to cause these events as an illocutionary act of the words themselves, just as they are presumed to work within the text's narrative.

The Apocalypse of Elijah thus seems to have functioned as a ritual execration of the Lawless One, a formalized curse against an image of cosmic evil. Clear evidence also appears in the similes it offers to describe the Lawless One's death:

> Elijah and Enoch . . . pursue the Lawless One. They kill him without his being able to utter a word. In that time he will dissolve in their presence as ice dissolves in fire. He will perish like a serpent with no breath in it. They will say to him, Your time has passed by. Now indeed you will perish with those who believe in you [5:32-34].

The similes of "ice in fire" and "lifeless serpent" occur before Elijah and Enoch actually pronounce the Lawless One's death. The casual interpreter would ascribe this peculiar order to either sloppiness or interpolation; but there is reason to assume deliberate choice in the order. The very character of the similes explains why they would be uttered before the pronouncement of death: each recalls traditional analogies employed in Egyptian ritual curses to repulse and verbally "kill" the mythical adversaries of the cosmos.

The image of "melting," in the sense of dissolution (Greek, τήκειν),[99] was commonly used in the Greco-Roman period to refer to the earth in eschatological conflagration (2 Pt 3:12; *Apoc. Pet.* 5); and indeed, the *Book of the Watchers* and 2 *Clement* each attach a simile to strengthen the force of this verb: "and [the hills] shall melt [τακήσονται] like wax before a flame" (1 *En* 1:6 after Ps 97:5);[100] "and the whole earth (will be) like lead melting [τηκόμενος] in fire" (2 *Clem.* 16:3). While retaining this eschatological sense, however, the metaphor of ice dissolving in fire that we find in ApocEl 5:33, as applied to an individual, explicitly recalls the diverse

---

99. Coptic, ⲃⲱⲗ ⲉⲃⲟⲗ (Ach p. 42, ll. 16–17) is commonly used in ritual texts to invoke a power to "loosen"—cf. London Ms. Or. 6796, ll. 25, 40, 59 (= G in Kropp, 1:36–37). But it customarily translates τήκειν (cf. Crum, 32B, s.v. ⲃⲱⲗ §d), which was presumably used in the Greek text.

100. Greek text of 1 *En* 1:6, ed. R. H. Charles, in *The Book of Enoch or 1 Enoch* (Oxford: Clarendon, 1912), 274. In Micah 1:4, "the valleys will burst open [יתבקעו], like wax near [מפני] the fire." Cf. Ps 68:3.

melting and burning metaphors that appear in Greco-Roman and Greco-Egyptian "binding" and cursing spells, where such metaphors are intended either to obliterate the free will and resistance of a victim (e.g., for erotic purposes) or to destroy her or him altogether.[101] When we narrow our focus to Egyptian culture alone, we find the same imagery used for a purpose quite similar to that in ApocEl 5: burning and melting were the dominant metaphors used in the central rituals to curse Apophis and Seth, the demonic images of chaos in darkness and chaos in periphery and desert.[102] These rituals, which aimed to repulse Apophis from the sun and Seth from the ordered cosmos of Egypt, involved the molding and burning of wax images and required the continual utterance of detailed spells:[103]

> THIS SPELL IS TO BE SPOKEN OVER (a figure of) 'APEP drawn on a new sheet of papyrus in green ink, and there shall be made (an image of) 'APEP WITH WAXEN BODY WITH HIS NAME INSCRIBED ON IT IN GREEN INK, TO BE PUT ON THE FIRE that he may burn before Re. . . . Thou shalt do this very often against storm so that the sun may shine and 'APEP be felled in very truth.
>
> . . . FALL UPON THY FACE, O 'APEP, THOU FOE OF RE; the fire which issues from the Eye of Horus comes forth against thee . . . it presses on thee with a blast of flame, the fire comes forth against thee, and fierce is its flame against thy soul, thy spirit, thy magic, thy body and thy shade; the Mistress of Burning has power over thee, . . . she annihilates thy shape, she chastises thy form, . . .
>
> . . . The fire comes forth against you, ye foes of Re, ye who rebel against Horus, and against your souls, your bodies and your shades; the fire

101. Cf. P. Heidelberg 1681 (tenth cent. c.e.): "In the hour that I write your names, along with your figures and your amulets, on a potsherd, and light a fire under it until it is charred, (so may) you char the face of NN" (ll. 35–39, ed. Friederich Bilabel in idem and Adolf Grohman, *Griechische, koptische und arabische Texte zur Religion und religiösen Literatur in Ägyptens Spätzeit* [Heidelberg: Universitätsbibliothek, 1934], 401–2). See Ernst Kuhnert, "Feuerzauber," *Rheinisches Museum für Philologie* 49 (1894):37–58; Christopher A. Faraone, "Clay Hardens and Wax Melts: Magical Role-Reversal in Vergil's Eighth *Eclogue*," *CP* 84 (1989):294–300; "Binding and Burying the Forces of Evil: The Defensive Use of 'Voodoo Dolls' in Ancient Greece," *Classical Antiquity* 10 (1991):165–205, esp. 172–80; and, esp., idem, "Molten Wax, Spilt Wine and Mutilated Animals: Sympathetic Curses in Near Eastern and Early Greek Oaths," *JHS* 113 (1993, forthcoming). The goddess Artemis uses wax figures to destroy evil in an inscription published by Merkelbach, "Ein Orakel des Apollon für Artemis von Koloe," *ZPE* 88 (1991):70–72. The use of a wax-melting simile against "enemies" in Ps 68:3 suggests the influence or background of such execration rites.

102. See chap. 7, pp. 164–68.

103. See H. Te Velde, *Seth, God of Confusion*, tr. G. E. van Baaren-Pape (Leiden: Brill, 1977), 150–51; Maarten J. Raven, "Wax in Egyptian Magic and Symbolism," *Oudheidkundige mededelingen uit het rijksmuseum van oudheden te Leiden* 64 (1983):7–47, esp. 14, 24–26; and Ritner, "Mechanics of Ancient Egyptian Magical Practice," 93–111.

comes forth, it cooks you, its glow (?) bakes (?) you, its burning burns you, Wepes the great divides you, she devours you, she parches you.[104]

As for the wax, they make it into "enemies" to kill his [Seth's] name, to prevent his soul from leaving the place of execution. As for the wax, one molds it into figurines of "enemies" to destroy his name. . . .
The flame, the burning, the great lioness, the embracer. . . . (It is they) who cast fire against Seth and the Robbers. . . .
Mistress of the flame with powerful visage. . . . She whose flame is harmful. They recite the books of "repulsing the enemies," of "putting the enemies on the fire," of "pursuing the opponents," of "reducing the enemies to ashes."[105]

Such metaphors functioned as *persuasive analogies*, to use Tambiah's terminology. That is, the metaphorical images (burning, melting, and, in some classical texts, spearing and crushing), combined with the mimetic gestures, represent the desired and potential state of the object: Apophis, Seth, their "rebels"—or, in the Apocalypse of Elijah, the Lawless One. By invoking the images as metaphor, the speaker or author seeks to transfer that desirable state onto the object.[106] The speech act itself need not be explicitly in a jussive, subjunctive, or injunctive case—"Let it be that X becomes like Y"—as so often occurs in practical spells. Even in the representative or definite mode, the declarative utterance would function with illocutionary force akin to that of the curse.[107] Indeed, it can be argued that any prophetic description of the demise of an adversary, whether "real" or demonic, is grounded linguistically in the curse, the illocutionary transfer of these images of demise onto the object.[108]

---

104. P.Bremner-Rhind 22.24–23.2, 24.8-11, 25.4-5 (tr. R. O. Faulkner, "The Bremner-Rhind Papyrus—III–IV: D. The Book of Overthrowing ʿApep," *JEA* 23 [1937]:168, 169, 170).

105. P.Salt 825, V.4-5, X, XII (tr. Philippe Derchain, *Le papyrus Salt 825 (B.M. 10051): Rituel pour la conservation de la vie en Égypte*, Mémoires de l'académie royale de Belgique 58, 1a [Brussels: Palais des académies, 1965], 138, 141–42; cf. 78, 161–62.

106. Stanley J. Tambiah, "Form and Meaning of Magical Acts: A Point of View," *Modes of Thought: Essays on Thinking in Western and Non-Western Societies*, ed. Robin Horton and Ruth Finnegan (London: Faber & Faber, 1973), 199–229, esp. 205, 225.

107. See Daniel Lawrence O'Keefe on the "magical sentence" (*Stolen Lightning: The Social Theory of Magic* [New York: Vintage, 1982], 53–54.

108. Cf. Jeremiah 28 (woe oracles); Nm 10:35 (ritual curses); 1QH vi, 29–35; 1QM xii, xix (victory hymns describing demise of spiritual adversary's armies); Rv 20:7-10 (description of spiritual adversary's demise presented in past tense). Formal parallels between Egyptian execration and Hebrew prophetic discourse have been discussed by A. Bentzen, "The Ritual Background of Amos I, 2–II, 16," *Oudtestamentische Studiën* 8 (1950):83–99, and M. Weiss, "The Pattern of the 'Execration Texts' in the Prophetic Literature," *Israel Exploration Journal* 19 (1969):150–57. The ironic or "persuasive" use of the dirge form in Revelation 18 against Rome (as "Babylon") is analyzed by Yarbro

Therefore when the Apocalypse of Elijah describes the Lawless One as going to "dissolve as ice dissolves in fire," it is trying to cause the Lawless One, whose presence would have become as real as Seth or Apophis was for Egyptian priests, to dissolve also, at that moment, by the power of the lethal utterance itself.[109] Through the use of such analogies and descriptions, the Apocalypse of Elijah gains a ritual function approximating that of the traditional execration texts, but in a Christian setting.

Plutarch reports popular forms of curse rituals against Seth performed in Egypt as late as the early second century C.E.; and his testimony, taken with the presence, well through the Byzantine period, of general curse spells inscribed on papyrus and lead tablets, militates against any notion that these traditions had evaporated by the Roman period.[110] Once the concept of "execration" or curse has been applied to the last chapters of the Apocalypse of Elijah, and once it is admitted that the act of cursing Seth or Apophis and the act of cursing the Lawless One are similar ritual "goals," it is difficult to deny that the techniques and language of cursing a dominant mythical adversary would have persisted within Egyptian culture.[111] It is quite likely, therefore, that the author of the Apocalypse of Elijah is drawing on native execration traditions in his use of specific analogies for the Lawless One's death.

Collins, "Revelation 18: Taunt-Song or Dirge?" in *L'apocalypse johannique et l'Apocalyptique dans le Nouveau Testament*, ed. J. Lambrecht (Louvain: Louvain University Press, 1980), 185–204. On the variety of curse forms and their illocutionary intent, see general articles by A. E. Crawley, "Cursing and Blessing," *ERE* 4:367–74; and Lester K. Little, "Cursing," *ER* 4:182–85.

109. Note that a "completed" illocution in a curse, according to formal speech-acts analysis, would require the prior existence in reality of the victim, such that the victim could be transformed through the illocution. This would seem impossible in the cases under discussion, where the illocution is designated against what might be viewed as an imaginary victim, the spiritual or mythical adversary ("How would one gauge if the illocution were felicitous or not?"). Three points would qualify these objections: (1) within the worldview of the subjects, the victim or adversary is not imaginary; (2) the prescriptions of the ritual are otherwise fulfilled within cultural conventions, that is, the mythical adversary is not expected to be present as, for example, the priest is; (3) by Tambiah's participant-centered analysis of ritual language's effectiveness, the "completion" of the speech act is accomplished through the catharsis of the ritual (as if the locution were not outwardly but inwardly directed). Cf. Little, "Cursing," 184.

110. Plutarch *De Iside et Osiride* 30–31, which describes the ritual destruction of objects stamped with an image of a bound ass or a bound human, iconography that matches that in the Egyptian texts; see John Gwyn Griffiths, ed. and tr., *Plutarch: De Iside et Osiride* (Cardiff: University of Wales Press, 1970), 407–8, 411–12.

111. On the continuity of Seth imagery in Coptic demonology, see E. Amélineau, "The Rôle of the Demon in the Ancient Coptic Religion," 519–25; François Lexa, *La magie dans l'Égypte antique*, 2 vols. (Paris: Paul Geuthner, 1925), 1:151–52; Antoine Guillaumont, "La conception du désert chez les moines d'Égypte," *RHR* 188 (1975):11–15; and below, pp. 164–66.

The second metaphor compares the Adversary to "a serpent [δράκων] with no breath in it." The image suggests the draconine Satan of Revelation 12, and certainly an author with any acquaintance with the book of Revelation would recall this figure; there is evidence that early Copts held it in particular interest.[112] Because the Apocalypse of Elijah has hitherto described the Lawless One as essentially human, however, it makes less sense to import Revelation 12 as the key at this point in the text than to read the analogy in its functional sense in terms of the persuasive analogies directed at Apophis, a dragon, and Seth, who represented dangerous reptiles in general.[113]

A striking parallel to the second metaphor appears, coincidentally, in the context of a sustained diatribe against the devil from the fifth century, the work of the Coptic abbot Shenoute. In this famously complex sermon Shenoute begins a comparison of the devil to a serpent by describing the devil's far more extensive "poison": "Wither will the serpent throw (its) liquid? For perhaps (the poisons) reach as far as those (who are standing) near it. . . .But you, O impious one, your poisons reach those in the entire universe!"[114] The devil–serpent analogy established, Shenoute then declares the devil impotent by virtue of his primordial expulsion or fall, invoking, apparently, Gn 3:14 in combination with Is 14:12. The devil, he implies, can thus be compared to a serpent's harmless corpse. In the following passage one can hear the illocutionary force of Shenoute's declarations, such that his insistence on a *past* event (the devil's fall) would have functioned in the immediate, performative context as lethal speech—the "killing" of a quite real and pernicious enemy in the world of his audience:

> A serpent is really (only) like a piece of rope, rising and bending, quite easily destroyed, and whoever avoids its poison will not die from it. But you, you are indeed the enemy, and you have no other power than the poison of your sins, for you are cut up and scattered far beyond (?) the serpent,[115] not only because God has made you impotent[116] in this way,

112. See the (apotropaic?) illustration of a serpent next to Revelation 12 in the twelfth-century British Museum Ms. Oriental 6803, fol. 18ʳ, in E. A. Wallis Budge, *Coptic Biblical Texts in the Dialect of Upper Egypt* (London: British Museum, 1912; reprint, New York: AMS, 1977), 299.

113. *Pace* Rosenstiehl, 115n. *ad loc.*; Wintermute, 752 n. k3.

114. Inst. fr. Coptic 1, fol. 10.38–43, 50–55, ed. P. du Bourguet, "Diatribe de Chenouté contre le démon," *Bulletin de la société d'archéologie copte* 16 (1961/62):30; cf. 43, 51.

115. ⲉⲃⲟⲗ ⲡⲁⲣⲁ ⲡϩⲟϥ. Perhaps, "to a far greater extent than the serpent"?

116. ⲁⲁⲕ ⲛⲉⲃⲓⲏⲛ: the sense is analogous to the Lawless One's accused powerlessness in ApocEl 4:5; cf. Crum, 53A.

but also because your corporeal form is destroyed according to what is written and what we know of you by your weakness, whereas even the body of the serpent is whole so that it may be touched (?).[117]

Like the Apocalypse of Elijah, Shenoute invokes the analogy of devil to serpent (ϧⲟϥ) specifically in the context of declaring the devil's impotence, and in a type of speech where the *function* of declaration carries particular illocutionary force. In both cases the image of a dead or dying snake is invoked in order to "kill" the spiritual adversary at that moment by this illocutionary force of declaration. In Shenoute's case, the illocutionary act implicity carries the added force of the biblical declarations in Gen 3:14 and Isa 14:12. Finally, in both cases one can hear echoes of the exercration of the "serpents" Apophis and Seth.[118]

It has been argued here that both similes applied to the demise of the Lawless One in ApocEl 5—ice melting and a serpent dying—carried the illocutionary function of killing the Lawless One ritually through persuasive analogy: "*Let him* dissolve as ice melts in fire; *Let him* perish like a serpent with no breath." Moreover, we have seen that this illocutionary function is only an extension to the text as a whole of the symbolically lethal nature of the diatribes uttered by Tabitha, Elijah and Enoch, and the sixty righteous ones. Both concepts, we have seen, are deeply traditional to Egyptian religion and culture; and the cursing similes employed at the end of the text themselves draw on traditional Egyptian imagery used to curse equivalent cosmic adversaries. By virtue of its last chapters, therefore, the Apocalypse of Elijah may plausibly be viewed with the function of execration, and its performative setting with the function of curse ritual.[119]

In a way, to recognize that the Apocalypse of Elijah was designed to function as a ritual execration is merely to acknowledge that the text and its symbols, imagery, and names held many more types of power for a late antique Egyptian audience than for a modern one. "The very quality of the sounds and the [intonation] of the Egyptian words," the *Corpus*

---

117. ⲧⲁϧⲟϥ. Du Bourguet unnecessarily corrects to ⲧⲁⲕⲟϥ. Text: Inst. fr. Coptic 1, 12.35–13.9, ed. du Bourguet, "Diatribe de Chenouté contre le démon," 32; cf. 44, 51–52. I am deeply indebted to Jacques van der Vliet for discussion of this passage.

118. At the conclusion of an execration of Seth in the Edfu texts (Hellenistic period), "Seth turned himself into a Roaring Serpent . . . and was seen no more" (9, 9; tr. H. W. Fairman, in "The Myth of Horus at Edfu—I," *JEA* 21 [1935]:32). Seth's metamorphosis into a serpent at his death poses a striking parallel to ApocEl 5:33.

119. Ritual cursing, even as part of the liturgy, was common in Christian monastic tradition; see Lester K. Little, "La morphologie des malédictions monastiques," *Annales* 34 (1979):43–60.

Hermeticum claimed at roughly the same time, "carry in themselves the power of the things said. . . . Our speech is *not* mere talk; it is an utterance replete with workings."[120] As names and words continued to bear these special powers in Coptic religion, so the public utterance of the written word would have carried a potency that transcended the mere transmission of knowledge.[121]

Furthermore, the dramatized encounter with the Lawless One offered by the Apocalypse of Elijah could not have been a neutral event in the life of an Egyptian Christian audience in the second half of the third century, a period replete with persecutions and perceived persecutions, millennialist hopes and rumors, struggles between orthodoxies and heresies, and a general decline in the economic and political orders (subjects discussed in the last three chapters of this book). Where Jenks noticed "a pattern of increasingly dramatic accounts of the destruction of the Antichrist" in Christian literature of the late third century,[122] perhaps we may perceive communities in the act of reconciling the anxieties of this period through rituals of cursing the eschatological Adversary—the representative image of all the deception, conflict, and imperial power that they imagined to be poised in the cosmos. By describing his demise in the most specific terms imaginable, they would "experience" the end of evil and achieve catharsis in the knowledge that all things would be accomplished as described.

---

120. *Corp. Herm.* 16.1–2 (ed. A. D. Nock and A.-J. Festugière, *Corpus Hermeticum*, 2 vols. [2d ed.; Paris: Société d'Édition "Les Belles Lettres," 1960], 2:232; modified from translation by Walter Scott, *Hermetica*, 4 vols. [Oxford, 1924–36; reprint, Boston: Shambhala, 1985]), 1:265.

121. MacDermot, *The Cult of the Seer in the Ancient Middle East* (London: Wellcome Institute of the History of Medicine, 1971), 193–95; cf. Kropp, 3:116–39; L. Kákosy, "Remarks on the Interpretation of a Coptic Magical Text," *AOH* 13 (1961):325–28.

122. Jenks, *Antichrist Myth*, 97.

6

Exhortatio ad Martyrum:
The Apocalypse of Elijah and
the Lore of Martyrdom

The penultimate chapter of the Apocalypse of Elijah narrates a series of heroic martyrdoms, which are projected into the end times. The first two episodes, comprising the challenge, martyrdom, and resurrection of Tabitha and, then, of Elijah and Enoch, seem to have been composed out of popular eschatological traditions concerning the heroes of the end times. The story of the saints' persecution in ApocEl 4:20-33, however, seems to draw from other forms of Egyptian Christian lore. Because the composition of the Apocalypse of Elijah occurred in the second half of the third century, it is likely that experiences, rumors, and attitudes stemming from the Decian and Valerian edicts contributed to the martyrdom imagery and expectations. The following analysis, however, will commence by bracketing the question of historical reflection to examine how such imagery arose and functioned as literary themes.

MARTYRDOM AS A LITERARY THEME

After the martyrdom of Elijah and Enoch, the Lawless One turns his wrath upon the saints, and the text describes his procedures of torture with lurid detail (4:22-23). The interest with which later audiences held this passage may be evident in the manuscript divergences:

Sa³	*Ach*
	He will kill them,
	he will exterminate them
	[. . . . .]

Sa³	*Ach*
He will command that their eyes be **seared** with an iron **borer**	. . .] them; that their eyes be **put out** with **sticks** of iron; **He will remove the skin from their heads.**
He will remove their nails one by one.	He will remove their nails one by one.
He will command that vinegar with lime be **shoved** into their nostrils.	He will command that vinegar with lime be **put** in their nostrils.

The simplest interpretation of these references to martyrdom is that the author considered a recently experienced, historical persecution (e.g., under the Decian or Valerian edicts) to be a sign that the end was near: that is, that the above passage was designed as *vaticinium ex eventus*. Yet these references follow such mythopoeic episodes as the Nile running with blood (2:44) and the return of Tabitha and Elijah and Enoch (4:1-19), thus militating against an interpretation that assumes that everything preceding the persecution is "historical" and everything following it, eschatological myth. Instead of borrowing wholesale from contemporaneous experiences of persecution, Richard Bauckham has pointed out, "the Apocalypse of Elijah's series of martyrs seems rather to indicate a writer who is spinning a narrative of the reign of Antichrist out of various diverse traditional materials available to him."[1]

What types of materials, then, would prompt the lurid details in 4:22-23? Certainly the events of the third century in Egypt would have provided a context for the scenes' formulation and meaning to an audience; but a far more plausible context than actual historical experience would be the lore of martyrdom that developed in Greco-Roman Judaism, became a dominant theme in the early Jesus movement, and came to flourish wildly in Egypt.[2] Oral martyrological traditions stressed the lurid details of sufferings well before the grossly anti-Christian edicts of Diocletian; and this lore was as socially vital for Christian self-definition and consolation as it was historically dubious.[3]

---

1. Richard Bauckham, "Enoch and Elijah in the Coptic Apocalypse of Elijah," *Studia patristica* 16, 2 (1985):75.
2. See the list of martyrological parallels to ApocEl 4:22-23 that Oscar von Lemm collected ("Kleine koptische Studien—X.5 Bemerkungen zu einigen Stellen der koptischen Apokalypsen, 4–6," *Bulletin de l'académie impériale des sciences de St.-Pétersbourg* 13 [1900]:23–26).
3. In general see Judith Perkins, "The Apocryphal Acts of the Apostles and Early Christian Martyrdom," *Arethusa* 18 (1985):211–30; and Peter Brown, *The Cult of the Saints: Its Rise and Function in Latin Christianity* (Chicago: University of Chicago Press,

Cyprian reveled in such imagery: "Blood was flowing that might extinguish the fire of persecution (and) settle the flames and fires of Gehenna with glorious gore."[4] The fifth-century Coptic abbot Shenoute considered a gruesome end the criterion of a "true" martyr.[5] And the performative "world" in which such stories circulated was vibrant: not only the re*telling* of events and rumors, but letters and even songs described martyrs' deaths.[6] One early story is particularly significant in that it has come down to us in two distinct versions. Both Eusebius and Palladius received, independently, oral accounts of the martyr Potamiaena's execution by hot pitch during Severus's reign (193–211) and retold them with only the most basic elements in common—and yet with a common interest in drama and graphic details.[7] Indeed, Palladius claims a specific lineage to his version's transmission: that he received it from one Isidore, who in turn had heard it from the mouth of the hermit Antony himself. The important point we may derive from the coincidence of these stories is that the retelling of martyrdoms in graphic detail had become a peculiarly Christian tradition already in the third century, long before the actual production of martyrological texts.[8]

In the Apocalypse of Elijah, scenes of martyrdom and persecution function as "signs," marking and clarifying the course of the preeschatological woes for an audience that evidently needed such a map. We might well presume from this function that martyrdom and persecution

---

1981), 80–85. Saul Lieberman has suggested that many of the punishments that apocalyptic writers envisioned in hell were actually based on contemporaneous Roman punishments ("On Sins and Their Punishments," in idem, *Texts and Studies* [New York: Ktav, 1974], 48–50). Most of his evidence for these Roman practices, however, comes from materials whose interests in the details of torture are more lurid than objective: Eusebius, martyrologies, and ancient Christian art (cf. Lieberman, "Sins and Their Punishments," 46 n. 101, 50 nn. 122–23, 51 n. 130). Roman brutality notwithstanding, the historian must comprehend the martyrological interests in emphasizing this brutality—as with apocalyptists' interests in creating hell punishments—within their own ideological and social contexts.

4. Cyprian, *Epistle* 10.2.2 (in *Saint Cyprien: Correspondence*, ed. and tr. Le Chanoine Bayard, 2 vols. [Paris: Société d'Édition "Les Belle Lettres," 1925], 1:24), my trans.

5. On Shenoute's view of martyrs, see Jürgen Horn, *Studien zu den Märtyrern des nördlichen Oberägypten*, vol. 1: *Märtyrerverehrung und Märtyrerlegende im Werk des Schenute*, Göttinger Orientforschungen 4, Reihe: Ägypten 15 (Wiesbaden: Otto Harrassowitz, 1986), 8–9. Origen, *Exhortatio ad martyrum*, 23–24, dwells on lurid details in discussing 2 Maccabees 6.

6. Tertullian *Scorpiace* 7 (songs); Cyprian *Ep.* 31.2; cf. Dionysius of Alexandria in Eusebius, *Hist. eccles.* 6.41–42 (letters).

7. Eusebius, *Hist. eccles.* 6.5; Palladius *Historia Lausiaca* 3. Cf. Frances M. Young, *From Nicaea to Chalcedon* (Philadelphia: Fortress, 1983), 40–41.

8. On motivations behind such graphic imagery in martyrdom lore, see Donald W. Riddle, *The Martyrs: A Study in Social Control* (Chicago: University of Chicago Press, 1931), 66–69; and Brown, *Cult of the Saints*, 82–84.

had become components of the field of literary motifs used to construct eschatological scenarios, and that the audience would already have been familiar with the "eschatological" significance of martyrdom.

In fact, the tradition of sacred martyrdom to which the Apocalypse of Elijah alludes stems from a Jewish tradition associating the holiness and privilege of prophets with martyrdom.[9] "As early as the first century C.E.," Henry Fischel describes, "it had become a generally accepted teaching of Judaism that prophets had to suffer or even undergo martyrdom."[10] The teaching gained full literary representation in such texts as 2 and 3 Maccabees, the *Martyrdom of Isaiah* and other lives of the prophets, and rabbinic midrashim.[11] The residue of oral tradition in Q— "no prophet is accepted in his own country"[12] —and Mark—"they will deliver you up to councils; and you will be beaten in synagogues"[13]— shows that themes of persecution and martyrdom amounted to an ethic preached among itinerant prophets.

Through the book of Revelation (with whose ideas the Apocalypse of Elijah shows some familiarity), the martyrdom and persecution of prophets gain particular prominence as a sign—a constitutive stage—of the eschatological sequence: for example, the episode of the "two μάρτυροι" (probably Moses and Elijah) of Rv 11:3-13, which is expanded and dramatized in ApocEl 4:7-19 (the characters there identified as Elijah and Enoch).[14] The fact that the Apocalypse of Elijah places this episode (along with the martyrdom of Tabitha) as the first of a series of eschatological martyrdoms signifies that the episode had assumed an archetypal meaning by which the subsequent martyrdoms of the "saints" might be understood. Thus, as Elijah and Enoch's return and martyrdom were a distinctive sign of the eschaton (in the tradition of the

---

9. See, in general, Henry A. Fischel, "Martyr and Prophet (A Study in Jewish Literature)," *JQR* 37 (1947):265-80, 363-86; and George W. E. Nickelsburg, Jr., *Resurrection, Immortality, and Eternal Life in Intertestamental Judaism*, Harvard Theological Studies 26 (Cambridge: Harvard University Press, 1972), esp. 93-111.

10. Fischel, "Martyr and Prophet," 279; cf. Nickelsburg, *Resurrection, Immortality, Eternal Life*, 48-66, on the tradition of the wise man as martyred saint.

11. See Fischel, "Martyr and Prophet," 265-80.

12. Q/Lk 4:24 (// Gospel of Thomas 31; Jn 4:44b); cf. Mk 6:4b (// Mt 13:57b).

13. Mk 13:9 (// Mt 10:17-18; Lk 21:12-13).

14. Wilhelm Bousset, *The Antichrist Legend*, tr. A. H. Keane (London: Hutchinson, 1896), 208-11; R. H. Charles, *A Critical and Exegetical Commentary on the Revelation of St. John*, 2 vols. (Edinburgh: T. & T. Clark, 1920), 1:281-82; M. Black, "The 'Two Witnesses' of Rev. 11:3f. in Jewish and Christian Apocalyptic Tradition," in *Donum Gentilicium: New Testament Studies in Honour of David Daube*, ed. E. Bammel, C. K. Barrett, and W. D. Davies (Oxford: Clarendon, 1978), 227-37; and Bauckham, "Enoch and Elijah in the Coptic Apocalypse of Elijah," 69-76.

book of Revelation but orally as well), so also others' martyrdoms in the text were to be understood as distinctive signs of eschatological imminence.[15]

By the third century C.E., persecution and martyrdom were widely interpreted in apocalyptic and other eschatological literature as heralding the eschaton, suggesting that the martyr or righteous sufferer had come to represent a primary form of authority, power, and holiness for sectarian communities: the saints, as it were, must suffer; those who suffer must be saints; and the suffering of the saints signifies the beginning of the end times.[16]

By bracketing questions of historical experience and veracity behind the images of martyrdom in ApocEl 4, one can perceive the combination of two "literary" traditions in these passages: (1) the oral martyrological lore circulating in the wake of the Decian and Valerian edicts (and doubtless earlier); and (2) the tradition found in many apocalyptic texts (and also in oral circulation) that the collective martyrdom of the righteous would be a sign of the end times. The question therefore arises: How did the details of martyrs' suffering function socially, particularly as these details were framed in the Apocalypse of Elijah within an eschatological narrative?

EXHORTATIO AD MARTYRUM:
SOCIAL REFLECTION AND SOCIAL CONTROL
IN THE APOCALYPSE OF ELIJAH

The Social Function of
Predicting Martyrdom

Martyrdom lore functioned reflexively, to strengthen audiences' social cohesiveness, to console them, to reverse embarrassment through

---

15. W.H.C. Frend suggests, on the basis of the tradition of Elijah's premillennial return (Mal 4:5-6) and the fast growth in late antiquity of the tradition of his and Enoch's martyrdom, that Elijah in particular was the archetypal prophet–martyr (*Martyrdom and Persecution in the Early Church* [London: Basil Blackwell, 1965; reprint, Grand Rapids: Baker Book House, 1981], 58–59). He cites the LXX form of Sir. 48:10a, "You [Elijah] who are for reproofs [$\dot{\epsilon}\nu$ $\dot{\epsilon}\lambda\epsilon\gamma\mu o\hat{\imath}\varsigma$] at the appointed time," a verse whose significance is not quite clear. If correct, this hypothesis of Elijah's particular significance to early martyrs would provide an interesting link between the interest in martyrdom in ApocEl 4 and the text's very pseudepigraphy of Elijah.

16. Hippolytus *In Danielem* 4.51; Cyprian *Ep.* 67.7-8; Cyprian, *De mortem*. In general see Bousset, *Antichrist Legend*, 211–15; Gregory Jenks, *The Origins and Early Development of the Antichrist Myth*, BZNW 59 (Berlin: deGruyter, 1991), 64–67, cf. 185; and Frend, *Martyrdom and Persecution*, 46, 58–59.

heroization, to lend drama to community life and identity, and to define the community itself as select and sacred.[17] Like the telling of past martyrdoms, which habitually employed such motifs as the frustrations of the persecutors and the suffering and then apotheosis of the martyrs to dramatize reports,[18] a lurid account of eschatological martyrdom would draw an audience into active participation with the drama, but this time as a particular sign of the end. In ApocEl 4 such drastic future events in the lives of the saints constituted a sign to recognize and understand, a distinct stage in the progression toward parousia and millennium.

The book of Revelation again provides helpful parallels and sources for interpreting these motifs as they occur in ApocEl 4. In the history of martyrdom as an eschatological theme, Revelation had already expanded the motif from referring to single prophet–martyrs to embracing *and defining* a social body, presumably the first audience of Revelation who themselves may never have experienced persecution.[19] Using a homiletic aside similar to those in the Apocalypse of Elijah, John of Patmos indicates that an account of the fate of those seduced by an eschatological Adversary "is a call for the endurance of the saints. . . . And I heard a voice from heaven saying, 'Write this: Blessed are the dead who die in the Lord henceforth'" (Rv 14:12-13). Not only should the audience be inspired by the eventual destruction of the unrighteous, but they should imagine their own sanctification in execution. Wayne Meeks has aptly described the function of this collective anticipation of suffering as legitimizing sectarianism itself:

> The "cognitive dissonance" produced by that separation was sharply *emphasized*, not relieved, by the promise that they would be persecuted . . . the experience [of hostility] helps to make sense of the separation and thus to reinforce the boundaries between the group and the larger society.[20]

17. Cf. Nickelsburg, *Resurrection, Immortality, Eternal Life*, 93–111; Riddle, *Martyrs*, 53–76; Perkins, "Early Christian Martyrdom."

18. See Fischel's detailed folkloric analysis of the Jewish-Christian martyr legend in "Martyr and Prophet," 376–84.

19. See Leonard Thompson, "A Sociological Analysis of Tribulation in the Apocalypse of John," *Semeia* 36 (1986):147–74; cf. idem, *The Book of Revelation: Apocalypse and Empire* (New York: Oxford University Press, 1990), 172–74, 188–91. A collective body of "persecuted righteous" is a traditional Jewish literary theme from the post-Exilic period; see Nickelsburg, *Resurrection, Immortality, Eternal Life*, 11–111.

20. Wayne Meeks, "Social Functions of Apocalyptic Language in Pauline Christianity," *Apocalypticism in the Mediterranean World and the Near East*, David Hellholm, ed. (Tübingen: Mohr [Siebeck], 1983), 692; cf. 692 n. 19.

ApocEl 4 would likewise draw thick lines between those who would suffer and those who, implicitly, might be expected to obey the commands of the Lawless One. Most importantly, the collective nature of the eschatological martyrdoms that follow those of Tabitha, Elijah, and Enoch would subsume the fearsome individuality of the stories of torture and execution that were circulating in Christian lore.[21] Suffering would befall the "saints" as a whole, both demonstrating and rewarding them with their enthronement in heaven.

The Promise of Heavenly Rewards

It is typical of the literature of martyrdom to associate the gruesome process of suffering with the attainment of a heavenly status beyond that of normal humans. In the book of Revelation martyrs are envisioned under the very altar of the heavenly temple (6:9-10), and the vision of Saturus included in the *Martyrdom of Perpetua and Felicitas* actually identifies the martyrs who congregate around the throne of God in the heavenly temple by the names of recently executed Christians (chaps. 11–13). This theme of a martyr's heavenly rewards evidently derives from the prior association of prophetic status and martyrdom: that in martyrdom the prophet is so exalted as to be accepted into heaven and taught heavenly secrets (a point exemplified in the attachment of the *Ascension of Isaiah* to the earlier *Martyrdom of Isaiah*).[22]

The text's linking of martyrdom and heavenly rewards in such a way as to reconcile possible anxieties about gruesome executions with glorious promises may serve another overall function in its composition and public performance: the *exhortatio ad martyrum*. More properly regarded as a species of homily within a genre (such as a letter or a sermon) than as a literary genre itself, the *exhortatio ad martyrum* may in this case designate the overall design of the prophecy and its sequence of forms in the Apocalypse of Elijah.

At three points in the text a single passage links together four important themes of social definition: (1) identity within the primary sacred group, (2) resistance to the Lawless One, (3) ascent to heavenly status, and (consequently) (4) privilege over another social group. The first passage occurs in the beginning of the text and is obviously addressed to the intended audience:

---

21. The reduction of the Christian's individuality through the literature and process of martyrdom is one of Riddle's singular theses in *Martyrs;* cf. 21–26, 77–90.

22. Cf. Fischel, "Martyr and Prophet," 364–71. On heavenly rewards in Coptic martyrology, see MacDermot, *Cult of the Seer,* 184–88, 642–56.

Remember that he has prepared for you thrones and crowns in heaven. For everyone who will obey his voice will receive thrones and crowns. Among those who are mine, says the Lord, I will write my name upon their foreheads and seal their right hands. They will not be hungry, nor will they thirst, nor will the Lawless One prevail over them, nor will the Thrones hinder them, but they will go with the angels to my city. (1:8-10 [Sa³])

The author has not prefaced these promises with any explanation of why the audience should deserve them: Is this privileged destiny extended to the whole audience, to particular members, to every Christian? Or is it a formulaic "promise" used to exhort any congregation in an anxious state? The explanation must be found in the eschatological narrative itself, into which the audience has been projected as the "saints." We have seen this projection already in terms of recognizing the Lawless One's inability to resurrect (3:12-13; 4:31). The same language of heavenly promises is likewise repeated in the "rapture" scene in ApocEl 5:

In that time the Christ will have pity upon those who belong to him. . . . Those upon whose foreheads is inscribed the name of the Christ, upon whose right hand is the seal, from little to great, [the angels] will lift them up on their wings and carry them away before the wrath. . . . And they will neither hunger nor thirst, nor will the Lawless One have power over them. (5:2, 4, 6 [Sa³])

Although the movement from earth in this passage is horizontal (to a "holy land") rather than vertical (an ascent to heaven), we can see that the author's previous promises to the audience in ApocEl 1 pertain to the fate of "saints" here in ApocEl 5. In both cases the recipients of the promises are identified as "those who are the Lord's," for example, or "those who are Christ's." The imagery of ascent in the first passage, however, is crucial to the promises offered. And it is precisely this ascent imagery that the Apocalypse of Elijah promises to those who suffer the cruelties of the Lawless One:

They will arise and receive a place of rest. But they will not inhabit the kingdom of the Christ like those who have endured. But for those who have endured, says the Lord, I will appoint them to sit at my right hand. [They will receive favor over others (Ach).] They will triumph over the Lawless One. They will witness the destruction of heaven and earth. They will receive the thrones of glory and the crowns. (4:27-29 [Sa³])

This passage is linked to the first one by its rewards of thrones and crowns and its reference to triumphing over the Lawless One; parallels with the second passage, from ApocEl 5, include resilience to the Law-less One and probably also the references to heavenly status (kingdom or holy land), the witnessing of the eschaton (cf. 5:36-38; 2:1), and, most importantly, ascent to heaven: arising (Coptic ⲧⲱⲟⲩⲛ), entering the kingdom of Christ, enthronement at God's right hand, rewards of thrones and crowns.

Through the parallel promises of heavenly ascent and enthronement given to the audience, the martyrs, and the righteous who exit the earth before the judgment, the text inevitably equates these different groups. Continually beckoning toward heaven as the audience's true destination no matter what fate might befall them, the text is able to inculcate dissociation from and, thus, resistance to edicts, tortures, and other calamities that might come by way of the audience.[23]

This use of heavenly ascent was apparently typical to the propaganda of martyrs and their circles during the third century. "From your letters," the jailed confessors Moses and Maximus wrote to Cyprian of Carthage,

> we saw those glorious triumphs of the martyrs, and with our eyes we have virtually followed them ascending to heaven, and we have contemplated them established among the angels and powers and dominions of heaven. Even more, we have virtually sensed the Lord with our ears, giving, (even) returning to them his promised testimony before the Father. It is this, then, that raises our spirits every day, and inflames us to pursue such a level of honor.[24]

Cyprian later answered in like terms, imagining their very incarceration as opportunity for ascent: "Already hoping only in heavenly things and contemplating only divine matters, you ascend to greater and greater heights by the very delay of your martyrdom, and in the long extension of time you do not dissipate your glory, you increase it!"[25] Cyprian's image was hardly an ad hoc metaphor, as the visions recorded in *Perpetua and Felicitas* depend on precisely this notion of martyrs gaining their visionary and ascent powers even before death.

Origen, writing only a few decades before the proposed period of the Elijah Apocalypse, provides a scenario of heavenly ascent through martyrdom that strongly resembles the heavenly "promises" under discussion:

23. Cf. Riddle, *Martyrs*, 28–38.
24. Cyprian *Ep.* 31.2 (ed. Le Chanoine Bayard, *Saint Cyprien: Correspondence* 1:78–79), my trans.
25. Cyprian *Ep.* 37.1.3 (Bayard, *Saint Cyprien* 1:93), my trans.

If you believe that Paul was caught up to the third heaven, and was caught up to Paradise and heard unspeakable words which man cannot utter, you will accordingly realize that you will have immediate knowledge of more and greater matters than the unspeakable words revealed to Paul. For after receiving them he descended from the third heaven, whereas after you have acquired this knowledge you will not descend again. . . . And if you do not fall away from those who follow [Christ] you yourselves shall pass through the heavens, passing not merely above earth and the mysteries of earth, but even above the heavens and their mysteries. For in God there are treasured up much greater visions than these, which no being with a material body can perceive before it is separated from every contact with matter.[26]

Here is evidence that the fantastic promises and systematic details of ascent in the Apocalypse of Elijah derived from a general linking of martyrdom with apocalypticism among Egyptian Christians already existing in the beginning of the third century.

Moreover, by identifying themselves with the eschatological martyrs as "those belonging to the Lord," the audience of the Elijah Apocalypse could expect an imperviousness to the power of the Lawless One, offered explicitly as a facet of their ascent to heaven (1:10; 4:28; 5:6). This additional promise would reflect the scale of the threat posed by the Lawless One's illegitimate dominion in ApocEl 3–5 (cf. 2:41); but it also reflects the typically adversarial conception of martyrdom in the third century, as triumph over demonic forces: "You not only confessed," says Cyprian, "but by God's will you terrified the great serpent himself, the precursor of Antichrist, by these utterances and divine words that I know."[27] As presented in the Apocalypse of Elijah, the Lawless One acts as a superhuman, but human nevertheless; yet the text alternately labels him as akin to Lucifer (4:11), the devil (4:12), and a serpent (5:33). Although he is never drawn as distinctly demonic as is, for example, Revelation's "beast" (chap. 13), such epithets do serve to clarify the nature of the conflict in which the saints are supposed to be engaged.

This exhortation function of the Apocalypse of Elijah fits well with other observations made thus far on the design and performative effect of the text. The prophetic mode of the text itself and the implied nature of the speaker as a prophet would have carried particular authority in a milieu concerned with the visionary aspects of martyrdom. The signs in

---

26. Origen *Exhortatio ad martyrum* 13 (tr. Henry Chadwick, *Alexandrian Christianity*, Library of Christian Classics 2 [London: SCM, 1954]), 402.

27. Cyprian *Ep.* 22.1.2 (Bayard, *Saint Cyprien* 1:59–60), my trans.

the text, which function to prepare the audience to persist through the eschatological woes by its ability to recognize clues in the chaos of events, incorporate predictions of martyrdoms as the inevitable fate of the heroes and saints who can recognize the Lawless One. The audience sees itself in a role given sacred value already by the heroic martyrdoms of Tabitha, Elijah, and Enoch; indeed, the promise of Tabitha's healing blood (4:6) suggests the establishment of martyr-cults.[28] So also the extended description of the demise of the Lawless One, coupled with the repeated descriptions of the saints' victorious ascent, creates a sense of ultimate vindication and retribution. The anticipation and hope proffered by the Apocalypse of Elijah are meant to surpass anxieties for individual safety and yet to exhort the audience to deaths framed as the natural consequences of their allegiance and understanding.

Historical Implications of the *Exhortatio* Function

It is now appropriate to return to the bracketed question of historical reflection. Specifically, if the Apocalypse of Elijah exhorts or even merely prepares its audience for martyrdom with the promise of heavenly rewards, does it therefore indicate that the author or members of the audience had historical acquaintance with the events surrounding the Decian or Valerian edicts or that the text was written partly to prepare an audience to become martyrs? It has been suggested that the martyrdom descriptions circulated with an interest in lurid details that transcended simple accurate reportage—that there was, in fact, a folklore of martyrdom in third-century Egypt—and that the narrative representation of martyrdom had a social function, particularly in the context of eschatology. These observations allow us to regard the Apocalypse of Elijah's use of martyrdom materials—not only the prophecy of martyrdom for the "saints" but the lurid details themselves—as highly traditional, instead of necessitating immediate historical experience. Such traditionality would account for the text's great popularity over the fourth and fifth centuries, when precise historical references and experience-specific exhortations would have been lost on audiences ac-

---

28. Cf. Wintermute, 756 n. 4a; and David T. M. Frankfurter, "Tabitha in the Apocalypse of Elijah," *JTS* 41 (1990):19–20. The saints' role in maintaining the cosmos in ApocEl 5:18 recalls that of the pharaoh (see below, pp. 162–63), but in this context probably reflects a highly revered cult of martyrs. On the martyr-cult as a "promise" of eventual reverence by the group, see Riddle, *Martyrs*, 92–97.

customed to a legitimate religion in Christianity. If the Apocalypse of
Elijah indeed expresses the function of *exhortatio ad martyrum*, however,
then presumably some kind of martyrdom was such a historical possibility for author and audience that actual exhortation was thought
necessary. If the text may be safely dated to the second half of the third
century, the historical coincidence with the period of the Decian and
Valerian edicts would lead one to expect that rumors arising from these
edicts had some impact on the author's portrayal of the end times.[29]

EXTREMIST VIEWS AND MELITIAN ORIGINS

Chapter 4 of the Apocalypse of Elijah describes two groups of "martyrs": those who undergo the gruesome tortures of the Lawless One
(4:20-23), and those who flee into the desert and die—the ἀναχώρητες.
Although those who choose this latter path will be blessed in having
their bodies preserved "until the last day of the great judgment" and will
ultimately "rise and receive a place of rest," the Apocalypse of Elijah
makes clear that these fugitives from torture "will not be in the kingdom
of the Christ like those who have endured [ΝΕΝΤΑΥ2ΥΠΟΜΙΝΕ]" (4:27).
It is likely that, prior to the audience's encounter with such a hierarchy
between martyr and ἀναχώρητης, it already held an ideology about the
diverse responses to threat (real or perceived) and about martyrdom as
an ideal. Moreover, even this mild disparagement of *anachoresis* during
the third century, when even *lapsi* were forgiven, would have placed the
audience at an extreme ideological position in relation to other Egyptian
Christians.[30]

Yet it was a position for which there is some record. The *Shepherd of
Hermas* anticipates the Apocalypse of Elijah's hierarchy remarkably,
advising that those who bear "stripes, imprisonments, great afflictions,
wild beasts, for the sake of the Name" will sit "on the right hand of the

29. It is unlikely that the historical impact on the text came from the edicts
themselves, rather than from the response of certain Christian groups to these edicts,
because the edicts were not designed against Christians and probably did not affect
Christians of more moderate temperaments. On the motivations behind the edicts, see
below, pp. 249–50, 259–61.

30. See Eusebius *Hist. eccles.* 6.42.5, 44.4; Annick Martin, "La reconciliation des *lapsi*
en Égypte," *Rivista di storia e letteratura religiosa* 22 (1986):256–69; and Oliver
Nicholson, "Flight from Persecution as Imitation of Christ: Lactantius' Divine Institutes
IV.18, 1–2," *JTS* 40 (1989):48–65. The desire for martyrdom is criticized in the *Testimony
of Truth* (NHC IX, 3), 34.

Holiness . . . but for the rest there is the left side."[31] Cyprian wrote in the early 250s to defend as an equal martyr the Christian who "flees, leaving behind all his property, and staying in hiding-places and solitude falls among bandits, or dies from fever or fatigue," whereas his opponents claim such a person "dies without peace and without communion."[32] In the beginning of the third century, Tertullian composed an entire tract against flight from persecution, arguing that martyrdom is ordained by God and therefore inevitable.[33] And a century earlier the *Apocryphon of James* recalled Jesus exhorting his disciples to imitate his sufferings quite literally, a martyrdom that would certainly exclude death during *anachoresis*.[34]

However, *anachoresis* or escape were precisely the responses to civic persecution favored by the Alexandrian bishops Dionysius and Peter and, evidently, by many others.[35] It may therefore be possible to attach the Apocalypse of Elijah's explicit hierarchy of martyrs to cultural proclivities within Egypt. On the basis of Eusebius's testimony in the *Historia ecclesiastica* and the *Martyrs in Palestine*, scholars have long regarded Upper Egyptians of this period as particularly fanatical in their longing for martyrdom.[36] Coincidentally, recent scholarship on the social origins of the Melitians in Egypt has also focused upon conflicts of authority and culture between Alexandria and Upper Egypt. The Meli-

31. Herm. *Vis.* 3.2.1 (tr. Kirsopp Lake, *The Apostolic Fathers*, 2 vols., LCL [Cambridge: Harvard University Press, 1912], 2:29, 31). The *Shepherd* then takes a less partisan posture, that "both, whether they sit on the right or the left, have the same gifts, and the same promises, only the former sit on the right and have somewhat of glory."

32. Cyprian *Ep.* 57.4.3.

33. Tertullian *De fuga in persecutione*. The probability that he wrote this tract after joining the New Prophecy, or Montanist, movement does not by any means suggest that the sentiments expressed in *De fuga* were uncommon among the Christianities of his era.

34. *Apocalypse of James* (NHC I, 2) 5 (on dating the *Apocalypse of James* to the early second century, see Ron Cameron, *The Other Gospels* [Philadelphia: Westminster, 1982], 56). On analogous sentiments among the Novatian sect, see Eusebius *Hist. eccles.* 6.43; and Timothy Gregory, "Novatianism: A Rigorist Sect in the Christian Roman Empire," *Byzantine Studies* 2 (1975):1–18.

35. On Dionysius, see Eusebius *Hist. eccles.* 6.40; on Peter of Alexandria, see Tim Vivian, *St. Peter of Alexandria: Bishop and Martyr*, SAC (Philadelphia: Fortress, 1988), 18–20. Cf. Tertullian *De fuga in persecutione* 11, which refers to ecclesiastical authorities fleeing, thereby (according to Tertullian) setting a bad example for lay Christians.

36. E.g., A.H.M. Jones, *The Later Roman Empire, 284–602: A Social, Economic, and Administrative Survey*, 2 vols. (Oxford: Basil Blackwell, 1964; reprint, Baltimore: Johns Hopkins University Press, 1986), 1:74–75; after Eusebius *Hist. eccles.* 6.41.14–42.4 (Dionysius); 8.9; *Martyrs of Palestine* 8.1, 13; 11.6; Ammianus Marcellinus 22.16.23; on rural martyrs, see also Cyprian *Ep.* 27.1.

tians, in outraged response to the Alexandrian church's leniency toward Christians who had lapsed during Diocletian's persecution, established their own "Church of the Martyrs," which gained great popularity among Christians in Upper Egypt. Its popularity in Egypt throughout late antiquity—even to the point of forming its own monasteries (composed, it appears, predominantly of Copts)—strongly suggests that its ideology had underpinnings in Upper Egyptian cultural identity.[37]

Without drawing the rural–Alexandrian cultural differences too rigidly or simplistically, one is tempted nevertheless to view, in such a "rigorist" milieu as the Apocalypse of Elijah seems to reflect, the ideological and social roots of the Melitians. While not attacking "Alexandrian" ecclesiastical authorities in any explicit way, the Apocalypse of Elijah elsewhere demonstrates ideological tendencies in polemic with those we can reconstruct as Alexandrian.[38] Because the Melitian schism represents the first major split within the church dominated by Dionysius and Peter, it is entirely likely that its origins would lie in tensions between the Alexandrian bishops and the Christian communities of outlying areas during the second half of the third century.

CONCLUSIONS

If the Apocalypse of Elijah is read as a response to later third-century millennialist interpretations of the imperial edicts, as having the function of exhorting its audience toward a heavenly identity resistant to earthly persecutions, as offering people already well acquainted with the gruesome folklore of Egyptian martyrdoms a preview of their eschatological victory, then its references to martyrdom provide the first internal correlation to a specific historical period—the time of Decius and Valerian and shortly thereafter. As an eschatological discourse the

---

37. See, esp., Vivian, *St. Peter of Alexandria*, 36–38; and C. Wilfred Griggs, *Early Egyptian Christianity: From Its Origins to 451 C.E.*, Coptic Studies 2 (Leiden: Brill, 1990), 121–30; and, in general, H. Idris Bell, *Jews and Christians in Egypt* (London: British Museum, 1924; reprint, Westport, Conn.: Greenwood, 1972), 38–99; Frend, *Martyrdom and Persecution*, 539–41; and Annick Martin, "Athanase et les mélitiens (325–335)," in *Politique et théologie chez Athanase d'Alexandrie*, ed. Charles Kannengiesser, Théologie historique 27 (Paris: Beauchesne, 1974), 31–61. Theodoret *Historia ecclesiastica* 1.9.14, enigmatically describes Melitian monks as following "practices corresponding to the madnesses of Samaritans and Jews" (text in Bell, *Jews and Christians in Egypt*, 42 n. 1), perhaps alluding to the non-Alexandrian sympathies of the movement.

38. E.g., the pronounced millennialism of the text (cf. chapter 10), the homily on fasting (cf. chapter 11), and the use of traditional anti-Alexandrian oracles (chapter 8, pp. 205–6, 213–14).

Apocalypse of Elijah offers no specific reflection of historical events of the later third century; and one must postulate a historical period on the tentative basis of the manuscripts themselves before seeking other, external reasons for assigning it to this period. Having done this, however, it is possible to find a number of important correlations between the contents of the text and historical and social situations of the second half of the third century. The method therefore does not proceed by way of the identification of *vaticinia ex eventus* but by reading the text's images generally as comprehensible within a particular historical period.

PART TWO

ENVISIONING THE COLLAPSE OF THINGS: THE CONVERGENCE OF EGYPTIAN AND CHRISTIAN WORLDVIEWS IN THE APOCALYPSE OF ELIJAH

7

Chaosbeschreibung:
The Literary and
Ideological Background
of the Apocalypse of Elijah

This and the following chapter serve two related points, vital for understanding the genesis of a document like the Apocalypse of Elijah in Roman Egypt. First, the motifs and language of much of the Apocalypse of Elijah arise and draw meaning from an Egyptian literary tradition of great antiquity. Second, because the motifs and language can be understood within this literary context, the interpretation of the text as a cryptic reflection of historical events—as *vaticinia ex eventus*—becomes impossible to maintain.

In the history of its interpretation, the Apocalypse of Elijah has occasionally been viewed as heir to the traditions of Egyptian oracular literature.[1] If one sets apart the vividly Christian beginning and end, a considerable portion of the Apocalypse of Elijah (designated as the second chapter in Jean-Marc Rosenstiehl's and subsequent translations) closely resembles a type of prophecy that had circulated in Egypt for several thousand years. This same type of prophecy was, moreover, adapted to the Roman experience in several texts contemporaneous with the Apocalypse of Elijah: the *Potter's Oracle* (which originated as a nationalist tract during the Ptolemaic period);[2] a related, anti-Jewish

---

1. Gaston Maspero, review of *Die Apokalypse des Elias*, by Georg Steindorff, *Journal des savants* (1899):41–43; Ludwig Koenen, "The Prophecies of a Potter: A Prophecy of World Renewal Becomes an Apocalypse," in *Proceedings of the 12th International Congress of Papyrology*, ed. Deborah H. Samuel, American Studies in Papyrology 7 (Toronto: Hakkert, 1970), 254; Françoise Dunand, "L'Oracle du Potier et la formation de l'apocalyptique en Égypte," in *L'Apocalyptique*, ed. Marc Philonenko, Études d'histoire des religions 3 (Paris: Paul Geuthner, 1977), 54–56; Rollin Kearns, *Das Traditionsgefüge um den Menschensohn* (Tübingen: Mohr [Siebeck], 1986), 97–99.
2. See Ludwig Koenen, "Die Prophezeiungen des 'Töpfers,'" *ZPE* 2 (1968):178–209

oracle (which may have originated as a response to the Jewish messianic revolution of 116–117 C.E.);[3] and the *Perfect Discourse*, probably composed during the third century C.E. and then included in the Hermetic tractate *Asclepius*, whence it came to Lactantius as an authoritative prophecy.[4] There are also extant remains of other oracles in circulation at this time that used similar prophetic forms, images, and mythology.[5] Both the Apocalypse of Elijah and these analogous texts belonged to a living native literary tradition with consistent ideology and forms of expression.

This chapter reviews the foundations, development, and characteristics of this native prophetic literature as it evolved from the twelfth dynasty (early second millennium B.C.E.) through the Byzantine period, in order to ground historically the contention in chapter 8 that the

---

(critical text and discussion); *ZPE* 3 (1968):137–38; idem, "Bemerkungen zum Text des Töpferorakels und zu dem Akaziensymbol," *ZPE* 13 (1974):313–17 (corrections); idem, "A Supplementary Note on the Date of the Oracle of the Potter," *ZPE* 54 (1984):9–13 (discussion); C. C. McCown, "Hebrew and Egyptian Apocalyptic Literature," *HTR* 18 (1925):397–400 (translation of text P[2], with brief discussion); Jonathan Z. Smith, "Wisdom and Apocalyptic," in *Religious Syncretism in Antiquity*, ed. Birger A. Pearson (Missoula, Mont.: Scholars Press, 1975), 144–54 (discussion); Dunand, "L'Oracle du Potier," 41–67 (extensive discussion); Stanley M. Burstein, ed., *The Hellenistic Age from the Battle of Ipsos to the Death of Kleopatra VII* (Cambridge: Cambridge University Press, 1985), 136–39 (English translation of text P[2]); cf. Richard Reitzenstein and H. H. Schaeder, *Studien zum antiken Synkretismus aus Iran und Griechenland* (Leipzig: Teubner, 1926), 39–40; and C. H. Roberts, "The Oracle of the Potter," *Oxyrhynchus Papyri* 22 (1954):89–99 (= P.Oxy 2332; first edition of text P[3] and detailed discussion of traditions).

3. PSI 982 (ed. Georg V. Manteuffel, "Zur prophetie in *P.S.I.*," VIII.982," *Mélanges Maspero* 2, Memoires publiés par les membres de l'institut français d'archéologie orientale du Caire 67 [Cairo: IFAO, 1934], 119–24); Menahem Stern, "A Fragment of Graeco-Egyptian Prophecy Bearing on Jews," *CPJ* 3:119–21 (= CPJ 520). Ludwig Koenen has shown me the text of an unpublished Oxyrhynchus fragment that is almost identical to CPJ 520 and that demonstrates both the currency of this prophecy and (by shared vocabulary) its ideological proximity to the *Potter's Oracle*.

4. *Asclepius* 24–27 = NHC VI, 8, 70–76; cf. A. D. Nock and A.-J. Festugière, *Corpus Hermeticum*, 2 vols. (2d ed.; Paris: Société d'Édition "Les Belles Lettres," 1960), 2:288–90; Jean-Pierre Mahé, *Hermès en Haute-Égypte*, 2 vols., Bibliothèque copte de Nag Hammadi 3 and 7 (Quebec: Presses de l'université Laval, 1978–82), 2:47–61; Garth Fowden, *The Egyptian Hermes* (Cambridge: Cambridge University Press, 1987), 38–44, 205–9.

5. PSI 760 (third/fourth century), in *Papiri Greci e Latini* 7 (Florence: Ariani, 1925), 45–46; P.Cairo 31222 (Roman period), in George R. Hughes, "A Demotic Astrological Text," *JNES* 10 (1951):256–64; P.Oxy 2554 (third century), in John Rea, "Predictions by Astrology," *Oxyrhynchus Papyri* 31 (1966):77–83; P.Stanford G93bv (second century), in John C. Shelton, "An Astrological Prediction of Disturbances in Egypt," *Ancient Society* 7 (1976):209–13; P.Tebt. Tait 13 (second century), in W. J. Tait, *Papyri from Tebtunis in Egyptian and in Greek (P.Tebt. Tait)* (London: Egypt Exploration Society, 1977), 45–48; and Vienna lunar omina papyrus (late second/early third centuries), in Richard A. Parker, *A Vienna Demotic Papyrus on Eclipse- and Lunar-Omina* (Providence, R.I.: Brown University Press, 1959), 35–52.

oracles of the Apocalypse of Elijah constitute not *vaticinia ex eventus*, as many scholars have hitherto assumed, but an ideal or typical tableau of times of distress in Egypt. Such tableaus, to which I refer under Jan Assmann's term *Chaosbeschreibung*,[6] arose out of the kingship ideology of traditional Egypt and the literary forms used by scribes to glorify and define the accession of kings. With the decline of the kingship in the Late period and increased controversy over its authority in the Hellenistic period, scribes from various (and often conflicting) temples began to appeal nostalgically to the legendary past for paradigms of true kingship and optimistically to the future for a "messianic" pharaoh. Both perspectives cast a gloomy light on the present times, the times of illegitimate or absent kingship; and scribes began to describe "this present chaos" with the vocabulary and motifs traditionally employed for characterizing the interregnal period: *Chaosbeschreibung*. Therefore the resurgence in ApocEl 2 of many of the ancient prophetic *topoi* confirms an important historical point: that the process of scribal composition during the Roman period was founded upon the ancient texts and legends and involved deliberate and continual updating.

The historical span covered in this chapter, perhaps striking non-Egyptological readers as excessive, should clarify that the scribal traditions that the Apocalypse of Elijah ultimately inherited were founded upon a tremendous conservatism.[7] Indeed, through the vicissitudes of Egyptian history during the Late, Hellenistic, Roman, and Byzantine periods, we find the same literary form, *Chaosbeschreibung*, emerging to address new historical situations in traditional ways. The Middle Kingdom roots of this form receive discussion largely to indicate its underlying ideology and the relationship of its "prophecies" to historical events: Were they understood to be *vaticinia ex eventus* or *sine eventibus*? These roots, however, also witness to a strong archaism in Egyptian literature, consistently pulling writers of the Greco-Roman period back to the language, symbols, and myths of classical Egypt. The classical

---

6. Jan Assmann, "Königsdogma und Heilserwartung: Politische und kultische Chaosbeschreibung in ägyptischen Texten," in *Apocalypticism in the Mediterranean World and the Near East*, ed. David Hellholm (Tübingen: Mohr [Siebeck], 1983), 345–77.

7. Note that scholars of Roman Egypt have customarily studied the prophecies of this period in continuity with those of classical Egypt: McCown, "Egyptian Apocalyptic Literature," 367–405; Jean Doresse, "Visions méditerranéennes," *La table ronde* 110 (1957):29–35; Koenen, "Prophecies of a Potter," 251–54; Mahé, *Hermès en Haute-Égypte* 2:69–81; Assmann, "Königsdogma und Heilserwartung," passim; and, esp., Jan Bergman, "Introductory Remarks on Apocalypticism in Egypt," in *Apocalypticism in the Mediterranean World*, ed. Hellholm, 53–55.

backgrounds of other, related literary or mythological traditions that persisted in Egyptian culture of the Roman period, such as that of the demonic adversaries Apophis and Seth, also contribute to the understanding of their appearances in late antiquity, even within a Christian matrix.

EGYPTIAN KINGSHIP IDEOLOGY

The axial symbol of Egyptian religion from earliest times through the Greco-Roman period was the figure of the pharaoh. Through the pharaoh's accession, presence, and dramatic enactment of festal rituals, two Egypts were united,[8] the sun rose, the Nile flowed, crops were fertile, people were healthy, children were born, families stayed together, the young respected their elders, economic and caste distinctions were maintained, invaders avoided the borders of Egypt, venomous snakes and desert beasts stayed away from people, the gods were propitiated, the deceased were properly disposed of and attained a pleasant afterlife, and so on. The pharaoh established *Ma'at*, order and justice, in Egypt; indeed, he symbolized its very presence and operation.[9]

The king was also the highest religious functionary, who adjured the various divinities of Egypt through public rituals to maintain the con-

8. Henri Frankfort has argued that the unification of an Upper and Lower Egypt in the person of the pharaoh and his crown did not represent a political unification of two distinct cultural entities but "expressed in political form the deeply rooted Egyptian tendency to understand the world in dualistic terms as a series of pairs of contrasts balanced in unchanging equilibrium" (*Kingship and the Gods* [Chicago: University of Chicago Press, 1948], 19, cf. 19–23).

9. Cf. Philippe Derchain, "Le rôle du roi d'Égypte dans le maintien de l'ordre cosmique," in *Le pouvoir et le sacré*, Annales du Centre d'étude des religions 1 (Brussels: Université libre de Bruxelles, 1962), 61–73. In Frankfort's words, "Nature itself could not be conceived without the king of Egypt. . . . Kingship in Egypt remained the channel through which the powers of nature flowed into the body politic to bring human endeavor to fruition . . . He exercises a never ending mysterious activity on the strength of which daily, hourly, nature and society are integrated" (*Kingship and the Gods* 33, 34, 60). Georges Posener, who otherwise argues for a less idealized kingship in Egypt, observes that in the ancient Egyptian worldview "lines of participation bind the cosmic order to the Egyptian community *at whose heart is the Pharaoh*. What affects social life reverberates in the universe. The human collectivity and nature are in solidarity and obey a law of similarity: like invokes like" (*De la divinité du pharaon*, Cahiers de la société asiatique 15 [Paris: Imprimerie nationale, 1960], 56; emphasis mine). On kingship and *Ma'at*, see also Henri Frankfort, *Ancient Egyptian Religion: An Interpretation* (New York: Columbia University Press, 1948; reprint, New York: Harper, 1961), 49–58; and, in general, John Baines, "Society, Morality, and Religious Practice," in *Religion in Ancient Egypt: Gods, Myths, and Personal Practice*, ed. Byron E. Shafer (Ithaca, N.Y.: Cornell University Press, 1991), 127–28.

tinuity of cosmos and society. He administrated the exchange of offerings and natural beneficences between the realms of humans and gods.[10]

In these roles the pharaoh was alternately identified with the gods Horus, Osiris, and Re.[11] As Horus he symbolized the king of both gods and people, the mediator between the divine order and the social and political order of Egypt, and the conqueror of Seth, the god of the periphery. As Osiris (a role assumed at the pharaoh's death) he symbolized chthonic and regenerative power;[12] and just as Osiris was father to Horus, so the dead pharaoh was the mythical "father" of the new pharaoh.[13] Finally, as "Son of" Re, the sun god (and the mythical father of *Ma'at*), the pharaoh was the creator of order, the opponent of chaos (both in creation and continually, with the rising of the sun), and the archetypal king of the heavens:[14]

> His eyes seek out every body.
> He is Re who sees with his rays,
> Who lights the Two Lands more than the sun-disk,
> Who makes verdant more than great Hapy,
> He has filled the Two Lands with life force.
> Noses turn cold when he starts to rage,
> When he is at peace one breathes air.
> He gives food to those who serve him,
> He nourishes him who treads his path.
> The king is sustenance, his mouth is plenty,
> He who will be is his creation.[15]

10. Posener, *De la divinité du pharaon*, 39–42, 61; Serge Sauneron, *The Priests of Ancient Egypt*, tr. Ann Morrissett, Evergreen Profile Book 12 (New York: Grove Press, 1960), 31–34.

11. The actual cultural equation of the Egyptian king and Egyptian divinities has given rise to considerable debate, the two sides generally being represented by Frankfort *(Kingship and the Gods)*, who emphasizes the pharaoh's divinity, and Posener *(De la divinité du pharaon)*, who argues that historical kings were consistently understood as humans as well as embodiments of the sacred office. Egyptologists tend to agree with Posener's argument: see David P. Silverman's discussion of the *status questionis* ("Divinity and Deities in Ancient Egypt," in *Religion in Ancient Egypt*, ed. Shafer, 58–73). Because the present section frames the *mythology* of kingship as background to the "messianic" oracles of the Greco-Roman period, I have sought to review common points and functions of kingship in Frankfort's and Posener's works.

12. Cf. Frankfort, *Kingship and the Gods*, 181–95.

13. Frankfort observes, "Kingship is conceived in its profoundest aspect, on the plane of the gods, as involving two generations . . . the actual occupancy of the throne creates a fusion of the late king and his successor" (ibid., 33). Cf. Posener, *De la divinité de la pharaon*, 20.

14. Cf. Frankfort, *Kingship and the Gods*, 148–61.

15. Stela of Sehetepibre (Cairo Museum 20538), verso, ll. 12–15 (tr. Lichtheim, 1:128).

THE DEMONIC OPPOSITION TO KINGSHIP

The created order and the pharaoh who maintained it owed some of their symbolic force to two distinct mythological systems of opposition in which order was threatened by chaos and finally triumphed. Seth and Apophis, two personifications of "evil"—chaos—in Egyptian literature, became particularly important in Greco-Egyptian magical texts but continued to maintain their ancient significance in the discussion and representation of threats to the land and cosmos of Egypt.

Seth

Seth can be most generally characterized as a god of things that dwell on the margins of Egypt: the desert and its life forms, foreigners, and chaos, as the limits of Egypt were considered the limits of civilization and *Ma'at*. In myths his functions were more vividly portrayed: Seth dismembers Osiris and scatters or drowns the pieces; Horus attacks Seth to avenge his father; Seth succeeds in removing Horus's eye; but finally, Horus triumphs. In another episode Seth sends a scorpion to sting the infant Horus while his mother Isis wanders through the marshes of the Delta.[16]

In Greco-Roman times Seth carried two principal functions in Egyptian culture: at the level of the priesthood and the royal cult, Seth was regarded as the divine power behind foreigners, particularly invading foreigners; and at a more popular or quotidian level, Seth was regarded as the threat posed by the desert and its dangerous inhabitants—reptiles, scorpions, demons.[17] The common symbolism at both levels is marginality. Seth was the god of Egypt's periphery and, therefore, of the periphery of the cosmos itself. Consequently, as periphery, he intrinsically threatened the interior, the order of the Egyptian cosmos—fertility, social harmony, the continuity of religion and cult—in much the same way as the Seth of mythology threatened Osiris and Horus, the images of order in the cosmos.[18]

Over the course of the Late and Hellenistic periods, Seth became explicitly associated with every nation that had invaded or was invading

16. See J. Gwyn Griffiths, *The Conflict of Horus and Seth* (Liverpool: Liverpool University Press, 1960); H. Te Velde, *Seth, God of Confusion*, tr. G. E. van Baaren-Pape (Leiden: Brill, 1977).

17. See L. Keimer, "L'horreur des égyptiens pour les démons du désert," *Bulletin de l'institut d'Égypte* 26 (1944):135–47.

18. Cf. Te Velde, *Seth*, 117.

Egypt: Assyria, Persia, and (in some temples) Greece. Translated into Greek as Typhon, Seth even became identified with the Jews in some priestly quarters.[19] More importantly, Seth was cursed in special rituals both for invasions past and to prevent invasions future, through the media of iconography (especially the image of a bound ass), inscriptions, priestly rituals, and public dramas, which often involved the king himself as Horus. Papyrus Jumilhac presents a typical execration of Seth from the late Ptolemaic period: Horus is invoked to "exterminate [Seth's] allies, destroy his towns and nomes, erase his name from the land, [and] shatter his statues in all the nomes."[20] The myth of Seth thus came to articulate a sweeping and hostile Egyptian xenophobia.[21]

The second, "quotidian" level at which Seth was understood also involved ritual and thus would have both assumed and promoted the mythology of Seth beyond the priesthood. Formulas and narratives describing Horus's snakebite or scorpion sting at Seth's behest and his suffering and subsequent cure at the hands of the goddesses Isis and Selket were engraved on stelae and statues and undoubtedly chanted over real victims.[22] The stelae themselves, which were carved in great abundance throughout the Greco-Roman period and placed by temples and in homes, portrayed the child Horus standing on crocodiles and victoriously grasping beasts traditionally associated with the desert and Seth: antelopes, scorpions, snakes. The Horus stelae functioned in a manner both curative (through water washed over them) and apotropaic: they warded off the powers of Seth in the form of reptiles and scorpions.[23]

There is considerable evidence beyond the Horus stelae that Seth's role as disturber of the cosmos was not just a priestly trope but also had

19. See below, pp. 189–90.
20. P.Jumilhac XVII.10–11 (tr. Jacques Vandier, *Le Papyrus Jumilhac* [Paris: Centre national de la recherche scientifique, 1961], 129; cf. 108–9). The classic exposition of a ritual drama against Seth is H. W. Fairman, *The Triumph of Horus* (London, 1974).
21. See, in general, Étienne Drioton, "Le nationalisme au temps des pharaons," in idem, *Pages d'égyptologie* (Cairo: Editions de la Revue de Caire, 1957), 375–86; J. Gwyn Griffiths, "Egyptian Nationalism in the Edfu Temple Texts," in *Glimpses of Ancient Egypt: Studies in Honour of H. W. Fairman*, ed. John Ruffle, G. A. Gaballa, and Kenneth Kitchen (Warminster: Aris & Phillips, 1979), 174–79.
22. See texts in Borghouts, 59–76.
23. See M. G. Daressy, *Textes et dessins magiques*, Catalogue général des antiquités égyptiennes du musée du Caire nos. 9401–449 (Cairo: IFAO, 1903); A. Moret, "Horus sauveur," *RHR* 72 (1915):213–87; P. Lacau, "Les statues 'guérisseuses' dans l'ancienne Égypte," *Académie des inscriptions et belles-lettres, Commission de la fondation Piot: Monuments et mémoires* 25 (1921–22):189–209; Keith C. Seele, "Horus on the Crocodiles," *JNES* 6 (1947):43–52.

meaning at a deeply popular level. Plutarch gives vivid descriptions of local execration rituals, including an annual mass slaughter of crocodiles in the town of Apollonopolis.[24] Greco-Egyptian ritual ("magical") texts, in which Seth–Typhon was often transvalued as an appeasable *daimôn*, nevertheless preserved the essence of his traditional functions: in a Greek section of the third-century C.E. Demotic magical papyrus of London and Leiden, Seth is addressed as "you who cause destruction and desolation, you who hate a stable household, you were driven out of Egypt and have roamed[25] foreign lands, you who shatter everything and are not defeated."[26] And the anti-Jewish violence that arose in Memphis and elsewhere in the Roman period is probably attributable to a popular notion of "Typhonian" peoples, a concept that certain priesthoods applied to Jews.[27]

Up through the Late period there existed actual temples of Seth, where he was propitiated as the foreigners' divinity, lord of the desert, thunder god, and powerful defender of Re against the dragon Apophis.[28] It is evident (although strange) that in a few quarters this cult continued even into the Roman period, when Seth had reached an almost exclusively negative status. A second-century C.E. papyrus lists, among a series of festivals celebrated in an Upper Egyptian town, one seemingly devoted to Typhon.[29] It remains unclear whether this festival or procession actually would have constituted a veneration of Seth–Typhon in any sense or a national exorcistic or apotropaic rite (to expel Seth–Typhon). The word—actually in dative plural, τυφωνίοις ("for the Typhonians")—might have been a priestly (and negative) term for the regular rites of a certain community of foreigners living in the area, in which the particular priest in the papyrus was asked to participate.

Apophis

Apophis was considered not a god, like Seth, but a great serpent in pursuit of Re, the sun; Seth is called upon in his capacity as god of

24. Plutarch *De Iside et Osiride* §§30–31, 50 (John Gwyn Griffiths, *Plutarch: De Iside et Osiride* [Cardiff: University of Wales Press, 1970], 411, 490–93).

25. ἐπενόμασθης: cf. LSJ 649A, s.v. ἐπίνομος.

26. P.London and Leiden col. XXIII, ll. 10–12 (tr. Janet Johnson in Betz, *Greek Magical Papyri*, 232).

27. CPJ 141; CPJ 520; cf. Roger Rémondon, "Les antisémites de Memphis," *Chronique d'Égypte* 35 (1960):244–61; and, esp., Jean Yoyotte, "L'Égypte ancienne et les origines de l'antijudaïsme," *RHR* 163 (1963):133–43. See also discussion below, pp. 189–91.

28. Te Velde, *Seth, God of Confusion*, 124–40.

29. P.Heid. inv. 1818ᵛ l.9 (in Herbert C. Youtie, "The Heidelberg Festival Papyrus: A Reinterpretation," in idem, *Scriptiunculae*, vol. 1 [Amsterdam: Hakkert, 1973], 514–45, esp. 525–28).

"confusion" to help repel Apophis from harrassing Re.[30] Apophis threatens to destroy the sun in its daily circuit through the sky; and insofar as the sun, Re, is the image of *Ma'at*, Apophis represents both darkness and chaos hypostasized. Consequently, the conflict cycle of Apophis and Re approximates that between Seth and Horus in expressing the accession of order and the triumph over chaos in all its manifestations. The myth also reflects another dimension, that of cosmogony, for Re is a creator–god and Apophis the hypostasization of primordial chaos and darkness. Thus as the king is "Son of Re" and the image of Re on earth, the repulsion of Apophis reflects the repulsion of the king's enemies.[31]

Apophis's mythological relevance arises almost exclusively in the context of ritual and iconographic cursing: the Bremner-Rhind papyrus gives extensive descriptions of the many Egyptian gods (imagined as riding in Re's barque) combining their powers to destroy Apophis.[32] The text is punctuated with declarations against Apophis and instructions for burning his images and names. By their ritualized reading, therefore, the descriptions of Apophis's destruction and Re's triumph would actually aid the sun in its circuit, replay the cosmogony, and thus reestablish *Ma'at* in the cosmos.

Whereas Seth and Apophis remained completely distinct ideas within the traditional mythology, occasional merging began to appear in the Late period, continuing as an occasional phenomenon of Greco-Egyptian ritual ("magical") texts.[33]

Conclusion

Two discrete schemes of mythological opposition were associated with Egyptian kingship ideology and, in the later period, came to reflect more general and critical oppositions in Egyptian experience, particularly in nationalist propaganda. Seth evolved from a "god of for-

---

30. See Te Velde, *Seth, God of Confusion,* 99–108.

31. Frankfort, *Kingship and the Gods,* 150; cf. Siegfried Morenz, *Egyptian Religion,* tr. Ann E. Keep (Ithaca, N.Y., and London: Cornell University Press, 1973), 168–69.

32. R. O. Faulkner, "The Bremner-Rhind Papyrus III–IV: D. The Book of Overthrowing 'Apep," *JEA* 23 (1937):166–75; 24 (1938):41–53. This drama is also described in the *Book of the Dead,* chap. 39.

33. Cf. Philippe Derchain, "A propos d'une stèle magique du musée Kestner," *REg* 16 (1964):19–23, Pl. 2 ("Seth cursed and iconographically bound for attacking sun"); Arthur S. Hunt, "An Incantation in the Ashmolean Museum," *JEA* 15 (1929):155–57, Pl. 31, 1 ("Typhon adversary of sun"); H. I. Bell, A. D. Nock, and Herbert Thompson, "Magical Texts from a Bilingual Papyrus in the British Museum," *Proceedings of the British Academy* (1931):252, 255, 275–79 (lizard, a Sethian animal, hated by the Sun and all the gods).

eigners" and of the desert to a "god of the chaotic, invading Foreigner," and in this evolution he became progressively demonized as the symbol of all historical forces that opposed the traditional order of Egypt. Apophis, by contrast, maintained a more abstract function as the antagonist of Re and concretization of chaos itself. There is scant evidence that these myths overlapped; such as there is derives largely from the Hellenistic period.

KINGSHIP PROPAGANDA AND
THE PORTRAYAL OF ANTIKINGSHIP

In the beginning of the second millennium B.C.E. a text was written describing—as prophecy—a cataclysmic decline in Egypt, including details of famine, social disintegration, and invasions from the East:

> Dry is the river of Egypt. . . . Foes have risen in the East, Asiatics have come down to Egypt . . . I show you the land in turmoil, what should not be has come to pass. Men will seize weapons of warfare, the land will live in uproar. . . . I show you the son as enemy, the brother as foe, a man slaying his father. . . . The land is ruined, its fate decreed, deprived of produce, lacking in crops. . . . The land is shrunk—its rulers are many, it is bare—its taxes are great; . . . Re will withdraw from mankind: Though he will rise at his hour, one will not know when noon has come.[34]

Concluding these descriptions was this "messianic" oracle:

> Then a king will come from the South, Ameny, the justified, by name, . . . He will take the white crown, he will wear the red crown; he will join the Two Mighty Ones, . . . Rejoice, O people of his time, the son of man will make his name for all eternity! The evil-minded, the treason-plotters, they suppress their speech in fear of him; Asiatics fall to his sword, Libyans will fall to his flame, rebels to his wrath, traitors to his might, . . . Then Order will return to its seat, while Chaos is driven away.[35]

The text, entitled the *Prophecy of Neferti*, has long been recognized as propaganda for the reign of Amenhemet I during the twelfth dynasty (1991–1783 B.C.E.); and therefore, as "prophecy," it was meant to function as *vaticinium ex eventu*.[36] This fact has led scholars to assume that, as the

---

34. *Neferti* (tr. Lichtheim, 1:141–43).
35. *Neferti* 57–70 (tr. Lichtheim, 1:143–44).
36. Cf. Georges Posener, *Littérature et politique dans l'Égypte de la XIIe dynastie* (Paris: Librarie ancienne Honoré Champion, 1956), 16–60, 145–57; and idem, "Literature," in *The Legacy of Egypt*, ed. J. R. Harris (2d ed.; Oxford: Clarendon, 1971), 231–32; and see summary of text in McCown, "Egyptian Apocalyptic Literature," 383–86.

messianic king Ameny represented the recently enthroned Amenhemet, so also the catastrophes in Egypt that precede Ameny's advent must have represented a real historical situation in Egypt at that time.[37] S. Luria, however, in a 1929 discussion of revolutionary reversal imagery, suggested that such descriptions of woes and chaos in Egyptian literature could be taken as formulaic and imaginative, rather than as reflective of historical events—indeed, that the theme of social reversal and catastrophe were literary *topoi* arising from Egyptian royal ideology.[38] Consequently, Egyptologist Miriam Lichtheim has argued that scribes of the twelfth dynasty in Egypt were drawing on a literary theme of "national distress," of which two components could be observed:

> The first is the infiltration of the Delta by Asiatics; the second is civil war among Egyptians. This second topic is described by means of three *topoi* . . . : indiscriminate bloodshed, indifference to suffering, and the reversal of the social order, by which the rich become poor and the have-nots become the masters.[39]

Whereas Lichtheim drew a fairly strict line between the literary *topos* and the historical events of the period, Raymond Weill in 1918 and Assmann in 1983 sought to reconcile the literary nature of these portrayals of catastrophe (which obviously drew their imagery from the sphere of historical detail) with a historical reality that was itself often incomprehensible without the ideological and articulative force of propaganda.[40] Weill saw the persistence of a "theme of disorder" in Egyptian literature, a "tableau of desolation" whose ahistorical components crystallized and even achieved a measure of historicity during the calamitous Late and Greco-Roman periods.[41] Assmann, classifying a broad range of such tableaus, employs the evocative term *Chaosbeschreibung*, which usefully indicates the mythological underpinnings of these ideas and of their roots in kingship ideology.

Chaosbeschreibung was, essentially, the idealized representation of Egypt without a pharaoh; discourses employing this form would thus

37. E.g., Posener, *Littérature et politique*, 45–59, which is otherwise the most complete and detailed study of the *Prophecy of Neferti* in its historical context.

38. S. Luria, "Die Ersten werden die Letzten sein (zur 'sozialen Revolution' im Altertum)," *Klio* 22 (1929):405–31.

39. Lichtheim, 1:144 n. 9.

40. Lichtheim, 1:134–35, 139, 149–50; Assmann, "Königsdogma und Heilserwartung," 345–77, esp. 349–50.

41. Raymond Weill, *La fin du moyen empire égyptienne* (Paris: Imprimerie nationale, 1918), 22–145, esp. 35–37, 65, 118, 125.

pertain intrinsically—that is, regardless of historical events—to both the interregnal periods and the actual lapses of kingship (such as those that occurred repeatedly over the course of the Late period). By kingship's very nature as the axis of order, its imagined absence must cause catastrophe in all the domains into which the pharaoh's integrative powers extend: religious structure, social structure, national boundaries, and fertility. *Chaosbeschreibung* acted as a trope to laud kingship by describing its symbolic antitheses. Thus *Chaosbeschreibung* discourses appear in ritual ("magical") spells to describe the cosmos in decline following Osiris's death or Horus's illness from snakebite or even the gods' refusal to obey the ritual demands of a priest, whose professed urgency was supposed to reflect the urgency and instability of the cosmic order under the threat of Seth.[42] As a literary form, *Chaosbeschreibung* was conceived to function as propaganda in praise of a present king, rather than as a chronicle of actual events.[43] Indeed, it effectively presented the

42. E.g., P.Turin 137, 1–4: "On the night that the wife of Horus shall bite thee, I suffer not the Nile to beat upon its bank, I suffer not the sun to shine upon the earth, I suffer not the seed to grow" (tr. Alan Gardiner, "Magic [Egyptian]," *ERE* 8:265A); P.Salt 825, I.2–5: "The earth is devastated, the sun does not leave, the moon tarries—it does not exist. Nun [the primeval ocean] is disturbed, the earth turns upside-down; the river is no longer navigable . . . the whole world groans and weeps" (French tr. Philippe Derchain, *Le papyrus Salt 825 [B.M. 10051]: Rituel pour la conservation de la vie en Égypte*, Mémoires de l'académie royale de Belgique 58, 1a [Brussels: Palais des académies, 1965], 137); cf. P.Leiden I, 348ᵛ II, 5–8 (in François Lexa, *La magie dans l'Égypte antique*, 2 vols. [Paris: Geuthner, 1925], 2:62); PGM V.284–89; PGM LXII.13–14. In general, on "magical" uses of *Chaosbeschreibung*, see Serge Sauneron, "Aspects et sort d'un thème magique égyptien: Les menaces incluant les dieux," *Bulletin de la société française d'égyptologie* (November 1951):11–21; and Siegfried Schott, "Altägyptische Vorstellungen vom Weltende," *Analecta biblica* 12 (1959):319–30, esp. 325–29; Derchain, *papyrus Salt 825*, 24–28, 146–47; and Assmann, "Königsdogma und Heilserwartung," 369–71.

43. Cf. Assmann, "Königsdogma und Heilserwartung," 350–51. Posener sees a series of stages evident in the evolution of *Chaosbeschreibung* as employed in the service of a present king. The prototype of the form lay in the "complaint" genre, epitomized by the *Admonitions of Ipuwer* (discussed below, pp. 171–72), which described a "present" state of social and cosmic chaos. The contemplation of present chaos then came to be juxtaposed to a mythical period of order (a paradise of sorts), and the disjunction between *illud tempus* and the present was accounted for by a myth of the "fallen state of the world," which is reflected in several early texts (Posener, *Littérature et politique*, 28). Basic images of this myth seem to be the departure of the primeval gods from earth, the arrival of Seth, the beginnings of environmental evils (such as serpents), the decline of human life spans, and the loss of Ma'at (cf. L. Kákosy, "Ideas about the Fallen State of the World in Egyptian Religion: Decline of the Golden Age," *AOH* 17 [1964]:205–16. The transposition of the mythical period of order to the "future" kingship, Posener argues, first took place in the composition of *Neferti* and was motivated by the political agenda of creating the most effective propaganda (*Littérature et politique*, 28–29).

king as salvific, even "messianic," as he restored an Egypt in deep disintegration.[44]

Neferti may be justly regarded as "the prototype of all subsequent political *Chaosbeschreibung*."[45] The discourse and its motifs came to be used to characterize the period before any pharaoh's accession: Hatshepsut, for example, claimed to have expelled invaders and restored order and religion in Egypt, when in fact her rule followed no such disasters;[46] and in 196 B.C.E. Ptolemy V, in manifest imitation of this tradition, would proclaim in the archaic phrases of the Rosetta Stone his defeat of rebels, preservation of temples from destruction, and general beneficence and order.[47]

Several centuries after *Neferti* there appeared another extended discourse, titled the *Admonitions of Ipuwer*,[48] whose prophetic motifs included social reversal ("See the judges of the land are driven from the land, ⟨the nobles⟩ are expelled from the royal mansions. See, noble ladies are on boards, Princes in the workhouse"); mass death ("There's blood everywhere, no shortage of dead, the shroud calls before one comes near it, the stream is the grave, the tomb became stream"); the encroachment of desert and invaders ("Lo, the desert claims the land, the nomes are destroyed, foreign bowmen have come into Egypt"); and the striking image of a bloody Nile ("Lo, the river is blood, as one drinks from it one shrinks from people and thirsts for water").[49] These vivid images of catastrophe convinced Egyptologist Alan Gardiner that "it is the picture of a real revolution . . . the condition of the country which it discloses is one which cannot be ascribed to the imagination of a romancer," whereas Lichtheim has more circumspectly viewed the text

44. The use of the word "messianic" is appropriate in this particular case because of the necessarily royal concept of the savior figure in Egyptian nationalistic prophecy. To clarify that the word is imported from another ideological context, however, I employ quotation marks.

45. Assmann, "Königsdogma und Heilserwartung," 360.

46. Weill, *La fin du moyen empire*, 40–44 (with further examples of *Chaosbeschreibung* as propaganda for specific kings, 45–60); see also Assmann, "Königsdogma und Heilserwartung," 364–68; Silverman, "Divinity and Deities," 70–71.

47. Cf. Ludwig Koenen, "Die Adaptation ägyptischer Königsideologie am Ptolemäerhof," in *Egypt and the Hellenistic World*, ed. E. Van 't Dack, P. van Dessel, and W. van Gucht, Studia hellenistica 27 (Louvain, 1983), 143–90, esp. 170–71.

48. Arguing against the scholarly consensus, on the basis of *Ipuwer*'s ahistoricity, Lichtheim classifies it "as a work of the Late Middle Kingdom [i.e., ca. 1750–1650 B.C.E.] and of purely literary inspiration" (1:149).

49. *Ipuwer* (tr. Lichtheim, 1:151–55). See the selection and discussion in McCown, "Egyptian Apocalyptic Literature," 370–82.

as "the last, fullest, most exaggerated and hence least successful, composition on the theme 'order versus chaos.'"[50]

Over the course of the second millennium B.C.E., *Ipuwer* and *Neferti* were continually recopied as classical literature of kingship.[51] These texts bear close similarities, except for the manner in which they are presented—that is, their genres. The *Chaosbeschreibung* discourse of *Ipuwer* appears to lack any narrative context and has therefore been classified as a "complaint."[52] Arising as it did in the archival milieus of Egyptian wisdom scribes, the text might well have served as a synthetic gathering of the *Chaosbeschreibung* motifs selectively deployed in propaganda for particular kings, as if to teach future scribes the components of effective propaganda. Weill likewise saw in *Ipuwer*

> the theme of disorder [giving] place to a veritable treatise on government and the administration of Egypt, in which each prescription results indirectly from the image of the calamity which occurs from what is not followed. Consequently the book contains a complete collection of social misfortunes of which Egyptians at this time had [at some point] the experience or the idea.[53]

The genre of *Neferti*, in contrast, was presented as the prophecy of the scribe and "great lector priest of Bastet," Neferti, before King Snefru. Both characters lived during the fourth dynasty and by the twelfth dynasty (the period of the text) had become legendary. The "prophecy" of a King Ameny during the reign of King Snefru therefore gained the authority of tradition through the literary comparison of the present and legendary kings.[54]

The technique of framing a discourse or plot within the life of a king in his court demonstrates the influence of the *Königsnovelle*, a favorite literary genre in ancient Egypt:

> In the fixed form of this historiographical genre, an important historical event is described as the result of an action taken by the king. A dream, a message, or some other event prompts the king to discuss the matter first

50. Alan Gardiner, *Egypt of the Pharaohs* (London: Oxford University Press, 1961), 109; Lichtheim, 1:150.

51. Cf. Posener, *Littérature et politique*, 30 n. 9; Lichtheim, 1:139 (*Neferti*); 1:149–50 (*Ipuwer*).

52. Cf. Assmann, "Königsdogma und Heilserwartung," 347–57. McCown believes that the text once had a narrative frame and ending ("Egyptian Apocalytic Literature," 371–72).

53. Weill, *Le fin du moyen empire*, 134.

54. See Posener, *Littérature et politique*, 29–36.

in an assembly of advisors, princes, or even workers; he then issues orders for the execution of his plans. These lead to a wide variety of historical actions. Warfare is undertaken; temples, sanctuaries, or wells are built or renewed; a statue of a god is transported; sacrifices are established, rituals performed, and provisions issued for workers; or prophecies about the unhappy future of Egypt and its final restoration under a new ruler are made and written down in the presence of the king.[55]

The genre or device may be compared to the Jewish court-romances of Ahikar, Joseph, Esther, and Daniel, the last of which likewise frames prophecy within the context of court narrative.[56] In the continuation of the *Chaosbeschreibung* form into the Roman period, the *Königsnovelle* was often used in Egyptian literary tradition as a framing narrative in order to identify the period of the prophecy and to legitimize it as the word of a legendary prophet.[57] Jonathan Z. Smith has labeled the two forms in combination—(1) a legendary seer's prophecy to a legendary king of (2) catastrophes and their reconciliation—as an "apocalypse," because of the resemblance to Jewish apocalypses (whose occasional eschatological discourses are often framed within courtly or other narratives).[58] The importation of this genre label, however, does not add to the understanding of either frame or *Chaosbeschreibung*;[59] further, apart from the literary need to contextualize a discourse with narrative, there is no intrinsic relationship between *Königsnovelle* and *Chaosbeschreibung*.[60]

55. Ludwig Koenen, "The Dream of Nektanebos," *BASP* 22 (1985):172–73; cf. Alfred Hermann, *Die ägyptische Königsnovelle*, Leipziger Ägyptologische Studien 10 (Glückstadt: Augustin, 1938). Koenen does express "doubts as to whether the *Königsnovelle* represents a genre or rather a narrative technique" ("Dream of Nektanebos," 173 n. 6).

56. See John J. Collins, "The Court-Tales in Daniel and the Development of Apocalyptic," *JBL* 94 (1975):218–34; Susan Niditch and Robert Doran, "The Success Story of the Wise Courtier: A Formal Approach," *JBL* 96 (1977):179–93; and John W. B. Barns, "Egypt and the Greek Romance," *Mitteilungen aus der Papyrussammlung der österreichischen Nationalbibliothek* 5 (1956):29–36.

57. The *Königsnovelle* was similarly used as a frame narrative for other purposes, e.g., to render a healing spell authoritative and powerful: "to cure whomever [suffers] physically from his illness, after His Majesty had seen a book of protection from the [time] of the ancestors" (P.Berlin 3049, 18.6–19.1; tr. Pascal Vernus, "Un Décret de Thoutmosis III relatif à la santé publique," *Orientalia* 48 [1979]:177; cf. 183–84 on use of *Königsnovelle*).

58. Smith, "Wisdom and Apocalyptic," 141–44.

59. Bergman, e.g., uses "apocalyptic" in an exclusively eschatological sense in his "Remarks on Apocalypticism in Egypt," 51–60.

60. Cf. Collins ("Court-Tales"), who suggests literary and historical associations between Daniel's court stories and the book's prophecies. In the case of Egyptian prophetic texts, one might argue that the nostalgia involved in setting the prophecies in the court of a legendary king is connected to the anticipation or adulation of "right"

THE USE OF *CHAOSBESCHREIBUNG* IN
THE HELLENISTIC PERIOD

During the Late period (712–332 B.C.E.), Egypt suffered repeated invasions from Assyrians and Persians; legends of these depredations continued well into the Coptic period. Thus we find in the later literature of *Chaosbeschreibung* greater precision in identifying the foreigners who, according to the kingship ideology, might enter Egypt unrepelled by the power of the pharaoh: they are now specifically denoted as Persians and Assyrians.[61] In the beginning of the Hellenistic period we also find that the legend of Nektanebos, the last native pharaoh before the coming of Alexander, is brought into the service of the *Königsnovelle* frame. He represents the paradigmatic king of yore and is even claimed as the secret father of the world emperor Alexander.[62]

The *Demotic Chronicle*

Nektanebos is exalted as the model Egyptian king in an important prophetic work of the early Hellenistic period, referred to as the *Demotic Chronicle*.[63] The structure of the text is a series of brief, enigmatic oracles—apparently based on those delivered in the oracle temple of Harsaphes in Herakleopolis—followed by brief commentaries applying the terms of the oracle to historical events.[64] The reference to Nektanebos

---

kingship in the prophecy. But this coincident "royal orientation" of the two literary forms expresses the social context of literature in Egypt (i.e., in the service of the king; see Smith, "Wisdom and Apocalyptic") rather than an intrinsic relationship of the literary forms.

61. See, e.g., Jacques Schwartz, "Les conquérants perses et la littérature égyptienne," *BIFAO* 48 (1949):65–80.

62. See Martin Braun, *History and Romance in Graeco-Oriental Literature* (Oxford: Blackwell, 1938), 19–25; B. E. Perry, "The Egyptian Legend of Nectanebus," *TPAPA* 97 (1966):327–33; Reinhold Merkelbach, *Die Quellen des griechischen Alexanderromans* (Munich: C. G. Beck'sche, 1977), 77–88; Alan B. Lloyd, "Nationalist Propaganda in Ptolemaic Egypt," *Historia* 31 (1982):46–50; idem, "The Late Period: 664–323 B.C.," in *Ancient Egypt: A Social History*, ed. B. G. Trigger et al. (Cambridge: Cambridge University Press, 1983), 291–92; and Koenen, "Dream of Nektanebos," 171–94.

63. McCown, "Egyptian Apocalyptic Literature," 387–92. The fullest discussion is by Janet H. Johnson, "Is the Demotic Chronicle an Anti-Greek Tract?" in *Grammata Demotika*, ed. Heinz-J. Thissen and Karl-Th. Zauzich (Würzburg: Gisela Zauzich, 1984), 107–24. Translations of the *Demotic Chronicle* can be found in Eugène Revillout, "Second extrait de la Chronique Démotique de Paris: Les prophéties patriotiques," *Revue égyptologique* 1 (1880):145–53; 2 (1881):1–10, 52–62; and Wilhelm Spiegelberg, *Die sogennante Demotische Chronik* (Leipzig: Hinrichs, 1914).

64. Cf. Janet H. Johnson, "The Demotic Chronicle as an Historical Source," *Enchoria* 4 (1974):1–17. François Daumas cogently compared this format to the Qumran *pesher* mode of millennialist exegesis of prophecy ("Littérature prophétique et exégétique

and systematic allusions to other kings of the Late period suggest not only that these "oracles" are a literary fiction but that the text was meant to offer a clear description of the ideal pharaoh, one who expels foreign invaders (notably the Persians) and mounts the throne with proper ritual.[65] As with the "king from the South" in the *Prophecy of Neferti,* the *Demotic Chronicle* envisions a realization of this ideal pharaoh—a "messianic" king to come from Herakleopolis (coincidentally the milieu of the *Demotic Chronicle*).

In the case of the *Demotic Chronicle* and other Egyptian kingship propaganda composed under the Ptolemies, the question arises whether the ideological function of *Chaosbeschreibung,* with its inevitable messianic conclusion, was nationalistic—that is, anti-Hellenistic. The legend of Nektanebos's fatherhood of Alexander is only one example of the many ways in which Egyptian priests used the native kingship ideology and its literary forms to compose propaganda for the Ptolemies.[66] Because the last king in the *Demotic Chronicle* is envisioned as succeeding the Greeks and apparently is meant to recall the native kings of the Dynastic period, however, it would seem that the author does not consider the Ptolemaic administration a legitimate reflection of Egyptian kingship. But the Greeks hardly receive the execration in the *Demotic Chronicle* that the Persians do. This may suggest that the priestly milieu that predicted a "messianic" native king remained fairly close to those milieus that advertised the Ptolemies as legitimate, as if the text were claiming, "The Ptolemies are better rulers than the Persians, but still not legitimate according to the traditional form."[67]

It is conceivable, however, that the author aimed at a protective subtlety, to prophesy against the Ptolemies but not to antagonize them directly.[68] A major theme of the text is the invasion of the foreigner, a

---

égyptienne et commentaires esséniens," in *A la rencontre de Dieu* [Mémorial Albert Gelin], Bibliothèque de la faculté catholique de théologie de Lyon 8 [Le Puy: Éditions Xavier Mappus, 1961], 203–21).

65. See Janet H. Johnson, "The Demotic Chronicle as a Statement of a Theory of Kingship," *Journal of the Society for the Study of Egyptian Antiquities* 13 (1983):66–72.

66. Braun suggests that the Alexander romance of Pseudo-Callisthenes is a deliberate extension of a nationalistic "Nektanebos romance" composed during the Persian period (*History and Romance,* 23–24). On priestly propaganda in favor of Ptolemies, see Koenen, "Die Adaptation ägyptischer Königsideologie," 143–90; Johnson, "Anti-Greek Tract?" 115–20; and Griffiths ("Edfu Temple Texts," 174–79), who discusses the evidence at the Upper Egyptian temple of Edfu for a xenophobic propaganda used in support of the Ptolemies and their military protection of Egypt.

67. Johnson, "Anti-Greek Tract?" 107–24.

68. Note that this text remains in Demotic, whereas other prophecies, both pro- and anti-Ptolemy, were translated into Greek. The use of Demotic would ensure that the text could not circulate outside the priesthood.

persistent theme of the lapse of kingship in *Chaosbeschreibung*; and it is quite likely that Greeks are implicitly included as members of this class, for a final oracle about "dogs" probably refers to them. One sees, then, in muted form, the use of traditional ideology in tension with contemporary political realities. The *Demotic Chronicle* is not "anti-Greek" per se but sets up an ideal contrast to Ptolemaic rule, which implicitly casts the latter as "a time of foreign domination," and thus as illegitimate.[69]

The rebellion, the messianic king from Herakleopolis, and the Egypt that he will purify of foreigners all constitute a prediction of an ideal scenario. These traditional themes represent an author's attempt at using *Chaosbeschreibung* to separate kingship ideology from the real, illegitimate administration of Egypt, by projecting a series of "revolutionary" events into a future context. Presumably, the *Sitz-im-Leben* of such a novel use of kingship ideology would have been the rivalry of the Herakleopolis oracle priesthood with the Memphis priesthood (which benefited substantially from Ptolemaic rule).[70]

The Oracles of the Lamb and the Potter

In contrast to the muted anti-Hellenism of the *Demotic Chronicle*, a series of oracles emanating from the temples of the god Khnum during the uprisings of the mid-second century B.C.E. articulated the religious nationalism of the kingship ideology in increasingly stronger terms, applying the images of *Chaosbeschreibung* specifically to the dominion of the Ptolemies.

The priesthoods of Khnum, whose chief centers were Herakleopolis (the source of the *Demotic Chronicle*) and Elephantine, had actively circulated oracular propaganda with explicitly nationalist overtones since the Late period.[71] Khnum was revered as the mythical potter and

---

69. Cf. J. Gwyn Griffiths, "Apocalyptic in the Hellenistic Era," in Hellholm, ed., *Apocalypticism in the Mediterranean World*, 279–80, 283; and Lloyd, "Nationalist Propaganda," 41–45. Johnson argues that the Greeks are criticized here as not ruling in accordance with *Ma'at*, but not simply because they were foreign ("Anti-Greek Tract?" 122–244; cf. idem, "Theory of Kingship," 72).

70. Lloyd, "Nationalist Propaganda," 41, 45. See also Dorothy J. Thompson, "The High Priests of Memphis under Ptolemaic Rule," in *Pagan Priests*, ed. Mary Beard and John North (Ithaca, N.Y.: Cornell University Press, 1990), 97–116.

71. Cf. Lloyd, "Nationalist Propaganda," 41, 45; Dunand, "L'Oracle du Potier," 61; L. Kákosy, "Prophecies of Ram Gods," *AOH* 19 (1966):341–56; J. F. Borghouts, "The Ram as a Protector and Prophesier," *REg* 32 (1980):33–46. The Elephantine papyri disclose violent conflicts between the Jewish temple of Elephantine and the priests of Khnum around the time of the invasion of Cambyses (ca. 525 B.C.E.); cf. Lloyd, "Late Period," 317.

creator, symbolized as a ram, whence arose a tradition around the Mediterranean world of a ram, or lamb, often four-headed, that uttered prophecies.[72] From this tradition arose *Königsnovelle* "frames" for oracles circulated under the authority of Khnum: Khnum was represented either as a lamb speaking before the legendary king Bocchoris (in the *Oracle of the Lamb*) or as a potter disclosing the future of Egypt before another legendary king, Amenhotep (as in the *Oracle of the Potter*).[73] Within such traditional narrative settings a *Chaosbeschreibung* discourse was delivered; but it now was presented as a prophecy for an Egypt that lacked a legitimate pharaoh and suffered under the sway of foreign rulers.

This latter scenario marks a significant contrast to and development from that of *Neferti*, whose prophecy of disintegration and reconstitution before the legendary king Snefru bore no connection with the reign of King Snefru himself. With stories such as that of Bocchoris, the prophecy itself is supposed to take place during a period of national catastrophe (e.g., Egypt under King Bocchoris), rather than during a neutral or glorious period in which it predicts calamities to come.[74] This new interconnection between the frame narrative and the tableaus of *Chaosbeschreibung* appears throughout Egyptian literature of the Hel-

72. Manetho frag. 64 and 65: "The twenty-fourth dynasty: Bochchoris of Sais . . . in his reign a lamb spoke," ed. W. G. Waddell, *Manetho*, LCL [Cambridge and London: Harvard University Press, 1940]; Aelian (*De nat. animal.* 12.3) describes the oracular lamb as eight feet tall, with two tails, two heads, and four horns. The god Amun, whose principal temple was in Thebes, was also represented as a lamb and also produced oracles—the most famous of which was the god's "recognition" of Alexander in the oasis shrine of Siwah; see Kákosy, "Prophecies of Ram Gods"; and Borghouts, "Ram as Protector and Prophesier." The Theban priesthood was quite active in sparking nationalistic rebellion against Ptolemaic rule during the second century B.C.E.; cf. Claire Préaux, "Esquisse d'une histoire des révolutions égyptiennes sous les Lagides," *Chronique d'Égypte* 22 (1936):530–32, 549–52; Maurice Alliot, "La Thébaïde en lutte contre les rois d'Alexandrie sous Philopator et Épiphane (216–184)," *Revue belge de philologie et d'histoire* 29 (1951):422–23, 432, 438; Edwyn R. Bevan, *House of Ptolemy* (Chicago: Ares, 1985), 335–37.

73. On the *Oracle of the Lamb*, see Weill, *La fin du moyen empire*, 114–19; McCown, "Egyptian Apocalytic Literature," 392–97; Griffiths, "Apocalyptic in the Hellenistic Era," 286–87; and the new edition and translation by Karl-Theodor Zauzich, "Das Lamm des Bokchoris," in *Papyrus Erzherzog Rainer (P.Rainer Cent.)* (2 vols.; Vienna: Verlag Brüder Hollinek, 1983), 1:165–74. Lysimachus also refers to a Bocchoris legend in his account of the "Invasion of the Impure," cited in Josephus, *Against Apion* §§304–11). On the use of the Khnum tradition in the *Potter's Oracle*, see P.Graf 29787 (= text P¹), in Koenen, "Prophezeiungen des 'Töpfers,'" 195–98 (and discussion, 182–86). The *Potter's Oracle* makes explicit use of the *Lamb's Oracle* in P³, ll. 33–34 ("(He) is the one who will bring the evils to the Greeks, as the Lamb announced to Bacharis [sic]"); on this verse, see Koenen, "Supplementary Note," 9–13.

74. Cf. Weill, *La fin du moyen empire*, 117.

lenistic period. In one story, reported by the first-century C.E. priest Manetho, the legendary king Amenophis discovers a written prophecy that during his reign Egypt will be invaded and despoiled by an impure people associated with Seth–Typhon. Accepting the fate as divinely ordained, Amenophis gathers all the sacred images and retreats to Memphis.[75] In the *Alexander Romance* of Pseudo-Callisthenes, King Nektanebos, himself blessed with clairvoyance (and therefore without need of a secondary prophet), learns that Egypt will be imminently invaded by hordes from many nations and, indeed, that this was the gods' design. He escapes to Macedonia, leaving Egypt with nothing but an oracle that "'this king who has fled will come again to Egypt, not in age but in youth, and our enemy the Persians he shall subdue'"[76]—that is, to wit, Alexander the Great.

The *Chaosbeschreibung* discourse of the *Oracle of the Lamb* concludes with explicit references to the Assyrian invasions and a deportation of images (analogous to King Amenophis's removal of holy images to Memphis before the invasion of the impure). Strikingly, order is restored not in connection with a king but through the Egyptians' rescue of the images after a nine-hundred-year period. Although the "latest" foreign power mentioned in the text is the "Medes," this does not imply that the text was written before the Ptolemaic period.[77] The extension of the times of distress over a nine-hundred-year period means that the foreign dominations might also be understood as relevant to a reader (or audience) of Ptolemaic or Roman times.[78] Indeed, the *Lamb's Oracle* is a good example of a typological use of Assyria and Persia as archetypal enemies, a status that was never attained by ῾Ελληνικοί.[79]

75. Manetho, frag. 54 (= Josephus *Apion* §§236–50); cf. Weill, *La fin du moyen empire*, 77–78, 118–20, on the use of traditional motifs in this story.

76. Pseudo-Callisthenes *Alexander Romance* 1.1–3 (tr. Ken Dowden, "Pseudo-Callisthenes: The Alexander Romance," in *Collected Ancient Greek Novels*, ed. B. P. Reardon [Berkeley: University of California Press, 1989], 656).

77. *Or. Lamb* 2.21–23: "And it will happen that the Mede who had turned his sight upon Egypt will depart after Foreigners and their other places. Injustice will perish. Right and Order will be established again in Egypt" (Ger. tr. Zauzich, "Der Lamm," 168).

78. Cf. Koenen, "Supplementary Note," 11 n. 12: "The passage seems to have been written without knowledge of, or without acknowledging, the Greek rule in Egypt. . . . The latter might have been possible before such oracles turned decisively anti-Greek in the 2nd cent. B.C." It is difficult to agree with his argument that Manetho's reference to an oracular Lamb (frag. 64/65) provides a *terminus ante quem* for the extant *Oracle of the Lamb*, for Manetho gives no indication that he was familiar with more than a tradition (or, at most, a *Vorlage* text) of the Lamb prophesying to Bocchoris about a "990 years" (frag. 64, ed. Waddell, *Manetho*, 164).

79. Although cf. P.Tebt. Tait 13, l. 7, in Tait, *Papyri from Tebtunis*, 47 and note j. The *Potter's Oracle* uses ζωνοφόροι ("girdle-wearers") to refer to Greeks, on which see

Salvation from the present chaos is therefore precluded during the time of the Greeks because of the excessively long waiting period of nine hundred years. This period, which Ludwig Koenen calculated to last until approximately 139 C.E., was meant to coincide with the turning of the Sothis period, a solar cycle that implied the renewal of the world.[80] The reintegration of Egypt was meant to occur not so much through the accession of any particular king as by the turn of the eons (so it would appear from the extant text in the manuscript). The solar associations of the Sothis tradition clarify the "royal" implications of the end of chaos, for the return of the royal sun god, Re, is the primary myth here. It is only in the briefest allusion that the *Oracle of the Lamb* prophesies the messianic pharaoh: "He of the 55 (years?) (is) our crowned one(?)."[81] In general, the Bocchoris story anticipates a single, culminative "millennium" of Re—a marked development from the cycle of *Chaosbeschreibung* and reconstitution in *Neferti*, which was understood to reflect any pharaoh's accession at any time.

Because of its long "premillennial" period, the *Lamb's Oracle* might appear to have been impractical as propaganda for a particular pretender to the throne of Egypt during the Hellenistic period. The *Potter's Oracle*, however, uses the *Oracle of the Lamb* in such a way as to suggest that revolutionary propaganda was historically composed on the basis of the *Lamb's Oracle*. Indeed, the *Potter's Oracle*—now extant in three Greek papyri[82]—appears to be a response to propaganda issued, in the name of Khnum or Amun, in support of one Harsiesis, a "counterpharaoh" around whom a rebellion began in the Thebaid around 130 B.C.E., to be crushed by Ptolemy Euergetes II in 129.[83]

Roberts, "Oracle of the Potter," 91 n. 3; and Koenen, "Prophezeiungen des 'Töpfers,'" 187. On the significance of "Mede" in Egypt, see David F. Graf, "Medism: The Origin and Significance of the Term," *JHS* 104 (1984):22–24. On the typological use of Assyria and Persia in the *Lamb's Oracle*, see Weill, *La fin du moyen empire*, 116; Arnaldo Momigliano, "Some Preliminary Remarks on the 'Religious Opposition' to the Roman Empire," in *Opposition et résistances à l'empire d'Auguste à Trajan* (Geneva: Vandoeuvres, 1986), 113; and, more generally, below, chap. 8, pp. 216–22.

80. Koenen, "Prophecies of a Potter," 253. Previous scholars have viewed the resulting date as the historical time of the redactor; cf. Weill, *La fin du moyen empire*, 116.

81. *Or. Lamb* 2.5 (Ger. tr. Zauzich, "Der Lamm," 168).

82. P¹ (= P.Graf 29787), from the second century C.E., has only the *Königsnovelle* frame introduction; P² (= P.Rainer 19 813), from the third century C.E., contains the prophecy and the conclusion to the frame story; P³ (= P.Oxy 2332), from the later third century C.E., resembles P² but lacks the frame ending and appears to have undergone several interpolations.

83. Koenen, "Prophezeiungen des 'Töpfers,'" 186–91. Harsiesis's success in the Thebaid was such that one papyrus has a date based on his kingship years (P.Kakara I, II; cited in ibid., 191).

On the basis of the other Egyptian kingship propaganda we have surveyed and from the material in the extant *Potter's Oracle*, we may conclude that this Harsiesis propaganda must have consisted of: (1) a *Chaosbeschreibung* discourse that, referring implicitly to the present state of Egypt, effectively denigrated the Ptolemies; (2) (within the latter material) specific references to Greeks and Greek domination as Typhonic (that is, associated with the Seth–Typhon), to clarify the immediate nature and the cause of chaos in Egypt; (3) the advent of a true pharaoh (as the fifty-five-year ruler of the *Lamb's Oracle*), described in such a way as to indicate Harsiesis with certainty; and (4) a prophecy of this king's expulsion of the foreigners, reestablishment of shrines, and restoration of *Ma'at* throughout the land. The genre of presentation would have been an oracle in the name of Amun or Khnum.

According to Ludwig Koenen's analysis, the *Oracle of the Potter* was composed specifically to denigrate Harsiesis's claims to kingship, to portray him as a foreigner, and to redirect expectations of the "fifty-five-year ruler" to an ideal pharaoh in the future, "sent from Helios" (that is, Re) and established by Isis.[84] Then, in a subsequent recension of the *Potter's Oracle* (represented in an Oxyrhynchus papyrus, designated as P³), an editor shifted the prophetic expectation from the "messianic" pharaoh to the renewal of the Sothis cycle itself.[85] Through this scheme, the *Potter's Oracle* "returns" to the eschatology of the *Lamb's Oracle* to imply (1) that it is the cosmos's renewal that allows the reestablishment of kingship, rather than (2) that the establishment of kingship per se renews the cosmos. *Chaosbeschreibung* and its salvific resolution thus become entirely prophetic visions of an eschaton.[86]

---

84. The *Potter's Oracle* describes Harsiesis's career in the mode of *vaticinium ex eventus*: "From Ethiopia there will arise [. . .] he from among the profane ones [ἀνοσίων] (will come) to Egypt, and he will settle [in the city, which] will afterwards be deserted— and he (was) our man of two years . . . and Amun spoke well" (*Or. Pot.* P² 16–20 [= P³ 30–31]; ed. Koenen, "Prophezeiungen des 'Töpfers,'" 202–3). This Ethiopian is almost certainly Harsiesis and the "city," Panopolis, which Harsiesis chose as his stronghold but which was destroyed with his defeat and no longer permitted to be rebuilt (Koenen, "Prophezeiungen des 'Töpfers,'" 188; and Bevan, *House of Ptolemy*, 317). In labeling him an "Ethiopian" the scribe implicitly denigrates him as a foreigner, a slight perhaps explicable by the fact that Ethiopia dominated the Thebaid during the Late period. The "two years" reference, however, was taken from the *Lamb's Oracle*, which prophesied "he of the 2 (years?), which (?) is not our (crowned one?)" to precede the true king of fifty-five years; in the *Potter's Oracle* it has been applied to Harsiesis's two-year reign as if it had been predicted (Koenen, "Supplementary Note," 12).

85. *Or. Pot.* ms. P³ interpolates: "[That man] was not ours; the one who is ours of the fifty-five years will bring the evils to the Greeks which the Lamb announced to Bacharis" (ll. 31–34; ed. Koenen, "Prophezeiungen des 'Töpfers,'" 203).

86. Koenen ("Prophecies of a Potter," 253–54) and Smith ("Wisdom and Apocalyptic,"

As in the *Lamb's Oracle*, the *Oracle of the Potter* focuses on the deportation and salvific return of religious images ("the divine statues [ἀγάλματα] of Egypt, which were transported there, will return to Egypt again").[87] Other traditional themes drawn from the *Chaosbeschreibung* tradition include abandonment of the land ("the land will fall into confusion, and not a few of those inhabiting Egypt will abandon their homes (and) go forth to foreign lands");[88] invasion by typical Eastern armies ("A king will come from Syria, who will be hateful to all men . . . the city which was founded by the foreigners[89] will be deserted, and these things will take place at the end of the evils [of the time] when hordes [φυλλόροια] of foreign men came into Egypt");[90] and celestial problems, the decline of fertility, and social strife:

> The sun will be blotted out [ἀμαυρωθήσεται] (as it will be) unwilling to behold the evils (occurring) in Egypt. The earth will not respond to seeds; these things will be part of its blight; the farmer will be charged for taxes on what he did not (even) plant, and they will fight in Egypt among each

---

152–53) propose that the *Potter's Oracle* thereby became an "apocalypse," because the eschatology was cosmic, as opposed to nationalist–millennialist propaganda for a specific person, and because the vision itself seems to have circulated without the frame (in the case of the two third-century papyri, P² and P³). Because the definition of the genre "apocalypse" has been disengaged from the criterion of eschatology (by such scholars as Rowland and Himmelfarb; see above, p. 41 n. 30), Koenen's and Smith's observations merely show that the *Oracle of the Potter* came to circulate as a solitary *Chaosbeschreibung* discourse, rather than in the literary frame of the *Königsnovelle*, and that the priestly eschatology of its authors, like that of most eschatological visionaries of the Greco-Roman period, came to synthesize and emphasize concepts of astrological determinism; cf. Franz Cumont, "La fin du monde selon les mages occidentaux," *RHR* 103 (1931):29–96.

87. *Or. Pot.* P² 34f (= P³ 57–58), ed. Koenen, "Prophezeiungen des 'Töpfers,'" 206–7. This motif of *Chaosbeschreibung* may also reflect traditions or experiences of the priesthood of Khnum. Koenen views the "passive" return of images to Egypt in the *Potter's Oracle* as significant of the impotence of real kings—that the heroic king desired would bring them back himself (ibid., 181), as Amenophis presumably would in the legend of the impure invaders. But as Griffiths observes, a military return of icons is not the case in the *Oracle of the Lamb* either, for there the people bring them back ("Apocalyptic in the Hellenistic Era," 290 n. 80). It is probable that the statues would be returned by virtue of the king's establishment of *Ma'at*, which would reconcile all things generally. Cf. also Mahé, *Hermès en Haute-Égypte*, 2:97–100, on the concept of sacred statuary in Greco-Roman Egypt.

88. *Or. Pot.* P² 21–23 (ed. Koenen, "Prophezeiungen des 'Töpfers,'" 202–4).

89. Literally: "The city of the foreigners, which was founded."

90. *Or. Pot.* P² 16–17, 30–32 (= P³ 30–31, 53–54); ed. Koenen, "Prophezeiungen des 'Töpfers,'" 202–3, 206–7. Roberts and Koenen are convinced that the "king from Syria" is an *ex eventu* reference to Antiochus Epiphanes, who invaded and occupied Egypt between 170 and 168 B.C.E. (Roberts, "Oracle of the Potter," 92, 98 n. 30; Koenen, "Prophezeiungen des 'Töpfers,'" 187); but this interpretation is unnecessary, for by this time the invasion of Syrians was a prophetic *topos*.

other because of their need for food; for what they plant another reaps and runs off (with it).[91]

Finally, with the departure of Ἀγαθὸς Δαίμων (the spirit of civic fortune) from the city of the foreigners (Alexandria) and its reinstatement in Memphis,[92] and as the city is abandoned and diminishes to the status of a fishing village,[93] a king "descended from Helios" will appear, "established by the greatest goddess Isis."[94] Under this king's reign all things return to order even to the point that "the living might pray that the deceased rise up to share in the prosperity."[95]

Conclusion

Thus, from the *Demotic Chronicle* through the *Potter's Oracle*, the *Chaosbeschreibung* discourse is increasingly applied to "current times" in Egypt, to characterize experience—whatever its realities—as an interregnal period that is by nature chaotic and awaiting the accession of a "King from Re, installed by Isis."

In a wider sense, however, the Nektanebos literature, the legends of Khnum, and the intertextuality of the prophecies themselves all reflect a scribal culture actively engaged in the collection, reworking, and dissemination of classical themes and legends. As Rome took control and the priesthoods became increasingly alienated from the government, we

91. *Or. Pot.* P² I, 7–10 (= P³ I, 18–23), ed. Koenen, "Prophezeiungen des 'Töpfers,'" 200–203).
92. *Agathos Daimon* represents the "divine blessing" upon Alexandria. However, the fact that it leaves Alexandria, the artificial city of the Hellenists, for Memphis (P² 29 [= P³ 52]), the traditional seat of priestly and pharaonic power, suggests that the author wants to portray a traditional Egyptian divine force: Psai, a native chthonic deity. See W. W. Tarn, "The Hellenistic Ruler-Cult and the Daemon," *JHS* 48 (1928):215–16, 218–19; P. M. Fraser, *Ptolemaic Alexandria*, 3 vols. (Oxford: Clarendon, 1972), 1:210–11.
93. *Or. Pot.* P² 35 (= P³ 59), ed. Koenen, "Prophezeiungen des 'Töpfers,'" 206–7. McCown is probably correct in understanding this phrase in the sense of Ez 26:5, 14 (LXX), "a place for the spreading of nets" (McCown, "Egyptian Apocalyptic Literature," 398 n. 79), because the author obviously wants to give as great a contrast as possible to the bustling merchant city of Alexandria.
94. Isis rose in both popular and politico-religious domains to virtually monolatrous status during the Greco-Roman period. In classical Egyptian religion, Isis was identified with the throne of the pharaoh. During the Hellenistic period she absorbed the symbolism and function of the goddess *Maʾat* (cosmic order and justice as mediated through the pharaoh), came to signify the maintenance of social and familial relationships, and—as enforcer of cosmic order—was identified with goddesses around the Mediterranean as an international *kosmokratrix*. The context in which Isis would have been understood to "install" a messianic pharaoh by (especially Memphite) priests of this period has been exhaustively studied by Jan Bergman, *Ich bin Isis: Studien zum memphitischen Hintergrund der griechischen Isisaretalogien*, Acta Universitatis Upsaliensis, Historia Religionum 3 (Uppsala: Uppsala University Press, 1968); see also notes by J. Z. Smith, "Native Cults in the Hellenistic Period," *HR* 11 (1971):236–49.
95. *Or. Pot.* P² 28–43 (= P³ 50–71), ed. Koenen, "Prophezeiungen des Töpfers,'" 204–7.

see the "Houses of Life," the temple scriptoria, working ever more feverishly to disseminate nostalgic accounts of great kings, angry accounts of invasions, pessimistic views of the present, and fantastic prophecies of a messianic pharaoh. A. Moret has well expressed the growing archivism of the priesthoods in connection with Egypt's historical vicissitudes:

> The most critical moments of national life were those where legends spontaneously flourished: at the time of the Ethiopian invasion the death of Bocchoris, at the time of the Persian invasion the disappearance into Egypt of Nectanebo II, made these last national Pharaohs enter the kingdom of legend whence they would perpetually return, armed with all the resources of magic, to correct situations and prepare the future resurrection of Egypt.[96]

Excursus: The Prophetic Motifs
of *Chaosbeschreibung*

The *Chaosbeschreibung* form in the history of Egyptian literary tradition involved a limited spectrum of motifs, all of which were inspired by authors' contemplations of the land and the cosmos without the integrating power of the pharaoh. As the mythical function of Egyptian kingship changed little between the second millennium B.C.E. and the Roman period (if anything, it gained a more idealized character), so the contemplation of that kingship's opposite—disorder and catastrophe—retained a constant selection of motifs (if anything, it gained greater detail over time). On the basis of the literature discussed so far, then, one may typologize *Chaosbeschreibung* into the following categories of motifs. They are listed here in the order of the importance the literature seems to attribute to them; however, in the texts themselves the categories and motifs are all interwoven. (It should be noted that the second and third categories, Chaos in Earth and Collapse of Borders, fall under the rubric of "threats of Seth–Typhon," demonstrating *Chaosbeschreibung*'s basis in mythology as well as kingship ideology.)

    1. Chaos in Society: Disintegration of the Social Order[97]
       a. interruption of family structure and life
          (1) suicide
          (2) strife among blood relatives
          (3) cessation of childbirth
          (4) infanticide
          (5) improper mortuary practices
       b. internal social strife and rebellions

---

96. Moret, "Horus sauveur," 286.
97. Assmann has emphasized social reversal and disintegration as axial to the entire ideology of *Chaosbeschreibung* ("Königsdogma und Heilserwartung," 357, 357 n. 55); cf. Posener, *De la divinité du pharaon*, 56–57.

      c. abandonment of villages and cities

      d. disintegration of religious cult

         (1) destruction of temples

         (2) disclosure of priestly secrets

         (3) removal of sacred icons

         (4) departure of gods[98]

   2. Chaos in Earth: Fertility and the Nile

      a. encroachment of desert

         (1) approach of desert animals[99]

         (2) activity of reptiles and scorpions[100]

      b. agricultural decline[101]

         (1) famine

         (2) drought

      c. drying of Nile

         (1) Nile running with blood (instead of water)[102]

---

98. The explicit description of the departure of the gods only appears in literature of the Greco-Roman period, particularly in the *Perfect Discourse;* however, J. Gwyn Griffiths has found another, etiological version of this *Chaosbeschreibung* motif which involves Seth (who pursues the Egyptian gods) and shows the motif's more ancient roots ("The Flight of the Gods before Typhon: An Unrecognized Myth," *Hermes* 88 [1960]:374–76). Cf. the *Potter's Oracle,* in which the *Agathos Daimon* of Alexandria departs to be reinstated in Memphis.

99. *Neferti* predicts that "desert flocks will drink at the river of Egypt, take their ease on the shores for lack of one to fear" (ll. 35–37; tr. Lichtheim, 1:141). The *Book of Overthrowing Apep* instructs the priests to make "an antelope bound and fettered, and it shall be thus inscribed: 'Apep, the Fallen'" (P.Bremner-Rhind 32.52–53; tr. Faulkner, "Bremner-Rhind Papyrus—IV," 53). In the Horus stelae (see above, p. 165), the child Horus holds "Sethian" animals in each hand, including antelopes, while a terra-cotta image of the protective god Bes shows him seated, victoriously, upon an antelope: see the discussion by Jean LeClant, "A propos d'une terre cuite de Bès à l'Oryx," *Hommages à Lucien Lerat,* 2 vols., ed. Hélène Walter, Centre de recherches d'histoire ancienne 55 (Paris: "Les Belles Lettres," 1984), 1:409–19. Antelopes were probably classed as dangerous not only by reason of their desert habitat but also because they could damage crops.

100. See n. 99, above. Just as "the serpent did not bite in the age of the primeval gods," according to a classical Egyptian cosmogony (*Urk.* 8.81; tr. Kákosy, "Fallen State of the World," 206), so in the last days, according to the *Apocalypse of Shenoute,* "wild animals will leave their caverns and crags; they will bite disobedient people; and these bites will make them suffer for six months, just as when a scorpion stings a person" (tr. E. Amélineau, *Monuments pour servir à l'histoire de l'Égypte chrétienne aux IV^è et V^è siècles, Memoires publiés par les membres de la mission archéologique française au Caire* 4 [Paris: Ernest Leroux, 1888], 344). Note the presence of scorpions and serpents to represent demonic danger in *Vita Antonii* chaps. 9, 12, 23, 24, 39. In chap. 41, Satan echoes Seth in complaining to Antony, "I no longer have a place"—he has been thwarted by the "new," Christian power of order, through the agency of Antony.

101. See Jacques Vandier, *La famine dans l'Égypte ancienne* (Cairo: IFAO, 1936); cf. the Byzantine apocalyptic uses of this motif cited in Wilhelm Bousset, *The Antichrist Legend,* tr. A. H. Keane (London: Hutchinson, 1896), 195–200.

102. In both *Ipuwer* and the *Perfect Discourse,* this image is associated with social strife and an excess of corpses (i.e., social chaos) rather than with drought.

3. Collapse of Borders
  a. invasion of "foreigners"
     (1) invasion of (Seth–)Typhonians
     (2) invasion of Asiatics[103]
        (a) invasion of Assyrians or Syrians
        (b) invasion of Persians[104]
        (c) invasion of "girdle-wearers"[105]
        (d) invasion of Jews
4. Chaos in the Heavens: Breakdown of the Celestial Order[106]
  a. disappearance (or darkening) of sun[107]
  b. disappearance (or darkening) of moon[108]

PRIESTHOOD AND ORACLES IN
THE ROMAN PERIOD

The *Demotic Chronicle*, the *Oracle of the Lamb to Bocchoris*, and the *Oracle of the Potter* all vividly mark the transition of the *Chaosbeschreibung* discourse from royal propaganda for a particular king (which demonstrated by contrast the integrative power he imposed in Egypt) to prophecies of calamity, referring to the present or imminent times, in anticipation of a "messianic" pharaoh. But whereas the *Demotic Chronicle* and the *Oracle of the Lamb* were composed and circulated for the most part in Demotic Egyptian—and therefore almost exclusively within priestly culture—the *Potter's Oracle* was translated into Greek, whence we have our complete versions.[109] As the medium of such

103. In *Neferti* (32–34) and *Ipuwer* (3.1), the invading foreigners were denoted by a general term for Oriental peoples.

104. Including "Medes"; cf. Graf, "Medism," 22–24.

105. ζωνοφόροι apparently denoting some aspect of military attire, this term is used to designate Greeks in the *Oracle of the Potter* and in the new Oxyrhynchus fragment of CPJ 520; cf. Roberts, "Oracle of the Potter," 91 n. 3; Koenen, "Prophezeiungen des 'Töpfers,'" 187.

106. This is a subsidiary motif of *Chaosbeschreibung* (which more reflects the effects of the lapse of kingship on land). By the Greco-Roman period, however, traditions of celestial portents became integrated into prophetic portrayals of eschatological chaos, as shown in the *Sibylline Oracles*.

107. For the significance of the solar eclipse in ancient Egypt, see primary sources in Ricardo A. Caminos, *The Chronicle of Prince Osorkon*, Analecta orientalia 37 (Rome: Pontifical Biblical Institute, 1958), 88–89; and Naphtali Lewis, *The Interpretation of Dreams and Portents* (Toronto: Stevens, 1976), 139–50. Cf. Posener, *De la divinité du pharaon*, 55–57. The darkening of the sun signified cosmic catastrophe or disorder in many Mediterranean cultures; see Jo Ann Hackett, *The Balaam Text from Deir ʿAllâ*, HSM 31 (Chico, Calif.: Scholars Press, 1984), 29, 75–76.

108. According to the Vienna Demotic lunar omina text (second/third centuries C.E.), odd moon phases or colorings generally correspond to invasions and social chaos in Egypt; see Parker, *Demotic Papyrus on Eclipse- and Lunar-Omina*, esp. 35–36.

109. Roberts includes a transcription of an extremely lacunose Greek papyrus, P.

translations from Demotic to Greek could only have been the priesthood, it is apparent that nationalist elements within the Egyptian priesthood had an interest in circulating these prophetic tracts outside their own enclaves.[110] By the Roman period in Egypt (and throughout the eastern Mediterranean world), Greek had become the major language not only for legitimizing one's native traditions and mythologies in a cosmopolitan mode but also for articulating anti-Greek, nationalist sentiments.[111] The translation and circulation of the *Potter's Oracle* in Greek also suggests that its compositional elements may have carried meaning and force outside Egyptian priestly circles. The presence in the *Third Sibylline Oracle* of a "King from Helios" prophecy (*Sib. Or.* 3.652–56), for example, shows the adoption of Egyptian forms of *Chaosbeschreibung* by Egyptian Jews.[112] The *Sibylline Oracles* themselves express a deliberate syncretization of various local prophetic traditions and motifs from around the Greco-Roman world, which authors accumulated and combined to draw the most effective eschatological scenarios.

The promulgation of the *Potter's Oracle* through the third century C.E., however, as well as of the Demotic text of the *Lamb's Oracle* (preserved

---

Trinity College Dublin 192b, which bears some similarities to the *Potter's Oracle* and which he believes might be a pre-250 B.C.E. copy of the same text ("Oracle of the Potter," 92 n. 3); but, given its condition, the relationship has yet to be shown. Most scholars believe the *Potter's Oracle* was originally written in Egyptian (e.g., Bevan, *House of Ptolemy*, 240; J.W.B. Barns, "Alexandria and Memphis: Some Historical Observations," *Orientalia* 46 [1977]:31; Lloyd, "Nationalist Propaganda," 50; *pace* Momigliano, "'Religious Opposition' to the Roman Empire," 111). The fragmentary Demotic prophecy P.Tebt.Tait 13 resembles the *Potter's Oracle*'s anti-Greek and pro-Memphite perspective; see Tait, *Papyri from Tebtunis*, 48; cf. also Eve A. E. Reymond, "Demotic Literary Works of Graeco-Roman Date in the Rainer Collection of Papyri in Vienna," in *Papyrus Erzherzog Rainer (P.Rainer Cent.)*, 2 vols. (Vienna: Verlag Brüder Hollinek, 1983), 1:50, on P.Vindob. D 9906/6758.

110. Cf. Koenen: "In all likelihood, the transmission of such prophecies was, in part, oral, with private copies made from hearsay and earlier private copies" ("Supplementary Note," 9 n. 2).

111. Cf. Fowden, *Egyptian Hermes*, 37, 43–44; and, esp., Glen W. Bowersock, *Hellenism in Late Antiquity* (Ann Arbor: University of Michigan Press, 1990).

112. John J. Collins has proposed that a Jewish courtier of Ptolemy VI may have viewed this king in such a salvific light that he used an Egyptian nationalist oracle to argue this perspective in local terms (*The Sibylline Oracles of Egyptian Judaism*, SBLDS 13 [Missoula, Mont.: Scholars Press, 1974], 41–44). Although an ingenious suggestion, it is based on no historical evidence other than the use of Egyptian kingship ideology to legitimize the Ptolemies. A more apt conclusion from the location the "King from Helios" oracle in a Jewish composition is that the oracle's "messianic" overtones held appreciable power among Jewish as well as Memphite circles. It is unnecessary to assume that traditional motifs such as this one must always refer to historical persons or events.

on a papyrus roll dated to ca. 7–8 c.e.), was also part of a movement of archaism and preservationism on the part of priesthoods.[113] Assessing the scribal character of the extant Demotic texts, Eve Reymond once suggested

> that there may even have been a general movement among members of the Egyptian priesthood towards building an archive of native literary traditions and works, one that continued into Roman times . . . a systematical collecting and copying of Egyptian historical romances written at various earlier dates. . . .
> . . . what has come down to us demonstrates the continuity of the literary traditions inspired by the events which followed the collapse of the New Kingdom. The subject-matters of the Fayyum narratives deal with war, civil wars, and, in particular with the war with the Assyrians.[114]

Thus, as much as the *Chaosbeschreibung* form and the *Königsnovelle* genre merged with other, similar forms and genres of the Mediterranean world, they also held a revered traditional status in the writing culture of Egypt throughout the Greco-Roman period.

Therefore it comes as little surprise to find, even in the period of the Apocalypse of Elijah, a profusion of Egyptian oracular texts composed— or merely copied—in imitation of the classical prophetic forms. A second-century Greek papyrus fragment combines the astrological specificity of lunar phases with a prediction of "disturbance" [ταραχή] in Egypt and has what appears to be an *ex eventu* reference to the *boukoloi*, a revolutionary bandit organization of the Roman period.[115] A second-century Demotic collection of "lunar omina" correlates lunar phases with invasions of Egypt, social breakdown, and the actions of the pharaoh.[116] A third-century Greek papyrus prophesies, in the manner of *Neferti*, class reversal combined with social strife, "famine and sickness," the trauma of royal abdication, and, finally, a time when "the king will be

---

113. See Dunand, *Religion populaire en Égypte romaine*, 126–27, 160. On the ideology of archaism, see E. J. Hobsbawm, "The Social Function of the Past: Some Questions," *Past and Present* 55 (1972):6–9.

114. Reymond, "Demotic Literary Works," 48; cf. 50, on *Oracle of the Lamb*. A similar phenomenon may be inferred from the Demotic magical texts of Roman date, e.g., the Demotic Magical Papyrus of London and Leiden.

115. P.Stanford G93bv (in John C. Shelton, "An Astrological Prediction of Disturbances in Egypt," *Ancient Society* 7 [1976]:209–13). On *boukoloi*, see ibid., 211; Jack Winkler, "Lollianos and the Desperadoes," *JHS* 100 (1980):175–81; Jean-Marie Bertrand, "Les Boucôloi ou le monde à l'envers," *REA* 90 (1988):139–49. The *ex eventu* prediction might refer to the anti-Roman revolt under Isidoros mentioned by Cassius Dio, *Historia* 72.4.

116. Parker, *Demotic Papyrus on Eclipse- and Lunar-Omina*, 35–52.

great and punish his adversaries."[117] A Demotic papyrus of the Roman period, bearing marked resemblances to the *Potter's Oracle*, envisions the destruction of Memphis in connection with "Greeks."[118] Another Demotic papyrus, of unspecified Roman date, organizes by astrological and Sothis phases predictions of rebellion, agricultural prosperity, Syrian military movements, and the defensive or beneficial activities of the pharaoh.[119] A third/fourth-century Greek papyrus, PSI 760, seems to prophesy disorder in all forms, from crocodiles to fire.

It is to such a general stream of Egyptian prophetic literature during the Roman period, and to the familiarity with the literary forms and motifs of Egyptian prophecy that this stream exemplifies, that we can ascribe the "core" prophecy of the Hermetic *Perfect Discourse*, a text that draws deeply from the *Chaosbeschreibung* tradition:[120]

> For all divinity will leave Egypt and will flee upward to heaven. And Egypt will be widowed; it will be abandoned by the gods. For foreigners will come into Egypt, and they will rule it. . . . And in that day the country that was more pious than all countries will become impious. No longer will it be full of temples but it will be full of tombs. . . . And Egypt will be made a desert by the gods and the Egyptians. And as for you, River, there will be a day when you will flow with blood more than water. . . . And he who is dead will not be mourned as much as he who is alive. . . . Darkness will be preferred to light and death will be preferred to life. No one will gaze into heaven. . . . In those days the earth will not be stable, and men will not sail the sea, nor will they know the stars in heaven. . . . And the lords of the earth will withdraw themselves. And they will establish themselves in a city that is in a corner of Egypt and that will be built toward the setting of the sun.[121]

117. P.Oxy 2554 (tr. Rea, in idem, "Predictions by Astrology," 81). The frame of this oracle is, strikingly, instructions for a magical rite (presumably integrating the oracle papyrus) to guarantee prosperity. The *Sitz-im-Leben* of the text would certainly have been private (although the source of the oracle proper may well have been oral-performative); cf. Koenen, "Supplementary Note," 9 n. 2.

118. P.Tebt. Tait 13 (in Tait, *Papyri from Tebtunis*, 45–48).

119. P.Cairo 31222 (in Hughes, "A Demotic Astrological Text," 256–64).

120. Mahé, *Hermès en Haute-Égypte*, 2:69–72 (on inactuality of historical references), 2:111–13 (on relationship of composition to Egyptian sources); *pace* Walter Scott, *Hermetica*, 4 vols. (Oxford, 1924–36; reprint, Boston: Shambhala, 1983), 1:61–76. Cf. also Jacques Schwartz, "Note sur la 'Petite Apocalypse' de l'*Asclepius*," *Revue d'histoire et de philosophie religieuse* 62 (1982):165–69; and Fowden, *Egyptian Hermes*, 37–44. On *Perfect Discourse* and Egyptian oracle tradition in general, see Dunand, "L'Oracle du Potier," 57–59; and Mahé, *Hermès en Haute-Égypte*, 2:72–97. Mahé rightly criticizes Dunand's supposition ("L'Oracle du Potier," 59) that the *Perfect Discourse* is dependent on the *Potter's Oracle*, as based on few textual parallels (Mahé, *Hermès en Haute-Égypte*, 2:78 n. 106, 79).

121. *Asclepius* 24–27 (= NHC VI, 8.70–75; tr. James Brashler, Peter A. Dirkse, and

Here and throughout Hermetic literature, one finds two other themes from the classical literature of *Chaosbeschreibung* that carry special emphasis: the decline of religion and ritual accuracy, and the exposure of ancient priestly secrets.[122] The crisis that would have inspired such sentiments of ritual decline, particularly in the Roman period, can be compared to the motivations behind the literary archaism of the priesthood: in both cases one can infer that the religious elite of Roman Egypt, no longer supported by the rulership, sensed a gradual diminishing of their authority, temples, and crafts.

Papyrus CPJ 520, a prophecy of the Roman period directed specifically against Jews, demonstrates another tradition from the Egyptian kingship ideology: that of identifying the *Chaosbeschreibung* motifs of invading foreigners and encroaching desert as manifestations of Seth–Typhon. Manetho and Chaeremon, Egyptian priests and national apologists from the third century B.C.E. and first century C.E. respectively, each responded to Jewish exodus accounts with a revisionist version from their own tradition, casting the Hebrews as defiled people who worshiped Seth, who were deliberately expelled from Egypt, and who then invaded Egypt, ravaging the countryside and (in particular) despoiling temples.[123] The apparent narrative basis to this story consisted of a

---

Douglas M. Parrott, *NHL*, 334–36). The city "in a corner of Egypt" is not necessarily Alexandria, an interpretation that would assume a subtly pro-Hellenistic bent to a prophecy that demonstrates a chauvinistic critique of Hellenism; cf. Mahé, *Hermès en Haute-Égypte*, 2:252; and B. Van Rinsveld, "La version copte de l'Asclépius et la ville de l'âge d'or," in *Textes et études de papyrologie grecque, démotique, et copte*, Papyrologica Lugduno-Batava 23 (Leiden: Brill, 1985), 233–42 (who assumes it is Alexandria).

122. Cf. *Corp. Herm.* 16.2: "As far as it is in your power, King, and you are powerful in all things, preserve the discourse [λόγος] from being translated, so that such great mysteries do not go to the Greeks, lest the arrogant, careless, fancy speech of the Greeks cause the meaning, the strength, and the empowered utterance of the words to be forgotten" (ed. Nock and Festugière, *Corpus Hermeticum*, 2:232). The Hermetic *Discourse on the Eighth and Ninth* (NHC VI, 6) instructs the novice to inscribe teachings in hieroglyphs on turquoise tablets "and write an oath in the book, lest those who read the book bring the language into abuse, and not (use it) to oppose the acts of fate" (*Disc.* 8–9, 61.25–31, tr. James Brashler, Peter A. Dirkse, and Douglas M. Parrott, *NHL*, 326–27). The same sentiments are reflected in *Ipuwer*: "The private chamber, its books are stolen, the secrets in it are laid bare. Lo, magic spells are divulged, spells are made worthless through being repeated by people" (*Ipuwer* 6.6–8, tr. Lichtheim, 1:155).

123. Manetho frag. 54 (= Josephus *Apion* 1.26 §§227–50), ed. Waddell, *Manetho*, 113–31; and Chaeremon frag. 1 (= Josephus *Apion* 1.26 §§218–92), ed. Pieter Willem Van Der Horst, in idem, *Chaeremon: Egyptian Priest and Stoic Philosopher*, EPRO 101 (Leiden: Brill, 1984), 8–9 (cf. 49–50 nn. 1–8, on use of Egyptian nationalist tradition). Egyptian nationalist anti-Judaism is also referred to by Plutarch *De Iside et Osiride* 31; cf. Griffiths, *Plutarch: De Iside et Osiride*, 418–19. A similar story seems to have been promulgated by the Alexandrian author Lysimachus (*apud* Josephus *Against Apion* 1. §§304–11).

legend of an invasion by an impure, impious people who had destroyed
Egyptian temples and pillaged Egypt. This legend was essentially a
retrojection into the mythical past of the *Chaosbeschreibung* invasion
topoi and of traditional accounts of historical invasions, all framed as a
prophecy once given to the legendary king Amenophis.[124] But Manetho
(or a subsequent editor)[125] and Chaeremon identified these ancient impure invaders as the Jews. Chaeremon included the vital detail that it
was the goddess Isis who had instructed the pharaoh to expel them,
presumably an idea already part of the tradition.

This image of Isis as militant national savior, which stems from her
role as installer of the king in the *Potter's Oracle* prophecy, becomes a
focal myth in CPJ 520: the Jews are "lawbreakers [παράνομοι] once
expelled from Egypt by the wrath of Isis."[126] "Attack the Jews!" the
prophecy then proclaims, for "impious people will despoil your temples
[τὰ ἱερα]" and "your largest temple will become sand for horses (or
crocodiles? [ἵππων])."[127] Indeed, the text warns that the Jews "will inhabit
the City of Helios."[128]

The papyri themselves come from the third century C.E.—roughly
contemporaneous with both of the *Potter's Oracle* manuscripts and the
Apocalypse of Elijah; and with both of these texts CPJ 520 shares
vocabulary and motifs.[129] However, it was more likely composed in

---

124. See Weill, *La fin du moyen empire*, 120–45; Yoyotte, "L'Égypte ancienne," 133–43;
and Stern, "Fragment of Graeco-Egyptian Prophecy," 119–20.

125. E.g., during the Alexandrian tensions of the mid-first century C.E. See John G.
Gager, *Moses in Greco-Roman Paganism*, SBLMS 16 (Nashville: Abingdon, 1972), 115–18;
cf. 119–20.

126. On Isis's militant nationalistic function in the Hellenistic period, see Bergman,
Ich bin Isis, 121–71; and Louis V. Zabkar, *Hymns to Isis in Her Temple at Philae*
(Hanover, N.H., and London: University Press of New England/Brandeis University
Press, 1988), 58–73.

127. Koenen, review of *CPJ*, vols. 2–3, ed. Victor Tcherikover and Alexander Fuks,
Gnomon 40 (1968):258; cf. Manteuffel, ed., "Zur Prophetie," 121, suggesting the meaning
"hippopotamus."

128. CPJ 520 (= PSI 982). I use a corrected reconstruction of this text, graciously
provided by Ludwig Koenen and based on an unpublished Oxyrhynchus papyrus.

129. A crucial "intertextual" link between the *Potter's Oracle* and CPJ 520 appears in
the new Oxyrhynchus fragment's use of the word ζωνοφόροι ("girdle-wearers") as a
metaphor for Greeks as invading foreigners.

Koenen understands an exhortation, "Don't let your city be depopulated," to refer to
Alexandria—that is, in a positive sense (review of *CPJ*, 258). This would indicate a
Greek milieu for author and audience, rather than one hostile to Alexandria in the first
place (as in the case of the *Potter's Oracle*). Because the Alexandrian mob was
responsible for much anti-Jewish activity and propaganda during the first century (see
Philo *Against Flaccus*; Josephus *War* 2:494–98; H. Idris Bell, *Jews and Christians in Egypt*

response to the Jewish messianic revolt of 116–117, when Jewish culture and activities had a far greater impact on Greco-Egyptian life than in the third century and when Egyptian peasants themselves were actively engaged in the defense of temples (CPJ 438).[130] Its recopying during the third century may be understood in connection with another papyrus fragment, CPJ 450, which attests to a local festival continuing in the late second century in Oxyrhynchus that celebrated victory over the Jews.[131] The discourse of this festival almost certainly articulated the (now legendary) victory of Egyptians over Jews in terms of the eradication of Typhonians. Even beyond this local ritual context for this oracle's continued significance, however, its recopying shows once again that oracles composed in the traditional manner—even for such specific circumstances—were valued, reread, and probably subjected to new interpretations in later times.[132]

[London: British Museum, 1924; reprint, Westport, Conn.: Greenwood, 1972], 10–21; idem, "Anti-Semitism in Alexandria," *JRS* 31 [1941]:10–21; Alan K. Bowman, *Egypt after the Pharaohs* [Berkeley: University of California Press, 1986], 209–17; Maria Pucci Ben Ze'ev, "Greek Attacks against Alexandrian Jews during Emperor Trajan's Reign," *JSJ* 20 [1989]:31–48), Koenen's interpretation is plausible; but the city likely refers to Memphis, whose priests would be more likely to use such a traditional prophecy to incite action. CPJ 439 is evidence that Memphis's defending army in 117 was able to defeat the Jews; in such circumstances the Memphite priesthood's use of such a hortatory prophecy would be understandable.

130. On the military services of the peasantry, see Alexander Fuks, "The Jewish Revolt in Egypt (A.D. 115–117) in the Light of the Papyri," *Aegyptus* 33 (1953):145, 153–54; idem in *CPJ* 2:236–38; and A. Kasher, "Some Comments on the Jewish Uprising in Egypt in the Time of Trajan," *JJS* 27 (1976):147–58. Under these circumstances, and considering the consequent wholesale extermination of Jews in Egypt, it is likely that priests were involved in the call to arms, as I argue in "Lest Egypt's City Be Deserted: Religion and Ideology in the Egyptian Response to the Jewish Revolt (116–117 C.E.)," *JJS* 43 (1992):203–20, a scenario that would allow a precise historical context for this oracle. Rémondon has discussed anti-Jewish ideology in the priestly center of Memphis in the first century B.C.E. ("Les antisémites de Memphis," 244–61); and CPJ 439 shows that the defenders of this city had a major victory over the Jews (because of the Memphite priesthood's exhortations?—cf. *Sib. Or.* 5.60–70). The association between CPJ 520 (= PSI 982) and the Jewish revolt was first suggested by Manteuffel, ed., "Zur Prophetie," 123–24.

131. On the native Egyptian participants in this festival, see Fuks, "Jewish Revolt in Egypt," 153–54; and idem in *CPJ* 2:260, note for ll. 30–35.

132. Therefore Stern may be incorrect in assuming that CPJ 520 is "evidence for anti-Jewish feelings in third-century Egypt" ("Fragment of Graeco-Egyptian Prophecy," 120); the reason for its recopying and preservation may have been its status as a traditional Egyptian prophecy. The social and economic decline of the third century C.E. may also account for the profusion of new and old oracles during this period (as is discussed below, chap. 9, pp. 249–57).

CONTINUITY OF *CHAOSBESCHREIBUNG* IN
LATE ROMAN EGYPT AND THE LITERARY CONTEXT
OF THE ELIJAH APOCALYPSE

As Egyptian priestly scribes and their counterparts in Coptic monasteries continued to copy, translate, interpret, and reapply the classical literary corpus through the Byzantine period, the motifs of *Chaosbeschreibung* found their way into a diverse range of texts: not only apocalypses and prophecies but also legends and historical romances.

Cambyses, the Persian king who invaded Egypt in 525 B.C.E., had been progressively demonized in Egyptian scribal memory and propaganda since the Hellenistic period. But in the Coptic Cambyses legend (pre-seventh century C.E.) and the *Chronicle of John of Nikiu* (ca. 690) this demonization reaches its apex.[133] The Cambyses legend demonstrates a thorough acquaintance with classical Egyptian genres, such as the fable and *Königsnovelle*, as well as traditionally "nationalist" views of foreign invasion. Both the Cambyses legend and the *Chronicle of John* strengthen their typically demonic view of Cambyses by identifying him with the biblical Nebuchadnezzar.[134] The *Chronicle of John* describes Cambyses as deporting Egyptians and—a familiar theme from *Chaosbeschreibung* tradition—the land of Egypt as consequently becoming desert. These texts have particular relevance for the use of "Persians" as the archetypal invaders in late antique Egyptian literature.

Chaosbeschreibung motifs also informed the representation of invasions and terrestrial catastrophe in the *Apocalypse of Shenoute*, which was added to Besa's *Life of Shenoute* near the time of the latter's translation into Arabic (ca. 685–690 C.E.). Here, too, the Arab invasion is cast in traditional terms as invasion by the "Persians," following which the Antichrist appears and the earth lurches into chaos and drought.[135]

---

133. See H. Ludin Jansen, *The Coptic Story of Cambyses' Invasion of Egypt*, Avhandlinger utgitt af det Norske Videnskaps-Akademi i Oslo 2, Hist.-Filos. Klasse 1950, 2 (Oslo: Jakob Dybwad, 1950); cf. Leslie S. B. MacCoull, "The Coptic Cambyses Narrative Reconsidered," *Greek, Roman, and Byzantine Studies* 23 (1982):185–88, which attempts a perhaps too exact reconstruction of this text's situation of origin; and R. H. Charles, *The Chronicle of John*, Texts and Translations Society 3 (London, 1916; reprint, Amsterdam: APA-Philo Press, 1981). Note that this increasing emphasis on the person of the "invader–king" and his "rule" continues a classical theme describing the state of royalty before the accession of the "savior–king"; cf. Weill, *La fin du moyen empire*, 45–68, 111–18.

134. These similarities suggest the possibility of common sources; cf. Jansen, *Coptic Story of Cambyses' Invasion*, 27.

135. Tr. Amélineau, in idem, *Monuments*, 338–48; cf. Rosenstiehl, 40–42; and above, pp. 25–26.

An eschatological discourse found among the Coptic Manichaean homilies and contemporaneous with the Apocalypse of Elijah makes broad use of Egyptian *Chaosbeschreibung* imagery, along with other traditions from the Mediterranean world.[136] Essential Egyptian *topoi* are used to describe both the decline of the world and its eschatological reintegration under "Jesus the Splendor." While there is no reason to expect the author made use of actual Egyptian texts in this case, the discourse demonstrates the spread of imagery that was once sensible only within Egyptian kingship ideology through the whole Mediterranean world, a process already found in the *Sibylline Oracle* collections. Yet the presence of such imagery in a missionary text translated for native Egyptian consumption can hardly have been coincidental, for these motifs were part of the *langue* of the Egyptian religious mentality.

Another text, the Arabic legend of an antediluvian king of Egypt, Surid, to whom Copts ascribed the building of the pyramids, drew on both *Chaosbeschreibung* and the classical *Königsnovelle* genre.[137] According to this legend, Surid had the pyramids built to house treasures and books of wisdom after priests reported to him a prophecy of the decline of Egypt, culminating in a flood and conflagration. Surid's preservation of holy objects in response to a prophecy of doom bears strong parallels to the legend of Amenophis, who removes all the holy animals and images to Ethiopia in response to a prophecy he reads concerning the invasion of the impure. The content of Surid's prophecy—conflagration, flood, cosmic portents—integrated many of the cosmic regeneration ideas of the Mediterranean world.[138]

In drawing on such a broad range of sources for their images of catastrophe—and, in the case of the Cambyses legend, referring his evil to a biblical archetype, Nebuchadnezzar—the scribes of the Byzantine period demonstrated a commitment to updating the old traditions, to appealing to new forms of authority and symbolism, and, by the same

---

136. Jakob Polotsky, *Manichäische Handschriften der Sammlung Chester Beatty* (Stuttgart: Kohlhammer, 1934), homily 2, 7.8–42.7; see Franz Cumont, "Homélies manichéennes," *RHR* 111 (1935):119–21; Doresse, "Visions méditerranéennes," 43–47; Ludwig Koenen, "Manichaean Apocalypticism at the Crossroads of Iranian, Egyptian, Jewish, and Christian Thought," in *Codex Manichaicus Coloniensis: Atti del Simposio Internazionale,* ed. Luigi Cirillo (Cosenza: Editore Marra, 1986), 285–332, esp. 321–26.

137. See A. Fodor, "The Origins of the Arabic Legends of the Pyramids," *AOH* 23 (1970):335–63, esp. 347–53; Sándor Fodor, "The Origins of the Arabic Surid Legend," *ZÄS* 96 (1970):103–9, esp. 107–9. S. Fodor suggests a late third-century C.E. date for a hypothetical Greek *Vorlage* of this legend ("Arabic Surid Legend," 107, 109).

138. See A. Fodor, "Arabic Legends of the Pyramids," 359–60; cf. 340–41, on the use of Enoch traditions in a similar etiology of the pyramids.

account, to comprehending new problems in traditional terms. This is evident in Mani's revelations in the case of the Coptic homily, the Arab invasion in the case of the *Apocalypse of Shenoute*, the phenomenon of the pyramids in the case of Surid, and the connection between biblical events and Egyptian history in John of Nikiu and Surid.

The Greek, Demotic, Coptic, and Arabic literature of the Roman period demonstrates the native character and cultural importance of *Chaosbeschreibung* as a form of discourse and a spectrum of *topoi*, applicable to a variety of immediate purposes but invariably expressive of the same perspective: the fragile stability of the relevant cosmos—society and fertility in Egypt—and its sensitivity to the vicissitudes of rulers. Within this context, it is clear that the Apocalypse of Elijah represented one more attempt to describe chaos and distress in Egypt and their resolution with the advent (in Egypt) of a "messianic" king.[139] Most importantly, the Elijah Apocalypse's composition would be fairly directly contemporaneous with the *Perfect Discourse*, CPJ 520, and a variety of other fragments of prophecy, including versions of the *Potter's Oracle*. The Apocalypse of Elijah stands apart not so much by its obviously Christian passages as by its addition of another period of sorrows and decline after the accession of a "king from the sun" (ApocEl 5:7-21, following 2:46-53). It is, therefore, Christ whom the text envisions as the real solar pharaoh (3:3).

---

139. See Wolfgang Kosack, *Die Legende im Koptischen: Untersuchungen zur Volksliteratur Ägyptens*, Habelts Dissertationdrucke, Reihe klassische Philologie 8 (Bonn: Habelt, 1970), 47–48, 92–93.

8

Vaticinia Sine Eventibus: The Use of Egyptian Chaosbeschreibung Tradition in the Apocalypse of Elijah

The last chapter presented a traditional "catalog" of motifs in Egyptian prophetic literature for envisioning social, national, terrestrial, and cosmic breakdown, motifs which were interlinked within the native ideology of kingship and its antithesis. During the second and third centuries C.E., both "pagan" and Christian Egyptian writings continued to employ this *Chaosbeschreibung* tradition to cast current oracles and legends in imagery of archaic resonance. These writings included copies (or recensions) of texts essentially composed during the Ptolemaic period (such as the *Potter's Oracle*) and texts composed during the Roman period in response to, or to incite activity in response to, specific events or circumstances (such as the Jewish revolt of 116–117).

ApocEl 2 can be understood as an extension of this literature, although integrated with the prophetic sentiments of Christians rather than those of (or beyond those of) the native priesthood. This chapter shows that the selection of motifs, dramatis personae of the preeschatological woes, and the "sphere of relevance" in ApocEl 2—Egypt, kingship, local religious sites—all bespeak the author's intentional continuity with traditional Egyptian prophetic literature.

Previous observations of this continuity notwithstanding, however, the history of scholarship on the Apocalypse of Elijah has sought to identify precise historical references in the course of the narrative, taking (for example) the references to "Persian" and "Assyrian" armies in

The nucleus of this chapter was delivered as a paper in the SBL Pseudepigrapha Group, November 1988, under the title "The Eschatological Discourse of the Apocalypse of Elijah: *Ex Eventu* or Imaginary?"

Egypt as literally reflecting historical events of some period.[1] The dating of texts is a necessary component of historical and textual scholarship, and often this must be accomplished through the use of internal (narrative) evidence. The assumption upon which such scholars' historical hypotheses rest, however, is that the symbolism of oracular literature has the essential function of "replacing" historical elements with other terms.

This assumption has been criticized in recent scholarship on the "historical" discourses in Jewish and Christian apocalypses, whose symbols—and the structures in which those symbols interact—manifestly reflect ancient Near Eastern mythological cycles.[2] John Collins has pointed out that "a literary allegory does not consist merely of a set of isolated correspondences, but tells its story in such a way that it reflects the pattern of a venerated older story."[3] Even in the the case of the *Sibylline Oracles*, *vaticinia ex eventus* are mixed with *vaticinia* that have no identifiable historical antecedent in the ancient world: "If one should consider the *Sibylline Oracles* a book of 'keys,'" observes Marcel Simon, "one ought well to recognize that some 'false keys' can be found there, which do not open any door."[4]

There are cases where historical antecedents to symbols can be identified, but in such cases the symbols themselves are often arranged in such a manner as to reflect mythological order rather than a chronicle's endeavor toward identifiability. Apocalypses and oracles of the Greco-Roman period tended especially toward numerological arrangements. Kings or animals would appear and interact in groups of four, seven, ten, twelve, or multiples of these. Because history itself does not unfold in such neat numerological arrangements, scholars have rightly examined the preference for certain numbers and the traditions that lay

---

1. See above, chap. 1, pp. 10–17.

2. Cf. Paul Ricoeur, "Foreword" to André Lacocque, *The Book of Daniel*, tr. David Pellauer (rev. ed., Atlanta: John Knox, 1979), xvii–xxvi; John J. Collins, *The Apocalyptic Vision of the Book of Daniel*, HSM 16 (Missoula, Mont.: Scholars Press, 1977); Paul A. Porter, *Metaphors and Monsters: A Literary-Critical Study of Daniel 7 and 8*, Coniectanea Biblica, Old Testament Series 20 (Lund: Gleerup, 1983), esp. 5–12; and John J. Collins, "Apocalyptic Literature," in *Early Judaism and Its Modern Interpreters*, ed. Robert A. Kraft and George W. E. Nickelsburg (Atlanta: Scholars Press, 1986), 349–52.

3. Collins, *Apocalyptic Vision*, 113–14.

4. Marcel Simon, "Sur quelques aspects des Oracles Sibyllines juifs," in *Apocalypticism in the Mediterranean World and the Near East*, ed. David Hellholm (Tübingen: Mohr, 1983), 224; cf. 222–24; and, in general, John J. Collins, "The Development of the Sibylline Tradition," in *ANRW* 2.20.1 (1987), 421–59.

behind them.[5] Both seven and twelve have ancient roots in Hebrew traditions of self-definition and cosmology; but by the Greco-Roman period, other cultures' speculations on the zodiac, the planets, and the Greek vowels would have been thoroughly synthesized into the symbolism of these numbers. Four, the cardinal number of directions and elements, had already in the Greco-Roman period achieved mythological status as the number of world empires preceding cosmic renewal; by this scheme, there must always be four empires and then a fifth "millennial" empire, however one actually identifies those empires with historical kingdoms.[6] The ancient world was replete with such numerological systems for arranging narrative; but it may be most useful to remember that these systems' origins lie not in specific scripture but in that same human penchant for "perfect" numbers and for ordered repetition of story that has always operated in folktales and epics.[7]

Numerology and numerological arrangement had a general function in casting a sense of order and certainty upon the world when there was, in actuality, none "out there."[8] Lars Hartman has likewise concluded that apocalyptic "timetables" such as those in Daniel 12, *Apocalypse of Abraham* 28–32, and 1 *Enoch* 93–105 had a *perlocutionary* ("practical") function in conveying to reader or audience a sense of identity or eschatological imminence, rather than a *locutionary* ("theoretical") function, "which would give precise answers to the 'what and when' concerning the future."[9] Both Hartman and Leonard Thompson have questioned the historicity of the tribulations prophesied in Mk 13:9-13 and the book of Revelation, on the basis that the theme of "tribulation" was both a

5. See Adela Yarbro Collins, "Numerical Symbolism in Jewish and Early Christian Apocalyptic Literature," in *ANRW* 2.21.2 (1984):1221–87.

6. Joseph Ward Swain, "The Theory of the Four Monarchies: Opposition History under the Roman Empire," *CP* 35 (1940):1–21: "The theory of four monarchies and a fifth included three elements: (1) it made each monarchy a world-empire; (2) it minimized everything else (e.g., pre-Alexandrian Greece and ancient Egypt); and (3) it declared that the fifth monarchy—which might or might not have appeared as yet—would be vastly superior to all its predecessors and last forever" (ibid., 13). Cf. David Flusser, "The Four Empires in the Fourth Sibyl and in the Book of Daniel," *Israel Oriental Studies* 2 (1972):148–75; and A. Yarbro Collins, "Numerical Symbolism," 1239–41.

7. Cf. Alex Olrik, "Epic Laws of Folk Narrative," tr. Jeanne P. Steager, in *The Study of Folklore*, ed. Alan Dundes (Englewood Cliffs, N.J.: Prentice-Hall, 1965), 132–36, 139–40; Max Lüthi, *The European Folktale: Form and Nature*, tr. John D. Niles (Bloomington: Indiana University Press, 1982), 32–33, 79; Jan Vansina, *Oral Tradition as History* (Madison: University of Wisconsin Press, 1985), 132–33.

8. As cogently suggested by Yarbro Collins, "Numerical Symbolism," 1224.

9. Lars Hartman, "The Functions of Some So-called Apocalyptic Timetables," *NTS* 22 (1976):12; cf. 2–3.

literary theme of early Jewish prophecy (Hartman) and a symbol of community self-definition with no verifiable historical basis (Thompson).[10] Robert Hodgson has also shown that Paul's lists of his tribulations—apparently sketching his various historical sufferings—actually had the illocutionary function of expressing his authority in the traditional terms of Greco-Roman heroes and holy men, with no intentional historical assertions.[11] It is clear that, for such religious texts, historical accuracy is not nearly as important as rhetorical or perlocutionary effect on an audience or community.

The problem in the interpretation of ApocEl 2 is therefore to ascertain which symbols or motifs might designate historical events in the life of the author and which function as "merely" ideal images in the tradition of *Chaosbeschreibung*, forming a literary pastiche of chaos. Because virtually all the symbols in that chapter of the Apocalypse of Elijah derive from the literary tradition of *Chaosbeschreibung*, this "identification" process must rely largely on guesswork, plausibility, and coincidence between the text and its historical period. Because the prophetic use of *Chaosbeschreibung* (in the *Potter's Oracle* as well as ApocEl 2) is supposed to describe future events, the function of such a discourse and its pseudohistorical configuration of motifs might very well be to lend a powerful verisimilitude to the prophetic reality. Indeed, the prophetic description of future events in the form of "signs" intrinsically casts a secret order and determinism over the imminent catastrophes, to offer the audience the sense of foreknowledge and preparation. Like the "woe" discourse in Mark 13, ApocEl 2 constitutes a series of warnings and signs, a predetermined layout of events whose eventual unfolding would appear chaotic to those "uninitiated."

By a different scheme, ApocEl 2 might be viewed as an a priori apocalyptic composition—in the words of Bernard McGinn, "making use of the already established apocalyptic scenario to interpret current

---

10. Lars Hartman, *Prophecy Interpreted: The Formation of Some Jewish Apocalyptic Texts and of the Eschatological Discourse Mark 13 Par.*, tr. Neil Tomkinson (Lund: Gleerup, 1966), esp. 145–77; cf. M. D. Hooker's suggestion "that the phrases [which Hartman perceives to be employed in Mark 13] are not Old Testament 'quotations,' connected by a concealed catch-phrase, but reflect a use of *traditional eschatological motifs*" (review of *Prophecy Interpreted*, by Lars Hartman, *JTS* 19 [1968]:265; emphasis mine); and see also David E. Aune, *Prophecy in Early Christianity and the Ancient Mediterranean World* (Grand Rapids: Eerdmans, 1983), 185; Leonard Thompson, "A Sociological Analysis of Tribulation in the Apocalypse of John," *Semeia* 36 (1986):147–74.

11. Robert Hodgson, "Paul the Apostle and First Century Tribulation Lists," *ZNW* 74 (1983):59–80.

events"—in contrast to an a posteriori composition, which reacts "to political and social change by expanding the scenario to include transcendentalized versions of recent events, thus giving final validation to the present by making a place for it at the end."[12] The a priori apocalyptic mode is tradition-oriented, whereas the a posteriori mode is the more creative and innovative. Granted, a strict separation between these modes would ignore the intrinsic creativity by which traditional symbolic systems lend themselves to "expansion," where new symbols are integrated into the traditional frameworks with no greater historical specificity.[13] McGinn's working distinction, however, properly characterizes ApocEl 2 in light of Egyptian *Chaosbeschreibung* and in contrast to certain *ex eventus* passages of the *Sibylline Oracles* (which could be called a posteriori by their use of historical detail). "Inherited apocalyptic language," McGinn states, "was a readily available, or *a priori*, way of interpreting contemporary events, especially conflict situations,"[14] by articulating contemporary issues in terms of ancient apocalyptic symbols and also by "realizing" the symbols themselves in the implied antecedent issues. One of the problems faced in the interpretation of ApocEl 2 is whether such a conflict situation is reflected analogically in the narrative or whether it lies behind the text as a whole, inspiring the author to invoke the *Chaosbeschreibung* tradition as an a priori image of reality.

For several reasons, then, one would expect the content of ApocEl 2 by its very nature to lie in tension with historical realities. Thus it is useful to state three presuppositions from which the identification of any of its historical antecedents must proceed: (1) One must look at literary precedents and traditions before seeking historical reflections,

---

12. Bernard McGinn, *Visions of the End: Apocalyptic Traditions in the Middle Ages*, Records of Civilization Sources and Studies 46 (New York: Columbia University Press, 1979), 33.

13. An example of this symbolic "expansion" would be the image of the Endtyrant, which is a synthesis of legendary events in the history of Israel (e.g., Nebuchadnezzar, Antiochus IV Epiphanes) with more contemporaneous "historical" legends (Nero) and traditional demonology (Belial). Gregory C. Jenks traces the development of this image into the Christian "Antichrist myth" (*The Origins and Early Development of the Antichrist Myth*, BZNW 59 [Berlin: de Gruyter, 1991], 153–68, 175–83, 199–327). Its manifestations in the New Testament vividly demonstrate its "historical" verisimilitude—its pretense to certainty—and yet its utter fantasy: Mk 13:14; 2 Thessalonians 2; Revelation 13. The important aspect of the Endtyrant tradition in any historical period was its ready applicability to leadership, emperors, or simply the times at hand—to render experience more meaningful by interpreting it as the realization of a priori tradition.

14. McGinn, *Visions of the End*, 35.

on the basis that the former will inevitably dominate and give meaning to the latter. (2) The prophetic discourse is a complex literary form whose performative function is more often illocutionary—establishing a perspective and reifying an ideological or social system (such as the predetermined structure of the eschaton for those who are blessed)—than locutionary—conveying a body of information (such as a chronicle of events). (3) Oracles, *Chaosbeschreibung*, and other kinds of "woe" descriptions might be encountered, "realized," and meaningful, in performance or private reading, without the necessity that the audience or reader attempt systematic correspondences between the predictions and immediate politics.[15]

OUTLINE OF APOCEL 2: THE DISCOURSE ON SIGNS OF WOE

§A The Assyrian King (2:2-5)[16]

§B The King of Peace (2:6-16)
(a) Introduction: Vengeance on Egypt (vv. 6-9)
(b) Beneficence to Egypt (vv. 10-11)
(c) Secret activities (vv. 12-14)
(d) Deportation of people to "Metropolis by sea" (vv.15-16)

§C The Sons of the King of Peace (2:17-28)
(a) Introduction: Two sons (vv. 17-19)
(b) Establishment of Memphite temple; woes begin (vv. 20-23)
(c) Religious oppression (vv. 24-28)

§D Social Woes under the Evil King (2:29-38)
(a) Introduction: Woe upon Egyptian rulers (vv. 29-30)
(b) Urban decline (v. 31)
(c) Distress and suicide (vv. 32-34)
(d) Oppression of nursing mothers (v. 35)

15. Cf. Robert Doran, "The Non-Dating of Jubilees: Jub 34–38; 23:14–32 in Narrative Context," *JSJ* 20 (1989):1–11. On the concept of symbols' autonomy from antecedents in the real world, see Peter L. Berger and Thomas Luckmann, *The Social Construction of Reality* (Garden City, N.Y.: Doubleday, 1966); and Roy Wagner, *Symbols That Stand for Themselves* (Chicago: University of Chicago Press, 1986).

16. The verse numbers in parentheses correspond to the standard chapter and verse divisions used in the Appendix and in Wintermute. This discussion of ApocEl 2, however, refers to sections, designated by capital and small letters both in this outline and in the translation in Appendix.

(e) Military conscription of children (v. 36)

(f) Lament of mothers and joy of virgins (vv. 37-38)

§E Political Signs in Brief Oracles (2:39-43)

(a) Persian invasion; deportation of Jews (v. 39)

(b) Signs from Jerusalem (v. 40)

(c) The Lawless One (v. 41)

(d) War between Persia and Assyria (v. 42)

(e) Depredations of war (v. 43)

§F Terrestrial Woes: The Nile Running with Blood (2:44-45)

§G The Advent of the King from the Sun (2:46-50)

(a) Appearance of king (v. 46)

(b) Flight to Memphis (vv. 47-48a)

(c) Destruction of Pagan shrines and erection of Christian (?) shrines (v. 48)

(d) Support of Christian (?) shrines (vv. 49-50)

§H A Deceptive Peace (2:51—3:1)

(a) King acclaimed as savior (v. 51)

(b) Reprieve of taxes (v. 52a)

(c) Social prosperity (vv. 52b-53)

(d) Appearance of false Christ (3:1)

GENERAL IMPLICATIONS OF APOCEL 2

A distinctive structure pervades this sequence of prophecies: the period of preeschatological decline is envisioned through a cyclical alternation of evil kings and (ostensibly) beneficial kings, with their corresponding dominions of woe and prosperity, from the introduction of the king of the Assyrians in §A to the advent of the solar Christ at the very end of the Apocalypse of Elijah (cf. 3:3).

Comparing this structure of alternating kingships to the kingship ideology behind the *Chaosbeschreibung* tradition, one can see that the author of the Apocalypse of Elijah is addressing traditional Egyptian conceptions of woe and prosperity. Woes begin with the arrival of the king of the Assyrians (§A) and continue through the beginning of the reign of the King of Peace (§B.a), before he reverses Egypt's fortune and causes prosperity (§B.b–c). With the accession of the latter's son with the demonic face, however, prosperity ends (§C.b–c),[17] and the inhabitants of Egypt enter a period of horrible suffering (§§C.c–D, F). Then there arises a King from the "city which is called 'the City of the Sun'"—a manifest reflection of the King from Helios–Re in the *Potter's Oracle*—and Egypt enters a period of hitherto unknown prosperity and peace (§§G–H). This penultimate savior in the Apocalypse of Elijah no doubt forms one of the major sources of the "Last Emperor" tradition in Byzantine apocalypticism: a human ruler whose beneficent accession and dominion would paradoxically usher in the period of the Antichrist.[18]

Indeed, it is at this point that the Lawless One arises, whose dramatic rise and fall are narrated in ApocEl 3–5; and it is significant that the author calls him a "king" at one point too (4:24). His dominion, which has dreadful consequences only for the "saints," apparently (it is not specified) maintains the prosperity of Egypt until angels rescue the saints (5:1-6). Then Egypt enters a period of unparalleled drought and decline: the sun darkens, birds and plants die, all moisture disappears. Then Christ arrives (5:36)—whom the text has already described as appearing "like the sun which shines from the east to the west" (3:3)—and the millennium is inaugurated.

There are clear instances of repetition in this structure: the king from "the City of the Sun" repeats the acts of the King of Peace in his benefits to saint-shrines (§G.c–d; cf. §B.b), allegiance to the monolatrous slogan "The name of God is One" (§G.c; cf. §B.b), his apparent acts of trickery (the ambush of the Assyrians in §G.b, as with the incognito tour of Egypt in §B.c), and, more generally, his dominion of beneficence and prosperity. It is evident that the author constructed his prophecy of times of distress and recovery in a cyclical pattern, making use of a limited repertoire of prophetic "plots."[19]

Whereas *Chaosbeschreibung* arose in Egypt to portray the decline of

17. To a certain extent, prosperity, or the king's benevolence toward Egypt, ends with §B.c–d; however, the precise meaning for a third-century Egyptian Christian of these verses and of the judgment they cast upon the king is unclear; see below, pp. 205–6, 229–30.

18. The earliest digression on the Last Emperor appears in the Latin Tiburtine Sibyl, whose *Vorlage* seems to have been dependent on the Apocalypse of Elijah. See above, pp. 24–25; and Paul J. Alexander, "The Diffusion of Byzantine Apocalypses in the Medieval West and the Beginnings of Joachimism," in *Prophecy and Millenarianism: Essays in Honour of Marjorie Reeves*, ed. Ann Williams (Essex: Longman, 1980), 58–59, 63–64.

19. Cf. Rosenstiehl, 30–31, 36–37. Schrage (217–20) has aptly argued that the use of parallels and doublets in composition is not an indication of source and redaction but rather of compositional style (*pace* Wintermute, 721, 725–26).

the cosmos during a lapse of kingship or in interregnal periods, this cyclical structure of alternating dominions portrays chaos as occurring at the hands of kings (e.g., §§C.d and D.d–e). The reason for this evolution in *Chaosbeschreibung* may be historical. The literary acknowledgment of "bad" kingship in Egyptian literature (when previously kingship was good per se) appears to have begun in the Late and early Hellenistic periods, a product of diverse calamities and, as J. Gwyn Griffiths has argued, Jewish influence.[20] It is conceivable that the ruthless taxation and socioeconomic decline of the *chora* under the Roman emperors would have contributed to the evolution of this concept of bad kingship to one of predatory kingship.

CHAOSBESCHREIBUNG MOTIFS IN APOCEL 2

The clearest instance of the author's use of native Egyptian prophetic tradition appears in §F. The surreal image of the Nile running with blood not only is anticipated in the classical *Admonitions of Ipuwer* but also occurs in the *Perfect Discourse*, demonstrating its continued symbolic power throughout the history of Egyptian literature.[21] An ancient fascination with this unique image of traumatic disorder can be seen in the legend of Moses' turning the Nile to blood (Ex 7:14-24); and it is significant that Philo of Alexandria, who was probably acquainted with the Egyptian prophecies, extends the scriptural account of the biblical legend with lurid detail: "And the opened 'veins' [φλέβας] gushed forth jets of blood as in a hemorrhage, such that not a transparent trickle could be seen."[22] But the Jewish use of the motif may be a case of counterpropaganda (attributing to YHWH the power to effect this most traditional

20. Alan B. Lloyd, "The Late Period: 664–323 B.C.," in *Ancient Egypt: A Social History*, ed. B. G. Trigger et al. (Cambridge: Cambridge University Press, 1983), 298–99; Janet H. Johnson, "The Demotic Chronicle as a Statement of a Theory of Kingship," *Journal of the Society for the Study of Egyptian Antiquities* 13 (1983):68–72; J. Gwyn Griffiths, *The Divine Verdict: A Study of Divine Judgement in the Ancient Religions*, NumenSupp 52 (Leiden: Brill, 1991), 176–83.

21. *Ipuwer* 2.10–11 (tr. Lichtheim, *AEL* 1:151; *Perfect Discourse: Asclepius* 24 (= NHC VI, 71.17–20). S. Luria used the currency of this image to question the historicity of "distress" prophecies in *Ipuwer* and *Neferti* ("Die Ersten werden die Letzten sein [zur 'sozialen Revolution' in Altertum]," *Klio* 22 [1929]:414–15).

22. Philo of Alexandria *De vita Mosis* 1.99 (ed. and tr. Roger Arnaldez, Claude Mondésert, Jean Pouilloux, and Pierre Savinel, *De vita Mosis I–II*, Les oeuvres de Philon d'Alexandrie 22 [Paris: Éditions du Cerf, 1967]). An analogous image of mountain ravines filled with corpses and flowing blood in torrents in *Sib. Or.* 3.682–84 appears to recall instead Ez 38:22 (cf. Hartman, *Prophecy Interpreted*, 91–94, esp. 93).

horror of Egyptians). Both *Ipuwer* and the *Perfect Discourse*, for example, associate the image with the excess of corpses that come from internal strife and brigandage.[23] Thus the *topos* combines the idea of the disintegration of fertility with that of the disintegration of social and political structure, as if it were by the blood of slaughtered neighbors that the Nile lost its potential to irrigate.

The traditional use of drought imagery to express chaos on earth appears not only in ApocEl 2 (cf. 2:31) but also in ApocEl 5, in the description of the earth's decline after the departure of the saints (5:7-9, 12, 14):

> Then, in that time, the earth will tremble; the sun will darken. Peace will be removed from upon the earth and under heaven[. . .]The trees will be uprooted and topple over. Wild beasts and farm animals will die in a catastrophe. Birds will fall on the ground dead. The earth will parch, and the waters of the sea will dry up. . . . [The sinners left on the earth under the dominion of the Lawless One complain:] See, now we will die in a famine and tribulation! . . . We went to the depths of the sea and we found no water. We dug in the rivers and papyrus reeds and we found no water.[24]

Although this situation arises in response to the absence of "saints" (and to the dominion of the Lawless One) rather than to the absence of a pharaoh, the author nevertheless considers the details of drought and famine to epitomize cosmic disintegration as might precede the eschatological judgment and parousia. This choice of imagery suggests that the author is drawing upon epichoric traditions of *Chaosbeschreibung*, which were also probably the most meaningful for an Egyptian audience acquainted with the realities of drought.

Terrestrial chaos is combined with images of social chaos in §§D.a–f. Indeed, a number of motifs in this section of ApocEl 2 have precise literary precedents in Egyptian oracle tradition. For example, §D.c, which appears to repeat the last part of §A, describes people so desperate in the times of distress that they seek to commit suicide but for some reason are unable to succeed: "Death flees from them." Suicide is a *Chaosbeschreibung* motif in *Ipuwer* ("Lo, great and small ⟨say⟩, 'I wish I were dead,' little children say, 'He should not have made me live!'")[25]

---

23. *Ipuwer* 2.6–7; *Perfect Discourse: Asclepius* 24 (= NHC VI, 71.19–21).
24. Taken from Sahidic texts; see Appendix for notes on translation and manuscript conditions.
25. *Ipuwer* 4.3 (tr. Lichtheim, 1:153).

and, with the addition of death's "flight," this oracular logion seems to have become a standard motif of eschatological distress in the Greco-Roman period, occurring in only slightly divergent forms in the *Sibylline Oracles* (2.307-8; 8.353-54; 13.116-18) and the book of Revelation (9:6).[26]

The prophecy in §D.b of the abandonment of the "cities of Egypt" belongs to the same tradition as the appellation "metropolis by the sea" in §B.d. Alexandria, so-named in the *Potter's Oracle*, is there prophesied to become "a refuge for fishermen."[27] An extension of the repertoire of *Chaosbeschreibung* motifs describing terrestrial chaos, the image of the decline of a great "City by the Sea" arose especially during the Hellenistic period as a response to Alexandria and to the alien phenomenon of the polis in general.[28] The particular version in §D.b, however, recalls the traditional image of the encroaching desert (along with the third-century reality of abandoned villages and the recession of arable land).[29] Significantly, this prophetic motif reappears in a positive antithesis in §H.a, where the King of Righteousness is sent "so that the land will not

26. Because Rv 9:6 has nothing intrinsically to do with the attack of the locusts in Revelation 9 (cf. R. H. Charles, *A Critical and Exegetical Commentary on the Revelation of St. John*, 2 vols. [Edinburgh: T. & T. Clark, 1920], 1:243: "The writer has here passed from the role of the Seer to that of the prophet"), it is likely that John took the phrase from elsewhere, rather than coining it himself. The parallelism between the first two lines and chiasmus between the second two suggests that the verse is a *logion* of independent circulation. Close parallels to the "flight of death" motif occur in Ovid *Ibis* 123; Seneca *Troades*; Cornelius Gallus *Elegies* 1; and Sophocles *Electra* 1007-8 (see Charles, *Revelation of St. John*, 243–44).

27. Or a "place for fisherman to hang their nets." See above, p. 182 n.93.

28. Cf. *Perfect Discourse: Asclepius* 27 (= NHC VI, 75.28-33): "And the lords of the earth will withdraw themselves. And they will establish themselves in a city that is in a corner of Egypt and that will be built toward the setting of the sun. Every man will go into it, whether they come on the sea or on the shore" (tr. Brashler et al., *NHL*, 336); see discussion in Jean-Pierre Mahé, *Hermès en Haute-Égypte*, 2 vols., Bibliothèque copte de Nag Hammadi 3 and 7 (Quebec: Presses de l'université Laval, 1978–82), 2:79, 252. The motif is used again in the Manichaean *Homilies* 2.14.11 ff: see translation and commentary in Ludwig Koenen, "Manichaean Apocalypticism at the Crossroads of Iranian, Egyptian, Jewish and Christian Thought," in *Codex Manichaicus Coloniensis: Atti del Simposio Internazionale*, ed. Luigi Cirillo (Cosenza: Editore Marra, 1986), 322. Striking is the exhortation in CPJ 520, "Don't let your city be depopulated," which Koenen sees as referring to Alexandria but which could also refer to Memphis. Christian Cannuyer has aptly demonstrated indigenous roots to this motif in classical Egyptian idealizations of the city in Egyptian wisdom literature: "Variations sur le thème de la ville dans les maximes sapientiales de l'ancienne Égypte," *Chronique d'Égypte* 64 (1989):44–54.

29. The Greek Tiburtine Sibyl's version of the Elijah Apocalypse passage more vividly reflects this tradition, reading "the cities of the East will become deserts, . . . and [the king] will hiss and say: 'Was there ever a city here?'" (198–200; in Paul J. Alexander, *The Oracle of Baalbek: The Tiburtine Sibyl in Greek Dress*, Dumbarton Oaks Studies 10 [Washington, D.C.: Dumbarton Oaks, 1987], 21, 28).

become desert." Such images provide glimpses of the author's debt to a traditional ideology that associated terrestrial and social prosperity directly with kingship.

§D.d–f may also be classified under "social chaos," in that these verses describe the disastrous effects of evil kingship (and chaos in general) upon human fertility and procreation. It is "antithetical" to the proper status and function of a little boy for the military to conscript him, as occurs in §D.e. The poem in §D.f laments motherhood and praises virginity in the time of these woes, in considerable opposition to traditional Egyptian values, which would laud motherhood and procreation as an extension of the ordering power of Ma'at and Isis (mediated, ultimately, through the symbol of the king).[30] The terrible image in §D.d describes the evil transformation of the magical symbols of breasts, breast milk, and blood in the time of woe; these magical "fields" should be understood as extensions of human fertility.

The variety of eschatological uses to which the symbolism of childbearing and motherhood have been put, both in Egyptian and Jewish literature, suggests that the continuity or arrest of normal maternity represented for these cultures a gauge of social prosperity or disintegration—a vivid symbol of order or chaos. While *Ipuwer* laments motherhood during the time of woe—"If only this were the end of man, no more conceiving, no births! Then the land would cease to shout, tumult would be no more!"[31]—the *Oracle of the Lamb* (3.3) and deutero-Isaiah prophesy happiness for barren women in the new age: "Sing, O barren one, who did not bear; break forth into singing and cry aloud, you who have not been in labor! For the children of the desolate one will be more than the children of her that is married!" (Is 54:1).[32]

Yet a curious encratite ideology emerges in some early Jewish literature that reverses the traditional sentiments toward normal childbearing.[33] The notion of being "blessed" in current childlessness (Is 54:1b) changes into a notion of childlessness as a desirable eschatological state

30. See Françoise Dunand, *Religion populaire en Égypte romaine*, EPRO 77 (Leiden: Brill, 1979), 60–73.

31. *Ipuwer* 6.1–2 (tr. Lichtheim, 1:154).

32. Cf. *Or. Lamb:* "The barren woman will rejoice *and* she who has a child will be glad, because of the good things which happen in Egypt" (3.3; Ger. tr. Zauzich, "Das Lamm des Bokchoris," 168, my emphasis). The precise reason for the barren woman's gladness is unstated but one might assume it would be her conception of a child.

33. I use "encratite" in the sense of Robert Murray's conservative definition: "the rejection of marriage and the evaluation of sexual union as evil and defiling" (*Symbols of Church and Kingdom* [Cambridge: Cambridge University Press, 1975], 11). Obviously only the first aspect is an undeniable inference from this passage in the Apocalypse of Elijah.

(*2 Bar.* 10:13–15; Lk 23:29). Consequently, the Egyptian-Jewish text *Wisdom of Solomon* praises barrenness in this world as a form of purity, holding out "fruit" as a reward for the time of "examination of souls" (3:13).[34]

This is evidently the sentiment of the poem in §D.f. Whereas lines 1 through 6 obviously use the sorrow of mothers to express the trauma of the time (in continuity with *Chaosbeschreibung*),[35] the author—or his source (for the strophes can be separated form-critically)—adds a "condition" by which the women of the audience may avoid such sorrows: the barren woman and the virgin will be "insulated" from the anguish of mothers during the times of woe and, moreover, are promised "children in heaven."

The tyrannical role of the evil king in §D.d indicates that the passage must be understood as further depredations on maternity in this period of chaos. The image of women forced to suckle snakes, however, had a wider currency in Egypt than simply *Chaosbeschreibung* imagery, suggesting a special symbolism indigenous to Egyptian culture.[36] Its sig-

---

34. See the discussion in David Winston, *The Wisdom of Solomon*, AB 43 (Garden City, N.Y.: Doubleday, 1979), 131–32. Philo describes the monastic women of the Therapeutae as "yearning not for mortal but for immortal offspring, to which only the divinely beloved soul can give birth" (*De vita contemplativa* 68). Although Philo nowhere suggests this ideology arose as part of a millennialist attitude, this passage shows that the idea of "heavenly children"—in this case, ἀθάνατοι ἐκγόνοι—may have circulated more widely. See *De vita contemplativa*, ed. and tr. François Daumas, Les oeuvres de Philon d'Alexandrie 29 (Paris: Éditions du Cerf, 1963), 128–29; and Ross Kraemer, "Monastic Jewish Women in Greco-Roman Egypt: Philo Judaeus on the Therapeutrides," *Signs* 14 (1989):352–55. A similar ethos in Philo (*Deus* 13–15) enlarges the meaning of barrenness and motherhood so that these concepts might represent states in his mystical system (in Winston, *The Wisdom of Solomon*).

35. The use in line 5 of the Egyptian phrase ϩⲙⲟⲟⲥ ⲉⲧⲱⲃⲉ ("sit on a brick") for the birth process would have been received, even in the original Greek, as a composition of traditional Egyptian images; see Wintermute, 742 n. s2; Schrage, 246 n. g.

36. Cf. *Apoc. Pet.* 8; and Coptic Tebtunis paintings published by Colin C. Walters, "Christian Paintings from Tebtunis," *JEA* 75 (1989): pls. 26, 28; and discussion, 201–2. In general, see Martha Himmelfarb, *Tours of Hell: An Apocalyptic Form in Jewish and Christian Literature* (Philadelphia: University of Pennsylvania Press, 1983), 97–100. Although Himmelfarb accounts for the image in Christian visions of hell by *lex talionis* (measure-for-measure punishment), the currency of the image in Egypt may have preceded Jewish and Christian traditions. In his life of Antony (§86), Plutarch reports the legend that "Cleopatra had given orders that the reptile [θηρίον] might fasten itself upon her body . . . and baring her *arm* [τὸν βραχίονα] she held it out for the bite"; and then that "an image of Cleopatra herself with the asp clinging to her was carried in [her funeral] procession" (in Bernadotte Perrin, tr. *Plutarch's Lives*, LCL [London: Heinemann, 1920], 9:328–29). But the uncertain reference to her arm may be a mere case of "displacement outward"; it can hardly be a coincidence that Shakespeare reverts to the traditional Coptic theme of the serpent biting the *breast* in *Antony and Cleopatra*, act 5, sc. 2, ll. 243–310 (in ll. 311–13 she applies another serpent to her arm). Considering that Cleopatra modeled herself after the goddess Isis (cf. P. M. Fraser, *Ptolemaic Alexandria*,

nificance to an audience of Roman Egypt may be broached through analyzing the symbolism of serpents, breasts, breast milk, blood, and poison.

It is the mention of poison that first alerts us that the meaning of §D.d may lie in the context of Egyptian ritual ("magical") spells. The Coptic word ⲕⲁⲟ referred to a vegetable poison, as opposed to, for example, snake venom, and thus to the type of substance collected and purveyed by an expert.[37] The Greek word used by the Tiburtine Sibyl—and presumably, that used by the Greek original of the Apocalypse of Elijah[38]—is φάρμακον, which was used equally for medical remedies and for the diverse types of potions concocted by magical professionals in ritual.[39]

A survey of Egyptian ritual spells from the classical through the Greco-Roman periods reveals an overwhelming interest in averting snakebite and in the repulsion of snakes in general.[40] Such spells occasionally subsumed this interest within the more mythopoeic scope of the repulsion of Apophis but more often took the view of snakes as an extension of the peripheral sphere of Seth–Typhon.[41] The snake

---

3 vols. [Oxford: Clarendon, 1972], 1:244) and that a dominant form of Isis iconography in the Greco-Roman period was Isis *lactans*—that is, suckling Horus—one may presume that her processional image followed this iconographic convention and that the snake (rather than Horus) was attached to her breast, not her arm. On the Egyptian symbolism in Cleopatra's suicide (by *two* snakes!) in general, see J. Gwyn Griffiths, "The Death of Cleopatra VII," *JEA* 47 (1961):113–18, pl. 9.

37. Oscar von Lemm, "Kleine koptische Studien—X: Bemerkungen zu einigen Stellen der koptischen Apokalypsen, 4," *Bulletin de l'académie impériale des sciences de St. Pétersbourg* 13 (1900):11–22; Crum, 102B; cf. A. Lucas, "Poisons in Ancient Egypt," *JEA* 24 (1938):198–99. Von Lemm specifically notes Coptic legends in which a *magos* uses ⲕⲁⲟ along with other substances ("Kleine koptische Studien—X.4," 12–14). In the Coptic the use of ⲕⲁⲟ rather than ⲙⲁⲧⲟⲩ (snake venom) adds a further "miraculous" sense to the passage: whereas the audience might expect the biting serpents to produce ⲙⲁⲧⲟⲩ in the blood of the women, the result is instead ⲕⲁⲟ, vegetable poison! The message of the Coptic scribe, therefore, is that in the eschaton such terrible miracles as ⲕⲁⲟ from serpents will occur.

38. See Alexander, *Oracle of Baalbek*, 38–39.

39. Cf. LSJ 1917A–B, esp. §1.1, 3, 4. On the inclusion of poison in the magical repertoire, see Wolfhart Westendorf, "Gifte," *Lexikon der Ägyptologie* 2 (Wiesbaden: Otto Harrassowitz, 1977), 596–97.

40. E.g., the Metternich Stela (tr. in Borghouts, nos. 93–95) and associated Horus stelae and magical statue bases; the Turin magical papyrus (tr. in Borghouts, nos. 92, 102, 106, 108, 111, 115, 138); P.Vatican 19a (ed. and tr. in P. E. Suys, "Le papyrus magique du Vatican," *Orientalia* 3 [1934]:63–87); P.Yale 1792 (in George M. Paráossoglou, "A Christian Amulet against Snakebite," *Studia Papyrologica* 13 [1974]:107–10); the discussion of *ḥf3w* in Jan Zandee, *Death as an Enemy according to Ancient Egyptian Conceptions*, NumenSupp 5 (Leiden: Brill, 1960), 101–2; and the representative collection in Borghouts, 91–94 (nos. 136–43; cf. 51–85 [nos. 84–123] on scorpions, and p. ix).

41. Cf. spell 6 on the magical statue base, published by Adolf Klasens, *A Magical*

emerges from such traditions as a highly symbolic figure: the archetypal danger in the Egyptian landscape.[42]

Breasts symbolized the most vulnerable part of the woman in her capacity as mother. A detailed spell from the ritual–medical corpora invokes a *historiola* of Isis as mother of Horus in order to protect a woman's breasts from "a male dead and a female dead"[43]—that is, two specific demons—and it is probably within this sphere of ritual that a spell from the Coffin Texts should be read: "That a woman may not be eaten by a snake."[44] Hence the forcible application of serpents to breasts would have constituted an "unimaginable horror," such as might occur in the times of woe under an evil kingship.

By itself, blood had highly symbolic value as a magical substance in Egyptian ritual symbolism.[45] The Apocalypse of Elijah refers to the blood of the eschatological heroine–martyr Tabitha as "a healing [oγxλι] for the people [λλoc]" (4:6), which probably continues an older tradition of the scorpion goddess Ta-Bitjet, by whose blood Horus was invoked to cure scorpion venom.[46] Breast milk also was considered powerful.[47] But the replacement of breast milk with blood—although both sacred substances in their own rights—was horrifying: "Do not produce blood!" commands one spell to protect the breasts.[48] It is this horror that presumably led to the invention and transmission of a curious legend in the Arabic *History of Alexandrian Patriarchs*, in which a woman baptizes her children by cutting her breast and anointing them

Statue Base (Socle behague) in the Museum of Antiquities at Leiden (Leiden: Brill, 1952), 59, 99.

42. See also the *Life of Jeremiah the Prophet* 1–7, where the prophet is credited with expelling snakes (a power that persists after his death through the dust from his tomb); and the *Life of Adam and Eve*, where Eve's wailing at the child Seth's snakebite (chap. 37) and Seth's subsequent ritual rebuke of the snake (chap. 39) recall vividly the Isis–Horus drama invoked in Egyptian healing spells.

43. P.Ebers 95.1–14 (tr. Borghouts, 40–41 [= no. 64]). Borghouts, 41–44 (nos. 65–70), are likewise meant to protect a baby's continued feeding from the breast.

44. Coffin Texts, spell 717 (tr. in Zandee, *Death as an Enemy*, 101).

45. E.g., the *Tjet* amulet in ancient and Greco-Roman Egyptian tradition (see *Book of the Dead,* spell 156); William H. Worrell, "Coptic Magical and Medical Texts," *Orientalia* 4 (1935):7–8, 11 (= P.Mich. inv. 1190ʳ, l. 33): "Find strength from this blood, which is under NN"; PGM IV.2484: "It is she, NN, who said, 'I saw [the goddess] drinking blood'"; and Kropp, 2:93 (= no. XXVIII), ll. 112–15.

46. See Borghouts, 72–73 (= nos. 97–98, 100); and David T. M. Frankfurter, "Tabitha in the Apocalypse of Elijah," *JTS* 41 (1990):14–23.

47. See Borghouts, 24–25, 34 (= nos. 34–35 [for burns], 51 [for catarrh]). Spell no. 34 invokes Isis, who says, "Show me my way that I may do what I know (to do), that I may extinguish it for him with my milk, with the salutary liquids from between my breasts."

48. Borghouts, 41 (= no. 64).

with drops of her blood.[49] As in the *Apocalypse of Peter*, which describes as sour the milk produced by women in hell whose breasts are tortured by animals, the positive maternal symbolism of breast milk is negated in this martyrdom legend: it is blood that becomes the sacred substance. In these two contexts—symbolic baptism and hell—blood or sour milk from breasts is appropriate. In contrast, §D.d of ApocEl 2 attributes an entirely negative significance to the drawing of blood from breasts. The power of this image in ApocEl 2 and its evocation of the *Chaosbeschreibung* tradition arises precisely because under the "demon-faced" king's reign, blood would replace breast milk—because such an inversion as is acknowledged in the stories of the baptizing mother and the hell of the *Apocalypse of Peter* might actually happen in Egypt under a cruel king.

The use of *Chaosbeschreibung* in ApocEl 2 is therefore both explicit and implicit. That these terrors stem directly from vicissitudes in the kingship implies a continuity of Egyptian kingship ideology into the description of woes in the Apocalypse of Elijah. The details of the fate of women and maternity in these times also recall a basic motif of social chaos in *Chaosbeschreibung;* although it must be acknowledged that §D.f bears a form-critical resemblance to some contemporaneous Jewish literature concerning the eschaton.

Explicit uses of *Chaosbeschreibung* appear in the Nile, drought, and famine imagery; the abandonment of cities (especially Alexandria) and their return to dust; and the suicide motif (which also has wider parallels in the Greco-Roman world). These images were traditional to Egypt; they constituted the primary symbols within Egyptian literary culture for social and cosmic breakdown, and they were the symbols to which a predominately nonliterate Egyptian culture was accustomed in its reception and understanding of oracles and oracular propaganda (such as the *Potter's Oracle* and CPJ 520).[50] In the Greco-Roman period, the

---

49. "She cut her right breast with the knife, and took from it three drops of blood, with which she made the sign of the cross on the foreheads of her two children, and over their hearts, in the name of the Father, the Son, and the Holy Ghost; and she dipped them in the sea" (in B. Evetts, tr., "History of the Patriarchs of the Coptic Church of Alexandria, VI: Peter the First," *Patrologia orientalis* 1 [1907]:386). The application of cross marks with sacred substances, and the manual cruciform gesture in general, had manifestly "magical" value in late antique Christianity (cf. Athanasius *Vita Antonii* 13, 78, and passim; *Vita Symeon Stylites* [Syr.] passim).

50. On literacy in ancient Egypt, see John Baines and C. J. Eyre, "Four Notes on Literacy," *Göttinger Miszellen* 61 (1983):65–72; Griffiths, *Divine Verdict*, 215–16. On Greco-Roman Egypt, see below, pp. 273–75.

traditional language of *Chaosbeschreibung* functioned to situate material in the lives, sentiments, and symbolic world of Egyptians.

INTEGRATION OF
LEGENDS WITH *CHAOSBESCHREIBUNG*

Archaic symbolism is not the only material with which an Egyptian audience might have been familiar in listening to the Apocalypse of Elijah. The author seems to have employed legends of Hellenistic rulers to establish types for the composition of the kingship cycles in §§A–C.

Legends as such, however, cannot be considered to have been recognizable *vaticinia ex eventus*. Such a view would presuppose that the audience could identify the figures in the legends and thereby date their own historical position vis-à-vis the chronology of the text. Legends such as ApocEl 2 employs have an ambivalent relationship to historical events: although they may arise from particular historical episodes or experiences, their development occurs independently of these episodes and depends upon the traditions and immediate context of the culture and of those who tell the legends. Legends function not to replicate historical episodes (as might chronicles) but to express basic themes or ideologies through the dramatic arrangement of the motifs. There is no evidence that the author of ApocEl 2 intended a consistent representation of a historical period. Rather, he made use of stories which had arisen in the folklore surrounding particular rulers, stories which characterized those rulers as beneficial or evil and which eventually had come to circulate as types of beneficial or evil rulership—such as one might plausibly expect in a prophecy of future kings—independent of the rulers themselves.

The "King of Peace" who arises in the West (§B.a), runs over the sea like a lion (§B.a), and founds a "city by the sea" (§B.d) is clearly modeled upon traditions of Alexander the Great.[51] In Hellenistic tradition, Alexander was the successor of the four "Asian" empires, the salvific conqueror "from the west."[52] As the four Asian empires were themselves a motif of Greco-Roman prophetic literature, so Alexander and the

51. As first recognized and discussed by Franz Kampers, *Alexander der Grosse und die Idee des Weltimperiums in Prophetie und Sage* (Freiburg: Herdersche Verlagshandlung, 1901), 152–73; cf. Schrage, 212.

52. In his retelling of Dn 2:36, Josephus speaks of Alexander as "another (king) from the west" (ἀπὸ τῆς δύσεως; *Ant.* 10.209).

Greeks were construed as the final empire, those who would put an end to Asian dominion.[53]

Egypt in particular revered Alexander as a savior–king.[54] The popular (if dubious) Egyptian tradition that Alexander paid homage to a Libyan Ammon shrine was given a fantastic background in the *Alexander Romance* of Pseudo-Callisthenes. This text, which gained great popularity in the Greco-Roman and medieval worlds, clearly derives from Egyptian priestly propaganda in favor of Alexander.[55] In the *Romance*, Alexander appears as the true son of Nektanebos, the last native pharaoh and a legendary magician–prophet, who escaped to Macedon in the face of massive foreign invasion and, taking the form of the god Ammon, impregnated Philip's wife in the form of the god Ammon.

The relevance of the Alexander tradition for ApocEl 2, §B.a, is evident at the beginning of the *Romance*. In the birth narrative Alexander is given leontomorphic attributes: "This child who is going to be born," a seer reports to Philip, "will reach the rising sun, waging war with all— like a lion"; and at his birth Alexander has "the mane of a lion [λεοντοκόμου] . . . and teeth as sharp as a serpent's; he displayed the energy of a lion. And there was no doubt of how his nature would turn out."[56] Underlying this symbolism is a wealth of Mediterranean, includ-

53. Cf. *Sib. Or.* 4.88–101, which puts Macedonia as the final of four kingdoms (in the original, Hellenistic oracle; cf. J. Collins, "Development of the Sibylline Tradition," 427). It is striking that Greece is never posed as the fifth "millennial" kingdom per se but rather as a more general successor to Asian empires. Both Swain ("Theory of the Four Monarchies") and Flusser ("Four Empires") have shown that this mythic structure of history was developed in the Greco-Roman Near East as popular propaganda against Hellenism. In Egypt, however, a distinction between Egypt and Greece was rarely made (e.g., *Sib. Or.* 11.186–260, in which Egypt follows Macedonia in world dominion, before Rome). Therefore from the Asian—or, more exactly, Persian—perspective the four-empires scheme functioned as propaganda against Greece and for "predicting" Rome as the "millenial" fifth kingdom that would expel the Greeks.

54. Stanley Burstein has argued for the circulation of Egyptian propaganda against Alexander ("Alexander in Egypt: Continuity and Change" [paper presented to the Conference of the American Research Center in Egypt, Berkeley, Calif., 1990]).

55. Cf. E. A. Wallis Budge, *The History of Alexander the Great* (Cambridge: Cambridge University Press, 1889), xxxv–li; Reinhold Merkelbach, *Die Quellen des griechischen Alexanderromans* (Munich: C. G. Beck'sche, 1977), 77–88; and Ludwig Koenen, "The Dream of Nektanebos," *BASP* 22 (1985):192–93. It may not be a coincidence that the Alexander traditions revolve around the authority of the god Ammon; the priests of this Ram god were responsible for producing many propagandistic oracles.

56. Pseudo-Callisthenes *Alexander Romance* 1.8.5, 13.3 (tr. Ken Dowden, "Pseudo-Callisthenes: The Alexander Romance," in *Collected Ancient Greek Novels*, ed. B. P. Reardon [Berkeley: University of California Press, 1989], 660, 662). On Alexander's leontomorphism, see also Plutarch, *De fort. Alex.* 2.2 (335C); Kampers, *Alexander der Grosse*, 170–71; Friedrich Pfister, *Alexander der Grosse in den Offenbarungen der Griechen, Juden, Mohammedaner, und Christen* (Berlin: Akademie-Verlag, 1956), 19, 21.

ing Jewish and Egyptian, traditions of comparing heroes and victors to lions, and a third-century audience would probably not have heard this simile as evocative of any one culture.[57] The image of the king's "running upon the sea" signified—in oracular parlance—the act of conquering from across the Mediterranean.[58] It may be concluded that, in general, the attributes of the King of Peace in §B.a derive from Egyptian Alexander traditions.

Whereas §B.a employs "positive" Alexander traditions for an image of a beneficial king, §B.d shows quite the opposite view of the same king: by his order "wise men" are "seized" (ⲥⲉ6ⲱⲡⲉ) and deported to a "city by the sea."[59] But Alexander traditions lie behind the latter passage too. The "city by the sea," as noted, is Alexandria. In referring this way to Alexandria, prophecies such as the *Potter's Oracle* portray the city in a negative, resentful light, for Alexandria had displaced the priestly city Memphis as an administrative, economic, and religious power in

57. During the Roman period, several major Egyptian gods were compared to lions in their victorious manifestations: Re (PGM III.511; IV.1667); Horus (PGM IV.939; XX.9), Isis (PGM IV.2129, 2302), and, with particular vividness, Khnum at Esna: "His majesty appeared shining under the form of a lion with valorous power; he had been put in the world like a lion with ferocious visage, vigorous, brave, frightening, . . . filling the mountains with his roars" (*Esna* 127.5–6; Serge Sauneron, tr., in idem, *Les fêtes religieuses d'Esna aux derniers siècles du paganisme*, Esna 5 [Cairo: IFAO, 1962], 375). On Egyptian lion symbolism, see Constant De Wit, *Le rôle et le sens du lion dans l'Égypte ancienne* (Leiden: Brill, 1951), esp. 16–36, and Ludwig Koenen, "Die brennende Horosknabe: Zu einem Zauberspruch des Philinna-Papyrus," *Chronique d'Égypte* 37 (1962):172. On Jewish uses of leonine symbolism (e.g., for a messiah), see Gn 49:8-12; Dt 33:22; 4 Ezr 11–12, esp. 12:31-32; 4QSb 5:29; Rv 5:5; cf. 1 Macc 3:4; and the short discussion by Richard Bauckham, "The *Figurae* of John of Patmos," in *Prophecy and Millenarianism: Essays in Honor of Marjorie Reeves*, ed. Ann Williams (Essex: Longman, 1980) 113–15. Cf. also Brian McNeil, "Coptic Evidence for Jewish Messianic Beliefs," *RSO* 51 (1977):39–45, whose limited scope leads him to make these Jewish traditions proof of this passage's Jewish background. Hippolytus applies leonine attributes to the Antichrist (who thereby imitates Christ) in his treatise *On Christ and Antichrist* 6–14, but he draws this image exegetically from Gn 49:8-12 and Dt 33:22 and does not use it as a singular point of identification (in chap. 14 he identifies the Antichrist as a serpent).

58. Figures rise out of the sea in Dn 7:3-4 (leonine), 4 Ezr 13:3, and Rv 13:1-2, but they are never said to traverse it in this way. The royal goddess Isis, who is described in a second-century C.E. inscription as "Queen of seamanship—I make the navigable and unnavigable when it pleases me" (Kyme aretalogy; tr. Frederick C. Grant, in idem, *Hellenistic Religions* [Indianapolis: Bobbs-Merrill, 1953], 133), is imagined as "walking upon the face (of) the water of the Syrian sea" in a Hellenistic dream-oracle (texts 1 and 47; tr. J. D. Ray, *The Archive of Hor* [London: Egypt Exploration Society, 1976], 11, 112; cf. 13–14, 156). On Isis as nautical goddess, see J. Gwyn Griffiths, *Apuleius of Madauros: The Isis-Book*, EPRO 39 (Leiden: Brill, 1975), 31–47.

59. Wintermute is clearly wrong in stating that "in the present text, the hostility [toward Alexandria] is removed" (730). It is quite difficult both etymologically and contextually to derive a positive meaning from ⲥⲱⲡⲉ (see Crum, 826A).

Egypt.[60] The Apocalypse of Elijah has taken the idea of displacement one step further, though, in drawing upon a tradition (reported in Pseudo-Aristotle's *Economica*) that Alexander had forcibly deported the market, the merchants, and even the priesthood of the Delta town Canopus to his new city foundations in order to establish the latter's financial and hierocratic authority.[61] Thus the Apocalypse of Elijah has employed negative as well as positive Hellenistic traditions, both of which derived from Egyptian priestly lore and culture.

These negative traditions continue into §C, whose details recall incidents of the Diadochoi. The "left–right" symbolism in §C.a is revealed through an oracle in the *Demotic Chronicle:* "Left will be exchanged for right—right is Egypt; left is the land of Syria."[62] Although this oracle may originally have referred to an episode between one of the early Ptolemies and a native pretender–king,[63] for the present purposes it clearly demonstrates that in Egyptian oracle tradition "right–left" stood for "West–East," and more precisely, "Egypt–Syria."[64] Thus, if the "Righ-

60. A sentiment clearly voiced in the *Oracle of the Potter;* in general, see J.W.B. Barns, "Alexandria and Memphis: Some Historical Observations," *Orientalia* 46 (1977), 24–33; Fraser, *Ptolemaic Alexandria,* 1:251–54; and Dorothy J. Thompson, "The High Priests of Memphis under Ptolemaic Rule," in *Pagan Priests,* ed. Mary Beard and John North (Ithaca, N.Y.: Cornell University Press, 1990), 113–14. The *Alexander Romance* of Pseudo-Callisthenes preserves traces of native distrust of Alexandria: Alexander himself is supposed to have been warned "not to found the city on so great a scale, 'because you will not be able to find enough people to fill it; and even if you do, the administration will be unable to supply the food it would need. In addition, the inhabitants of the city will be at war with each other because of its excessive and boundless size'" (31; tr. Dowden, "Alexander Romance," 674). Jerome also recalls Egyptian priestly diatribes when he cast the hermit Paul of Thebes as prophesying, "Woe to thee Alexandria, who dost worship monsters in room of God. Woe to thee, harlot city, in whom the demons of the earth have flowed together" (*Vita Paul* 8, PL 23:25; tr. Helen Waddell, *The Desert Fathers* [London: Constable, 1936; reprint, Ann Arbor: University of Michigan Press, 1966], 33).

61. Pseudo-Aristotle *Economica* 2.33C (ed. B. A. Van Groningen, *Aristote: Le second livre de l'économique* [Leiden: Sijthoff, 1933], 18–19 (cf. 186–87). See translation and discussion in Edwyn R. Bevan, *House of Ptolemy* (Chicago: Ares, 1985), 16–17. The source of the tradition may have been Egyptian propaganda that credited native Egyptians as being the first inhabitants of Alexandria. But it is probably untrue; Robin Lane Fox points out that "the citizen body was exclusive rather than commercial. Macedonian veterans, Greeks and prisoners, perhaps too a contingent of Jews, were detailed as the new citizens, and native Egyptians were mostly added as men of lesser status" (*Alexander the Great* [London: Futura, 1973], 198). Furthermore, Fraser notes that "this synoecism [of local peoples in Alexandria], if historical, was physical, and not merely constitutional—that is, the inhabitants of the area are said to have taken up residence in the new city" (*Ptolemaic Alexandria,* 1:41).

62. *Dem. Chr.* 2.12 (tr. Janet H. Johnson, in idem, "Is the Demotic Chronicle an Anti-Greek Tract?" in *Grammata Demotika,* ed. Heinz-J. Thissen and Karl-Th. Zauzich [Würzburg: Gisela Zauzich, 1984], 110).

63. Cf. Johnson, "Anti-Greek Tract?" 110–13.

64. Cf. Griffiths, *Divine Verdict,* 225, on mythological use of right–left.

teous King" in the first section of the Apocalypse of Elijah recalled Alexander, his "two sons" would depict the Diadochoi, Ptolemy and Seleucus.[65]

A further indication that the "demon-faced" son "on the right" recalls Ptolemy I appears in §C.b, where the son sails up to Memphis to build a temple. Historically, Ptolemy I inaugurated the Sarapis cult in Memphis, exploiting the authority and power of the priestly city to legitimize this new, syncretistic religion of the Greeks.[66] This tradition of Ptolemy I (like that in §C.a) could only have originated in a milieu hostile to Sarapis and Hellenism.[67] Such a milieu would have been Memphite in locale (to account for the interest in this city and the disdain for Alexandria in the previous section) and priestly but extraordinarily conservative in its priestly outlook.[68] Thus, along with his generally "Christian" ideology, the author has—with no apparent sense of contradiction—integrated Memphite priestly traditions of early Hellenism.[69]

That the text recalls historical figures without reflecting their historical existence is not a contradiction in terms. As an image of the future—of what has not yet happened—the eschatological discourse must depend on mythology and legend to create a scenario of events that are both plausible and meaningful. In Egyptian literature the transhistorical, mythic representations of ideal kingship were combined with anecdotal attributes of legendary kings such as Amenophis or Nektanebos. Thus the author of the Apocalypse of Elijah uses legendary attributes of Hellenistic kings in combination with the mythological ramifications of kingship in Egypt to build a coherent royal sequence or cycle for the future times of woe. One could only call such recollections *ex* (or *post*) *eventus* in the sense that they are drawn from the legends surrounding figures of the past who made considerable impacts upon

65. The memory of the early Hellenistic kings in oracles was not favorable: *Sib. Or.* 11.225 views the Diadochoi as "kings who are devourers of people and overbearing and faithless" (tr. John J. Collins, in idem, "Sibylline Oracles," *OTP* 1:440).

66. On Ptolemy I and the Sarapis cult in Memphis, see Fraser, *Ptolemaic Alexandria,* 1:252–54.

67. Cf. H. Idris Bell, *Cults and Creeds in Greco-Roman Egypt* (Liverpool: Liverpool University Press, 1953; reprint, Chicago: Ares, 1975), 20; however, P. M. Fraser has argued that in the second century B.C.E. the Sarapis cult had significant appeal among native Egyptians ("Two Studies on the Cult of Sarapis in the Hellenistic World," *Opuscula Atheniensia* 3 [1960]:9, 15–17).

68. Note that pro-Memphite, anti-Alexandrian sentiments characterize other Egyptian prophecies circulating in the Roman period, e.g., the *Potter's Oracle* (P² ll. 28–30 [= P³ ll. 50–53, 60]) and P.Tebt. Tait 13 (see W. J. Tait, *Papyri from Tebtunis in Egyptian and in Greek [P.Tebt. Tait]* [London: Egypt Exploration Society, 1977], 45–48).

69. See above, pp. 101–2. To have such knowledge and interest in these priestly traditions might suggest the author's prior training in the priesthood.

Egyptian culture; but it would be incorrect to view such recollections as references, as if the audience were likely to pick out Alexander and Ptolemy to mark points in time by which they might situate themselves.

THE QUESTION OF HISTORICAL ANTECEDENTS TO APOCEL 2

Early scholarship on the Apocalypse of Elijah displayed a concerted interest in connecting the various episodes in ApocEl 2 to historical events in the Greco-Roman world. As more elements in this discourse have been identified as traditional Egyptian literary motifs and types, however, the necessity of seeking historical antecedents has become more difficult to maintain. The author is obviously heir to the Egyptian *Chaosbeschreibung* tradition and to Hellenistic-Egyptian "types" of rulers, which had originally circulated as legends of Alexander and the Ptolemies. One gains the impression that the author's primary interest was—again in the tradition of *Chaosbeschreibung* literature—to create a literary pastiche of alternating times of prosperity and woe, which reflected both an archaic coherence and a certain verisimilitude.

Two components of ApocEl 2, however, have often been regarded as analogical reflections of current history: (1) the battles between Assyrians and Persians in Egypt (§§E and G), and (2) the accession of the "king from the city which is called 'The City of the Sun'" (§G). It is methodologically appropriate to assess the traditions behind these literary components before seeking historical antecedents.

Before the Assyrians appear as opponents of Persians in §§E.d and H.b, a King of the Assyrians is mentioned in §A. Georg Steindorff perceived in this Assyrian King the distant reflection of Antiochus Epiphanes and the Seleucid invasion of Egypt; Jean-Marc Rosenstiehl saw him as Pompey, in his capacity as "King from the North."[70] Either interpretation assumes that the author intended such attributes as "Northern" and "Assyrian" to be understood literally and historically.

By the Hellenistic period, however, the word *assyrioi* had assumed a largely unspecific and literary significance in oracles and other literature. "Assyrians" in the *Sibylline Oracles* signifies groups as diverse as Jews (e.g., 11.29, 80), Babylonians (3.99, 268–70, 809–10), Antiochenes (12.135), Eastern peoples in general (11.159–61; 12.107–9), and even

70. Steindorff, 75 n. 7; Rosenstiehl, 72.

Persians (5.336; 11.179; 12.266).[71] In *Sib. Or.* 11.81–82, an "Assyrian King" seems to denote Solomon.[72] In the book of Judith, Nebuchadnezzar rules over "Assyrians" rather than Babylonians (1:1 and passim). The word, therefore, seems to have had an essentially symbolic value, signifying Eastern "hordes."

In Egyptian prophetic literature, however, "Assyrians" had an exclusively negative meaning, denoting one of the typical invading armies of "foreigners"—peoples of Seth–Typhon.[73] Even Athanasius uses the Assyrian army of biblical legend (2 Kings 19) in the *Life of Antony* as an example of demonic hordes, against which the divine angels are victorious.[74] The *Chronicle of John of Nikiu* and the Coptic Cambyses legend apparently used a source that identified Cambyses as Nebuchadnezzar.[75] Because all these texts come from the Roman period, it is not surprising that the Apocalypse of Elijah should follow the same tradition of viewing "Assyrians" as a type of evil invader, a component of the *Chaosbeschreibung* tradition. Indeed, the author has made this symbolic value clear in identifying the Assyrian King both as "from the North" (a biblical attribute of the evil invader: Jer 1:14; 4:6; Jl 2:20; Ez 38:15) and as "the Unrighteous King"; and his invasion is followed by traditional "signs of distress": the groaning land, the seizure of children, the longing for death. It is therefore doubtful that a particular figure or army of historical Assyrian (or Syrian) nationality is intended; rather, it is a motif of *Chaobeschreibung*: the invasion of Typhonian people.

The symbolic value of "Assyrians" continues in §§E and G, where they are opposed by "Persians" in battles that range over Egyptian soil. Obviously, Persian and Assyrian armies were at no time so engaged

---

71. See David Potter, *Prophecy and History in the Crisis of the Roman Empire: A Historical Commentary on the Thirteenth Sibylline Oracle* (Oxford: Clarendon, 1990), 197–99; and Th. Nöldeke, "ASSYRIOS SYRIOS SYROS," *Hermes* 5 (1871):443–68.

72. See J. Collins, "Development of the Sibylline Tradition," 438–39.

73. Cf. *Or. Lamb* 2.24; and *Or. Pot.* P³ 30f (although Ludwig Koenen understands this also to refer *ex eventu* to Antiochus Epiphanes—"Die Prophezeiungen des 'Töpfers,'" *ZPE* 2 [1968], 187). P.Cairo 31222 uses "Syrian" consistently to represent hostile lands outside Egypt, as a reflection of domestic chaos; see George R. Hughes, "A Demotic Astrological Text," *JNES* 10 (1951):258–59. See also Arnaldo Momigliano, "Some Preliminary Remarks on the 'Religious Opposition' to the Roman Empire," in *Opposition et résistances à l'empire d'Auguste à Trajan,* Entretiens sur l'antiquité classique 33 (Geneva: Vandoeuvres, 1986), 113.

74. Athanasius *Vita Antonii* 28.

75. See H. Ludin Jansen, *The Coptic Story of Cambyses' Invasion of Egypt,* Avhandlinger utgitt av det Norske Videnskaps-Akademi i Oslo 2, Hist.-Filos. Klasse 1950, 2 (Oslo: Jakob Dybwad, 1950), 27–29.

within Egypt. Therefore just as "Assyrians" functions as a "type" of invader in this text, so also must "Persian."

By the first century C.E., Persia had already become the backdrop to the myth of Nero *redivivus*. In this myth the emperor Nero did not die but fled to Persia, whence he would return at some future time, supported by the Persian army, to conquer the Roman Empire.[76] The image of Persian invasion is an important corollary theme of the myth: "For the Persian will come onto your soil like hail, . . . with a full host numerous as sand, bringing destruction on you. And then, most prosperous of cities [= Alexandria], you will be in great distress."[77] As, in popular tradition, the Persians were supposed to install Nero, so the Persian invasion in ApocEl 2 culminates in the installation of the king from "the City of the Sun" in §G. It is apparent that "Persians" as an invading force constituted a popular literary backdrop to mysterious kings in the composition of oracles in the Greco-Roman world.

In Egypt, after the invasion of Cambyses, the image of "Persians" carried an overwhelmingly negative significance (like "Assyrians"). Cambyses' invasion was continually retold through the Roman period in harsh, martyrological scenes, becoming a paradigm for understanding the Arab invasion of the seventh century.[78] "Persian" was used in Hel-

---

76. Cf. John J. Collins, *The Sibylline Oracles of Egyptian Judaism*, SBLDS 13 (Missoula, Mont.: Scholars Press, 1974), 80–81. The tradition of his return with the Persians appears most explicitly in *Sib. Or.* 5.94–105, 143–54; 8.139–59. On the Nero *redivivus* myth, in general, see Larry Kreitzer, "Hadrian and the Nero *Redivivus* Myth," ZNW 79 (1988):92–115; and Martin Bodinger, "Le mythe de Néron de l'Apocalypse de Saint Jean au Talmud de Babylone," RHR 206 (1989):21–30. Both scholars note that the myth originally developed as a prophecy in the eastern Mediterranean of the eventual supplanting of Rome by the Asian kingdoms—that is, as anti-Roman nationalist propaganda. The Jewish prophecies of Nero as an evil antihero in *Sibylline Oracles* books 4, 8, and 12 and in Revelation may well be counterpropaganda against such popular hopeful views of Nero and Persia. These prophecies' circulation throughout the Roman world is shown by the several "false Neros" who managed to gain considerable followings (see Albert Earl Pappano, "The False Neros," *Classical Journal* 32 [1937]:385–92). E.g., *Sib. Or.* 8.153–57 expresses itself in the form of an argumentative warning: "*Celebrate, if you wish,* the man of secret birth, riding a Trojan chariot from the land of Asia with the spirit of fire. *But when he* cuts through the isthmus glancing about, going against everyone, having crossed the sea, then dark blood will pursue the great beast" (tr. J. Collins, "Sibylline Oracles," *OTP* 1:421), emphasis mine.

77. *Sib. Or.* 5.93, 97–98 (tr. J. Collins, "Sibylline Oracles," *OTP* 1:395). Note the equation of a Persian invasion with woe upon Alexandria (the "City by the Sea").

78. See Jacques Schwartz, "Les conquérants perses et la littérature égyptienne," BIFAO 48 (1949):65–80; Samuel K. Eddy, *The King Is Dead* (Lincoln: University of Nebraska Press, 1961), 261–67; Lloyd, "Late Period," 286–88; Jansen, *Coptic Story of Cambyses' Invasion*, 45–49; cf. *Chronicle of John of Nikiu* 51. Lloyd has found evidence in Herodotus that the earliest priestly recollections of Cambyses were mixed, with some constituencies attributing to him an Egyptian lineage (as the *Alexander Romance* of Pseudo-Callisthenes did with Alexander the Great): see Alan B. Lloyd, "Herodotus on

lenistic Egypt as a fictional nationality, apparently denoting a legal status of inferiority; and it is likely that the choice here of "Persian" also derived from a popular memory of Persian depredations.[79] Finally, the *Testament of Job* displays its Egyptian provenance in having the devil disguise himself as the king of the Persians.[80]

Yet it is striking that ApocEl 2 does not entirely follow this traditional Egyptian view of Persians as a typical evil. Although in §G.b "the Persians will take vengeance [ⲛⲁ.ⲭⲓ ⲙ̄ⲡⲉⲕⲃⲁ] on the land," they are also imagined as ridding the land of Jews[81] and Assyrians and installing the penultimate savior, the king from "the City of the Sun"—a reversal of the traditional Egyptian sentiments toward Persians. Because an Egyptian audience with an "Egyptian" identity would have understood "Persian" with its traditionally negative value, this reversal might have led to a certain dissonance between the textual symbol and the traditional symbol.

The simplest resolution of this contradiction in the meaning and function of "Persian" has been to take "Assyrian" and "Persian" as having represented each other in a historical prophecy of the imminent future; then one might conceivably come up with a historically accurate conflict of the third century.[82] "Assyrians," that is, might be said to represent the Sassanid Persians under Ardashir and Shapur I, who threatened the Roman empire and its ally Palmyra (under Odenath) for much of the third century C.E.; whereas "Persians" could represent the Palmyrene (Syrian) army of Odenath and, subsequently, Zenobia.[83] Palmyra and Persia had actually engaged in frequent battles during the

---

Cambyses: Some Thoughts on Recent Work," in *Achaemenid History*, vol. 3: *Method and Theory*, ed. Amélie Kuhrt and Heleen Sancisi-Weerdenburg (Leiden: Nederlands Instituut voor het nabije Oosten, 1988), 55–66, esp. 62. By the later Hellenistic period, however, the negative interpretations of Cambyses seem to have dominated (see Eddy, *King Is Dead*, 261–63; and Lloyd, "Herodotus on Cambyses," 62, 65–66), culminating in the Cambyses legend, which is preserved in Coptic but probably derived from a Hellenistic *Grundlage* (see Jansen, *Coptic Story of Cambyses' Invasion*, 33, 49).

79. Bevan, *House of Ptolemy*, 109–11.

80. *T. Job* 17; cf. John J. Collins, "Structure and Meaning in the Testament of Job," SBLSP (1974), vol. 1, ed. George MacRae (Cambridge, Mass.: SBL, 1974), 50. It is rather striking that an Egyptian Jew would follow the Egyptian hatred of Persians, for in Jewish memory the Persians were generally salvific.

81. A beneficial act in Egyptian nationalist tradition; see below, pp. 226–28.

82. It might be suggested that, as the subsequent King of Peace recalls traditions of Alexander, so the Unrighteous King (ApocEl 2:2-5) recalls (without actually reflecting) Cambyses, from whose legendary depredations upon Egypt (and consequent Persian domination) Alexander was once viewed as a savior. Ἀσσύριοι seems to have been used for "Persian" in Strabo 16.743; cf. *Sib. Or.* 5.336; 11.179.

83. Cf. Schrage, who suggests that "Assyrian" denoted a contemporary great power that included both Persia and Rome (224).

middle of the third century, although in Syria, not Egypt. Zenobia herself entered Upper Egypt in 269 C.E., allegedly at the invitation of a Greco-Egyptian merchant and dissident from Roman rule, Timagenes.[84] Indeed, Zenobia's apparent attempts at conciliating local and priestly sentiments in Egypt could conceivably be related to the "nationalist" elements of ApocEl 2.[85]

The argument for ApocEl 2's analogical reflection of third-century history continues further. Zenobia (or, according to Rollin Kearns, her son Waballath)[86] would become the king from the "City of the Sun," for Palmyra did have a solar religion. The Jewish authorship of a putative *Vorlage* of the Apocalypse of Elijah would presumably explain the text's high regard for Zenobia as the restorative king, because she may have restored a synagogue in Upper Egypt.[87] Thus the Apocalypse of Elijah, in some redactional phase, would emerge as deliberate (albeit allusive) propaganda for Zenobia's "messianic" authority.

But these arguments at best rely on the historical coincidence of Zenobia's invasion with the *terminus ante quem* of the text of the Apocalypse of Elijah; and at worst they rely upon the untenable assumption that the Apocalypse of Elijah was written by a Jew. The assumption that these episodes in §§E and G were meant to be read allegorically—as direct reflections of immediate history—is belied by the overwhelmingly typical (or "literary") nature of ApocEl 2 as a whole. Indeed, the classic *Chaosbeschreibung* image of the Nile running with blood appears in the midst of these allegedly "historical" sections.

It is also in §E that one finds a profusion of stereotyped numerological indicators: three kings (§E.a), four kings versus three kings (§E.d), three years (§E.e). A survey of the use of numbers in ApocEl 2 reveals that they are all multiples of three or four: "four kings" (2:20), "30th year" (2:21), "three kings" (2:39, 42), "four (kings)" (2:42), "three years" (2:43), "three days" (2:44), "sixth year" (2:47), "three years and six months" (2:52),[88] "fourth year" (3:1). It is doubtful that any period of history could

84. Zosimus *Historia nova*, 1.44; see below, chapter 9, pp. 262–64.

85. Cf. Arthur Stein, "Kallinikos von Petrai," *Hermes* 58 (1923):454–55; Jacques Schwartz, "Les palmyréniens et l'Égypte," *Bulletin de la société archéologique d'Alexandrie* 40 (1953):76–77; and Glen W. Bowersock, "The Miracle of Memnon," *BASP* 21 (1984):31–32.

86. Rollin Kearns, *Das Traditionsgefüge um den Menschensohn* (Tübingen: Mohr [Siebeck], 1986), 96–100.

87. See Rosenstiehl, 64–67; cf. Schwartz, "Les palmyréniens et l'Égypte," 77.

88. The use of "three years and six months" in passage §H.b is drawn directly from a popular apocalyptic numerological system assigned to times of eschatological distress:

conform to such numerological regularity. Therefore it is likely that the numbers three and four constituted the author's numerical formulas, the fixed units he used to denote amounts that carried cultural and performative relevance. ApocEl 2 is arranged on the basis of threes and fours (and the early Jewish "three years and six months"), just as an epic or folktale might unfold in threes, fours, sevens, or hundreds.

Finally, the supposed reference to Zenobia as "king" not only crosses gender lines but is so vague in terms of historical veracity that it could only be written considerably after the Palmyrene invasion—that is, close to the turn of the century. It would thereby lose its significance as *ex eventu* oracular propaganda for her authority and dominion; the reason for referring to her would consequently be lost; and, most importantly, the composition of the Greek text itself would be pushed problematically close in time to the date of its first Coptic recensions in the early fourth century.

The interpretation of §§E and G as referring to events of the third century C.E. therefore loses much of its basis. Yet one still must account for the positive view of Persians in a text that otherwise cleaves closely to a literary tradition with fundamentally xenophobic views of invading foreigners. Insofar as invading Persians held an almost neutral (and occasionally beneficial) significance in the wider Mediterranean world as the prophesied supporters of Nero *redivivus* against Rome (and, perhaps more notably, as the destroyers of Alexandria in *Sib. Or.* 5.98), there may have been a standard expectation of eschatological Persian invasions (and oriental triumph in general) among Greek-speakers in Roman Egypt, separate from the traditional Egyptian view of Persian invasions. The Greek-comprehending audience of the Apocalypse of Elijah may have understood this more general sense of "Persians." The Persian expulsion of Jews and installation of the king from "The City of the Sun," however, would have had an ironic significance to an audience with the slightest knowledge of the Egyptian negative valuation of

cf. Dn 7:25; 12:7 (= "a time, [two] times, and half a time"); Rv 11:2; 13:5 ("forty-two months"); 11:3; 12:6 ("one thousand, two hundred, and sixty days"); Commodian *Carmen apologeticum* ll. 885–86 ("three years and a half"; ed. and tr. Antonio Salvatore, *Commodiano: Carme apologetico* [Torino: Societa Editrice Internazionale, 1977], 102–3). Charles notes also the effect of this numerological system on Luke's retelling of Elijah's drought in 1 Kgs 18:1: where the biblical legend assigns the drought to roughly three years, Lk 4:25 puts three and a half years. See Charles, *Revelation of St. John*, 1:279–80; Hermann Gunkel, *Schöpfung und Chaos in Urzeit und Endzeit* (Göttingen: Vandenhoeck & Ruprecht, 1895), 257–58, 266–72, 330, 395.

Persians. To such an audience, the Persians' accomplishment of such beneficial acts would mean that these acts (and the king's beneficial dominion) should *not* be understood as permanent or ultimate. Rather, the symbolic inversion of the Persians expresses the chaos of the pre-eschatological era, when evil forces accomplish ostensibly positive acts.

How, then, may we understand the "king from the city which is called 'The City of the Sun'" in §G.a? The solar connotations of this penultimate great king closely resemble the prophecy in the *Potter's Oracle* of a messianic "king descended from Helios," designating a final, perfect pharaoh who would express the restorative and ordering powers of the sun god, Re.[89] The term is also used in the Egyptian Jewish *Third Sibylline Oracle*, although subordinated to YHWH:

> And then God will send a King from the sun who will stop the entire earth
> from evil war, . . . and he will not do all these things by his private plans
> but in obedience to the noble teachings of the great God.[90]

Collins has explained the Jewish use of such a traditional Egyptian motif as propaganda for Ptolemy VI: that a Jewish courtier might have viewed this king in such salvific terms that he took an Egyptian term to express this sentiment in local symbolism (although phrasing it mono-theistically: it is God who sends the king).[91] Whether or not this oracle had a particular historical reference, however, it provides evidence of the circulation of "King from Re" prophecies or expectations beyond simply that of the *Potter's Oracle*.[92] The extended form in which the prophecy appears in §G.a would reflect the Hellenistic-Egyptian priestly tradition that the savior–pharaoh would arise in Heliopolis, the ancient sacred city of Re, near Memphis.[93]

An analogous prophecy of "solar" figures appears in the *Thirteenth Sibylline Oracle*, but it is divided into a "priest . . . sent from the sun" (l. 151), a "city of the sun" (l. 153), and a terrible lion "sent from the sun" (ll. 164–65). This section of the *Thirteenth Sibylline Oracle* has been shown

---

89. Note that, in the frame narrative of the *Potter's Oracle*, the story of the potter's oracle to King Amenophis concludes with the latter burying the visionary potter ἐν ʿΗλίου πόλει (*Or. Pot.* P² ll. 51–52; in Koenen, "Prophezeiungen des 'Töpfers,'" 208).

90. *Sib. Or.* 3.652-56 (tr. J. Collins, "Sibylline Oracles," *OTP* 1:376).

91. J. Collins, *Sibylline Oracles*, 41–44.

92. Cf. Raymond Weill, *La fin du moyen empire égyptien* (Paris: Imprimerie nationale, 1918), 131–32 on the role of Heliopolis in the ancient Egyptian *Königsnovelle* about the impure invaders.

93. Cf. CPJ 520, which expresses the fear that the Jews (i.e., Typhonian foreigners) "will inhabit the City of Helios."

to refer to events surrounding the cities of Emesa and Palmyra in Syria, whose religious iconography did have a solar theme.[94] Ironically, it is in light of these particular Syrian parallels that many scholars have taken §G.a in ApocEl 2 to reflect a Palmyrene monarch.[95]

Yet it is a problematic move to take the language (and historical antecedents) of an oracle composed in Syria to interpret a similar motif in an Egyptian Christian text, when the same motif can be found in other, contemporaneous Egyptian literature. The solar king in ApocEl 2 manifestly reflects the Egyptian tradition: he is associated specifically with the increase of arable land in §H.a (implying that he is conceived by the author as fulfilling traditional pharaonic functions), and he is the last beneficial king before the parousia of Christ.

Indeed, it is likely that the presence in the *Thirteenth Sibylline Oracle* of analogs of the "King from Re" motif actually reflects an importation of the Egyptian tradition, whose centrality in Egyptian prophetic literature (and widening circulation through such media as the *Third Sibylline Oracle* and copies in late antiquity of the *Potter's Oracle*) led to its inclusion in the Greco-Roman *oikumenê* of oracular motifs. The author of the *Thirteenth Sibylline Oracle* found in the "King from Re" motif and its analogs (such as the "City of the Sun") fitting allegorical symbols for Palmyra and Emesa and their solar connotations. Similarly, the editor of the Greek Tiburtine Sibyl used the solar king of the Apocalypse of Elijah to prophesy the preeschatological rise of the Syrian city of Heliopolis.[96]

Historical events of the third century, one may conclude, are not signified allegorically in ApocEl 2. The text was intended to be meaningful and plausible as a prophetic vision without the audience's perception of past history through its symbols and episodes. The period of the audience, in the chronological spectrum of the Apocalypse of Elijah, lies back in ApocEl 1:13 and following—the "deceivers" who "oppose fasting"—therein rendering all of ApocEl 2 as true prediction, rather than an account of past history.[97]

---

94. The "priest" is Uranius Antoninus II and his Elagabalus cult (see A. T. Olmstead, "The Mid-Third Century of the Christian Era," *CP* 37 [1942]:406–8). The "lion" is clearly Odenath (ibid., 420; cf. Saul Lieberman, "Rabbinic Parallels to the Thirteenth Sibylline Book," *JQR* 37 [1947]:37–38). J. Collins incorrectly identifies both as Odenath ("Sibylline Oracles," *OTP* 1:458).

95. E.g., Wilhelm Bousset, "Beiträge zur Geschichte der Eschatologie: Die Apokalypse des Elias," *ZKG* 20 (1899):106.

96. Greek Tiburtine Sibyl l. 205 (shortened to "a king will arise from the city of the sun"). On the author's interest in Heliopolis, see Alexander, *Oracle of Baalbek*, 44–47.

97. See chap. 11.

This interpretation of ApocEl 2 as using an essentially a priori signification can be verified by assessing the understandings of the text
expressed by subsequent editors who used the Apocalypse of Elijah to
compose new texts. Did such author–editors interpret its predictions of
woes as meant to happen during immediate history or eschatologically?
The first witness to the text, Didymus the Blind, did not consider the
legend of Tabitha either a reference to an individual of his day or a
"type" to be interpreted abstractly, but rather an authoritative proof text
for the use of the name "Shameless One" for the figure of "Antichrist."[98]

A more complex case is the Greek Tiburtine Sibyl, which is constructed of prophecies in such obviously allegorical form and systematic
arrangement that one may assume the text's audiences viewed them as
vaticinia ex eventus. Yet the text depends on the Apocalypse of Elijah
exclusively for its imaginary portrayal of the eschaton.[99] That is, it reads
the Apocalypse of Elijah again as an ideal—not *ex eventus*—prophecy of
woes. Because of its consistent references to a Heliopolis (in this case,
evidently, the Syrian city) and the building of its temples, Paul J.
Alexander has argued that the Greek Tiburtine Sibyl "was compiled in
or near Heliopolis" and that the author had a strong interest in this city's
status in the last days.[100] It cannot be a coincidence, therefore, that the
author has allowed his text to culminate with the Apocalypse of Elijah's
"King from the Sun" prediction. Indeed, the author changes "a king from
the city which is called 'The City of the Sun,'" as both Sa[3] and Ach
articulate the oracle, to "a king from the City of the Sun [ἀπὸ ἡλίου
πόλεως]," which perhaps more easily reflected Syrian Heliopolis.[101] The
manifest interest in this city must account for the use of the Apocalypse
of Elijah in the first place: the author sought an oracular text that might
be read to express the ultimate glory of Heliopolis and found such a text
in the Apocalypse of Elijah. His disregard for the *ex eventus* value of the
Apocalypse of Elijah's oracles is expressed in that he actually rearranged
many of the episodes for his new eschatological prophecy.

98. Didymus the Blind *Comm. Eccles.* 235.24–28 (ed. and tr. Johannes Kramer and
Bärbel Krebber, *Didymos der Blinde: Kommentar zum Ecclesiastes [Tura-Papyrus]*, vol. 4:
Kommentar zu Eccl. Kap. 7–8, 8, PTA 16 [Bonn: Rudolf Habelt, 1972], 136–37).

99. Grk. Tib. Sib. 173–227.

100. Alexander, *Oracle of Baalbek*, 44–47; the bulk of the references are in ll. 76–88,
referring to Antiochus. There are no "King from Heliopolis" references in the Latin
Tiburtine Sibyl.

101. Grk. Tib. Sib. 205. Alexander is incorrect in stating that the author interpolated
the oracle here as an expression of his interest in the city (*Oracle of Baalbek*, 47). Rather,
the author is epitomizing ApocEl 2, the culmination of which is this very oracle.

Therefore, in the case of the Greek Tiburtine Sibyl, the Apocalypse of Elijah was read and appropriated out of an interest in one particular oracle in its text. Yet this oracle was not then understood historically; in the Tiburtine Sibyl it remained an entirely eschatological vision of a savior–king.[102] The hermeneutic difference lies in the author's localization of the oracle, so that it would pertain to civic interests. This was effected through the composition of the rest of the Tiburtine Sibyl.

The last text that shows clear knowledge of the Apocalypse of Elijah is the *Apocalypse of Shenoute*. This late seventh-century expansion of the *Vita* composed by Besa, Shenoute's own disciple, adds to the earlier text an eschatological revelation from Christ that begins with a prophecy *ex eventus* of the Arab invasions.[103] Like the Apocalypse of Elijah, this prophecy uses "Persian" as a type for invaders (in this case, the Arabs), mixing such allusive language with more explicit references to bishops, Christians, and monasteries.[104] The eschatological imagery, however, grows increasingly fantastic, compiled largely from the book of Revelation, and at this point the author evidently added motifs from the Apocalypse of Elijah: the women who are suckled by serpents and produce poison (§D.d), the sufferers' appeal to the rocks to fall upon them (§D.c), *anachoresis* (ApocEl 4:24-26), and others.[105] The author not only is drawing on the Apocalypse of Elijah as a source for eschatological imagery (as opposed to the description of immediate history) but is using the text in a haphazard way, drawing from different sections without regard for their order in the text of the Apocalypse of Elijah.[106] Thus in the late seventh century, in the mind of at least one monastic scribe, the images of the Apocalypse of Elijah referred to the eschaton rather than to proximate events in Late Roman and Byzantine Egyptian history.

The evidence of subsequent readings of the Apocalypse of Elijah would not support an assumption that audiences heard and understood its oracles in light of political events of their own day. This evidence

---

102. Cf. Rosenstiehl, 37–40, 42.

103. Ed. E. Amélineau, *Monuments pour servir à l'histoire de l'Égypte chrétienne aux IVe et Ve siècles, Mémoires publiés par les membres de la mission archéologique française au Caire* 4 (Paris: Ernest Leroux, 1888), 338–51.

104. In ibid., 340–41.

105. In ibid., 342–44.

106. Cf. Rosenstiehl, 40–42. It is a likely inference that this prophecy was composed from the *memory* of various scriptural descriptions of the eschaton rather than with Revelation, the Apocalypse of Elijah, and (later in the text) Mark 13 on the scribe's very desk.

therefore supports my contention that ApocEl 2 was intended as prophecy—as a compilation of ideal (though traditional) oracles.

THE MEANING OF REFERENCES TO JEWS AND JERUSALEM

The references to Jews and Jerusalem in §E.a–b pose a different sort of
question, that of the social location of the author (although one scholar
has suggested that these passages too were *vaticinia ex eventus*, describing the restoration of Jerusalem after the Babylonian Exile).[107] Earlier
scholars assumed that the reference to Jews returning to Jerusalem in
§E.a represented a Jewish writer's own expectation of a premillennial
restoration, which would create a deceptive sense of peace, as §E.b
describes. The problem with this assumption is not only the profound
dearth of evidence for Egyptian Jewry in the late third century[108] but also
the verb that describes the Jews' return to Jerusalem: $αἰχμαλωτίζειν$
("take captive"). This word, employed previously in ApocEl 1:3 to
describe the "captivity [$αἰχμαλωσία$] of this age," can hardly express a
salvific act for Jews on the part of the Persians. What §E.a describes is
the Persians' deportation of the Jews from Egypt and the resettlement of
Jerusalem with Jews, both of which are eschatological "signs."

The first act, the Jews' removal from Egypt, can be understood in the
context of CPJ 520, the anti-Jewish oracle that predicted the expulsion
from Egypt of the Jews as Typhonians, foreigners who worshiped Seth–
Typhon, "by the anger of Isis." Although CPJ 520 was probably composed as native propaganda against the Jewish revolt of 116–17, the
extant papyri derive from the third century—that is, roughly contemporaneous to the Apocalypse of Elijah. Thus the Apocalypse of
Elijah's §E.a belongs to the "tradition" of Egyptian nationalist anti-
Judaism, which arose primarily in the Hellenistic period.

The Jewish resettlement of Jerusalem as a sign of the end of days,
such as §E.a–b describes, appears prominently in Eastern Christian
apocalyptic literature only after the third century C.E.[109] This idea com-

---

107. Oscar von Lemm, "Kleine koptische Studien, XXVI Bemerkungen zu einigen
Stellen der koptischen Apokalypsen 14," 46.

108. See Tcherikover and Fuks, *CPJ* 1:94–96.

109. Cf. Cyril of Jerusalem *Catecheses* 15.15; *Vita Shenoute* (Arabic), in Amélineau,
Monuments, 341; Greek *Apocalypse of Daniel* 8. Cf. also Wilhelm Bousset, *The Antichrist
Legend*, tr. A. H. Keane (London: Hutchinson, 1896), 162–63; and Paul J. Alexander, *The
Byzantine Apocalyptic Tradition*, ed. Dorothy deF. Abrahamse (Berkeley: University of
California Press, 1985), 206.

bined early Jewish (and Christian) prophecies that the Antichrist would "take his seat in the temple of God" (2 Thes 2:4) with Jewish hopes in late antiquity that the Messiah would rebuild the Jerusalem temple.[110] Thus in Hippolytus "the antichrist . . . is also the one who will raise up the kingdom of the Jews."[111] Although Robert L. Wilken has shown that many Christian authorities of the first three centuries held little regard for the terrestrial Jerusalem (preferring instead the heavenly Jerusalem or an altogether allegorical understanding of the holy city),[112] there is some evidence for "Jewish" Christians who continued to hold reverence for the city as a holy place and the site of many eschatological events.[113] Both §E.a and §E.b seem to reflect this position in describing Jerusalem as the site of two (deceptively) "blessed" events, the return of the Jews and the rumor of peace.[114] The association between "security" in Jerusalem and the imminent arrival of the Destructive One shows that the author imagines Jerusalem only as an eschatological barometer—when things appear pleasant there, then the eschatological Adversary will arise in "the holy places."[115]

110. See sources in Bousset, *Antichrist Legend*, 160–62 (the Apocalypse of Elijah draws on this tradition from 2 Thessalonians in describing the Lawless One as "taking his stand in the holy places"—e.g., ApocEl 2:41, 4:1-2). On late antique Jewish traditions of the restoration of Jerusalem and the temple, see Joseph Klausner, *The Messianic Idea in Israel*, tr. W. F. Stinespring (3d Ger. ed.; New York: MacMillan, 1955), 513–14. In the fourth century there was a Christian millennialist movement whose tenets included the rebuilding of the temple; Basil of Caesarea writes disapprovingly of this "base" interpretation of biblical prophecies in *Epistles* 263 and 265, whereas Jerome's commentaries on Ezekiel, Isaiah, and Daniel take seriously Jewish expectations of restoration; see Robert L. Wilken, "The Restoration of Israel in Biblical Prophecy: Christian and Jewish Responses in the Early Byzantine Period," in *"To See Ourselves as Others See Us": Christians, Jews, "Others" in Late Antiquity*, ed. Jacob Neusner and Ernest S. Frerichs (Chico, Calif.: Scholars Press, 1985), 443–71. The sixth and seventh centuries saw an increase of Jewish apocalyptic prophecies of the temple rebuilt: see *Sefer Zerubbabel* and *Sefer Eliahu* (in both of which the temple descends from heaven, as in Revelation 21); Wilken, "Restoration of Israel," 453–61; and Salo Wittmayer Baron, *Social and Religious History of the Jews*, 18 vols. (2d ed.; New York: Columbia University Press, 1957), 5:139–50.

111. Hippolytus *On Christ and Antichrist* 25.2 (ed. Enrico Norelli, *Ippolito: L'Anticristo* [Nardini Editore, 1987], 94).

112. Robert L. Wilken, "Early Christian Chiliasm, Jewish Messianism, and the Idea of the Holy Land," in *Christians among Jews and Gentiles*, ed. George W. E. Nickelsburg and George W. MacRae (Philadelphia: Fortress, 1986), 298–307.

113. E.g., Irenaeus *Adv. haer.* 1.26.2; see Wilken, "Early Christian Chiliasm," 299, 301; and idem, "Restoration of Israel."

114. In ApocEl 4:2-3, Jerusalem is juxtaposed to "the region of the sunset"—that is, the Egyptian land of the dead. It is conceivable that this juxtaposition represented a Christian extension of the mythological geography that separated the land of the dead from the land of the sunrise.

115. "Holy places" in plural may signify either the diverse holy sanctuaries of

The references to Jews and Jerusalem derive both from Egyptian nationalist anti-Judaism—a theme of *Chaosbeschreibung* in its Hellenistic and Roman development—and from early Christian millennial ideology of the preeschatological restoration of Israel and Jerusalem. They do not reflect the author's own Jewish background or sympathies.

THE SYNTHESIS OF NATIVE AND CHRISTIAN TRADITIONS

The Apocalypse of Elijah 2 §D.f combines what is probably a traditional Near Eastern—Egyptian and Jewish—concept of childbirth as a gauge of eschatological woes or prosperity with an encratite ideology, unique to ascetic Judaism of the Greco-Roman period and its Christian offshoots, praising virginity and barrenness. Both the assurance of "heavenly" children to the childless in this poem and the addition of παρθένος to a traditional saying that originally pertained to *inadvertent* childlessness suggest that the passage was expressing a current ethos or ideal of sexual renunciation in the author's milieu. Indeed, the "promise" of heavenly children suggests that the author himself advocated this ethos to his audience.[116]

A different reflection of popular Christian sentiments appears in the references to "saints" in ApocEl 2. Their function both in the narrative and, presumably, in the life of the audience is clarified outside ApocEl 2, in 5:2-20; the author makes clear that when Egypt ("the earth") falls into rapid decline under the Lawless One, this happens because of the departure of the saints—"for because of them the earth gives fruit, for because of them the sun shines upon the earth, for because of them the dew falls upon the earth" (5:18). Such powers were attributed in an equally causal manner to the pharaoh in traditional kingship ideology, as demonstrated earlier (chap. 7, pp. 162–63); yet in the Apocalypse of Elijah the integrative force of the cosmos has shifted to the saints (who were evidently a combination of deceased and venerated martyrs and the intended audience of the text projected into the future).

Jerusalem or the multiple saint-shrines of Egypt. This is the only place where Ach and Sa mss. agree on the number of these places. Elsewhere, where Sa³ has "place" (meaning Jerusalem?) Ach has "places" (ApocEl 3:5), and vice versa (4:7); cf. 4:1, where Sa¹ has "place" and Ach and Sa³ have "places."

116. The precedent in the *Wisdom of Solomon* should warn us not to view this ethos as uniquely or originally Christian, although, at the time of the composition of the Apocalypse of Elijah, we might justly assume it to be primarily Christian.

This harmony of native Egyptian tradition and a distinctly local Christian understanding of the charisma of saints and shrines pervades ApocEl 2. The explicit beneficiaries of the King of Peace's apparent benevolence in §B.b–c are the "saints," the "priests," and the "holy places," all of whom are juxtaposed to the "pagans" and their "idols." In the prophecy of the king from "the City of the Sun" (§G), prosperity is likewise equated with the fate of saint-shrines; and as the King of Peace favors shrines and "saints"—compounding traditional Egyptian images of royal benevolence with Christian images—so also the king from "the City of the Sun" wipes out "pagans" and reestablishes Christian shrines in §G.c–d. Indeed both figures utter the motto "The name of God is One!" (§§B.b, G.d).

Although the slogan "The name of God is One" (§B.b) has Jewish roots, it would not have seemed particularly strange to traditional Egyptians; indeed, the slogan gained great notoriety in popular Egyptian Christian tradition, as is witnessed by Saint Mark's legendary encounter with an Alexandrian cobbler who used the motto, as well as diverse amulets on which the motto functioned apotropaically.[117] In the third-century Apocalypse of Elijah, the motto would have indicated the King of Peace's (apparent or initial) sympathy for Christian identity: it functioned as a slogan of allegiance.[118]

In §C.c the author has evidently intended to make as vivid a contrast as possible between the dominions of the King of Peace (§B) and his son

117. Egyptian literature displays a tendency toward henotheism—a preference for venerating "unity" while implicitly acknowledging plurality; cf. Siegfried Morenz, *Egyptian Religion*, tr. Ann E. Keep (Ithaca, N.Y., and London: Cornell University Press, 1973), 135–49. On the Mark legend, see Birger Pearson, "Earliest Christianity in Egypt: Some Observations," in *The Roots of Egyptian Christianity*, ed. Birger A. Pearson and James E. Goehring, SAC 1 (Philadelphia: Fortress, 1986), 140–45. Among magical texts, cf. Dierk Wortmann, "Neue magische Texte," *Bonner Jahrbücher* 168 (1968):105, 107 (= #7, 10). On the slogan in general, see Eric Peterson, *HEIS THEOS* (Göttingen: Vandenhoeck & Ruprecht, 1926).

118. §B.c suggests that this "King of Peace" will become unfavorable to Christians. Although the precise sentiments of this passage are not clear, the author seems to imagine a situation in which a ruler will travel up the Nile in disguise to assess the value of religious property, perhaps for the purpose of later confiscation. The folkloric theme of a ruler in disguise is widespread, although in Hellenistic Egypt it was given literary prominence in Pseudo-Callisthenes' *Alexander Romance*: Nektanebos escapes Memphis and sails to Macedon in disguise (1.3.2–6). In the *Thirteenth Sibylline Oracle*, the priest ἡλιόπεμπτος (ll. 151–52; identified with Uranius Antoninus II of Emesa) is said to "accomplish everything with deceit [δόλῳ]." It is likely that the attribute of deceptiveness, both in the *Thirteenth Sibylline Oracle* and in the Elijah Apocalypse, made structural sense as the *opposite* of the correct understanding of signs with which the reader or audience of the text is endowed through hearing its oracles.

with the "demonic face." This is most clear when the demon-faced son recalls "every gift which my father gave you": there is a simple exchange between the activities of the "King of Peace" and the demon-faced son. The explicit reference to performing "sacrifices and abominations," however, may reflect the imperial sacrifice edicts from the mid-third century. Likewise, the seizure of saints and priests and the shutting of the shrines suggests depredations specifically against Christians, whether imagined or experienced. Thus one realm of tradition and lore to which the author appeals in casting this second image of eschatological woes is that of third-century persecution against Christians, or perhaps the lore emanating from the Christian response to the religious edicts. Although one cannot deduce that the demon-faced son historically represents Decius or Valerian, there is the suggestion here, as in the materials discussed above in chapter 6, that persecution traditions and fantasies that arose in the third century affected the author's image of evil kingship.

It is likely that the author intended the obscure image of the son "appear[ing] beneath the sun and the moon" (§C.c, 2:27)[119] as an explanation for the son's anti-Christian depredations. Although Schrage interpreted the image as a euphemism for self-exaltation (in the spirit of Is 14:13-14 and Dn 8:10-11),[120] it gains greater contextual meaning when interpreted within Egyptian Christian cultural categories, as allegiance to the sun and the moon as cosmic powers in the Greco-Egyptian sense and therefore as emblems of the son's primary allegiance to a high ritual "paganism"—the antithesis of Christianity in third-century Egypt. "Appearing beneath" in this sense could signify either iconographic representation (e.g., on stelae or amulets) or a public ritual. The use of "sun and moon" as emblems of "high" paganism would therefore belong to the *interpretatio Graeca* of Egyptian religious cosmology: Re and Thoth as successive lords of the sky, whose counterparts in Greco-Egyptian ritual spells received considerable devotion.[121] That early Egyptian Christians considered typical "paganism" to be sun-, moon-, and star-worship may be implied in the beginning of the *Apocalypse of Paul*, where each celestial body complains to God about human impiety and asks to punish mankind "so that they may know that you *alone* are God"

---

119. ⲞⲨⲰⲚϨ ⲈⲂⲞⲖ ϨⲀ. Wintermute translates "appear *before*" (741).

120. Schrage, 244 n. d.

121. See Hans Georg Gundel, *Weltbild und Astrologie in den griechischen Zauberpapyri* (Munich: Beck, 1968), 3–17, 25–26; Patrick Boylan, *Thoth: The Hermes of Egypt* (London, 1922; reprint, Chicago: Ares, 1987), 62–68; Garth Fowden, *The Egyptian Hermes* (Cambridge: Cambridge University Press, 1987), 22–27.

(4–6).[122] The attitude emerges clearly in a Coptic sermon from the Byzantine period, which imagines sun, moon, and idols standing at the judgment seat of God and describing how humans worshiped them in spite of their lowliness in the heavens.[123] In late antiquity such polemics would not have been directed at the royal cult per se but at the Greco-Roman expressions of Re and Thoth in the cults, cosmologies, and ritual spells of the Roman period.[124] Thus, by describing the son as "appearing beneath the sun and moon," the author was implying that this demonic figure was a concerted pagan, a worshiper of heavenly bodies—and that this is why he launched a persecution of the saints.

The solar associations of the king from "the City of the Sun" (§G), who functions as penultimate benefactor to the "saints" and their shrines, reflect a syncretism pervading the Apocalypse of Elijah—and no doubt much of early Egyptian Christianity—at the broadest level: that is, the conceptualization of Christ and the eschatological Adversary in terms of classical Egyptian mythology. It has been noted that Christ's parousia follows upon a series of alternating cycles between woe and beneficence; this makes Christ the ultimate restorer of the order, fertility, and power that the King from the City of the Sun approximated and the Lawless One subsequently banishes. Christ's function reflects native traditions of a salvific restoration of the cosmos after a period of chaos—traditions that derived from the kingship ideology.

As the pharaoh was "son of Re," the terrestrial emblem of the sun, so the penultimate salvific king was to come from the City of the Sun—and so also does Christ come "like the sun which shines from the east to the west" (ApocEl 3:3). This simile distantly recalls the Synoptic Sayings Source in its comparison of the parousia to lightning (Lk 17:24 [= Mt 24:27]), an image considerably fleshed out by a second-century Egyptian Christian in the *Apocalypse of Peter*:

> The coming of the Son of God will not be manifest, but like the lightning which shines from east to the west, so shall I come on the clouds of heaven with a great host in my glory, with my cross going before my face will I

---

122. Latin; the Greek omits this clause. The text continues with similar testimonies from sea, (fresh) waters, and earth.

123. Pierpont Morgan ms. 595, fol. 105ᵛ-106ʳ (in J. B. Bernardin, "A Coptic Sermon Attributed to St. Athanasius," *JTS* 38 [1937]:124–25). Cf. Jer 8:2.

124. Cf. Ramsay MacMullen, *Paganism in the Roman Empire* (New Haven: Yale University Press, 1981), 84–88.

come in my glory, shining seven times as bright as the sun will I come in my glory, with all my saints, my angels.[125]

Whether or not the author of the Apocalypse of Elijah remembered this particular passage or an oral condensation of it, it is quite significant that he imagined the sun as the most appropriate simile for Christ's return. From the Synoptic Sayings Source to the Apocalypse of Elijah, therefore, the symbol of the parousia has changed from lightning to sun; and it cannot be a coincidence that this change occurred with its progressive Egyptianization.[126]

The same indigenous perspective on Christian motifs can be seen in the representation of the devil. In reviewing the "execration" function of the last chapters of the Apocalypse of Elijah, it becomes apparent that the Adversary himself is imagined in the merged role of Seth–Typhon and Apophis (the opponent of the sun in Egyptian tradition). Like Seth–Typhon in Egyptian mythology, the Adversary in the Elijah Apocalypse causes the decline of fertility and irrigation after the departure of the saints (5:7-14); like both Seth–Typhon and Apophis, he dies "like a serpent with no breath in it" (5:33); and, most vividly recalling Apophis, the devil is announced in ApocEl 1 as having "desired to prevent the sun from rising over the earth and"—evidently meant as a corollary threat— "to prevent the earth from bearing fruit" (1:4).

By the Roman period the traditional cosmic threats of Seth–Typhon and Apophis often merged; thus, in two love spells from the second or third century C.E., the following evidently well-known *historiola* is twice tapped to bring lovers together: "As Typhon is the adversary [$\dot{\alpha}\nu\tau\acute{\iota}\delta\iota\kappa\sigma$] of the sun, so also inflame [the proposed beloved]."[127] The scribe draws on "Typhon's" perpetual, obsessive pursuit of Re to invoke the same kind of power for erotic ends.[128] The author of the Apocalypse of Elijah

---

125. *Apocalypse of Peter* 1 (Eng. tr. Hill [Ger. tr. Maurer and Duensing], *NTA* 2:668).

126. Cf. Julian Hills, *Tradition and Composition in the Epistula Apostolorum*, 100–106, 110. Christ is dubbed "the sun of righteousness" in a discourse attributed to Shenoute, Cairo ostracon 44674.125, ed. and trans. W. E. Crum, in idem and H. G. Evelyn White, *The Monastery of Epiphanius at Thebes*, 2 vols. (New York: Metropolitan Museum of Art, 1926), 2:13–14 (txt), 2:163–64 (trans.) (= no. 56). See in general G. Michaïlidès, "Vestiges du culte solaire parmi les chrétiens d'Égypte," *Bulletin de la société d'archéologie copte* 14 (1950):37–110.

127. PGM XXXIIa (in Arthur S. Hunt, "An Incantation in the Ashmolean Museum," *JEA* 15 [1929]:155–57 and pl. 31, fig. 1); and P. Cairo 60636 (in O. Guéraud, "Deux textes magiques du musée du Caire," in *Mélanges Maspero*, 2 vols., Mémoires de l'IFAO 67 [Cairo: IFAO, 1934–37], 2:201–6).

128. PGM XXXVI.77–82 invokes the ritual burning of an image or inscribed name of Apophis or Seth in priestly execration rites, in order to "burn" the beloved's heart. See

in a similar case has imagined the devil's paradigmatic activity in the cosmos as threatening the sun, like Apep, and fertility, like Seth–Typhon.[129]

One could conceptualize the intermediary steps and cultural paths between the still-continuing Egyptian temples and the Christian author of the Apocalypse of Elijah as (1) the trade in ritual ("magical") spells, by which priestly materials continually entered popular culture and application; or (2) what Griffiths has called the "rather fluid adoption of sayings from one category to another" among the literate cultures of Roman Egypt—a matrix of shared perspectives, as it were, among those who wrote for Egyptian audiences;[130] or (3) a more general concept of an Egyptian "mentality" that tended to imagine cosmic dynamics and forces within a limited, traditional range of symbols and motifs. But whatever means allowed for continuity of traditions into the world of the Apocalypse of Elijah, one must be prepared to recognize a thorough syncretism in the theological perspective of the author, one that is both Christian and Egyptian. In Egypt the sun was the archetypal symbol of divinity and order; and as the two cosmic adversaries, Seth–Typhon and Apep, merged in the practical mythologies of the Roman period, the singular demonic result posed a convenient reflection of, and therefore source for, the image of evil transmitted through Christian texts. As a creator, a synthesizer, then, the author of the Apocalypse of Elijah has demonstrated that Christian sentiments and Egyptian mythological images were fundamentally harmonious.

A similar harmony can be perceived in the alternation of details concerning "pagans" and "saints": as the pagans had their idols, so the saints now have their "holy places." These "holy places" reflect the author's consciousness of some network of shrines dispensing power that would be acceptable to Christians. It may be that the author is

---

Guéraud's review of erotic uses of Typhon mythology ("Deux textes magiques," 204–5). Note that another ritual text from the Roman period, the Demotic magical text from London and Leiden, continues the traditional concept of *Apophis* against the sun (col. XIX, 1.37).

129. Even if this introductory section was based upon a prior fragment, the "original" form of this particular verse is invisible behind the quite different versions in ApocEl and ApocPaul. See parallel translation in Appendix 1.

130. Griffiths, *Divine Verdict*, 220–21. This would be a "literary" analog to Walter Burkert's concept of "religious craftsmanship": those ritual techniques whose neutral ideological value allows fluid importation into other religions ("Craft vs. Sect: The Problem of Orphics and Pythagoreans," in *Jewish and Christian Self-Definition*, vol. 3: *Self-Definition in the Roman World*, ed. B. F. Meyers and E. P. Sanders [Philadelphia: Fortress, 1982], 1–22, 183–89, esp. 6–8).

transposing a fantasy of Palestine, the "holy land" (cf. ApocEl 5:5 Sa), upon Egypt, whose network of indigenous temples and pilgrimage sites remained in active use during the third century.[131] It is also conceivable that "holy places" signify actual martyr-shrines, perhaps generated over the course of the third-century's executions, although real evidence for Christian cult-structures and for devotion to martyrs' relics does not appear in Egypt before the fourth century.[132] But native Egyptian popular religion was based on local shrines; and either alternative would express the fact that in the Apocalypse of Elijah the "world" of Christian piety follows traditional, epichoric forms: shrines, holy men, priesthood, the awareness of kingship, and the integrity of land and society as the relevant factors of the cosmos. It is hardly unique to Egypt, however, that the conversion of the countryside should proceed through the exchange of healing shrines.[133]

131. On the holy sites of Palestine (specifically the tombs of prophets), see Marcel Simon, "Les saints d'Israël dans la dévotion de l'église ancienne," *Revue d'histoire et de philosophie religieuses* 34 (1954):106–12; idem, "Les pèlerinages dans l'antiquité chrétienne," *Les pèlerinages, de l'antiquité biblique et classique à l'occident médiéval*, Études d'histoire des religions 1 (Paris: Geuthner, 1973), 97–104; Eric M. Meyers and James Strange, *Archaeology, the Rabbis, and Early Christianity* (Nashville: Abingdon, 1981), 162–64; and esp. John Wilkinson, "Jewish Holy Places and the Origins of Christian Pilgrimage," *The Blessings of Pilgrimage*, ed. Robert Ousterhout, Illinois Byzantine Studies 1 (Urbana/Chicago: University of Illinois Press, 1990), 41–53. The classic evidence for these tomb-shrines is Mt 23:29; 27:52-53; and Lk 11:47-48. Alexander of Cappadocia is the first recorded (pre-213 C.E.) Christian visitor to Palestinian holy sites (see Eusebius *Hist. eccl.* 6.11.2), although opinions differ on calling him a "pilgrim" (P.W.L. Walker, *Holy City, Holy Places?* [Oxford: Clarendon, 1990], 12, to the affirmative; Pierre Maraval, *Lieux saints et pèlerinages d'orient* [Paris: Éditions du Cerf, 1985], 25–27, to the contrary). On Egyptian holy sites and pilgrimage, see Jean Yoyotte, "Les pèlerinages dans l'Égypte ancienne," *Les pèlerinages*, Sources orientales 3 (Paris: Éditions du Seuil, 1960), 54–57; H. Idris Bell, *Cults and Creeds in Graeco-Roman Egypt* (Liverpool: Liverpool University Press, 1953; reprint, Chicago: Ares, 1975), 68–69; Alan K. Bowman, *Egypt after the Pharaohs* (Berkeley: University of California Press, 1986), 171–72; and note "Osiris shrines" mentioned by Strabo *Geography* 17.1.23. Roger S. Bagnall ("Combat ou vide: christianisme et paganisme dans l'Égypte romaine tardive," *Ktema* 13 [1988]:285–96) observes a decline in the general superstructure of Egyptian religion during the third century, almost certainly due to Roman taxation and inflation, on which see below, pp. 242–49.

132. See Athanasius *Vita Antonii* 90; and Athanasius's festal letters for 369 and 370 C.E. Cf. discussion by L. Th. LeFort, "La chasse aux reliques des martyrs en Égypte au IVe siècle," *La nouvelle Clio* 6 (1954):225–30, esp. 227 n. 1; Alfred C. Rush, *Death and Burial in Christian Antiquity*, Catholic University of America Studies in Christian Antiquity 1 (Washington, D.C.: Catholic University Press, 1941), 117–25. On the record of martyr-shrines in Egypt see Hippolyte Delehaye, *Les origines du culte des martyrs*, Subsidia Hagiographica 20 (2d ed.; Brussels: Société des Bollandistes, 1933), 43, 46–47; and, on Alexandria, Annick Martin, "Les premiers siècles du christianisme à Alexandrie: Essai de topographie religieuse (IIIe–IVe siècles)," *Revue des études augustiniennes* 30 (1984):211–25.

133. Ramsay MacMullen, *Christianizing the Roman Empire* (A.D. 100–400) (New Haven and London: Yale University Press, 1984), 77, 152 n. 13.

The particular combination of Christian and native Egyptian traditional elements in ApocEl 2 (as elsewhere in the text) obviously posed no contradiction in the mind of the author or his subsequent readers. Rather than an ideology that simply demonized and extirpated indigenous categories, therefore, the Christianizing Apocalypse of Elijah espoused an ideology of replacement or extension—founding Christian ideas upon native traditions.[134] While seldom so vividly represented in early Egyptian Christian literature outside of martyrologies, this mode of Christianization seems to have been characteristic of Egypt, at least as far as the most fundamental traditions of the native religion are concerned (i.e., those through which Christianity was situated in the culture).[135] Outright conflicts between Christian mobs (such as those led by Shenoute of Atripe) and indigenous religion seem to have occurred largely in connection with issues of relative authority: authority of leadership, authority under which a local site was sacred, or authority under which a local ritual was practiced.[136] It was in these latter cases

134. Cf. Pierre Canivet, *Histoire d'une entreprise apologétique au Ve siècle* (Paris: Bloud & Gay, 1957), 108.

135. The old debate on the continuity of mythological motifs in Coptic apocryphal literature, waged by E. A. Wallis Budge ("Egyptian Mythology in Coptic Writings," in idem, *Coptic Apocrypha in the Dialect of Upper Egypt* [London: British Museum, 1913], lvi–lxxii), Frank Hudson Hallock ("Christianity and the Old Egyptian Religion," *Egyptian Religion* 2 [1934]:6–17), O.G.E. Burmester ("Egyptian Mythology in the Coptic Apocrypha," *Orientalia* 7 [1938]:355–67), and Ernst Hammerschmidt ("Altägyptische Elemente im koptischen Christentum," *Ostkirchliche Studien* 6 [1957]:233–50), has been superseded by more nuanced studies on the continuity of traditions and structures: see A. Piankoff, "La descente aux enfers dans les textes égyptiens et dans les apocryphes coptes," *Bulletin de la société d'archéologie copte* 7 (1941):33–46; Jean Doresse, *Des hiéroglyphes à la croix: Ce que le passé pharaonique a légué au Christianisme* (Istanbul: Nederlands Historisch-Archaeologisch Instituut, 1960); Violet MacDermot (*The Cult of the Seer in the Ancient Middle East* (London: Wellcome Institute of the History of Medicine, 1971), 108–201; Jan Zandee, "Traditions pharaoniques et influences extérieures dans les légendes coptes," review of *Die Legende im Koptischen: Untersuchungen zur Volksliteratur Ägyptens*, by Wolfgang Kosack, *Chronique d'Égypte* 46 (1971):211–19; Theofried Baumeister, *Martyr Invictus,* Forschungen zur Volkskunde 46 (Münster: Regensberg, 1972); Wolfgang Schenkel, *Kultmythos und Märtyrerlegende: Zur Kontinuität des ägyptischen Denkens*, Reihe: Ägypten 5 (Wiesbaden: Harrassowitz, 1977); Torgny Säve-Söderbergh, "The Pagan Elements in Early Christianity and Gnosticism," in *Colloque international sur les textes de Nag Hammadi*, ed. Bernard Barc, Bibliothèque copte de Nag Hammadi, section "Études" 1 (Quebec: Université Laval, 1981), 71–85; and Douglas M. Parrott, "Gnosticism and Egyptian Religion," *Novum Testamentum* 29 (1987):73–93.

136. See Jean Maspero, "Horapollon et la fin du paganisme égyptien," *BIFAO* 11 (1914):163–95; Roger Rémondon, "L'Égypte et la suprême résistance au Christianisme (V^e–VIIe siècles)," *BIFAO* 51 (1952):63–78; Walter Kaegi, "The Fifth-Century Twilight of Byzantine Paganism," *Classica et Mediaevalia* 27 (1966):249–58; and Ewa Wipszycka, "La christianisation de l'Égypte aux IVe–VIe siècles: Aspects sociaux et ethniques," *Aegyptus* 68 (1988):117–65. See further the Coptic primary sources listed in Doresse, *Des hiéroglyphes à la croix*, 19 n. 46.

that Christian bishops and monks alike viewed the "pagan" element as synonymous with "demonic."[137] But even then the marauding Christians would reestablish the local cult in purified but functionally similar form. In the words of Shenoute himself,

> Thus then at the site of a shrine to an unclean spirit, it will henceforth be a shrine to the Holy Spirit. And at the site of sacrificing to Satan and worshipping and fearing him, Christ will henceforth be served therein, and He will be worshipped, bowed down to and feared. And where there are blasphemings, it is blessings and hymns that will henceforth be therein.
>
> And if previously it is prescriptions for murdering man's soul that are therein [i.e., the fearsome magical power of hieroglyphs which he proceeds to describe] . . . where these are, it is the soul-saving scriptures of life that will henceforth come to be therein, fulfilling the word of God with His name inscribed for them and His son Jesus Christ and all His angels, righteous men and saints (portrayed), that everywhere what is therein may give instruction concerning every good thing, especially purity.[138]

So also, in the Apocalypse of Elijah, it was not the principle of ancient holy places that was rejected and opposed during the "conversion" of rural Egypt; for indeed, this principle underlay the secure hold Christianity achieved in Egypt by the sixth century.[139] Rather, what was rejected as demonic was that temple or shrine whose local dominance threatened or otherwise could not be integrated into the local Christian establishment.

CONCLUSION: THE PERSPECTIVE OF APOCEL 2

When one considers carefully the various symbols, images, and "events" of the second chapter of the Apocalypse of Elijah, the assumption that the author is referring—systematically and allegorically—to precise historical events in the life of his audience(s) becomes untenable. The author has compiled a series of traditional Egyptian and Greco-Roman oracles from memory or, occasionally, from literary sources and from his own imagination—itself informed by the symbolic

---

137. See also André-Jean Festugière, *Les moines d'Orient*, vol. 1: *Culture ou sainteté* (Paris: Éditions du Cerf, 1961), 23–39.

138. Michigan ms. 158 (tr. Dwight W. Young, in idem, "A Monastic Invective against Egyptian Hieroglyphs," in *Studies Presented to Hans Jakob Polotzky*, ed. D. W. Young (Beacon Hill, Mass.: Pirtle & Polson, 1981), 353–54.

139. Cf. Doresse, *Des hiéroglyphes à la croix*, 22–23, 30–33; Baumeister, *Martyr Invictus*, 65–67.

world and the forms of expression of traditional Egyptian prophecy—to describe cycles of woe and beneficence in Egypt preceding the advent of the eschatological Deceiver. The typical chaos–order structure of these cycles and their correspondence and (often) dependence upon the ideal figure of the king (whether beneficial or predatory) show the dependence of the chapter's macrostructure upon Egyptian kingship ideology. The smaller, precise details, such as the advance of the desert, the King from the Sun (and the solar Christ), the longing for death, the expulsion of the Jews, and the Nile running with blood, show the author's debt to the actual literary tradition of Egyptian nationalist prophecy, whether or not he knew the texts directly.

What is the ideological context for an extensive prophecy of imaginary (albeit historically plausible) events in the land of Egypt? Michael Barkun has argued that millennialist movements (such as Christianity, in its nascent centuries) generally develop in connection with a disaster.[140] Because disasters are relative to the impact an event might have upon a group, however, it is the circumstances and "mentality" of the group that determine the "disastrous" nature of a particular event.[141] One aspect of this "mentality," which paves the way for millennialist response, observes Barkun, is

> a general, nonspecific sense of dread. It is quite possible for large numbers of people to believe that some fearful event is imminent, without knowing its type, specific time of occurrence, or the kind of measures that may be taken against it. The sense of impending doom may have very little basis in fact. It may, on the other hand, serve in some subtle fashion as a self-fulfilling prophecy which drags in train the very dreaded events themselves. . . . Some periods seem to fantasize disasters more than others. . . . These prophecies may become self-fulfilling because they encourage a particular reading of events . . . the existence of disaster itself may come from the connotations given to ambiguous events.[142]

Such anxiety can be cogently inferred for many groups, both Christian and traditional, in late Egypt and North Africa of antiquity on the basis of the promulgation of the native oracles of the Roman period; the Christian writings of Tertullian, Hippolytus, Cyprian, Lactantius, and Commodian; and the behavior of the martyrs. The literature of the second and—even more—third centuries C.E. prophesied or envisioned

---

140. Michael Barkun, *Disaster and the Millennium* (New Haven: Yale University Press, 1974; reprint, Syracuse, N.Y.: Syracuse University Press, 1986).

141. Ibid., 51–90.

142. Ibid., 59, 60.

contemporary decline in terms drawn from indigenous traditions and typologies, with little attention to the concrete occurrences around it. Such visions, in the words of Ramsay MacMullen,

> could be set in motion by a civil war, invasion, or natural disaster, and any one such event drew up to the surface of popular consciousness an accompaniment of many happenings quite unconnected or, from a sense of appropriateness, invented out of whole cloth. . . . No difference was discerned between political instability and plague: both fell upon the empire according to some cosmic or divine order. . . .
> . . . Millenary myth gave shape to present experiences and projected them into a future of cosmic collapse; or they were referred into the past, into eras variously chosen but, by agreement, better . . . none of the responses to crisis is new in kind. What alone is new is at most a greater frequency of traditional responses, inevitable in the circumstances.[143]

The Apocalypse of Elijah thereby takes its historical and ideological position not only beside the *Perfect Discourse*, the manuscripts of the *Potter's Oracle*, and CPJ 520 but, more generally, beside the epistulary and homiletic interpretations of the age given by millennialist Christian authors, both outside of Egypt—Cyprian's letters, Hippolytus on the Antichrist, Lactantius on the details of the eschaton—and inside— Nepos of Arsinoë, the subject of chapter 10.

143. Ramsay MacMullen, *The Roman Government's Response to Crisis*, A.D. 235–337 (New Haven: Yale University Press, 1976), 6–7, 12.

PART THREE

A SILHOUETTE
OF THE MILLENNIUM:
TOWARD A HISTORICAL
AND SOCIAL CONTEXT FOR
THE APOCALYPSE OF ELIJAH

9

The First Level: Egypt in the Third Century C.E.

Woe to you, rulers of Egypt, at that time,
 because your time has passed!
The violence of the poor will turn against you,
 and they will seize your sons as plunder!
 —*ApocEl 2:29-30*

If the Apocalypse of Elijah provides little in the way of *vaticinia ex eventus* to locate its precise date of composition, it certainly reflects the turbulence and anxiety of some immediate historical situation. The above woe oracle displays a remarkable lust for revolution. The poor either hold an incipient animosity toward the rulers, imminently to be ignited, or are ready to turn the violence they have suffered at the hands of the rulers back against them—shades of medieval peasant revolts. The plural apostrophe "rulers"—using the Greek, ἄρχων, instead of Coptic, ⲚⲢⲞ—could be read as a sarcastic reference to the non-Egyptian background of an Egyptian administration. Evidently, we are in an era when the "Romanness" of Egypt's overlords was particularly noticed and viewed as particularly oppressive.

In reconstructing this era and its implications for the composition of the Apocalypse of Elijah, one must be aware that historical circumstances had significance only as mediated through the ideological perspectives of author, milieu, and immediate culture. The text, as demonstrated so far, synthesizes a millennialist ideology out of native Egyptian traditions of *Chaosbeschreibung*, Christian eschatological tradition, and local Egyptian Christian lore and piety. As "other-worldly" as millennialism tends to be, however, it invariably responds to stresses in its perceived environment. As one seeks to understand the origins of the text, one must comprehend not only this millennialist ideology but also its religious milieu and its environment—not only the "historical facts" of this environment but how members of the movement read these facts.

THE SOCIOECONOMIC DECLINE IN
EGYPT IN THE THIRD CENTURY

The immediate context in which *Chaosbeschreibung* would have had meaning in third-century Egypt has been aptly summarized in the words of Pierre Jouguet: "The third century was a disastrous epoch, where the crisis of central power aggravated, if not created, social troubles and economic misery."[1] H. I. Bell has also described the decline of third-century Egypt by,

> on the one hand, the impoverishment of the urban middle-class and, on the other hand, the development of the process which eventually, by the beginning of the fifth century, reduced the bulk of the peasantry to the semi-servile dependents of a limited number of great landowners possessing an almost feudal authority.[2]

This marked decline in the economy—especially rural—during the third century C.E. and the concomitant increase in the general exploitation of both peasant and middle classes can be illustrated and explained by a combination of factors. On the most general level, multiplying hostilities along the various borders of the empire required increased military funding, and Rome had long looked to the agricultural *richesse* of the Nile Valley to sustain its imperial coffers. The shift in imperial power to the military by the beginning of the third century, as has often been recognized, resulted in the imposition of particularly extreme burdens on all of the provinces (and especially on Egypt) to pay the armies or to bribe them not to revolt.[3] Of considerable importance for the economic life of Egyptians during this period was the drastic decline in the value of currency, beginning with Caracalla's institution

1. Pierre Jouguet, *La domination romaine en Égypte aux deux premièrs siècles après Jésus-Christ* (Alexandria: Société archéologique d'Alexandrie, 1976), 62.
2. H. Idris Bell, "Roman Egypt from Augustus to Diocletian," *Chronique d'Égypte* 13 (1938):360.
3. See Mikhail Rostovtzeff, *The Social and Economic History of the Roman Empire*, 2 vols. (2d ed.; Oxford: Clarendon, 1957), 1:394–432, 487–88, 496–97; and A. R. Birley, "The Third Century Crisis in the Roman Empire," *BJRL* 58 (1975–76):253–81.

of the *Antoninianus* in the beginning of the century and leveling out under the reigns of Aurelian and Diocletian.[4]

A social or economic decline in a country is invariably signaled by changes in the bureaucratic system of taxation—for example, new laws, new positions, or new calculations—as a sort of prelude to catastrophe. Bell suggested, indeed, that it was not the amount of taxes that increased with Roman domination "but the very efficiency of the Romans [that] made [their taxes] more burdensome,"[5] whereas F. Oertel observed that the increased levies, a hallmark of the empire of the third century, consisted "not in an increase in the normal items of taxation (land-taxes, poll-taxes, trade-taxes, etc.) corresponding to the devaluation of the currency—which such a step would have made plain to see—but in supplementary taxation."[6]

The tax system had already changed considerably with Roman rule through the development of the liturgical system of tax farming. Under this system, "free-lance" tax collectors bought—increasingly under coercion—the right to collect a set amount of taxes in a region, regardless of the year's earnings of the populace. Their ability to break even or turn a profit hence depended on their efficiency in collecting. From the beginning of the Roman period, there is evidence that in times of drought or agricultural decline such tax farmers would resort to extreme and violent methods of extortion to collect the requisite sum.[7]

Papyri from the reign of Philip (244–249 c.e.), however, disclose innovations even in this liturgical system, illustrating the correlation between economic innovation and exploitation. P. J. Parsons found references both to new tax quotas levied in response to (or regardless of) a general economic decline and to a new bureaucratic position to oversee taxation. He connected these innovations both to the greater financial needs of the empire under Philip and to a situation of drastically reduced resources in mid-third-century Egypt. Roman authorities, in a pattern of continued exploitation, indeed had responded to economic decline with

4. Allan Chester Johnson, *Egypt and the Roman Empire*, The Jerome Lectures, 2d series (Ann Arbor: University of Michigan Press, 1951), 42–51; Rostovtzeff, *Social and Economic History*, 1:470–73; and Michael Crawford, "Finance, Coinage, and Money from the Severans to Constantine," in *ANRW* 2.2 (1975):569–71, 575–77.

5. H. Idris Bell, "Egypt under the Early Principate," *CAH* 10 (1934):314.

6. F. Oertel, "The Economic Life of the Empire," *CAH* 12 (1939):262.

7. Philo *De Spec. Leg.* 2.92; 3.30; on the legality of such practices see Naphtali Lewis, *Life in Egypt under Roman Rule* (Oxford: Clarendon, 1983), 226 n. 5 and, in general, 159–67; H. Idris Bell, "The Byzantine Servile State in Egypt," *JEA* 4 (1917):89–93; idem, "The Economic Crisis in Egypt under Nero," *JRS* 28 (1938):1–8.

heavier and more efficient taxation.[8] The direct victims of this exploitation were, coincidentally, a middle class that the Roman administration had largely created to expand the tax base; and it is the precarious fate of this middle class that may provide a context for new religious movements in third-century Egypt.

As the imperial administration changed land tenure, in the beginning of Roman rule, from a free royal serfdom and collective responsibility for taxation to private land ownership and individual responsibility for taxes, a village petite bourgeoisie[9] developed, consisting of Greco-Egyptians, formerly of peasant classes, who could now own their own land and enter the ranks and responsibilities of a propertied class.[10] This bourgeoisie also consisted of Greco-Egyptians in the lower civil positions, who, during the latter half of Ptolemaic rule, had begun to occupy civil and military offices originally created by and for Greeks. Simultaneously, Greeks already in this middle class increasingly assimilated with the native population. Thus already by the beginning of Roman rule a sizable, ethnically mixed intermediate class existed in Egypt;[11] and while Rome established firm class divisions through the imposition of the poll tax, the Roman taxation itself singled out individual achievement and status.

Private landholding and its "privileges" were a two-faced gift; and this tendency to expand honors to the ironic detriment of a lower middle

8. P. J. Parsons, "Philippus Arabs and Egypt," *JRS* 57 (1967):134–41.
9. In using this term I am referring to a number of economic positions in Roman Egypt that were associated as a "class" distinct from the peasantry, as well as from a Greek elite whose economic means were based outside of Egypt proper (e.g., in Mediterranean shipping or Roman concerns). The following pages define the class's nature further. However, I do not imply by the use of this term any particular economic theory about the relationship between classes or the dynamics of classes.
10. For a summary of "classes" in Roman Egypt, see Lewis, *Life in Egypt*, 39–51, 66–67; Alan K. Bowman, *Egypt after the Pharaohs* (Berkeley: University of California Press, 1986), 100–101. The ethnic designation "Greco-Egyptian" here refers to (1) persons of native background who spoke Greek, participated in Hellenistic culture (inevitable for most Egyptians during the Roman period), or even considered themselves Greek; and (2) those of Greek background who identified themselves within traditional Egyptian cultural terms. The term is an analytic convenience, however, not a historical self-reference; see Koen Goudriaan, *Ethnicity in Ptolemaic Egypt*, Dutch Monographs on Ancient History and Archaeology 5 (Amsterdam: J. C. Gieben, 1988), esp. 117–19. "Greek" will therefore designate the main Alexandrian populace (and certain individuals in the larger Egyptian cities such as Oxyrhynchus), which did not consider itself "Egyptian" in any way and was not so viewed by others.
11. Françoise Dunand, "Grecs et égyptiens en Égypte lagide: Le problème de l'acculturation," in *Modes de contacts et processus de transformation dans les sociétés anciennes*, Collection de l'école française de Rome 67 (Pisa and Rome: École française de Rome, 1983), 69–70. Cf. S. Davis, *Race Relations in Ancient Egypt: Greek, Egyptian, Hebrew, Roman* (New York: Philosophical Library, 1952), 56; Bowman, *Egypt after the Pharaohs*, 122.

class and the relative profit of the imperium emerges even more clearly in 212 C.E., when Caracalla expanded the actual Roman citizenship to all those above the lowly *dedicatii*, a status of unclear parameters but which essentially consisted of unpropertied peasants. The result (and certainly the motive) was the imposition and collection of even more taxes from those in the country towns who could barely pay.[12] Furthermore, with the dubious honor of Roman citizenship people with minor land-holdings and economic means became subject to the liturgical system of public service, and their financial responsibilities to the government had to be met individually.[13] During hard times, the tax farmers tended to concentrate their efforts on those who could pay more rather than on peasants who clearly had nothing. Conversely, in the beginning of the third century, those who had been at one time so privileged as to hold public office in a town and to be subject to λειτουργία suddenly found themselves forced to buy a post—tax collection—for which there would be no possible compensation; people were unable to pay or had fled.[14] In the midst of the innovations of Philip (250 C.E.), one finds a record of a trial before the Roman prefect, in which a group of villagers in Arsinoë complain that they have been illegally pressed into performing liturgies for the city. A representative of the Arsinoite senate pleads:

> By law you are judging citizens of Arsinoë, formerly a numerous body, but now going to ruin if they hold office for two days only; . . . One of them, making a declaration to be put on record before the strategus, said "Let him have my property and fulfil the liturgy"; the man who said this sustained the office, this very man who had abandoned his property.[15]

A liminal class was thus caught between the large landholders of the cities and the impoverished peasantry.[16] As the latter classes continued

12. Rostovtzeff, *Social and Economic History*, 1:418–19.

13. Bell, "Byzantine Servile State," 88–90; Rostovtzeff, *Social and Economic History*, 1:292–97.

14. See Arthur E. R. Boak, "Village Liturgies in Fourth Century Karanis," *Mitteilungen aus der Papyrussamlung der österreichischen Nationalbibliothek* 5 (1956):37–40.

15. P.Lond. 2565, ll. 93ff (in T. C. Skeat and E. P. Wegener, "A Trial before the Prefect of Egypt, Appius Sabinus, c. 250 A.D.," *JEA* 21 [1935]:237; cf. 246). The testimony describes a villager who actually sold off all his property in order to avoid the λειτουργία but was forced into office anyway. Severus (193–211 C.E.) himself had made it illegal to press villagers into the service of the city; thus the papyrus shows that by the mid-third century Severus's laws protecting the lower classes from undue exploitation were commonly being abrogated. In this case the Arsinoites argue unsuccessfully that he had ordained this law "while the cities were still prosperous." Cf. Rostovtzeff, *Social and Economic History*, 1:409; Lewis, *Life in Egypt*, 48–49.

16. See Bell, "Byzantine Servile State," 93 (cf. 100); idem, "Early Principate," 314; Jouguet, *Domination romaine*, 63–64; Lewis, *Life in Egypt*, 49–50, 163. It is interesting to note Sarah Pomeroy's theory "that under Roman rule women gained in economic and

at roughly the same level—the more cunning landholders occasionally expanding their estates, the peasants simply leaving in greater numbers—a town and village bourgeoisie was raised and crushed over the course of the century.[17] The position of this bourgeoisie itself was precarious: failure to perform liturgy or pay taxes would result in public humiliation through confiscation of property, reduction in rank to peasant, and, quite often, corporal punishment.[18]

When one compounds these facts of third-century petite bourgeois life with the cultural composition of a class created largely of successful, "upwardly mobile" Greco-Egyptians and a lower class of Greeks, it is apparent that insecurity of economic position would have been merely the foundation of a general social insecurity: cultural, ethnic, and—insofar as the economic vicissitudes of the bourgeoisie became a function of the existence and well-being of peasants and the continued fertility of their fields—local.[19] Having inspired the resentment of the peasantry (who now largely constituted the militia in Egypt)[20] and gradually losing their holdings to an urban elite, the Egyptian village and town bourgeoisie of the third century was caught between two hostile worlds of identity and culture.[21] Nowhere does this appear more clearly than in Caracalla's 215 edict expelling all ethnic Egyptians from Alexandria:

> Genuine Egyptians [he advises] can easily be recognized among the linenweavers by their speech, which proves them to have assumed the appearance and dress of another class; moreover, their mode of life, their far from civilized manners reveal them to be Egyptian country-folk.[22]

---

legal capacity while the prosperity of Egypt as a whole declined" ("Women in Roman Egypt: A Preliminary Study Based on Papyri," in *Reflections of Women in Antiquity*, ed. Helene P. Foley [New York: Gordon & Breach, 1981], 318).

17. This is not to understate the plight of the peasantry, who suffered equally from taxation and yet who were bound to their land increasingly by Roman laws. See Oertel, "Economic Life," 264, 268; Bell, "Byzantine Servile State."

18. Rostovtzeff, *Social and Economic History*, 1:486–89; Lewis, *Life in Egypt*, 161–66.

19. Rostovtzeff, *Social and Economic History*, 1:496–97; cf. Lewis, *Life in Egypt*, 48–50; and Bowman, *Egypt after the Pharaohs*, 105, on economic interdependence.

20. On Egyptian peasants in the Roman army, see Rostovtzeff, *Social and Economic History*, 425, 498–501; A. Kasher, "Some Comments on the Jewish Uprising in Egypt in the Time of Trajan," *JJS* 27 (1976):151–58; Lewis, *Life in Egypt*, 20–21, 27–28; J. F. Gilliam, "Enrollment in the Roman Imperial Army," in idem, *Roman Army Papers*, Mavors Roman Army Researches 2 (Amsterdam: J. C. Gieben, 1986), 163–72. On religious developments in this native military "subculture," see Françoise Dunand, *Religion populaire en Égypte romaine*, EPRO 77 (Leiden: Brill, 1979), 81–82, 107, 110, pls. 91–93.

21. Cf. Oertel, "Economic Life," 264.

22. P.Giessen 40, II.28–30 (ed. and tr. F. M. Heichelheim, "The Text of the *Constitutio*

Along with the simple, peasant ἀναχωρῆτες were quite a number of tradespeople and propertied individuals—members of the Greco-Egyptian petite bourgeoisie—who fell under the edict as "assuming the appearance and dress of another class."[23]

These factors are important for understanding millennialist activity in Egypt of this period. Although many scholars of millennialism have noted a consistently peasant base for such movements, often religious movements of the most systematically "other-worldly" character arise among liminal or middle classes.[24] The reason most commonly offered for this phenomenon is that the subversion of the middle class's economic status results in the deprivation of critical aspects (and symbols) of their social status, such as access to institutions of the dominant culture and the various means of social identity.[25] Furthermore, a socioeconomic transition within a single culture from (relative) collectivization to individualization has implications for the status of the individual person: identity ceases to be dependent on locale and on collective life and traditions and becomes more contingent on means of acquiring status that distinguish and must be maintained by the individual. In the terms coined by Mary Douglas, the social structure of Greco-Roman Egypt (or at least of the bourgeoisie) would have turned from a relatively "high grid" (integrated and interdependent) system

---

Antoniniana and the Three Other Decrees of the Emperor Caracalla Contained in Papyrus Gissensis 40," *JEA* 26 [1940]:12–13).

23. Apparently some Egyptians were allowed to stay, presumably those who appeared to conform to Caracalla's exception for those "who congregate here with the object of viewing the glorious city of Alexandria or come down for the sake of enjoying a more civilized life [or] for incidental business" (P.Giessen 40, II.25–27; tr. Heichelheim, "Constitutio Antoniniana," 13). Dionysius mentions Egyptians among the first martyrs in the Alexandrian pogrom of 249 (in Eusebius, *Hist. eccles.* 6.41.19, 21).

24. See Max Weber, *The Sociology of Religion,* tr. by Ephraim Fischoff (Boston: Beacon Press, 1963), 98–99, 106–8. Cf. E. J. Hobsbawm, *Primitive Rebels: Studies in Archaic Forms of Social Movement* (New York: Frederick Praeger, 1959; reprint, New York: W. W. Norton, 1965), 71–72, 83, 85; Michael Barkun, *Disaster and the Millennium* (New Haven: Yale University Press, 1974; reprint, Syracuse, N.Y.: Syracuse University Press, 1986), 36, 94–95. On economic aspects of millennialism, see Kenelm Burridge, *New Heaven, New Earth: A Study of Millenarian Activities* (Oxford: Basil Blackwell, 1969), 41–46, 108–15.

25. On the symbols of middle-class identity in Roman Egypt—names, benefits of citizenship, cultural institutions—see Bowman, *Egypt after the Pharoahs,* 124–26. On the instability of maintaining these symbols, see Mary Douglas, *Natural Symbols* (New York: Pantheon, 1973), 103–4; John Gager, *Kingdom and Community* (Englewood Cliffs, N.J.: Prentice-Hall, 1975), 94–96. Norman Cohn has stressed the impact of rapid social and economic change in producing a mentality conducive to millennialist expectation (*The Pursuit of the Millennium* [rev. ed.; London: Temple Smith, 1970], 53–60); see also Hobsbawm, *Primitive Rebels,* 67, 80.

under Ptolemaic rule to a "low grid" (individualistic and competitive) system under Roman rule.[26] Consequently, the rapid disintegration of both the urban and the epichoric bourgeoisie from Caracalla through Diocletian would have isolated the members of this class still more, as it became progressively impossible for the individual to maintain class status and cultural identity under the weight of imperial exploitation.[27] Under these circumstances, the rapid flight to a millennialist sect whose sights were set purely on eschatological events can be explained as a flight by people bereft of socioeconomic status and cultural identity (as a result of third-century oppression), whose self-definition was largely individualistic, to a social situation of purely collective identity—again, in Douglas's terms, "the high group, low grid" situation.[28] The individual status, lost in the vicissitudes of the Egyptian economy, becomes moot in the experience of the millennialist sect: one is simply a "Christian" (or, in the terms of the Apocalypse of Elijah, a "saint" or a "righteous one"). One might also draw a correlation between the "fractured individual" of the third-century Egyptian bourgeoisie and the "pathological yearning for martyrdom" apparent among Egyptian martyrs in the Diocletianic persecution.[29] In assuming biblical names and volunteering for tortures

26. Egyptian society maintained a relatively consistent stratification through the Ptolemaic period; see Dunand, "Grecs et égyptiens," 67–68. Although it is difficult to gauge "group"—Douglas's spectrum of collective versus individual identity—in historical cultures, it would seem evident that at this time in Egypt the progressive individualization of identity and responsibility indicates a transition to "low group" status. In a similar vein, Henry A. Green attributed the individualism of early Egyptian Gnosticism to this very transition from Ptolemaic to Roman economic administrations and their effect on pre-115 Judaism (*Economic and Social Origins of Gnosticism*, SBLDS 77 [Atlanta: Scholars Press, 1985]; and idem, "The Socio-Economic Background of Christianity in Egypt," in *The Roots of Egyptian Christianity*, ed. Birger A. Pearson and James E. Goehring, SAC 1 [Philadelphia: Fortress, 1986], 110–11).

27. This portrait of misery is not to gainsay the glorious attempts made by emperors and cities alike to invoke civic pride and divert the populace with games; cf. Robin Lane Fox, *Pagans and Christians* (New York: Alfred A. Knopf, 1987), 578.

28. Cf. Kenelm Burridge, "Millennialisms and the Recreation of History," in *Religion, Rebellion, Revolution*, ed. Bruce Lincoln (New York: St. Martin's, 1985), 230: "The tensions between too much and too little freedom for the self to realize itself, brought about by politico-economic conditions with a strong moral component in which an alternative moral order is suggested, seem to me to form the armature of millennialisms." Such conditions in Roman Egypt would presumably have been the extension of citizenship by Caracalla.

29. The phrase is G.E.M. de Ste. Croix's ("Why Were the Early Christians Persecuted?" in *Studies in Ancient Society*, ed. M. I. Finley [London and Boston: Routledge & Kegan Paul, 1974], 234–37); see also Donald W. Riddle, *The Martyrs: A Study in Social Control* (Chicago: University of Chicago Press, 1931), 60–69. The paramount example of this "pathological yearning" is Tertullian's *Scorpiace* 7.

and execution, the latter were sacrificing all sense of themselves as individuals to an eschatological identity and to pain.[30]

REBELLION, RELIGION, AND IDEOLOGY IN THIRD-CENTURY EGYPT

Ideological Responses to Decline

The rumbling of the empire's foundations was not experienced only on the level of immediate livelihood and subsistence. Prophets and ideologues on all sides also saw the decline in a wider and more ominous perspective: that the world itself was collapsing.[31]

For example, it was in the third century that the religious requirements imposed on the populace of the empire changed most markedly from the cultural ecumenism of the Hellenistic world to obligations of conformity. Whether it arose from the imperium's own pessimistic self-reflection or from genuinely new ideas about what should constitute an imperial religion, the concept developed that certain forms of piety were anarchic and criminal. Hence the Roman period witnessed paranoid hunts for evidence of "magic"[32] and the imperial edicts on sacrifice.

On the one hand, then, it was understood both by the state and by considerable numbers of people that the integrity of the empire was being threatened by insufficient ritual homage and by subversive cults actively working against it: "If the Tiber floods the town or the Nile fails to flood the fields," proceeds Tertullian's famous complaint, "if the sky stands still or the earth moves, if famine, if plague, the first reaction is 'Christians to the lion!'"[33] In the eyes of the populace and the mobs, the

30. Eusebius *Martyrs in Palestine* 11. On masochism as the subordination and diminishment of the ego, see Esther Menaker, "Masochism–A Defense Reaction of the Ego," *Psychoanalytic Quarterly* 22 (1953):205–20; cf. Theodor Reik, *Masochism in Sex and Society* (New York: Grove Press, 1962), 349–59.

31. See, in general, E. R. Dodds, *Pagan and Christian in an Age of Anxiety* (Cambridge: Cambridge University Press, 1965; reprint, New York: Norton, 1970); Ramsay Mac-Mullen, *The Roman Government's Response to Crisis, A.D. 235–337* (New Haven and London: Yale University Press, 1976), chap. 1; Peter Brown, *The Making of Late Antiquity* (Cambridge: Harvard University Press, 1975), 99–101.

32. See Peter Brown, "Sorcery, Demons, and the Rise of Christianity from Late Antiquity into the Middle Ages," in *Witchcraft Confessions and Accusations,* ed. Mary Douglas (London: Tavistock, 1970), 17–45; and Morton Smith, *Jesus the Magician* (San Francisco: Harper & Row, 1978), 68–93.

33. Tertullian *Apologia* 40 (ed. T. Herbert Bindley, *Tertulliani apologeticus adversus gentes pro christianis* [Oxford: Clarendon Press, 1889], 124–25); see also Dodds, *Pagan and Christian,* 114–15; MacMullen, *Roman Government's Response,* 24–47; Robert L. Wilken, *The Christians as the Romans Saw Them* (New Haven: Yale University Press, 1984), 50, 59–69.

atheism and anarchism that appeared intrinsic to Christianity would result in the departure of the gods and *tychē* from the inhabited cosmos.[34] On the other hand, the third century witnessed a great outpouring of Christian millennialist literature, articulating almost the same view from a different perspective: that the weakening of the empire and the onset of persecutions signaled the imminent end of the world and the beginning of the reign of Christ.[35]

Rebellion, Religion, and Nationalism

In the context of this "culture of anxiety" and in response to the social and economic breakdown in Egyptian society and to the economic and racial oppression of Roman administration, a series of violent revolts characterizes the third century in both Egypt and Alexandria. The history of these revolts is assessed here with particular attention to their ideological ramifications, for I propose that the Apocalypse of Elijah can be read as a Christian synthesis of such general oppositional sentiments as motivated these revolts. However, it is useful to clarify the terminology and presuppositions involved in assessing the ideologies of rebellious social groups. Most problematic is the term "nationalism."

In classical Egypt, a typical hierocratic kingdom, religious and political discourses were fundamentally indistinguishable. Indeed, the self-definition of Egypt and its pharaoh as against the nations of its known world was symbolized and understood within the mythological antithesis of Horus and Seth, leading Egyptologists such as Étienne Drioton to characterize the ancient Egyptian mythological perspective as nationalistic.[36]

The validity of this term becomes clear in the Late and Hellenistic periods, as members of the Egyptian priesthood sought alternately (and often in competition with each other) to discredit and to legitimize pharaohs of foreign descent by framing them in relationship to nostalgic visions of the past, chief among which was the ability of legitimate pharaohs to expel foreigners and quell revolt. Disliked forces or leaders (such as Cambyses and various Ptolemies) were thereby objectified

---

34. See de Ste. Croix, "Why Were the Early Christians Persecuted?" 238–42.

35. See Jean Gagé, "Commodien et le moment millénariste du IIIe siècle (258–262 ap. J.-C.)," *RHPR* 41 (1961):355–78; Géza Alföldy, "The Crisis of the Third Century as Seen by Contemporaries," *GRBS* 15 (1974):89–111; MacMullen, *Roman Government's Response,* 1–23.

36. Étienne Drioton, "Le nationalisme au temps des pharaons," in idem, *Pages d'égyptologie* (Cairo: Éditions de la Revue du Caire, 1957).

symbolically as Typhonian—as people of Seth—and opposed to *Ma'at*—cosmic order and social integrity. Both Samuel K. Eddy and Alan B. Lloyd have shown in detail the nationalist character of the various movements of the Hellenistic period that opposed the foreign kingships, while J. Gwyn Griffiths, Janet H. Johnson, and Ludwig Koenen have argued for a similar "king versus foreigner" ideology having been deployed in support of the Ptolemies.[37] Therefore it would seem that "nationalism" is a coherent and appropriate term for the ideology of native opposition or rebellion during the Greco-Roman period, indicating a numinous sense of Egypt as a relative geographical unit that was defending its boundaries against "invasion."

A problem arises, however, in applying to social trends in an ancient agrarian society a term conceived in modern times to represent modern ethnic or political movements, as Ernest Gellner has argued most articulately.[38] Theoretically, the traditionally and deeply local character of peasant lives, as is manifested in kinship boundaries and language dialects, should create a virtually autonomous symbolic world, one both separate from the symbolic worlds of other (even neighboring) local cultures and "beneath" any sort of national consciousness that might cross these many parochial worlds. By this view, which assumes a primitive region unaffected by wars, invasions, or political propaganda, a "national consciousness" would be neither relevant nor accessible to the lives of village peasants.[39] The ruling elite (including the priesthood) in such a society would express its cultural self-definition not in terms of nationalist alliance with these dispersed peasant classes (from whom they would have a long-standing hierarchical interest in distinguishing themselves) but rather in terms of caste status.[40] If peasants are viewed as fundamentally local in identity and aspirations and the priesthood—

---

37. Samuel K. Eddy, *The King Is Dead* (Lincoln: University of Nebraska Press, 1961), chaps. 10–11; Alan Lloyd, "Nationalist Propaganda in Ptolemaic Egypt," *Historia* 31 (1982):33–55; J. Gwyn Griffiths, "Egyptian Nationalism in the Edfu Temple Texts," in *Glimpses of Ancient Egypt: Studies in Honour of H. W. Fairman*, ed. John Ruffle, G. A. Gaballa, and Kenneth Kitchen (Warminster: Aris & Phillips, 1979), 174–79; Ludwig Koenen, "Die Adaptation ägyptischer Königsideologie am Ptolemäerhof," in *Egypt and the Hellenistic World*, ed. E. Van 't Dack, P. van Dessel, and W. van Gucht, Studia Hellenistica 27 (Louvain, 1983), 143–90; Janet H. Johnson, "Is the Demotic Chronicle an Anti-Greek Tract?" in *Grammata Demotika*, ed. Heinz-J. Thissen and Karl-Th. Zauzich (Würzburg: Gisela Zauzich, 1984), 107–24.

38. Ernest Gellner, *Nations and Nationalism* (Ithaca, N.Y.: Cornell University Press, 1983), 8–18.

39. Ibid., 12–13.

40. Ibid., 16.

the actual instrument of elite political propaganda—as fundamentally hierarchical in identity (i.e., as opposing itself to the lower classes), then, according to Gellner, there should be "little incentive or opportunity for [such agrarian] cultures to aspire to the kind of monochrome homogeneity and political pervasiveness and domination for which later, with the coming of the age of nationalism, they eventually strive."[41]

Although the image of rigidly distinct cultural worlds would aptly characterize Egypt in pharaonic (and even early Ptolemaic) times because of the culture's powerful, complex priesthood and differing cultural regions, by the Roman period this ideal scenario collapses, for three significant reasons: (1) the issue of ethnic distinctions and racism, which became a source of considerable identification and conflict during the Roman period;[42] (2) the increasing conflict among elements of the priesthood during the Greco-Roman period, often regional in identification and public sway (e.g., Memphis, Thebes, Esna, Edfu, and Elephantine); and (3) the public (or even "popular") role of the local priesthood, whose oracles might be used to inspire rebellious sentiments or violence, often across a considerable region.[43] It must furthermore be remembered that the status and authority of priests and temples diminished considerably under Roman administration, eliminating the intrinsic alliance between economic and religious (or cultic) authorities that had developed over the course of the Hellenistic period: now the priesthoods were essentially on their own, exploited for funds like the rest of Egypt.[44] Therefore Glen Bowersock has argued that "at the center of provincial subversion

41. Ibid., 13.
42. A point argued at length by Davis, *Race Relations in Ancient Egypt*, esp. 113–65. Cf. Dunand, "Grecs et égyptiens en Égypte," passim.
43. See Dunand, *Religion populaire*, 118–34; idem, "Grecs et égyptiens," 71–74; cf. Claire Préaux, "Equisse d'une histoire des révolutions égyptiennes sous les lagides," *Chronique d'Égypte* 22 (1936):529, 545–52. On the popular authority of the Egyptian priesthood in the Roman period through administration of oracles, see Ammianus Marcellinus, *Hist.* 19.12 (Bes oracle thriving in 359 C.E.); W. Schubart, "Orakelfragen," *ZÄS* 67 (1931):110–15; A. Henrichs, "Zwei Orakelfragen," *ZPE* 11 (1973):115–19; Adam Bülow-Jacobsen, "P. Carlsberg 24: Question to an Oracle," *ZPE* 57 (1984):91–92; P.Oxy 2554 (ed. John Rea, "Predictions by Astrology," *Oxyrhynchus Papyri* 31 (1966):77–83; P.Yale 299 (second century C.E.); ed. George M. Parássoglou, "Circular from a Prefect: Sileat omnibus perpetuo divinandi curiositas," in *Collectanea Papyrologica*, Festschrift H. C. Youtie, ed. Ann Ellis Hanson [Bonn: Rudolf Habelt, 1976], 261–74; and John Rea, "A New Version of P.Yale inv. 299," *ZPE* 27 (1977):151–56; plus materials in chap. 7.
44. Dorothy J. Thompson, "The High Priests of Memphis under Ptolemaic Rule," in *Pagan Priests*, ed. Mary Beard and John North (Ithaca, N.Y.: Cornell University Press, 1990), 115–16; Lewis, *Life in Egypt*, 91–92; H. Idris Bell, *Cults and Creeds in Graeco-Roman Egypt* (Liverpool: Liverpool University Press, 1953; reprint, Chicago: Ares, 1975), 54–55.

[during the Roman period] stood the local temples, . . . [which were] far more vital than many have thought."[45]

Moreover, rural villagers in Roman Egypt, subject as they were to ethnic discrimination, invasions, revolts, and the universalizing ideology of Hellenistic language and culture, were hardly immune to national or multiregional alliances. Bruce Lincoln has discussed latent configurations of identity that become activated, even at the most local level, under certain historical circumstances and which effectively unite people across prior local divisions.[46] Under certain kinds of real or perceived stress, the most localized and conservative communities may redefine themselves in much more expansive and powerful terms than those in which they ordinarily lead their lives—here is a dualism that divides (or, respectively, unites) everything in its view.[47] Clifford Geertz perceives this phenomenon as a function of ideology itself:

> It is when neither a society's most general cultural orientations nor its most down-to-earth "pragmatic" ones suffice any longer to provide an adequate image of political process that ideologies begin to become crucial as sources of sociopolitical meanings and attitudes.[48]

Primitive nationalism is hence a form of latent social identity aroused under extreme circumstances, a phenomenon of organization, sentiment, and discourse that essentially cuts across our modern distinctions of religion and politics. It is basically a "regionalism," expanded and intensified against perceived invasion or impurity through the use of religious propaganda, which is invariably wielded by figures in positions of highly traditional authority, especially priests. Nationalism conceived

45. Glen W. Bowersock, "The Mechanics of Subversion in the Roman Provinces," in *Opposition et résistances à l'empire d'Auguste à Trajan*, Entretiens sur l'antiquité classique 33 (Geneva: Vandoeuvres, 1986), 315; cf. comments by M. Giovannini in "Discussion," in *Opposition et résistance*, 319.

46. Bruce Lincoln, *Discourse and the Construction of Society* (New York: Oxford University Press, 1989), 3–50. Lincoln's approach is not entirely incompatible with Gellner's, as most of his examples come from urban, industrial societies, the cultural point at which Gellner finds the social basis of nationalism.

47. See Georg Simmel, *Conflict and the Web of Group-Affiliations*, tr. Kurt H. Wolff and Reinhard Bendix (New York: Free Press, 1955), 98–107. This widely dualistic worldview arises particularly with millennialist movements that draw on the cosmic and otherworldly terms of Christian scripture; see Peter Worsley, *The Trumpet Shall Sound: A Study of "Cargo" Cults in Melanesia* (2d ed.; New York: Schocken, 1968), 245–46; cf. Barkun, *Disaster and the Millennium*, 84–86, on indigenous structures from which prophets and their communities can synthesize millennialist worldviews.

48. Clifford Geertz, "Ideology as a Cultural System," in idem, *The Interpretation of Cultures* (New York: Basic Books, 1973), 219.

in this way can encompass the oppositional sentiments of both native and immigrant groups, of both an underclass and an elite, of both mobs and militias. Although admitting the problematic nature of such a modern term in reference to the ideal and static agrarian society, one can profitably apply it to certain ideological trends that express an exceptionally wide identity in opposition to a perceived foreign presence and that articulate xenophobic sentiments vis-à-vis the land. Such ideologies tend to arise in those agrarian cultures that have been subject to ethnic division; economic exploitation; popular, often insurgent priestly leadership; or prior multiregional alliances or identities. Roman Egypt epitomizes these circumstances, from city to *chora*. The motivations among the participants in the sequence of anti-Roman revolts over the course of the third century cannot otherwise be understood. The regional character of these revolts as well as the evidence of priestly leadership implies that the participants understood themselves as defenders of a culture against perceived aliens—a culture whose ordering structure was the temple and a view of the land as resisting Seth–Typhon in his many forms. Thus we may aptly call the sequence of revolts and their violent prophecies "nationalistic."

Viewing nationalism in Roman Egypt in this way furthermore allows the critic to see a continuity between "secular" revolts (which might use no apparent mythological discourse) and overtly religious texts such as the Apocalypse of Elijah. E. J. Hobsbawm has shown in detail that religious–secular distinctions are anachronistic with regard to popular movements of rebellion, which customarily involved both mythological and economic types of rhetoric.[49]

Therefore one must dismiss such assertions as Ramsay MacMullen's that "the religious attachments of the Egyptians had been much weakened over the first three hundred years of Roman occupation, and had been to some extent withdrawn from other aspects of culture,"[50] or

49. Hobsbawm, *Primitive Rebels*, esp. 66: "The kinds of community which produced millenarian heresies are not the ones in which clear distinctions between religious and secular things can be drawn." More recently, Hobsbawm has derived the popular "proto-nationalist" mentality even in modern times from *religious* understandings of land and people (*Nations and Nationalism since 1780: Programme, Myth, Reality* [Cambridge: Cambridge University Press, 1990], esp. 50–51, 67–79).

50. Ramsay MacMullen, "Nationalism in Roman Egypt," *Aegyptus* 44 (1964):191. It should be noted that MacMullen is responding to J. Grafton Milne, "Egyptian Nationalism under Greek and Roman Rule," *JEA* 14 (1928):226–34, an article guilty of some excessive assertions about the monolithic character of Greco-Roman Egyptian religion.

A.H.M. Jones's "that there was no conscious survival of the old Egyptian nationalism in the Christian period."[51] In circumstances of popular revolt, a religious character must be assumed and articulated critically, rather than assessed doubtfully through anachronistic criteria.

Three Kinds of Nationalism in Roman Egypt

It is useful to delineate the spheres of nationalistic activity that characterize third-century Egypt and its cultures; for it would be incorrect to say that all the revolts of the third century reflected the popular sentiments of either the peasantry or the declining middle class of Greco-Egyptians.

First, since the beginning of Roman domination, Greek Alexandria, which was infamous among Romans for its mobs and collective demonstrations,[52] had developed its own form of nationalism—of city-state identity and pride—and this "nationalism" of the elite shows itself persistently from Caracalla to Diocletian.

The chief literary witness for a Greek social entity that asserted its identity in opposition to native Egyptians and Egypt as a whole, Jews (and ultimately Christians), and Roman power and the pretensions of emperors is the corpus of disparate papyri known as the *Acta Alexandrinorum*.[53] This literature appears in the form of stylized trial protocols, composed over a period from the early first century through the third century C.E., and exhibits the struggles of the gymnasiarchs of Alexandria against a prejudiced imperium and (in their view) haughty Jews.[54] The tone is defensive; the authors were clearly composing propaganda to justify popular Greek sentiments of persecution and hostility. Although arising from and referring to the first century, the papyri on which the *Acta* are preserved are dated to the second and third centuries, showing that these tracts captured enough minds to be copied con-

---

51. A.H.M. Jones, "Were Ancient Heresies National or Social Movements in Disguise?" *JTS* 10 (1959):287. Cf. John Gwyn Griffiths, "Egyptian Influences on Athanasius," in *Studien zu Sprache und Religion Ägyptens*, vol. 2: *Religion* (Göttingen: F. Junge, 1984), 1023–37.

52. See Meyer Reinhold, "Roman Attitudes toward Egyptians," *Ancient World* 3 (1980):97–103; cf. H. Idris Bell, "Anti-Semitism in Alexandria," *JRS* 31 (1941):1–18.

53. See Herbert A. Musurillo, *The Acts of the Pagan Martyrs* (Oxford: Clarendon, 1954).

54. An animosity toward the Jews is apparent in several of the *Acta* (e.g., *Acta Isidori*), reflecting political and ethnic struggles over gaining Roman citizenship in the first century C.E.

tinually through the third century.[55] That they were found in Upper Egypt also shows that propaganda concerning Alexandrian self-definition was being used to galvanize anti-Roman sentiments among Greeks living outside Alexandria. "We can easily picture," suggests Naphtali Lewis, "the more literate and affluent of the Alexandrians and metropolites nursing the political grievances of their classes by perusing these books in the privacy of their libraries or reading them aloud in gatherings of friends."[56]

Second, there was the "nationalism" of a Roman Empire coming apart at its seams, whose apologists understood this decline quite religiously, in terms of anarchic elements both beyond and within its borders.[57] But organized violence among self-defined Romans often evolved along military lines; in an empire that was increasingly dependent upon and governed by armies, there was the tendency for the military commanders to revolt, along with the Roman citizens of a region, against the emperor.

Finally, there is evidence for Egyptian nationalistic uprisings in the third century, expressed in the *Potter's Oracle* manuscripts, the *Perfect Discourse*, and the briefer oracular materials in Demotic and Greek, discussed above (pp. 185–91). In this period Egyptian nationalism may be characterized as focusing on a "millennial" reconstitution of the Egyptian kingship, which would simultaneously restore fertility to the land, create order among the people of the land, and expel foreigners from the borders of Egypt. It is probable that the major social class to have sought refuge and identity in Egyptian nationalism by the middle of the third century was the Greco-Egyptian bourgeoisie, a new class in Roman Egypt whose members were gradually losing economic subsistence and access to the institutions of the dominant culture.[58] The

---

55. Rostovtzeff (*Social and Economic History*, 1:418) follows the theory of A. von Premerstein (*Zu den sogennanten alexandrinischen Märtyrerakten*, Philologus Supp. 16:2 [Leipzig: Dietrich, 1923], 73–75) that the *Acta Alexandrinorum* were actually collected into a single tract just before Caracalla's massacre, signifying an increase in Alexandrian nationalist fervor. Unfortunately, the diverse fragments cannot be attributed at any time to a single editorial project; see Musurillo, *Acts of the Pagan Martyrs*, 264–66.

56. Lewis, *Life in Egypt*, 200–201.

57. See de Ste. Croix, "Why Were the Early Christians Persecuted?" 210–49.

58. Zbigniew Borkowski, "Local Cults and Resistance to Christianity," *JJP* 20 (1990):25–30, has recently called attention to a preference on the part of the village lower-aristocracies for local, distinctly Egyptian cults. This and the evidence discussed by Françoise Dunand (*Religion populaire en Égypte romaine*, esp. 146–58), concerning popular Egyptian preference for "Hellenistic" forms of indigenous deities, suggest a Greco-Egyptian cultural syncretism at the village level in Egypt, implying an Egyptian identity that could be galvanized through priestly propaganda like the *Potter's Oracle*.

circulation of the *Potter's Oracle* in Greek indicates that a Greek-speaking milieu found no contradiction in expressing anti-Greek feelings and expectations in this language—that, indeed, it had become the "native" language of a sizable population of Egyptians.

Although Egyptian nationalism was opposed to Greeks and Romans (and occasionally Jews); Alexandrian nationalism to Egyptians, Romans, and Jews; and Roman nationalism to groups of individuals in its midst who advocated (or prayed for) the end of the empire and its gods, all shared, in the vicissitudes of their respective crises, a pathological attribution of all negative events to alien, impure elements within the social and geographical boundaries defining each one's "nation."

ALEXANDRIAN REVOLTS OF
THE THIRD CENTURY

In 215 C.E., responding to what seems to have been a direct affront on the part of the elite elders and youth of Alexandria, the emperor Caracalla had his troops massacre a sizable portion of the city's population. The Alexandrines' initial actions seem to have been inspired by a combination of Caracalla's own particular pretensions, his exploitative economic innovations, and their general anti-Roman sentiments.[59]

Although the victims of the massacre came predominately from the elite of the Greek population, a considerable number of Egyptians and Greco-Egyptians, refugees from the *chora*, also fell to Caracalla's army. These natives seem to have played some role in Alexandrian insurgency, for Caracalla expelled them from Alexandria by edict in 215 for "agitating the city."[60] In light of the Egyptian nationalist view of the "city by the sea" as the seat of the foreigner, destined for destruction, Alexandria at this point undoubtedly took on greater negative significance for Egyptians, because native Egyptians—in particular, those fleeing taxation or drought in the *chora*—could no longer enter the city.[61]

59. Cassius Dio *Historia* 78.22–23; J. Grafton Milne, *History of Egypt under Roman Rule*, A History of Egypt 5 (3d ed.; London: Methuen, 1924), 63–64; P. Benoît and J. Schwartz, "Caracalla et les troubles d'Alexandrie en 215 après J.-C.," *Études de papyrologie* 7 (1948):17–33; Rostovtzeff, *Social and Economic History*, 1:417–18; and Fergus Millar, *A Study of Cassius Dio* (Oxford: Clarendon, 1964), 156–58, who views the obscurity of these events as "an object lesson in how little our sources help us to understand particular events" (156).

60. P.Giessen 40, II.20; see Heichelheim, "Text of the *Constitutio Antoniana*," 10–22; cf. Benoît and Schwartz, "Caracalla et les troubles d'Alexandrie," 30 n. 2, 31. Obviously, much of this agitation derived from the Greek Alexandrines' own ethnic prejudices. Origen was apparently among those expelled.

61. On peasant *anachoresis* to Alexandria, see Claire Préaux, "L'attache à la terre:

The next period revealing evidence of religious–nationalistic activity is the transition from Philip to Decius, from 244–251 C.E. It has been noted above that the reign of Philip represented perhaps the lowest point in the Egyptian economy and the period of the most serious social disintegration during the whole Roman administration of Egypt. Papyrus evidence from this period shows both a greater earnestness in collecting taxes (with a new post: taxation overseer) and the desperate abrogation of laws that Severus had designed specifically to protect the village economy.[62] One can assume that resentment among all classes was running high at this time.

David Potter has pointed to Philip's celebration of Rome's thousand-year anniversary with lavish festivals and games as an act that many in the empire would have taken as portentous of some imminent change of great proportions.[63] As Zosimus describes, such celebrations on even a hundred-year scale had the power to "bring about cures for plagues, decay, and diseases," and their neglect might have dire consequences for the empire.[64] So an imperial celebration of the turning point of the millennium, at the same time as others (such as Cyprian) were defining the age in terms of a more violent, cataclysmic turning point,[65] may have struck some people in Alexandria and Egypt as an event of critical proportion, requiring collective action.[66]

Between the newly compounded burden of Rome and this spate of propaganda, it is therefore not surprising to find, in the letters of Dionysius of Alexandria, the report of a *mantis* attracting the Alexandrian crowds in the winter of 248, with the message that a new religion that was denying the gods was responsible for the woes around them. In Dionysius's perspective, this

Continuités de l'Égypte ptolémaïque à l'Égypte romaine," in *Das römisch-byzantinische Ägypten*, Aegyptiaca Treverensia 2 (Mainz: Philipp von Zabern, 1983), 2–3.

62. Parsons, "Philippus Arabs and Egypt"; Skeat and Wegener, "Trial before the Prefect of Egypt."

63. David Potter, *Prophecy and History in the Crisis of the Roman Empire: A Historical Commentary on the Thirteenth Sibylline Oracle* (Oxford: Clarendon, 1990), 236–40. Cf. W. Ensslin, "The Senate and the Army," *CAH* 12 (1939):91–92; Robert M. Grant, *Augustus to Constantine: The Rise and Triumph of Christianity in the Roman World* (New York: Harper & Row, 1970), 167–68.

64. Zosimus *Historia nova* 2.1, 7.

65. MacMullen, *Roman Government's Response*, chaps. 1 and 2; Alföldy, "Crisis of the Third Century."

66. Awareness of imperial or foreign events may have been restricted to urban and trade populations, whose economic spheres were culturally wider than rural and peasant populations. The fullest account of Philip's games appears only in Orosius's fifth-century history of Rome, *Contra paganos*, in which he associates the magnificence of the games with Philip's (traditionally alleged) Christianity (chap. 20).

creator of evils for this city, whoever he was, was beforehand in stirring and inciting the masses of the heathen [ἐθνῶν] against us, fanning anew the flame of their native superstition. Aroused by him and seizing upon all authority for their unholy deeds, they conceived that this kind of worship of their gods—the thirsting for our blood—was the only form of piety.[67]

It is interesting that Dionysius views the rhetoric of the *mantis* as appealing to "native" superstition (τὴν ἐπιχώριον αὐτοῦ δεισιδαιμονίαν), because this implies that he was using terminology and motifs that the audience could appreciate as rooted in the traditions and self-definition of the city. In the act of "prophesying," the *mantis* was expressing the audience's genuine experience of the times in terms of the myth of Alexandrian culture and persecution and identifying the *christianoi* as a gross danger to their cultural and cosmic integrity. Therefore Stewart Oost has aptly compared the resulting pogrom to that against the Jews under Flaccus in the first century, for the Jews also became the scapegoats of anti-Roman sentiment.[68] It was clear to the crowd that the malaise of the times and the depredations by the imperium were a direct result of the bizarre practices of a cult that (to them) made a point of denying the city's holy *tychē*.[69] Thus the initial performance of the *mantis* and the ensuing pogrom were a response both to Roman authority and to the peculiar behavior of the Christians, while the forms of speech the *mantis* used articulated these "dangerous entities" in the clear terms of local prophetic expectation.

Philip's reign and administrative innovations provoked such animosity in Alexandria that his overthrow by Decius in 249 must have

67. Dionysius of Alexandria, in Eusebius *Hist. eccles.* 6.41.1 (tr. J.E.L. Oulton, *Eusebius: The Ecclesiastical History*, LCL [London: William Heinemann, 1932], 2:101).

68. Stewart Irvin Oost, "The Alexandrian Seditions under Philip and Gallienus," *CP* 56 (1961):2, 4.

69. Many scholars have suggested that the mob (or the *mantis*, as "soul" of the mob) would have picked the Christians out of the many religions in Alexandria because Philip himself, according to legend, carried on a mild flirtation with Christianity, allegedly even receiving a letter from Origen (see Eusebius *Hist. eccles.* 6.34, 36; Oost, "Alexandrian Seditions," 4–5; W.H.C. Frend, *Martyrdom and Persecution in the Early Church* [London: Basil Blackwell, 1965; reprint, Grand Rapids: Baker Book House, 1981], 404–5; Fox, *Pagans and Christians*, 452–54; and, esp., Hans A. Pohlsander, "Philip the Arab and Christianity," *Historia* 29 [1980]:463–71). The mobs, then, were taking out their resentment for the emperor's policies on representatives of the emperor's religion. This is pure conjecture, however, and attributes the wrong sort of rationality to the Alexandrian mob. It is far more likely that the Alexandrians' "local superstitions"—in Dionysius's own terms—were the motivating elements: a traditional hatred of Roman authority and the pretenses of its emperors; a deep reliance on *Agathos Daimon*—in indigenous terms, the presence of the holy in the city of Alexandria and the performances that kept its protection—and a strong sense of their own cultural identity in Egypt.

been greeted with some relief by Greeks in Egypt.[70] Decius's religious respect for the Roman order and *tychē* doubtless galvanized sentiments of some parties in Alexandria, who temporarily transcended their anti-Roman nationalism to identify themselves within the larger sphere of the empire and its cosmos. The evidence of the *libelli*, the affidavits of public sacrifice, shows that Decius's understanding of the relationship between regional piety and the maintenance of the empire was unprecedented in Roman history, yet highly nostalgic in motivation. In Potter's words:

> The evidence of [Decius's] actions suggests that he was deeply conservative, that he was deeply pious, that he possessed a ferocious temper, and that he was quite stupid. He seems to have yearned for the days when the empire appeared to be invincible, and he appears to have cherished the memory of Trajan and the other emperors who had made Rome great. Thus one of his first acts after assuming the throne was to take the name Trajan for himself and to issue an edict ordering all the inhabitants of the empire to sacrifice to the ancestral gods for the safety of the state.[71]

Through Decius's institutions, therefore, the religious anxieties of the Alexandrians (concerning civic fortune, presence of gods, tradition, and cosmic stability)—which complemented and partly motivated their ethnic nationalism—were allayed through an ecumenical revival of religious values and cult, uniting the pantheism of the empire with the most localized guardian deities. The edicts of sacrifice seem to have been worded in sufficiently general terms ("to the gods") to evoke these divergent sentiments of the need for divine presence and accessibility in the land.[72] That is, such a requirement as public sacrifice for the maintenance of the imperium and its world was comprehensible to a variety of nationalist ideologies, particularly during the political catastrophes of the mid-third century.[73]

70. Cf. Parsons, "Philippus Arabus and Egypt," 140–41; Grant, *Augustus to Constantine,* 168; Fox, *Pagans and Christians,* 452.

71. Potter, *Prophecy and History,* 41–42; cf. John R. Knipfing, "The Libelli of the Decian Persecution," *HTR* 16 (1923):357; Oost, "Alexandrian Seditions," 7; Frend, *Martyrdom and Persecution,* 405–6; and the perceptive discussion by Hans A. Pohlsander, "The Religious Policy of Decius," *ANRW* 2.16.3 (1986):1826–42.

72. Knipfing, "Libelli," 353. See, in general, Brown, *Making of Late Antiquity,* 99–101 and passim.

73. Coincidentally, our evidence for the people who conformed to this edict in Upper Egypt comes mostly from the class of Egyptian and Greco-Egyptian bourgeoisie discussed above, whose members had become citizens through Caracalla's decree and yet had been frequently dislocated during this period, probably owing to the oppression of new taxes; see Knipfing, "Libelli," 358; cf. 356.

The persecution of Christians becomes clearly an expression of religious and nationalist sentiments under Valerian in 257 C.E. The decision to harass Christians seems to have been conceived in the wake of a surge of disasters across the empire—clear demonstration to the Greco-Roman mind of impiety within the borders.[74]

The letters of Dionysius indicate that the instigator of the persecution was the chief financial minister to the emperor, Macrianus, who later replaced Valerian as emperor.[75] It is true that, in his official role, Macrianus's commitment to the persecution could only have been his responsibility for the sacrifice registry.[76] It is scarcely possible, however, that Dionysius is merely scapegoating Macrianus for being the executor of Valerian's plan. Macrianus must have demonstrated a particular interest in the choice of Christians, because he was acting as a religious leader concerned for the *tychē* of the city and empire, as invoked and symbolized in the loyalty of citizens to the divine benefactors—"the gods," the deputy prefect of Egypt admonished Dionysius, "who save the Empire."[77] That Macrianus's anti-Christian ideology echoed local and perhaps even epichoric anxieties about anarchic foreigners and their threat to the cosmos is shown by the fact that his—and then his son's— claim to the throne was recognized both in Alexandria and well into Upper Egypt.[78] Thus, once again, several nationalist ideologies could become allied on one major religious point, the extermination of impurity.

In the Alexandrian uprising of 260 there is the first suggestion of a synthesis of Christian and Alexandrian nationalistic sentiments. In 260, in support of the pretenders Macrianus and Quietus (the sons of Macrianus the financial minister) and in opposition to Gallienus (who had recently defeated them and would imminently restore Roman rule), a

74. See Christopher J. Haas, "Imperial Religious Policy and Valerian's Persecution of the Church, A.D. 257–260," *CH* 52 (1983):138; cf. Pohlsander, "Religious Policy of Decius."
75. In Eusebius *Hist. eccles.* 7.10.4; cf. Oost, "Alexandrian Seditions," 7–9, who probably goes too far in seeing Macrianus as the Roman appointed ἀρχιερεύς, acting in this capacity to start the persecution.
76. See H.-G. Pflaum, *Les carrières procuratoriennes équestres sous le haut-empire romain*, 4 vols. (Paris: Geuthner, 1960), 2:930–32.
77. Dionysius, in Eusebius *Hist. eccles.* 7.11.7. See Michael M. Sage, "The Persecution of Valerian and the Peace of Gallienus," *Wiener Studien* 17 (1983):139–42. Sage's observation that the persecution focused on wealthy Christians and on Christians' property suggests that there may have been a socioeconomic element in the performance of persecution in Alexandria.
78. Oost, "Alexandrian Seditions," 8, 17 n. 43; see also Sage, "Persecution of Valerian," 137–41.

considerable body of Alexandrians barricaded themselves into one part of the city. Moreover, although Gallienus himself declared the end of Valerian's persecution, a number of Christians joined the anti-Roman forces there.[79] Oost suggests that their opposition to Gallienus was inspired by their lack of conviction that the persecution was over; but it is more likely that the ideology of certain Christian groups at this point and in this milieu actually incorporated Alexandrian anti-Roman nationalism.[80] Nonetheless, a body of Christians from this anti-Roman side escaped over the line, intent on enjoying a Roman-sanctioned "Peace of the Church" and surviving to suffer the plague that racked Alexandria the following spring (262 C.E.).

This participation of Christians, suggesting a synthesis of Christian and Alexandrian nationalist attitudes, provides a comparative type to the milieu of the Apocalypse of Elijah, which synthesizes Christian and *Egyptian* nationalism. Therefore the participation of the Alexandrian Christians in the uprising becomes an important indicator of an ideologically complex series of Christianities during the third century. Indeed, it provides reason to believe that the millennialist overtones of third-century Christianity offered a more expansive ideology to those people who hoped for social, religious, and civic renewal in a nationalist or otherwise militant vein.

To what extent did these uprisings and their ideologies and propaganda influence the *chora?* A cultural continuity between Alexandria and such Upper Egyptian centers of Greek economic life as Oxyrhynchus has long been recognized, and the presence of copies of the *Acta Alexandrinorum* in the rubbish heaps of these towns proves that nationalist propaganda was in circulation up the Nile.[81] But the only event that clearly affected Alexandria and Egypt together was the invasion of the

---

79. Dionysius describes the Christians as "separated into one or the other part of the faction" (Eusebius *Hist. eccles.* 7.21.1; cf. 7.32.6–13, ed. Oulton and Lawlor, *Eusebius* 2:178); see Oost, "Alexandrian Seditions," 10–11, 19 n. 52.

80. The recollection of Rome's favors to Jews may well have become a shared propaganda between this new apocalyptic sect and those who continued to believe in the *tychē* of Alexandria.

81. Barkun argues that millennialist ideology generally cannot take root among urban social groups, insofar as their economic and social identities are too diversified and more accustomed to rapid change and misfortune in their immediate environment (*Disaster and the Millennium,* 66–74). It is likely, however, that when nationalist ideologies are transmitted out into the countryside, they may effect the growth of millennialism there. See the interaction between "political" and typically "religious" sentiments in rural Italy and Spain (nineteenth–twentieth centuries), discussed by Hobsbawm (*Primitive Rebels,* 57–107, esp. 62–63, 87–89).

Palmyrene army under Zenobia in 269 C.E., an incident that many scholars have viewed as the inspiration for the Apocalypse of Elijah.

The immediate occasion for this invasion, according to the historian Zosimus, was an invitation from Timagenes, a Greco-Egyptian, whose obvious desire was to expel the Romans—who were at this time progressively losing hold on the countryside—by the only means possible: an invasion by the only army at that time equal to the Roman forces.[82] Although one can only *infer* that Timagenes' motives were nationalistic and that he represented a sizable constituency among Greco-Egyptians of means, it is known that Zenobia devoted considerable propaganda to establishing herself in Egyptian tradition; indeed, she presented herself as the new Cleopatra.[83] Under these circumstances, we must view this invasion as working specifically in conciliation of Egyptian nationalist sentiments. If it is correct to assume that Timagenes represented an "Egyptian" anti-Roman leadership that had coalesced during the previous decade, then it would appear once again that the socioeconomic locus of these nationalist sentiments was still largely bourgeois.

The effect of this invasion on Upper Egyptian cultures must have been considerable, even if there is no notice of it in early Christian literature. Yet local response to the invasion was evidently not unequivocally positive, for at one point the Roman general Probus was able temporarily to expel the Palmyrene garrison with an army composed of Egyptians and Africans.[84] Nevertheless, Rome did not fully regain control over Upper Egypt until the end of the century. By this time the Blemmyes, a nomadic tribe from the south that had harried Egyptian towns from the beginning of the third century, had become allies against Rome for the growing Egyptian resistance; and the Blemmyes joined the Palmyrene army in its conquest of Egypt.[85]

Zenobia's claim on Alexandria in 270 was more of a compromise with

82. Zosimus *Historia nova* 1.44.

83. See Arthur Stein, "Kallinikos von Petrai," *Hermes* 58 (1923):454–55; Jacques Schwartz, "Les palmyréniens et l'Égypte," *Bulletin de la société archéologique d'Alexandrie* 40 (1953):76–77; Glen W. Bowersock, "The Miracle of Memnon," *BASP* 21 (1984):31–32.

84. Zosimus *Historia nova* 1.44. The immediate effectiveness of this ad hoc army recalls the battles of 117 C.E., when a Roman army of Egyptian conscripts effectively quelled the Jewish revolt and annihilated most of Egyptian Jewry. If Probus's army understood its defensive purpose similarly, there may well have been propaganda in circulation describing the Palmyrenes as "Typhonic" despoilers of Egypt, a view Zenobia herself would have sought actively to counter.

85. On the Blemmyes, see Ladislas Castiglione, "Diocletian und die Blemmyes," *ZÄS* 96 (1970):90–102.

Rome. She set up her son, Waballath, as a puppet ruler and established his power as *corrector orientis* by minting coins showing both him and the Roman emperor Aurelian.[86] But the compromise was short-lived; Aurelian did not accept Waballath's illegitimate title, and Zenobia declared herself and her son not only independent but *Augusti* in 272.[87] In response, Aurelian launched a new campaign against the Palmyrene army and succeeded that very year in expelling them from Egypt.[88]

The Alexandrian Greeks, with their growing hatred of the imperium, had also regarded the Palmyrenes as liberators; and immediately upon the expulsion of Zenobia, a rebellion started under the leadership of Firmus, a prominent merchant whose ties extended far up the Nile and who had allied himself with both Palmyra and the Blemmyes. This rebellion was crushed, however, along with a considerable portion of Alexandria itself, by Aurelian's army in 273.

THE EVIDENCE FOR REBELLIONS IN EGYPT

The *chora* underwent its share of sufferings during the third century, but the evidence for revolt there is much sparser than for Alexandria. The years 260–261 saw repeated raids by the Blemmyes into Upper Egypt; and, as part of their pro-Egyptian rule, Macrianus and Quietus sent a momentarily successful campaign against them.[89] Dionysius writes that during these years the Nile alternately ran exceedingly low and too high, causing severe famine in the *chora*.[90] Such circumstances, along with the Alexandrian battles and plague, continued flight from land, and the depredations of bandits (formed of these very fugitives and soldiers, give foundation to Mikhail Rostovtzeff's view of this period as one of depopulation.[91]

In 278 there is evidence for revolts in Ptolemais and Coptos, this time supported by the Blemmyes; and in the early 290s there appears to have been general uprising throughout Upper Egypt, once again in con-

86. On Waballath's role, see Schwartz, "Palmyréniens et l'Égypte," 75–76.
87. Henri Seyrig, "VHABALATHVS AVGVSTVS," in *Mélanges offerts à K. Michalowski* (Warsaw: Pánstwowe Wydawn, 1966), 659–62; J.-P. Rey-Coquais, "Syrie romaine, de Pompée à Dioclétien," *JRS* 68 (1978):59–60.
88. Seyrig, "VHABALATHVS AVGVSTVS"; Potter, *Prophecy and History*, 61.
89. It should be noted that in the early 270s Egyptian nationalists and the Palmyrene army looked to the Blemmyes for support against Rome.
90. In Eusebius *Hist. eccles.* 7.21.5–6.
91. Rostovtzeff, *Social and Economic History*, 1:476.

junction with the Blemmyes. The latter uprising was apparently not finally crushed until the end of the century.[92]

It is probable that a number of different ideologies combined in the uprising of the last decade of the third century. The revolt's acclaimed leaders, Achilleus and Domitius, sought an Egypt independent of Rome but predominately for Greek and Roman inhabitants—that is, in the tradition of Alexandrian nationalism.[93] But a critical area of the revolt in Upper Egypt was the region of Thebes and Coptos, a traditional priestly center.[94] This location would suggest that priestly propaganda might have played a role in galvanizing the uprising in the *chora;* and this propaganda would have recalled traditional Egyptian religious nationalism. This is only conjecture, however; the many Egyptian nationalist–prophetic documents dated to the third century cannot necessarily be ascribed to this period.

EPICHORIC RESPONSES
TO THIRD-CENTURY DECLINE:
HISTORICAL IMPLICATIONS FOR THE CONTEXT
OF THE APOCALYPSE OF ELIJAH

The third century in Egypt may be seen as a series of incremental catastrophes, and the cultures that suffered these catastrophes seem to have boiled almost constantly, in one revolt or another, over the course of this period. It would be possible, therefore, to view any millennialist uprising during the middle or the latter half of the century as a natural response to objective "deprivation"—that is, as an entirely economic movement, only couched in religious terms. But this kind of assessment of a millennialist group's historical self-understanding must necessarily ignore those catastrophes to which the group may not respond, and it may not be able to account for the often minor environmental stimuli that can trigger the formation of millennialist groups. Barkun observes:

92. See W. Seston, "Achilleus et la révolte de l'Égypte sous Dioclétien d'après les papyrus et l'*Histoire Auguste*," *Mélanges d'archéologie et d'histoire* 55 (1938):184–200; Allan Chester Johnson, "Lucius Domitius Domitianus Augustus," *CP* 45 (1950):14–16; Alan K. Bowman, "The Military Occupation of Upper Egypt in the Reign of Diocletian," *BASP* 15 (1978):26–33; and idem, "Two Notes: I. The Revolt of Busiris and Coptos," *BASP* 21 (1984):33–36.

93. See Johnson, "Lucius Domitius," 17–19.

94. See Bowman, "Revolt of Busiris and Coptos."

There is no reason to assume that the disaster syndrome is wholly dependent upon the presence of objective criteria. For the most part, of course, it is brought on by radical changes in the environment. Yet to a certain extent the very perception of these changes depends upon an individual's mental set. *This is particularly apt to be the case where there has been a long, slow erosion of familiar patterns and institutions,* changes which have gone largely unnoticed. In such circumstances, the catalytic event may appear relatively insignificant in itself, but it *suddenly brings together in the mind of the perceiver a sense of the interconnectedness of previously discrete events and a concomitant sense of loss and dread.*[95]

The preoccupation with signs of persecution and martyrdom in the Apocalypse of Elijah and the reference to saints being commanded "to perform sacrifices and abominations" (2:26) imply that in the historical self-definition of this particular millennialist Christian milieu, the edicts of Decius and perhaps also that of Valerian formed just such a catalytic event. Chapter 11 will discuss a more immediate catalytic event in the life of the group, which inspired the composition of the text. If, however, one takes these focal aspects of the Apocalypse of Elijah with the martyrdom lore that was widely current through Egypt by the end of the third century, a scenario develops of a minor civil requirement with no consistent enforcement and varying penalties that was almost immediately transformed among many Egyptian Christian groups into a series of wild legends of horrible persecution and torture—and of the holiness of those bodies that endured.[96]

That Decius's edict had a catalytic effect in the formation and galvanization of millennialist Christian groups, and that this "catalysis" must be viewed in the context of third-century decline, can also be seen in the transformation of the practice of *anachoresis* over the century. Popular *anachoresis* began as a check on the exploitation of peasants in Ptolemaic times: peasants might flee to local temples, from whose asylum they could safely negotiate with landlords. During the early Roman period, flight became a popular means to avoid taxes, and peasants would invariably make their way to Alexandria (whence Caracalla attempted to expel them in 215) or—less often—join bands of robbers in the marshes of the Nile Delta.[97] Not surprisingly, *anachoresis*

95. Barkun, *Disaster and the Millennium*, 81–82 (emphasis mine).
96. Fox aptly shows the difference between the reality of the edict's enforcement and its immediate use in Christian martyrological lore (*Pagans and Christians*, 455–60). Cf. Sage, "Persecution of Valerian," 137–59.
97. Cf. the revolt of the *boukoloi* under the priest Isidoros in 172 c.e. (although this probably did not have such official military roots as Milne [*History of Egypt*, 52] attests).

became epidemic in the third century as the economy collapsed; the Theadelphia papyri describe entire villages abandoned.[98]

A different form of social "disengagement" seems to have been practiced in first-century Judaism: the *Epistle of Barnabas* mentions individual retreat as an extreme form of response to eschatological imminence.[99] There may well be a relationship between this early rationale for escape from society and what one finds in the late-third-century *chora* of Antony, where a country town might have a number of hermits living right on its outskirts.[100] Their motivations may have been to imitate Elijah, as chapter 3 has discussed; both Antony and Paul of Thebes seem to have had religious motivations in their solitary escapes into the desert and may historically have considered themselves to be "waiting out" the judgment of the world (much like Elijah in 1 Kgs 17:1-7).[101] Later hermits' views of the desert and its monstrous inhabitants vividly recall the native Egyptian perception of the "region of Seth."[102]

In Jerome's recollection, however, Paul was also supposed to have abandoned his civic life to avoid "persecution" under the Decian edict.[103]

It is neither useful nor historically accurate to make a categorical distinction between ancient banditry and ancient rebellion; see Eric Hobsbawm, *Bandits* (rev. ed.; New York: Pantheon, 1981).

98. On the history of Greco-Roman Egyptian *anachoresis*, see Henri Henne, "Documents et travaux sur l'anachôrésis," *Mitteilungen aus der Papyrussammlung der österreichischen Nationalbibliothek* 5 (1956):59–66; Françoise Dunand, "L'éxode rural en Égypte à l'époque hellénistique," *Ktema* 5 (1980):137–50; Préaux, "L'àttache à la terre"; cf. Georges Posener, "L'ANACHORESIS dans l'Égypte pharaonique," in *Le monde grec: Hommages à Claire Préaux*, ed. Jean Bingen, Guy Cambier, and Georges Nachtergael (Brussels: Éditions de l'université de Bruxelles, 1975), 663–69. On abandonment of villages in Theadelphia, see P.Theadelphia, 20 (= P.Cairo 10889), in Pierre Jouguet, *Papyrus de Théadelphie* (Paris: Fontemoing, 1911), 123–26.

99. *Ep. Barn.* 4:10b. The "social disengagement" of the Therapeutae that is described by Philo (*De vita contemplativa*) is really an alternative community, not a response to anticipated catastrophe or flight from oppressive society.

100. *Vita Antonii* 3; cf. *Bohairic Life of Pachomius* 127: Antony says, "When I became a monk, there was as yet no *koinōnia* on earth to make it possible for me to live in a *koinōnia*. There were only a few people who used to withdraw a little way outside their village and live alone" (Armand Veilleux, tr. and ed., *Pachomian Koinonia*, 3 vols., Cistercian Studies Series 45–47 [Kalamazoo, Mich.: Cistercian Press, 1980–82], 1:184).

101. Paul's execration of Alexandria—"Woe to thee, Alexandria, . . . who dost worship monsters in room of God. Woe to thee, harlot city, in whom the demons of all the earth have flowed together." (Jerome *Vita Paul* 8 [*PL* 23:23f]; in Helen Waddell, tr., *The Desert Fathers* [London: Constable, 1936; reprint, Ann Arbor: University of Michigan Press, 1988], 33)—recalls the *Potter's Oracle*, which anticipates the city's destruction.

102. L. Keimer, "L'horreur des égyptiens pour les démons du désert," *Bulletin de l'institut d'Égypte* 26 (1944):135–47; cf. Antoine Guillaumont, "La conception du désert chez les moines d'Égypte," *RHR* 188 (1975):1–21.

103. Jerome *Vita Paul* 3–4 (*PL* 23:19–20).

Here one turns naturally to the considerable evidence for *anachoresis* as a response to perceived persecution. In 249, Dionysius wrote of "the multitude of those who 'wandered in deserts and mountains' [Heb 11:38], perishing from hunger and thirst and frost and diseases and bandits and wild beasts."[104] Whereas Dionysius implies that the plight of these refugees was a catastrophe in itself, both Annick Martin and Oliver Nicholson have recently discussed the attitude, popular during Dionysius's time, that flight to the desert was considered a noble, alternative form of martyrdom, even a deliberate imitation of biblical figures such as Elijah, John the Baptist, or Christ.[105] Such *anachoresis* resembles traditional Egyptian flight insofar as it functioned as an escape from civic responsibility and the penalties for disobedience; but it also resembles the "religious" *anachoresis* of the hermits insofar as the refugees often seem to have considered themselves to be awaiting the "appointed time."

CONCLUSION

At the first level of the historical and social context of the Apocalypse of Elijah, then, a profound decline in the Egyptian economy and concomitant increase in economic oppression during the century in which the text was written constitute the most general circumstances in which millennialist movements and their ideologies flourish. The context of a new and suffering middle class and economic innovations that put the maintenance of status and identity onto the individual provides a basis for sect formation. The persistent revolts and their ideological bases (occasionally explicit, as in the case of the *mantis* who sparks the anti-Christian pogrom in 249) show that types of "revolutionary behavior" similar to that of millennialism were endemic to the period. Moreover, the consistently nationalistic basis of these revolts parallels the archaic Egyptian nationalism underlying the *Chaosbeschreibung* motifs employed in the Apocalypse of Elijah. The continuity of culture and materials between Alexandria and the *chora* argues that the countryside (or at least its cities) was by no means insulated from events in Alexandria; and the inevitable rumors of these events must have attributed to them a

104. In Eusebius *Hist. eccles.* 6.42.2 (ed. Oulton and Lawlor, *Eusebius* 2:110).
105. See Annick Martin, "La reconciliation des *lapsi* en Égypte," *Rivista di storia e letteratura religiosa* 22 (1986):258–61; and Oliver Nicholson, "Flight from Persecution as Imitation of Christ: Lactantius' Divine Institutes IV.18, 1–2," *JTS* 40 (1989):48–65.

nationalistic significance appreciable by epichoric folk. Indeed, it would have been just such a rural, impoverished, nationalistic perspective that would coin and respond to the woe oracle of ApocEl 2 with which this chapter began: the foreign-born rulers of Egypt are damned as oppressive and apostrophically warned of incipient revolution.

Finally, this chapter has pressed the martyrological data discussed in chapter 6 to propose that the Decian edict provided a possible catalytic event for the historical self-definition of millennialist groups. The importance of the edict may be seen in the transformation of the meaning of *anachoresis* in Christian lore.

10

The Second Level:
Evidence for Millennialism in
the Egyptian *Chora*, Ca. 260–270 C.E.

Chapter 9 addressed the context in which a millennialist movement would be comprehensible in Egypt at the time of the composition of the Apocalypse of Elijah. Under the circumstances outlined, it is hardly a coincidence to find evidence for millennialist activity in a region of the Fayyum about a decade after the period of the Decian edict.

In a letter titled "On Promises," which largely concerns the interpretation of the book of Revelation, Dionysius of Alexandria refers to a group of Christians in Arsinoë who were following the ideas of Nepos, a local bishop, and Coracion, a Christian prophet of sorts. Nepos had written a treatise on Revelation called *Refutation of Allegorists*, on which, Dionysius complained, his followers "rely completely as proving incontrovertibly that Christ's kingdom will be here on earth."[1] Dionysius's account of his encounter and conflict with this group discloses a microcosm of millennialist sentiment during the catastrophic decline of the third century:

> When I arrived in the district of Arsinoë, where as you know this notion
> had long been widely held, so that schisms and secessions of entire
> churches had taken place, I called a meeting of the presbyters and teachers

---

1. Dionysius, in Eusebius *Hist. eccles.* 7.24.4 (ed. Oulton and Lawlor, *Eusebius: The Ecclesiastical History*, 2 vols. [London: Heinemann, 1932], 2:192). Eusebius himself summarizes their hope as "a kind of millennium on this earth devoted to bodily indulgence" (*Hist. eccles.* 7.24.1), but this "antinomian" interpretation probably reflects his own prejudices against millennialism; see Clementina Mazzucco, "Eusèbe de Césarée et l'*Apocalypse* de Jean," *Studia patristica* 17, 1 (1982):317–24; and Frank S. Thielman, "Another Look at the Eschatology of Eusebius of Caesarea," *VigChr* 41 (1987):226–37.

of the village congregations, with any laymen who wished to attend, and urged them to thrash out the question in public. So they brought me this book as positive and irrefutable proof, and I sat with them for three days on end from dawn to dusk, criticizing its contents point by point. In the process I was immensely impressed by the essential soundness, complete sincerity, logical grasp, and mental clarity shown by these good people, as we methodically and good-temperedly dealt with questions, objections, and points of agreement. We refused to cling with pig-headed determination to opinions once held even if proved wrong. There was no shirking of difficulties, but to the limit of our powers we tried to grapple with the problems and master them; nor were we too proud, if worsted in argument, to abandon our position and admit defeat: conscientiously, honestly, and with simple-minded trust in God, we accepted the conclusions to be drawn from the proofs and teachings of Holy Writ. In the end, the author and originator of this doctrine, Coracion by name, in the hearing of all present assured and promised us that for the future he would not adhere to it, argue about it, mention it, or teach it, as he was completely convinced by the arguments on the other side. Of the rest, some were delighted with the discussion, and with the all round spirit of accommodation and concord.[2]

Apparently, the book of Revelation had gained some popularity in Nepos's region, either before or after Coracion had begun teaching the text publicly as a scenario of imminent events. The text's popularity was due specifically to its promises of an imminent, terrestrial eschaton and installation of the kingdom of God. Coracion's interpretation attracted many followers, because (one might assume) he phrased his exegesis in the immediate terms and concerns of his audience and probably added corollary prophecies for their benefit. As the movement grew, however, some of its members became aware that the Alexandrian school of allegorical exegesis had been promoting a different interpretation of prophetic and apocalyptic texts, which effectively denied the imminent reality of Revelation's "promises." These members were undoubtedly of a social status that would have been aware of Alexandrian trends, for example, the Greco-Egyptian landed classes discussed in chapter 9.

Nepos was one of these literate and cultured participants. As bishop of the region, he may well have had more secure contacts with Alexandria than the others who followed Coracion and may have considered himself dependent upon Alexandria for his authority. Nepos proceeded to write a treatise explaining and justifying Coracion's interpretation of

---

2. Eusebius *Hist. eccles.* 7.24 (in G. A. Williamson, tr., *Eusebius: The History of the Church* [Harmondsworth: Penguin, 1965], 307–9).

Revelation; and in calling the treatise *Refutation of Allegorists*, he was directing it specifically at the Alexandrian school, of which Dionysius himself was head. Nepos was therefore a self-appointed apologist for a religious movement, attempting to defend a local "development" against the disapproval of outsiders. This scenario begins to reveal a fundamental conflict between Alexandrian and epichoric Greco-Egyptian religious cultures, one similar to that seen in the Elijah Apocalypse's "rigorist" perspective on proper martyrdom.[3]

From the popularity of Coracion's movement throughout the region, its attraction for both literate and nonliterate Greco-Egyptians in Arsinoë, and the explicitly eschatological nature of its ideology, we may cogently infer its "millennialist" character.[4] Furthermore, the large rural and peasant base that apparently characterized the movement (e.g., as indicated by the reference to its spread among the "villages" [κώμαι]) recalls the typically peasant roots of millennialist movements reviewed in cross-cultural studies.[5] Indeed, many of the congregations seem to have been led by people of rustic backgrounds: in Dionysius's view of the Arsinoite believers, Coracion's teachings "do not allow our simpler [ἁπλουστέρους] brethren to have lofty noble thoughts . . . they persuade them to expect in the Kingdom of God what is trifling and mortal and like the present."[6] This condescension stands in contrast to Dionysius's admitted respect for Nepos's own abilities, suggesting that the believers had a significantly lower cultural background than Nepos.[7]

With this kind of following, Coracion's millennialist teachings must have tapped deep epichoric sources, which would not have evaporated in intellectual argument with an Alexandrian bishop.[8] Dionysius himself informs his readers that when he arrived in the Arsinoite nome in the early 260s, "this doctrine had long been widely held, so that both

3. See above, chap. 6, pp. 152–54. In general, on socioeconomic origins of Egyptian clergy, see Annick Martin, "Aux origines de l'église copte: L'implantation et le développement du christianisme en Égypte (Iᵉ–IVᵉ siècles)," *REA* 83 (1981):48–51.

4. Dionysius's description of the Arsinoites as τοὺς ἀντιδιατιθεμένους ("militant opponents"; Eusebius *Hist. eccles.* 7.24.5 [ed. Oulton and Lawlor, *Eusebius* 2:192]), a polemical term inherited from 2 Tm 2:25, may also imply that they tended toward a certain fanaticism.

5. See Michael Barkun, *Disaster and the Millennium* (New Haven: Yale University Press; reprint, Syracuse, N.Y.: Syracuse University Press, 1986), 66–74, 92–97.

6. In Eusebius *Hist. eccles.* 7.24.5 (ed. Oulton and Lawlor, *Eusebius* 2:192).

7. Cf. W.H.C. Frend, *Martyrdom and Persecution in the Early Church* (London: Basil Blackwell, 1965; reprint, Grand Rapids: Baker Book House, 1981), 466.

8. Cf. Gerhard Maier, *Die Johannesoffenbarung und die Kirche*, WUNT 25 (Tübingen: Mohr [Siebeck] 1981), 87–96, who overemphasizes the intellectual aspect of the conflict.

schisms and secessions of whole congregations had taken place";[9] and he carefully avoids the claim that he quelled the entire movement, restricting the account of his dogmatic successes in Arsinoë to the one small meeting he held with Coracion and a few local leaders. Indeed, it is doubtful that even these representatives remained convinced for long after Dionysius returned to Alexandria. Their respective cultural worlds were too different, and Dionysius's allegorical use of Revelation too abstract and impractical in the face of present and immediate calamities for the movement simply to cease. What is more, an Alexandrian bishop at this time would hardly have had the authority in rural Egypt to dictate orthodoxy, as Dionysius wants to claim.[10]

If one may believe Dionysius's portrayal of this millennialist movement as essentially defining itself through Scripture, this focus must be reconciled with the predominant illiteracy of the *chora* during this period.[11] Indeed, Dionysius himself remarks on the rarity and, in his mind, the danger of such ideas as Coracion's being presented in written form:

> If [Nepos] were here now and putting forward his ideas in speech alone [ψιλῷ λόγῳ], conversation with nothing in writing would suffice, using question and answer as means to persuade and win over our militant opponents. But a work has been published [γραφῆς δὲ ἐκκειμένης] which some people find most convincing.[12]

How, then, was the ideology communicated and understood? What kind of hierarchy was responsible for dissemination of ideas?

The followers themselves are clearly rural and illiterate. Dionysius claims that he held a meeting to debate Nepos's views with "the presbyters and teachers of the brethren in the villages [ταῖς κώμαις]"—sug-

---

9. In Eusebius *Hist. eccles.* 7.24.6 (ed. Oulton and Lawlor, *Eusebius* 2:194).

10. C. Wilfred Griggs, *Early Egyptian Christianity: From Its Origins to 451 C.E.*, Coptic Studies 2 (Leiden: Brill, 1990), 100; see 86–88 on the Coracion–Nepos controversy. Philip Rousseau's image of a united Egypt (*Pachomius: The Making of a Community in Fourth-Century Egypt* [Berkeley: University of California Press, 1985], 3–13) is clearly inapplicable to the mid-third century.

11. On the predominance of nonliteracy and semiliteracy during this period, see Herbert C. Youtie, "AGRAMMATOS: An Aspect of Greek Society in Egypt," *HSCP* 75 (1971):161–76; idem, "BRADEOS GRAPHON: Between Literacy and Illiteracy," in idem, *Scriptiunculae*, 2 vols. (Amsterdam: Hakkert, 1973), 2:629–51; idem, "HYPOGRAPHEUS: The Social Impact of Illiteracy in Graeco-Roman Egypt," *ZPE* 17 (1975):201–21; Naphtali Lewis, *Life in Egypt under Roman Rule* (Oxford: Clarendon, 1983), 62, 81–82; and William V. Harris, *Ancient Literacy* (Cambridge: Harvard University Press, 1983), 190, 278–80, 316.

12. Dionysius, in Eusebius *Hist. eccles.* 7.24.4 (tr. Williamson, *Eusebius*, 308).

gesting rural and peasant audiences, if not also leadership. In Dionysius's description of the debate, he nowhere mentions these representatives' ability to read either Nepos's book or the Scripture on which it was based:

> They brought me this book as positive and irrefutable proof, and I sat with them for three days on end from dawn to dusk, criticizing its contents point by point. In the process I was immensely impressed by the essential soundness, complete sincerity, logical grasp, and mental clarity shown by these good people, as we methodically and good-temperedly dealt with questions, objections, and points of agreement.[13]

The language carefully describes a situation of *oral* interaction, in which even the book itself is viewed (by the congregants) only as a concrete demonstration of their beliefs: (1) they bring him the book, apparently as proof in and of itself; (2) Dionysius is the only character described as making use of the book itself ("I sat with them . . . criticizing its contents [τὰ γεγραμμένα]"); (3) the "intellectual" attributes that Dionysius imputes to them do not require literacy, only the ability to comprehend ideas; (4) any mention of a single congregant's ability to read or point out passages is conspicuously missing.[14] Indeed, by Dionysius's testimony not even Coracion has facility with letters: he is only mentioned as ἀρχηγὸς καὶ εἰσηγητής,[15] he does not debate Dionysius on different terms from the "presbyters and teachers," and he is instructed to refrain not from writing millennialist ideology, only from discussing (διαλέξεσθαι), mentioning (μεμνῆσθαι), or teaching (διδάξειν) it. It is more likely that Nepos or others with the ability to read had presented the text of the *Refutation of Allegorists* orally and in parts than that each congregant had read and contemplated the text.

Nepos, then, may well have been the first member of the Arsinoite movement to put its ideology into writing (thereby attracting the notice of the Alexandrian authorities). One might assume, however, that others like him—literate, conversant with Alexandrian Greek culture, and perhaps also viewing Alexandria as a source of philosophical and

---

13. Dionysius, in Eusebius *Hist. eccles.* 7.24.7–8a (ibid.).

14. Dionysius's statement that "a book has been published (that is) most convincing, so it seems to certain people" (in Eusebius *Hist. eccles.* 7.24.5; ed. Oulton and Lawlor, *Eusebius* 2:192) does not require that these "certain people" (τίσιν) had actually read it themselves. Certainly, Nepos's work may have made it to Alexandria, thus earning a more direct readership and "convincing" some people there of millennialist bent. Neither case, however, implies the literacy of Coracion's followers in Arsinoë.

15. In Eusebius *Hist. eccles.* 7.24.9 (ed. Oulton and Lawlor, *Eusebius* 2:194).

ecclesiastical authority—were involved among the millennialist congregations, at least in the positions of copyist, lector, and public interpreter of Scripture.[16]

Because the movement seems to have arisen in connection with a text, the book of Revelation, even though the majority of its adherents would have been illiterate, it is likely that the charismatic leadership of the movement consisted of those able to read and interpret this particular text.[17] This capacity might also imply three tiers of interaction: leaders, subsidiary teachers, and audience–adherents. In this situation the leaders belonged to such socioeconomic milieus as promoted literacy on a general level; the partial literacy of the subsidiary teachers would have stood in contrast to their audiences' basic illiteracy and dependence on these teachers for access to Scripture.[18] Thus the "literary" character of the movement would have positioned teachers and audiences, leaders and congregations, in different positions (perhaps thereby implying different socioeconomic backgrounds).

It has often been noted that charismatic leadership in millennialist movements, even those of the poorest socioeconomic classes, tends to come from those holding "marginal" status in society: individuals who are—and who express to their audience a status of being—conversant with the dominant culture but still fundamentally allied with the culture of the audience.[19] Nepos certainly conforms to this type: an educated Gɪeco-Egyptian bishop sympathetic to rural millennialism and able to

16. On the increasing literacy of the clergy in subsequent centuries, see Ewa Wipszycka, "Le degré d'alphabétisation en Égypte byzantine," *Revue des études augustiniennes* 30 (1984):288–91.

17. On the integral presence of charismatic leadership in millennialist movements, see, e.g., Peter Worsley, *The Trumpet Shall Sound: A Study of "Cargo" Cults in Melanesia* (2d ed.; New York: Schocken, 1968), ix–xxi; Yonina Talmon, "Pursuit of the Millennium: The Relation between Religious and Social Change," *Archives européennes de sociologie* 3 (1962):133–35; Barkun, *Disaster and the Millennium*, 39–40, 86–90.

18. Cf. the North African martyr Lucian, who is "less well trained in holy scripture," according to Cyprian of Carthage (*Epistles* 27.1; in *Saint Cyprien: Correspondence*, ed. and tr. Le Chanoine Bayard, 2 vols. [Paris: Société d'Édition "Les Belles Lettres," 1925], 1:65), but nevertheless can prepare crude certificates of absolution in the names of fellow martyrs (*Ep.* 27.2; ed. Bayard, *Correspondence* 1:65). On partial literacy in Roman Egypt, see Youtie, "BRADEOS GRAPHON," 2629–51; and Annick Martin, "Aux origines de l'église copte," 48–49; idem, "L'église et la khôra égyptienne au IVᵉ siècle," *Revue des études augustiniennes* 25 (1979):15–17, on recruitment of lower, nonliterate classes in Christian priesthood.

19. Kenelm Burridge, *New Heaven, New Earth: A Study of Millenarian Activities* (Oxford: Basil Blackwell, 1969), 153–63; Bruce Lincoln, "Notes toward a Theory of Religion and Revolution," in idem, ed., *Religion, Rebellion, Revolution* (New York: St. Martin's, 1985), 274–75.

write a literary *apologia* for it. Coracion too, whether fully or partially literate, would have had to display an unusual knowledge of Scripture and prophetic lore to have galvanized a millennialist movement; thus he also is placed in a marginal position in relation to his illiterate audience. It is interesting to note that the author of the Apocalypse of Elijah also betrays a considerable acquaintance with certain scriptural texts, as well as an "oral" culture of quoted and epitomized Scripture. At no point, however, does the Elijah Apocalypse's author make an explicit distinction between scriptural quotations and his own statements in "biblicalese," which suggests that the audience itself may not have been able to tell the difference.

Here one should consider the singular role of Revelation in the teachings of Coracion and Nepos and, presumably, in the ideology of the movement as a whole. It is unlikely that this was the only text with which Coracion and his followers would have been familiar. The abundant circulation of apocalyptic and liturgical texts during this time is reflected in the libraries of Wadi Natrun and the White Monastery of Shenoute; and Jerome's description of an eschatological discourse in a fourth-century monastic liturgy would explain the interest in and need for texts of an eschatological bent.[20] Among the other texts in circulation in Upper Egypt during the third century that might have had popularity in congregations of millennialist bent are the *Shepherd of Hermas*, the *Apocalypse of Peter*, and parts of the Enochic corpus.[21] However, Coracion's (apparently) central use of Revelation in Arsinoë: corresponds to the Apocalypse of Elijah's special familiarity with this text among other books of Scripture. Moreover, it would make the Arsinoite movement "genuinely" millennialist (as per Rev 20:2-10). Although the relationship between text and religious movement is always highly complex, Arsinoë provides an early example of what was to become in history a typical colonial phenomenon: the use of an essentially alien text to comprehend local anxieties and inequities and to motivate behavior in response.[22]

The papyrus record for Arsinoë during the 260s is diverse. From what

20. Jerome *Epistles* 22.35.3; discussed above, pp. 79–80.
21. See George W. E. Nickelsburg, Jr., "Two Enochic Manuscripts: Unstudied Evidence for Egyptian Christianity," in *Of Scribes and Scrolls: Studies on the Hebrew Bible, Intertestamental Judaism, and Christian Origins Presented to John Strugnell*, ed. Harold W. Attridge, John J. Collins, and Thomas H. Tobin, College Theology Society Resources in Religion 5 (Lanham, Md.: University Press of America, 1990), 251–60.
22. See esp. Burridge, *New Heaven, New Earth*, 15–22, 108, on Te Hua, prophet of the New Zealand *Hauhau* movement of 1862.

is known of this period, the overall situation could only have become worse over the decade since Philip's reign. It was just over ten years since the senate of this very nome tried to force villagers into assuming the urban liturgies, claiming that the metropolitan citizens themselves were being ruined.[23] By the end of the third century, according to the Theadelphia papyri, the arable land in the southwestern part of the nome had vastly receded before the desert, and whole villages had been abandoned.[24] By contrast, one of the earliest Christian papyri is a letter from a wealthy Greek Christian concerning trade between Arsinoë, Alexandria, and Rome and reflecting a well-endowed, urban, Greek congregation in Arsinoë during the late 260s.[25] It is quite evident, then, that there was economic diversity in the Arsinoite nome of the mid-third century but that suffering was more general in the *chora*, and some prosperity existed among those elite Greeks who were not economically attached to Arsinoë and its decline.[26] The Christian papyrus also gives evidence for congregations of an Alexandrian-identified merchant class that may have been less inclined to join millennialist ideologies of the countryside. Perhaps it was just such a class of Christians that first alerted Dionysius to Nepos's activities.

One may therefore conclude that sometime in the late 250s or early 260s,[27] in the aftermath of Valerian's edicts and concurrent with Alexandrian seditions and profound despair in Egypt, a Christian millennialist movement spread among villagers in the Arsinoite *chora*. Although its ideology was based on public interpretations of apocalyptic texts in circulation at that time, which were administered by literate members of the Egyptian or Greco-Egyptian middle class, there also developed an oral form of interpretation and exhortation among congregations led by semiliterate or nonliterate "presbyters and teachers."

23. P.London inv. 2565 (in T. C. Skeat and E. P. Wegener, "A Trial before the Prefect of Egypt Appius Sabinus, c. 250 A.D.," *JEA* 21 [1935]:224–47 and pl. 28).

24. See Pierre Jouguet, *Papyrus de Théadelphie* (Paris: Fontemoing, 1911), esp. nos. 16–17, 20.

25. P.Amherst 3(a); in Herbert Musurillo, "Early Christian Economy: A Reconsideration of P.Amherst 3(a) (= Wilcken, Chrest 126)," *Chronique d'Égypte* 31 (1956):124–34.

26. See Henry A. Green, "Socio-Economic Background of Christianity in Egypt," in *The Roots of Egyptian Christianity*, ed. Birger A. Pearson and James E. Goehring, SAC 1 (Philadelphia: Fortress, 1986), 105.

27. This trip was one of Dionysius's final acts before he died in 264 and may be dated to the period after his return from exile under Valerian (ca. 262). However, the Arsinoite millennialist movement apparently had begun considerably before his arrival and probably did not expire so soon thereafter.

Indeed, there is papyrological evidence that literacy was not a require-ment for Christian liturgical leadership in the Roman period.[28]

What is most important at this point, however, is the historical cor-relation between agricultural, economic, political, and social disinte-gration and a millennialist movement of the poor and disenfranchised. One cannot deduce the extent to which Egyptian nationalist ideology had an effect in this movement; the schism with Alexandrian authority and the rural, Greco-Egyptian social makeup of the movement only give reason to expect that this millennialist ideology bore elements of Egyp-tian nationalism or nativism.

Although the dates of this millennialist movement correspond to the period in which the Apocalypse of Elijah was written, and although the movement evidently extended over a considerable area in the Fayyum, it would be premature to view Coracion and Nepos's milieu as *the* historical situation from which the Apocalypse of Elijah derived.[29] This would be to rest on the assumption that there were no other similar millennialist movements in Upper Egypt during this period. On the contrary, the existence of rebellions throughout the third century, the ideological continuum that has been argued to have existed among the various rebellions and among their respective propagandas, and the sporadic growth of Christianity in the *chora*[30] all would suggest that behind the silence arose other such millennialist movements. Cross-culturally, the addition of Christian eschatological doctrine to situations of socioeconomic stress has led quite often to millennialism over broad regions.[31] The Arsinoite movement, therefore, must be regarded as representing a *type* of religious situation that occurred often around Egypt during the third century and in which the Apocalypse of Elijah was written.

28. P.Oxy 2673; see Youtie, "AGRAMMATOS," 163, 163 n. 6; cf. Ewa Wipszycka, "Un lecteur qui ne sait pas écrire ou un chrétien qui ne veut pas se souiller? (P.Oxy. XXXIII 2673)," ZPE 50 (1983):117–21.

29. It is interesting to note that Hugh G. Evelyn White assigned to this very movement of Coracion and Nepos a fragment of an "Apocalyptic Gospel" containing some significant parallels to the Apocalypse of Elijah (Hugh G. Evelyn White, ed., The Monasteries of Wadi 'N Natrûn, vol. 1: New Coptic Texts from the Monastery of Saint Macarius [New York: Metropolitan Museum of Art, 1926], 18).

30. See Ewa Wipszycka ("La christianisation de l'Égypte aux IVè–VIè siècles. Aspects sociaux et ethniques," Aegyptus 68 [1988]:117–65), who argues, against Roger S. Bagnall ("Religious Conversion and Onomastic Change in Early Byzantine Egypt," BASP 19 [1982]:105–23), that conversion occurred exceedingly slowly on the popular level, and then only in mass conversions of villages.

31. Cf. Sylvia L. Thrupp, "Millennial Dreams in Action: A Report on the Conference Discussion," in idem, ed., Millennial Dreams in Action: Studies in Revolutionary Religious Movements (New York: Schocken, 1970), 11–27.

11

The Third Level:
A Sect in the Crossfire of
Asceticism Debates, Ca. 260–290 C.E.

In the scheme of historical analysis set out in these final chapters, the first level represented the most general context for the composition of a text like the Apocalypse of Elijah: historical, economic, social, and ideological circumstances within which a millennialist movement and its literary compositions would be comprehensible. The second level of historical–social context demonstrated that Christian millennialism did arise during this period, probably out of the catastrophes of the mid-third century. This level also suggested the instrumental use of the book of Revelation in focusing and legitimating popular Christian millennialism. Finally, there is reason to expect that rumors of persecution could have catalyzed the formation of a millennialist movement, to whose members the Apocalypse of Elijah was subsequently addressed, even though the text gives no indication that the martyrdoms it narrates point to an immediately critical incident. We are thus moving closer to a hypothetical historical, social, and religious scenario in which the Apocalypse of Elijah makes sense as a literary phenomenon.

Early Christian texts were often composed in direct response to specific ideological conflicts. Indeed, one might suggest that the desire to put ideology into literary form tends to arise from disagreements of such magnitude that oral preaching and debate simply cannot carry enough authority in the conflict. The exalted literary frames of prophecy and apocalypse encapsulate ideas often of the most ephemeral importance, cast as the words of angels or even of God.

What particular conflict might therefore have motivated the literary composition of the Apocalypse of Elijah, which is presented in the form

of an authoritative discourse from God? Between the parenetic introduction to the Apocalypse of Elijah and the eschatological discourse
proper there is a substantial passage concerned with fasting and its
benefits but, more specifically, with a group of "deceivers" who oppose
fasting (1:13-22). This passage contains its own introduction ("Hear now,
you wise men"), suggesting its fundamental independence from the
opening passages of the Elijah Apocalypse; it is presented as a singularly
important thought. In form the passage is clearly hortatory, punctuated
with imperatives and second-person addresses. Its function as exhortation seems to have been both polemical and apologetic.

Insofar as the passage is hortatory, addressing a particular audience
in the second person, it continues the rhetorical mode of the introduction of the Apocalypse of Elijah, focusing its parenetic concerns on
the issue of fasting. However, insofar as the issue of fasting is introduced
with an alert to the audience regarding "deceivers who will multiply *in
the end time*," the passage also functions as the immediate frame for
understanding the entire subsequent eschatological discourse: the warning about opponents of fasting becomes the "reason" for the eschatological discourse itself and its description of eschatological deception.

Could the specific form in which this section is presented and its
central importance for the rest of the text reflect a real historical situation—a controversy over fasting—in reaction to which the text was
composed? Although this study has argued in detail for the ahistoricity
of most of ApocEl 2, on the basis of prior literary traditions behind
ostensibly historical references, this particular theme—eschatological
opponents of fasting—does not have a literary tradition behind it.[1]

THE CONCEPT OF FASTING IN THE
APOCALYPSE OF ELIJAH

The homily in ApocEl 1:13-22 stresses the purifying function of fasting. Fasting seems to cultivate a para-angelic state in the individual,
symbolized especially in the allusion to incense rising to the throne of

1. On fasting in general, see E.C.E. Owen, "Fasting in the Eastern Church," *CQR* 126
(1938):95–110; Rudolf Arbesmann, "Fasting and Prophecy in Pagan and Christian
Antiquity," *Traditio* 7 (1949–51):1–71; idem, "Fasten," in *Reallexikon für Antike und
Christentum*, ed. Theodor Klauser (Stuttgart: Anton Hiersemann, 1950-), 7:474–82;
Herbert Musurillo, "The Problem of Ascetical Fasting in the Greek Patristic Writers,"
Traditio 12 (1956):1–64.

God. But fasting also had a concrete function for the author's milieu: it cultivated a force that was both *apotropaic* (against demons and diseases) and *connective*. The verb ἐνεργεῖν signifies the control of some sort of natural force or power, and the comparisons to incense and ointment make clear that this power was conceived quite concretely.[2]

The apotropaic fast, which was aimed at thwarting disease and demons through avoiding food, was based on the notion that demons resided in or might enter into food (or certain foods).[3] Although the extensive demonology of Egypt would certainly have provided rich soil for this notion, the fullest discussion of demons' use of food to enter bodies is found in the Pseudo-Clementine texts.[4] Naturally, there was but a short step between the idea of food as prone to demonic habitation (which has parallels in many local traditions outside Egypt of late antiquity) and the idea that food—especially meat—was by its very nature demonic. Although this belief achieved special status among Manichaeans, sparking such ecclesiastical responses as the Synod of Ancyra's canon 14 (requiring all clerics at least to taste meat at feasts),[5] it is likely that any community practicing extreme fasting regimes might arrive at the conclusion that eating itself was an unholy act. For the Montanist Tertullian, the refusal of food restored the purity lost through Adam's eating of the fruit.[6] A fourth- or fifth-century Egyptian monk who managed to put off eating for an entire day saw a demon rise out of himself in smoke and was rewarded with the disappearance of all his hunger.[7]

2. On the attainment of sacred power through fasting, see Roland Crahay, "Le jeûne comme symbole charismatique," in *Eschatologie et cosmologie*, Annales du centre d'étude des religions 3 (Brussels: Université libre de Bruxelles, 1969), 137, 142, 152–54.

3. See Musurillo, "Ascetical Fasting," 19–23; Otto Böcher, *Dämonenfurcht und Dämonenabwehr: Ein Beitrag zur Vorgeschichte der christlichen Taufe*, BWANT 5, 10 (Stuttgart: Kohlhammer, 1970), 273–88. Cf. Athanasius, *Vita Antonii* 23.

4. Pseudo-Clementine *Homilies* 9.10; *Recognitions* 4.16–19, 32–34; see discussion in Musurillo, "Ascetical Fasting," 20–21.

5. Cf. Synod of Gangra, Canon 2: "If any one condemns one who eats meat, though he abstains from blood, idolatrous sacrifices, and things strangled, and is faithful and devout, as if in so doing he had no hope of salvation, let him be anathema" (tr. Charles Joseph Hefele, in idem, *History of the Councils of the Church*, vol. 2: A.D. 326 to A.D. 429, tr. and ed. Henry Nutcombe Oxenham [Edinburgh: T. & T. Clark, 1896; reprint, New York: AMS, 1972], 328).

6. Tertullian, *De Ieiunio* 3.

7. *Apophthegmata patrum* (Anon.) no. 145 in F. Nau, ed., "Histoires des solitaires égyptiens," *Revue de l'orient Chrétien* 13 (1908):50 = no. 13 in Benedicta Ward, tr., *The Wisdom of the Desert Fathers* (Fairacres, Oxford: SLG Press, 1986], 4). In another story, desert monks on a mission to Alexandria are unwittingly served meat; when this is revealed to them they refuse to eat any more (*Apophthegmata patrum* [Anon.] no. 162, in

Fasting in rural Egypt represented no abstract withdrawal or discipline as part of the philosopher's life, but rather a quite concrete attainment of apotropaic and divine power. Indeed, the concreteness of the early Egyptian ascetics' concept of fasting is reflected in the terse lists of the fast's powers that are found in both the Apocalypse of Elijah and a later treatise on virginity attributed to Athanasius:[8]

ApocEl 1:21-22	Pseudo-Athanasius
For [the holy fast (Sa³)] releases sin,	You see what the fast does:
heals diseases,	it heals diseases,
	it dries up bodily discharges,
casts out demons,	it exorcises demons,
	it expels evil thoughts,
	it makes the mind clearer,
	it purifies the heart,
	it cleanses the body
	and it sets a person
exerts power up to the throne of God as an ointment, [as incense, (Sa³)] as a remission of sin through a holy prayer	by the throne of God.

In Jewish apocalyptic tradition, there was a close relationship between fasting and heavenly visions;[9] and early Christian uses of the apocalypse model, such as the *Shepherd of Hermas*, show that the preparation for mystical vision by fasting was widely noted as a literary theme if not attempted as a practice.[10] It is therefore striking that the Apocalypse of Elijah lacks any mention of the use of fasting as preparation for visionary experiences. Perhaps this particular tradition of mystical practice was not a constitutive part of the religious life of the sect behind the Apocalypse of Elijah—that its ascetic ideology focused exclusively on purity and concrete effects such as exorcism.

Nau, ed., "Histoires des solitaires égyptiens," 53 = no. 30 in Ward, *Wisdom of the Desert Fathers*, 7).

8. Pseudo-Athanasius, *On Virginity* 7 (*PG* 28:260).

9. E.g., 4 Ezr 5:13; 6:35; 2 *Bar.* 9:2; 12:5; cf. Dn 10:3.

10. *Herm. Vis.* 2.2.1; 3.1.2; 3.10.6–7. See the discussion in Arbesmann, "Fasting and Prophecy," 52–71, esp. 57–59.

THE NATURE OF THE CONFLICT
IN APOCEL 1:13-19

The passage 1:13-19 describes a situation in which certain individuals are preaching "against" the fast, whereas the author or speaker of the text and his audience believe strongly in the practice of fasting and have high claims for its various effects.[11] Yet the extreme positioning of opponents and defenders probably masks a more complex situation: the opponents, it may be, are criticizing *the type or extent of fasting* practiced by the author and community. One should also consider the historical identity of the opponents in relation to the nature of polemic in general: simply put, distinctions are drawn more vividly and polemic is phrased more bitterly the closer the opponents are in categories other than that under contention—in Georg Simmel's words, "Where enough similarities continue to make confusion and blurred borderlines possible, points of difference need an emphasis not justified by the issue but only by that danger of confusion."[12] Early Christianity is replete with examples of authors labeling their intimate opponents with the strongest available terms: Antichrist, sons of darkness, Satan.[13] Thus the "deceivers" were probably not so ideologically alien to the home audience as the author wants to indicate. It is quite improbable that the passage originated, for example, as a Jewish defense of Yom Kippur fasting against Christians.[14] The author was undoubtedly faced with (at least) two groups of Christians.[15]

---

11. It might also be suggested that the author is attempting to convince a *neutral* audience of the value of fasting, against "deceivers" who preach against fasting. As I show shortly, however, the debate cannot be between opponents and proponents of fasting per se (for fasting was common to all types of Christians) but rather would be between different degrees and ideologies of fasting. The radical distinctions would make little sense to outsiders, who would see both groups as advocating some sort of fasting. Hence the author must be defending a practice already current in the community, which has been brought under criticism by outside parties. That is, the text arises out of a situation common to both author and audience.

12. Georg Simmel, *Conflict and the Web of Group-Affiliations*, tr. Kurt H. Wolff and Reinhard Bendix (New York: Free Press, 1955), 48.

13. On the use of demonological categories to label religious opponents, see Neil Forsyth, *The Old Enemy: Satan and the Combat Myth* (Princeton: Princeton University Press, 1987), 309–14; Gregory C. Jenks, *The Origins and Early Development of the Antichrist Myth*, BZNW 59 (Berlin: de Gruyter, 1991), 60–64, 115; and cf. 2 Cor 11:13-15; 1 Jn 2:18-19; Rv 2:9, 20.

14. Cf. Steindorff, 19; Rosenstiehl, 83 n. *ad loc;* followed by Wintermute, 737 n. q2.

15. Cf. Schrage, 235 n. b.

The question then arises, What "types" of Christians might represent the respective sides? Two alternatives might be advanced: (1) "gnostic antinomian" (or "extremist Pauline") Christians who were opposed to all fasting (as a demonic component of the "law") when fasting per se was normative to Egyptian and Alexandrian Christianity; or (2) Alexandrian ecclesiastical authorities who were opposed to the extreme fasting in practice among certain sects in the *chora* but not opposed to fasting per se. Because the only evidence for "gnostic antinomians" who opposed all fasting is a short reference in Epiphanius's *Panarion* (1.26.5.8), a notoriously fantastic account of heresies from the fourth century, and because the Alexandrian attitude toward asceticism apparently tended to "spiritualize" and to endorse moderation in fasting,[16] it would seem more historically probable to posit the second alternative as the scenario behind the Apocalypse of Elijah. That is, the "deceivers" envisioned by the Elijah Apocalypse correspond best to orthodox Alexandrian Christians.

EXCURSUS:
FASTING IN THE GOSPEL OF THOMAS

The *Gospel of Thomas*'s strange admonitions regarding religious fasting might be construed as opposing the practice altogether, so that the first alternative mentioned above would be a possible context for the fasting passage.[17] Because Thomas circulated early and—in light of the papyrus fragments—profusely among Egyptian Christians, it is worth considering its logia as potential contradictions to the fasting ideology in the Apocalypse of Elijah.

The most enigmatic of these logia, 14, states quite directly that "if you fast, you will beget sin for yourselves," elaborating further: "For what goes into your mouth will not defile you, but what comes out of your mouth, that is what will defile you." The context in which it occurs, however, militates against an overly literal interpretation: "If you pray you will be condemned, and if you give alms, you will do evil to your spirits." The latter directions function as paradoxes, aimed to raise the understanding of religious practices to a higher or more

16. See Clement of Alexandria, *Strom.* 6.12; 7.12. *Barnabas* 3 quotes Is 58:3-7, a post-Exilic assault on such fasting as might have excluded social compassion (cf. also Justin, *Dial.* 15). *Barnabas*'s subsequent critique of millennialist *anachoresis*—"do not live alone, retiring by yourselves, as if already perfected" (4:10b)—allows the possibility that *Barnabas* 3 is directed against first-century hermits who were fasting in preparation for the eschaton. On "spiritual fasting" in general, see Musurillo, "Ascetical Fasting," 35–42; and J. A. McGuckin, "Christian Asceticism and the Early School of Alexandria," *Monks, Hermits, and the Ascetic Tradition*, ed. W. J. Sheils (Oxford: Blackwell, 1985), 30–38.

17. Cf. Frank Williams (*The Panarion of Epiphanius of Salamis*, NHS 35 [Leiden: Brill, 1987], 87 n. 20), who refers to logia 14 and 104 as potential evidence for Epiphanius's image of alleged gnostic opposition to fasting.

spiritual level. The text therefore allows that fasting is not wrong per se but absurd in its "literal," concrete form.

Logion 27, which is also extant in Greek (P.Oxy 1, ll. 4–11), instructs: "If you do not fast *from the world* [ЄПКОСМОС; Greek, τὸν κόσμον], you will not find the kingdom." The *Gospel of Thomas* thus tends to abstract the notion of fasting from "mere" abstention from eating food to a more general disengagement from certain worldly effects, an interpretive move similar to the attitudes of the Alexandrian allegorical school.[18]

Finally, logion 104 answers an invitation to pray and fast with the command "(Only) when the bridegroom comes out of the bridal chamber, *then* [τότε] let them fast and let them pray." This is obviously a multiform of Mk 2:19-20 (// Mt 9:15; Lk 5:34-35), concerning Jesus' historical difference from John the Baptist on the question of fasting. The Markan saying served to justify fasting among early Christians in spite of the tradition that Jesus himself did not fast during his lifetime (Q/Lk 7:33-34). The *Gospel of Thomas* saying, in contrast, sets the time of not fasting during the period when the bridegroom is "in the bridal chamber"— evidently the period of the text's reading—rather than the period of Jesus' life (as in Mark): that is, the reader ought not to fast until the time when Jesus "comes out of the bridal chamber."[19]

Taken in all, the *Gospel of Thomas* betrays an incipient distrust of the practice of fasting; but an interpretation that would take this distrust as evidence of the authors' and audiences' liberal attitude toward food would run up against not only the text's own ascetic tendency (e.g., *Gos. Thom.* 29, 110) but also the entire ascetic tenor of its Syrian background.[20] *Thomas* does not advocate fasting as a deliberate ascetic act—and, indeed, logion 14 demonstrates the text's earnest desire to subvert the whole notion of "deliberate" piety—but it does couch fasting within a general self-abnegatory stance: as the Greek version of logion 36 teaches, "Do not be concerned from morning until evening and from evening until morning, either about your food, what you eat, or your clothes, what you wear."[21]

The *Gospel of Thomas* demonstrates that, even in manifestly ascetic texts, the gnostic attitude toward fasting tended to oppose concrete regimens, and therefore to resemble the "spiritual fast" of the Alexandrian church. Although the

18. Cf. Clement of Alexandria, *Strom.* 6.12; 7.12.

19. It may not even be clear that the reader is meant here, for the final third-person exhortation, "Let *them* fast and let *them* pray," contrasts with the disciples' initial question, "Let *us* pray today and let *us* fast," and Jesus' "What sin have *I* committed?" If such a contrast were intended, then it would again place fasting and praying as acts of "surface" piety, which "they" do in contrast to "our" pure piety.

20. See Sebastian Brock, "Early Syrian Asceticism," *Numen* 20 (1973):1–19, esp. 4–5; cf. Arthur Vööbus, *History of Asceticism in the Syrian Orient*, vol. 2: *Early Monasticism in Mesopotamia and Syria*, CSCO 197, Subsidia 17 (Louvain: CSCO, 1960), 261–64. Striking evidence of Syrian interest in fasting appears in Matthew's addition of the specific term νηστεύειν to Jesus' acts in the wilderness of the temptation (Mt 4:2; cf. Lk 4:2).

21. P.Oxy 655, ll. 1–7. I take the reconstruction as established and therefore have eliminated brackets; see *Nag Hammadi Codex II, 2–7*, NHS 20, ed. Bentley Layton (Leiden: Brill, 1989), 121.

religious meaning and value of "spiritual fasts" may have differed considerably between worldly Alexandrians and gnostic communities, the rejection of Jewish scriptural traditions of self-denial as shallow continued between these Christian cultures. "Nevertheless," as the Valentinian Ptolemy informs a neophyte in the late second century C.E.,

> fasting as to the visible realm *is* observed by our adherents, since fasting, if practiced with reason, can contribute something to the soul, so long as it does not take place in imitation of other people or by habit or because fasting has been prescribed (for) a particular day. Likewise, it is observed in memory of true fasting, so that those who are not yet able to observe true fasting might have a remembrance of it from fasting according to the visible realm.[22]

Taking into account, then, the late-third-century date of the Elijah Apocalypse's composition and its Egyptian milieu, one ought to seek the events reflected in the fasting passage during this half-century. More specifically, we seek evidence of inter-Christian controversies over fasting practice in this period that would have an impact on a group in Upper Egypt. Indeed, it must have been an impact of catastrophic proportions if, as seems likely, the composition of the extant Apocalypse of Elijah sprang from the fasting passage (ApocEl 1:13-22) as an ad hoc defense of community religious practices against outside opponents. For the author of this passage and of the subsequent eschatological discourse effectively set his audience on the threshold of an eschatological countdown, simply by the fact that the audience would recognize those very "deceivers" who opposed their fasting regimens.

A HISTORICAL CONTEXT FOR
INTERNECINE CONFLICT OVER ASCETICISM

The only documentary evidence concerning Egyptian Christians' fasting practices in the third century appears in Dionysius of Alexandria's letter to Basilides, tentatively dated to 247–248 C.E.[23] Asked to establish some rules about Paschal fasting when, it seems, Romans and Pentapolitans followed different customs for this period, Dionysius in

---

22. Letter to Flora (= Epiphanius, *Panarion* 33.5.13–14); in Bentley Layton, tr., *The Gnostic Scriptures* (Garden City, N.Y.: Doubleday, 1987), 312.

23. See Charles Lett Feltoe, *The Letters and Other Remains of Dionysius of Alexandria* (Cambridge: Cambridge University Press, 1904), 91–105; translation in idem, *St. Dionysius of Alexandria: Letters and Treatises* (London: SPCK, 1918), 76–81. The date is uncertain, but Feltoe (*Letters and Other Remains*, 92) locates it in the period when Dionysius was both bishop and administrator of the Alexandrian catechetical school.

this letter rules that everyone should try his or her best to continue beyond midnight to Easter morning. Those who could not make it even this far would be censured; those who continue on to the fourth watch are praised; but "all do not continue during the six days of the fast either equally or similarly." Dionysius's interests are clearly not in forcing a resistant congregation to go beyond its capabilities; rather, he attempts "gentle coercion" of adherents to follow the very rudiments of the annual ritual.

The letter would suggest that at this point in the third century when Dionysius was bishop, and specifically in Alexandria, there was little threat perceived from communities and individuals who practiced a more extreme form of asceticism than that advocated by Dionysius. There were undoubtedly ascetic hermits at this time; the *Life of Antony* mentions "local" ascetics living on the outskirts of villages in the late third century (chap. 3). And it is clear that Dionysius himself was not loath to censure forms of piety he considered incompatible with his own churches (as he did in the conflict with Coracion and Nepos some fifteen years later). But the situation Dionysius is witnessing in Alexandria appears to be a tendency to "underfast" rather than to fast in extreme degrees. Although a regional conflict over fasting is not evident at this point in the third century, one can see the bishop's desperation to cajole even a slightly self-abnegating attitude out of his flock, a need that might turn to capitulation to (and justification of) their laxity under extreme circumstances. A controversy between Alexandria and rural ascetics over the issue of fasting would therefore have had to have taken place after the middle of the third century.

It was precisely in this period (250–300) that a determined Manichaean mission to Upper Egypt was already establishing cenobitic communities. This mission to Egypt was facilitated through the translation of Manichaean materials from Aramaic immediately into Coptic. This tactic allowed Manichaeism to bypass Alexandrian Greek culture and head directly to the countryside, where encratite sects with a Syrian Christian basis had apparently been flourishing for a century or more.[24]

---

24. See W. Seston, "L'Égypte manichéenne," *Chronique d'Égypte* 14 (1939):362–72; Robert M. Grant, "Manichees and Christians in the Third and Early Fourth Centuries," in *Ex Orbe Religionum (Studia Geo Widengren)*, NumenSupp 21 (Leiden: Brill, 1972), 430–39; Ludwig Koenen, "Manichäische Mission und Klöster in Ägypten," in *Das römisch-byzantinische Ägypten*, Aegyptiaca Treverensia 2 (Mainz am Rhein: Philipp von Zabern,

As Alexandrian authorities became aware of Manichaeism's growth and attraction in Egypt, they began to lash out against its ascetic practices. A papyrus fragment from the late third century shows that one of the first issues addressed in the polemic against Manichaeism was its renunciation of marriage.[25] But Manichaeism brought with it a particularly exalted view of fasting and its powers. The Coptic collection of Manichaean teachings known as the *Kephalaia* describes the purifying functions of fasting in great detail, even asserting that when *Electi* fast they generate angels (chap. 81).[26] Nevertheless, even these views would not have differed substantially from the ascetic attitudes of many Jewish–Christian sects and desert hermits. Consequently, anxious as they were to identify and decry Manichaeism in its rise even when Egyptian Manichaeans were essentially indistinguishable from other Christian ascetics, it was inevitable that Alexandrian bishops would notice and strike at every group practicing extreme degrees of asceticism.

Parallels abound from the fourth century. Jerome remarks bitterly that when certain Christian women of his town "see a woman with a pale sad face, they call her 'a miserable Manichaean nun': and quite logically too, for on their principles fasting is heresy."[27] In Jerome's desperate defense of a strict encratism and asceticism he had continually to defend himself against charges of Manichaeism, which had become, in the words of Robert Markus, "part of the standard vocabulary of denigration frequently hurled especially at ascetics and their defenders."[28] A pathological fear of Manichaean *electi* in church ranks led the Synod of Ancyra in 314 to decree the mandatory tasting of meat:

1983), 93–108; Gedaliahu G. Stroumsa, "Monachisme et marranisme chez les manichéens d'Égypte," *Numen* 29 (1982):184–201; idem, "The Manichaean Challenge to Egyptian Christianity," in *The Roots of Egyptian Christianity*, ed. Birger A. Pearson and James E. Goehring, SAC 1 (Philadelphia: Fortress, 1986), 307–19; C. Wilfred Griggs, *Early Egyptian Christianity: From Its Origins to 451 C.E.*, Coptic Studies 2 (Leiden: Brill, 1990), 95–96.

25. P.Rylands III.469; see Grant, "Manichees and Christians," 432; and Stroumsa, "Manichaean Challenge," 311–15, who notes the Manicheans' successful endeavors to appear like Christians. It is interesting to note that renunciation of marriage was also a dominant issue in the Synod of Gangra: the "Eustathians" are said not only to have forbidden marriage but to have avoided the homes of married people and to have despised married priests.

26. On Manichaean fasting, see extracts of the *Kephalaia* in Michael H. Browder, "Coptic Manichaean: Kephalaia of the Teacher (Selections)," in Vincent H. Wimbush, ed., *Ascetic Behavior in Greco-Roman Antiquity: A Sourcebook*, SAC 6 (Minneapolis: Fortress, 1990), 190, 193.

27. Jerome, *Epistles* 22.13 (ed. and tr. F. A. Wright, *Select Letters of Jerome* [Cambridge: Harvard University Press, 1933], 81).

28. Robert Markus, *The End of Ancient Christianity* (Cambridge: Cambridge University Press, 1990), 48; cf. 37–39.

even those *presbyteroi* or *diakonoi* who customarily avoided flesh must demonstrate their good faith by taking a bit at special feasts, or they would "be excluded from the ranks of the clergy." The test would efficiently discover those clerics whose ascetic rigidity embarrassed the wider church. And in Egypt, where the *Life of Antony* states unequivocally that the hermit refused to converse with Manichaeans (chap. 68), Robert Grant has argued that Athanasius would not have made the point "unless there had been some suspicion that Antony's asceticism was like that of his opponents."[29]

Manichaeism continued to grow in popularity around the Mediterranean world throughout the fourth century, although its infamy was legislated by the time of Diocletian's 297 edict of repression.[30] Therefore one cannot say that the late third century was the only time Manichaeism would have irritated Alexandrian authorities to such a degree that they would have lashed out against rural ascetics. However, other social and political problems of the late third century thus far observed—extreme inflation, banditry, invasions, the disintegration of towns, and a fanatical Christian culture in the *chora* comprised of refugees from the edicts and persecutions—might have contributed to the anxiety of certain bishops in their encounter with Manichaeism during this particular period.

Indeed, the "crisis" of Manichaean success in the *chora* may have merely crystallized a wider tension between the charismatic ascetic figures in the countryside and the Alexandrian bishops, who were still struggling to gain authority outside the city during the third century. The bishops had to contend not only with the charismatic potential of such *prophetae redivivi* as were discussed in chapter 3 but also with a sustained influx of Syrian Christian texts and missionaries with strongly ascetic tendencies, whose teachers claimed broad powers of *gnosis* and vision.[31] As its sizable Coptic remains show, the Manichaean mission itself could only have followed well-trodden paths into the countryside, to communities already sympathetic to the Manichaean denigration of the flesh.[32] Michael Williams is doubtless correct to read the *Life of*

29. Grant, "Manichees and Christians," 438–39.
30. Cf. *Codex Theodosianus* 16.5; and see discussions in Stroumsa, "Monachisme et marranisme," 190, 194; and idem, "Manichaean Challenge," 309–13.
31. On Syrian Christianity in Egypt, see Helmut Koester, *History and Literature of Early Christianity* (Philadelphia: Fortress, 1982), 222–25.
32. See, esp., Peter Brown, "The Diffusion of Manichaeism in the Roman Empire," in idem, *Religion and Society in the Age of Saint Augustine* (London: Faber & Faber, 1972), 97, 103–5; cf. Seston, "L'Égypte manichéenne," 366–67; Stroumsa, "Manichaean Challenge," 310–11.

Antony in this light, not as a manifesto for the anchorite life but as an instrument of polemic and refutation *against* rural holy men in Egypt who were locally honored for their zealous asceticism and regarded as having charismatic powers. Throughout the *Life*, Williams has shown, Athanasius is domesticating Antony, creating a hermit who would work with, rather than in conflict with, Alexandrian Christianity.[33]

Even the *Apocalypse of Paul*, whose visionary ambitions might otherwise have conflicted with Alexandrian ecclesiastical sensibilities, imagines that, hung on trees outside the heavenly Jerusalem, there are

> those who fasting day and night have zealously practised renunciation, but they have had a heart proud beyond that of other men in that they have glorified and praised themselves and done nothing for their neighbours. . . . All the time these spent on earth serving God they humbled themselves shamefacedly during that time because men confounded and reproached them, but they were not sorry nor did they repent in order to desist from the pride which was in them.[34]

The early movement against Egyptian Manichaeism gave direction and purpose to Alexandria's struggle for authority in the *chora;* therefore the identifying criteria and accusatory label of "Manichaeism" or "heresy" were wielded haphazardly and vehemently. Within this context, the Apocalypse of Elijah's fasting passage makes eminent sense. Just as Dionysius, alerted by the circulation of Nepos's apologetic tract, sailed up to Arsinoë in an attempt to quell a millennialist movement, so another group of Alexandrian ecclesiarchs may have traveled through the *chora* to seek out and warn against Manichaeism, thinking they could identify its members by their rigorous ascetic practices and thus distinguish them from orthodox Christians. The special fasting ideology and, presumably, practices of the milieu of the Apocalypse of Elijah may have attracted the attention and suspicions of these ecclesiastical agents in their anxious search to root out Manichaeism in Egypt—and, in a wider sense, to enforce the authority of the Alexandrian church. The Alexandrians' criticisms of the sect apparently had a devastating effect on the community, for these ecclesiarchs were seen as "deceivers who

33. Michael A. Williams, "The *Life of Antony* and the Domestication of Charismatic Wisdom," in idem, ed., *Charisma and Sacred Biography*, JAAR Thematic Studies 48, 3–4 (Chico, Calif.: Scholars Press, 1982), 23–45.

34. *Apoc. Paul* 24 (Eng. tr. Best [Ger. tr. Duensing], NTA 2:775–76). On dating, see R.P. Casey, "The Apocalypse of Paul," *JTS* 34 (1933):28; and Martha Himmelfarb, *Tours of Hell: An Apocalyptic Form in Jewish and Christian Literature* (Philadelphia: University of Pennsylvania Press, 1983), 18–19.

will multiply in the end time," who preached that "the fast does not exist, nor did God create it." The latter phrase is merely typical hyperbole for teaching that fasting as this sect performed it was extreme, incompatible with Alexandrian church practice, and suggestive of Manichaean motivations.

AN ANALOGOUS SCENARIO:
TERTULLIAN'S *DE IEIUNIO*

In the second half of the second century c.e., there arose a religious movement that, its unique origins notwithstanding, may be justly and profitably compared to any subsequent ecstatic millennialist movement that espoused Christian ideology. This was Montanism; its location, the backcountry of Asia Minor; and its "doctrine," the return of authoritative oral prophecy, the imminence of the eschaton, and the necessity of severe asceticism to bring on ecstasy and hasten the end.[35] As the movement spread west and gained popularity in North Africa, a Carthaginian church official named Tertullian converted (in the early third century c.e.) and became a sophisticated spokesman for Montanist ideology.

One of Tertullian's last extant works, which he wrote as a Montanist, is an apology for the sect's severe fasting regimes, titled *De Ieiunio*. It has particular relevance to the fasting passage of the Apocalypse of Elijah because it demonstrates the type of rhetoric a member of a millennialist sect might use to defend his community's radical fasting practices against the criticisms and admonishments of moderation from representatives of an unconverted ecclesiastical "orthodoxy."[36]

As the Apocalypse of Elijah describes its opponents as "people whose god is their belly," so Tertullian addresses the detractors of Montanism:[37]

35. On Montanism as a millennialist movement, see D. H. Williams, "The Origins of the Montanist Movement: A Sociological Analysis," *Religion* 19 (1989):331–51.

36. Timothy D. Barnes might well be correct that "Tertullian no longer harboured any real hope of persuading those who rejected the New Prophecy. He was writing rather to justify, to vindicate and to encourage the Montanists alone" (*Tertullian: A Historical and Literary Study* [Oxford: Oxford University Press, 1971], 135); however, this begs the question of the function and *Sitz-im-Leben* of any polemical or apologetic tract as an extramural document.

37. The characterization of "people whose god is their belly" probably derives from a popular accusation of gluttony in the Greco-Roman period, used against other Jesus believers in Phil 3:19; cf. 3 Macc 7:11; Euripides *Cyclops* 334–35. There is little reason to assume that its use demonstrates knowledge of Philippians as a whole; rather, it was part of the *langue* of religious polemic among early Christians.

For to you your belly is god, and your lungs a temple, and your paunch a sacrificial altar, and your cook the priest, and your fragrant smell the Holy Spirit, and your condiments spiritual gifts, and your belching prophecy.[38]

Other polemical terms of this controversy also anticipate those of the Apocalypse of Elijah: Montanists, according to Tertullian, have been labeled not only *haeretici* but also *pseudoprophetae* (*De Ieiun.* 12). Moreover, among his arguments for radical fasting, Tertullian places fasting in the context of Genesis exegesis (*De Ieiun.* 3) and states on the basis of Christian Scripture that "fasts are to be the weapons for battling with the more direful demons,"[39] paralleling the rationales for fasting in the Apocalypse of Elijah. Of particular interest are Tertullian's consistent references to the story of Elijah, "for Elijah," he explains, "insofar as he had invoked a famine, already devoted himself enough to fasts."[40]

Although the dates and the cultural and religious contexts are quite distinct, the polemical situation that spawned *De Ieiunio* and the rhetoric used to argue it approximate what one can surmise of the Apocalypse of Elijah's background to such an extent that Tertullian's situation offers a social and historical type for illuminating the text's situation. Both *De Ieiunio* and the Apocalypse of Elijah apparently concern a sectarian response to authoritative outsiders' criticisms of fasting practice. Both sects espouse millennialist ideology. The rhetoric of debate in one case parallels that of the other. Therefore *De Ieiunio* constitutes a comparative scenario for the background of the fasting passage in the Apocalypse of Elijah and for the hypothesis that it was directed not toward "gnostic antinomians" but against a centralized ecclesiastical administration that was uncomfortable with severe asceticism.

THE SEVERITY OF EGYPTIAN
ASCETIC FASTING

The hypothesis that an epichoric Egyptian Christian group may have practiced a more extreme degree of fasting than Alexandrian (and other urban Greek) groups is corroborated by the reputation of Egyptian desert hermits in the fourth and subsequent centuries and by the Egyptian incorporation of lengthy fasts into normalized Christian practice.

38. Tertullian *De Ieiun.* 16 (tr. Thelwall, *ANF* 4:113).
39. Tertullian *De Ieiun.* 8 (tr. Thelwall, *ANF* 4:107).
40. Tertullian *De Ieiun.* 6 (my trans.); cf. 7, 9.

Athanasius's festal letters of the early fourth century show a much greater emphasis on the importance of fasting and in normalizing extensive fasts than does Dionysius's letter to Basilides. The festal letter of 329, for example, while advocating only a five-day fast, exalts the practice of fasting with *exempla* from the stories of Moses, Elijah, and Daniel and with some specific exhortations that recall those of the Apocalypse of Elijah.[41] With references to the rules for holy war in Numbers 10, Athanasius compares fasting with preparation for battle (chap. 2);[42] it separates the pure and the impure (chap. 4). The food of the impure is demonic (chap. 5), whereas the food of the pure "prepares the saints, and raises them above the earth" (chap. 5). In the context of these exhortations to popular fasting, we may understand the preparation of the *Life of Antony*, which associated fasting specifically with purity and resistance to demons (e.g., chap. 23).

Fourth-century literature from within the ascetic communities is even more explicitly favorable toward radical fasting. The monastic canon of Pseudo-Hippolytus institutes a forty-day fast as part of the annual cycle, along with fasts on Wednesday and Friday; furthermore, "whoever should add to this (schedule) will receive recompense" (canon 20).[43] It was probably Athanasius who first publicly recommended the forty-day fast as an official practice in the 330s,[44] but in doing so he was drawing on a practice already traditional (and unique) to Egyptian ascetics: imitating Jesus' forty-day temptation as a fasting period.[45] A certain Abba James is said to have starved himself secretly for forty days to stave off the demon of fornication, breaking the fast only when another hermit visited him with the holy communion.[46]

The exhaustive lore of the Egyptian hermits in Palladius's *Historia Lausiaca* and in the various *Apophthegmata patrum* contain numerous

41. On *exempla*, see Musurillo, "Ascetical Fasting," 5–6.
42. Cf. ApocEl 1:23-24 (which directly follows the fasting passage): "Who among you would go out to the field, taking pride in his skill, but without a tool in his hand? Or who is it that who would go to war [to fight (Ach)] without a breastplate on? If he is discovered will they not kill him, because he despised the service [ὀφφίκιον] of the king?"
43. René-Georges Coquin, tr., "Les canons d'Hippolyte, *Patrologia Orientalis* 31, 2 (1966):387.
44. Cf. Athanasius *Festal Letter* 10 (338 C.E.), 12.
45. Coquin, "Canons d'Hippolyte," 328–30. As Mt 4:2 already adds νηστεύσας to Mk 1:13, the interpretation of the temptation as a fasting period could have drawn on a primitive Syrian Christian tradition.
46. E.g., *Apophth. patr.* (Alphabetical), Phocas 2.

laudatory stories of extreme ascetic practices, starvation fasts, and demonstrations of the purificatory and exorcistic effects of fasting.[47] Although these stories are difficult to date, many certainly come from the fourth century and earlier and thus provide some background and explanation for the fourth-century institutionalization of long fasts in Egyptian Christianity. Athanasius and Pseudo-Hippolytus were reflecting epichoric tendencies in ascetic practice, and so their rationales for fasting drew upon a lore of asceticism's concrete powers, a lore that apparently came from the hermits themselves.[48] The ideology of fasting promoted by the Apocalypse of Elijah was actually quite regular in the context of rural Egyptian asceticism, as demonstrated by the Pseudo-Athanasius treatise on virginity, quoted above (p. 282).

Extreme fasting was also retrojected into presentations of biblical lore. In a curious extension of the concept of the didactic *exemplum*, the *Testament of Isaac* states:

> Now our father Isaac had made for himself a bedroom in his house; and when his sight began to fail he withdrew into it and remained there for a hundred years, fasting daily until evening. . . . And he kept three periods of forty days as fasts each year, neither drinking wine nor eating fruit nor sleeping on his bed. And he prayed and gave thanks to God continually.[49]

The author of this text apparently made structural use of the *Testament of Abraham*, an Egyptian Jewish or Christian text from about the first century C.E.; the focus on the cycles of forty-day fasts, however, implies a monastic milieu of the fourth or later centuries. To be sure, the regimen of daily (dawn to dusk) fasting, plus three forty-day cycles annually of (presumably) more severe fasting, that is ascribed to Isaac may be merely the sort of exaggerated feat one normally attributes to a hero or patriarch (such as the extended life span). The way the regimen is specifically dictated in this passage, however, suggests that, even if superhuman, it would not have been much more severe than those regimens followed by the intended audience of the *Testament of Isaac*.[50]

---

47. E.g., *Apophth. patr.* (Alphabetical): Theodora 6; Cassian 1. See Arbesmann, "Fasting and Prophecy," 33–35; Musurillo, "Ascetical Fasting," 28–32. Cf. also Eusebius's account of the Egyptian martyr Procopius's severe diet (*Martyrs of Palestine* [Syr.] 3).

48. In a judgment scene on the wall of the Coptic Abydos chapel dating from the tenth century, there is a figure specified as "he who breaks the fast before the appointed time [ⲡⲉⲧⲃⲁⲗ ⲛⲙⲏⲥϯⲁ ⲉⲃⲟⲗ ⲙⲡⲁⲧⲉⲥϣⲱⲡⲓ]" (in C. C. Walters, "Christian Paintings from Tebtunis," *JEA* 75 [1989]:203 and pl. 28, 2).

49. *T. Isaac* 5:3, 5–7 (Sahidic; tr. K. H. Kuhn, *AOT* 431); cf. Stinespring's translation from Arabic in *OTP* 1:907.

50. The actual differences implied between the daily and forty-day fasts are unclear

The retrojection of monastic or anchoritic fasting practices into the life of a biblical figure suggests, once again, the fundamental importance of the biblical tradition for establishing religious paradigms in Egyptian ascetic Christianity, whether in formal *exempla* or in contemplation and private imitation. There may indeed be a relationship between the centrality of fasting in the milieu of the Apocalypse of Elijah and the figure of Elijah himself, because Elijah was consistently brought up as a paradigm of religious fasting, with or without seclusion.[51]

Regardless, however, of these rural ascetic currents promoting infinite fasting, certain ecclesiastical quarters continued to criticize what they perceived as excesses. A story about Athanasius, included in the Arabic *History of the Patriarchs*, tells of some nuns who complained to him that some of their members fasted "six days of the week continuously" and therefore were unable to work. Athanasius is said to have replied,

> Believe me my sisters, I have never fasted for two whole days together, without breaking my fast during the day; but I only ate in moderation, and neither wearied my soul nor punished my body. For it is good that fasting should be in moderation, and drinking in moderation, and sleep in moderation. For if a man eats as he ought, he is strong for prayer; and so likewise if he sleeps in moderation; but to food there should be a limit, and to drink a limit, and to sleep a limit. So tell them to break their fast in moderation, and to work, for everything is good in moderation, that words may not be multiplied, and the beginning of them may not be forgotten.[52]

Just as the biblical patriarch Isaac is brought into service of severe asceticism in *Testament of Isaac* 4, the Alexandrian patriarch Athanasius, who himself systematized fasting among Egyptian lay Christians, is here

and may have ranged from the addition or subtraction of bread or meat at dusk to the addition or subtraction of water itself. Fasting practices among the desert hermits were entirely irregular and even among cenobitic communities of the late fourth century, Jerome indicates there were problems in the various degrees of fasting; for, he romanticizes, "long fasts help no one here [in his Palestinian monastery]. Starvation wins no deference, and the taking of food in moderation is not condemned" (*Ep.* 46.10, tr. W. H. Freemantle, *NPNF* 6:64). On the diversity of fasting practices, see Owen, "Fasting in the Eastern Church," 96–97, 102–5.

51. Tertullian *De Ieiun.* 7, 9; Athanasius, Festal Letter 1 (329 c.e.), 6; *Vita Antonii* 7; *Vita Paul* 10, 13; cf. *1 Clem.* 17:1.

52. Arabic *History of the Patriarchs*: Athanasius (B. Evetts, ed. and tr., "History of the Patriarchs of the Coptic Church of Alexandria—II," *Patrologia orientalis* 1 [1907]):405. L.-Th. LeFort discerns a historical basis to this encounter of Athanasius and the nuns ("Athanase, Ambroise, et Chenoute: 'Sur la virginité,'" *Le Muséon* 48 [1935]:55–73, esp. 67–68).

brought into the service of those Christian authorities who censured severe asceticism.

In a Coptic encomium on Elijah from the Byzantine period, this prototype of radical desert asceticism is finally domesticated. The encomium exhorts the audience to

> keep the feast of the holy Elijah, each one according to his ability. For he requires nothing from us beyond our power, but only bread whereon we shall feast together with him on the day of his commemoration. If we give a cup of cold water according to our power, we shall make ourselves worthy of the holy Elijah.[53]

This stress on individual limits marks a far cry from the competitive self-denials of the desert anchorites.

Fasting in the Egyptian *chora* was practiced to extreme degrees from at least the fourth century, whereas the Alexandrian perspective on fasting continued to emphasize moderation and to disapprove of ascetic "athletics." It is plausible to infer from these later materials that the milieu of the Apocalypse of Elijah followed an earlier form of these fasting regimens (or the ascetic ideology behind them), thus earning the attention and confused censure of Alexandrian authorities in the later third century.[54]

CONCLUSION: FASTING AND THE APOCALYPSE OF ELIJAH

Therefore, from the passage on fasting in the Apocalypse of Elijah, one can make the following hypotheses concerning the historical circumstances of the text's composition.

Members of the collective body for which the extant Apocalypse of Elijah was composed practiced an extreme regimen of fasting, such as was practiced by the desert hermits of later Egyptian ascetic literature.

53. Cairo ms. 53 (tr. Hugh G. Evelyn-White, in idem, ed., *The Monasteries of the Wadi 'N Natrûn*, vol. 1: *New Coptic Texts from the Monastery of Saint Macarius* [New York: Metropolitan Museum of Art, 1926], 72). The text is attributed to John Chrysostom and is evidently a recension of the Pseudo-Chrysostom encomium published by E. A. Wallis Budge, "On the Fragments of a Coptic Version of an Encomium on Elijah the Tishbite, attributed to Saint John Chrysostom," *Transactions of the Society of Biblical Archaeology* 9 (1893):384 (text), 404 (translation).

54. Cf. the ascetic Christian milieu proposed for the *Ascension of Isaiah* by Antonio Acerbi, *Serra lignea: Studi sulla fortuna dell'Ascensione di Isaia* (Rome: A.V.E., 1984), 40–53; see also A. Camplani, *Le lettere festali di Atanasio di Alessandria: Studio storico-critico* (Rome: C.I.M., 1989), 277–78.

The practice of fasting held considerable symbolic importance for this group. It expressed the exorcism of demons, purification toward an angelic status, and—of greatest importance—imitation of the saints of biblical legend.

During the same period that this group was practicing (or at least espousing) its fasting regimes—a useful range might be 260–290 C.E.— Manichaean missions were growing in size and influence in Upper Egypt. The group under consideration was not itself Manichaean, for the Apocalypse of Elijah does not show any Manichaean influence; but the ideology of radical asceticism may ultimately derive from Syrian Christianity, along whose missionary tracks Manichaeism followed.

Ecclesiastical authorities based in Alexandria, becoming aware of the Manichaean mission, viewed it as a considerable threat. In seeking to cast the differences between Manichaeism and Alexandrian Christianity in the sharpest terms and to prevent any overlap in allegiance, they chose to focus upon the religious styles that they considered most alien to their own practices, specifically, radical asceticism. These authorities consequently set out to the *chora* to find and censure whatever groups of Christians practiced severe asceticism.

The milieu of the Apocalypse of Elijah fell under such censure and perhaps even ruptured under it, as often happens with religions in situations of rival doctrine and authority. At this point, indeed, the social body to whom the Apocalypse of Elijah was addressed might be considered a "sect," for strong boundaries against the world seem to be established first in regard to the fasting dispute. Moreover, because the dominant theme of the Apocalypse of Elijah after the fasting passage concerns the problem of deceitful leadership in the end times, it is likely that the author was especially sensitive to the power of rival authority. The Alexandrian authorities who criticized the severity of the sect's fasting regimen were thus seen as "deceivers" who denied fasting altogether.[55]

A literate member of the sect or an individual with "prophetic" pretensions, who was acquainted with apocalyptic literature, composed the fasting passage—perhaps initially as a spontaneous discourse—to be a

---

55. It is equally likely that only one ecclesiastical official had arrived and opposed the sect's fasting, because the plural in the prophecy of "deceivers" attributes the necessary determinism to the arrival of even one "deceiver." The plural also functions to reduce the personal charisma of the "deceiver" (such as the Lawless One is endowed with) and makes him or them merely instruments of a "deceptive" doctrine.

defense of fasting, an exposition of the ascetical ideology of the sect, and perhaps an expression of the effect of these deceivers on the sect. Assuming that the text was meant for or derived from public presentation, its composition in Greek implies that the sect consisted of individuals who could understand Greek.

For the sect, the ecclesiastical censure may have represented a final, "catalytic" event, signifying the imminence of preeschatological woes and a millennium sure to follow—that is, the point at which the third-century decline, the rumored persecutions of Christians, and the millennialist teachings to which they had been exposed in such texts as Revelation all "suddenly made sense." Insofar as the author placed the fasting passage immediately before the eschatological discourse, the former comes to function as a threshold of recognizable events before the onset of unfamiliar eschatological woes and signs. In this position, the fasting passage becomes the historical validator of the events of the eschatological discourse, in spite of the fact that the events themselves do not systematically reflect historical events of the late third century. The link between the fasting passage and the eschatological discourse is reinforced by the consistent emphasis in the latter on illegitimate and deceitful leadership, culminating in the account of the Lawless One. This emphasis intrinsically recalls "the deceivers who will multiply in the end time . . . who say 'the fast does not exist.'"

The fate of the sect that spawned the Elijah Apocalypse can only be imagined. It seems plausible that its opposition to the Alexandrian ecclesiarchy would have continued through the persecutions of Diocletian, perhaps to form one root of the Melitian schism. The emphasis on exalted martyrdom in the Apocalypse of Elijah, however, makes it nearly certain that members of the sect would have been counted among the more fanatical Egyptian martyrs during the Diocletianic persecution.[56]

---

56. See Maureen A. Tilley, "The Ascetic Body and the (Un)Making of the World of the Martyr," *JAAR* 59 (1991):467–79, who proposes that preparation for martyrdom derived from ascetic activity already common to Christian sects.

The Text of the Apocalypse of Elijah in English

INTRODUCTION

The three most recent translations of the Apocalypse of Elijah, those of Wolfgang Schrage, K. H. Kuhn, and O. S. Wintermute, followed Georg Steindorff's original opinion that the Achmimic manuscript represented the best reading of the text, and indeed that the extant Sahidic manuscripts might themselves be translations from the Achmimic.[1] The splendid and, by now, standard translations these scholars prepared therefore depended primarily on Ach, referring to the Sahidic manuscripts to correct corruptions and fill lacunae.

The particular value of these translations over their predecessors, those of Steindorff and Jean-Marc Rosenstiehl, came from their inclusion of the Chester Beatty manuscript, Sa[3], to "complete" the text of the Apocalypse of Elijah. However, they used this manuscript almost solely to fill in lacunae (such as ApocEl 2:16-30) rather than to offer a more general perspective on the Sahidic and Achmimic recensions. Rosenstiehl had provided just such a perspective in his 1972 commentary (prepared, unfortunately, without access to the vital Sa[3]): a parallel translation of Sahidic and Achmimic texts, by which one might see the nature of the variations between these manuscripts. Rosenstiehl recog-

---

1. Cf. Steindorff, 17; Carl Schmidt, "Der Kolophon des Ms. orient. 7594 des Britischen Museums," *Sitzungsberichte der preussischen Akademie der Wissenschaften, Philosophisch-Historisch Klasse* (1925):318; cf. Pietersma, 14; and Jean-Marc Rosenstiehl, "L'Apocalypse d'Élie," *Le Muséon* 95 (1982):272–73.

nized and then reasserted in 1982 that each Coptic text must be regarded as an independent lineage or family from the Greek, and that it is therefore misleading to focus on one or another manuscript or recension as "better."[2]

It is out of respect for the Coptic recensions as "families" that I have chosen to follow Rosenstiehl's example and offer a parallel translation.[3] Indeed, the reader will find that very few of the divergences in wording and content (printed in boldface) can reasonably be ascribed to "corruptions" one way or the other. When such a corruption can be traced, it is noted; but in general the reader will encounter the divergences as testimony to the fluidity of copying and transmission in Roman Egypt (see chapter 2, pp. 27–29).

It is perhaps dishonest, then, to place the Sahidic recension as a unit to the left and the Achmimic to the right, because the Sahidic manuscripts themselves present some divergences. However, the textual analysis prefacing the recent critical edition of Sa[3] has demonstrated that there are fewer divergences within the Sahidic family than between any of the Sahidic manuscripts and Ach, and, furthermore, that the Sahidic texts may follow the Greek more faithfully than Ach.[4] I have therefore chosen to compile a "best" Sahidic text on the left, following Pietersma in endowing Sa[3] with somewhat more authority but noting "variations" either in the translation (also in boldface, where Sa[3] and Ach agree: cf. ApocEl 4:8; 5:9) or in notes, according to the importance I assign to the variation.

Those lacunae for which reconstructions have been fairly established are not marked with brackets, so that the reader may derive a sense for the *text* of the Apocalypse of Elijah rather than merely for its manuscripts in their original states. In those places where lacunae are unbreachable I have placed brackets, separated approximately the length of line missing. The notes cover those instances where reconstructions have been debated.

Chapter and verse numbers follow Wintermute's translation, on the basis that five chapters are easier to work with than three (as in Rosen-

2. Rosenstiehl, "L'Apocalypse d'Élie," 272–74.
3. It is hoped that a future edition of the Coptic texts of the Apocalypse of Elijah will also employ parallel columns, rather than keying all divergences to a single text as Albert Pietersma, Susan Turner Comstock, and Harold A. Attridge did.
4. Pietersma, 12–18.

stiehl and Kuhn) and any chapters and verses are better than keying a complete translation to the pages and line numbers of a single manuscript (as in Pietersma and Schrage). To link the text more conveniently to discussions in the rest of this book, however, the text has been completely arranged with subject headings and, in the case of ApocEl 2, lettered paragraphs, many of which overlap Wintermute's verse numbers.

As the translation is not meant as a commentary, discussion of content has been kept to a minimum in the notes, although the notes will key particular passages to relevant discussions in the book. For the reasons outlined in chapter 2 (pp. 31–39), scriptural and apocryphal parallels are not provided unless they have immediate historical or literary relevance to the understanding of a passage. Rosenstiehl and Schrage provide an abundance of motif and verbal parallels in early Jewish and Christian literature. The present translation and this study are not meant to present the Elijah Apocalypse as simply a matrix of parallels and influences.

The translation opens in three columns, to incorporate the introduction to *Apocalypse of Paul* 3, with which the Apocalypse of Elijah bears a definite literary relationship.

THE APOCALYPSE OF ELIJAH

Prophetic Introduction[5]

Sa	*Ach*	*Apoc. Paul 3–4*[6]
1.1. The word of the Lord came to me thus: Say to this people, why do you sin and add sin to your sins, angering the Lord God who created you?	**1**.1. The word of the Lord came to me thus: **Son of Man,** say to this people, why do you add sin to your sins, angering the Lord God who created you?	The word of the Lord came to me thus: Say to this people, how long will you **transgress**[7] and multiply sin and anger the God who created you? . . . [3a]

5. See discussion, pp. 82–86.
6. On the relationship to the Apocalypse of Elijah of this passage from the *Apocalypse of Paul*, see pp. 28–29.
7. Latin: *delinquetis (= delinquentes)*; Greek: ἁμαρτάνετε.

Sa	*Ach*	*Apoc. Paul 3–4*
2. Do not love the world, nor what is in the world, for the pride of the world and its destruction are of the devil.[8]	2. Do not love the world, nor what is in the world, for the pride of the world and its destruction are of the devil.	
3. Remember that the Lord who created everything had mercy on you,	3. Remember that the Lord **of Glory** who created everything had mercy on you,	Remember and know that all creation is subject to God. . . . [3b]
so that he might rescue us from the captivity of this age.	so that he might rescue us from the captivity of this age.	

The Reason for Christ

Sa	*Ach*	*Apoc. Paul 3–4*
4. For many times the devil desired to prevent[9] the sun from rising over the earth and to prevent the earth from giving fruit,[10]	4. For many times the devil desired to prevent the sun from rising over the earth and to prevent the earth from giving fruit,	. . . For many times the sun, the great light, has objected to God saying: O Lord God almighty, I look upon the impiety and injustice of men. [4]

Sa	*Ach*
wishing to swallow people like fire that runs through straw, wishing to swallow them like water.	wishing to swallow people like fire that runs through straw, wishing to swallow them like water.
5. And because of this the God of glory had mercy on us: He **will send** his son into the world so that he might rescue us from the captivity.	5. And because of this the God of glory had mercy on us. He **sent** his son into the world so that he might rescue us from the captivity.

---

8. Cf. 1 Jn 2:15-17; but the scribe has apparently invoked the verse from memory: see discussion, pp. 34–35, 83.

9. Sa: ⲉⲧⲙ̅ⲕⲁ ⲡⲣⲏ; Ach: ⲁⲧⲙ̅ⲕⲁⲡⲣⲓ. I am following Pietersma (21) in taking this in an active sense; cf. Wintermute: "not to let" (736).

10. See discussion, pp. 232–33.

Sa	*Ach*
6. He did not inform an angel when he came to us, nor an archangel, but he changed himself to be like a man, when he came to us, so that he might rescue us from the flesh,[11]	6. He did not inform an angel when he came to us, nor an archangel, **nor any principality,** but he changed himself to be like a man, when he came to us, so that he might rescue us. . . .
7. **so that** you might thus become children to him as he becomes a father to you.	7. **Therefore,** become children to him as he becomes a father to you.

Heavenly Rewards and Punishments[12]

8. Remember that he has prepared for you [pl.] thrones and crowns in heaven. For everyone who will obey **his voice** will receive thrones[13] and crowns. 9. Among those who are mine, says the Lord, I will write my name upon their foreheads and seal their right hands. They will not be hungry, nor will they thirst, 10. nor will the Lawless One have power over them, nor will the Thrones hinder them, but they will go with the angels to my city.	8. Remember that he has prepared for you [pl.] thrones and crowns in heaven. For everyone who will obey **me** will receive thrones and crowns. 9. Among those who are mine, says the Lord, I will write my name upon their foreheads and seal their right hands. They will not be hungry, nor will they thirst, 10. nor will the Lawless One have power over them, nor will the Thrones hinder them, but they will go with the angels to my city.
11. But as for those who sin, they will not pass by the Thrones, but the Thrones of death will seize them and exert power over them, because the angels do not trust them,[14] 12. and they have estranged themselves from his dwelling places.	11. But as for those who sin, **they will be shamed;** they will not pass by the Thrones, but the Thrones of death will seize them and exert power over them because the angels do not trust them, 12. and they have estranged themselves from his dwelling places.

11. Cf. Phil 2:6-8; Heb 1:4-6; *Asc. Is.* 10; *Epis.Apost.* 13. See discussion, p. 35.

12. See discussion, pp. 147–51.

13. Note that θρόνοι is used both for such physical rewards (cf. 4:10) and for the intermediary angels who obstruct the impure from entering heaven (1:10-11). See discussion, pp. 35–37.

14. ⲡⲓⲑⲉ (= πείθεσθαι). On hostile Thrones as gatekeepers of heaven, see pp. 35–37.

Sa   *Ach*

A Discourse on Fasting[15]

13. Hear now, you wise men of the land, concerning the deceivers who will multiply in the end time, because they will adopt teachings that are not of God. They will put aside God's law—**these people whose god is their belly**—who say, "The fast does not exist, nor did God create it"—who make themselves like strangers to the covenant of God, and rob[16] themselves of glorious promises. 14. These ones are never established in firm faith. So do not let those people deceive you!

15. Remember that the Lord made fasting from (the time of) his creation of the heavens as a benefit to mankind on account of the passion and **changing** desires that oppose you, so that the evil one will not **deceive you.** 16. But a holy fast is what **he** has established. The Lord says,[17] 17. He who fasts **continually** will never sin, although envy and strife are in him. 18. But he who is holy, let him fast. He who fasts, (however,) without being holy angers the Lord and also the angels, 19. and he harms his own soul.

Furthermore, he gathers up wrath for himself for the Day of Wrath.

13. Hear now, you wise men of the land, concerning the deceivers who will multiply in the end time, because they will adopt teachings that are not of God. They will put aside God's law—**those who have made their belly their god**—who say, "The fast does not exist, nor did God create it"—who make themselves like strangers to the covenant of God, and rob themselves of glorious promises. 14. These ones are never established in firm faith. So do not let those people deceive you!

15. Remember that the Lord made fasting from (the time of) his creation of the heavens as a benefit to mankind on account of the passion and desires that oppose you, so that the evil one will not **consume** you. 16. But a holy fast is what **I** have established, the Lord says, 17. He who fasts will never sin, even though there be in him envy and strife. 18. But he who is holy, let him fast. He who fasts, (however,) without being holy angers the Lord and also the angels, 19. and he harms his own soul.

He gathers up wrath for himself for the Day of Wrath.

---

15. See discussion, chap. 11.
16. Sahidic mss. use Coptic ϥⲱϭⲉ; Ach uses Greek ἀποστερεῖν.
17. Sa² ends at this point.

Sa

20. A holy fast is what **the Lord** established with pure heart and pure hands. 21. For **the holy fast** releases sin, heals [θεραπεύειν] diseases, casts out demons, 22. exerts power [ἐνεργεῖν] up to the throne of God, as an ointment, **as incense,** as a remission of sin through a holy prayer.[18]

Ach

20. A holy fast is what **I** established with pure heart and pure hands. 21. For it releases sin, heals [θεραπεύειν] diseases, casts out demons, 22. exerts power [ἐνεργεῖν] up to the throne of God, as an ointment, as a remission of sin through a holy prayer.

On Single-Mindedness

23. **For** who among you would go out to the field, taking pride in his skill, but without a tool in his hand? Or who is it that would go to war without a breastplate on?

23. Who among you would go out to the field, taking pride in his skill, but without a tool in his hand? Or who is it that would go to war **to fight** without a breastplate on?

24. If he is discovered will they not kill him, because he despised the service of the king? 25. Likewise, it is impossible for anyone to enter the holy place while in doubt. 26. He who doubts in prayer is darkness to himself, and even the angels do not trust him.

24. If he is discovered will they not kill him, because he despised the service of the king? 25. Likewise, it is impossible for anyone to enter the holy place while in doubt. 26. He who doubts in prayer is darkness to himself, and even the angels do not trust him.

27. **If you are** always single-minded in the Lord, **be wise to the Time,** so that you might comprehend [νοεῖν] all things **2.**1 concerning the Assyrian kings and the destruction of heaven and earth.[19]

27. **Therefore, be** always single-minded in the Lord, so that you might comprehend [νοεῖν] all things. **2.**1. **Therefore,** concerning the Assyrian kings and the destruction of heaven and earth **and the things under the earth:**[20]

---

18. There is a similar list of benefits to fasting preserved in the Pseudo-Athanasian *On Virginity* 7. See p. 282.

19. It is not entirely clear whether "concerning the Assyrian kings," etc., should be understood as the reference of "know all things"; Rosenstiehl (87), Wintermute (739, 739 n. a), and Kuhn (764) all believe on the basis of Ach that a distinctively new chapter begins right here with a summarizing incipit.

20. In the addition of this reference to "the things under the earth," the Achmimic scribe may be demonstrating his acquaintance with contemporaneous "tours" of hell—supposed to disintegrate in the eschaton (cf. Rv 20:13-14; *Apoc. Pet.* 5).

Sa   *Ach*

The Discourse on the Signs of Woe[21]

§A. The Assyrian King

a) 2. **Those who are mine** will not be overcome, says the Lord, nor will they fear in battle.

2. **Now, therefore,**[22] **they** will not be overcome, says the Lord, nor will they fear in battle.

b) 3. And when they see a king who has arisen in the north they will call him the King of the Assyrians and the Unrighteous King. He will increase his wars and disturbances against Egypt. 4. The land will groan together. Your children will be seized. 5. Many will desire death at that time.

3. And when they see a king who has arisen in the north they will call him the King of the Assyrians and the Unrighteous King. He will increase his wars and disturbances against Egypt. 4. The land will groan together. Your children will be seized. 5. Many will desire death at that time, **but death will flee from them.**[23]

§B. The King of Peace

a) 6. Then a king will arise in the west, whom they will call the King of Peace. 7. He will run upon the sea like a roaring lion. 8. He will kill the Unrighteous King. **Vengeance will be taken**[24] upon Egypt with war, and there will be much bloodshed. 9. At that time **he will command** peace in Egypt and a worthless gift.

6. Then a king will arise in the west, whom they will call the King of Peace. 7. He will run upon the sea like a roaring lion. 8. He will kill the Unrighteous King. **He will take vengeance** upon Egypt with war, and there will be much bloodshed. 9. At that time he **commanded** peace in Egypt and a worthless gift.

b) 10. He will grant peace to the saints.[25] He will proceed to say, "The

10. He will grant peace to the saints. He will proceed to say, "The name of

---

21. See discussion, chap. 8.

22. ⲧⲓⲛⲟⲩ ⳓⲉ. Rosenstiehl (87 n. *ad loc*), after Steindorff (76 n. 1), took this as a corruption of the corresponding words ⲛⲉⲧⲉ ⲛⲟⲩⲉⲓ ⲛⲉ in the Sahidic mss.

23. This phrase appears also in 2:32, at which point Sa³ also continues "but death will flee from them." The phrase was evidently widely known, as it appears also in Rv 9:6. Because Sa³ and Sa¹ agree in not including the second part of the phrase in 2:5, it is conceivable that the Achmimic scribe made the addition to 2:5 on the basis of 2:32.

24. The difference between the recensions here gives a somewhat different cast to the king's character; if deliberate, Sa³ may be removing any "negative" aspects to the king's character, or Ach may be ensuring that this king not be seen as entirely salvific.

25. The same root, ⲟⲩⲁⲁⲃ ("holy"), is used for "saints" (ⲛⲉⲧⲟⲩⲁⲁⲃ) and "priests" (ⲛⲟⲩⲏⲏⲃ)—serving to designate both native and Christian hierophants. The resulting ambiguity surrounding the type or authority of "holiness" under discussion probably reflects a continuity in the concept of the holy in the world of the Apocalypse of Elijah's author. See discussion, pp. 99–101.

Sa	*Ach*
name of God is One!" 11. He will give honor to the **priests of God.** He will exalt the **holy places.**	God is One!" 11. He will give honors to the **s[aints].** He will exalt the **places of the saints.**

c) 12.[26] He will give worthless gifts to the house of God. 13. He will circulate among the cities of Egypt with deception, without (their) knowing. 14. He will take count of the holy places. He will weigh the idols of the Pagan [ἔθνος]. He will take count of their wealth. He will appoint priests for them.

12. He will give worthless gifts to the house of God. 13. He will circulate among the cities of Egypt with deception, without (their) knowing. 14. He will take count of the holy places. He will weigh the idols of the Pagan [ἔθνος]. He will take count of their wealth. He will appoint priests for them.

d) 15. He will command that the wise men of the land be seized, along with the great ones of the people, to be taken to **a** metropolis by the sea, as he says, "There is but one language!" 16. But when you hear "Peace and Joy exist!" I will . . .[29]

15. He will command that the wise men of the land be seized, along with the great ones of the people, to be taken to **the** metropolis[27] by the sea, as he says . . .[28]

§C. The Sons of the King of Peace[30]

a) 17. . . . for here are his signs. I will tell you so you will recognize him:[31] 18. For he has two sons, one on his right and one on his left. 19. Now the one on the right will get a demonic

---

26. There is an indentation here in Sa³ ms. p. 6; cf. Pietersma, 74.

27. Here Sa¹ agrees with Ach against Sa³ in giving the definite article. Cf. *Oracle of the Potter:* ἡ παραθαλάσσιος πόλις (P² 35 = P³ 59); and the contrasting sense in *Asclepius* 27: ογπολιc εϲϫῑ ογκοος ῏ντε κημε [NHC VI,75, 28–29]. On the use of this term, see pp. 205, 213–14.

28. Both Ach and Sa¹ break off here.

29. One line illegible in Sa³. See facsimile in Pietersma, 74.

30. Although this section has dropped out of the Achmimic leaves of the Apocalypse of Elijah, its use in the Greek Tiburtine Sibyl (ll. 190–98; ed. Paul J. Alexander, in idem, *The Oracle of Baalbek: The Tiburtine Sibyl in Greek Dress,* Dumbarton Oaks Studies 10 [Washington, D.C.: Dumbarton Oaks, 1967], 20–21) makes it certain that it was part of the original Greek text.

31. The antecedent of "his (signs)" must be the son who gains a "demonic face," whereas the "he" who has two sons (2:18) must refer to the "King of Peace" described in the preceding passage.

| *Sa* | *Ach* |

face.[32] He will abandon the name of
God.

b) 20. For four kings come from that
king. 21. But in his thirtieth year he
(will) come up to Memphis; he will
build a temple in Memphis at that
time.[33] 22. His son will arise against
him and kill him. 23. The whole land
will tremble.

c) 24. At that time he[34] will issue a
decree over all the land that the
priests of the land and all the saints
be seized, saying "Every gift which
my father gave you, and all the good
things, you will return two-fold!" 25.
He will shut the holy places. He will
take their homes. He will take their
sons as prisoners. 26. He will command (that they)[35] perform sacrifices
[θυσία] and abominations and bitter
acts upon the land. 27. He will
appear beneath the sun and the
moon. 28. At that time the priests of
the land will tear their garments.

§D. Social Woes under the Evil King

a) 29. Woe to you, rulers of Egypt, at
that time, because your time has
passed! 30. The violence of the poor[36]

---

32. The corresponding king in the Greek Tiburtine Sibyl "has a changed shape
[μορφὴν ἔχων ἠλλοιωμένην]" (l. 191; ed. Alexander, *Oracle of Baalbek,* 20, 28). If this
phrase is original to the Apocalypse of Elijah in Greek, it would imply that this king is
a precursor to the polymorphic Lawless One in ApocEl 3:16-17 (see ibid., 113, 113 n.
54). It is perhaps to make explicit this implication that the Coptic translator has used
διάβολος for his features here.

33. The corresponding king in the Greek Tiburtine Sibyl "will rebuild the altars of
Egypt" (l. 192; ed. Alexander, *Oracle of Baalbek,* 21, 28), apparently an abstraction from
the Apocalypse of Elijah text.

34. In spite of the previous prediction of his death at the hands of his own son, the
text is apparently still discussing the demon-faced son of the King of Peace. The latter is
a more likely candidate to be the donor of "gifts and good things" in v. 24.

35. Wintermute reads this conjunctive clause as passive (741), but the previous
sentences also contain an unstated plural party who must also be the antecedents here.

36. ⲡⲭⲓⲛ[ϭⲟ]ⲛⲥ ⲛ̄ⲛ̄ϩ ⲏ ⲕ ⲉ. The sense is either that the violence that the rulers have
committed against the poor will turn back against the rulers, or that the incipient

Sa

will turn against you, and they will seize your sons as plunder [ἁρπαγή].

b) 31. The cities of Egypt will groan at that time, and there will no longer be heard the voice of the buyer or seller in the markets [ἀγορά] of the cities of Egypt. They will collect dust.

c) 32. Then those who are in Egypt will weep together. They will desire death, yet death (will) flee from them. 33. They will climb up rocks and leap off them, saying "Fall down on us!"—and (yet) they (will) not die, **but death flees from them.** 34. A double affliction (will) multiply around the land **at that time.**

d) 35. In that time the king will command that all the nursing women be seized and be brought to him bound to suckle serpents [δράκων], that their blood be sucked from their breasts to be given as poison for arrows.[37]

e) 36. Because of the constraint [ἀνάγκη][38] of **war** [πόλεμος] he will

Ach

30 . . . , sons as plunder [ἁρπαγή].

31. The cities of Egypt will groan at that time, and there will no longer be heard the voice of the buyer or seller in the markets [ἀγορά] of the cities of Egypt. They will collect dust.

32. Then those who are in Egypt will weep together. They will desire death, yet death (will) flee from them. 33. **In that time** they will climb up rocks and leap off them, saying "Fall down on us!"—and (yet) they (will) not die. 34. A double affliction (will) multiply around the land.

35. In that time the king will command that all the nursing women be seized and be brought to him bound to suckle serpents [δράκων], that their blood be sucked from their breasts to be given as poison for arrows.

36. Because of the desperation [ἀνάγκη] of the **cities** [πόλις][39] he will

resentment of the poor will erupt into revolutionary violence against the rulers. The former interpretation is more likely, inasmuch as it allows a "reversal" sense to the woe oracle.

37. Sa³: ⲛ̅ⲥⲉⲧⲁⲁⲩ ⲛ̅ⲕⲗⲟ ⲛ̅ⲥⲟⲧⲟ (cf. Ach: ⲥⲉⲧⲉⲟⲩⲉ ⲁⲛⲕⲗⲟ ⲛ̅ⲛ̅ⲥⲁⲧⲉ). Oscar von Lemm identified ⲕⲗⲟ as a specific Egyptian poison ("Kleine koptische Studien—X: Bemerkungen zu einigen Stellen der koptischen Apokalypsen, 4–6," *Bulletin de l'Académie impériale des Sciences de St. Petersbourg* 13 [1900]: 11–28). The modifier to the poison could be a variation of Sahidic ⲥⲁⲧⲉ ("fiery") or Achmimic ⲥⲁⲧⲉ or Sahidic ⲥⲟⲧⲉ ("arrow"). Unfortunately, the two forms of ⲥ*ⲧ* in Ach and Sa³ are not precise variants of each other. But the virtually parallel section in the Greek Tiburtine Sibyl has διὰ τὰ φάρμακα τῶν βελῶν (l. 196; in Alexander, *Oracle of Baalbek*, p. 21), implying that the final ⲟ in Sa³'s ⲥⲟⲧⲟ should be ⲉ: ⲥⲟⲧⲉ. See Steindorff, 80 n. 4; Wintermute, 741 n. m2; and the extensive discussion in Alexander, *Oracle of Baalbek*, 37–40.

38. Both Pietersma (37) and Wintermute (741) translate ἀνάγκη with the sense of "anguish, distress"; but the author clearly imagines that the forced draft is a response to the necessities of war (see Kuhn 765, 765 n. 12).

39. This is a plausible scribal corruption of πόλεμος, which makes more sense in the context. Rosenstiehl argues convincingly that the corruption had already occurred at the

Sa	*Ach*
command that every young boy twelve years and younger be seized and be taught to shoot arrows.	command that every young boy twelve years and younger be seized and be taught to shoot arrows.

f) 37.[40] The midwife of the land
   shall mourn **in that time,**
And she who has given birth
   shall cast her eye to heaven and
   say,
"Why did I sit upon the birthstool[41]
To bear a child on the earth?"

37. The midwife of the land
   will mourn **in that time,**
And she who has given birth
   will cast her eye to heaven and
   say,
"Why did I sit upon the birthstool
To bear a child on the earth?"

38. The barren woman and the virgin
   shall rejoice:
"It is the time for us to rejoice,
For we have no children on the
   earth,
But our children are in the
   heavens."[42]

38. The barren woman and the virgin
   shall rejoice:
"It is the time for us to rejoice,
For we have no children on the
   earth,
But our children are in the heavens."

§E. Political Signs in Brief Oracles

a) 39. At that time three kings will arise from Persia, capturing [αἰχμαλωτίζειν] the Jews who are in Egypt, to take them to Jerusalem and inhabit it with them again.

39. At that time three kings will arise from Persia, capturing [αἰχμαλωτίζειν] the Jews who are in Egypt, to take them to Jerusalem and inhabit it with them again.

b) 40. Then if you should hear that there is security and safety[43] in Jeru-

40. Then if you should hear that there is security and safety in Jeru-

---

Greek stage, because from τὴν ἀνάγκην τῶν πόλεμων to τὴν ἀνάγκην τῶν πόλεων requires a change of merely one letter ("L'Apocalypse d'Élie," 273–74; cf. Alexander, *Oracle of Baalbek*, 39).

40. The verb tenses in Sa³ change in this section from first to third future. Because there are also formal devices of parallelism and repetition (earth vs. heaven), Wintermute has suggested that the section originated as an independent poem (742 n. p2).

41. Lit. ⲧⲱⲃⲉ ("brick"). Cf. Ex 1:16; and see Wintermute, 742 n. s2.

42. [ⲥ̣]ⲛ̄ⲙ̄ⲡⲏⲟⲩⲉ (cf. Ach: ϩⲛ̄ⲛ̄ⲡⲏⲩⲉ). It is thus likely that the text originally read "heavens," regardless of Sa³'s singular article.

43. ⲡⲱⲣⲝ . . . ⲙⲛ̄ ⲧⲁⲥⲫⲁⲗⲓⲁ are synonymous, as Wintermute notes (742 n. w2), but were obviously compounded to achieve rhetorical effect. Pietersma reads ⲡⲱⲣⲝ without an article—"dissension"—but then must contort the meaning to account for ἀσφάλεια (39). The message is obviously that what is apparently peace is only a foreshadowing of greater troubles, a theme paralleled in 2:48-53. Rosenstiehl makes a cogent comparison to 1 Thes 5:3—"When they say, 'There is peace and security [Coptic: ϫⲉ ϯⲣⲏⲛⲏ ⲙⲛ̄ ⲡⲱⲣⲝ],' then sudden destruction will come upon them"—although there is no basis for assuming immediate textual influence ("L'Apocalypse d'Élie," 279).

Sa	*Ach*

Sa

salem, tear your garments, O priests of the land, because the Destructive One will not be long in coming!

c) 41. Immediately the Lawless One will appear in the holy places, at that time.

d) 42. The kings of Persia will flee at that time and they will stand to fight(?)[44] with the kings of the Assyrians; four kings (will) fight with three.

e) 43. They will spend three years in that place, until they have taken the wealth in that place.

§F. Terrestrial Woes (Nile)

44. Blood will flow from Kos to Memphis: the river of Egypt will become blood, so that no one can drink from it for three days. **45.** Woe to Egypt and to those who are **in Egypt!**

§G. The Advent of the King from the Sun

a) 46. At that time a king will arise in the city which is called "The City of the Sun." **At that time** the whole land will tremble.

b) 47. He will flee up to Memphis in the sixth year **of the kings of the Persians. He** will lay an ambush in Memphis. **He** will kill the Assyrian

Ach

salem, tear your garments, O priests of the land, because the Destructive One will not be long in coming!

41. Immediately the Lawless One will appear in the holy places, at that time.

42. The kings of Persia will flee at that time and they will stand to fight(?)[45] with the kings of the Assyrians; four kings (will) fight with three.

43. They will spend three years in that place, until they have taken the wealth **of the temple** in that place.[46]

44. Blood will flow from Kos to Memphis: the river of Egypt will become blood, so that no one can drink from it for three days. **45.** Woe to Egypt and to those who are **in it!**

46. At that time a king will arise in the city which is called "The City of the Sun," **and** the whole land will tremble.

47. He will flee up to Memphis in the sixth year. **The kings of the Persians will** lay an ambush in Memphis.[47] **They** will kill the Assyrian

---

44. The top of this page of Sa³ is lacunose: the remaining letters of the section in question—which somewhat resemble the remaining Ach words—are: [. . . . . . .] Ϩⲡⲓⲧ.

45. ⲁϨⲣϨⲁⲡⲓⲧ (= [ⲥⲉ]ⲁϨⲉ ⲁⲣⲉⲧⲟⲩ [ⲁⲙⲓϨⲉ]—"and they will stand to fight" (Oscar von Lemm, "Kleine koptische Studien—XXVI: Bemerkungen zu einigen Stellen der koptischen Apokalypsen, 14," *Bulletin de l'académie impériale de sciences de St. Pétersbourg* 21 [1904], 46); but this does not seem to match the remaining text of Sa³. See Wintermute, 743 n. d3.

46. It is unclear whether this reference to a temple is original. Robbing temples is a consistent motif in ApocEl 2.

47. The Achmimic recension clearly deemphasizes the (Egyptian?) king's role in this

Sa	*Ach*
kings. 48. The Persians will take vengeance upon the land.	**king.**[48] 48. The Persians will take vengeance upon the land.
c) He will command that the Pagans and the Lawless Ones be killed. **He will command that the temples of the Pagans be plundered and their priests destroyed. He** will command that the shrines[49] of the saints be rebuilt.	**And they** (will) command that the Pagans and the Lawless Ones be killed. **They** will command that the shrines of the saints be rebuilt.
d) 49. **He** will give double gifts to the House of God. **He** will say: "The name of God is One!" 50. The whole land will hail the Persians.	49. **They** will give double gifts to the House of God. **They** will say: "The name of God is One!" 50. The whole land will hail the Persians.

§H. A Deceptive Peace

a) 51. And even the remnant who did not die under the calamity [$\pi\lambda\eta\gamma\acute{\eta}$] will say "It is a King of Righteousness whom the Lord has sent to us, so that the land might not become desert!"	51. And even the remnant who did not die under the calamity [$\pi\lambda\eta\gamma\acute{\eta}$] will say "It is a King of Righteousness whom the Lord has sent to us, so that the land might not become desert!"
b) 52. He will command that no royal (taxes)[50] be given for three years and six months.	52. He will command that no royal (taxes) be given for three years and six months.
c) The land will be full of prosperity in great abundance. 53. The living will go say to the dead, "Arise and remain with us in this rest!"	The land will be full of prosperity in great abundance. 53. The living will go say to the dead, "Arise and remain with us in this rest!"

---

sequence of events; and Wintermute rightly argues that this tendency would be secondary to the Sahidic recension's focus upon this king (743 nn. 13, n3).

48. The plural, "kings," in Sa[3] continues the narrative from v. 43. The singular in Ach has a number of possible explanations: (1) to correspond with the Unrighteous Assyrian King in v. 1; (2) to imply a reference to Odenath or another historical person of the late third century; (3) to represent a literary shift in focus from plural dramatis personae to individual dramatis persona (such as the Lawless One), which commences with ApocEl 3.

49. I have translated as "shrines" ⲛⲉⲣⲡⲏⲩⲉ the same word that designates "temples."

50. Sa[3]: ⲛⲉⲩϯ ⲗⲁⲁⲩⲉ ⲛ̅ⲣⲣⲟ. The sense has been construed in diverse ways, from the absence of a king per se (Pietersma, 43) to a relaxation of royal taxes (Kuhn, 767 n. 18; Wintermute, 744 n. q3). The latter seems to be the original sense, for the Tiburtine Sibyl seems to copy the text of the Elijah Apocalypse here fairly directly: καὶ δώσει ἀτέλειαν εἰς ὅλας τὰς χώρας ἐπὶ ἔτη τρία καὶ μῆνας ἕξ ("And he will grant a tax-exemption to entire countries for three years and six months" [ll. 206–7]; ed. Alexander, *Oracle of Baalbek*, 21; translation, 29).

Sa	*Ach*

d) 3.1. In the fourth year of that king there will appear **someone** saying "I am the Christ." But he is not—do not believe him!

3.1. In the fourth year of that king there will appear **the Lawless One** saying "I am the Christ." But he is not—do not believe him!

Interlude on Signs of the Parousia[51]

2. **For** [de] when the Christ comes he will come like a **covey**[52] of doves, with his crown of doves surrounding him, as he traverses the clouds[53] of heaven with the sign of the cross going before him.

2. When the Christ comes he will come like a **brood** of doves, with his crown of doves surrounding him, as he traverses the clouds of heaven with the sign of the cross going before him.

3. The whole world **sees** him like the sun which shines from the east to the west.

3. The whole world **will see** him like the sun which shines from the east to the west.

4. This is the way that **the Christ** comes: with all his angels surrounding him.

4. This is the way **he** comes: with all his angels surrounding him.

The Signs of the Lawless One: Miracles[54]

5. The Lawless One will again[55] begin to stand in the holy **place**.[56]

5. The Lawless One will again begin to stand in the holy **places**.

---

51. See discussion, pp. 231–32.

52. Sa³: ⲙⲉϩⲁⲗ (cf. Crum 208A, s.v. ⲙⲁϩ); Ach: ⲥⲁⲙⲛⲧ (cf. Crum 339B). See in general Wintermute, 744 n. e on the sense of the two words. Because of their proximity in meaning it is more likely that such a divergence arose in translating Greek νοσσιά into Coptic than in a Coptic scribe's "correction" of another Coptic word.

53. Sa³: [ⲃ]ⲏⲡⲉ = Ach: ⲕⲏⲡⲉ, following Rosenstiehl's reconstruction ("L'Apocalypse d'Élie," 274–75 n. 24); *pace* Pietersma, 42–43: [ⲕ]ⲏⲡⲉ ("vaults" of heaven).

54. See discussion, pp. 112–17.

55. ⲟⲛ; the sense of repetition is unclear, as both prior references to the Lawless One's advent (2:40; 3:1) refer to this as a single event. However, because the description of his advent is broken by a parenthetical image of the parousia (3:2-4), ⲟⲛ might be read to mean: "Again: the Lawless One will begin. . . . "

56. The singular form must refer to the temple in Jerusalem, a site of eschatological events in Christian eschatology of late antiquity (see pp. 226–27). Indeed, the Latin Tiburtine Sibyl reads: *tunc revelabitur manifeste Antichristus et sedebit in domo Domini Ierusalem* (ed. Ernst Sackur, in idem, *Sibyllinische Texte und Forschungen* [Halle: Max Niemeyer, 1898], 186). The plural form in Ach, used by all mss. throughout ApocEl 2, seems to refer to saint-shrines (vv. 14, 25, 48b). It would make sense that the first author would have intended this more exotic location for the appearance of the Lawless One, and that later scribes changed the articular prefix in light of their reverence for local shrines (and perhaps unintentionally). In 4:1, however, Sa¹ alone has the singular, "holy place," whereas both Ach and Sa³ have "holy places."

Sa	*Ach*

Sa

6. He will say to the sun,
"Fall," and it will fall;
"Darken!" and it does so.
"Shine!" and it does so.

8. He will accompany them[57]
through the sky,[58]
saying, "Walk upon the sea and the
rivers as if upon dry land."[59]

9. He will make the lame walk,
He will make the deaf hear,
He will make the dumb speak,
He will make the blind see,
10. Lepers he will purify,
The sick he will heal,
The demons he will cast out—

11. He will multiply his signs and
wonders in the presence of
everyone.

Ach

6. He will say to the sun,
"Fall," and it will fall;
He will say, "Shine!"—it does so.
He will say, "Darken!"—it does so.

7. He will say to the moon, "Become
blood!"—it does so.

8. He will accompany them through
the sky.
He will walk upon the sea and the
rivers as if upon dry land.

9. He will make the lame walk,
He will make the deaf hear,
He will make the dumb speak,
He will make the blind see,
10. Lepers he will purify,
The sick he will heal,
The demons he will cast out—

11. He will multiply his signs and
wonders in the presence of
everyone.

---

57. Both Sa³ and Ach have a plural object pronoun here; only Ach has identified both sun *and* moon as its antecedents. Therefore it is possible to conclude that the reference to the moon somehow dropped out of Sa³ during copying. See Pietersma, 16.

58. ϥⲛⲁⲃⲱⲕ ⲙ̄ⲛ̄ⲙⲁⲩ ⲉⲃⲟⲗ ϩ̄ⲛ̄ ⲧⲡⲉ. Both Rosenstiehl (97) and Schrage (252) translate with the sense that he *removes* them from the sky, an image that would conform to popular images of the eschatological adversary (cf. Rv 12:4; Wilhelm Bousset, *The Antichrist Legend*, tr. A. H. Keane [London: Hutchinson, 1896], 175–76) but which is confused by the prepositional phrase *"with"* them" (ⲙ̄ⲛ̄ⲙⲁⲩ). It is possible that it bears some relation to an enigmatic prophecy in ApocEl 2 that the demon-faced son "will appear beneath [ⲉⲃⲟⲗ ϩⲁ] the sun and the moon" (2:27), for this figure bears some functional resemblances to the Lawless One (cf. 2:27 and 3:16-17). It is tempting to take the image of "accompanying" the sun and the moon "through the sky" as recalling the classical Egyptian tradition of the barque of Re, the sun god and a chief national deity in Egypt even in the Greco-Roman period. In this barque ride the other major gods and goddesses of Egypt, who all participate in warding off Apep, demon of chaos and darkness. To accompany the sun (and moon—Thoth) might mean that the Lawless One is raised to the mythological position of passenger on the celestial barque of the gods.

59. This miracle makes little sense as a command from the Lawless One to the sun (and moon). As in other miracle lists (see above, pp. 113–16), the miracle of walking upon the water belongs to the same group as the healing and exorcism miracles that follow it.

Sa	Ach
12. He will do the things which the Christ **did**,[60] except only for raising a corpse—	12. He will do the things which the Christ did, except only for raising a corpse—
13. by this you will know that he is the Lawless One: he has no power to give life![61]	13. by this you will know that he is the Lawless One: he has no power to give life!

The Signs of the Lawless One: Physiognomy[62]

14. For behold, I will tell you his signs so that you might recognize him:	14. For behold, I will tell you his signs so that you might recognize him:
15. He is a small *pelēc*, thin-legged, tall,[63] with a tuft of grey hair on his forehead, which is bald,[64] while his	15. He is a small *pelēc*, thin-legged, tall, with a tuft of grey hair on his forehead, which is bald, while his

60. Sa³; Sa¹: "will do."

61. Sa³: ⲘⲚ ⲄⲞⲘ ⲘⲘⲞϤ ⲉϯ ⲚⲞⲨⲮⲨⲬⲎ; Sa¹, Ach: . . . ⲉϯ ⲮⲨⲬⲎ. In the context, "life" is a clearer translation than "soul." Steindorff (91, 121), Rosenstiehl (98), Schrage (253), and Kuhn (768) all take ⲉϯ as a preposition and article—"[power] over the [soul]"—whereas Pietersma (45) and Wintermute (745) read it as a verb with infinitive marker—"[power] to give." The former interpretation corresponds to a claim made by Tabitha in the subsequent narrative when she resurrects herself: "You have no power over my soul [ⲉⲦⲀⲮⲨⲬⲎ] nor over my body [ⲟⲩⲆⲉ ⲡⲀⲤⲰⲘⲀ]" (4:5b); but it does not make sense in the context of the Lawless One's signs (where power "over" souls does not make as much difference as power "to give" life). The addition of the object marker and indefinite article in Sa³ clarifies that it is the Lawless One's inability to give life that is at issue.

62. See discussion, pp. 117–25.

63. These words have confounded translators and editors; a thorough discussion of the interpretative problems can be found in Wintermute, 746 n. w. Jean-Marc Rosenstiehl's attempt to connect ⲡⲉⲗⲏⲋ (Sa³, Ach; Sa¹: ⲡⲉⲗⲏⲕ) to an Essene name for Hyrcanus II ("house of Peleg": CD 20.22; 4QpNah 3.9; cf. Rosenstiehl, 68–69, 98; and idem, "Un sobriquet essénien dans l'Apocalypse copte d'Élie," *Semitica* 15 [1965]:97–99) has not met with much agreement; but this word—presumably a noun—has not since found other interpretations.

Crum (333A) suggests the interpretation of ⲥⲀⲗⲀϣⲉⲓⲉ (missing in Ach and assumed for the lacuna in Sa³ ms. p. 13) be "tall" or even "monstrously tall" (148A), a detail that would correspond to other adversary physiognomies, such as that of the Greek *Apocalypse of Daniel:* "The height of his stature (will be) fifteen feet" (tr. G. T. Zervos, *OTP* 1:767); and even that of *Sefer Eliahu:* "his stature is extremely tall" (ed. Eben-Shmuel, *Midrᵉshei Gᵉulah* [Jerusalem: Mosad Bialik, 1954]). See Jean-Marc Rosenstiehl, "Le portrait de l'antichrist," in *Pseudépigraphes de l'ancien testament et manuscrits de la mer morte*, ed. Marc Philonenko (Paris: Presses universitaires, 1967), 54.

64. On the interpretation of ⲚⲄⲀⲗⲟⲨⲂⲒⲒ (Sa) and ⲚϣⲀⲦⲘⲉ2Ⲏⲗ (Ach), see von Lemm, "Kleine koptische Studien—XXVI:16," 229–30; Crum, 211B.

Sa	*Ach*

eye**lids**[65] reach to his ears, (and) there is a leprous spot on the front of his hands.

16. He will transform himself before **you:**
at one time he will be an **old man;**
but at another time he will be **a young boy.**

17. He will transform himself in **every sign,**[66]
but the sign of his head he will not be able to change.

18. By this you will know that he is the Lawless One!

eye**brows** reach to his ears, (and) there is a leprous spot on the front of his hands.

16. He will transform himself in the presence of **those who see him:**
at one time he will be a **young boy**
but at another time he will be an **old man.**

17. He will transform himself in every sign,
but the sign of his head he will not be able to change.

18. By this you will know that he is the Lawless One!

The Legend of Tabitha

4.1. The virgin whose name is Tabitha[67] will hear that the Shameless One has made his appearance in the holy places.[68]

She will put on her garment of linen, 2. and hurry up to Judea, reproving him as far as Jerusalem, saying **to him,** "O Shameless One, O Lawless One, O you who are hostile to all the saints!"

4.1. The virgin whose name is Tabitha will hear that the Shameless One has made his appearance in the holy places.

She will put on her garment of linen, 2. and hurry **after him** up to Judea, reproving him as far as Jerusalem, saying, "O Shameless One, O Lawless One, O you who are hostile to all the saints!"

65. Ach is preferred on this divergence; Sa[3] makes little sense in the context, which concerns the hair arrangement of the Lawless One. Cf. Wintermute, 746 n. z.

66. Sa[3]; Sa[1]: "in his signs."

67. Evidently not the Tabitha (Dorcas) of Acts 9 (*pace* Steindorff, 92–93 n. 1; Wintermute, 746 n. 4a). Rather, this eschatological Tabitha is a combination of Bithia, the daughter of Pharaoh, who was viewed in early Egyptian Judaism as a righteous Gentile who entered heaven alive (Ex 2:5-10; 1 Chr 4:17; *Exod. Rab.* 1.26, 18.3; *Lev. Rab.* 1.3; *Der. Er. Zut.* 1.18) and would return in the eschaton (cf. *History of Joseph the Carpenter* [Arabic] 32), and Ta-Bitjet, wife of the god Horus and scorpion goddess, by whose blood poisons were adjured in traditional Egyptian magic (cf. Borghouts, nos. 97–98, 101; cf. Baudouin van de Walle, "L'Ostracon E 3209 des Musées Royaux d'Art et d'Histoire mentionnant la déesse scorpion Ta-Bithet," *Chronique d'Égypte* 42 [1967]:13–29). The appearance of a Tabithia with Isiac characteristics in the Coptic ritual text London Hay 10391 (= Kropp, vol. 1, text M), ll. 50–77, suggests that traditions of Ta-Bitjet continued within ritual traditions of the goddess Isis. In general, see David T. M. Frankfurter, "Tabitha in the Apocalypse of Elijah," *JTS* 41 (1990):13–25.

68. Sa[3]; Sa[1]: "holy places."

Sa   *Ach*

3. Then the Shameless One will be
angered at the virgin. He will pursue
her towards the west.

He will suck her blood in the evening 4. and toss her up onto the
temple, and she will become a healing[69] for the people.

5. At dawn she will rise up alive and
rebuke him, saying, "You Shameless
One—you have no power over my
spirit[70] or my body, because I live in
the Lord always! 6. And even my
blood which you cast upon the
temple has become a healing for the
people!"

The Return of Elijah and Enoch

7. Then when Elijah and Enoch hear
that the Shameless One has made
his appearance in the holy places[71]
they will come down to do battle
with him, saying,

8. Are you not ashamed that you are
always estranged **[when you associate yourself with the saints (Sa¹)]**?

9. [72] You have become an enemy to
the heavenly ones and you have
acted against those on earth.

10. You are an enemy of the angels
and the Thrones.[73] You are always a
stranger.

---

69. ⲟⲩⲝⲁⲓ. Cf. the "healing" (θεραπεύειν) of the fast in 1:21.
70. ψυχή, translated "life" above (3:13).
71. Again, Sa¹ maintains "place" in the singular.
72. See discussion of this diatribe, pp. 130–32.
73. Sa³; Sa¹ reverses: "the Thrones and the angels."

Sa	*Ach*

11. You have fallen from heaven like the morning star. You changed (and) **your**[74] lineage[75] became dark to you.

12. Are you not indeed ashamed, as you establish yourself against God? —You, O Devil![76]

13. The Shameless One will hear and be angered and do battle with them in the market of the great city.[77] He will spend seven days fighting with them **and kill them**;

14. and they will spend three and a half days dead in the market while all the people look upon them.

15. **But** on the fourth day they will rise **again**[78] and reprove him, saying: O Shameless One,

                                                   "O Shameless One,
                                                  O Lawless One,

Are you not indeed ashamed, you who deceive the people of God for whom you have not suffered? Do you not know that we live in the Lord **so that we may rebuke you?**

                     Are you not indeed ashamed, you who deceive the people of God for whom you have not suffered? Do you not know that we live in the Lord?"

74. Sa³; Sa¹: *"the* lineage."

75. ⲧⲉⲕⲫⲩⲗⲏ. Because the preceding strophe refers to the Lucifer myth (Is 14:12), it is likely that this strophe should be read as continuing the myth (cf. Rosenstiehl, 101 n. *ad loc*; and K. H. Kuhn, review of *The Apocalypse of Elijah*, by Albert Pietersma, *Journal of Semitic Studies* 27 [1982]:315). Thus the adversary's "lineage," "race," or "tribe" would be angelic. Note that the *Book of the Watchers* refers to the fallen angels as "lawless ones" (ἄνομαι; 1 En 7:6).

76. Sa¹ clearly has ⲟⲩⲇⲓⲁⲃⲟⲗⲟⲥ; Sa³ has a lacuna here, but the stem of some letter that could not be ⲟⲩ- is visible immediately before the break (cf. Pietersma, 83 [facsimile of ms. p. 15]). Although Pietersma reads this letter as ⲡ- (thus: "you are *the* devil; 48], it appears more likely to be a *dalda*, the first letter of ⲇⲓⲁⲃⲟⲗⲟⲥ. The use of ⲛ̄ⲧⲟⲕ in the last two lines is an intensification of the primary noun.

77. Although commentators have rightly signaled the basis of this scene in Rv 11:2-12 (cf. Richard Bauckham, "The Martyrdom of Enoch and Elijah: Jewish or Christian?" *JBL* 95, 3 [1976]:457–58; idem, "Enoch and Elijah in the Coptic Apocalypse of Elijah," *Studia patristica* 16, 2 [1985]:72–73), where the "great city" is clearly Jerusalem, Wintermute also rightly notes that the term has a more general significance as "the metropolis of a detested enemy" (748 n. w). In this case, the use of ἀγορά, echoing the oracle in 2:31, suggests a synthesis between Rv 11:8 and a nationalistic Egyptian view of Alexandria, the "great city" of Egypt at this time and certainly the most proximate stereotype of a great urban marketplace for a third-century Egyptian writer.

78. Sa³: "But . . . again"; Sa¹ omits.

Sa

16. Whenever you say, "I have overpowered them,"[79] we will lay down the flesh **of this body** and kill you, as you are powerless to speak on that day, for we **live** in the Lord always, but[81] you are always an enemy!

17. The Shameless One will listen, infuriated, and do battle with them. 18. The whole city will surround them.

19. On that day they will shout aloud to heaven, shining, while the whole world watches them, **and** the Lawless One will not overpower them.

Ach

16. When the words were spoken they overpowered him,[80] **saying,** "We will lay down the flesh **for the spirit** and kill you, as you are powerless to speak on that day, for we **are strong** in the Lord always, but you are always an enemy **of God!**

17. The Shameless One will listen; **he will be angry** and do battle with them. 18. The whole city will surround them.

19. On that day they will shout aloud to heaven, shining, while **all the people and** the whole world watch them. The Lawless One will not overpower them.

Martyrdoms[82]

20. He will grow angry at the land and will seek to sin against the people.

20. He will grow angry at the land and will seek to sin against the people.

21. He will pursue all of the saints. They will be brought back in chains, along with the priests of the land.

22. He will kill them. He will exterminate[83] **them [............] them,** that their eyes be **put out** with **sticks** of iron;

22. He will command that their eyes be **seared** with an iron **borer.**

---

79. Following syntax suggested by Wintermute, 748 n. c2.

80. ⲉⲩϫⲟⲩ ⲛ̄ϣⲉϫⲉ ⲁⲩϭⲛ̄ϭⲁⲙ ⲁⲣⲁϥ ⲉⲩϫⲟⲩ ⲙ̄ⲙⲁⲥ. Wintermute alone has rendered the sense of these lines (748 n. c2); other translators have ignored them as corrupt (Steindorff, 93 n. 3; Kuhn, 769 n. 22). Presumably the Achmimic scribe received fragmentary words ("overpower," "saying") from a Greek or Sahidic original that read more closely to what is here translated as Sa. In giving meaning to these fragments, however, the scribe evidently synthesized a traditional Egyptian magical image, that of "words" that themselves might "overpower." See above, pp. 129–30.

81. Sa[1]: ϫⲉ; cf. Ach: ⲗⲉ. I take the Sahidic as a corruption of the Greek preserved in Ach.

82. See discussion, chap. 6, pp. 141–47.

83. ⲉⲓⲣⲉ + Greek ὀλέκω.

Sa	*Ach*
	23. **He will remove the skin from their heads.**[84]
23. He will remove their nails one by one. He will command that vinegar with lime be **shoved** into their nostrils.	He will remove their nails one by one. He will command that vinegar with lime be **put** in their nostrils.

The Heavenly Rewards of Martyrdom[85]

24. But those who are unable to bear the tortures of that king will take **their** gold and flee to the ferries, **saying, "Ferry us to the desert."**	24. But those who are unable to bear the tortures of that king will take gold and flee to the ferries, **to places in the desert.**
They will lie down like one asleep, 25. **while** the Lord will take up to himself their spirits and their souls.	They will lie down like one asleep. 25. The Lord will take up to himself their spirits and their souls.
26. Their flesh will become like rock;[86] no wild animals will eat them until the last day of the great judgment.	26. Their flesh will become like rock; no wild animals will eat them until the last day of the great judgment.
27. They will arise and **receive** a place of rest. But they will not inhabit the Kingdom of the Christ like those who have endured.[87]	27. They will arise and **find** a place of rest. But they will not inhabit the Kingdom of the Christ like those who have endured.
But for those who have endured, says the Lord, I will appoint them to sit at my right hand.	**For** the Lord says, I will appoint them to sit at my right hand. 28. **They will receive favor over others.**
28. They will triumph over the Lawless One. They will witness the destruction of heaven and earth. 29. They will receive the thrones of glory and the crowns.	They will triumph over the Lawless One. They will witness the destruction of heaven and earth. 29. They will receive the thrones of glory and the crowns.

84. Here Ach and Sa¹ agree against Sa³.

85. See discussion, pp. 147–51.

86. Sa¹ and Sa³ have ⲡⲉⲣⲛⲁ ("ham"), but this is obviously a corruption of Greek πέτρα, preserved in Ach; cf. Rosenstiehl, "L'Apocalypse d'Élie," 281; Wintermute, 749 n. r2.

87. Greek ὑπομένειν. A hierarchical difference between those who flee and those who suffer is indicated; see discussion above, pp. 152–54.

Sa	*Ach*

The Challenge of the Sixty Righteous Ones

30. In that time sixty righteous ones, prepared for that hour, will hear. 31. They will gird themselves with the breastplate of God. They will run to Jerusalem, fighting[88] with the Shameless One, saying:	30. In that time sixty righteous ones, prepared for that hour, will hear. 31. They will gird themselves with the breastplate of God. They will run to Jerusalem, fighting with the Shameless One, saying:
Every feat[89] which the prophets performed, you have performed, **but** you were **quite** unable to raise a corpse, because you lack the power. By this we have recognized that you are the Lawless One!	Every feat which the prophets performed **from the beginning** you have performed, (but) you were unable to raise a corpse, because you lack the power **to give life.** By this we have recognized that you are the Lawless One!
32. **The Shameless One** will hear **and be angered and command** 33. that the Righteous Ones be bound and heaped up **on altars** and burned.	32. **He** will hear. **He (will) be angered: He (will) command that altars be lit,** 33. that the Righteous Ones be bound, heaped up, and burned.

In illo tempore: The Evacuation of the Saints

5.1. And in that time the hearts of many will **turn away and withdraw** from him, saying, This is not the Christ! **For** the Christ does not kill the Righteous, nor does he pursue people of truth. **Will he not (rather) seek to** persuade them with signs and wonders?[90]	**5.**1 And in that time the hearts of many will **harden and they will flee** from him, saying, This is not the Christ! The Christ does not kill the Righteous, nor does he pursue people **when he will seek (them), but he persuades** them with signs and wonders.
2. In that time the Christ will have pity upon those who are his.	2. In that time the Christ will have pity upon those who are his.

---

88. Sa[3], Ach: ⲉⲩⲙⲓϣⲉ; Sa[1] seems to preserve the original Greek with ⲉⲩⲡⲟⲗⲉⲙⲓ.

89. The focus of discussion here, Coptic ⲃⲟⲙ, has been variously translated "feat" and "power."

90. Pietersma's reconstruction of Sa[3] here (18, ll. 19–21) does not require an interrogative sense, but the alternative translation—"he *will not* try to persuade them"— poses an enormous theological contradiction to the other recensions, a tendency not elsewhere implied in Sa[3]. Sa[1] introduces a parallel negative interrogative with the Greek μή and strengthens the sense with ⲛ̄ϩⲟⲩⲟ, "all the more" (ms. p. 10, ll. 29–30; in Steindorff, 134).

Sa	*Ach*
He will send his angels from heaven to the number of sixty-four thousand, each with six wings.[91] 3. Their sound will move heaven and earth as they bless and glorify.	He will send his angels from heaven to the number of sixty-four thousand, each with six wings. 3. Their sound will move heaven and earth as they bless and glorify.
4. Those upon whose forehead is inscribed the name of the Christ, upon whose right hand is the seal—from little to great—they will lift them up on their wings and carry them away before the **wrath.**	4. **Now** those upon whose forehead is inscribed the name of the Christ, upon whose right hand is the seal—from little to great—they will lift them up on their wings and carry them away before **his fury.**
5. Then Gabriel and Uriel will make a pillar of light[92] **and lead them until they bring them** into the holy land[93] 6. and grant them to eat from the tree of life and to wear the white **garment;** and the angels watch over	5. Then Gabriel and Uriel will make a pillar of light, **leading them** into the holy land 6. and granting them to eat from the tree of life, and to wear white **garments;** and the angels watch over them.[94] And they will not

91. This image of seraphim as warrior or rescue angels is unique, as their role as guardians of the throne of God and singers of the heavenly *trisagion* (Isaiah 6:1-3) remained relatively circumscribed throughout apocalyptic literature (*2 En* 21:1; *Apoc. Ab.* 18; Rv 4:8); and even the mid-fourth-century Egyptian liturgy ascribed to Serapion of Thmuis maintains the seraphim's specialized function: "Beside Thee stand thousand thousands and ten thousand times ten thousands of angels, archangels, thrones, dominations, principalities, powers: by Thee stand the two most honourable six-winged Seraphim, with two wings covering the Face and with Two the Feet and with two flying, and crying 'Holy'; with whom receive also our cry of 'Holy' as we say, Holy, holy, holy" (tr. Gregory Dix, in idem, *The Shape of the Liturgy* [San Francisco: Harper & Row, 1945], 163). In the following verse (ApocEl 5:4), the author has drawn on the tradition of the seraphim's loud, unearthly voices (*Apoc. Ab.* 18:2-3; cf. Ez 1:24) to portray the cosmos as filled with the throne liturgy during this period of the last days. The immensity of the signs preceding the rescue of the righteous might be compared to 1 Thes 3:16 and Mt 24:30-31.

92. The imagery is drawn from Ex 13:21-22, but translators have differed in how to take the archangels' role here: as themselves the pillar (Wintermute; Kuhn; Pietersma), or as the creators of the pillar (Steindorff; Rosenstiehl; Schrage). These differences arise from the ambiguous Coptic ειρε. Uriel might plausibly be identified with the biblical pillar of fire (Hebrew: אוריאל ["light of God"]), and in *Rossi Tractate* 8.6 an angel Iôriêl is invoked "by the cloud [6нпе] of light which is with the Father, in which he was hidden before he created anything." Gabriel is only associated with such a pillar in *Rossi Tractate* 15.1—"I invoke you, Gabriel, by the grea[t p]illar of l[ight]"—but is generally not endowed with such symbols in Coptic tradition: cf. Kropp, 3:81-83; Origen, *De princip.* 1.8.1 (Gabriel supervises wars).

93. Sa³; Sa¹ = "the holy place [пма етоуллв]." The variation offers additional reason to take "holy land" as an idealized Palestine. "The holy place" was a common euphemism for the Jerusalem temple: *Ep. Aristeas* 81; 2 Macc 5:17–20; 3 Macc 1:9, 23.

94. Ach becomes extremely lacunose in this section, but Schmidt ("Der Kolophon," 321) improved immensely upon Steindorff's reconstruction; cf. Wintermute, 750 n. q.

Sa

them. And they will **neither hunger** nor thirst, nor will the Lawless One have power over them.

Ach

thirst, nor will the Lawless One have power over them.

The Decline of the Earth[95]

7. Then, in that time, the earth will tremble; the sun will grow dark. Peace will be removed from upon the earth and under heaven [. . . . .][96] The trees will be uprooted and topple over. Wild beasts and farm animals will die in a catastrophe.[97] 8. Birds will fall on the ground dead,
9. **[The earth will parch (Sa¹),]** and the waters of the sea will dry up.

7. Then, in that time, the earth will tremble; the sun will grow dark. Peace will be removed from upon the earth.

9. The earth will parch, and the waters of the sea will dry up.

10. The sinners will lament on the earth, What have you done to us, Lawless One, saying "I am the Christ" when you are the **Lawless One?** 11. But you are powerless to save yourself so that you might save us. You performed **vain** signs in our presence until you estranged us from the Christ who created **every one.** Woe to us, for we listened to you!

10. The sinners will lament on the earth, What have you done to us, Lawless One, saying "I am the Christ" when you are the **Devil?** 11. But you are powerless to save yourself so that you might save us. You performed signs in our presence until you estranged us from the Christ who created **us.** Woe to us, for we listened to you!

12. See, now we will die in a famine[98] **and tribulation.**
Indeed, where now is the footprint of a righteous person that we should worship **you,** or where is our teacher, that we might appeal to him?

12. See, now we will die in a famine.

Indeed, where now is the footprint of a righteous person that we should worship **him,** or where is our teacher, that we might appeal to him?

95. See discussion, p. 204.

96. One and a half lines are missing from Sa³, but because Sa¹ proceeds immediately to the following lines, it is impossible to determine what is missing from Sa³.

97. ϣⲧⲟⲣⲧⲣ̅, the same word translated above as "tremble," here with indefinite article. Naphtali Lewis provides a helpful picture of the world of farm animals (ⲧ̅ⲃⲛⲟⲟⲩⲉ), as a third-century Egyptian might imagine their demise by this verse (*Life in Egypt under Roman Rule* [Oxford: Clarendon, 1983], 130–33).

98. Although the mss. agree in the reading ⲟⲩϩⲉ ⲃⲱⲱⲛ—"evil way"—Pierre Lacau suggested convincingly that this be restored ⲟⲩϩⲉ ⲃⲱⲱⲛⲉ—"famine" ("Remarques sur le manuscrit akhmimique des apocalypses de Sophonie et d'Élie," *JA* 254 [1966]:191; cf. Crum, 643A; Wintermute, 751 n. e2; and Rosenstiehl, "L'Apocalypse d'Élie," 278).

Sa	*Ach*
13. Now we will be destroyed in wrath, because we disobeyed God.	13. Now we will be destroyed in wrath. . . . [one leaf missing]
14. We went to the depths of the sea and we found no water. We dug in the rivers and papyrus reeds[99] and we found no water.	
15. Then the Shameless One will weep[100] in that time, saying, Woe is me, too, for my time has passed away![101] I was saying that my time would not pass away, 16. (but) my years have become months, my days have passed like dust blowing away.[102] Now indeed I will perish like you!	
17. Now, indeed, flee to the desert! Seize robbers and kill them![103] 18. Bring up the saints—[104]	

99. The ingenious translation "papyrus reeds" from ⲙ̄ⲛ̄ⲁⲥⲉ ⲙ̄ⲙⲁϩⲉ (v. 14b) comes from Wintermute (751 n. i2); Steindorff's translation, "sixteen cubits" (141), is followed by Pietersma (59), Kuhn (772), and Schrage (268). Rosenstiehl (111) justifies this reading with a quotation from Pliny, that the height of the Nile is sixteen cubits (*Nat. Hist.* 5.57–58); but because the Nile flooded at radically inconsistent levels during the Roman period (cf. Lewis, *Life in Egypt,* 114–15, on the second century), it is scarcely possible that the author of the Elijah Apocalypse could have known this "fact" from Pliny.

100. Sa³ has room for another line of text before "in that time," but the condition of the manuscript gives no clue as to what words would have been there (cf. Pietersma, 58, 88).

101. Sa³ ends here, and the scribe has completed the page with line fillers (cf. Pietersma, 88).

102. ⲟⲩⲱⲧⲃ, the dominant verb in these laments, translated here so as to preserve the simile.

103. This command seems to be a non sequitur in the context. It should probably be read as the suddenly penitent Lawless One's attempt to rid the land of chaotic elements (other than himself), just as he tries to reestablish fertility in the following verse. Schrage reads the opposite sense, however (269 n. h; cf. 268 n. g): ⲥⲟⲟⲛⲉ does not mean "robbers" but *Herumstreichenden,* presumably the desert refugees of 4:24, and Schrage refers to *Pss. Sol.* 17:17-18, where desert refugees are harried by "lawless ones." Besides the improbable derivation of ⲥⲟⲟⲛⲉ from the verb ⲥⲓⲛⲉ ("pass through"), this interpretation would require the preceding command to "flee" (ⲡⲱⲧ) to be, rather, "run out" (with the intent of hunting down the remaining Righteous Ones). Finally, unless this command is meant to "flashback" to the end of ApocEl 4, it is unclear what Righteous Ones would be left on the earth after 5:6.

104. ⲁⲛⲉⲧⲟⲩⲁⲁⲃ ⲁⲛⲓⲥⲟⲩ ⲁϩⲣⲁⲓ. ⲉⲓⲛⲉ ⲉϩⲣⲁⲓ clearly means "bring up" (Crum, 80A). But in the Apocalypse of Elijah the saints are either in the desert (4:24-26), heaven (4:28-29), or in "the holy land" (5:5). The strange reference here to an underworld of

Sa   Ach

For because of them the earth gives
 fruit,
For because of them the sun shines
 upon the earth,
For because of them the dew falls
 upon the earth!

19. The sinners will weep, saying,
You have made us enemies of God.
If you have the power, rise and run
after them!

The Last Battle

20. Then he will take to his wings of
fire and fly after the saints. He will
do battle with them again.[105]

21. The angels will hear, come down,
and do battle with him, fighting with
many swords.

22. It will happen at that time that
the Lord will hear and give a command in great wrath: that the heaven
and the earth spew out fire, 23. and
the fire will overcome the earth (to a
depth of) seventy-two cubits. It will
consume the sinners and the devils
like straw.[106]   . . . . . stra]w

The Last Judgment

24. **There will be** a true judgment at 24. . . . **in** a true judgment. At that
that time. 25. The mountains and the time 25. the mountains and the earth
earth will let forth their voices. **At** will let forth their voices.
that time [. . .[107]

---

saints may derive from popular rather than received apocalyptic tradition, just as the
following, parallel descriptions of saints' functions draw on popular traditions.

105. "Again" (ON) must refer to the Lawless One's battle with the sixty Righteous
Ones, 4:30-33.

106. Notice the repeat of the simile in 1:4, here reversed: rather than the devil
consuming men like fire in straw, the fire consumes devils like straw.

107. Sa[1] ends here.

Sa	*Ach*
	The roadways[108] will say to each other, Have you heard today the voice of a man who walks who does not go before the judgment of the Son of God?[109]
	26. The sins of each one will stand against him in the place where they were committed, whether of the day or of the night.[110]
	27. The Righteous Ones and the [. . . .] will see the sinners in punishment, along with those who persecuted them and those who delivered them over to die. 28. Then the sinners [. . . . . . .] will see the place of the Righteous Ones; 29. and thus there will be grace.[111]

108. ⲛ2ⲟⲟⲩ = ⲛ2ⲓⲟⲟⲩⲉ (cf. Wintermute, 752 n. w2).

109. The awkward use of circumlocutions in this question has the ring of a wisdom-saying, such as those popular in both Egyptian scribal traditions and monastic literature (as well as the Bible itself). It might be paraphrased: "Can you conceive of a single human who won't find him- or herself being judged in the afterlife?" Wisdom sayings on the inevitability of judgment after death were popular in Egypt: cf. *Merikare* ll. 50-57, where life is similarly symbolized as "striding"; and Abba Orsisius's simple admonition that, however pure a monk is, "even so we shall scarcely escape the judgment of God" (*Apophthegmata Patrum:* alphabetical: Orsisius 1; tr. Benedicta Ward, in *The Desert Christian: The Sayings of the Desert Fathers* [New York: Macmillan, 1980], 161).

110. Cf. the judgment scene in the Coptic *Apocalypse of Paul:* "O Lord God Almighty, I am the angel of this soul, and I brought unto thee its deeds, both those belonging to the day and those belonging to the night; judge it according to its judgment." The image is subsequently explained to Paul: "When [souls] appear before the throne of God, the sins of each man, as well as his good deeds, become manifest" (fols. 25ʳ, 26ʳ; in E. A. Wallis Budge, tr., *Miscellaneous Coptic Texts in the Dialect of Upper Egypt* [London: British Museum, 1915], 1045, 1046; [text] 558, 559). In general, see Budge, *Miscellaneous Coptic Texts,* clxii–lxiii; R. P. Casey, "The Apocalypse of Paul," *JTS* 34 (1933):10–14. A similar image may be alluded to in *Wisdom of Solomon:* "Their lawless deeds will convict them to their face" (4:20).

111. The image of the condemned and righteous in view of each other was a widespread theme in Greco-Roman Jewish literature, epitomized in the tale of Lazarus (Lk 16:23-26), which bears important parallels to the ancient Egyptian story of Setne-Khamwas and Si-Osire (see Lichtheim, 3:25–26, 38–42; Martha Himmelfarb, *Tours of Hell: An Apocalyptic Form in Jewish and Christian Literature* [Philadelphia: University of Pennsylvania Press, 1983], 79–81; Richard Bauckham, "The Rich Man and Lazarus: The Parable and the Parallels," *NTS* 37 [1991]:225–46). The vividly "gloating" force of this image suggests its literary function must be continuous between the Elijah Apocalypse

[Sa]

Ach

In that time what the Righteous request will be given to them many times over.[112]

30. In that time the Lord will judge heaven and earth:
he will judge the transgressors in heaven,

Grk

. . . the shepherds of the people:

and those who acted thus on earth.
31. He will judge the shepherds of the people:

he will ask them about the flock of sheep;
and they will be handed over[113] without deceit.

he will ask them about the flock of sheep;
and they will be given to him without **deadly** deceit.

Eschaton and Millennium

32. After these things Elijah and Enoch will come down. They will put aside the flesh of the world and put on the "flesh" of the spirit

32. After this Elijah and Enoch (will) come down. They (will) lay aside the flesh of this world (and) put on the "flesh" of the spirit.

They will pursue the Lawless One.
. . .

They (will) pursue the Lawless One.
They (will) kill him without his being able to utter a word.

33. In that time he will dissolve in their presence as ice dissolves in fire. He will perish like a serpent with no breath in it.[114]

---

and its parallels in Jewish sectarian texts (*Jub* 23:30; 1 [Parables] *En* 62:11; 1 [Epistle of] *En* 108:14-15), to experience vicariously the reversal of a present situation in which opponents (or persecutors) are empowered to the (perceived) detriment of the author and audience.

112. By its position, ⲛ̄ϩⲁϩ ⲛ̄ⲥⲁⲡ should modify "request" (ⲣ̄ ⲁⲓⲧⲉⲓ), as translators have customarily taken it; but sense is restored by reading it with "it will be given to them [ⲥⲉⲛⲁⲧⲉⲉϥ]."

113. παραδοθήσονται: Pietersma's suggested reconstruction of part of missing line (92).

114. The content and use of these two similes is strongly evocative of the similes in Egyptian, Greco-Egyptian, and Coptic curses and binding spells, suggesting a more-than-narrative function to this passage. See chap. 4, pp. 133–39.

Sa   *Ach*

34. They will say to him, Your time
has passed by! Now indeed you will
perish with those who believe in
you!

35. They will be thrown into the
bottom of the pit and it will be closed
over them.

36. In that time the Christ (will)
descend from heaven—the king
with all his saints. 37. He (will) burn
this earth. He (will) spend one thousand years on it, 38. because the
sinners ruled it (before). He will
make a new heaven and a new earth.
There will be no devil . . .[115] in them.
39. He will rule with the saints, (and
they will be) ascending and descending, along with the angels, with
the Christ for a thousand years.

The Apocalypse
of Elijah

---

115. . . . ⲱⲩ. Rosenstiehl (116 n.) suggests ⲙⲟⲩ ("death"): thus "neither devil nor
death," which Wintermute has corrected to "deadly devil" on syntactical grounds (753 n.
r3). Schrage and Kuhn have dismissed the reconstruction entirely (cf. Schrage, 274 n. 1).

Bibliography

THE APOCALYPSE OF ELIJAH

Texts

Bouriant, Urbain. "Les papyrus d'Akhmim (Fragments de manuscrits en dialectes bachmourique et thébain)." *Mémoires publiés par les membres de la mission archéologique française au Caire.* Vol. 1, Fasc. 2 (1885):243–304.

Budge, E. A. Wallis, ed. *Coptic Biblical Texts in the Dialect of Upper Egypt.* Translated by E. A. Wallis Budge. London: British Museum, 1912. Reprint. New York: AMS, 1977.

Pietersma, Albert, Comstock, Susan Turner, and Attridge, Harold A. *The Apocalypse of Elijah.* SBLTT 19. Missoula, Mont.: Scholars Press, 1981.

Schmidt, Carl. "Der Kolophon des Ms. orient. 7594 des Britischen Museums." *Sitzungsberichte der preussischen Akademie der Wissenschaften, Philosophisch-Historisch Klasse* (1925):312–21.

Steindorff, Georg. *Die Apokalypse des Elias, eine unbekannte Apokalypse, und Bruchstücke der Sophonias-Apokalypse.* Leipzig: J. C. Hinrichs'sche, 1899.

Translations and Commentaries

Houghton, Herbert Pierrepont. "The Coptic Apocalypse." *Aegyptus* 39 (1959):40–91, 179–210.

Kuhn, K. H. "The Apocalypse of Elijah." In *AOT* 753–73.

Rosenstiehl, Jean-Marc. *L'Apocalypse d'Élie: Introduction, traduction, et notes.* Textes et Études 1. Paris: Paul Guethner, 1972.

Schrage, Wolfgang. "Die Elia-Apokalypse." In *Apokalypsen,* ed. Werner Georg Kümmel et al. Jüdische Schriften aus hellenistisch-römischer Zeit 5. Gütersloh: Gerd Mohn, 1980, 195–288.

Wintermute, O. S. "Apocalypse of Elijah." In *OTP* 1:721–53.

Studies

Aranda, Gonzalo. "Ideas escatológicas judías en el Apocalipsis copto de Elías." In *Simposio biblico español,* ed. N. Fernandez Marcos et al. Madrid: Universidad Complutense, 1984, 663–79.

Bauckham, Richard. "Enoch and Elijah in the Coptic Apocalypse of Elijah." *Studia patristica* 16, 2 (1985):69–76.

Beaux, Nathalie. "Pour une paléographie du papyrus Chester Beatty 2018." In *Études coptes 3*, Cahiers de la bibliothèque copte 4. Louvain: Peeters, 1988, 46–49.

Bousset, Wilhelm. "Beiträge zur Geschichte der Eschatologie: Die Apokalypse des Elias." *ZKG* 20 (1899):103–12.

Frankfurter, David T. M. "Tabitha in the Apocalypse of Elijah." *JTS* 41 (1990):13–25.

Kuhn, K. H. Review of *The Apocalypse of Elijah based on P.Chester Beatty 2018*, by Albert Pietersma et al. *Journal of Semitic Studies* 27 (1982):313–16.

Lacau, Pierre. "Remarques sur le manuscrit akhmimique des apocalypses de Sophonie et d'Élie." *JA* 254 (1966):170-95.

McNeil, Brian. "Coptic Evidence of Jewish Messianic Beliefs." *RSO* 51 (1977):39–45.

Maspero, Gaston. Review of *Die Apokalypse des Elias*, by Georg Steindorff. *Journal des savants* (1899):31–43.

Rosenstiehl, Jean-Marc. "L'Apocalypse d'Élie." *Le Muséon* 95 (1982):269–83.

von Lemm, Oscar. "Kleine koptische Studien—X: Bemerkungen zu einigen Stellen der koptischen Apokalypsen, 4–6." *Bulletin de l'Académie impériale des Sciences de St. Pétersbourg* 13 (1900):11–28.

———. "Kleine koptische Studien—XXVI: Bemerkungen zu einigen Stellen der koptischen Apokalypsen, 13–18." *Bulletin de l'Académie impériale des Sciences de St. Pétersbourg* 21 (1904):227–32.

Associated Texts and Translations

Alexander, Paul J. *The Oracle of Baalbek: The Tiburtine Sibyl in Greek Dress.* Dumbarton Oaks Studies 10. Washington, D.C.: Dumbarton Oaks, 1967.

Amélineau, E. *Monuments pour servir à l'histoire de l'Égypte chrétienne aux IVᵉ et Vᵉ siècles.* Mémoires publiés par les membres de la mission archéologique française au Caire 4. Paris: Ernest Leroux, 1888.

Apophthegmata patrum (Alphabetical). Edited by J.-P. Migne. *PG* 65:71–440.

Apophthegmata patrum (Alphabetical). Translated by Benedicta Ward. In idem, *The Desert Christian: The Sayings of the Desert Fathers.* New York: Macmillan, 1980.

Apophthegmata patrum (Anonymous). Edited by F. Nau. "Histoires des solitaires égyptiens." *Revue de l'orient chrétien* 13 (1908):47–66, 266–97; 14 (1905):357–79; 17 (1912):204–11, 294–301; 18 (1913):137–46.

Apophthegmata patrum (Anonymous). Translated by Benedicta Ward. In idem, *The Wisdom of the Desert Fathers.* Fairacres, Oxford: SLG Press, 1975.

Athanasius. *Letters.* Edited and translated by L.-Th. LeFort. *S. Athanase: Lettres festales et pastorales en copte.* 2 vols. CSCO 150–51, Scriptores Coptici 19–20. Louvain: Imprimerie orientaliste, 1955.

———. *Vita Antonii* (Grk.). Translated by Robert T. Meyer. *St. Athanasius: The Life of Saint Antony.* Ancient Christian Writers 10. Westminster, Md.: Newman Press, 1950.

————. *Vita Antonii* (Syr.). Edited and translated by René Draguet. *La vie primitive de S. Antoine.* CSCO 418, S. Syri 184. Louvain: Secrétariat du CSCO, 1980.

Besa. *Life of Shenoute.* Translated by David N. Bell. *The Life of Shenoute by Besa.* Cistercian Studies Series 73. Kalamazoo, Mich.: Cistercian Press, 1983.

Betz, Hans Dieter, ed. *The Greek Magical Papyri in Translation.* Chicago: University of Chicago Press, 1986.

Borghouts, J. F., tr. *Ancient Egyptian Magical Texts.* Nisaba 9. Leiden: Brill, 1978.

Budge, E. A. Wallis. "On the Fragments of a Coptic Version of an Encomium on Elijah the Tishbite, Attributed to Saint John Chrysostom." *Transactions of the Society of Biblical Archaeology* 9 (1893):355–404.

Buttenweiser, Moses. *Die hebräische Elias-Apokalypse.* Leipzig: Eduard Pfeiffer, 1897.

Chaeremon. Collected and translated by Pieter Willem Van Der Horst. *Chaeremon: Egyptian Priest and Stoic Philosopher.* EPRO 101. Leiden: Brill, 1984.

Charlesworth, James H., ed. *The Old Testament Pseudepigrapha.* 2 vols. Garden City, N.Y.: Doubleday, 1983–85.

Commodian. *Carmen apologeticum.* Edited and translated by Antonio Salvatore. *Commodiano: Carme apologetico.* Torino: Societa Editrice Internazionale, 1977.

Crum, W. E., and Evelyn White, H. G. *The Monastery of Epiphanius at Thebes.* 2 vols. New York: Metropolitan Museum of Art, 1926.

Cyprian of Carthage. *Letters.* Edited and translated by Le Chanoine Bayard. *Saint Cyprien: Correspondance.* 2 vols. Paris: Société d'Édition "Les Belles Lettres," 1925.

Didymus the Blind. *Commentary on Ecclesiastes.* Edited and translated by Johannes Kramer and Bärbel Krebber. *Didymos der Blinde: Kommentar zum Ecclesiastes (Tura-Papyrus).* Vol. 4: *Kommentar zu Eccl. Kap.7–8, 8.* PTA 16. Bonn: Rudolf Habelt, 1972.

Dio Cassius. *Historia.* 9 vols. Edited by Herbert Baldwin Foster. Translated by E. Cary. LCL. Cambridge: Harvard University Press, 1915–27.

Dionysius of Alexandria. *Letters.* Edited by Charles Lett Feltoe. *The Letters and Other Remains of Dionysius of Alexandria.* Cambridge: Cambridge University Press, 1904.

Dioscorus of Alexandria (attrib.). *Panegyric on Macarius of Tkôw.* Edited and translated by D. W. Johnson. *A Panegyric on Macarius, Bishop of Tkôw, Attributed to Dioscorus of Alexandria.* 2 vols. CSCO 415–16, Scriptores Coptici 41–42. Louvain: Sécrétariat du CSCO, 1980.

Eben-Shmuel, Yehudah, ed. *Midrᵉshei Gᵉulah.* Jerusalem: Mosad Bialik, 1954.

Epiphanius of Salamis. *Panarion.* Translated by Frank Williams. *The Panarion of Epiphanius of Salamis, Book I (Sects 1–46).* NHS 35. Edited by James M. Robinson. Leiden: Brill, 1987.

Eusebius of Caesarea. *Historia ecclesiastica.* Edited and translated by Kirsopp Lake. *Eusebius: The Ecclesiastical History.* Vol. 1. LCL. Cambridge: Harvard University Press, 1926.

————. *Historia ecclesiastica.* Edited and translated by J.E.L. Oulton and H. J.

Lawlor. *Eusebius: The Ecclesiastical History.* Vol. 2. LCL. London: William Heinemann, 1932.

———. *Martyrs of Palestine* (Grk.). Edited and translated by Gustav Bardy. *Eusèbe de Césarée: Histoire ecclésiastique, livres VIII–X et les martyrs en Palestine.* SC 55. Paris: Éditions du Cerf, 1958.

———. *Martyrs of Palestine* (Syr.). Edited and translated by William Cureton. *History of the Martyrs in Palestine by Eusebius of Caesarea.* London: Williams & Norgate. 1861.

———. *Historia Ecclesiastica.* Translated by G. A. Williamson. *Eusebius: The History of the Church.* Harmondsworth: Penguin Books, 1965.

Evelyn White, Hugh G., ed. *The Monasteries of Wadi 'N Natrûn.* Vol. 1: *New Coptic Texts from the Monastery of Saint Macarius.* New York: Metropolitan Museum of Art, 1926.

Faulkner, R. O. "The Bremner-Rhind Papyrus, III–IV: D. The Book of Overthrowing 'Apep." *JEA* 23 (1937):166–75; 24 (1938):41–53.

———. *The Ancient Egyptian Book of the Dead.* 2d ed. Translated by Carol Andrews. London: British Museum, 1985.

Geffcken, Johannes, ed. *Die Oracula Sibyllina.* Leipzig: J. C. Hinrichs'sche, 1902.

Heichelheim, F. M. "The Text of the *Constitutio Antoniniana* and the Three Other Decrees of the Emperor Caracalla Contained in Papyrus Gissensis 40." *JEA* 26 (1940):10–21.

Hennecke, Edgar. *New Testament Apocrypha.* 2 vols. Edited by Wilhelm Schneemelcher. English translation edited by R. McL. Wilson. Philadelphia: Westminster Press, 1963–65.

Herbert, Máire, and McNamara, Martin, eds. *Irish Biblical Apocrypha: Selected Texts in Translation.* Edinburgh: T. & T. Clark, 1989.

Hippolytus of Rome. *De antichristo.* Edited and translated by Enrico Norelli. *Ippolito: L'Anticristo.* Nardini Editore, 1987.

Historia Monachorum in Aegypto. Edited and translated by André-Jean Festugière. Subsidia Hagiographica 53. Brussels: Société des Bollandistes, 1971.

———. Translated by Norman Russell. *The Lives of the Desert Fathers.* Introduction by Benedicta Ward. London and Oxford: Mowbray, 1980.

Hughes, George R. "A Demotic Astrological Text." *JNES* 10 (1951):256–64.

James, Montague Rhodes. *The Testament of Abraham.* Texts and Studies 2, 2. Cambridge: Cambridge University Press, 1892.

———. *Apocrypha Anecdota.* Texts and Studies 2, 3. Cambridge: Cambridge University Press, 1893.

———. *The Apocryphal New Testament.* Oxford: Clarendon Press, 1924.

Jansen, H. Ludin. *The Coptic Story of Cambyses' Invasion of Egypt.* Avhandlinger utgitt av det Norske Videnskaps-Akademi i Oslo 2. Hist.-Filos. Klasse 1950, 2. Oslo: Jakob Dybwad, 1950.

John, Bishop of Nikiu. *Chronicle.* Translated by Robert Henry Charles. *The Chronicle of John.* Text and Translation Society 3. London, 1916. Reprint. Amsterdam: APA Philo Press, 1981.

Jouguet, Pierre. *Papyrus de Théadelphie.* Paris: Fontemoing, 1911.

Knipfing, John R. "The Libelli of the Decian Persecution." *HTR* 16 (1923):345–90.

Koenen, Ludwig. "Die Prophezeiungen des 'Töpfers.'" *ZPE* 2 (1968):178–209.

_____. "Bemerkungen zum Text des Töpferorakels und zu dem Akazien-symbol." *ZPE* 13 (1974):313–19.

Kropp, Angelicus M. *Ausgewählte koptische Zaubertexte*. 3 vols. Brussels: Fondation reine Élisabeth, 1931.

Lactantius. *Divinae institutae*. Translated by Mary Francis McDonald. *Lactantius: Divine Institutes*. The Fathers of the Church 49. Washington, D.C.: Catholic University Press, 1964.

Lewis, Naphtali. *The Interpretation of Dreams and Portents*. Toronto and Sarasota, Fla.: Samuel Stevens, 1976.

Lexa, François. *La magie dans l'Égypte antique*. 2 vols. Paris: Paul Geuthner, 1925.

Lichtheim, Miriam. *Ancient Egyptian Literature*. 3 vols. Berkeley: University of California Press, 1973–80.

Mahé, Jean-Pierre. *Hermès en Haute-Égypte*. 2 vols. Bibliothèque copte de Nag Hammadi 3 and 7. Quebec: Presses de l'Université Laval, 1978–82.

Manetho. Translated by W. G. Waddell. *Manetho*. LCL. Cambridge and London: Harvard University Press, 1940.

Manteuffel, Georg V. "Zur Prophetie in *P.S.I., VIII.982.*" In *Mélanges Maspero*. Vol. 2. Mémoires publiés par les membres de l'Institut français d'archéologie orientale du Caire 67. Cairo: IFAO, 1934, 119–24.

Musurillo, Herbert A. *The Acts of the Pagan Martyrs*. Oxford: Clarendon, 1954.

Nau, F. "Révélations et légendes: Méthodius—Clément—Andronicus." *JA* 9 (1917):415–71.

Nock, Arthur Darby, and Festugière, André-Jean. *Corpus Hermeticum*. 2 vols. 2d ed. Paris: Société d'Édition "Les Belles Lettres," 1960.

Oulton, John Ernest Leonard, and Chadwick, Henry, trs. *Alexandrian Christianity*. Library of Christian Classics 2. London: SCM Press, 1954.

Palladius. *Historia Lausiaca*. Translated by Robert T. Meyer. *Palladius: The Lausiac History*. Ancient Christian Writers 34. Westminster, Md.: Newman Press, 1965.

Parker, Richard A. *A Vienna Demotic Papyrus on Eclipse- and Lunar-Omina*. Providence, R.I.: Brown University Press, 1959.

Pearson, Birger A. "The Pierpont Morgan Fragments of a Coptic Enoch Apocryphon." In *Studies on the Testament of Abraham*, ed. George W. E. Nickelsburg. Septuagint and Cognate Studies 6. Missoula, Mont.: Scholars Press, 1972, 227–84.

Philo of Alexandria. *De vita Mosis*. Edited and translated by Roger Arnaldez, Claude Mondésert, Jean Pouilloux, and Pierre Savinel. *De vita Mosis I–II*. Les oeuvres de Philon d'Alexandrie 22. Paris: Éditions du Cerf, 1967.

Plutarch. *De Iside et Osiride*. Edited and translated by John Gwyn Griffiths. *Plutarch: De Iside et Osiride*. Cardiff: University of Wales Press, 1970.

Polotsky, Hans Jakob, ed. *Manichäische Homilien*. Manichäische Handschriften der Sammlung A. Chester Beatty 1. Stuttgart: Kohlhammer, 1954.

Pseudo-Callisthenes. *Alexander Romance*. Edited by William Kroll. *Historia Alexandri Magni*. Vol. 1. Berlin: Wiedmann, 1926.

_____. *Alexander Romance*. Translated by Ken Dowden. "Pseudo-Callisthenes:

The Alexander Romance." In *Collected Ancient Greek Novels*, ed. B. P. Reardon. Berkeley: University of California Press, 1989, 650–735.

Rea, John. "Predictions by Astrology [P.Oxy 2554]." *Oxyrhynchus Papyri* 31 (1966):77–83.

Reitzenstein, R., and Schaeder, H. H. "Das Töpferorakel." In idem, *Studien zum antiken Synkretismus aus Iran und Griechenland*. Leipzig: Teubner, 1926, 38–51.

Roberts, C. H. "The Oracle of the Potter [P.Oxy 2332]." *Oxyrhynchus Papyri* 22 (1954):89–99.

Robinson, James M., ed. *The Nag Hammadi Library*. 3d ed. San Francisco: Harper & Row, 1988.

Robinson, Stephen Edward. *The Testament of Adam*. SBLDS 52. Chico, Calif.: Scholars Press, 1982.

Sackur, Ernst. *Sibyllinische Texte und Forschungen*. Halle: Max Niemeyer, 1898.

Scott, Walter. *Hermetica*. 4 vols. Oxford, 1924–36. Reprint. Boston: Shambhala, 1985.

Shelton, John C. "An Astrological Prediction of Disturbances in Egypt." *Ancient Society* 7 (1976):209–13.

Simpson, William Kelly, ed. *The Literature of Ancient Egypt*. 2d ed. New Haven and London: Yale University Press, 1973.

Skeat, T. C., and Wegener, E. P. "A Trial before the Prefect of Egypt Appius Sabinus, c. 250 A.D. (P.Lond. Inv. 2565)." *JEA* 21 (1935):224–47 and pl. 28.

Sobhy, George P. G., ed. and tr. *Le martyre de saint Hélias et l'encomium de l'évêque Stéphanos de Hnès sur saint Hélias*. Bibliothèque d'études coptes 1. Cairo: IFAO, 1919.

Sparks, H.F.D., ed. *The Apocryphal Old Testament*. Oxford: Clarendon Press, 1984.

Stone, Michael E., and Strugnell, John. *The Books of Elijah, Parts 1–2*. SBLTT 18. Missoula, Mont.: Scholars Press, 1979.

Tait, W. J. *Papyri from Tebtunis in Egyptian and in Greek (P.Tebt. Tait)*. London: Egypt Exploration Society, 1977.

Tcherikover, Victor A, Fuks, Alexander, and Stern, Menahem. *Corpus papyrorum Judaicarum*. 3 vols. Cambridge: Harvard University Press, 1957–64.

Veilleux, Armand, ed. and tr. *Pachomian Koinonia*. 3 vols. Cistercian Studies Series 45–47. Kalamazoo, Mich.: Cistercian Press, 1980–82.

Vermes, Geza, tr. *The Dead Sea Scrolls in English*. 2d ed. Harmondsworth: Penguin, 1975.

Waddell, Helen, tr. *The Desert Fathers*. London: Constable, 1936. Reprint. Ann Arbor: University of Michigan Press, 1966.

Wimbush, Vincent L., ed. *Ascetic Behavior in Greco–Roman Antiquity: A Sourcebook*. SAC 7. Minneapolis: Fortress Press, 1990.

Young, Dwight W. "A Monastic Invective against Egyptian Hieroglyphs." In *Studies Presented to Hans Jakob Polotsky*, ed. D. W. Young. Beacon Hill, Mass.: Pirtle and Polson, 1981, 348–60.

Zabkar, Louis V. *Hymns to Isis in Her Temple at Philae*. Hanover, N.H., and London: University Press of New England/Brandeis University Press, 1988.

Zauzich, Karl-Theodor. "Das Lamm des Bokchoris." In *Papyrus Erzherzog Rainer (P.Rainer Cent.)*. 2 vols. Vienna: Verlag Brüder Hollinek, 1983, 1:165–74.

Zosimus. *Historia nova*. Edited and translated by François Paschoud. *Zosime: Histoire nouvelle*. 3 vols. Paris: "Les Belles Lettres," 1971.

―――. *Historia nova*. Translated by Ronald T. Ridley. *Zosimus: New History*. Byzantina Australiensia 2. Melbourne: Australian Association for Byzantine Studies, 1982.

SECONDARY LITERATURE A:
HISTORICAL AND TEXTUAL WORKS

Acerbi, Antonio. *Serra lignea: Studi sulla fortuna della Ascensione di Isaia*. Rome: A.V.E., 1984.

Achtemeier, Paul J. *"Omne verbum sonat:* The New Testament and the Oral Environment of Late Western Antiquity." *JBL* 109 (1990):3–27.

Aland, Kurt. "The Problem of Anonymity and Pseudonymity in Christian Literature of the First Two Centuries." *JTS* 12 (1961):39–49.

Alexander, Paul J. "The Diffusion of Byzantine Apocalypses in the Medieval West and the Beginnings of Joachimism." In *Prophecy and Millenarianism: Essays in Honour of Marjorie Reeves*, ed. Ann Williams. Essex: Longman, 1980, 55–106.

―――*The Byzantine Apocalyptic Tradition*. Edited by Dorothy deF. Abrahamse. Berkeley: University of California Press, 1985.

Alföldy, Géza. "The Crisis of the Third Century as Seen by Contemporaries." *GRBS* 15 (1974):89–111.

Alliot, Maurice. "La Thébaïde en lutte contres les rois d'Alexandrie sous Philopator et Épiphane (216–184)." *Revue belge de philologie et d'histoire* 29 (1951):421–43.

―――. "La fin de la résistance égyptienne dans le sud sous Épiphane." *REA* 54 (1952):18–26.

Amélineau, E. "Le christianisme chez les anciens coptes." *RHR* 14 (1886):308–45; 15 (1887):52–87.

―――. "The Rôle of the Demon in the Ancient Coptic Religion." *The New World* 2 (1893):518–35.

Arbesmann, Rudolph. "Fasting and Prophecy in Pagan and Christian Antiquity." *Traditio* 7 (1949-51):1–71.

―――. "Fasten." In *Reallexikon für Antike und Christentum*. Ed. Theodor Klauser. Stuttgart: Anton Hiersemann, 1969, 7:447–93.

Assman, Jan. "Königsdogma und Heilserwartung: Politische und kultische Chaosbeschreibung in ägyptischen Texten." In *Apocalypticism in the Mediterranean World and the Near East*, 345–77. See Hellholm, David, ed.

Aune, David E. *Prophecy in Early Christianity and the Ancient Mediterranean World*. Grand Rapids: William B. Eerdmans, 1983.

―――. "The Apocalypse of John and the Problem of Genre." *Semeia* 36 (1986):65–96.

Bagnall, Roger S. "Religious Conversion and Onomastic Change in Early Byzantine Egypt." *BASP* 19 (1982):105–23.

―――. "Conversion and Onomastics: A Reply." *ZPE* 69 (1987):243–50.

————. "Combat ou vide: christianisme et paganisme dans l'Égypte romaine tardive." *Ktema* 13 (1988):285–96.

————. "Greeks and Egyptians: Ethnicity, Status, and Culture." In *Cleopatra's Egypt: Age of the Ptolemies*. Brooklyn, N.Y.: The Brooklyn Museum, 1988, 21–28.

Baines, John, "Society, Morality, and Religious Practice." In *Religion in Ancient Egypt*, 123–200. See Shafer, Byron E., ed.

Baines, John, and Eyre, C. J. "Four Notes on Literacy." *Göttinger Miszellen* 61 (1983):65–96.

Balogh, Josef. "'Voces Paginarum': Beiträge zur Geschichte des lauten Lesens und Schreibens." *Philologus* 82 (1926):84–109, 202–40.

Barb, A. A. "Mystery, Myth, and Magic." In *The Legacy of Egypt*, 138–69. See Harris, J. R., ed.

Bardy, Gustav. "Les premiers temps du christianisme de langue copte en Égypte." In *Mémorial LaGrange*. Paris: J. Gabalda, 1940, 203–16.

————. "Le souvenir d'Élie chez les pères grecs." In *Élie le prophète*, vol. 1: *Selon les écritures et les traditions chrétiennes*. Bruges: Les études carmélitaines, 1956, 131–58.

Barnard, L. W. "Judaism in Egypt, A.D. 70–135." In idem, *Studies in the Apostolic Fathers and Their Background*. Oxford: Basil Blackwell, 1966, 41–55.

Barnes, T. D. "Angel of Light or Mystic Initiate? The Problem of the *Life of Antony*." *JTS* 37 (1986):353–68.

————. "Trajan and the Jews." *JJS* 40 (1989):145–62.

Barns, John Wintour Baldwin. "Egypt and the Greek Romance." *Mitteilungen aus der Papyrussammlung der österreichischen Nationalbibliothek* 5 (1956):29–36.

Barr, David L. "The Apocalypse of John as Oral Enactment." *Interpretation* 40 (1986):243–56.

Barr, James. "Jewish Apocalyptic in Recent Scholarly Study." *BJRL* 58 (1975):9–35.

Bauckham, Richard. "The Martyrdom of Enoch and Elijah: Jewish or Christian?" *JBL* 95, 3 (1976):447–58.

————"The Apocalypses in the New Pseudepigrapha." *JSNT* 26 (1986):97–117.

————. "Early Jewish Visions of Hell." *JTS* 41 (1990):355–85.

Bauer, Walter. *Orthodoxy and Heresy in Earliest Christianity*. 2d ed. Translated by Philadelphia Seminar on Christian Origins. Edited by Robert A. Kraft and Gerhard Krodel. Philadelphia: Fortress Press, 1971.

Baumeister, Theofried. *Martyr Invictus*. Forschungen zur Volkskunde 46. Münster: Regensberg, 1972.

Baynes, Norman H. "St. Antony and the Demons." *JEA* 40 (1954):7–10.

Bell, H. Idris. "The Byzantine Servile State in Egypt." *JEA* 4 (1917):86–106.

————. *Jews and Christians in Egypt*. London: British Museum, 1924. Reprint. Westport, Conn.: Greenwood Press, 1972.

————. "The Economic Crisis in Egypt under Nero." *JRS* 28 (1938):1–8.

————. "Roman Egypt from Augustus to Diocletian." *Chronique d'Égypte* 13 (1938):347–63.

————. "Anti-Semitism in Alexandria." *JRS* 31 (1941):1–18.

————. "Evidences of Christianity in Egypt during the Roman Period." *HTR* 37 (1944):185–208.

————. "Popular Religion in Graeco-Roman Egypt, 1: The Pagan Period." *JEA* 34 (1948):82–97.

————. *Cults and Creeds in Graeco-Roman Egypt.* Liverpool: Liverpool University Press, 1953. Reprint. Chicago: Ares, 1975.

Benoît, P., and Schwartz, J. "Caracalla et les troubles d'Alexandrie en 215 après J.-C." *Études de papyrologie* 7 (1948):17–33.

Bentzen, A. "The Ritual Background of Amos I, 2–II, 16." *Oudtestamentische Studien* 8 (1950):85–99.

Bergman, Jan. *Ich bin Isis: Studien zum memphitischen Hintergrund der griechischen Isisaretalogien.* Acta Universitatis Upsaliensis, Historia Religionum 3. Uppsala: Uppsala University Press, 1968.

————. "Introductory Remarks on Apocalypticism in Egypt." In *Apocalypticism in the Mediterranean World and the Near East,* 551–60. See Hellholm, David, ed.

Bernardin, J. B. "A Coptic Sermon Attributed to St. Athanasius." *JTS* (1937):113–29.

Betz, Hans Dieter. "The Formation of Authoritative Tradition in the Greek Magical Papyri." In *Jewish and Christian Self-Definition.* Vol. 3: *Self-Definition in the Greco-Roman World,* ed. Ben F. Meyer and E. P. Sanders. Philadelphia: Fortress Press, 1982, 161–70, 236–38.

Bevan, Edwyn R. *The House of Ptolemy.* Chicago: Ares, 1985. Previously published as *A History of Egypt under the Ptolemaic Dynasty.* London, 1927.

Bingen, Jean. "L'Égypte greco-romaine et la problematique des interactions culturelles." In *Proceedings of the Sixteenth International Congress of Papyrology,* edited by Roger S. Bagnall, Gerald M. Browne, Ann E. Hanson, and Ludwig Koenen. American Studies in Papyrology 23. Chico, Calif.: Scholars Press, 1981, 3–18.

Birley, A. R. "The Third Century Crisis in the Roman Empire." *BJRL* 58 (1975–76):253–81.

Black, M. "The 'Two Witnesses' of Rev. 11.3f. in Jewish and Christian Apocalyptic Tradition." In *Donum Gentilicium: New Testament Studies in Honour of David Daube,* ed. E. Bammel, C. K. Barrett, and W. D. Davies. Oxford: Clarendon Press, 1978, 227–37.

de Blois, L. "Odaenathus and the Roman-Persian War of 252–264 A.D." *Talanta* 6 (1975):7–23.

Boak, Arthur E. R., and Youtie, Herbert C. "Flight and Oppression in Fourth-Century Egypt." In *Studi in Onore di Aristide Calderini E Roberto Paribeni.* 2 vols. Milan: Ceschina, 1957, 2:325–37.

Bodinger, Martin. "Le mythe de Néron de l'Apocalypse de Saint Jean au Talmud de Babylone." *RHR* 206 (1989):21–40.

Borghouts, J. F. "The Ram as a Protector and Prophesier." *REg* 32 (1980):33–46.

Borkowski, Zbigniew. "Local Cults and Resistance to Christianity." *JJP* 20 (1990):25–30.

Botte, D. B. "Une fête du prophète Élie en Gaule au VIᵉ siècle," *Cahiers sioniens* 3 (1950):170–77.

Bousset, Wilhelm. *The Antichrist Legend*. Translated by A. H. Keane. London: Hutchinson, 1896.

———. "Antichrist." In *ERE* 1:578–81.

Bowersock, Glen W. "The Miracle of Memnon." *BASP* 21 (1984):21–32.

———. "The Mechanics of Subversion in the Roman Provinces." In *Opposition et résistances à l'empire d'Auguste à Trajan*. Entretiens sur l'antiquité classique 33. Geneva: Vandoeuvres, 1986, 291–317; discussion, 318–20.

———. *Hellenism in Late Antiquity*. Ann Arbor: University of Michigan Press, 1990.

Bowman, Alan K. "The Military Occupation of Upper Egypt in the Reign of Diocletian." *BASP* 15 (1978):25–38.

———. "Two Notes: I. The Revolt of Busiris and Coptos." *BASP* 21 (1984):33–36.

———. *Egypt after the Pharaohs*. Berkeley: University of California Press, 1986.

Braun, Martin. *History and Romance in Graeco-Oriental Literature*. Oxford: Basil Blackwell, 1938.

Brennan, Brian. "Athanasius' Vita Antonii: A Sociological Interpretation." *VC* 39 (1985):209–27.

Brockington, L. H. "The Problem of Pseudonymity." *JTS* 4 (1953):15–22.

Brown, Peter. "Approaches to the Religious Crisis of the Third Century A.D." *English Historical Review* 83 (1968):542–58.

———. "Sorcery, Demons, and the Rise of Christianity from Late Antiquity into the Middle Ages." In *Witchcraft Confessions and Accusations*, ed. Mary Douglas. London: Tavistock, 1970, 17–46.

———. *The World of Late Antiquity, A.D. 150–750*. London: Thames & Hudson, 1971. Reprint. New York: Harcourt Brace Jovanovich, 1978.

———. "The Diffusion of Manichaeism in the Roman Period." In idem, ed. *Religion and Society in the Age of Saint Augustine*. London: Faber & Faber, 1972, 94–118.

———. *The Making of Late Antiquity*. Cambridge: Harvard University Press, 1975.

———. *The Cult of the Saints: Its Rise and Function in Latin Christianity*. Chicago: University of Chicago Press, 1981.

Budge, E. A. Wallis. *Egyptian Magic*. Books on Egypt and Chaldea. Vol. 2. London: Kegan Paul, Trench, Trübner, 1901. Reprint. New York: Dover, 1971.

———. "Egyptian Mythology in Coptic Writings." In idem, *Coptic Apocrypha in the Dialect of Upper Egypt*. London: British Museum, 1913, lvi–lxxii.

Burmester, O. G. E. "Egyptian Mythology in the Coptic Apocrypha." *Orientalia* 7 (1938):355–67.

Buttenweiser, Moses. *Outline of the Neo-Hebraic Apocalyptic Literature*. Cincinnati: Jennings & Pye, 1901.

Cannuyer, Christian. "Variations sur le thème de la ville dans les maximes sapientiales de l'ancienne Égypte." *Chronique d'Égypte* 64 (1989):44–54.

Casey, R. P. "The Apocalypse of Paul." *JTS* 34 (1933):1–32.

Černý, J. "Language and Writing." In *The Legacy of Egypt*, 197–219. See Harris, J. R., ed.

Charles, R. H. *A Critical and Exegetical Commentary on the Revelation of St. John.* 2 vols. Edinburgh: T. & T. Clark, 1920.

Charlesworth, James H. "Christian and Jewish Self-Definition in Light of the Christian Additions to the Apocryphal Writings." In *Jewish and Christian Self-Definition.* Vol. 2: *Aspects of Judaism in the Greco-Roman Period,* ed. E. P. Sanders, with A. I. Baumgarten and Alan Mendelson. Philadelphia: Fortress, 1981, 27–55, 310–15.

———. *The Pseudepigrapha and Modern Research, with a Supplement.* Septuagint and Cognate Studies 7. Chico, Calif.: Scholars Press, 1981.

———. *The New Testament Apocrypha and Pseudepigrapha: A Guide to Publications, with Excurses on Apocalypses.* ATLA Bibliography Series 17. Metuchen, N.J., and London: ATLA/Scarecrow, 1987.

Cleopatra's Egypt: Age of the Ptolemies. Brooklyn, N.Y.: The Brooklyn Museum, 1988.

Collins, Adela Yarbro. "The Early Christian Apocalypses." *Semeia* 14 (1979):61–121.

———. "Revelation 18: Taunt Song or Dirge?" In *L'Apocalypse johannique et l'Apocalyptique dans le Nouveau Testament,* ed. J. Lambrecht. Bibliotheca Ephemeridum Theologicarum Lovaniensium 53. Louvain: Louvain University Press, 1980, 185–204.

———. "Numerical Symbolism in Jewish and Early Christian Apocalyptic Literature." In *ANRW* 2.21.2:1221–87.

———. "Introduction: Early Christian Apocalypticism." *Semeia* 36 (1986):1–11.

Collins, John J. *The Sibylline Oracles of Egyptian Judaism.* SBLDS 13. Missoula, Mont.: Scholars Press, 1974.

———. "The Court-Tales in Daniel and the Development of Apocalyptic." *JBL* 94 (1975):218–34.

———. "Jewish Apocalyptic against Its Hellenistic Near Eastern Environment." *BASOR* 220 (1975):27–36.

———. *The Apocalyptic Vision of the Book of Daniel.* HSM 16. Missoula, Mont.: Scholars Press, 1977.

———. "Pseudonymity, Historical Reviews, and the Genre of the Revelation of John." *CBQ* 39 (1977):329–43.

———. "Introduction: Towards the Morphology of a Genre." *Semeia* 14 (1979): 1–19.

———. "The Genre Apocalypse in Hellenistic Judaism." In *Apocalypticism in the Mediterranean World and the Near East,* 531–48. See Hellholm, David, ed.

———. *The Apocalyptic Imagination.* New York: Crossroad, 1984.

———. "Apocalyptic Literature." In *Early Judaism and Its Modern Interpreters,* ed. Robert A. Kraft and George W. E. Nickelsburg. Atlanta: Scholars Press, 1986, 345–70.

———. "The Development of the Sibylline Tradition." In *ANRW* 2.20.1:421–59.

Coptic Egypt. Papers read at a symposium held under the joint auspices of New York University and the Brooklyn Museum, February 15, 1941. Brooklyn, N.Y.: The Brooklyn Museum, 1944.

Crahay, Roland. "Le jeûne comme symbole charismatique." In *Eschatologie et cosmologie*. Annales du Centre d'étude des religions 3. Brussels: Université libre de Bruxelles, 1969.

Crawford, Dorothy J. "Ptolemy, Ptah, and Apis in Hellenistic Memphis." In *Studies on Ptolemaic Memphis*. Studia Hellenistica 24. Louvain: Studia Hellenistica, 1980, 1–42.

Crawford, Michael. "Finance, Coinage, and Money from the Severans to Constantine." In *ANRW* 2.2:560–93.

Crum, W. E. *A Coptic Dictionary*. Oxford: Clarendon Press, 1939.

Daumas, François. "Littérature prophétique et exégétique égyptienne et commentaires esséniens." In *A la rencontre de Dieu (Mémorial Albert Gelin)*. Bibliothèque de la faculté catholique de théologie de Lyon 8. Le Puy: Éditions Xavier Mappus, 1961, 203–21.

Davis, S. *Race Relations in Ancient Egypt: Greek, Egyptian, Hebrew, Roman*. New York: Philosophical Library, 1952.

Dehandschutter, B. "Les Apocalypses d'Élie." In *Élie le prophète: Bible, tradition, iconographie*, ed. Gerard F. Willems. Louvain: Peeters, 1988, 59–68.

De Jonge, Marinus. "The Testaments of the Twelve Patriarchs: Christian and Jewish." In idem, *Jewish Eschatology, Early Christian Christology, and the Testaments of the Twelve Patriarchs*. Leiden: Brill, 1991, 233–43.

Delehaye, Hippolyte. *Les martyrs d'Égypte*. AnBoll 40. Brussels: Société des bollandistes, 1922.

_____. *Les origines du culte des martyrs*. Subsidia Hagiographica 20. 2d ed. Brussels: Société des Bollandistes, 1933.

Denis, Albert-Marie. *Introduction aux pseudépigraphes grecs d'ancien testament*. SVTP 1. Leiden: Brill, 1970.

Derchain, Philippe. "Le rôle du roi d'Égypte dans le maintien de l'ordre cosmique." In *Le pouvoir et le sacré*. Annales du Centre d'étude des religions 1. Brussels: Université libre de Bruxelles, 1962, 61–73.

_____. *Le papyrus Salt 825 (B.M. 10051): Rituel pour la conservation de la vie en Égypte*, Mémoires de l'Académie royale de Belgique 58, 1a. Brussels: Palais des académies, 1965.

Der Nersessian, Sirarpie. "Some Aspects of Coptic Painting." In *Coptic Egypt*, 43–50. See *Coptic Egypt*.

de Ste. Croix, G.E.M. "Aspects of the 'Great' Persecution." *HTR* 47 (1954):75–113.

_____. "Why Were the Early Christians Persecuted?" In *Studies in Ancient Society*, ed. M. I. Finley. London and Boston: Routledge & Kegan Paul, 1974, 210–55.

Dodds, E. R. *Pagan and Christian in an Age of Anxiety*. Cambridge: Cambridge University Press, 1965. Reprint. New York: W. W. Norton, 1970.

Doresse, Jean. "Visions méditerranéennes." *La table ronde* 110 (1957):25–47.

_____. *Des hiéroglyphes à la croix: Ce que le passé pharaonique a légué au Christianisme*. Istanbul: Nederlands Historisch-Archaeologisch Instituut, 1960.

Dottin, G. "Les deux chagrins du royaume du ciel." *Revue celtique* 21 (1909):349–87.

Drioton, Étienne. "Le nationalisme au temps de pharaons." In idem, *Pages d'égyptologie*. Cairo: Éditions de la revue du Caire, 1957, 375–86.

Droge, Arthur J., and Tabor, James D. *A Noble Death: Suicide and Martyrdom among Jews and Christians in the Ancient World*. San Francisco: Harper Collins, 1991.

Dunand, Françoise. "L'Oracle du Potier et la formation de l'apocalyptique en Égypte." In *L'Apocalyptique*, ed. Marc Philonenko. Études d'histoire des religions 3. Paris: Paul Geuthner, 1977, 39–67.

_____. *Religion populaire en Égypte romaine*. EPRO 77. Leiden: Brill, 1979.

_____. "L'exode rural en Égypte à l'époque hellénistique." *Ktema* 5 (1980):137–50.

_____. "Grecs et égyptiens en Égypte lagide: Le problème de l'acculturation." In *Modes de contacts et processus de transformation dans les sociétés anciennes*. Collection de l'École française de Rome 67. Pisa and Rome: École française de Rome, 1983, 45–87.

_____. "Religion populaire et iconographie en Égypte hellénistique et romaine." *Visible Religion* 3 (1984):18–42.

Eddy, Samuel K. *The King Is Dead*. Lincoln: University of Nebraska Press. 1961.

Élie le prophète. Vol. 1: *Selon les écritures et les traditions chrétiennes*. Bruges: Les études carmélitaines, 1956.

Élie le prophète: Bible, tradition, iconographie. Edited by Gerard F. Willems. Louvain: Peeters, 1988.

Evans, Elizabeth Cornelia. "Roman Descriptions of Personal Appearance in History and Biography." *HSCP* 46 (1935):43–84.

_____. "The Study of Physiognomy in the Second Century A.D." *TPAPA* 72 (1941):96–108.

Fallon, Francis T. "The Gnostic Apocalypses." *Semeia* 14 (1979):123–58.

Faraone, Christopher A. "Binding and Burying the Forces of Evil: The Defensive Use of 'Voodoo Dolls' in Ancient Greece." *Classical Antiquity* 10 (1991):165–205

_____. "Molten Wax, Spilt Wine and Mutilated Animals: Sympathetic Curses in Near Eastern and Early Greek Oaths." *JHS* 113 (1993), forthcoming.

Festugière, André-Jean. *Les moines d'Orient*. Vol. 1: *Culture ou sainteté*. Paris: Éditions du Cerf, 1961.

Fischel, Henry A. "Martyr and Prophet (A Study in Jewish Literature)." *JQR* 37 (1947):265–80, 363–86.

Flusser, David. "The Four Empires in the Fourth Sibyl and in the Book of Daniel." *Israel Oriental Studies* 2 (1972):148–75.

Fodor, A. "The Origins of the Arabic Legends of the Pyramids." *AOH* 23 (1970):335–63.

Fodor, Sándor. "The Origins of the Arabic Surid Legend." *ZÄS* 96 (1970):103–9.

Forsyth, Neil. *The Old Enemy: Satan and the Combat Myth*. Princeton: Princeton University Press, 1987.

Foucart, George. "Names (Egyptian)." *ERE* 9:151–55.

Fowden, Garth. *The Egyptian Hermes.* Cambridge: Cambridge University Press, 1987.

Fox, Robin Lane. *Pagans and Christians.* New York: Alfred A. Knopf, 1987.

Frankfort, Henri. *Ancient Egyptian Religion: An Interpretation.* New York: Columbia University Press, 1948. Reprint. New York: Harper, 1961.

———. *Kingship and the Gods.* Chicago: University of Chicago Press, 1948.

Frankfurter, David. "Lest Egypt's City Be Deserted: Religion and Ideology in the Egyptian Response to the Jewish Revolt." *JJS* 43 (1992):203–20.

Fraser, P. M. *Ptolemaic Alexandria.* 3 vols. Oxford: Clarendon, 1972.

Frend, W.H.C. "The Winning of the Countryside." *JEH* 18 (1967):1–14.

———. "The Christian Period in Mediterranean Africa." In *The Cambridge History of Africa.* Vol. 2: *From c. 500 B.C. to A.D. 1050,* ed. J. D. Fage. Cambridge: Cambridge University Press, 1978, 410–89.

———. *Martyrdom and Persecution in the Early Church.* London: Basil Blackwell, 1965. Reprint. Grand Rapids: Baker Book House, 1981.

———. "Nationalism as a Factor in Anti-Chalcedonian Feeling in Egypt." In *Religion and National Identity,* ed. Stuart Mews. Studies in Church History 18. Oxford: Basil Blackwell, 1982, 21–38.

Friedman, Florence D., ed. *Beyond the Pharaohs: Egypt and the Copts in the Second to Seventh Centuries A.D.* Providence, R.I.: Rhode Island School of Design, 1989.

Fuks, Alexander. "Aspects of the Jewish Revolt in A.D. 115–117." *JRS* 51 (1961):98–104.

Gagé, Jean. "Commodien et le moment millénariste du IIIe siècle (258–262 ap. J.-C.)." *RHPR* 41 (1961):355–78.

Gager, John G. *Moses in Greco-Roman Paganism.* SBLMS 16. Nashville: Abingdon Press, 1972.

Ginzberg, Louis. *The Legends of the Jews.* 7 vols. Philadelphia: Jewish Publication Society, 1909–38.

Goudriaan, Koen. *Ethnicity in Ptolemaic Egypt.* Dutch Monographs on Ancient History and Archaeology 5. Amsterdam: J. C. Gieben, 1988.

Goyon, Jean-Claude. "Ptolemaic Egypt: Priests and the Traditional Religion." In *Cleopatra's Egypt: Age of the Ptolemies.* Brooklyn, N.Y.: The Brooklyn Museum, 1988, 29–40.

Grabar, André. *Martyrium: Recherches sur le culte des reliques et l'art chrétien antique.* 2 vols. Paris: Collège de France, 1946.

Graf, David F. "Medism: The Origin and Significance of the Term." *JHS* 104 (1984):15–30.

Graham, William A. *Beyond the Written Word: Oral Aspects of Scripture in the History of Religion.* Cambridge: Cambridge University Press, 1987.

Grant, Robert M. *Augustus to Constantine: The Rise and Triumph of Christianity in the Roman World.* New York: Harper & Row, 1970.

———. "Manichees and Christians in the Third and Early Fourth Centuries." In *Ex Orbe Religionum (Studia Geo Widengren).* NumenSupp 21. Leiden: Brill, 1972, 430–39.

Green, Henry A. *The Economic and Social Origins of Gnosticism.* SBLDS 77. Atlanta: Scholars Press, 1985.

_____. "The Socio-Economic Background of Christianity in Egypt." In *The Roots of Egyptian Christianity,* 100–113. See Pearson, Birger A., and Goehring, James E., eds.

Griffiths, J. Gwyn. "The Flight of the Gods before Typhon: An Unrecognized Myth." *Hermes* 88 (1960):374–76.

_____. "Egyptian Nationalism in the Edfu Temple Texts." In *Glimpses of Ancient Egypt: Studies in Honour of H. W. Fairman,* ed. John Ruffle, G. A. Gaballa, and Kenneth Kitchen. Warminster: Aris & Phillips, 1979, 174–79.

_____. "Apocalyptic in the Hellenistic Era." In *Apocalypticism in the Mediterranean World and the Near East,* 273–93. See Hellholm, David, ed.

_____. "Egyptian Influences on Athanasius." In *Studien zu Sprache und Religion Ägyptens.* Vol. 2: *Religion.* Göttingen: F. Junge, 1984, 1023–37.

_____. *The Divine Verdict: A Study of Divine Judgement in the Ancient Religions.* NumenSupp 52. Leiden: Brill, 1991.

Griggs, C. Wilfred. *Early Egyptian Christianity: From Its Origins to 451 C.E.* Coptic Studies 2. Leiden: Brill, 1990.

Gruenwald, Ithamar. *Apocalyptic and Merkavah Mysticism.* Arbeiten zur Geschichte des antiken Judentums und des Urchristentums 14. Leiden: Brill, 1980.

Guillaumont, Antoine. "La conception du désert chez les moines d'Égypte." *RHR* 188 (1975):1–21.

_____. "Gnose et monachisme: Exposé introductif." In *Gnosticisme et monde hellénistique,* ed. Julien Ries, Yvonne Janssens, and Jean-Marie Sevrin. Publications de l'institut orientaliste de Louvain 27. Louvain: Catholic University of Louvain, 1982, 301–10.

Haas, Christopher J. "Imperial Religious Policy and Valerian's Persecution of the Church, A.D. 257–260." *CH* 52 (1983):133–44.

Hallock, Frank Hudson. "Christianity and the Old Egyptian Religion." *Egyptian Religion* 2 (1934):6–17.

Hammerschmidt, Ernst. "Altägyptische Elemente im koptischen Christentum." *Ostkirchliche Studien* 6 (1957):233–50.

Hanson, John S. "Dreams and Visions in the Graeco-Roman World and Early Christianity." In *ANRW* 2.22.2:1395–1427.

Hardy, Edward Rochie. *Christian Egypt: Church and People.* New York: Oxford University Press, 1952.

Harris, J. R., ed. *The Legacy of Egypt.* 2d ed. Oxford: Clarendon Press, 1971.

Harris, William V. *Ancient Literacy.* Cambridge: Harvard University Press, 1989.

Hartman, Lars. *Prophecy Interpreted: The Formation of Some Jewish Apocalyptic Texts and of the Eschatological Discourse Mark 13 Par.* Translated by N. Tomkinson. Coniectanea Biblica. New Testament Series 1. Lund: Gleerup, 1966.

_____. "The Functions of Some So-called Apocalyptic Timetables." *NTS* 22 (1976):1–14.

_____. "Survey of the Problem of Apocalyptic Genre." In *Apocalypticism in the Mediterranean World and the Near East,* 329–43. See Hellholm, David, ed.

Hayek, Michel. "Élie dans la tradition syriaque." In *Élie le prophète*. Vol. 1: *Selon les écritures et les traditions chrétiennes*. Bruges: Les études carmélitaines, 1956, 159–78.

Hefele, Charles Joseph. *A History of the Councils of the Church*. Vol. 1: *To the Close of the Council of Nicaea, A.D. 325*. Translated and edited by William R. Clark. Edinburgh: T. & T. Clark, 1894. Reprint. New York: AMS, 1972.

———. *A History of the Councils of the Church*. Vol. 2: *A.D. 326 to A.D. 429*. Translated and edited by Henry Nutcombe Oxenham. Edinburgh: T. & T. Clark, 1896. Reprint. New York: AMS, 1972.

Hellholm, David, ed. *Apocalypticism in the Mediterranean World and the Near East*. Tübingen: Mohr, 1983.

Hengel, Martin. "Anonymität, Pseudepigraphie und 'Literarische Fälschung' in der jüdisch-hellenistischen Literatur." In *Pseudepigrapha I*, ed. Kurt von Fritz. Entretiens sur l'antiquité classique 18. Geneva: Vandoeuvres, 1972, 231–308; discussion, 309–29.

———. "Messianische Hoffnung und politischer 'Radikalismus' in der 'jüdisch-hellenistischen Diaspora'." In *Apocalypticism in the Mediterranean World and the Near East*, 665–86. See Hellholm, David, ed.

Henne, Henri. "Documents et travaux sur l'anachôrésis." In *Mitteilungen aus der Papyrussamlung der österreichischen Nationalbibliothek* 5 (1956):59–66.

Hervé de l'Incarnation, P. "Élie chez les pères latins." In *Élie le prophète*. Vol. 1: *Selon les écritures et les traditions chrétiennes*, 179–207. See *Élie le prophète*.

Hills, Julian. *Tradition and Composition in the Epistula Apostolorum*. HDR 24. Minneapolis: Fortress Press, 1990.

Himmelfarb, Martha. *Tours of Hell: An Apocalyptic Form in Jewish and Christian Literature*. Philadelphia: University of Pennsylvania Press, 1983.

———. "The Experience of the Visionary and Genre in the Ascension of Isaiah 6–11 and the Apocalypse of Paul." *Semeia* 36 (1986):97–111.

———. "Heavenly Ascent and the Relationship of the Apocalypses and the Hekhalot Literature." *HUCA* 59 (1988):73–100.

Hodgson, Robert. "Paul the Apostle and First-Century Tribulation Lists." *Zeitschrift für neutestamentliche Wissenschaft* 74 (1983):59–80.

Hyde, Douglas. "Mediaeval Account of Antichrist." In *Medieval Studies in Memory of Gertrude Schoepperle Loomis*. Paris: Champion, 1927, 391–98.

James, Montague Rhodes. *The Lost Apocrypha of the Old Testament: Their Titles and Fragments*. London: SPCK, 1920.

Janssens, Yvonne. "Apocalypses de Nag Hammadi." In *L'Apocalypse johannique et l'Apocalyptique dans le Nouveau Testament*, ed. J. Lambrecht. Bibliotheca Ephemeridum Theologicarum Lovaniensium 53. Louvain: Louvain University Press, 1980, 69–75.

Jenks, Gregory C. *The Origins and Early Development of the Antichrist Myth*. BZNW 59. Berlin: de Gruyter, 1991.

Jeremias, Joachim. "Ἡλ(ε)ίας." Edited by Gerhard Kittel. Translated and edited by Geoffrey W. Bromiley. In *TDNT* 2:928–41. Grand Rapids: Eerdmans, 1964.

Johnson, Allan Chester. "Lucius Domitius Domitianus Augustus." *CP* 45 (1950):13–21.

————. *Egypt and the Roman Empire*. The Jerome Lectures. 2d series. Ann Arbor: University of Michigan Press, 1951.

Johnson, Janet H. "The Demotic Chronicle as a Statement of a Theory of Kingship." *Journal of the Society for the Study of Egyptian Antiquities* 13 (1983):61–72.

————. "Is the Demotic Chronicle an Anti-Greek Tract?" In *Grammata Demotika*, Festschrift for E. Lüddeckens, ed. Heinz-J. Thissen and Karl-Th. Zauzich. Würzburg: Gisela Zauzich, 1984, 107–24.

Jones, A.H.M. "Were Ancient Heresies National or Social Movements in Disguise?" *JTS* 10 (1959):280–98.

————. *The Later Roman Empire, 284–602: A Social, Economic, and Administrative Survey*. 2 vols. Oxford: Basil Blackwell, 1964. Reprint. Baltimore: Johns Hopkins University Press, 1986.

Jouguet, Pierre. "Les lagides et les indigènes égyptiens." *Revue belge de philologie et d'histoire* 2 (1923):419–45.

————. *La domination romaine en Égypte aux deux premièrs siècles après Jésus-Christ*. Alexandria: Société archéologique d'Alexandrie, 1976.

Judge, E. A. "The Earliest Use of MONACHOS for 'Monk' (P.Coll. Youtie 77) and the Origins of Monasticism." *JAC* 20 (1977):72–89.

————. "Fourth-Century Monasticism in the Papyri." In *Proceedings of the Sixteenth International Congress of Papyrology*, ed. Roger S. Bagnall, Gerald M. Browne, Ann E. Hanson, and Ludwig Koenen. American Studies in Papyrology 23. Chico, Calif.: Scholars Press, 1981, 613–20.

————. "The Magical Use of Scripture in the Papyri." In *Perspectives on Language and Text: Essays and Poems in Honor of Francis I. Andersen's Sixtieth Birthday*, ed. Edgar W. Conrad and Edward G. Newing. Winona Lake, Ind.: Eisenbrauns, 1987, 339–49.

Kaegi, Walter E. "The Fifth-Century Twilight of Byzantine Paganism." *Classica et Mediaevalia* 27 (1966):243–75.

Kákosy, L. "Remarks on the Interpretation of a Coptic Magical Text." *AOH* 13 (1961):325–28.

————. "Ideas about the Fallen State of the World in Egyptian Religion: Decline of the Golden Age." *AOH* 17 (1964):205–16.

————. "Prophecies of Ram Gods." *AOH* 19 (1966):341–58.

Kampers, Franz. *Alexander der Grosse und die Idee des Weltimperiums in Prophetie und Sage*. Freiburg: Herder, 1901.

Kasher, A. "Some Comments on the Jewish Uprising in Egypt in the Time of Trajan." *JJS* 27 (1976):147–58.

————. "The Jewish Community of Oxyrhynchus in the Roman Period." *JJS* 32 (1981):151–57.

Kearns, Rollin. *Das Traditionsgefüge um den Menschensohn*. Tübingen: Mohr [Siebeck], 1986.

Keimer, L. "L'horreur des égyptiens pour les démons du désert." *Bulletin de l'institut d'Égypte* 26 (1944):135–47.

Klijn, A.F.J. "Jewish Christianity in Egypt." In *The Roots of Egyptian Christianity*, 161–75. See Pearson, Birger A., and Goehring, James E., eds.

Koenen, Ludwig. Review of *Corpus Papyrorum Judaicarum*, vols. 2–3, edited by Victor Tcherikover and Alexander Fuks. *Gnomon* 40 (1968):256–59.

———. "The Prophecies of a Potter: A Prophecy of World Renewal Becomes an Apocalypse." In *Proceedings of the Twelfth International Congress of Papyrology*, ed. Deborah H. Samuel. American Studies in Papyrology 7. Toronto: Hakkert, 1970, 249–54.

———. "Die Adaptation ägyptischer Königsideologie am Ptolemäerhof." In *Egypt and the Hellenistic World*, Studia Hellenistica 27, ed. E. Van 't Dack, P. Van Dessel, and W. Van Gucht. Louvain: Studia Hellenistica, 1983, 143–90.

———. "Manichäische Mission und Klöster in Ägypten." In *Das römisch-byzantinische Ägypten*. Aegyptiaca Treverensia 2. Mainz am Rhein: Philipp von Zabern, 1983, 93–108.

———. "A Supplementary Note on the Date of the Oracle of the Potter." *ZPE* 54 (1984):9–13.

———. "The Dream of Nektanebos." *BASP* 22 (1985):171–94.

———. "Manichaean Apocalypticism at the Crossroads of Iranian, Egyptian, Jewish, and Christian Thought." In *Codex Manichaicus Coloniensis: Atti del Simposio Internazionale*, ed. Luigi Cirillo. Cosenza: Editore Marra, 1986, 285–332.

Kosack, Wolfgang. *Die Legende im Koptischen: Untersuchungen zur Volksliteratur Ägyptens*. Habelts Dissertationsdrucke. Reihe klassische Philologie 8. Bonn: Habelt, 1970.

Kreitzer, Larry. "Hadrian and the Nero *Redivivus* Myth." *ZNW* 79 (1988):92–115.

LeFort, L.-Th. "La chasse aux reliques des martyrs en Égypte au IVᵉ siècle." *La nouvelle Clio* 6 (1954):225–30.

Lewis, Naphtali. *Life in Egypt under Roman Rule*. Oxford: Clarendon Press, 1983.

Lieberman, Saul. "On Sins and Their Punishments." In idem, *Texts and Studies*. New York: Ktav, 1974, 29–56.

Lloyd, Alan B. "Nationalist Propaganda in Ptolemaic Egypt." *Historia* 31 (1982):33–55.

———. "The Late Period: 664–323 B.C." In *Ancient Egypt: A Social History*, ed. B. G. Trigger et al. Cambridge: Cambridge University Press, 1983, 279–348.

———. "Herodotus on Cambyses: Some Thoughts on Recent Work." In *Achaemenid History*. Vol. 3: *Method and Theory*, ed. Amélie Kuhrt and Heleen Sancisi-Weerdenburg. Leiden: Nederlands Instituut voor het nabije Oosten, 1988, 55–66.

Long, Burke O. "Reports of Visions among the Prophets." *JBL* 95 (1976):353–65.

Luria, S. "Die Ersten werden die Letzten sein (zur 'sozialen Revolution' im Altertum)." *Klio* 22 (1929):405–31.

McCown, C. C. "Hebrew and Egyptian Apocalyptic Literature." *HTR* 18 (1925):357–411.

MacDermot, Violet. *The Cult of the Seer in the Ancient Middle East*. London: Wellcome Institute of the History of Medicine, 1971.

McGinn, Bernard. *Visions of the End: Apocalyptic Traditions in the Middle Ages*. Records of Civilization, Sources and Studies 46. New York: Columbia University Press, 1979.

———. "Portraying Antichrist in the Middle Ages." In *The Use and Abuse of*

Eschatology in the Middle Ages, ed. Werner Verbeke, Daniel Verhelst, and Andries Welkenhuysen. Mediaevalia Lovaniensia Series 1. Studia 15. Louvain: Louvain University Press, 1988, 1–48.

MacLean, Arthur John. "Fasting (Christian)." In *ERE* 5:765–71.

MacMullen, Ramsay. "Nationalism in Roman Egypt." *Aegyptus* 44 (1964):179–99.

———. *Enemies of the Roman Order*. Cambridge: Harvard University Press, 1966.

———. *Roman Government's Response to Crisis*, A.D. *235–337*. New Haven and London: Yale University Press, 1976.

———. *Christianizing the Roman Empire (*A.D. *100–400)*. New Haven and London: Yale University Press, 1984.

———. "The Preacher's Audience (A.D. 350–400)." *JTS* 40 (1989):503–11.

Maier, Gerhard. *Die Johannesoffenbarung und die Kirche*. WUNT 25. Tübingen: Mohr [Siebeck], 1981.

Martin, Annick. "Athanase et les mélitiens (325–335)." In *Politique et théologie chez Athanase d'Alexandrie*, ed. Charles Kannengiesser. Théologie historique 27. Paris: Beauchesne, 1974, 31–61.

———. "L'église et la khôra égyptienne au IVe siècle." *Revue des études augustiniennes* 25 (1979):3–26.

———. "Aux origines de l'église copte: L'implantation et le développement du christianisme en Égypte (I^e–IVe siècles)." *RÉA* 83 (1981):35–56.

———. "Les premiers siècles du christianisme à Alexandrie: Essai de topographie religieuse (IIIe–IVe siècles)." *Revue des études augustiniennes* 30 (1984):211–25.

———. "La reconciliation des *lapsi* en Égypte." *Rivista di storia e letteratura religiosa* 22 (1986):256–69.

Mazzucco, Clementina. "Eusèbe de Césarée et l'*Apocalypse* de Jean." *Studia patristica* 17, 1 (1982):317–24.

Merkelbach, Reinhold. *Die Quellen des griechischen Alexanderromans*. Munich: C. G. Beck'sche, 1977.

Metzger, Bruce. "Literary Forgeries and Canonical Pseudepigrapha." *JBL* 91 (1972):3–24.

Michaïlidès, G. "Vestiges du culte solaire parmi les chrétiens d'Égypte." *Bulletin de la société d'archéologie copte* 14 (1950):37–110.

Milne, J. Grafton. *A History of Egypt under Roman Rule*. A History of Egypt 5. 3d ed. London: Methuen, 1924.

———. "Egyptian Nationalism under Greek and Roman Rule." *JEA* 14 (1928):226–34.

Momigliano, Arnaldo. "Some Preliminary Remarks on the 'Religious Opposition' to the Roman Empire." In *Opposition et résistances à l'empire d'Auguste à Trajan*, 103–29; discussion, pp. 130–33. Entretiens sur l'antiquité classique 33. Geneva: Vandoeuvres, 1983.

Morenz, Siegfried. *Egyptian Religion*. Translated by Ann E. Keep. Ithaca, N.Y., and London: Cornell University Press, 1973.

Musurillo, Herbert. "Early Christian Economy: A Reconsideration of P.Amherst 3(a) (= Wilcken, Chrest. 126)." *Chronique d'Égypte* 31 (1956):124–34.

———. "The Problem of Ascetical Fasting in the Greek Patristic Writers." *Traditio* 12 (1956):1–64.

Nicholson, Oliver. "Flight from Persecution as Imitation of Christ: Lactantius' Divine Institutes IV.18, 1-2." *JTS* 40 (1989):48–65.

Nickelsburg, George W. E., Jr. *Resurrection, Immortality, and Eternal Life in Intertestamental Judaism*. Harvard Theological Studies 26. Cambridge: Harvard University Press, 1972.

_____. "Two Enochic Manuscripts: Unstudied Evidence for Egyptian Christianity." In *Of Scribes and Scrolls: Studies on the Hebrew Bible, Intertestamental Judaism, and Christian Origins Presented to John Strugnell*, ed. Harold W. Attridge, John J. Collins, and Thomas H. Tobin. College Theology Society Resources in Religion 5. Lanham, Md.: University Press of America. 1990, 251–60.

Nock, Arthur Darby. "Later Egyptian Piety." In *Coptic Egypt*, 21-29. See *Coptic Egypt*.

Nordheim, Eckhard von. "Das Zitat des Paulus in 1 Kor 2⁹ und seine Beziehung zum koptischen Testament Jakobs." *ZNW* 65 (1974):112–20.

Oost, Stewart Irvin. "The Alexandrian Seditions under Philip and Gallienus." *CP* 56 (1961):1–20.

Orlandi, Tito. "Coptic Literature." In *The Roots of Egyptian Christianity*, 51–81. See Pearson, Birger A., and Goehring, James E., eds.

Owen, E.C.E. "Fasting in the Eastern Church." *CQR* 126 (1938):95–110.

Pappano, Albert Earl. "The False Neros." *Classical Journal* 32 (1937):385–92.

Parrott, Douglas M. "Gnosticism and Egyptian Religion." *Novum Testamentum* 29 (1987):73–93.

Parsons, P. J. "Philippus Arabus and Egypt." *JRS* 57 (1967):134–41.

Pearson, Birger A. "Egyptian Seth and Gnostic Seth." In SBLSP 1977. Edited by Paul J. Achtemeier. Missoula, Mont.: Scholars Press, 1977, 25–43.

_____. "Earliest Christianity in Egypt: Some Observations." In *The Roots of Egyptian Christianity*, 133–59. See Pearson, Birger A., and Goehring, James E., eds.

_____. *Gnosticism, Judaism, and Egyptian Christianity*. SAC 5. Minneapolis: Fortress Press, 1991.

Pearson, Birger A., and Goehring, James E., eds. *The Roots of Egyptian Christianity*. SAC 1. Philadelphia: Fortress Press, 1986.

Perry, B. E. "The Egyptian Legend of Nectanebus." *TPAPA* 97 (1966):327–33.

Perkins, Judith. "The Apocryphal Acts of the Apostles and the Early Christian Martyrdom." *Arethusa* 18 (1985):211–30.

Piankoff, A. "La descente aux enfers dans les textes égyptiens et dans les apocryphes coptes." *Bulletin de la société d'archéologie copte* 7 (1941):33–46.

Pohlsander, Hans A. "Philip the Arab and Christianity." *Historia* 29 (1980):463–73.

_____. "The Religious Policy of Decius." In *ANRW* 2.16.3:1826–42.

Porten, Bezalel. "The Diaspora, D. The Jews in Egypt." In *The Cambridge History of Judaism*. Vol. 1: *Introduction: The Persian Period*, ed. W. D. Davies and Louis Finkelstein. Cambridge: Cambridge University Press, 1984, 372–400.

Posener, Georges. *Littérature et politique dans l'Égypte de la XII^è dynastie*. Paris: Librairie ancienne Honoré Champion, 1956.

————. *De la divinité du Pharaon*. Cahiers de la société asiatique 15. Paris: Imprimerie nationale, 1960.

————. "Literature." In *The Legacy of Egypt*, 220–56. See Harris, J. R., ed.

————. "L'ANACHORESIS dans l'Égypte pharaonique." In *Le monde grec: Hommages à Claire Préaux*, ed. Jean Bingen, Guy Cambier, and Georges Nachtergael. Brussels: Éditions de l'université de Bruxelles, 1975, 663–69.

Potter, David. *Prophecy and History in the Crisis of the Roman Empire: A Historical Commentary on the Thirteenth Sibylline Oracle*. Oxford: Clarendon Press, 1990.

Préaux, Claire. "Esquisse d'une histoire des révolutions égyptiennes sous les lagides." *Chronique d'Égypte* 22 (1936):522–52.

————. "L'attache à la terre: Continuités de l'Égypte ptolémaïque à l'Égypte romaine." In *Das römisch-byzantinische Ägypten*. Aegyptiaca Treverensia 2. Mainz: Philipp von Zabern, 1983, 1–5.

Prigent, Pierre. "Ce que l'oeil n'a pas vu, I Cor.2,9: Histoire et préhistoire d'une citation." *TZ* 14 (1958):416–29.

Raven, Maarten J. "Wax in Egyptian Magic and Symbolism." *Oudheidkundige mededelingen uit het rijksmuseum van oudheden te Leiden* 64 (1983):7–47.

Rees, B. R. "Popular Religion in Graeco-Roman Egypt, 2: The Transition to Christianity." *JEA* 36 (1950):86–100.

Reinhold, Meyer. "Roman Attitudes toward Egyptians." *Ancient World* 3 (1980):97–103.

Rémondon, Roger. "L'Égypte et la suprême résistance au christianisme." *BIFAO* 51 (1952):63–78.

————. "Les antisémites de Memphis." *Chronique d'Égypte* 35 (1960):244–61.

————. "L'église dans la société égyptienne à l'époque byzantine." *Chronique d'Égypte* 47 (1972):254–77.

Rey-Coquais, J.-P. "Syrie romaine, de Pompée à Dioclétien." *JRS* 68 (1978):44–73.

Reymond, Eve A. E. "Demotic Literary Works of Graeco-Roman Date in the Rainer Collection of Papyri in Vienna." In *Papyrus Erzherzog Rainer (P.Rainer Cent.)*. 2 vols. Vienna: Verlag Brüder Hollinek, 1983, 1:42–60.

Reymond, E.A.E., and Barns, J.W.B. "Alexandria and Memphis: Some Historical Observations." *Orientalia* 46 (1977):1–33.

Riddle, Donald W. *The Martyrs: A Study in Social Control*. Chicago: University of Chicago Press, 1931.

Rinsveld, B. Van. "La version copte de l'Asclépius et la ville de l'âge d'or." In *Textes et études de papyrologie grecque, démotique et copte*, ed. P. W. Pestman. Papyrologica Lugduno-Batava 23. Leiden: Brill, 1985, 233–42.

Ritner, Robert K. "The Mechanics of Ancient Egyptian Magical Practice." Ph.D. diss., University of Chicago, 1987.

Roberts, Colin H. *Manuscript, Society and Belief in Early Christian Egypt*. London: British Museum, 1979.

Rosenstiehl, Jean-Marc. "Le portrait de l'antichrist." In *Pseudépigraphes de l'ancien testament et manuscrits de la mer morte*, ed. Marc Philonenko. Paris: Presses Universitaires, 1967, 45–60.

————. "Les révélations d'Élie: Élie et les tourments des damnés." In *La lit-*

térature intertestamentaire: Colloque de Strasbourg. Strasbourg: Presses universitaires de France, 1985, 99–107.

Rostovtzeff, M. *The Social and Economic History of the Roman Empire*. 2 vols. 2d ed. Revised by P. M. Fraser. Oxford: Clarendon Press, 1957.

Rousseau, Philip. *Pachomius: The Making of a Community in Fourth-Century Egypt*. The Transformation of the Classical Heritage 6. Berkeley: University of California Press, 1985.

Rowland, Christopher. *The Open Heaven: A Study of Apocalyptic in Judaism and Early Christianity*. New York: Crossroad, 1982.

Russell, D. S. *The Method and Message of Jewish Apocalyptic*. Philadelphia: Westminster Press, 1964.

Sage, Michael M. "The Persecution of Valerian and the Peace of Gallienus." *Wiener Studien* 17 (1983):137–59.

Saldarini, Anthony J. "Apocalypses and 'Apocalyptic' in Rabbinic Literature." *Semeia* 14 (1979):187–205.

Sauneron, Serge. "Aspects et sort d'un thème magique égyptien: Les menaces incluant les dieux." *Bulletin de la société française d'égyptologie* 8 (November 1951):11–21.

_____. *The Priests of Ancient Egypt*. Translated by Ann Morrissett. Evergreen Profile Book 12. New York: Grove Press, 1960.

Säve-Söderbergh, Torgny. "The Pagan Elements in Early Christianity and Gnosticism." In *Colloque international sur les textes de Nag Hammadi*, ed. Bernard Barc. Bibliothèque copte de Nag Hammadi, section "Études" 1. Quebec: Université Laval, 1981, 71–85.

Schott, Siegfried. "Altägyptische Vorstellungen vom Weltende." *Analecta biblica* 12 (1959):319–30.

Schürer, Émil. *Geschichte des jüdischen Volkes in Zeitalter Jesu Christi*. 3 vols. 4th ed. Leipzig: J. C. Hinrichs'sche, 1909.

_____. *The History of the Jewish People in the Age of Jesus Christ*. Revised and edited by Geza Vermes, Fergus Millar, and Martin Goodman. 3 vols. Edinburgh: T. & T. Clark, 1973-87.

Schwartz, Jacques. "Les conquérants perses et la littérature égyptienne." *BIFAO* 48 (1949):65–80.

_____. "Les palmyréniens et l'Égypte." *Bulletin de la société archéologique d'Alexandrie* 40 (1953):63–81.

_____. "Note sur la 'Petite Apocalypse' de l'*Asclepius*." *RHPR* 62 (1982):165–69.

Scott-Moncrieff, Philip David. *Paganism and Christianity in Egypt*. Cambridge: Cambridge University Press, 1913.

Seston, W. "Achilleus et la révolte de l'Égypte sous Dioclétien d'après les papyrus et l'*histoire Auguste*." *Mélanges d'archéologie et d'histoire* 55 (1938):184–200.

_____. "L'Égypte manichéenne." *Chronique d'Égypte* 14 (1939):362–72.

Séyrig, Henri. "VHABALATHVS AVGVSTVS." In *Mélanges offerts à K. Michalowski*. Warsaw: Pantswawe Wydawn, 1966, 659–62.

Shafer, Byron E., ed. *Religion in Ancient Egypt: Gods, Myths, and Personal Practice*. Ithaca, N.Y.: Cornell University Press, 1991.

Shore, A. F. "Christian and Coptic Egypt." In *The Legacy of Egypt*, 390–433. See Harris, J. R., ed.

Silverman, David P. "Divinity and Deities in Ancient Egypt." In *Religion in Ancient Egypt*, 7–87. See Shafer, Byron E., ed.

Simon, Marcel. "Sur quelques aspects des Oracles Sibyllines juifs." In *Apocalypticism in the Mediterranean World and the Near East*, 219–33. See Hellholm, David, ed.

Smith, Jonathan Z. "Native Cults in the Hellenistic Period." *HR* 11 (1971):236–49.

―――. "Wisdom and Apocalyptic." In *Religious Syncretism in Antiquity*, ed. Birger A. Pearson. Missoula, Mont.: Scholars Press, 1975, 131–56. Reprinted in idem, *Map Is Not Territory: Studies in the History of Religions*. Studies in Judaism in Late Antiquity 23. Leiden: Brill, 1978, 67–87.

―――. "Towards Interpreting Demonic Powers in Hellenistic and Roman Antiquity." In *ANRW* 2.16.1:425–39.

Smith, Morton. "Pseudepigraphy in the Israelite Literary Tradition." In *Pseudepigrapha I*, ed. Kurt von Fritz. Entretiens sur l'antiquité classique 18. Geneva: Vandoeuvres, 1972, 191–215; discussion, 216–27.

―――. "On the History of ΑΠΟΚΑΛΥΠΤΩ and ΑΠΟΚΑΛΥΠΣΙΣ." In *Apocalypticism in the Mediterranean World and the Near East*, 9–20. See Hellholm, David, ed.

Sparks, H.F.D. "1 Kor 2⁹: A Quotation from the Coptic Testament of Jacob?" *ZNW* 67 (1976):269–76.

Speyer, Wolfgang. "Religiöse Pseudepigraphie und literarische Fälschung im Altertum." *JAC* 8/9 (1965–66):88–125.

Stein, Arthur. "Kallinikos von Petrai." *Hermes* 58 (1923):448–56.

Stevenson, Jane. "Ascent through the Heavens, from Egypt to Ireland." *Cambridge Medieval Celtic Studies* 5 (1983):21–35.

Stone, Michael Edward. *Fourth Ezra: A Commentary on the Book of Fourth Ezra*. Hermeneia. Minneapolis: Fortress Press, 1990.

Stroumsa, Gedaliahu G. "Monachisme et marranisme chez les manichéens d'Égypte." *Numen* 29 (1982):184–201.

―――. "The Manichaean Challenge to Egyptian Christianity." In *The Roots of Egyptian Christianity*, 307–19. See Pearson, Birger A., and Goehring, James E., eds.

Swain, Joseph Ward. "The Theory of the Four Monarchies: Opposition History under the Roman Empire." *CP* 35 (1940):1–21.

Tarn, W. W. "The Hellenistic Ruler-Cult and the Daemon." *JHS* 48 (1928):206–19.

Tcherikover, Victor A. "The Decline of the Jewish Diaspora in Egypt in the Roman Period." *JJS* 14 (1963):1–32.

Te Velde, H. *Seth, God of Confusion*. Translated by G. E. van Baaren-Pape. Leiden: Brill, 1977.

Thielman, Frank S. "Another Look at the Eschatology of Eusebius of Caesarea." *VigChr* 41 (1987):226–37.

Thompson, Dorothy J. "The High Priests of Memphis under Ptolemaic Rule." In *Pagan Priests*, ed. Mary Beard and John North. Ithaca, N.Y.: Cornell University Press, 1990, 97–116.

Till, Walter C. "Coptic and Its Value." *BJRL* 40 (1957):229–58.

Tilley, Maureen A. "The Ascetic Body and the (Un)Making of the World of the Martyr." *JAAR* 59 (1991):467–79.

Timbie, Janet Ann. "Dualism and the Concept of Orthodoxy in the Thought of the Monks of Upper Egypt." Ph.D. diss., University of Pennsylvania, 1979.

van den Broek, R. "Popular Religious Practices and Ecclesiastical Policies in the Early Church." In *Official and Popular Religion: Analysis of a Theme for Religious Studies*, ed. Pieter Hendrik Vrijhof and Jacques Waardenburg. Religion and Society 19. The Hague: Mouton, 1979, 11–54.

Veilleux, Armand. "Monasticism and Gnosis in Egypt." In *The Roots of Egyptian Christianity*, 271–306. See Pearson, Birger A., and Goehring, James E., eds.

Vielhauer, Philip. "Apocalypses and Related Subjects: Introduction." Translated by David Hill. In NTA 2:581–607.

Vivian, Tim. *St. Peter of Alexandria: Bishop and Martyr*. SAC 3. Philadelphia: Fortress Press, 1988.

Walters, Colin C. "A Vision of Hell from Tebtunis." In *Glimpses of Ancient Egypt: Studies in Honour of H. W. Fairman*, ed. John Ruffle, G. A. Gaballa, and Kenneth Kitchen. Warminster: Aris & Phillips, 1979, 190–95 and pl. 1.

———. "Christian Paintings from Tebtunis." *JEA* 75 (1989):191–208 and pls. 16–29.

Weill, Raymond. *La fin du moyen empire égyptien*. Paris: Imprimerie nationale, 1918.

Weinel, Heinrich. "Die spätere christliche Apokalyptik." In ΕΥΧΑΡΙΣΤΗΡΙΟΝ. Festschrift for Hermann Gunkel, ed. Hans Schmidt. Göttingen: Vandenhoeck & Ruprecht, 1923, 141–73.

Weiss, M. "The Pattern of the 'Execration Texts' in the Prophetic Literature." *Israel Exploration Journal* 19 (1969):150–57.

Westermann, Claus. *The Basic Forms of Prophetic Speech*. Translated by Hugh Clayton White. Philadelphia: Westminster Press, 1967.

Westermann, William Lynn. "On the Background of Coptism." In *Coptic Egypt*, 7–19. See *Coptic Egypt*.

Wiener, Aharon. *The Prophet Elijah in the Development of Judaism: A Depth-Psychological Study*. London: Routledge & Kegan Paul, 1978.

Wilken, Robert L. "The Restoration of Israel in Biblical Prophecy: Christian and Jewish Responses in the Early Byzantine Period." In *"To See Ourselves as Others See Us": Christians, Jews, "Others" in Late Antiquity*, ed. Jacob Neusner and Ernest S. Frerichs. Chico, Calif.: Scholars Press, 1985, 443–72.

———. "Early Christian Chiliasm, Jewish Messianism, and the Idea of the Holy Land." In *Christians among Jews and Gentiles*. Festschrift for K. Stendahl, ed. George W. E. Nickelsburg and George W. MacRae. Philadelphia: Fortress Press, 1986, 298–307.

Williams, Michael A. "The *Life of Antony* and the Domestication of Charismatic Wisdom." In *Charisma and Sacred Biography*, ed. Michael A. Williams. JAAR Thematic Studies 48, 3–4, pp. 23–45. Chico, Calif.: Scholars Press, 1982.

Wipszycka, Ewa. "Un lecteur qui ne sait pas écrire ou un chrétien qui ne veut pas se souiller? (P.Oxy. XXXIII 2673)." *ZPE* 50 (1983):117–21.

―――. "Le degré d'alphabétisation en Égypte byzantine." *Revue des études augustiniennes* 30 (1984):279–96.

―――. "La valeur de l'onomastique pour l'histoire de la christianisation de l'Égypte: À propos d'une étude de R. S. Bagnall." *ZPE* 62 (1986):173–81.

―――. "La christianisation de l'Égypte aux IVe–VIe siècles: Aspects sociaux et ethniques." *Aegyptus* 68 (1988):117–65.

Wisse, Frederik. "Gnosticism and Early Monasticism in Egypt." In *Gnosis*. Festschrift for Hans Jonas, ed. Ugo Bianchi et al. Göttingen: Vandenhoeck & Ruprecht, 1978, 431–40.

Youtie, Herbert C. "AGRAMMATOS: An Aspect of Greek Society in Egypt." *HSCP* 75 (1971):161–76.

―――. "The Heidelberg Festival Papyrus: A Reinterpretation." In idem, *Scriptiunculae*. 2 vols. Amsterdam: Hakkert, 1973, 1:514–45.

―――. "BRADEOS GRAPHON: Between Literacy and Illiteracy." In idem, *Scriptiunculae*. 2 vols. Amsterdam: Hakkert, 1973, 2:629–51.

―――. "HYPOGRAPHEUS: The Social Impact of Illiteracy in Graeco-Roman Egypt." *ZPE* 17 (1975):201–21.

Yoyotte, Jean. "L'Égypte ancienne et les origines de l'antijudaïsme." *RHR* 163 (1963):133–43.

Zandee, Jan. *Death as an Enemy, According to Ancient Egyptian Conceptions*. NumenSupp 5. Leiden: Brill, 1960.

―――. "Traditions pharaoniques et influences extérieures dans les légendes coptes." Review of *Die Legende im Koptischen: Untersuchungen zur Volksliteratur Ägyptens*, by Wolfgang Kosack. *Chronique d'Égypte* 46 (1971):211–19.

SECONDARY LITERATURE B:
COMPARATIVE AND METHODOLOGICAL WORKS

Abrahams, Roger D. "Introductory Remarks to a Rhetorical Theory of Folklore." *Journal of American Folklore* 81 (1968):143–58.

―――. "The Complex Relations of Simple Forms." In *Folklore Genres*, ed. Dan Ben-Amos. Publications of the American Folklore Society 26. Austin: University of Texas Press, 1976, 193–214.

Austin, J. L. *How to Do Things with Words*. Edited by J. O. Urmson and Marina Sbisá. 2d ed. Cambridge: Harvard University Press, 1975.

Baird, J. Arthur. "Genre Analysis as a Method of Historical Criticism." In *SBL Book of Seminar Papers*. 1972. 2 vols. Edited by Lane C. McGaughy, 2:385–411.

Barkun, Michael. *Disaster and the Millennium*. New Haven: Yale University Press, 1974. Reprint. Syracuse, N.Y.: Syracuse University Press, 1986.

Burridge, Kenelm. *New Heaven, New Earth: A Study of Millenarian Activities*. Oxford: Basil Blackwell, 1969.

―――. "Millennialisms and the Recreation of History." In *Religion, Rebellion, Revolution*, 219–35. See Lincoln, Bruce, ed.

Chatman, Seymour. *Story and Discourse: Narrative Structure in Fiction and Film.* Ithaca, N.Y., and London: Cornell University Press, 1978.

Cohn, Norman. *The Pursuit of the Millennium.* Revised edition. London: Temple Smith, 1970.

Doty, William G. "The Concept of Genre in Literary Analysis." In *SBL Book of Seminar Papers.* 1972. 2 vols. Edited by Lane C. McGaughy, 2:413–48.

Douglas, Mary. *Natural Symbols: Explorations in Cosmology.* New York: Pantheon, 1982.

Geertz, Clifford. *The Interpretation of Cultures.* New York: Basic Books, 1973.

Gellner, Ernest. "Notes towards a Theory of Ideology." *L'Homme* 18 (1978):69–82.

_____. *Nations and Nationalism.* Ithaca, N.Y.: Cornell University Press, 1983.

Grottanelli, Cristiano. "Archaic Forms of Rebellion and Their Religious Background." In *Religion, Rebellion, Revolution,* 15–45. See Lincoln, Bruce, ed.

Hirsch, E. D., Jr. *Validity in Interpretation.* New Haven and London: Yale University Press, 1967.

Hobsbawm, E. J. *Primitive Rebels: Studies in Archaic Forms of Social Movement.* New York: Frederick Praeger, 1959. Reprint. New York: W. W. Norton, 1965.

_____. "The Social Function of the Past: Some Questions." *Past and Present* 55 (1972):3–17.

Jansen, William Hugh. "Classifying Performance in the Study of Verbal Folklore." In *Studies in Folklore in Honor of Stith Thompson,* ed. W. Edson Richmond. Bloomington: Indiana University Press, 1957, 110–18.

Lincoln, Bruce. *Discourse and the Construction of Society.* New York: Oxford University Press, 1989.

_____. "Notes toward a Theory of Religion and Revolution." In idem, ed. *Religion, Rebellion, Revolution,* 266–92. See Lincoln, Bruce, ed.

_____, ed. *Religion, Rebellion, Revolution.* New York: St. Martin's Press, 1985.

Malinowski, Bronislaw. *Magic, Science and Religion, and Other Essays.* Garden City, N.Y.: Doubleday, 1954.

Olrik, Axel. "Epic Laws of Folk Narrative." In *The Study of Folklore,* ed. Alan Dundes. Englewood Cliffs, N.J.: Prentice-Hall, 1965, 129–41.

Ong, Walter J. *Orality and Literacy: The Technologizing of the Word.* London and New York: Methuen, 1982.

Searle, John R. "A Taxonomy of Illocutionary Acts." In *Language, Mind, and Knowledge,* ed. Keith Gunderson. Minnesota Studies in the Philosophy of Science 7. Minneapolis: University of Minnesota Press, 1975, 344–69.

Simmel, Georg. *Conflict and the Web of Group-Affiliations.* Translated by Kurt H. Wolff and Reinhard Bendix. New York: Free Press, 1955.

Talmon, Yonina. "Pursuit of the Millennium: The Relation between Religious and Social Change." *Archives européennes de sociologie* 3 (1962):125–48.

Tambiah, Stanley J. "The Magical Power of Words." *Man* 3 (1968):175–208.

_____. "Form and Meaning of Magical Acts: A Point of View." In *Modes of Thought: Essays on Thinking in Western and Non-Western Societies,* ed. Robin Horton and Ruth Finnegan. London: Faber & Faber, 1973, 199–229.

Thrupp, Sylvia L., ed. *Millennial Dreams in Action: Studies in Revolutionary Religious Movements.* New York: Schocken, 1970.

Weber, Max. *The Sociology of Religion.* Translated by Ephraim Fischoff. Boston: Beacon Press, 1963.

Worsley, Peter. *The Trumpet Shall Sound: A Study of "Cargo" Cults in Melanesia.* 2d ed. New York: Schocken, 1968.

Index of
Ancient Sources

EGYPTIAN LITERATURE

HEBREW BIBLE

EARLY CHRISTIAN TEXTS

OTHER ANCIENT AUTHORS AND TEXTS

Index of Subjects

Index of
Modern Authors